Western New York

Western New York

From Niagara Falls and Southern Ontario to the Western Edge of the Finger Lakes

Christine A. Smyczynski

with photographs by the author

The Countryman Press ✳ Woodstock, Vermont

FIRST EDITION

We welcome your comments and suggestions. Please contact Explorer's Guide Editor, The Countryman Press, P.O. Box 748, Woodstock, Vermont 05091, or e-mail countrymanpress@wwnorton.com.

ISBN 0-88150-655-9
ISSN 1552-6097

Maps by Moore Creative Design, © 2005 The Countryman Press
Book design by Bodenweber Design
Text composition by PerfecType, Nashville, TN
Cover photograph by Rudi Von Briel/Index Stock Imagery

Published by The Countryman Press
P.O. Box 748
Woodstock, Vermont 05091

Distributed by W. W. Norton & Company, Inc.
500 Fifth Avenue
New York, NY 10110

Printed in the United States of America

10 9 8 7 6 5 4 3 2 1

DEDICATION

To my family and all the people of Western New York: May you always enjoy exploring our vast region.

EXPLORE WITH US!

Welcome to the first edition of the most comprehensive guide to Western New York. All entries, including attractions, inns, restaurants and stores are chosen based on merit, not through paid advertising.

The layout of this guide has been kept simple to make it easy to read and use. Here are some pointers to help you get started.

WHAT'S WHERE

In the beginning of the book you'll find an alphabetical listing of special high-lights, important information, and items unique to Western New York. You'll find advice on everything from where to ski in winter, swim in summer, and find the best-tasting chicken wings.

LODGING

Places included in this book have been selected on merit alone. This is the only travel guide that tries to personally check every lodging property to assure quality accommodations. It is also one of the few that doesn't charge for inclusion. It is recommended that you make lodging reservations well in advance, especially during the peak tourist season.

PRICES

Please don't hold the author or innkeepers responsible for the prices listed as of press time in early 2005. Price changes are often inevitable. Note that the prices quoted do not include state and local taxes. In the "Southern Ontario" chapter, prices are quoted in Canadian funds.

SMOKING

Almost all Western New York inns, restaurants, and other establishments are smoke free, so if smoking is important to you, inquire about the smoking policy when you make a reservation.

RESTAURANTS

Note the distinction between "dining out" and "eating out." Restaurants listed under Eating Out are generally more casual and less expensive than those listed under Dining Out.

KEY TO SYMBOLS

- ♕   Special Value. The blue-ribbon icon appears next to lodging, restaurants, and attractions that combine quality and moderate prices.

- ✎   Child-Friendly. The crayon icon appears next to lodging, restaurants, and activities that appeal to families with young children.

♿   Handicapped Access. The wheelchair symbol appears next to establishments that are wheelchair accessible.

🐾   Pet Friendly. The dog paw symbol appears next to lodgings that accept pets. Not all establishments advertise the fact that they do accept pets, so be sure to inquire when making reservations if you are bringing a pet. Some establishments may charge a rather nominal fee, while others may charge quite a bit to accommodate a pet.

☂   Rainy-Day Activities. The umbrella symbol indicates activities and places that are appropriate on bad-weather days.

Ⓧ   Weddings. The wedding ring symbol appears next to wedding chapels and lodgings that specialize in weddings. The listings included in this book are all in the Niagara Falls area.

🍸   Nightlife. The martini glass icon appears in front of restaurants and other establishments with good bars.

✦   National Historic Landmark. This icon appears in front of designated National Historic Landmarks. Nearly 30 of these can be found in the Western New York area.

Keep in mind that as of press time, all information was current and accurate. However, as with anything in life, change is inevitable. Some new businesses will open, while others may close or change ownership. Stores and restaurants may change their hours. Please be sure to call ahead if you are traveling any distance to a particular establishment to avoid disappointment. If you happen to discover a business or attraction not reviewed in this book that you feel should be included, please let the publisher know so that it can be considered for inclusion in future editions. I would appreciate comments and corrections. Please write The Countryman Press, P.O. Box 748, Woodstock VT 05091 or e-mail countrymanpress@wwnorton.com.

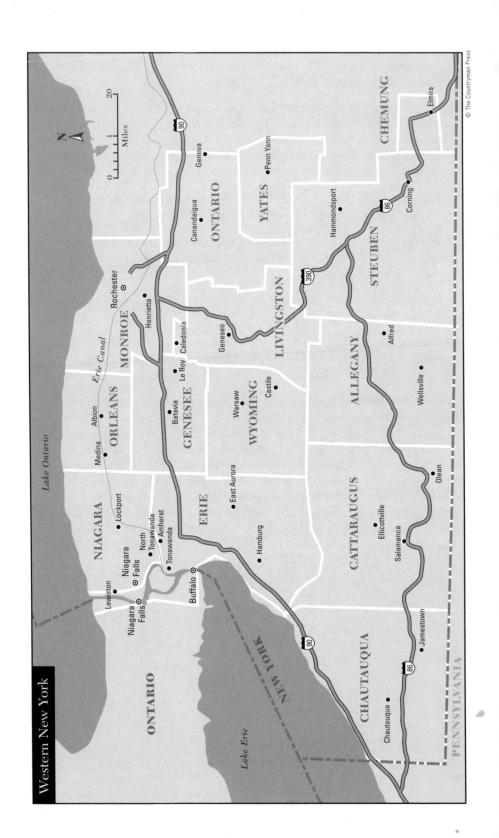

Western New York

© The Countryman Press

CONTENTS

ACKNOWLEDGMENTS

Of course, I couldn't have written a book of this magnitude without help. Friends, family, and strangers alike supplied me with moral support as well as information. I could fill a book just with the names of people who were so generous and accommodating in sharing information.

First and foremost, I'd like to thank God, for giving me the writing ability, as well as the strength and patience, to see this project through. On more than one occasion, I think divine intervention must have been at work as I did my research. Often I would enter a town, and the first person I would encounter would be exactly the right person I needed to talk to find out the information I was seeking.

Next, I'd like to thank my husband, Jim, and my children Andy, Peter, Jennifer, and Joey, who had to put up with me while I wrote this book. Many days they were virtually ignored and fed pizza or sandwiches for dinner, as I was too exhausted to cook. They also accompanied me on many of my adventures, especially my youngest, Joey, who has to be the most traveled toddler in western New York!

My special thanks to Jim, who offered encouragement and suggestions when I started losing focus and doubting my ability to write this book. I would have never completed it without his love and support.

Of course, I must thank my parents, Joseph and Adele Kloch, who sparked my interest in local travel when I was a young child and have encouraged me in my writing career.

I also have to thank my friends and relatives, especially Mary Dentinger, Linda Gebhardt, Maria Portera, Ann Marie Wik, John and Sandy Smyczynski, Alice Smyczynski, and Steve Wik, who either gave me tips on places to visit, accompanied me on some adventures, and/or provided babysitting services when needed.

My writing career would have never taken off if not for Kathryn Radeff, who introduced me to the field of freelance writing and is one of the best writing instructors around. A special thanks to Dr. Eva Shaw, whom I never met face to face, but who offered support and encouragement when I perfected my travel-writing skills in one of her online travel writing courses. I also have to thank Michele Miller, publisher and editor of *Western New York Family* magazine, who published my first of many travel articles. It was that first article, "Kid-Friendly Museums in western New York," that sparked the idea to write a travel guide to western New York. Other editors who helped and encouraged me along the way include Susan LoTempio, Gerald Goldberg, Rick Stanley, and Toni Ruberto from the *Buffalo News;* and Elizabeth Licata of *Buffalo Spree.* A special thanks to this book's project editor, Dale Evva Gelfand, for helping me make a good book even better.

The folks at local chambers of commerce and visitors bureaus as well as shopkeepers and owners of bed & breakfasts were invaluable. I would like to thank every single one of them by name, but space will not permit. Some people, however, went the "extra mile" when providing me with information, including Tom and Louise Yots of Park Place Bed & Breakfast in Niagara Falls, Elizabeth Davis of Niagara Tourism and Convention Corp., and Sue Macnaughton in Youngstown in Niagara County. In southern Ontario I'd like to thank Isabelle from the Parliament Cottage Bed & Breakfast in Niagara-on-the-Lake, Jane Davies and Jude Scott at the Fort Erie Museum, David Dimberio of Bridgeburg Antique Village in Fort Erie, Mia Russell in Crystal Beach, and Victor Ferraluolo, vice president of Niagara Falls Ontario Tourism. In Erie County I'd like to thank Nancy Vargo and Karen Kane at the Buffalo-Niagara Convention and Visitors Bureau, Jennifer Maynard and Diana Principe at the Mansion on Delaware, Julie Hallgren from North Park Florist, Anne Conable at the Buffalo and Erie County Historical Society, Mary Ann Anaka from the Akron Chamber of Commerce, Mary Holtz, Cheektowaga town clerk and historian, Jane Penvose from the Historical Society of the Tonawandas, and Daniel Kij, Lackawanna town historian. Kristen Saulsbury and August Jewison from the Orleans County Chamber of Commerce and Nancy Onesong from the Medina Stone Farm provided me with a lot of Orleans County information. I also must thank Tobi and Bruce Ahlquist, Lynn Nelson, Lin Baylis, Rebecca Brumagin, and Denise TeWinkle from Findley Lake, Cindy Ferraro from Chautauqua County Tourism, and Karen Kumpf at the Dunkirk Chamber of Commerce for information on Chautauqua County. In Cattaraugus County thanks goes out to Joelle Eddy at the Salamanca Chamber of Commerce; Jeremy, a tour guide at the Seneca Nation Museum; Sheila Lesniowski at Discover Ellicottville; and Kristen from Holiday Valley in Ellicottville. In Allegany County my thanks to Patience Reagan and Jesse Case from Allegany County Tourism, Patty Stalker, Fleurette Pelletier, and Pat Kaake from Angelica, Brien Learn from Cuba, and Bette Stockman, a researcher from Friendship. I also must thank Bonita Sheer, deputy county historian for Wyoming County; Becky Ryan from the Livonia Chamber of Commerce; and Cindy Smith from the Geneva Chamber of Commerce. Thanks also goes out to Margie Frungillo from the Hornell Chamber of Commerce. There are many, many more people I could thank who are not listed above. If you helped me in any way at all, I extend my sincere thanks.

INTRODUCTION

Y ou hold in your hands the first comprehensive book on the market to describe all there is to see and do in Western New York, from the grandeur of Niagara Falls to small out-of-the-way villages. Whatever your interest is, you can find it in western New York.

If history is your thing, there are hundreds of museums, both big and small, along with close to 30 designated National Historic Landmarks, including the site of a presidential inauguration. The area also has one of the oldest structures in the Great Lakes region, the French Castle at Old Fort Niagara.

Closely entwined with the region's history is its unique architecture, including Buffalo structures designed by three of the 19th century's most prominent architects, Frank Lloyd Wright, Louis Sullivan, and Henry Hobson Richardson. Buffalo and Rochester also have park systems designed by noted landscape architect Frederick Law Olmsted. Many of the small towns throughout the area have historic downtown business districts that have been virtually untouched since the early 1900s.

If you enjoy arts and culture, western New York offers a wide array of theaters, art galleries, and other cultural institutions. *American Style* magazine recently ranked the Buffalo-Niagara region fourth in the nation as an arts and cultural destination. This region also has the largest concentration of theaters in the state outside of New York City.

Western New York has a lot to offer in the way of outdoor recreational activities. With its abundance of lakes, rivers, and streams, it is a boaters'—as well as anglers'—paradise. In the spring, several of these rivers swell from the rain and melting snow to offers superb whitewater rafting. If you like getting close to nature, the area has numerous parks and nature centers, as well as campgrounds. You don't have to head south to enjoy good golfing since hundreds of top-rated courses are right in western New York. With the region's legendary winters, skiing is one of the most popular cold-weather activities. And just for the record, it's not always snowy and cold in Buffalo—there are four distinct seasons!

If you are inclined to more leisurely recreational activities, this book also describes over sixty wineries, which are prevalent in the Finger Lakes region, as well as in Niagara and Chautauqua Counties, and Southern Ontario. Other interesting places described include country stores, bed & breakfast inns, and of course, hundreds of restaurants, along with annual events and festivals.

This book was written with a wide audience in mind, including tourists and travelers to the area, who want to know what else there is to do once they've seen Niagara Falls and eaten chicken wings. Native western New Yorkers will also enjoy the book, as it describes many little-known, out-of-the-way places that they may wish to explore. Parents looking for places to take the kids on school breaks and summer vacations will appreciate the "kid-friendly" icons used throughout the book. If you are seeking a getaway without the kids, many romantic bed & breakfast inns and sophisticated restaurants are described. History buffs will enjoy the little-known historical facts presented in the introduction to each section, as well as the descriptions of the many museums located throughout the region. If you are a tour operator or plans trips for school, youth or senior citizen groups, you will find this book to be an invaluable resource.

While there are several general guides to New York State on the market that devote a chapter or two to western New York, Countryman Press's *Explorer's Guide to Western New York* is unique, as it is the first and only guidebook that focuses specifically on the western region of the state. While the other guidebooks are well-written and factual, the have only a limited amount of space to devote to this area, so they focus only on the well-known attractions. This book also describes these well-known attractions, but in addition, it takes you along the back roads to places not mentioned in any other travel guide; places like the unique antique shops in the tiny village of Angelica in Allegany county, the serenity of the Abbey of the Genesee in Livingston County and the scenic beauty of diminutive Findley Lake in Chautauqua County.

This book is set up so that each chapter covers one county in western New York, with the exception of Erie County, which is divided into three chapters: City of Buffalo, Northern Erie, and Southern Erie. The basic format of each chapter begins with an overview of that county—including a brief history and helpful contacts on where to go for guidance, travel directions, area newspapers, locations of hospitals, and where to park—as well as a brief history of the towns. (Note: If you wish to find out more about a certain town's history, the address and phone number of the local historical society is included under the museum sections.)

Each chapter is then broken down into sections that cover a specific town or group of towns. These sections describe things to see—such as museums and historic sites—and things to do—including boat excursions, golf courses, and family activities. Under Green Spaces, you will find parks, beaches, and nature centers. Each section also has descriptions of available lodging, restaurants, entertainment venues, and shops. I have personally visited or contacted each business listed and have included only those establishments that offer quality goods and services. Concluding each section are highlights of that county's annual events and festivals.

While I have tried to include as much information as possible about western New York, any travel guide has space limitations, so it would be impossible to include every town, attraction, restaurant, lodging, and store. I therefore picked places that have wide appeal and are generally welcoming to visitors. While some towns are wonderful places to live, they don't have much in the way of tourist attractions or other places of interest.

Writing this book took over a year, during which time I clocked more than 600 hours traveling around the region, adding 10,000 miles to my car's odometer, and sitting at my computer for 1,200 hours, typing and doing research. I also shot close to 100 rolls of film to come up with the photographs in this book. It was a lot of work, but the effort was more than matched by my enjoyment in discovering new places in the region in which I was born and raised.

Many thanks to the folks at Countryman Press (a division of W. W. Norton), including Kermit Hummel, for allowing me to write this guide for them. Readers comments, corrections, and suggestions are always welcome. Please contact Countryman Press by snail mail or e-mail, or use the postcard provided in this book.

Enjoy exploring western New York!

—Christine Smyczynski, Getzville, NY

WESTERN NEW YORK HISTORY: A BRIEF OVERVIEW

To fully appreciate western New York, you have to understand the rich history of the area, as the present and future are shaped by things of the past. According to archeologists, the first prehistoric inhabitants of western New York were believed to be Clovis people (10,000 B.C.) and Lamokas (2500 B.C.). Hopewellian "Mound Builders" then inhabited the region around 300 A.D. Later, the region was home to several tribes of Native Americans, who hunted, fished, and lived on the land for hundreds of years before European settlement. Historians suggest that in the 16th century, the Native American population in the region was larger than the population here today. The largest of these tribes, the Seneca, were known as the "Keepers of the Western Door." Their villages, located along rivers and lakes, were made up of bark longhouses.

The land was granted to the Massachusetts Bay Province by King Charles I in 1628, but Native Americans continued to live all over the region because pioneer settlement did not take place until much later. Massachusetts and New York both claimed the area that is now western New York, so in 1786 both states reached a compromise—subject to the tribes' agreement—that allowed both states to extend their boundaries westward. While New York had sovereignty over the land, Massachusetts would have the "preemptive" right to obtain title from the Indians. In 1788 Massachusetts sold about six million acres to a pair of land speculators, Oliver Phelps and Nathaniel Gorham, who purchased the tract for $1,000,000. After getting title to the land from the Native Americans, Phelps and Gorham ended up with a bit fewer than five million acres. They were only able to gain clear title to the portion east of the Genesee River.

However, Phelps and Gorham failed to extinguish Indian title and defaulted on payments in 1790; the preemptive right to the lands west of the Genesee River reverted back to Massachusetts. In 1790 the land east of the Genesee River was sold to Robert Morris of Philadelphia, a signer of the Declaration of the Independence and one of the richest men in America. Then in 1791 Morris purchased the land west of the Genesee River, nearly four million acres, from Massachusetts. Two years later Morris sold off 3.3 million acres to a group of Dutch investors, referred to as the Holland Land Company, but since this land was still occupied by the Seneca, land rights needed to be obtained. The Big Tree Treaty of 1797, which took place in what is now Geneseo in Livingston

County, allowed the Seneca Nation to retain 200,000 acres of the land, set aside for reservations. One of the most prominent Indian leaders involved in this negotiation was Red Jacket, who was a great orator.

Theophile Cazenove was hired as a general agent to oversee the land sale. In 1798 Joseph Ellicott, resident agent for the Holland Land Company, and his brother, Benjamin, along with 130 men, surveyed all the land in western New York, which was referred to as Ontario County. It is interesting to note that at the time, the United States did not have a standard unit of measurement. Joseph Ellicott—who was very concerned with accuracy—gathered several rulers and calculated the average length. After determining that 12 inches would equal one foot, he gave each surveyor a brass 12-inch ruler to ensure accurate results. Ellicott was one of the first people to use the 1-foot ruler that we use today. By the 1830s this standard of measure was put into law to prevent fraud. The first parcel of this land was sold in 1801 at $2 per acre to Asa Ransom, who built his house in what is now Clarence.

The Niagara Frontier—particularly northern Niagara County and southern Ontario in Canada—was an important battleground during the War of 1812. Old Fort Niagara in Youngstown, which played a role in that war, and in the earlier French and Indian War, has the oldest structure in the Great Lakes region. Once this war was over and the threat of British aggression removed, pioneer settlers began arriving in western New York.

As the area was settled, many factors influenced the region's growth, including the Erie Canal, which was completed in 1825. The canal opened up the western part of the state to settlement and allowed the movement of goods from the region to the Eastern Seaboard. The canal still serves the area as a recreational waterway.

By the mid- to late 1800s, the region prospered with growing industries, including agriculture, milling, cheese making, dairy farming, textiles, and salt mining. Around this time the railroad overtook the canal as the primary mode to transport goods as well as allowing people to travel more extensively throughout the region. Many European immigrants were attracted to western New York in the early 1900s, especially the Polish, Germans, Italians, and the Irish.

Many influential inventions were also developed in western New York, including fire hydrants (patented by noted Lockport inventor Birdsill Holly in 1863), the Brownie camera (invented in 1900 by George Eastman of Rochester, founder of Eastman Kodak, which brought photography to the common man), and air-conditioning (patented in Buffalo by Willis Haviland Carrier in 1902). Hammondsport aviation pioneer Glenn Curtiss was responsible for many early aeronautical developments.

Because of the close proximity to the power of Niagara Falls, the region was one of the first in the country to harness hydroelectric power to illuminate homes and businesses. The 1901 Pan-American Exposition, held in Buffalo, was a shining example of this power, and each evening the fair was illuminated, becoming "a city of light." Of course, the exposition had its dark side: the assassination of President William McKinley.

Because of the region's relative prosperity at the turn of the 20th century, especially in Buffalo and Rochester, wealthy residents were able to commission some of America's foremost architects—including Frank Lloyd Wright, Louis Sullivan, and H. H. Richardson—to design their homes and businesses. Many of these structures still stand today, giving us prime examples of late 19th- and early 20th-century architecture.

In the 20th century the steel industry as well as auto manufacturing played a big role in Buffalo's economy, while Rochester's economy focused on more white-collar industries, such as Eastman Kodak and Xerox. Agriculture still plays an important role in the more rural sections of the region with apple growing, maple syrup production, and daily farming some of the primary businesses. The region also has a growing tourism industry along with the presence of high-tech, banking, medical, educational, and industrial-related businesses. Many museums and cultural institutions in the region reflect its past. As you peruse through this book, be sure to read the introductions to each section, which contain many historical facts about highlighted towns and villages.

WHAT'S WHERE IN WESTERN NEW YORK

AREA CODE There are five area codes throughout the region. The area code in Erie, Niagara, Chautauqua, and Cattaraugus counties is 716. When calling southern Ontario, Canada, the area code is 905. For Orleans, Genesee, Wyoming, Allegany, Livingston, Ontario, and Monroe Counties, the area code is 585. The area code for Steuben County and eastern Allegany County is 607. The area code for both Yates County and eastern Ontario County is 315.

AFRICAN AMERICAN HISTORICAL AND CULTURAL SITES Western New York has many African American cultural sites that are significant both locally and nationally. The region played an important role in assisting escaping slaves on the Underground Railroad. The Niagara Movement, the forerunner of the NAACP, was founded in this region and they held their first conference in Niagara Falls Ontario in 1905. It was originally planned for Buffalo, but blacks had difficulty booking hotel rooms in Buffalo. Currently, the Michigan Avenue Preservation Corporation (716-282-1028) has several historic buildings which are under renovation, including the **Reverend J. Edward Nash House**, **Michigan Street Baptist Church,** and the **Colored Musicians Club**. Resources for information on African American Heritage include the North Jefferson Branch Library and Center for Local African American History, 332 E. Utica; the Langston Hughes Institute (716-881-3266) 25 High Street; the African American Cultural Center,(716-884-2013) 350 Masten Avenue; and the Africana Research Museum (716-891-4413), 699–701 Fillmore Avenue. The Buffalo–Niagara Convention and Visitors Bureau publishes an *African American Heritage Guide,* which highlights events and attractions that focus on the African American legacy.

AGRICULTURAL FAIRS During July and August each of the 13 counties covered in this book hosts an agricultural fair, the largest and most popular being the **Erie County Fair**, held in mid-August in Hamburg, just south of Buffalo. Check the Special Events listing at the end of each chapter for information on the other county fairs in the region.

AIRPORTS AND AIR SERVICE The two larger international airports in the region include the **Buffalo Niagara International Airport** (716-630-6000; www.buffaloairport.com) and the **Greater Rochester International Airport** (585-464-6020; www.rocairport.com), which are served by most major airlines. A few regional airports in western New York offer commuter and shuttle service. These include the **Chautauqua County Airport** (716-484-0204 or 800-428-4322) in Jamestown and the **Elmira-Corning Regional Airport** (607-739-5621), exit 51 off I-86 near Corning. There are also several other smaller airports, with landing strips for private planes, located throughout the region.

AMTRAK The train service has regularly scheduled stops at stations on Dick Road in **Depew** (716-683-8440), on Exchange Street in downtown **Buffalo** (716-856-2075), and in **Niagara Falls**. A stop is also made at the station at 320 Central Avenue in **Rochester** (585-454-2894). For detailed information, check out www.amtrak.com, or call 800-872-7245.

AMUSEMENT PARKS The region's largest amusement park, **Six Flags Darien Lake** (585-599-4641; www.sixflags.com/darienlake) in Genesee County has hundreds of rides and attractions, including a huge waterpark complex. Other parks in western New York include **Martin's Fantasy Island** (716-773-7591; www.martinsfantasyisland.com) on Grand Island, which is just the right size for families with young children; **Midway Park** (716-386-3165; www.midway-park.com) in Maple Springs in Chautauqua County, a classic, old-fashioned park that opened in 1898; **Seabreeze Amusement Park** (585-323-1900; www.seabreeze.com) lo-

cated along Lake Ontario's shores near Rochester; and **Marineland** (905-356 9565) in Niagara Falls, Ontario, which offers amusement rides along with live dolphin, seal, and whale shows.

ANTIQUES Hundreds of dealers are located throughout western New York, with large concentrations of shops in Clarence, Westfield, Lewiston, Canandaigua, Bloomfield, and Angelica, and on Elmwood Avenue and Hertel Avenue in Buffalo, A brochure produced by **Sunday Driver Directories** (716-353-4295; www.sundaydriver.com) offers a comprehensive list and driving map of dealers throughout western New York and the Finger Lakes Region.

APPLES New York State is the second largest apple-producing state—and is first in the number of varieties—and the Lake Ontario shore, particularly Niagara County, is one of the state's principal apple-growing regions. Locally grown apples and apple cider are available at farm markets and at u-pick farms throughout the region. For more information check out the **New York State Apple Association** Web site: www.nyapplecountry.com.

Courtesy Buffalo–Niagara Convention & Visitors Bureau and Murphy Orchards

AQUARIUMS The **Aquarium of Niagara**, (716-285-3575; www.aquariumofniagara.org) in Niagara Falls has over 1,500 types of aquatic animals including sharks, piranhas, moray eels, and even penguins. Across the border in Niagara Falls, Ontario, **Marineland** (905-356-2142; www.marinelandofcanada.com) is one of the largest aquariums in the world, featuring a huge variety of aquatic life.

ARCHITECTURE The works of many well-known architects can be found in western New York, including designs in the city of Buffalo by three leading 19th-century architects, Frank Lloyd Wright, H. H. Richardson, and Louis Sullivan. In Rochester the George Eastman house was designed by J. Foster Warner, while the Boynton House was designed by Frank Lloyd Wright. The Wings of Progress and Mercury are also interesting architectural elements in Rochester. Many of the small towns and villages that dot western New York have historic preservation districts with unique architecture to be found.

ART ASSOCIATIONS AND COUNCILS **Arts Council** (716-856-7520; www.artsbuffalo.com), 700 Main Street, Buffalo. This organization is the primary advocate for promoting arts and culture in Buffalo and Erie County. They offers support to local artists and art organizations, as well as grants and funding to art programs and projects. **Niagara Arts and Cultural Center** (716-282-7530; www.naccarts.net or www.thenacc.org) in Niagara Falls is home to over 70 visual and performing artists' studios. The **GO ART! Cultural Facility** (585-343-9313 or 800-774-7372; www.goart.org) in Batavia is headquarters for arts and culture in Genesee and Orleans Counties. **The Arts Council for Wyoming County** (585-237-3517; www.artswyco.org) organization promotes artistic and cultural events and programs throughout Wyoming County, including gallery exhibits, folk-art programs, and the popular Letchworth Arts and Craft show on Columbus Day Weekend. **The Arts Council for Chautauqua County** (716-664-2465) a county-wide organization was formed in 1979 to service art organizations and artists. They support art in education, organize community events, and assist cultural organization. Also in Chautauqua, the **Chautauqua Institution** (716-357-6200; www.ciweb.org) is a well-known center for performing and visual arts, education, religion, and recreation. The **Genesee Valley Council on the Arts** (585-243-6785; www.gvcaonline.org) is dedicated to supporting and promoting arts and culture in Livingston County. The **Rochester Contemporary** (585-461-2222; www.rochestercontemporary.org) has been promoting contemporary art in upstate New York for over twenty-five years. A large artist community in Allegany County belongs to the **Allegany Artisans** (800-521-0885; www.alleganyartisans.com).

ARTISTS AND GALLERIES The largest art center in Buffalo is **Hallwalls Contemporary Arts Center**, (716-835-7362; www.hallwalls.org). This arts center focuses on visual, performing, media, and literary arts. At least a dozen smaller galleries can also be found in Buffalo, many located in and around the Allentown and Elmwood Village areas. Lockport's **Kenan Center**, (716-433-2617; www.kenancenter.org)

is an arts, education, and recreation center. The **Market Street Art Center** (716-478-0083; www.market streetstudios.com or www.msgallery lockport.com), located in a historic building on the banks of the Erie Canal in Lockport, features several art galleries showcasing the work of Niagara County artists, along with 20 working artists' studios. Many other smaller galleries are located in both urban and rural areas throughout the region. When in Rochester, be sure to visit **Craft Company No. 6** and the **Oxford Gallery.**

ART MUSEUMS The larger museums in the region include the **Albright-Knox Art Gallery** (716-882-8700; www.albrightknox.org) on Elmwood Avenue in Buffalo. The gallery, which opened in 1905, is one of the nation's oldest public art organizations. Across the street, the **Burchfield-Penney Art Center** (716-878-6011; www .burchfield-penney.org) showcases the talents of western New York artists. The **Castellani Art Museum** (716-286-8200; www.niagara.edu/~cam), located on the campus of Niagara University, has works by Picasso and Dali, along with artwork depicting Niagara Falls. The 400-acre **Griffis Sculpture Park**, (716-257-9344 or 716-667-2808; www.griffispark.org) in East Otto contains over 200 sculptures created by local and national artists, displayed among ponds, forests, and meadows. The **Rockwell Museum** (607-937-5386; www.rockwell museum.org), located in Corning's restored 1893 city hall, houses the most comprehensive collection of Western art in the U.S. **Memorial Art Gallery** (585-473-7720; www .rochester.edu/mag), housed on the campus of the University of Rochester,

features 5,000 years of art, including works by some of the great masters.

AUTOMOBILE RACING Numerous racecar tracks throughout the region feature NASCAR, stock car, and other types of auto races. Some of these tracks include **Lancaster Speedway** (716-629-8531; www.lancasterracing .com); **Holland International Speedway** (716-537-2272; www .hollandspeedway.com); **Ransomville Speedway** (716-791-3602; www .ransomvillespeedway.com); **Wyoming County International Speedway** (585-237-2510, 585-237-2580; www.wyomingcountyinternational speedway.com) in Perry; and **Limerock Speedway** (585-538-2597) in Caledonia.

AVIATION MUSEUMS For a time the center of aviation in the United States was Buffalo, New York, where the world's largest aircraft plant was built in 1917. Several museums in western New York highlight aviation history. The **Niagara Aerospace Museum** (716-278-0060; www.niagaramuseum .org) in Niagara Falls features vintage aircraft and memorabilia as well as an overview of aviation history. The **Glenn Curtiss Museum** (607-569-2160; www.linkny.com/curtiss museum) in Hammondsport chronicles the contributions of aviation pioneer Glenn Curtiss, who was issued the first pilot's license in the U.S. The museum houses a collection of early aircraft, motorcycles, bicycles, and more. In Elmira, the **Wings of Eagles Discovery Center** (607-739-8200; www.wingsofeagels.com) has a display of vintage aircraft from World War II to Desert Storm, while the nearby **National Soaring Museum** (607-734-3128; www.soaringmuseum

.org) is home to the largest collection of gliders and sailplanes in the world.

BEACHES With two Great Lakes, abundant rivers, and numerous other large and small lakes throughout the region, you could go to a different beach every day of the summer and still not visit all the beaches in western New York. Some of the more popular ones include: **Ontario Beach Park** in Rochester, considered by many to be the best sand beach on the Great Lakes; **Beaver Island State Park** on the Niagara River; **Woodlawn Beach; Wendt Beach, Bennett Beach, Evangola, Sunset Bay;** and **Angola on the Lake** on Lake Erie; **Wilson Tuscarora** and **Olcott Beach** on Lake Ontario in Niagara County; and **Bay Beach, Crystal Beach, Crescent Beach, Thunder Bay,** and **Wavery Beach** in southern Ontario. Many other smaller beaches are located on lakes throughout the Finger Lakes Region.

BED & BREAKFASTS Hundreds of bed & breakfast inns can be found in

Christine A. Smyczynski

western New York, from fisherman's cottages to elegant and romantic resort spas. They range in price from less than $50 to over $300 nightly. These inns generally offer more individual attention than you would get by staying in a large hotel or chain motel. The innkeepers are knowledgeable about local attractions, shops, and restaurants and can advise you on the best spots to seek out. The following Web sites have links to many of the area's bed & breakfast inns: **Western New York Bed & Breakfast Association** (www.bbwny.com) and **Empire State Bed & Breakfast Association** (www.esbba.com). Many inns cater to couples or families with older children, so if you are traveling with very young children, be sure to call ahead to see if they will be able to accommodate you.

BICYCLING The **Greater Buffalo Niagara Regional Transportation Council** (GBNRTC) puts out a bicycle map of the Buffalo Niagara region. For additional information, contact GBNRTC, 438 Main Street, Suite 503, Buffalo, NY 14202; www.gbnrtc.org. Walking, hiking, and biking trails are listed under the *Green Space* heading of each section.

BOATING With its abundance of lakes, rivers, and streams, western New York is a boater's paradise. Public marinas are listed under *Green Space* in each section. For more information about boating in the state, check out the NYS Parks boating Web site: www.nysparks.com/boat

BOAT TOURS AND EXCURSIONS There are numerous scenic boat excursions to choose from across western New York including the

Courtesy Buffalo Niagara Convention & Visitors Bureau

Miss Buffalo/ Niagara Clipper in the City of Buffalo, the **Grand Lady** in Grand Island, the **Maid of the Mist** in Niagara Falls (U.S. and Canada), **Lockport Locks & Canal Cruises** in Lockport, the **Chautauqua Belle** in Mayville, the **Sam Patch** in Pitts-ford, the **Harbor Town Belle** and the **Keuka Maid** in and the Mary Jemison in Rochester, and the **Canandaigua Lady** and **Captain Grays Tours** on Canandaigua Lake.

BOOKS—FICTIONAL BOOKS SET IN WESTERN NEW YORK *Buffalo Winged* by Patricia Reilly. This romantic novel is set in the city of Buffalo.

City of Light by Lauren Belfer. This bestseller is a fictionalized account of events during the 1901 Pan-American Exposition in Buffalo.

The Falls by Joyce Carol Oates. This mystery novel, written by the noted author and western New York native, is set in Niagara Falls and revolves around a love story gone wrong.

First Desire by Nancy Reisman. This novel is set on Buffalo's Lancaster Avenue in the 1930s–1950s.

The Ghost and Me, Joey by Iris Drzewiecki. A ghost story for children about Lancaster's Hull House.

Journey to Nowhere, Frozen Summer, The Road to Home by Mary Jane Auch. These three novels, geared to children age 9–12, follow pioneer teenager Mem and her family as they travel from Connecticut to a new life in central New York.

Lake Effect by Ronald W. Adams. A murder mystery set in Buffalo and the Southtowns.

Too Close to the Falls by Catherine Gildiner. This New York Times bestseller is a coming-of-age memoir about growing up in the small town of Lewiston, near Niagara Falls, in the 1950s.

BOOKS—REGIONAL GUIDEBOOKS AND OTHER NONFICTION BOOKS ABOUT WESTERN NEW YORK AND VICINITY. Books marked with the # symbol can be purchased from Western New York Wares (www .buffalobooks.com), which specializes in regional books. Many of these books can also be found in local bookstores and museum shops.

Buffalo and Environs

Beautiful Buffalo: Preserving a City by Linda Levine and Maria Scrivani.

#Beyond Buffalo: A Photographic Journey and Guide to the Secret Natural Wonders of our Region by David Reade.

Big Russ and Me: Father and Son Lessons of Life by Tim Russert. Written by one of Buffalo's famous sons, Tim Russert, moderator of *Meet the Press*. It's a tribute to Russert's father, who still lives in South Buffalo., and explains how Russert grew up to become a well-known newscaster.

Buffalo's Best by Francis Basil. This book highlights some of Buffalo's best attractions and restaurants.

#*Buffalo's Brush with the Arts: from Huck Finn to Murphy Brown* by Joe Marren This book explores creative people and their connections to western New York.

#*Buffalo City Hall: Americanesque Masterpiece* by John Conlin.

Buffalo Good Neighbors, Great Architecture by Nancy Blumenstalk Mingus.

Buffalo Memories by George Kunz. One hundred fifty nostalgic tales about Buffalo's past accompanied by historic photos.

#*Buffalo Treasures: A Downtown Walking Guide* by Jan Sheridan with illustrations by Kenneth Sheridan. This book describes 25 major downtown buildings.

#*Buffalo's Waterfront: A Guidebook* by Tim Tielman.

#*Church Tales of the Niagara Frontier Legends, History & Architecture* by Austin Fox and illustrated by Lawrence McIntyre. History and folklore of sixty area churches.

#*Classic Buffalo-A Heritage of Distinguished Architecture* by Richard O. Reisem, photos by Andy Olenick. Beautiful photographs illustrated this book filled with historic information.

#*Daring Niagara: 50 Death-Defying Stunts at the Falls* by Paul Gromosiak.

Dispatches from the Muckdog Gazette by Bill Kaufman is about life in the small town of Batavia; it also profiles some notable Batavia natives.

#*The Erie Canal: The Ditch that Opened a Nation* by Dan Murphy historical information on the Erie Canal.

#*Erie Canal Legacy: Architectural Treasures of the Empire State* by Richard Reisem and photos by Andy Olenick.

#*Exploring Niagara: The Complete Guide to Niagara Falls and Vicinity* by Hans and Allyson Tammemagi.

Forest Lawn Cemetery—Buffalo History Preserved by Richard O. Reisem.

#*Frank Lloyd Wright's Darwin Martin House: Rescue of a Landmark* by Marjorie L. Quinlan details the rescue of the region's most architecturally significant home.

#*A Ghosthunter's Journal: Tales of the Supernatural and the Strange in Upstate New York* by Mason Winfield.

#*Great Lake Effects: Buffalo Beyond Winter and Wings* is a unique cookbook compiled by the Junior League of Buffalo.

#*John Larkin: A Business Pioneer* by Dan Larkin is a biography of a local business innovator.

The Mighty Niagara: One River, Two Frontiers by Greg Stein takes a look at the binational nature of the Niagara Region.

#*National Landmarks of Western New York: Famous People and Historic Places* by Jan Booth Sheridan is a guide to 30 National Historic Landmarks and Sites in western New York; and the Finger Lakes Region.

#*Nature's Niagara: A Walk on the Wild Side* by Paul Gromosiak highlights plants, animals, and geological formations at Niagara Falls.

#*Niagara Falls Q&A: Answers to the 100 Most Common Questions about Niagara Falls* by Paul Gromosiak.

#*The Rainbow City: Celebrating Light, Color and Architecture at the*

Pan American Exposition, Buffalo 1901 by Kerry S. Grant.

Second Looks and Glancing Back: A Pictorial History of Amherst, New York by Dr. Joseph Grand; www .marketstreetstudios.com.

Secret Places, Scenic Treasures of Western New York and Southern Ontario by Bruce Kershner is a guide to little-known treasures

#Shadows of the Western Door: Haunted Sites and Ancient Mysteries of Upstate New York by Mason Winfield.

#Spirits of the Great Hill: More Haunted Sites and Ancient Mysteries of Upstate New York by Mason Winfield.

#Symbol & Show: The Pan-American Exposition of 1901 by Austin Fox, with illustrations by Lawrence McIntyre.

#Victorian Buffalo: Images From the Buffalo and Erie County Public Library by Cynthia VanNess features images of 19th-century Buffalo.

#Water Over the Falls: 101 of the Most Memorable Events at Niagara Falls by Paul Gromosiak.

#Western New York Weather Guide by Tom Jolls.

#White Death: Blizzard of '77 by Erno Rossi chronicles the blizzard that hit Buffalo in 1977.

#Zany Niagara: The Funny Things People Say About Niagara Falls by Paul Gromosiak.

Finger Lakes Region

Persons, Places, and Things in the Finger Lakes Region by Emerson Klees.

Birding in Central and Western New York by Norman E. Wolfe.

200 Waterfalls in Central and Western New York by Rich and Sue Freeman.

Take a Hike! Family Walks in the Finger Lakes and Genesee Valley Region by Rich and Sue Freeman.

Take a Hike! Family Walks in the Rochester Area by Rich and Sue Freeman.

Take Your Bike: Family Rides in the Finger Lakes & Genesee Valley Region by Rich and Sue Freeman.

Take Your Bike: Family Rides in the Rochester Area by Rich and Sue Freeman.

Snow Trails: Cross-Country Ski and Snowshoe in Central and Western New York by Rich and Sue Freeman.

Legends and Stories of the Finger Lakes Region by Emerson Klees.

More Legends and Stories of the Finger Lakes Region by Emerson Klees.

200 Years of Rochester Architecture and Gardens by Richard O. Reisem, photos by Andy Olenick.

Mount Hope: America's First Municipal Victorian Cemetery by Richard O. Reisem.

Buried Treasures in Mount Hope Cemetery by Richard O. Reisem.

Rochester's Corn Hill: The Historic Third Ward by Michael Leavy chronicles Rochester's "Ruffled Shirt District" from its aristocratic beginnings to its current example of historic preservation.

Rochester Routes: Tours of Monroe County's Historic Places by Patricia Braus offers an overview of the historic architecture in Monroe County.

Also available on cassette and CD to listen to in your car.

Best Book of Rochester History by Blake McKelvey and Ruth Rosenberg Naparsteck, city historians for Rochester, brings to life Rochester's colorful past.

BUS SERVICE New York Trailways Bus Service operates throughout New York State (800-295-5555). **Greyhound** (800-231-2222; www .greyhound.com) also operates throughout the state. The **Niagara Frontier Transportation Authority (NFTA)** (716-855-7211; www.nfta), 181 Ellicott Street, Buffalo, operates buses in Buffalo, Niagara Falls, Lockport and their outlying suburbs. **Rochester-Genesee Regional Transportation Authority** (585-288-1700 or 800-288-3777; www.rgrta.org) has routes throughout Rochester, Monroe County, and surrounding counties. Livingston County also has limited bus service, **Livingston Area Transportation Service** (585-335-3344). The **Chautauqua County Regional Transit** (800-556-8553) serves Chautauqua County.

CAMPING Private, public, and state-run campsites abound in western New York. See *Other Lodging* in each chapter. For more information on camping in New York State parks, call 800-456-CAMP, or visit www.reserve america.com.

CANADIAN CUSTOMS For information on entering Canada, see the introduction to the "Southern Ontario" chapter.

CASINO GAMBLING While high-stakes casino gambling is not permitted in New York State per se, it is legal on Indian Reservations. The **Seneca Niagara Casino** in Niagara Falls is built on land purchased by the Seneca Nation of Indians. They also operate the **Seneca Allegany Casino** in Salamanca. High-stakes bingo can be found the Cattaraugus Indian Reservation in Irving. Across the border in Niagara Falls, Ontario, **Casino Niagara** and the new **Niagara Fallsview Casino Resort** draw patrons from both sides of the border. In Canada you must be at least 19 years old to enter a casino; in New York State, you must be 21.

CEMETERIES Cemeteries are not something usually listed in travel guides, but several notable resting places in Western New York are worth a trip—either for their artistic Victorian statuary or to visit the graves of notable Americans. Two of these sites include **Forest Lawn** in Buffalo and **Mount Hope** in Rochester.

Christine A. Smyczynski

CHICKEN WINGS Better known as "Buffalo wings," these are a must-taste item when visiting the region. No other culinary creation has put Buffalo on the map like the chicken wing. The once lowly wing, which was relegated to the stockpot in the past, has become wildly popular not only in Buffalo but throughout the United States, Canada, and many other countries.

This phenomenon started on a Friday night back in 1964 at Frank and Theresa Bellissimo's Anchor Bar in Buffalo. Their son, Dom, arrived with a bunch of hungry friends and he asked his mom to fix them something to eat. Theresa spotted a plate of chicken wings in the kitchen that were about to go into the soup pot. Thinking they looked too nice to be put into soup, she deep fried them, poured on some hot sauce, and, well, the rest is history. Chicken wings can be found on most menus throughout western New York. Some of the best known wing places include the **Anchor Bar** where Buffalo wings made their debut; **La Nova Pizzeria,** which is equally well-known for its pizza as it is for wings; and **Duffs**, a popular wing spot in the suburbs.

CHILDRENS' MUSEUMS There are several excellent children's museums in the region. The most well-known is the **Strong Museum** in Rochester. In the Buffalo area children can learn while they play at **Explore & More** in East Aurora.

COBBLESTONE CONSTRUCTION As you travel around in western New York, you may notice buildings constructed of cobblestones. This type of masonry, unique to the region, was

Christine A. Smyczynski

developed by rural masons shortly after constructing the Erie Canal. The majority of these structures can be found in counties that the canal flows through, including Niagara, Orleans, Monroe, and northern Ontario County. To learn more about cobblestone construction, visit the **Cobblestone Museum Complex** in Childs, just north of Albion in Orleans County.

COTTAGE RENTALS An alternative to staying in a hotel or other accommodation is to rent a cottage. This is especially popular if you are traveling with a large family. Rentals are numerous along Lake Chautauqua and in the Finger Lakes region. You'll find listings for rental properties under Other Lodging. A good website to find out about cottage rentals is Vacation Rentals by Owner, www.vrbo.com.

DINERS Several traditional, old-fashioned diners are located in Western New York. For a listing of diners in the state, check out www.geocities.com/cornwallace55/ buff.html. Some of the diners listed in this book include **Main Diner** in Westfield, **Highland Park Diner** in Rochester, **50's Diner** in Depew, the **Lake Effect Diner** in Buffalo, and the **Penn Yan Diner** in Penn Yan.

DOORS OPEN NIAGARA There are many architectural treasures on both sides of the Niagara River, yet the average person often does not have the opportunity to learn about the building's history or appreciate the significance of the structure. **Doors Open Niagara** (888-333-1987; www.doorsopenniagara.com) an annual binational, two-day heritage-tourism event held in mid-October offers locals as well as visitors a chance to peek inside many of the historic and architectural gems in western New York and southern Ontario that are normally closed to the public. Close to 100 buildings are open, including art galleries, mansions, churches, schools, Underground Railroad sites, lighthouses, inns, and private homes. Volunteers give tours and answer questions at each site. Admission is free.

EMERGENCIES Dial 911 from anywhere in western New York for emergencies.

EMPIRE PASSPORT This annual all-season park pass, which can be purchased from the New York State Parks for around $50, allows the purchaser access to 152 state parks, 50 forest preserves, and numerous boat launch sites. For New York State residents over 62, the Golden Park Program allows free access to state parks and fee reductions to state historic sites and state operated swim-

ming, golf, tennis, and boat rentals. For information, call 518-474-0456.

ERIE CANAL The Erie Canal, the most well-known canal in America, is a 350-mile waterway that threads its way through New York State from Buffalo to Albany. When it opened in 1825, it was considered the greatest engineering marvel of the world. It was originally 40 feet wide, four feet deep, and 363 miles long. It had 83 locks and 18 aqueducts over rivers. This new shipping route allowed goods to be moved quickly and inexpensively from the Great Lakes region to the Atlantic Ocean. It also allowed the westward movement of settlers. Over the years the canal has been widened, re-routed, and shortened. Today the waterway has 35 locks and four aqueducts remaining.

It is now part of the 524-mile New York State Canal System, which also includes the Cayuga Seneca Canal, Oswego Canal, Champlain Canal, and Hudson River. While transportation was the main application of the canal when it first opened, today's focus is on recreational boating, fishing, and tourism. Towns located along the canal, including Lockport, Medina, Brockport, Pittsford, and Fairport,

Christine A. Smyczynski

feature quaint shops, restaurants, and canalside parks and walking trails.

To learn more about the Erie Canal, request the brochure "The Best 100 Miles of the Erie Canal," published by the New York State Canal System (800-4CANAL4; www .canals.state.ny.us) Another good source of information about the canal is *Erie Canal Legacy: Architectural Treasures of the Empire State* by Richard Reisem, with photos by Andy Olenick, published by the Landmark Society of Western New York (www .eriecanallegacy.com). For information on the history of the canal, check out this Web site: www.eriecanal.org.

ESPECIALLY FOR CHILDREN
Attractions and dining establishments with special kid appeal are highlighted with the crayon symbol ✎.

EVENTS/FESTIVALS Special events and contact information are listed in each chapter.

FALL FOLIAGE Autumn in Western New York is an especially beautiful time, particularly in the southern part of the region, with its mountain peaks and valleys. Some of the more popular spots to view fall foliage are Letchworth State Park on the border of Wyoming and Livingston Counties, the Zoar Valley outside Gowanda, and Ellicottville in central Cattaraugus County.

FARMERS MARKETS New York State rates in the top five producers of many crops, including apples, cabbage, and pumpkins. Twenty-five percent of the state is designated farmland. There are literally hundreds of farms and farm markets in the western New York area, so just a fraction

of them can be highlighted in this book. For a complete guide to the farm markets in the Western Region, which includes Buffalo–Niagara and the western Finger Lakes, contact the New York State Department of Agriculture and Markets and request their publication *New York State Farm Fresh Guide* (800-554-4501; www.agmkt.state.ny.us).

FISH FRY If you're not originally from Western New York or are a visitor to the area, you'll probably wonder why so many restaurants are noted for their Friday-night fish fries. This tradition harkens back to the days when the largely Catholic population of western New York was required to abstain from eating meat on Fridays. Since the Second Vatican Council in 1962, abstinence needed only to be observed on Fridays during Lent and on Ash Wednesday and Good Friday, yet the tradition continues. Local bars and restaurants serve up over 100,000 pounds of fish, mainly haddock, each week. While other cities around the country serve fried fish, you can't beat a beer-battered western New York fish fry.

Christine A. Smyczynski

FISHING With its abundance of lakes, rivers, and streams, western New York is an angler's paradise, with catches including small- and large-mouth bass, walleye, trout, salmon, muskellunge, and pike. For updates on the fishing season and current conditions, call the fishing hotline at 716-844-1111, ext. 4142, or visit www .northeastoutdoors.com. New York State fishing licenses can be obtained at most county clerk's offices as well as at local sporting goods establishments. A state fishing license application can be downloaded from www .dec.state.ny.us/website/dfwmr/hunt fish.html.

FORTS History buffs will want to check out the historic forts located in the region. **Old Fort Niagara**, in Youngstown boasts the "French Castle," the oldest structure in the Great Lakes region. Across the Niagara River, **Fort George** and **Fort Mississauga** played important roles in the war of 1812. **Fort Erie** also features War of 1812 memorabilia.

GARDENS Horticulturists will enjoy the beautiful botanical gardens located throughout western New York, including the **Buffalo and Erie County Botanical Gardens** in Buffalo, **Sonnenberg Gardens** in Canandaigua, and the **Niagara Parks Botanical Gardens** in Niagara Falls, Ontario.

GREEN SPACES Beaches, nature preserves, parks, and waterfalls can be found in these sections.

GOLF Golf courses are listed under *To Do* sections. Some of the finest courses in the Northeast can be found in

Courtesy Buffalo–Niagara Convention & Visitors Bureau

western New York, and close to 150 golf courses are listed in this book. For further information on golf in the area, check out www.buff-golf.com or call the **Buffalo Region Annual Golf Guide** (315-622-9715).

GORGES Several large gorges are located in western New York, including the **Niagara Gorge**, which was formed by Niagara Falls; the **Genesee River Gorge**, which runs through Letchworth State Park; the **High Falls Gorge**, between the City of Rochester and Lake Ontario; and **Zoar Valley** in Cattaraugus County. White-water rafting is popular in Letchworth State Park and Zoar

Courtesy Buffalo–Niagara Convention & Visitors Bureau and Angel Art Ltd.

Courtesy Buffalo–Niagara Convention & Visitors Bureau and Erie County Botanical Gardens

Valley. The **Whirlpool Jet Boat Tours**, (888-438-4444; www .whirlpooljet.com) in Lewiston, take guests on a jet boat ride to the whirlpool through the world-famous Lower Niagara rapids in the Niagara Gorge.

HANDICAPPED ACCESSIBLE Look for the handicapped icon ♿ in the margin that identifies establishments that are accessible. While most new buildings are accessible, some of the older, historic sites described in this book may not be accessible or have only partial access.

HIKING AND BIKING TRAILS Numerous trails located are through Western New York. *Biking & Hiking in the Central Destinations of the Finger Lakes Region*, a brochure that includes suggested hikes and maps, can be obtained from by calling 800-228-2760 or from the Web site www .finger-lakes.com.

HISTORIC HOMES, MUSEUMS, AND HISTORIC SITES Almost every city, town and village in western New York has a historical society and historic homes, along with unique museums.

Some of the "must sees" for history buffs include: **Buffalo and Erie County Historical Society, Darwin Martin House, Theodore Roosevelt Inaugural Site,** and **Buffalo and Erie County Naval and Military Park** in Buffalo; **Graycliff** in Derby; and **Pedaling History Bicycle Museum** in Orchard Park; The **Niagara Historical Society** in Niagara-on-the-Lake, **Holland Land Office** in

Christine A. Smyczynski

Batavia, the **Cobblestone Museum Complex** in Childs, **Lucy-Desi Museum** in Jamestown, **Seneca-Iroquois Museum** in Salamanca; the **Strong Museum**, **George Eastman House**, and **Susan B. Anthony House** in Rochester; **Corning Museum of Glass** in Corning, and the **Glenn Curtiss Museum** in Hammondsport.

HORSE RACING Fans of horse racing will want to visit **Fairgrounds Gaming and Racing** in Hamburg, **Batavia Downs Racetrack** in Batavia, **Fort Erie Racing and Slots** in Fort Erie (Canada), and **Finger Lakes Racing and Gaming** in Farmington in the Finger Lakes Region.

HUNTING For questions on New York's hunting seasons and regulations, contact the DEC (800-933-2257; www.dec.state.ny.us) Licenses can be purchased over the counter at certain sporting goods stores, some major discount stores, and at town clerk's offices. Licenses can also be purchased by phone (866-933-2257) or by mail: WorldCom, P.O. Box 36985, Phoenix, AZ 85067-6985. A mail-order application form is available at www.dec.state.ny.us. When applying for a license by mail, you must include proof of residency and eligibility. Hunters younger than 16 must apply for a license in person and be accompanied by a parent or legal guardian.

INFORMATION Each county has its own visitors bureau; however, you can get regional information at the following information centers: **Buffalo Niagara Convention and Visitors Bureau** (800-BUFFALO), 617 Main

Street, Buffalo; **Chautauqua County Tourism** (800-242-4569; www .tourchautauqua.com) at the Main Gate of the **Chautauqua Institution;** and at the **Rochester Convention and Visitors Bureau** (800-677-7282; www.visitrochester.com), 45 East Avenue, Rochester. Refer to the heading marked Guidance near the beginning of each section for where-to-go for information.

LAKES Major lakes in the region include **Erie, Ontario, Chautauqua, Canandaigua, Keuka,** and **Seneca.** There are also many smaller lakes, which are described under Ponds and Lakes in the Green Space sections.

LAKE-EFFECT SNOW If you are visiting Western New York during the winter, you'll probably hear the words "lake-effect snow" uttered during a weather forecast on more than one occasion. This weather phenomenon, common in the Great Lakes Region from November through January, occurs when Lake Erie is not frozen. Cold arctic air moves over the relatively warm lake water and picks up moisture as it crosses Erie. This moisture is deposited as heavy snow on the downwind shores of the lake. This type of snowfall often comes down in narrow bands, resulting in heavy snowfall in one area and clear skies a few miles away. Most communities in western New York have the snow-fighting equipment to keep up with this heavy snowfall, but lake-effect snow is often responsible for hazardous driving conditions and school closings.

LIGHTHOUSES Several historic lighthouses dot the region, both public and privately owned. Along Lake Erie's shores you will find the privately owned **Barcelona** lighthouse along with the **Dunkirk** lighthouse. The **Buffalo Light** can be found at the Buffalo Harbor, while the **Fort Niagara Light** is on the grounds of Old Fort Niagara. Along Lake Ontario you'll find the **Thirty Mile Point Lighthouse** at Golden Hill State Park. The **Charlotte-Genesee Lighthouse** is along the Genesee River in the Port of Rochester. There are also several smaller lighthouses on Lake Chautauqua.

LOCAL CUISINE Besides the previously mentioned chicken wings, other western New York culinary favorites include beef on weck: thinly sliced beef served on a salty kimmelweck roll. When craving a hot dog, Buffalonians prefer Sahlens or Wardynski's, preferably topped with Webers Horseradish mustard, while folks in Rochester and the Finger Lakes region favor Zweigles "hots." Buffalo natives who now live in other parts of the country have been known to take home a care package from Buffalo after coming home to visit friends and relatives. Those coolers you see them toting on the plane are filled with Sahlens hot dogs and Webers mustard!

When visiting the Finger Lakes region, be sure to try salt potatoes: baby potatoes cooked in salt water and served with melted butter. "Garbage plates" piled high with hot dogs or hamburgers and assorted sides and topped with a meaty hot sauce are also popular here.

Another popular chicken in western New York is Chiavetta's chicken, which can be found at events and fund raisers throughout the summer.

Their famous BBQ marinade and salad dressings can be purchased at local supermarkets.

LODGING There are many choices listed under lodging, from cottages, to bed & breakfast inns to four-star resort hotels. Many of the bed & breakfast establishments have age restrictions for children, and most lodgings, except those noted with the 🐾 icon the margin, do not accept pets. Prices quoted don't include tax.

MAPLE SUGARING New York State is the third-largest maple producer in the world. About 17 percent of all syrup made in America—about 210,000 gallons—is produced in New York. Just over 10 years ago a group of Wyoming County maple producers decided to open their facilities to showcase the making of maple products. The event, referred to as **Maple Weekend** (Western New York Maple Producers, 585-535-7136;

Christine A. Smyczynski

www.mapleweekend.com) demonstrates the maple-sugaring process, from tapping the trees and collecting the sap to boiling it into syrup. Over three dozens producers across western New York participate in the event. Some also offer a variety of other activities that weekend, from pancake breakfasts to children's activities. Keep in mind that this event takes place on working farms, so dress according to the weather, and wear boots or old shoes since conditions are often muddy and visitors may have to walk a distance from their cars to the sugar shacks. For a listing of all the maple producers in the state, contact State of New York Department of Agriculture and Markets (518-474-2121), 1 Winners Circle, Albany, NY 12235.

MAPS The *MapWorks* digital atlas to Buffalo and Rochester has some of the best street maps available. They are well worth the approximately $20 investment. Maps can also be obtained for free or for a nominal charge from each county's tourism office.

NATIONAL HISTORIC LANDMARKS These sites are places where significant historical events occurred, where prominent Americans lived or worked, that represent important ideals of our past, or are outstanding architectural design. About 2,500 National Historic Landmarks can be found across the United States, and over two dozen are in the area covered by this book. National Historic Landmarks featured in this guide are marked with the ✪ symbol. For more information on National Historic Landmarks, check out www.cr.nps.gov.

NATIONAL REGISTER OF HISTORIC PLACES These are buildings and places that are considered cultural resources worthy of preservation. There are more than 75,000 nationwide, with numerous listings in Western New York.

NATIVE AMERICAN CULTURE A book about western New York would not be complete without mentioning Native American heritage and culture. All of New York State was once occupied by the Iroquois Nation. One of the five original Iroquois Nations, the Seneca Nation—known as the Keepers of the Western Door—lived in the western portion of the state.

There are eight clans among the Seneca: bear, beaver, turtle, wolf, deer, hawk, heron, and snipe. Animals and nature play an important role in Native American culture. The society is matrilineal, meaning that clan status is determined by a person's mother, and women play an important role in society.

After the Holland Land Purchase and the arrival of European settlers, life changed dramatically for the Seneca. Treaties had to be negotiated to protect Seneca lands. The Big Tree Treaty in 1797 established several reservations for the Native Americans. Today four Seneca reservation and one Tuscarora reservations are located in the western part of the state. Three Seneca reservations are the Tonawanda Reservation near Akron, the Cattaraugus Reservation near Gowanda, and the Allegany Reservation in Salamanca, the only city in the world located entirely on an Indian Reservation. The fourth is the Oil Springs Reservation near Cuba in Allegany County, a 1-mile-square area surrounding a natural oil spring that has a large amount of medicinal herbs growing nearby. The Tuscarora Reservation is located near Lewiston in Niagara County.

The Senecas on the Cattaraugus and Allegany Reservations established an elective form of government in 1848, while the people who live on the Tonawanda Reservation follow a more traditional chief system.

Today the Seneca Nation is best known for the casinos and gaming facilities that they operate in Irving, Salamanca, and Niagara Falls.

To learn more about the area's Native American culture, be sure to visit the Seneca-Iroquois National Museum in Salamanca. You can also learn about Seneca culture at Ganondagan State Historic Site in Victor, which was the site of a major 17th-century Seneca town.

NATURE PRESERVES AND WILDLIFE REFUGES Many areas in western New York have been set aside as nature preserves. These include **Tifft Nature Preserve** in Buffalo; **Buckhorn Island State Park** on Grand Island; **Reinstein Woods Nature Preserve**, a 300-acre preserve with undisturbed ancient forest; **Charles E. Burchfield Nature and Art Center** in West Seneca; **Penn Dixie Paleontological Site**, which has an abundance of fossils; **Bergen Swamp**, one of the nation's seven Natural History Landmarks; the **Iroquois National Wildlife Refuge**, the largest wildlife refuge in New York State; **Beaver Meadow Nature Center** in North Java; the **Jamestown Audubon Nature Center** and the **Roger Tory Peterson Institute** in Jamestown; **Goosehill Waterfowl Park** in Delevan, the second largest waterfowl

park in the world; **Pfeiffer Nature Center** in Olean; several nature preserves in Allegany County, including **Hanging Bog**, **Keaney Swamp**, **Moss Lake,** and **Rattlesnake Hill**; the **Cummings Nature Preserve** in Naples; and the **Spencer Crest Nature Preserve** in Corning.

NEWSPAPERS The two major daily newspapers in the area covered by this book are the *Buffalo News* and the *Democrat & Chronicle* in Rochester.

NIAGARA ESCARPMENT Throughout this book there is reference to the Niagara Escarpment, a ledge of solid rock that runs through New York State that created Niagara Falls and High Falls in Rochester. The city of Lockport is also located along the escarpment, which necessitated the construction of the "flight of five" locks to raise boats traveling west to the top of the escarpment. Route 104 is known as "the Ridge," being the ridge of the Niagara Escarpment. The ridge was once the shoreline of ancient Lake Iroquois, created by Canadian glaciers. Over time this lake receded to become present-day Lake Ontario.

OLMSTED Frederick Law Olmsted is considered to be the "Father of Landscape Architecture." Along with his business partner, Calvert Vaux, Olmsted took the idea of formal manicured gardens—very common in Europe—and evolved it into something distinctly American, creating parks and green spaces within urban, industrialized cities. His designs include several well-known parks: Boston's Fens, the grounds of the Biltmore Estate in North Carolina, and—most famously—New York City's Central Park. In western New York, Olmsted designed the Niagara Reservation State Park and Buffalo's park system, which was the first complete park system that he designed. His largest body of work, it is listed on the National Register of Historic Places. Olmsted also designed four parks and a parkway system in the city of Rochester. Many cities throughout the United States have Olmsted-designed parks, but only six have entire park systems designed by Olmsted: Buffalo, Rochester, Boston, Brooklyn, Chicago, and Louisville.

PAN-AMERICAN EXPOSITION The eyes of the world were focused on Buffalo in 1901, when the Pan-American Exposition took place. Three hundred fifty acres of farmland were converted into a wonderland of exhibits, midways rides, and unusual attractions. The centerpiece of the exposition was the nearly 400-foot-tall Electric Tower, which soared over the grounds. At night the exposition was transformed into a "city of light" as the buildings were illuminated. This was considered quite a feat at the turn of the 20th century, when electric lighting was considered a novelty. Buffalo's close proximity to the power-generating facilities in Niagara Falls made this possible.

The exposition was not without critics. Many felt that the fair had a negative attitude toward minorities, notably Native Americans and African Americans, who were often depicted as savage and uncivilized.

The exposition ended dramatically and tragically when President William McKinley was assassinated at the Temple of Music on September 5 by self-proclaimed anarchist Leon Czolgosz. McKinley died of his gunshot wounds little more than a week later on September 14, and Vice-President Theodore Roosevelt was sworn into office at the home of his friend Ansley Wilcox. To learn more about the Pan-American Exposition, visit the **Buffalo and Erie County Historical Society** (the only surviving building from the exposition) or the Theodore Roosevelt Inaugural National Historic Site (Wilcox mansion), which has an in-depth display on the assassination.

PARKS There are literally thousands of parks in western New York, from small neighborhood parks to huge state parks. Since it's impossible to list every single park, I have listed—in the Green Space sections—those that offer the most diverse recreational

Courtesy Buffalo and Erie County Historical Society

Christine A. Smyczynski

performs a summer season at the Chautauqua Institution.

RAILROAD EXCURSIONS AND MUSEUMS Rail fans can relive the glory days of the railroad at the following museums and historic train rides: **Arcade and Attica Railroad** in Arcade, **Medina Railroad Museum** in Medina, and the **New York Museum of Transportation/ Genesee Valley Railroad Museum** in Rush.

attractions, have the best scenery, are historic in nature, or just are great places to spend some free time. The more than 30 state parks are described in the Green Space sections. For detailed information on New York State parks, check out www.nysparks.com.

RAINY-DAY ACTIVITIES The ☂ icon indicates places that are good to visit when the weather is inclement.

RELIGIOUS SITES Those seeking the spiritual will want to visit these sites that offer solace and beauty, including **Our Lady of Victory Basilica** in Lackawanna, home of Father Baker; **Our Lady of Fatima Shrine** in Lewiston; and the **Abbey of the Genesee** in Piffard in Livingston County. The **Chautauqua Institute** also offers cultural and religious programs and speakers, while **Lily Dale** in Cassadaga is the world's largest center for Spiritualism. There are also many historic churches in the city of Buffalo, including **Saint Joseph's Cathedral**, **Saint Louis Church**, and **Saint Paul's Episcopal**, which is on the National Register of Historic Places. The **Hill Cumorah** site on the border of Wayne and Ontario Counties in the Finger Lakes region is the site of an annual religious pageant put on by the Church of the Latter-Day Saints (Mormons).

PETS Pet-friendly accommodations are indicated with the dog-paw symbol 🐾 Most charge an additional fee. Always call ahead when traveling with a pet.

PHILHARMONIC AND SYMPHONY ORCHESTRAS Numerous professional and semiprofessional orchestras reside in western New York. Find them under the Entertainment heading near the end of each section. Some of the larger orchestras include the **Buffalo Philharmonic** (800-699-3168), which performs in Kleihans Music Hall as well as other venues in the Buffalo area; the **Rochester Philharmonic** (585-454-2100), which performs at the Eastman Theatre as well as at the Finger Lakes Performing Arts Center in Canandaigua in the summer; and the **Chautauqua Symphony** (716-757-6250), which

RESTAURANTS—REGIONAL CHAINS. Several regional chain restaurants were founded in the area and have expanded to include multiple locations. Stop by one of these if you want to experience a true taste of western New York. Some of the popular chains in the Buffalo area include **John and Mary's**, which has specialized in submarine sandwiches, wings, and pizza for nearly 50 years; **Ted's Hot Dogs** (www.tedsonline.com) famous for their foot-long Sahlen's hot dogs as well as hamburgers for over 75 years; and **Anderson's** (www.andersons custard.com), known for roast beef on kimmelweck and soft custard. **DiBella's Old Fashioned Submarines** has two locations in Buffalo and seven in Rochester. Founded in 1918 in Rochester, DeBella's serves subs in an old-fashioned decor. In the Finger Lakes Region, choose from **Abbotts Frozen Custard**, which is noted for its ice cream treats, and **Tom Whal's** and **Bill Gray's**, known for hot dogs and burgers.

RATES—LODGING Please do not hold the innkeepers or author to the lodging rates listed in this book, as price increases are often inevitable, and prices may vary seasonally. Call ahead to confirm rates. Reservations are generally recommended, especially during peak seasons.

SEAWAY TRAIL This 454-mile scenic route runs parallel to Lake Erie, the Niagara River, Lake Ontario, and the Saint Lawrence River. The trail runs through ten counties and is the state's only National Scenic Byway. Clearly marked with green Seaway Trail signs, the trail takes you through quaint villages and other scenic sites that would be missed if you traveled on a superhighway. There are also 42 War of 1812 sites along the trail, marked with brown War of 1812 signs. Guided walking tours are offered in several communities located along the trail, including Westfield, Lewiston, and North Tonawanda. For more information call 800-SEAWAY-T (800-732-9298) or check out their web site www.seawaytrail.com.

SCENIC DRIVES Besides the previously mentioned **Seaway Trail**, several other roadways in the region offer scenic vistas, along with historic sites and unusual landmarks. If you're looking for a ride in the country, try **NY 104** from Niagara Falls to Rochester, where you'll pass farms, farm markets, and antiques stores as well as numerous homes of cobblestone construction. Looking for spectacular scenery? Take a drive along the 38-mile-long **Niagara Parkway** in Canada from Fort Erie to Niagara-on-the-Lake, once described by Winston Churchill as the "world's prettiest Sunday afternoon drive." To recapture the "glory days" of motoring, á la Route 66, try traveling **Routes 5 and 20** (www.routes5and20 .com) through the Finger Lakes Region, originally a Native American foot trail before becoming the main east-west highway in the state—until the New York State Thruway was constructed in the 1950s. Many of the places along this route have retained their small-town charm and offer travelers a slice of Americana. **Lake Ontario State Parkway**, part of the Seaway Trail, takes you along the shores of Lake Ontario, from Orleans County to Charlotte in Rochester. Several other shorter scenic drives are listed under the Green Space sections.

SKIING—CROSS COUNTRY Most larger state and county parks have cross-country trails. The following alpine ski resorts also have cross-country trails: **Holiday Valley, Holimont,** and **Peek 'n Peak**. **Bryncliff Resort** in Varysburg also offers cross-country skiing

SKIING—DOWNHILL Seven major ski resorts in Western New York offer downhill skiing: **Kissing Bridge** in Erie County, **Cockaigne** and **Peek 'n Peak** in Chautauqua County, **Holiday Valley** and **Holimont** in Ellicottville in Cattaraugus County, **Swain Ski and Snowboard Center** in Allegany County, and **Bristol Mountain** in Ontario County. For ski information, check out www.ski-guide.com. Several county and municipal parks also have small downhill slopes.

SNOWMOBILING One of the more popular winter activities in New York State is snowmobiling. Nearly 8,000 miles of state-funded snowmobile trails wind throughout the state, many in state parks. Riders under 18 are required to take a snowmobile safety course. For information on the course or for a trail map, call 518-474-0446, or write Snowmobiling, NYS Parks, Albany, NY 12238. You can also check out their Web site: www.nysparks .com/snow.

SPORTS You can find all sorts of sports in western New York, amateur, college, and professional. Some of the better-known pro teams that play here include the Buffalo Bills, Buffalo Bisons, Buffalo Sabres, and the Rochester Redwings. Some of the larger college teams hail from Niagara University, Canisius College, Saint Bonaventure, and SUNY at Buffalo. Check each chapter's Entertainment listings to find sports teams.

SUNDAYS AND MONDAYS Many shops and restaurants, along with some museums, may be closed on Sunday and/or Monday. If you'll be traveling any distance to a particular listing, always call ahead to check the hours because many establishments change their hours seasonally.

THEATER From summer stock to large professional companies, there are numerous theaters throughout the region. The Buffalo-Niagara region alone has the highest concentration of theaters in the state outside of New York City. You'll find theaters listed under the Entertainment heading, right after the restaurant listings.

TOURS Guided tours and tour companies are listed under the *To Do* section in each chapter.

TRAFFIC AND HIGHWAY TRAVEL TIPS Locals often joke that there are really only two seasons in western New York, winter and road construction. Allow extra time when traveling during the warmer months due to construction delays. In winter, the major roads are generally in good shape due to the region's top-notch snow-fighting equipment, but side

Courtesy Buffalo–Niagara Convention & Visitors Bureau and Angel Art Ltd.

streets—even in the cities—may prove challenging after a big storm.

Expect delays when returning from Canada in this post-9/11 climate, particularly on holidays or weekends, when there are long lines of traffic on bridges.

Frequent travelers on the New York State Thruway may want to apply for an EZ Pass, which allows you to pass through the toll booths more quickly. An application can be obtained at any Thruway toll booth, or call 800-333-8655 or visit www.e-zpassny.com.

UNDERGROUND RAILROAD

Underground Railroad was not an actual rail line but a series of safe houses where people escaping slavery in the South could find refuge along their path to freedom in Canada. With western New York's close proximity to Canada, there were many "stations" in the region. Organized tours of Underground Railroad sites are organized by **Motherland Connextions** (716-282-1028). Some noted sites include the **Michigan Street Baptist Church** in Buffalo, **Bertie Hall** in Fort Erie, and **Murphy Orchards** in Burt. Many slaves crossed the Niagara River on the ferry that operated from Broderick Park, at the foot of Ferry Street, to Fort Erie Canada. There were many more sites in the area, but since aiding runaway slaves was illegal, they are usually not well documented. Information on these places is usually passed down through oral history.

URBAN CENTERS Buffalo, Rochester, and Niagara Falls are the three major cities in the Western New York region. Some of the smaller cities include

Batavia, Lockport, Canandaigua, and Geneva.

WATERFALLS While **Niagara Falls** is by far the most well-known waterfall in the region, numerous other waterfalls throughout western New York offer scenic vistas. These falls were formed when water began to flow over the Onandaga Escarpment, a 67-mile-long rock layer running from Buffalo to Rochester. It is about 20 miles south of the Niagara Escarpment, which Niagara Falls flows over. If you like waterfalls, be sure to check out: **Glen Falls** in Williamsville, a 27-foot-high falls located in a beautiful park; **Akron Falls,** a 50-foot lower falls and a 20-foot upper falls over the escarpment in Akron Park; and **Indian Falls**, a 30-foot-high falls, in Tonawanda Creek near the Tonawanda Indian reservation ("Tonawanda" is the Iroquois word for Swift Water). Other waterfalls include **Holley Falls** in Orleans County and **High Falls** in Rochester.

WEATHER Western New York has four distinct seasons, despite its reputation as the snow capital of the nation. The area got the bad weather reputation as a result of a major blizzard that hit the Buffalo area in 1977. While the metro Buffalo area does get its fair share of snow in the winter— an average of 93 inches measured at the Buffalo Airport annually—the regions south of the city, where the ski resorts are located, usually get around 180 inches, making it one of the best ski areas in the northeast. Summers in western New York are beautiful, with temperatures in the 70s and 80s, lots of sunshine, and very low humidity. Spring and fall are cool but pleasant.

WEB SITES A good Web site that covers a lot of local information, especially on parks, recreation, and museums, is the **Western New York Regional Information Network** (www.wnyrin.com). The **Niagara Frontier Tourism Task Force** site (www.niagarafrontiertourism.com) has information about their large group of members, many of which are in tourism-related businesses. Each county's tourism office Web site also offers lots of information about the area. Check the Guidance section for the URLs of those sites.

WEDDINGS Several wedding chapels are located in both Niagara Falls, New York and Niagara Falls, Ontario. They are identified with the ⊗ symbol. Please note that wedding arrangements must generally be made well in advance—these are not Las Vegas–style elopement chapels—although some will perform ceremonies on short notice. Refer to the chapters that cover these cities for more information about obtaining a marriage license.

WHITEWATER RAFTING Several areas in the region lend themselves well to whitewater rafting. One of the more popular whitewater tour operators is **Adventure Calls** (585-343-4710; www.adventure-calls.com). Touting themselves as "western New York's premier river runners," they offer the safest beginner and intermediate levels of whitewater rafting possible. The licensed, experienced guides are among the best in the business, and they are dedicated to providing family fun. Whitewater rides are offered in three locations. Site one, the Genesee River, is perfect for novice paddlers and families. The Genesee, one of the few major rivers in the Northern Hemisphere to flow south to north, runs through the gorge at scenic Letchworth State Park. Site two, Cattaraugus Creek in Gowanda, is for more adventurous souls. A three-hour journey takes visitors on the most exciting raft ride in western New York. Site three, the Salmon River in Pulaski (north of Syracuse) also offers lots of excitement.

WINERIES More than 60 wineries in Western New York and southern Ontario are highlighted in this book. Many are located either near Lake Erie and Lake Ontario's shorelines or in the Finger Lakes region. Most offer tastings and sales of their products, and some offer also offer tours. The New York Wine and Grape producers want to remind you that ounces add up and to be aware of the amount of wine you consume at a wine tasting, especially if you are driving. A typical wine-tasting pour is 1–2 ounces. If you sample several wines at each winery and visit a few wineries in succession, your abilities may become legally impaired. In New York State a blood alcohol concentration of .08 is considered legally intoxicated. According to the New York Grape and Wine Producers, the average 135-pound woman will reach this level by consuming about 20 ounces of wine in a two hour period. A 170-pound man will reach the .08 level after about 25 ounces of wine in two hours.

WINE TRAILS Several wine trails—associations of wineries, retailers, inns and restaurants located in a particular area—run throughout western New York. These trails include **Niagara County Wine Trail, Chautauqua**

Wine Trail, Keuka Wine Trail, Canandaigua Wine Trail, Seneca Wine Trail, and the wineries of **Niagara-On-The-Lake** (www .winesofniagara.com).

WRIGHT, FRANK LLOYD Considered by many to be America's greatest architect, Wright designed more than 420 buildings during his illustrious career. Some of his nationally known designs include the Guggenheim Museum in New York City and Fallingwater in Pennsylvania. Wright is especially known for his Prairie Style buildings, which have low horizontal lines and pick up the features found in the surrounding landscape. He was the first U.S. architect to design homes with open spaces; often eliminating the walls between rooms. One of his most noted earlier works was the 1904 Larkin building in Buffalo. Unfortunately, this structure was demolished in 1950, during the urban-renewal movement. Fortunately, several other Wright-designed

Christine A. Smyczynski

structures in Buffalo and western New York remain intact, including the **Darwin D. Martin House** and **Graycliff,** which offer tours. To learn more about Wright and his work, check out this all-Wright Web site: http://www.geo cities.com/SoHo/1469/FLW.html.

ZOOS Places to observe wild animals include the **Buffalo Zoo, Seneca Park Zoo** in Rochester, and **Zooz** in Fort Erie, Canada.

CITY OF BUFFALO

Buffalo is one of New York State's best kept secrets. Those who have never visited may assume that it's just another aging "Rust Belt" city with wild winter weather, but those who live in or know the area consider Buffalo a shining jewel on the shores of Lake Erie.

The city is home to dozens of museums and cultural institutions, along with an abundance of parks and recreational activities. Buffalo has been ranked fourth in the nation as an arts and cultural destination by *American Style* magazine, ranking ahead of Los Angeles and Seattle. The city has the highest concentration of theaters in the state outside of New York City.

Buffalo has unique attractions that can't be found anywhere else in the country, including some of the finest architecture in the United States. Due to Buffalo's 19th-century industrial growth and subsequent prosperity, the wealthy were able to commission some of the finest architects of the day to construct their homes and businesses. Buffalo is the only city besides Chicago to have major works by the three greatest architects of the 19th and 20th centuries: Frank Lloyd Wright, H. H. Richardson, and Louis Sullivan. There are nine National Historic Landmark buildings within the city limits.

Buffalo's extensive parks and parkway system, designed by noted 19th-century landscape architect Frederick Law Olmsted, the "Father of Landscape Architecture," is not only beautiful, but historically significant, as well: It was Olmsted's first park system designed for any city. The parks, which are listed on the National Register of Historic Places, represent the largest body of Olmsted's work. Buffalo is one of only six cities nationwide that has an Olmsted park system still substantially intact.

If you like to eat, you'll love Buffalo. Hundreds of wonderful restaurants, from fine dining to casual eateries, offer locally inspired foods as well as cuisine from around the world. Fast-food junkies know Buffalo as the birthplace of that deep-fried delicacy, the Buffalo chicken wing, which is a must-try when visiting the city.

European settlement began in the region in the late 1700s. Prior to this, the area was home to several Indian tribes and was extensively traveled by fur traders. All of western New York west of the Genesee River was part of what is known as the Holland Land Purchase. Joseph Ellicott was hired by the Dutch Land Purchase Investors to survey the territory. In 1804 he established the

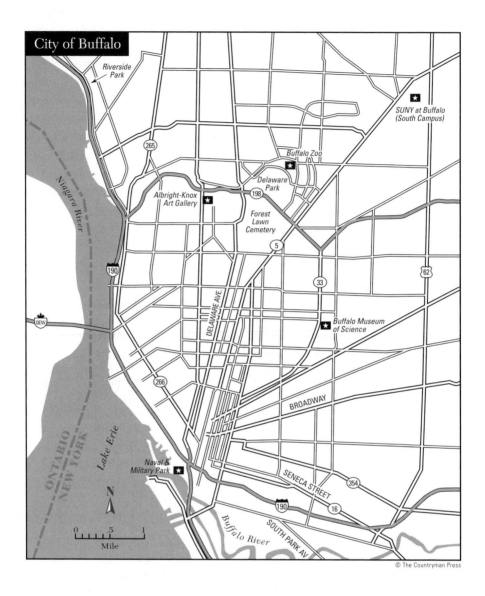

City of Buffalo

© The Countryman Press

gridlike street system of the new settlement at the crossroads of Lake Erie and the Buffalo River that he named—in honor of his employers—"New Amsterdam," which later was renamed Buffalo.

No one really knows for sure where the name "Buffalo" came from, though there are several theories. One is that Buffalo is a mispronunciation of the French *beau fleuve*, or beautiful river, referring to the scenic river. Another theory holds that an Indian named Buffaloe lived at the crossroads, and the area was known as "Buffaloe's Creek." While some may think the area was named after the American bison—or as it is more commonly known by its misnomer, buffalo—there is no evidence of these creatures ever roaming the area.

By 1809 there were over a dozen homes, two taverns, and several businesses in the village; by 1813, over 100 buildings. During the War of 1812, the area became a military post due to its strategic location. The village was burned by the British during the war. Only four buildings remained, and many residents fled to the nearby villages of Williamsville and Clarence. After the war the village slowly rebuilt. Buffalo was incorporated in 1822, and by 1825 there were over 400 structures in town.

The completion of the Erie Canal in 1825, which connected Lake Erie and points west with the Eastern Seaboard, contributed greatly to the city's growth. As the western terminus of the Erie Canal, Buffalo became the nation's busiest inland port by the turn of the 20th century. Finished goods or raw materials bound for factories would be transferred from the canal boats to freighters that sailed the Great Lakes and the eastern seaboard. Buffalo, officially incorporated as a city in 1832, was also the busiest grain transfer port in the world and the world's second largest milling center. It then became a national center for technology and industrial development. The grain elevator, which revolutionized the grain industry, was invented in Buffalo in 1842 by Joseph Dart. A number of these early elevators still line the Buffalo River.

Harnessing hydroelectric power from nearby Niagara Falls, beginning in 1896, made Buffalo one of the world's most technically advanced cities. The 1901 Pan-American Exposition brought national attention to the city and encouraged industrial progress, and the exposition was the largest-scale display of electrical illumination seen to that time. Unfortunately the Pan-American Exposition also brought about one of the most tragic events to befall the city, the assassination of President William McKinley. Vice-President Theodore Roosevelt took the presidential oath of office in Buffalo, making it one of only a handful of sites of a presidential inauguration outside of Washington, D. C.

Buffalo is also rich in African American history. Given its proximity to Canada, it was an important last stop on the Underground Railroad, a means for escaping slaves to reach freedom. The Niagara Movement, the forerunner to the NAACP, was founded in the city in 1905. Interest is high in heritage tourism, with many Black heritage sites currently under development.

By 1910 Buffalo was the eighth-largest city in the United States in terms of population and commerce. Some 60 millionaires resided in the city, more per capita than any other U.S. city. Numerous immigrants seeking new lives in the Midwest passed through Buffalo in the 19th and early-20th centuries, giving the city the nickname "Inland Ellis Island." Many of these immigrants remained in Buffalo and established neighborhoods that continue to flavor the city's traditions.

Starting in the 1950s, the city saw a marked decline, due to changes in transportation and industry. Fortunately, today's Buffalo is now on the upswing, a result of its cultural, historical, and architectural assets as well as its opportunities for growth in the high-tech, banking, medical, and education fields.

The city of Buffalo can be broken down into several identifiable sections, each with its own focus and flavor.

COMMUNITIES **Downtown/Center City** The downtown area is the business and financial heart of the city as well the Theatre and Entertainment District. It is easy to travel in this area, as the Light Rail Rapid Transit System travels aboveground along Main Street through the center of downtown. There is no fee to ride this portion of the rail system. There are numerous theaters as well as restaurants and bars, especially in the area centering around Main and Chippewa.

Elmwood Village Over 250 unique shops, art galleries, restaurants, and bars are located along Elmwood Avenue between the Albright-Knox Art Gallery and Virginia Street. For a map/brochure, contact Forever Elmwood (716-881-0707), 410 Elmwood Avenue, Buffalo, NY 14222; www.foreverelmwood.org. **Allentown** (716-881-1024; www.allentown.org or www.allenstreet.com), Allentown Association, 414 Virginia Street, Buffalo 14201); located on the southern end of the Elmwood Village, is an eclectic collection of art galleries, antique shops, bars, and restaurants. The neighborhood, which runs along Allen Street from Main to Wadsworth, and a few blocks to the north, south, and west of Allen, was named for Lewis Allen, the Uncle of Grover Cleveland, who lived in this area in the early 19th century. It is listed on the National Register of Historic Places and is one of the largest urban preservation districts in the nation. It is the site of the Allentown Art Festival in June.

North Buffalo/Hertel Avenue Hertel–North Buffalo Business Association (716-877-6607). Hertel Avenue is a walkable urban shopping area lined with an array of shops, restaurants, and other businesses. Since many of the residents in the area are of Italian decent, numerous Italian restaurants are here, and it's the site of the annual summer Italian Heritage Festival.

Museum District This area, which is located near Olmsted-designed Delaware Park, has three major Buffalo cultural institutions within its borders: the Albright-Knox Art Gallery, the Buffalo & Erie County Historical Society, and the Burchfield-Penney Art Center. The neighborhood is surrounded by spacious parkways lined with elegant mansions, including Lincoln Parkway and Nottingham Terrace. The district is also referred to as the **Olmsted Crescent**. Adjacent to this area is the **Parkside District,** which contains the acclaimed Frank Lloyd Wright–designed Darwin D. Martin House, along with tree-lined streets and restored homes of various architectural styles.

The **East Side**, **West Side**, **University District,** and **South Buffalo** are urban residential areas, with a sprinkling of restaurants, shops, and landmarks mixed in.

AREA CODE The area code for the city is 716.

GUIDANCE & **Buffalo Niagara Convention and Visitors Bureau** (716-852-0511 or 800-BUFFALO; www.buffalocvb.org), 617 Main Street, Suite 400, Buffalo. Open Monday–Friday 10–2. Numerous brochures about western New York attractions are available here as is a gift shop featuring Buffalo-themed items. The visitors bureau is located in the circa 1892 Market Arcade building, the best surviving 19th-century retail structure in Buffalo. The Convention and Visitors Bureau also operates another location at the Galleria Mall, exit 52 off the NYS Thruway. Open Monday–Saturday 11–7, Sunday 12–5.

GETTING THERE *By air:* **Buffalo Niagara International Airport** (716-630-6000; www.buffaloairport.com), 4200 Genesee Street, Buffalo. The airport, which averages about 100 flights daily, is served by most major airlines. Car rentals at the airport include **Alamo** (631-2044), Avis (632-1808), **Budget** (632-4662), **Enterprise** (565-0002), **Hertz** (632-4772), **National** (634-9220), and **Thrifty** (633-8500).

By bus: **Greyhound Lines** (716-855-7533 or 800-231-2222; www.greyhound.com) operates out of the Ellicott Street Bus Terminal, 181 Ellicott Street at North Division.

By car: There are several approaches to the city. From Rochester and east, take the New York State Thruway (I-90) to I-290 (Youngmann Expressway), where you can connect to either the 33 (Kensington Expressway) or the I-190. The 219 and the I-90 from Erie, Pennsylvania, approach the city from the south. From Canada, take the Queen Elizabeth Way (QEW) to the Peace Bridge. Special note: The Peace Bridge, built in 1927 to commemorate the long-standing friendship between the United States and Canada, is the sixth busiest international border crossing in North America.

By train: **Amtrak** (800-872-7245; www.amtrak.com) has two stations in the Buffalo area, one at 75 Exchange Street, Buffalo (716-856-2075), the other at 55 Dick Rd, Depew (716-683-8440).

GETTING AROUND Buffalo has been referred to as the "20-minute" city because that's how long it usually takes to get from the city to the outlying areas.

By car: The major streets in Buffalo branch out in a radial pattern from the downtown business district. Main Street is permanently closed to vehicular traffic, from the foot of Main Street to the Theater District, due to the Light Rail Rapid Transit.

By bus: **Niagara Frontier Transportation Authority** (716-855-7211; www.nfta.com), 181 Ellicott Street, Buffalo. Numerous routes run throughout the city and to the outlying suburbs, Niagara Falls, and Lockport. Check their Web site for a complete listing. NFTA also operates the metro rail system, the Buffalo and Niagara Falls International Airports, and the Buffalo Harbor.

By subway: **Light Rail Rapid Transit System** This system travels from the foot of Main Street to the Main Street campus of the University at Buffalo (www.nfta.com/metro). The train is free to ride in the aboveground downtown portion. There is a charge to ride it when it goes underground past the Theatre District.

By taxi: **Airport Taxi Service** (716-633-8294 or 800-551-9369; www.buffaloairporttaxi.com) serves major downtown hotels and the airport. Taxis are available 24 hours.

MEDICAL EMERGENCY Call 911

Buffalo General Hospital (716-859-5600; kaleidahealth.org), 100 High Street, Buffalo. **Erie County Medical Center** (716-898-3000; www.ecmc.edu), 462 Grider Street, Buffalo.

Mercy Hospital of Buffalo (716-826-7000; www.chsbuffalo.org), 565 Abbott Road, Buffalo.

Women's and Children's Hospital (716-878-7000; www.wchob.org), 219 Bryant Street, Buffalo.

Sisters of Charity Hospital (716-862-2000; www.chsbuffalo.org), 2157 Main Street, Buffalo.

Millard Fillmore Gates Circle Hospital (716-887-4600; http://gates.kaleida .health.org), 3 Gates Circle, Buffalo.

VA Healthcare System (716-834-9200), 3495 Bailey Avenue, Buffalo.

Roswell Park Cancer Institute (716-845-2300; www.roswellpark.org), Elm and Carlton Streets, Buffalo.

✳ To See

ART MUSEUMS AND GALLERIES The Buffalo-Niagara region has been ranked fourth in the nation as an arts and cultural destination by *American Style* magazine, ranking ahead of Los Angeles and Seattle, so it's not surprising that the area has a high concentration of art and history museums.

Arts Council In Buffalo and Erie County (716-856-7520; www.artscouncil buffalo.org), 700 Main Street, Buffalo. Open Monday–Friday 9–5. The Arts Council is an advocate for the arts, dedicated to promoting culture in the Buffalo-Niagara region along with building community and intellectual enrichment.

& ⬆ **Albright-Knox Art Gallery** (716-882-8700; www.albrightknox.org), 1285 Elmwood Avenue, Buffalo. Open Tuesday–Saturday 11–5, Sunday 12–5. Admission: $6 adults, $5 seniors and students, under 12 free. The gallery, which opened in 1905, is one of the nation's oldest public art organizations. The exhibits focus mainly on contemporary art, especially post-war American and European art. The collection includes a sampling of art throughout the centuries, including a Mesopotamian figure from 3000 BC, Renaissance paintings, and works by 19th-century artists, Gauguin, and van Gogh. Also represented are works by Picasso, Matisse, Pollock, and Warhol. If you have the opportunity, have lunch in the gallery's Garden Restaurant and be sure to check out the extensive gift shop.

HOME OF ONE OF THE WORLD'S FINEST COLLECTIONS OF MODERN AND CONTEMPORARY ART.

Christine A. Smyczynski

Anderson Gallery of the University at Buffalo (716-834-2579; www .artgallery.buffalo.edu), Martha Jackson Place, Buffalo. Open Tuesday–Friday 11–5, Saturday 12–5, closed holidays and the month of August. Free admission. Home to the university's permanent art collection. Exhibits include contemporary paintings, sculptures, and graphics.

Art Dialogue Gallery (716-885-2251; www.buffalo.com/NYAG-AD), 1 Linwood Avenue, Buffalo. Open

Tuesday–Friday 11–5, Saturday 11–3. Founded in 1985, the exhibits at this gallery feature the works of artists, composers, musicians, poets, and writers living in western New York.

Big Orbit Art Gallery (716-883-3209; www.bigorbitgallery.com), 30D Essex Street, Buffalo. Open Thursday–Sunday 12–5. Contemporary art created by Western New York artists featuring visual art, music, performance theater, video, and public art projects.

Buffalo Arts Studio (716-833-4450; www.buffaloartsstudio.org), Tri-Main Center, 2495 Main Street, Suite 500, Buffalo. Open Tuesday–Friday 11–5, Saturday 11–3. The Buffalo Arts Studio features two galleries exhibiting regional, national, and international artists. Forty-five resident artists specialize in painting, printmaking, photography, sculpture, pottery, metalworking, woodworking, and installations.

& **Burchfield-Penney Art Center** (716-878-6011; www.burchfield-penney .org), 1300 Elmwood Avenue, Buffalo. Open Tuesday–Saturday 11–5, Sunday 1–5, closed holidays. Admission: $5 adults, $4 over age 64, $3 children 6–18. This art museum showcases the talents of western New York artists. It contains nearly 6,000 works by artists who have lived in this region. Included in the collection are paintings, photographs, sculptures and folk art objects, including rare wallpaper samples in the M. H. Birge and Sons Wallpaper Company Collection. The museum also has the world's largest collection of works by renowned watercolorist Charles Burchfield, who was responsible for the creation of the museum in 1966. Between 1991 and 1994 art collector Charles Rand Penney gifted the center with more than 1,300 works by western New York artists, including works by Burchfield and by the Roycroft Arts and Crafts Community of East Aurora. Permanent exhibits include a recreation of Charles Burchfield's studio and the Metcalf Rooms, which were salvaged from a local mansion and restored. There are usually six major exhibits a year and 15 to 20 smaller, on-loan exhibits annually. There is also a hands-on gallery for children. In addition to the artwork, the center also presents concerts, literary readings, performances, and workshops.

& **CEPA Gallery** (716-856-2717; www.cepagallery.com), 617 Main Street, Suite 201, Market Arcade Complex, Buffalo. Open Monday–Friday 10–5, Saturday 12–4. The CEPA Gallery was founded in 1974 as a resource for photographic creation, education, and presentation. It is one of the largest galleries of its kind in North America. Facilities include an open-access darkroom and digital lab, Macintosh computer, Internet access, and more, which are open to the public for a nominal charge. In addition, photographic workshops are offered for every skill level.

College St. Gallery (882-9727; www.collegestreetgallery.tripod.com/college street.htm), 244 Allen Street, Buffalo. Open Thursday–Saturday 2–8, Sunday 2–5. This gallery was established in 1997 by Michael Mulley to give local artists a venue to display their work. The main focus of the gallery is photography, but they also welcome sculpture, paintings and other media. Many of these works are offered for sale. The gallery's permanent collection features rock and jazz photos by Mr. Mulley and other artists as well as urban street scenes and nature photography.

Hallwalls Contemporary Arts Center (716-835-7362; www.hallwalls.org), 341 Delaware Avenue, Buffalo. Open Tuesday–Friday 11–6, Saturday 1–4. Free admission. This arts center located in the restored Asbury Delaware United Methodist Church focuses on visual, performing, media, and literary arts. Their mission is to bring new and challenging contemporary art to the public. It's been recognized nationwide for it programming mix. Facilities include a performance theater, cinema, three galleries, and editing studios.

Impact Artists Gallery (716-835-6817 www.buffalo.com/impact), Tri-Main Building, 2495 Main Street, Suite 545, Buffalo. Open Tuesday–Friday 11–4. Impact focuses on the works of women artists, offering them a venue to display their work as well as space to teach, demonstrate, and produce works

Langston Hughes Institute (716-881-3266; http://africancultural.org/Langston Hughes.php; 25 High Street, Buffalo. Open Monday–Friday 9–5, Saturday 11–4. This institute was founded in 1968 to preserve African-American culture, arts, and music in the city of Buffalo. Numerous cultural and educational programs are offered, including African dance and drumming, painting, and drawing.

Tri-Main Center (716-835-3366; www.trimaincenter.com), 2495 Main Street, Buffalo. Building is open 7–9; studio hours vary for each individual gallery. This 1915 building, the former Trico Windshield Wiper manufacturing plant, houses numerous galleries and artist studios. See also **Buffalo Arts Studio** and **Impact Artist's Gallery.**

PUBLIC LIBRARY ♿ ⚑ ✐ **Buffalo and Erie County Public Library** (716-858-8900; www.buffalolib.org), 1 Lafayette Square, Buffalo. This modern library, headquarters to the 52-branch Buffalo and Erie County Public Library System, houses over 3 million books on 58 miles of shelves. The 40,000-square-foot building, which opened in 1964, covers more than two city blocks. The library has a Special Collections Department that houses noncirculating research materials, including the collection of the Western New York Genealogical Society, books on local history, atlases, maps, city directories, and access to Family Search, a vast genealogical collection put together by the Mormon Church. The library's Mark Twain Room features a rare-book collection, including Twain's *The Adventures of Huckleberry Finn* manuscript and other memorabilia. The Rare Book Room includes early print books and Bibles. There are 15 city branches plus 36 branches located in the outlying suburbs.

MUSEUMS AND HISTORIC HOMES ✪ ✐ ♿ **Buffalo & Erie County Historical Society** (716-873-9644; www.bechs.org), 25 Nottingham Court, Buffalo. Open Wednesday–Saturday 10–5, Sunday 12–5 (Museum shop is open Monday–Saturday 10–5, Sunday 12–5). Admission: $6 Adults, $4 seniors, $4.50 students 13–21, $2.50 children 7–12. The museum, which is one of the country's oldest regional historical institutions, is housed in the only remaining structure from Buffalo's 1901 Pan-American Exposition. The white Vermont marble, Greek Revival–style building, a National Historic Landmark, was designed by well-known Buffalo architect George Cary. Displays include the world's largest Pan-American exhibit, the area's largest textile collection, Native American displays, a War of 1812 exhibit, regional history, and Erie Canal history, as well as changing exhibits focusing on Buffalo and western New York. Be sure to check out the exhibit "Buffalo Made," which highlights products made and/or invented in western New York, including Cheerios, Keri Lotion, and the heart pacemaker. The historical society's resource center, located a short distance away at 459 Forest Avenue, features the Pan-American Centennial Exhibit, Spirit of the City: Imagining the Pan-American Exposition, which was created for the exhibits centennial celebration. The exhibit features artifacts and hands-on displays describing the exposition, including "the Little Building" the only surviving temporary structure built on the Pan-Am grounds. The Historical Society has a research library, with records accessible in person or online at www.wnylibraries.org.

✪ **Darwin D. Martin House** (716-856-3858; www.darwinmartinhouse.org), 125 Jewett Parkway, Buffalo. Docent-led tours by reservation only, times vary. Admission: $10 adults, $8 students. The structures located in this complex were designed by the well-known architect Frank Lloyd Wright in 1904 for one of his loyal clients, Darwin D. Martin, a wealthy industrialist. The prairie-style Martin House is regarded as one of the greatest residences in the world. The smaller Barton House was built for Martin's sister and her husband. After the Martin family moved out in 1938, the home sat vacant until 1954. It then changed hands several times until the 1980s, when the home was researched, surveyed, and given National Historic Landmark status. A gardener's cottage on the grounds is now a restored private residence. Restoration is an ongoing process, as the home is a valuable part of the region's heritage and a unique architectural masterpiece. With six public and private homes, the Buffalo area has the largest collection of Wright-designed structures east of the Mississippi. The visitors center, which will open in 2006, was designed by architect Tohiko Mori. Two nearby private residences, the **William R. Heath House** (76 Soldiers Place) and the **Davidson House** (57 Tillinghast Place), were also designed by Wright.

HISTORIC SITES Coit House, 414 Virginia Street, Buffalo. The Coit House, built by George Coit in 1814, is the oldest house in Buffalo. Coit, a prosperous businessman, built the two-story clapboard house on the corner of Pearl and Swan Streets after the fire that devastated the city during the War of 1812. The house was moved to its present location in the 1870s and changed hands numerous times until it was purchased by the Allentown Association in 1999. They plan to renovate the home and turn it into a museum.

THIS PRAIRIE-STYLE HOME DESIGNED BY FRANK LLOYD WRIGHT IS CONSIDERED ONE OF THE FINEST RESIDENCES IN THE WORLD. Courtesy Buffalo–Niagara Convention & Visitors Bureau

✪ *Edward M. Cotter* **Fireboat,** Foot of Ohio Street on the Buffalo River. The *Edward M. Cotter,* built in 1900, is the oldest operating fireboat in the United States; which has earned it a National Historic Landmark designation. The boat, which is used to fight fires on floating ships and in waterfront buildings, serves the Buffalo Harbor, Niagara River, and Lake Erie. The public can best view it during waterfront festivals or when welcoming visiting vessels and tall ships to the harbor.

Michigan Avenue Baptist Church, 511 Michigan Avenue, Buffalo. This brick church, built in 1845, was placed on the National Register of Historic Places in 1974. The church played an important role in the history of the African American community. It was a station on the Underground Railroad during the early 1800s, and many noted black abolitionists, like Frederick Douglass and William Wells Brown, made frequent stops here. It is the oldest property continuously, owned, operated, and occupied by African Americans in western New York.

Nash House, 36 Nash Street, Buffalo (Currently under restoration to become a museum; when open, it will feature documents, photos, books, and correspondence that relate to the Civil Rights movement.) This was the home of the Reverend J. Edward Nash (1868–1957) and his family from 1925 until 1987. Rev. Nash, pastor of the Michigan Avenue Baptist Church from 1892–1953, was influential in the Civil Rights Movement. In the early 20th century he was the best known African American in the city of Buffalo and was highly respected by both the black and white communities. Many Civil Rights leaders, including Booker T. Washington, W. E. B. Du Bois, and Rev. Adam Clayton Powell, frequently visited Nash in Buffalo. Mary Talbert, a member of the Michigan Avenue Baptist Church, along with Du Bois, planned the Niagara Movement, the forerunner of the National Association for the Advancement of Colored People (NAACP).

✪ **Theodore Roosevelt Inaugural National Historic Site** (716-884-0095; www.nps.gov/thri), 641 Delaware Avenue, Buffalo. Open Monday–Friday 9–5, Saturday–Sunday 12–5. Admission: $3 adults, $2 children 6–14 and seniors over 62. This National Historic Site, better known as the Wilcox Mansion, was the home of Ansley Wilcox, a close friend of Theodore Roosevelt. Following the assassination of President William McKinley at the 1901 Pan-American Exposition in Buffalo, Vice-President Roosevelt was sworn in as president in the library of this Victorian-era home. The home, which was originally brick, was built in 1838 as a barracks to house military offices. Over the years additions were made to the structure, which is one of the finest examples of Greek Revival architecture in the area. The site is operated as a museum by the National Parks Service. Docent-led tours are given of the home, which is decorated in period style. Educational programs are offered throughout the year for school groups and the general public. During the holidays the home is decorated in Victorian style for the annual Victorian Christmas celebration.

UNIQUE ARCHITECTURE

(✪ designates National Historic Landmark buildings)

Buffalo has one of the finest collections of late 19th- and early-20th-century buildings and homes in the country. There are nine National Historic Landmark

Buildings and sites within the city of Buffalo. Styles represented include Greek Revival, Gothic Revival, Romanesque Revival, Italianate, Queen Anne, and Prairie, just to name a few. It's one of only two cities in the nation that has structures designed by all three of America's greatest architects, Frank Lloyd Wright, Louis Sullivan, and H. H. Richardson. Be sure to take a stroll down Delaware Avenue between Gates Circle and North Street—dubbed "Millionaire's Row" during Buffalo's early days—to see numerous large mansions that now serve as corporate headquarters to local companies. A self-guided walking tour brochure, Downtown's Heritage, is available from the Convention and Visitors Bureau, along with a booklet, "Walk Buffalo" (www.walkbuffalo.org). Some architectural gems you don't want to miss include:

&. ↑ **Albright-Knox Art Gallery** (716-882-8700; www.albrightknox.org), 1285 Elmwood Avenue, Buffalo. Open Tuesday–Saturday 11–5, Sunday 12–5. Admission: $6 adults, $5 seniors and students, under 12 free. The gallery, which opened as the Albright Art Gallery in 1905, was designed by Edward B. Green, a distinguished Buffalo architect who also designed the Toledo Museum of Art and the Dayton Art Institute. The construction of the gallery was made possible because of a generous gift from Buffalo philanthropist John J. Albright. The newer wing, designed by Gordon Bunshaft, was dedicated in 1962. The name Knox was added because the addition was constructed thanks to a generous donation by the Seymour H. Knox, Jr., family.

Central Terminal (www.bfn.org/~bct, www.buffalocentralterminal.org), 495 Paderewski Drive, Buffalo. This train station, designed by Stewart Wagner and Alfred Fellheimer in 1929, is a prime example of art deco architecture that was popular during the 1920s and 1930s. The terminal, which is on both the National and State Registers of Historic Places, opened four months before the stock market crash in 1929 and closed in 1979. The 523,000-square-foot building has a massive 225-foot by 66-foot concourse that's just shy of 60 feet high. It is the tallest train station in the country, with its 17-story office tower that's 271 feet high. The station, which now stands in disrepair, has been vacant for several years and is not currently open to the public. However, there is much interest throughout the community in saving and using this historic structure. Note: This structure is

THE 1895 PRUDENTIAL BUILDING WAS THE FIRST STEEL-SUPPORTED CURTAIN-WALLED BUILDING IN THE WORLD.
Christine A. Smyczynski

located in a rather rundown area of town, so if you wish to view the building, visit during daylight hours.

"Electric Building": Niagara Mohawk Power Building, 535 Washington Street, Buffalo. The design for this 1912 structure was inspired by the Electric Tower at the 1901 Pan-American Exposition.

&. **Ellicott Square Building,** 295 Main Street, Buffalo. The Ellicott Square Building, designed by Burnham and Company, was the largest office complex in the world when it was completed in 1896. The building, which takes up a whole city block, was designed to resemble a 16th-century baroque palace. Built to commemorate Joseph Ellicott, the founder of Buffalo, the building is constructed around a large interior court with inlaid marble floors, one of the most ornate public spaces in the city.

&. **Erie Community College City Campus (Old Post Office Bldg.),** 121 Ellicott Street, Buffalo. The Flemish Gothic Revival structure, designed by James Knox Taylor, has a 245-foot central tower, complete with gargoyles and shallow gothic arched windows. The interior with its six-story skylighted courtyard is magnificent.

○ **H. H. Richardson Complex (Buffalo Psychiatric Center)**, 400 Forest Avenue, Buffalo. This structure, which has two 184-foot red Medina sandstone towers, was designed by noted architect Henry Hudson Richardson, who considered this building to be his greatest work. It was built between 1879 and 1896 to house New York State's fifth asylum for the insane. Frederick Law Olmsted designed the formal landscaping surrounding the buildings. At the present time it is not open to the public, although plans are in the works to restore it and convert it for public use.

○ **Kleinhans Music Hall** (716-883-3560; for Buffalo Philharmonic tickets and info: 716-885-5000 or 800-699-3168; www.bpo.org), 71 Symphony Circle, Buffalo. The permanent home of the Buffalo Philharmonic Orchestra, Kleinhans Music Hall is world-renowned for its acoustic excellence. This beautiful music hall, a designated National Historic Landmark, is a great setting for the many performances scheduled here throughout the year, including concerts by the BPO and an assortment of other local and national musical, dance, and variety acts. Designed by the architecture firms of F. J. and W. A. Kidd and Eliel and Eero Saarinen, it is considered one of the finest works by the Saarinens. While the Kidds designed the interior, the Saarinens were responsible for the graceful curves of the hall's exterior. The main auditorium, which seats 2,800, is semi-elliptical in shape. Its ceiling is built in a series of ridges that help to capture the sound and funnel it throughout the auditorium. The Mary Seaton Room, an elongated hemispherical chamber music hall featuring a parquet floor and zebra flexwood walls, seats 900. The exterior of the building is faced with Ohio Wyandotte brick enhanced with panels of veined sandstone.

Old County Hall, 92 Franklin Street, Buffalo. Built between 1871 and 1876, this Gothic Revival structure's most notable feature is the clock tower, with sculptures representing justice, agriculture, commerce, and mechanical arts.

✪ **Prudential Building (formerly the Guaranty Building),** 28 Church Street, Buffalo. This building, designed in 1895 by Louis Henry Sullivan, was cutting edge when it opened. The first steel-supported, curtain-walled building in the world, its features included steel frames, elevators, fireproofing, and electric lights. The outside of the building is decorated with intricate art nouveau red terra cotta ornaments.

St. Joseph Roman Catholic Cathedral (716-854-5844), 50 Franklin Street, Buffalo. Tours Wednesday and Friday at 1 PM. (716-687-1338 for tours) The Gothic Revival–style cathedral designed by prominent New York City architect Patrick Keeley was constructed of gray limestone between 1851–1862. One of the cathedral's interesting features is the three-story tall Hook & Hasting pipe organ that was originally built for the 1876 Centennial exposition in Philadelphia (the tour includes a demonstration of the organ), which the diocese purchased at the close of the exposition. It is believed to be one the oldest and largest church organs in the country.

St. Louis Church, Main and Edward Streets, Buffalo. This 1,900-seat church, which recently underwent a $1.5 million renovation, was built in 1889. The 14th-century-style Gothic church, one of the largest churches in the city, was modeled after a cathedral in Cologne, Germany. The parish actually was formed in 1829, when land was donated to the city for a church to be built on this spot. It is the oldest Catholic congregation in Buffalo. Several church buildings were erected before this landmark church was built.

✪ **St. Paul's Episcopal Cathedral** (716-855-0900; www.stpaulscathedral.org), 128 Pearl Street, Buffalo. On the second Saturday of the month at 10 AM, tours of both St. Paul's and St. Louis churches are offered. This Gothic Revival–style church, Buffalo's first national architectural landmark, was designed by Richard Upjohn in 1851 and is on the National Register of Historic Places. Upjohn, who also designed Trinity Episcopal Church in New York City, regarded St. Paul's as his finest church.

ARCHITECTURAL TOURS See *To Do—Guided Tours.*

SPECIAL INTEREST MUSEUMS ✪ **Buffalo & Erie County Naval and Military Park** (716-847-1773; www.buffalonavalpark.org), 1 Naval Park Cove, Buffalo. Open April–October daily 10–5, November Saturday and Sunday 10–4. Admission: $6 adults, $3.50 children 6–16 and seniors over 61. This six-acre waterfront site is the largest inland park of its kind in the nation. The museum features many exhibits representing all branches of the armed services. Start your tour by viewing video presentations about the park and about the on-site submarine, the U.S.S. *Croaker.* Visitors have the opportunity to climb aboard the cruiser U.S.S. *Little Rock* and the destroyer U.S.S. *Sullivans,* named after five brothers killed while serving during World War II. The U.S.S. *Sullivans* has been dedicated a National Historic Landmark. If you don't mind crawling into small enclosed spaces, tour the *Croaker.* (Safety note: Many ladders and tight spaces have to be navigated while touring the vessels; it is not recommended for children under age 5.) The museum offers tours for school and community groups as well as overnight encampments for scouts and other groups in the spring and fall.

🐾 **Buffalo Fire Historical Museum** (716-892-8400), 1850 William Street, Buffalo. Open Saturday 10–4 or by appointment. Free admission. Learn about the history of fire fighting in Buffalo from the 1800s until the present time. This museum has many photos and artifacts depicting the early days of the Buffalo Fire Department, including an 1893 parade carriage and an 1831 hand pumper. Visitors have an opportunity to pull an old-fashioned fire alarm box—a standard feature on street corners during the early 1900s and for decades after. Model and toy fire trucks are on display as well as an assortment of helmets and other fire-fighting equipment. One display is dedicated to the firefighters who lost their lives when a propane tank exploded in the city. The volunteers who run this museum are happy to give you a guided tour and answer any questions you might have about fire fighting in the city.

🐾 ⅚ ↑ **Buffalo Museum of Science** (716-896-5200; www.sciencebuff.org), 1020 Humboldt Parkway, Buffalo. Open Tuesday–Sunday 10–5, until 10 on Friday from September–April. Admission: $6 adults, $4 seniors, students and children 3–17. This Buffalo institution features over 600,000 exhibits on permanent display, from anthropology to zoology, along with short-term traveling exhibits. There are over a dozen exhibit halls, many with hand-on learning displays. It is the first museum in the U.S. to have a school on the premises (Drew Science Magnet).

↑ **Buffalo Transportation Pierce-Arrow Museum** (716-853-0084; www .pierce-arrow.com), 263 Michigan Avenue, Buffalo. Open Wednesday–Sunday 12–5. Admission: $7 adults, $6 seniors over 60, $3 children 6–17. Learn about Buffalo's transportation history, with special focus on the Buffalo-made Pierce-Arrow automobile. A visit to this 20,000-square-foot museum takes visitors back 100 years, to a time when Buffalo was a booming industrial center. On the opening day of the 1901 Pan-Am Exposition, inventor George Pierce drove his Pierce Motorette onto the grounds of the exposition, where thousands of people saw it and became interested in this new mode of transportation. Two years later Pierce introduced the Pierce-Arrow, the luxury car that would make him famous. This museum has several Pierce-Arrows on display, along with other classic cars like the Buffalo-made Thomas Flyer. Many of the vehicles on display are from the collection of museum founder James T. Sandoro; others are on loan from various collectors across the country. Also on display are other items related to the transportation history of Buffalo, including photos, literature, factory items, paintings, china, signs, and other memorabilia. A Frank Lloyd Wright–designed filling station to be constructed on the museum grounds is currently in the development stage.

Cofeld Judaic Museum (886-7150, ext. 24; www.tbz.org), Temple Beth Zion, 805 Delaware Avenue, Buffalo. Open Sunday–Friday 10–4, Saturday 11–noon. Free admission. This museum, which has the most comprehensive collection of Judaica between New York City and Chicago, has more than 1,000 Judaica artifacts dating from the 10th century to the present. The mission of the museum is to recognize important American Jewish achievements.

Iron Island Museum (716-892-3084; www.ironisland.com), 998 Lovejoy Street, Buffalo. This small neighborhood museum is located in the East Buffalo neighborhood of Lovejoy, or "Iron Island"—so dubbed because the area used to be surrounded by railroad tracks, so it is no surprise that railroad memorabilia is prominent. The museum also features a "Red, White and Blue" corner that salutes veterans and artifacts from days gone by, including many old photos of the New York Central Terminal, a dominant landmark in the neighborhood. Interesting note: Most of the land in this area was owned by Millard Fillmore from 1847–1850.

⬆ **Karpeles Manuscript Library Museum** (716-885-4139; www.karpeles .com), 453 Porter Avenue, Buffalo. Open Tuesday–Sunday 11–4. Free admission. Karpeles Manuscript Museums are the world's largest private holdings of important, original manuscripts and documents. There are eight such libraries across the country, including the one in Buffalo. Every three months the exhibits are rotated between the eight museums before being returned to the archive. The museum has over one million documents, including the original draft of the Bill of Rights and Einstein's Theory of Relativity. Adults as well as school-age children will find this museum interesting and educational. They also have a "mini museum" program in which reproductions of documents are taken to area schools.

Lower Lakes Marine Historical Society (716-849-0914), 66 Erie Street, Buffalo. Open Tuesday, Thursday, Saturday 10–3. Donation. This museum, located an 1896 building that once housed the Howard H. Baker Company ship chandlery, focuses on the maritime history of Buffalo and the Great Lakes region. There is an extensive collection of Erie Canal photos, along with models of many vessels that cruised the Great Lakes, the Buffalo River, and the Erie Canal.

LIGHTHOUSES Buffalo Main Light (716-856-6696), Buffalo Lighthouse Association, U.S. Coast Guard Base, 1 Fuhrmann Boulevard, Buffalo. This 76-foot octagonal lighthouse (built in 1823 to replace an 1818 lighthouse) is also known as "Chinaman's Light" after a turn-of the-20th-century pagoda-like tower that was located nearby and used to monitor the harbor for illegal immigrants. Although the light has not been in service since 1914, it has been maintained by the Buffalo Lighthouse Association since 1985. The tower is only open during festivals and special events. The grounds, located on U.S. Coast Guard

BUILT IN 1823, THIS LIGHTHOUSE HASN'T BEEN IN USE SINCE 1914.
Courtesy Buffalo–Niagara Convention & Visitors Bureau

property, are open daily dawn to dusk to the public. The lighthouse can also be viewed from the Erie Basin Marina.

✳ To Do

Boat excursions **Miss Buffalo/Niagara Clipper** (716-856-6696; www.miss buffalo.com), 79 Marine Drive, Buffalo. Open May–October, hours vary throughout the season. A unique way to view Buffalo's skyline, historic land-marks, and the Canadian shoreline, including Old Fort Erie: from the deck of a ship. The vessel cruises under the Peace Bridge and "locks through" the historic Black Rock Locks and Canal. During your two-hour narrated tour you'll see Buf-falo's lighthouse, the navy vessels U.S.S. *Sullivans* and U.S.S. *Little Rock,* and many other local landmarks.

CROSS-COUNTRY SKIING See **Tifft Nature Preserve** in *Green Space.*

FAMILY FUN ✑ **Buffalo City Hall Observation Deck** (716-851-5891), 65 Nia-gara Square, Buffalo. Open Monday–Friday 9–4, closed holidays. Free admis-sion. The observation deck of Buffalo City Hall offers one of the best views in the city. As you enter City Hall, take note of the building. This 32-story struc-ture, listed on the National Register of Historic Places, is an outstanding exam-ple of art deco architecture so popular in the 1920s and 1930s. The frieze above the building's entrance has figures illustrating different facets of the history of Buffalo. Take the elevator to the 25th floor; then go up three flights to the obser-vation deck, where you can view the city, Lake Erie, and the Niagara River from 330 feet up. On a clear day you can see the surrounding suburbs as well as across the river into Canada.

✑ ⅋ **Buffalo Zoo** (716-837-3900; www.buffalozoo.org), 300 Parkside Avenue, Buffalo. Open June 1–September 30 daily 10–5, October 1–May 31 daily 10–4. Admission: $7 adults, $3.50 children 2–14, $3 over 62. The 23-acre Buffalo Zoo—established in 1875, the third oldest zoo in the United States—has been undergoing major renovations over the course of the last several years. Animals are viewed in exhibit areas similar to their natural habitats as opposed to cages. Some of the more than 1,000 animals include lowland gorillas, polar bears, giraffes, and elephants as well as an aviary featuring exotic bird species. The zoo offers educational programs to schools and other youth groups. It also has one of the finest collections in the nation of porcelain animal sculptures created by artist and naturalist Edward Boehm.

FISHING The Buffalo–Niagara Region has some of the best fishing in the state. Catches include smallmouth bass, muskie king salmon, steelhead, walleye, and lake trout.

Bird Island Pier, end of West Ferry Street over bridge to Bird Island (see *Green Space—Walking and Hiking* trails). Other popular fishing spots include Lake Kirsty at Tifft Nature Preserve and the **Buffalo Small Boat Harbor (NFTA Boat Harbor),** 1111 Fuhrmann Boulevard, Buffalo.

GOLF **Cazenovia Golf Course** (716-825-9811), 1 Willink Avenue, Buffalo. A public 9-hole, par-3 course with a driving range located in Olmsted-designed Cazenovia Park.

Delaware Park (716-851-5806 or 835-2533), Delaware Park, Buffalo. A public 18-hole, par-71 course located in Buffalo's best-known park.

Grover Cleveland Park (716-836-7398), 3781 Main Street, Amherst. The clubhouse of this course was originally built by the Buffalo County Club in 1901. It was purchased by the city in 1925 and named after Grover Cleveland, former mayor of Buffalo, governor of New York, and president of United States. The 18-hole course is owned and operated by Erie County.

GUIDED TOURS **GrayLine-Niagara** (800-695-1603; www.grayline.com), Four-hour tours are offered Wednesday–Sunday, with departure from the Buffalo and Erie County Historical Society at 12:30. This "Best of Buffalo" tour highlights the city's history, architecture, and the Olmsted Crescent.

Historic Buffalo River Tours of the Industrial Heritage Committee, Inc. (716-856-6696—*Miss Buffalo* phone—for reservations; www.industrialheritage -buffalo.com). About six times a year the Industrial Heritage Committee offers two-hour narrated boat tours of the grain elevator district aboard the *Miss Buffalo*. The tour covers the invention of the grain elevator, their architectural significance, and the current uses of the structures. The committee also offers special members-only tours as well as charter tours for groups.

Landmark Society of the Niagara Frontier (716-852-3300; www.landmark -niagara.org), 617 Main Street, Buffalo. Scheduled tours and by appointment for groups. The Landmark Society offers a broad range of tours, including tours of Main Street buildings, Buffalo churches, and special tours of historic sites in the outlying suburbs. The line-up of tours changes from month to month.

Motherland Connextions (716-282-1028; www.motherlandconnextions.com), 176 Bridge Street Station, P.O. Box 176, Niagara Falls 14305. Fees and hours vary. The western New York area played a major role in the Underground Railroad—not an actual railway but roads and safe houses used by slaves seeking freedom in the 1850s. Motherland Connextions provides an educational and enlightening experience. "Conductors," dressed in period clothing, take groups to stops along the Underground Railroad in both western New York and southern Ontario. The tours are designed to be emotional as well as educational, encouraging participants to "stop and feel" the experience of those who risked their lives for freedom. This tour is not only about the slaves but also about the Native Americans and European settlers who helped them on their journey to freedom. Motorcoach tours start in downtown Buffalo and move to the Niagara Falls/Lewiston area.

Preservation Coalition of Erie County (716-885-3897 or 716-885-3899; www.preservationcoalition.org), 567 Lafayette Avenue, Buffalo. The purpose of the nonprofit Preservation Coalition is to promote the preservation, protection, and restoration of architecturally significant buildings, structures, neighborhoods, and parks in Erie County. Tours are offered to inform people about the history, culture, and architecture in western New York. These tours include house tours, boat cruises, bicycle tours, neighborhood walks, and more. Participants in the tours have the opportunity to visit homes designed by noted architect Frank Lloyd Wright as well as Buffalo's "grand mansions" on Delaware Avenue, notable churches, historic sites, and neighborhoods. Proceeds from the tours benefit historic preservation in Buffalo.

QRS Music Rolls (716-885-4600; www.qrsmusic.com) 1026 Niagara Street, Buffalo. Tours are offered Monday–Friday at 10 AM and 2 PM. Admission: $2 adults, $1 children under 12. They are limited to 15 people and are not recommended for young children. QRS is the world's only manufacturer of player-piano rolls.

Queen City Tours (716-652-3795) Research historians Michael Riester and Patrick Kavanagh offer Sunday-afternoon walking tours of Buffalo. Fees vary depending on tour. These include War of 1812 sites and historic homes in Buffalo, Parkside, or "Flint Hill" area tour and the "Pill Alley" tour of historic doctor's residences on Franklin Street. They also offer tours of Forest Lawn Cemetery, St. Louis Church, and Mount Calvary Cemetery.

Roam Buffalo (716-829-3543; www.wnyrin.com/s_infr/tran/tran_road/agen/roam_buff.html), Hayes Hall 143, 3435 Main Street, Buffalo. Fees vary depending on tour. Located on U. Buffalo's South Campus, Roam Buffalo offers tours of historic Buffalo—via walking, trolley, and bus—that include downtown Buffalo landmarks, the Theater District, Pan-Am sites, Buffalo churches, and more.

Way to Go Tours (716-693-0793) Fees vary depending on tour. This tour company, which is a member of the National Tour Association, has been in operation for over 20 years. They offer a variety of all-day tours, including architectural

AN OBSERVATION TOWER AT THE MARINA OFFERS A VIEW OF THE CITY, THE NIAGARA RIVER, AND LAKE ERIE.

Courtesy Buffalo–Niagara Convention & Visitors Bureau

tours of Buffalo. They also offer motor coach tours of the Finger Lakes region and Chautauqua County wineries to both groups and individuals.

MARINAS Erie Basin Marina (716-851-6503), 329 Erie Street, Buffalo. The Erie Basin Marina, located along Buffalo's waterfront, is a popular place to go during the warmer months. The city-owned marina has 278 slips used by a variety of boats, from fishing boats to pleasure crafts, along with a public boat launch. Even if you don't have a boat, the marina is a fun spot to people-watch or catch a pleasant breeze on a warm summer day. The marina has picnic tables, flower and rose gardens, and a casual waterfront restaurant, The Hatch. An observation tower located at one end of the marina offers a view of the city as well as the Niagara River and Lake Erie.

✳ Green Space

BEACHES AND POOLS Several **City of Buffalo parks** (716-884-9660) have pools that are open to residents and nonresidents alike. These include: **Allison Park** (Rees and Bradley Streets), **Cazenovia Park** (Cazenovia Street and Abbott Road), **JFK Recreational Center** (114 Hickory Street), **Kensington Park** (Kensington Avenue and Grider Street), **Lasalle Park** (Porter Avenue and Amvets Drive), Lovejoy Park (Lovejoy and Gold Streets), **MLK Jr. Park** (Best Street and Fillmore Avenue), **Massachusetts Park** (Massachusetts Avenue), **Masten Park** (Best Street and Masten Avenue) **Riverside Park** (Niagara and Vulcan), and **Stachowski/Houghton Park** (Clinton near Kelmer).

CEMETERIES Forest Lawn Cemetery & Garden Mausoleums (716-885-1600; www.forest-lawn.com), 1411 Delaware Avenue, Buffalo. Grounds open daily 8–5, until 6 PM Memorial Day–Labor Day. Forest Lawn is a place for peaceful repose for the departed and a place of beauty and tranquility for the living. It is such a lovely place that many newlyweds choose to have their wedding pictures taken here. The cemetery, which opened in 1849, has a number of prominent people buried here, including Millard Fillmore (1800–1874), the 13th president of the United States. President Fillmore's simple grave consists of a granite memorial marker inscribed with "MF." However, his family's plot is graced with a dignified obelisk of pink granite as a memorial to him. Other notables buried in the cemetery include aviation pioneer Lawrence Bell, philanthropist Maria Love, and Seneca chieftan Red Jacket. Among the many beautiful and interesting sculptures is the Blocher family memorial, a domelike structure unveiled in 1888 with four life-sized figures carved from marble: Nelson Blocher, who died at age 37 in 1884; his parents; and the figure of an angel. Nelson's tragic story has him falling in love with the family maid, whereupon his socially prominent parents sent him to Europe for a year, hoping that he would forget the girl. Instead, it has been said, he died of a broken heart. The cemetery recently opened the Blue Sky Mausoleum, which was constructed using a Frank Lloyd Wright design.

GARDENS 🦌 ✍ ♿ 🌳 **Buffalo and Erie County Botanical Gardens** (716-827-1584; www.buffalogardens.com), 2655 South Park Avenue, Buffalo. Open

Monday–Friday 9–4 (until 6 PM Wednesday), Saturday and Sunday 9–5. Free admission, donations accepted. The showplace of the gardens, a 100 year-old Victorian-style glass conservatory—350 feet long and 60 feet high—is listed on the New York State and National Register of Historic Places. Two smaller palm domes are connected to the central dome by glass growing ranges. The 11.3 acre site features plants from around the world, including cacti, fruit trees, palms, and many beautiful flowers. Located in South Park, the botanical gardens are part of the Buffalo Parks System designed by noted landscape artist Frederick Law Olmsted. Educational programs, children's workshops, and special events are held throughout the year.

NATURE PRESERVES ✐ ♿ **Tifft Nature Preserve** (716-825-1289), 1200 Fuhrmann Boulevard, Buffalo. Visitors center open Tuesday–Friday 9–2, Saturday 9–4, Sunday 12–4; grounds open daily, dawn to dusk. Donation. This 264-acre refuge run by the Buffalo Museum of Science is dedicated to environmental education and conservation. Located less than 3 miles from downtown Buffalo, it's great place to watch migrating birds and other wildlife, such as beaver and

---

OLMSTED PARKS

Buffalo's park and parkway system, designed in 1868 by America's first landscape architect, Frederick Law Olmsted, is made up of six parks linked with eight circles and eight landscaped parkways. Olmsted, often referred to as the "Father of Landscape Architecture," also designed New York's Central Park. Olmsted, along with Calvert Vaux, designed the parks not only to offer beautiful scenery but to offer people a place to walk and be active—especially important in an industrial city like Buffalo. The system of parks and parkways in Buffalo, which are listed on the National Register of Historic Places, are of historic significance because they represent the largest body of Olmsted's work and were the first of their kind in the nation. Seventy-five percent of the city's parkland is Olmsted-designed, and Buffalo is one of only five cities in the country that has an Olmsted park system that is still intact. The **Buffalo Olmsted Parks Conservancy** (716-838-1249; www.buffaloolmsted parks.org; 84 Parkside Avenue, Buffalo 14214), founded in 1978, is a not-for-profit organization that works with the city and community to ensure that the Olmsted-designed parks are preserved and maintained. The Conservancy sponsors a variety of events throughout the year including park cleanups, workshops, concerts, and more.

The parkways designed by Olmsted include **Lincoln, Bidwell, Chapin, Richmond, Porter, Red Jacket,** and **McKinley.** Humboldt Parkway was lost as a result of the construction of the Kensington Expressway. The seven circles are **Soldiers, Gates, Colonial, Ferry,** and **Symphony Circle,** all located near Delaware Park, and McClellan and McKinley Circles in South Buffalo.

deer. During the warmer months, get close to nature on 5 miles of hiking trails, and do some fishing along the preserve's Lake Kirsty. In winter, cross-country skiing and snowshoeing are popular (snowshoe rentals are available).

Times Beach Nature Preserve and South Buffalo Harbor, Off Fuhrmann Boulevard, Buffalo. Open daily dawn to dusk. Free admission. This 50-acre site, adjacent to the Coast Guard Station and the Buffalo Lighthouse, was once a disposal area for Buffalo Harbor sediment dredging. It's a good spot to view waterfowl in spring and fall.

PARKS, OLMSTED Cazenovia Park, Cazenovia and Abbott Roads, Buffalo. Open daily dawn to dusk. A 191-acre Olmsted Park, originally constructed in 1897, features a 9-hole golf course, indoor swimming pool, community center, sports fields, ice rinks, and outdoor spray pool. Cazenovia Creek is a popular launch site for canoe trips.

✣ **Delaware Park** (716-884-9660), Lincoln Parkway, Buffalo. Open daily dawn to dusk. This 350-acre park, the centerpiece of the Buffalo Parks system, was designed in the late 1800s by noted landscape architect, Frederick Law Olmsted. It was designed with three distinct features: a 42-acre lake, a large meadow, and several wooded areas. Over the years there have been changes to Olmsted's design. The meadow is now an 18-hole golf course, and the Buffalo Zoo, the Buffalo and Erie County Historical Society, and the Albright-Knox Art Gallery are located on what was originally park land. Today, visitors can enjoy the park's jogging and walking trails, tennis courts, softball diamonds, golf courses, and fishing venues. The park's Rose Garden features award-wining roses, along with a collection of antique roses dating back to the 1800s. During the winter, visitors can enjoy cross-country skiing and ice skating. Children's play areas are located throughout the park, as are picnic facilities. Special events held in the park include the Olmsted Winterfest in February and Shakespeare in the Park during the summer.

Front Park, Porter Avenue at the Peace Bridge. Open daily dawn to dusk. Originally known as "The Front," Front Park was considered the most formal of Olmsted's first three Buffalo parks (Front, Martin Luther King, and Delaware). When it was constructed in 1868, it had 32 acres and its main feature was its commanding view of the Niagara River, Lake Erie, and Canada. However, much of its parkland was lost due to the construction of the Peace Bridge in 1925 and the New York State Thruway in the 1940s and 1950s.

Martin Luther King Jr. Park (716-851-5806), Best Street and Fillmore Avenue, Buffalo. Open daily dawn to dusk. Also known as Humboldt Park, this 50-acre Olmsted park is adjacent to the Buffalo Museum of Science. The park was originally known as "The Parade," and was designed by Olmsted to be the site of military drills and large gatherings. It was later called Humboldt Park, then renamed Martin Luther King Jr. Park in 1977. Facilities include tennis courts, hockey rink, picnic shelters, and a 500-foot diameter wading pool.

Riverside Park (716-877-5972), 2607 Niagara Street, Tonawanda Street and Crowley Avenue, Buffalo. Open daily dawn to dusk. This 37-acre park was the final park designed in Buffalo by Olmsted. Originally the park overlooked the Erie Canal and the Niagara River, but it was cut off from the river by the Niagara section of the Thruway in the 1950s. Facilities include a swimming pool and a wading pool. The Riverwalk bike path also goes though the park.

South Park (716-838-1249; www.buffaloolmstedparks.com), South Park Avenue, South Buffalo. Open daily dawn to dusk. The design for South Park was first proposed by Olmsted in 1892, with its central feature being a circuit drive to enjoy views of the entire park—now popular with walkers, joggers, and in-line skaters, instead of carriage riders. Today the park features 155 acres of green space, including a shrub garden, a lake, and a golf course. The park's focal point is the circa 1900 Victorian glass conservatory, home to the Buffalo and Erie Country Botanical Gardens.

PARKS, OTHER **LaSalle Park** (716-884-9660), Porter Avenue at Amvets Drive, Buffalo. Open daily dawn to dusk. This 77-acre city park is located on Lake Erie at the mouth of the Niagara River. Facilities include a swimming pool, sports fields, snack bar, and picnic area. The Riverwalk Bike Path goes through it. LaSalle Park is a good place for bird watching. Several festivals and concerts are held at the park during the summer.

Cathedral Park, Main Street next to St. Paul's Cathedral, downtown Buffalo. A small, shady urban park, this is a popular spot for downtown office workers to eat lunch.

Numerous small neighborhood parks are located throughout the city. Contact the **Buffalo Parks Department** for more information (716-884-9660; www.ci .buffalo.ny.us) or check out the **Western New York Regional Information Network** (www.wnyrin.com), which lists the hundreds of parks found in the region.

WALKING AND HIKING TRAILS Besides those listed below, several hiking and biking trails are in the planning and construction phases in Buffalo and the surrounding communities.

Bird Island Pier (at the end of West Ferry Street, go over lift bridge to Bird Island). This path is on a 1-mile long cement barrier that separates the Black Rock Canal and the Niagara River. Walkers, joggers, and in-line skaters enjoy this trail, as do fishermen who try their luck from the rocks along the pier. This is also a good spot to watch rowers from the West Side Rowing Club on the Black Rock Canal.

Riverwalk Bike Path (716-858-8352). Riverwalk is a 14-mile county-owned paved pathway for walking, biking, jogging, and rollerblading. It starts on Commercial Street by the Naval Park in downtown Buffalo near the Erie Basin Marina, then travels along the Niagara River, through several parks, ending on Main Street in the City of Tonawanda along the Erie Canal. There is a concession stand near the Ontario Street boat launch.

See also **Tifft Nature Preserve**, **Delaware Park**, and **South Park** in *Green Space*.

☀ Lodging

INNS AND RESORTS ⅃ **The Mansion on Delaware Avenue** (716-886-3300; www.mansionondelaware.com), 414 Delaware Avenue, Buffalo. The 28 guest rooms in this 1869 Second Empire–style mansion have been carefully restored to reflect the inn's Victorian splendor. Each room is unique—some have fireplaces, others have bay windows, and some have 14-foot ceilings. Three of the rooms are fully handicap accessible. The building, known as "The House of Light" when it was first constructed, has over 175 windows, 14 of them large bay windows. Proprietors Gino and Diana Principe and their partner, Dennis Murphy of InnVest Lodging, have created a distinctive hotel that is not only a place to stay while visiting Buffalo but a destination in itself. They transformed it from a dilapidated, boarded-up place that had been vacant for over 25 years to a first-class luxury hotel that recently was awarded the AAA's prestigious Four-Diamond designation; placing the Mansion in the same class as the Waldorf-Astoria in New York City and the Ritz Carlton in Sarasota. The extraordinary amenities set this hotel apart from others, including 24-hour a day butlers, round-the-clock in-room dining, and an upscale complimentary continental breakfast. The hotel has been featured in articles in the *New York Times* and *Architectural Digest*. Visiting celebrities—including Hillary Clinton, Reba McEntire, and Faith Hill and Tim McGraw—as well as corporate executives choose the Mansion when they visit Buffalo. $145–$250. Reservations strongly recommended as this place is often fully booked.

MOTELS AND HOTELS ⅃ **Adams Mark** (716-845-5100; www.adamsmark.com), 120 Church Street, Buffalo. This waterfront hotel offers 486 guest rooms, including six multilevel suites. The hotel has an indoor pool, health club, 24-hour room service, and airport shuttle service. $89–$165.

⅃ **Comfort Suites Downtown**, (716-854-5500; www.choicehotels.com), 601 Main Street, Buffalo. Located in the heart of Buffalo's theater and entertainment district, this hotel offers 146 two-room suites, each with a king-sized bed, sofa bed, refrigerator, coffeemaker, and more. $99–$169

⅃ **Doubletree Club Hotel** (716-845-0112; www.doubletree.com), 125 High Street, Buffalo. One hundred spacious guest rooms located in Buffalo's medical corridor. Rooms include refrigerator, cable TV, and high-speed Internet access. Suites come equipped with a full-sized kitchen. A 24-hour fitness center is available. $109–$119.

THIS 1869 SECOND EMPIRE–STYLE MANSION IS NOW A FOUR-DIAMOND INN.

Christine A. Smyczynski

&. **Hampton Inn & Suites** (716-855-2223, 800-HAMPTON), 220 Delaware, Buffalo. This 137 room inn combines modern amenities with a historic feel, as it was constructed inside an existing vintage downtown building. In addition to regular rooms, the hotel has 31 suites, some as large as 1,500 square feet. It also has an indoor pool, Jacuzzi, workout area, and a complimentary weekday breakfast buffet. $105–$135.

&. **Hyatt Regency** (716-856-1234; www.buffalo.hyatt.com), 2 Fountain Plaza, Buffalo. This 395-room luxury hotel is located in the heart of the entertainment and business district and is connected to the Buffalo Convention Center by an enclosed walkway. It is unique in architecture, as the Hyatt Corporation utilized the 15-story circa-1923 Genesee Building, designed by E. B. Green and William Wicks, and added to it when building the hotel. The marble doorway of the old building serves as the entrance to the hotel's glass atrium. $89–$160.

BED & BREAKFASTS Beau Fleuve Bed & Breakfast (716-882-6116; www.beaufleuve.com), 242 Linwood Avenue (at Bryant), Buffalo. Hosts Rik and Ramona Whitaker offer five comfortable rooms in this circa 1881 grand Stick–style home, located in the Linwood Historic Preservation District. Interior features include an oak staircase and nine stained-glass windows. Each guest room reflects one of the ethnic groups that settled in the Buffalo area: French, Irish, German, Italian, and Polish. The French Room, which is decorated in shades of blue, has a private bath and a decorative fireplace; the German Room, which overlooks Linwood Avenue,

also has a private bath. The Irish Room, the inn's largest guest room, features a brass queen-sized bed, en suite bath, electric fireplace, and TV. The Polish and Italian Rooms share a bath that features an original sink dating back to the 1920s. The inn's common area, which has complimentary snacks and beverages for guests, is furnished in Craftsman style, with Native American artifacts. Start the day with an elegant breakfast that includes just-baked muffins, gourmet coffee, and entrées like veggie frittata, eggs Benedict, or Belgian waffles. Well-behaved children are welcome. $100–$145.

✳ Where to Eat

DINING OUT

Downtown/Center City/Delaware Avenue

Brownstone Seafood House & Oyster Bar (716-842-6800), 297 Franklin Street, Buffalo. Open for lunch Monday–Friday 11–4, dinner Monday–Thursday 4–10, Friday–Sunday 4–11. Reservations recommended. This upscale seafood restaurant features dining on two levels, amid brick walls and ironwork. The menu is dominated with seafood favorites, including oysters, crab, lobster, and mussels, along with numerous fish entrées. One of the most popular entrées, Chilean sea bass, is served with gingered carrots and mashed potatoes. Other selections include red snapper, blackened catfish, and tuna steak.

Buffalo Chop House (716-842-6900), 282 Franklin Street, Buffalo. Open Sunday–Thursday 4 PM–12 AM, Friday and Saturday 4 PM–2 AM. This steak house, located in a 1870 carriage house, is known for its large cuts of meat, like a 48-ounce porterhouse. The menu, modeled after the best steak houses in Manhattan, also offers chicken, pasta, and seafood if you are not in the mood for meat. The decor is luxurious, with natural brick, leather chairs, and heavy drapery.

& **E. B. Green's Steakhouse** (716-855-4870; www.ebgreens.com), 2 Fountain Plaza, Buffalo; in the Hyatt Hotel. Open daily 5–10. Specialties include porterhouse steak, filet mignon, prime rib, and Maine lobster. Generous portions and meat grilled to perfection are just two of the reasons why E. B. Green's is western New York's best steak house and was recently named one of America's top ten independent steak houses by Tom Horan's America's Top Ten Club.

& **Hutch's** (716-885-0074), 1375 Delaware Avenue (near Gates Circle), Buffalo. Open Monday–Thursday 5–10, Friday and Saturday 5–12, Sunday 4–9. This romantic eatery features cuisine with a hint of the southwest and Pacific Rim. With its brick walls adorned with posters and paintings, it has the feel of a European bistro. It is known for its seafood dishes, as well as pastas and meat selections. Rated four stars by the *Buffalo News*.

Ÿ **Lord Chumleys** (716-886-2220; www.lordchumleys.com), 481 Delaware Avenue, Buffalo. Open at 11:30. Elegant and romantic dining can be found in this gourmet restaurant located in a turn-of-the-20th-century townhouse. First off, the decor is breathtaking; its four-story atrium is designed to look like a cobblestone street at night, complete with lamp-posts and a starry sky. Start off your dining experience with Caesar salad, one of their specialties. Menu selections include chateaubriand, lobster,

ostrich, and frog legs, plus over 150 varieties of wine to choose from. Proper dress is required, including jackets for gentlemen.

Ÿ **Lotis** (716-332-4497; www.lotis lounge.com), 1389 Delaware Avenue (near Gates Circle), Buffalo. Open Monday–Saturday for dinner. This full-service restaurant features international nouveau cuisine, including steak, pasta, and seafood dishes, along with Southwest and Asian dishes. The decor is very modern, with low lights and a stainless steel-topped bar. The terrace, which has limited seating for dinner, includes an outdoor bar and lounge.

& **Park Lane** (716-881-2603; www .parklanerestaurant.com), 33 Gates Circle, Buffalo. Open for lunch Monday–Friday 11:30–3, dinner Monday–Saturday 5–10:30, Sunday brunch 10:30–2. Enjoy casual yet elegant dining in a restored landmark restaurant. Menu selections feature American cuisine, including prime beef, pasta, and Park lane's signature swordfish.

Rue Franklin (716-852-4416), 341 Franklin Street, Buffalo. Open Tuesday–Saturday 5:30–9:30. This beautifully decorated, intimate restaurant is the closest you can get to Paris without leaving Buffalo. Their French-inspired cuisine varies with the seasons and includes rib pork chops, braised veal, and filet of sole.

Shanghai Reds (716-852-7337), 2 Templeton Terrace, Buffalo. Open daily for dinner 5–10; call for lunch hours. This brand-new restaurant and banquet facility overlooks the Erie Basin Marina and the Buffalo waterfront. The menu features seafood, steaks, and pasta, plus several wok items.

Sphere Entertainment Complex (716-852-3900; www.spherebuffalo .com), 681 Main Street, Buffalo. Open for lunch Monday–Friday 11:30–2:30, dinner Wednesday–Saturday 4:30–9. This restaurant/theater/ nightclub is located on the site of the old Towne Casino, a popular nightspot during the 1950s. The menu features a variety of international dishes, including chicken cannelloni and mahimahi moquecca, a Brazilian clam dish.

West Side
Tempo (716-885-1594), 581 Delaware Ave., Buffalo. This upscale restaurant is located in a vintage home. Menu selections include seafood and steak with an Italian accent.

Ⴤ **Harry's Harbour Place Grille** (716-874-5400; www.harrysharbour .com), 2192 Niagara Street, Buffalo. Open for lunch and dinner. Reservations are recommended. Get a bird's-eye view of the Niagara River at this waterfront dining spot, just minutes from downtown Buffalo. The extensive menu features Continental cuisine, with selections like filet mignon, sea scallops, and grilled chicken breast. Harry's also offers an extensive wine list. It's a popular place to watch the sunset.

Left Bank (716-882-3509), 511 Rhode Island Street, Buffalo. Open Monday–Thursday 4–11, Friday–Saturday 5–12, Sunday brunch 11–2:30, dinner 4–10. This casually elegant American bistro is one of Buffalo's more popular dining spots. The menu features pastas, vegetarian steaks, and Mediterranean dishes. Signature dishes include pork tenderloins with a Grand Marnier sauce. Desserts are provided by Carriage Trade Pastries.

Roseland (716-882-3328), 490 Rhode Island Street, Buffalo. Open Monday–Thursday 5–10 PM, Friday and Saturday 5–11:30 PM, Sunday 3–9 PM. This popular Buffalo restaurant has been offering fine Italian dining since 1928. While spaghetti and red sauce will always be a popular dish in the cream-and-green dining room, patrons can also enjoy menu items with French, New England, and Mediterranean influences. One of their specialties is Caesar salad prepared tableside.

Elmwood Village/Allentown
Brodo (716-881-1117), 765 Elmwood Avenue, Buffalo. Open Monday–Saturday 11–11, Sunday 4–10. This café is best known for its homemade soups; the name of the restaurant loosely translates to mean broth or soup. Their signature soup, Dominic's brodo, is a tomato-based soup with pasta and sausage. In addition to soups, they also serve a selection of entrées.

&. **Fiddle Heads Restaurant & Wine bar** (716-883-4166), 62 Allen Street, Buffalo. Dinner Tuesday–Saturday 5–10. This upscale simple-but-elegant urban café features creative American dishes featuring pork, chicken, duck, and salmon. They are noted for their simple salad, as an appetizer to your meal.

Moka Gourmet (716-883-5888), 199 Allen St., Buffalo. Topen Tuesday–Thursday 7 am–11 pm, Friday and Saturday until midnight, and Sunday 8 am–4 pm. This newly opened restaurant in the heart of Allentown serves light fare including salads, panni sandwiches, and vegetarian dishes, along with a variety of coffees and sweets.

Nektar (716-881-1829), 451 Elmwood Ave., Buffalo. Open Monday–Saturday 11 am–2 am. This popular restaurant and martini bar recently re-opened after a devastating fire. Menu items include everything from hamburgers and sandwiches to shrimp, lobster, and steak.

& **Saigon Café** (716-883-1252), 1098 Elmwood Avenue, Buffalo. Open Monday–Thursday 11–10, Friday 11–11, Saturday 12–11, Sunday 12–9. This small, intimate restaurant, its tables adorned in white-linen tablecloths, cloth napkins, and fine china, offers diners fine Vietnamese and Thai cuisine. It has been rated the best Thai restaurant in Buffalo by *Artvoice*.

& **Sofra** (716-884-1100), 929 Elmwood Avenue, Buffalo. Open Tuesday–Thursday 11–9, Friday 11–10, Saturday 12–10, Sunday 12–9. Experience the taste of Turkey at this unique bistro, which is decorated in shades of gold and brown. Start your dining experience with hummus, tabouli, or eggplant salsa. For lunch you might choose a shish kebab sandwich or doner sandwich, while for dinner you may select lamb shank or karhiyarik (stuffed eggplant).

& **Toro** (716-886-9457; www.toro tapasbar.com), 492 Elmwood Avenue, Buffalo. Open Sunday 5–10 PM, Monday–Wednesday 5 PM–midnight, Thursday–Saturday 5 PM–2 AM. The menu at this trendy Elmwood Avenue eatery focuses on tapas, which are Spanish appetizers. Some of the more popular choices include baked oysters in phyllo and roasted beet carpaccio. If you're looking for something more substantial, dinner entrées are also served, including strip steak, lamb chops, and salmon.

North Buffalo/Hertel Avenue
& **Franks Sunny Italy** (716-876-5449; www.frankssunnyitaly.com),

2491 Delaware Avenue (one block north of Hertel), Buffalo. Open Monday 11–10, Tuesday–Saturday 11–11, Sunday 12–11. A casual, comfortable, sit-down family restaurant specializing in authentic Italian home cooking. Menu selections include veal chicken and pasta dishes, along with a large selection of pizzas. This restaurant has been operated since 1990 by the Sclafani family, who hail from Montemaggiore Belsitoa, small town in Sicily.

♉ & **The Hourglass Restaurant** (716-877-8788), 981 Kenmore Avenue, Buffalo. Open Tuesday–Saturday 4-9:30. A small, intimate restaurant featuring an extensive wine cellar and a large diverse menu of continental cuisine including double-cut lamb chops, fresh seafood, and roast duck Laperouse. Save room for their signature crème brûlée, their most requested dessert.

& **La Marina Seafood Market and Grille** (716-834-9681; www.lamarina online.com), 1503 Hertel Avenue, Buffalo. Open Tuesday–Thursday 11–9, Friday and Saturday 11–10. This popular restaurant is the only combination seafood market and restaurant in the Buffalo area. They serve the freshest seafood in town, creative pasta dishes, along with homemade soups and bread. Their Friday night fish fry is legendary and very popular; arrive early to avoid a long wait. Be sure to try their specialty, crab cakes.

North End Trattoria (716-446-0025), 1456 Hertel Avenue, Buffalo. Open Sunday, Monday, Wednesday, Thursday 5 PM–midnight, Friday and Saturday 5 PM–midnight; closed Tuesday. A small (seats only 36) intimate café, where you can actually see and smell the food being prepared. Menu choices include rack of lamb, steak, and osso buco, as well as chicken and seafood entrées. Reservations are recommended.

Oliver's (716-877-9662), 2095 Delaware Avenue, Buffalo. Open Monday–Thursday 5–10, Friday and Saturday 5–12, Sunday 4:30–9:30. This Buffalo restaurant has been a fine-dining destination for nearly 70 years. It's definitely a special-occasion restaurant, with its contemporary decor, distinctive entrées, and extensive wine list. Specialties include New York strip steak, seafood, and fresh fish.

Ristorante Lombardo (716-873-4291; www.ristorantelombardo.com), 1198 Hertel Avenue, Buffalo. Open for lunch Monday–Friday 11:30–2:30, dinner Monday–Thursday 5–10, Friday–Saturday 5–11. Enjoy lunch and dinner in a Tuscan-style dining room or outdoors in an intimate courtyard. Menu selections include penne and grilled veal, risotto con frutti di mare, and osso buco Milanese. They serve an authentic tableside Caesar salad and one of the best tiramisus in the city.

Tsunami (716-447-7915), 1141 Kenmore Avenue, Buffalo. Open Monday–Thursday 5–10, Friday and Saturday 5–11. An elegant restaurant with Asian-inspired cuisine. Entrées include seafood with a Pacific Rim flare, sushi, duck, and more. They also have a reputation for really good desserts.

EATING OUT

Downtown
♈ **Anchor Bar** (716-886-8920; www.anchorbar.com), 1047 Main Street, Buffalo. Open Monday–Thursday 11–11, Friday 11–1 AM, Saturday and

Sunday noon–1 AM. No trip to Buffalo is complete without a stop at the famous Anchor Bar, where Buffalo wings were first served back in 1964. While wings are the most popular menu item, a variety of other dishes are also offered, including pasta and veal parmigiana. While you're waiting for your wings, take a look at the photos of notable people and celebrities who have visited this Buffalo institution over the years. You can even take home a souvenir of your visit—a T-shirt, a hat, or a bottle of their famous hot sauce.

& **Bijou Grille** (716-847-1512; www.bijougrille.com), 643 Main Street, Buffalo. Open Monday 11-3, Tuesday–Saturday 11–midnight, Sunday 2–10. This theater-district eatery is decorated to resemble Hollywood in the 1950s. The menu has a decidedly California influence, along with many Mexican dishes.

♨ ♪ **Chefs** (716-856-9187; www.ilovechefs.com), 291 Seneca Street, Buffalo. Open Monday–Saturday 11:45–9. One of Buffalo's best-known Italian restaurants for over 80 years. Dine on red-and-white checkered tablecloths under grape chandeliers. Their red sauce, which can be purchased by the quart to take home, is one of the best in the city. Specialties include spaghetti parmigiana, lasagna, and ravioli. Desserts are baked fresh daily at a local bakery.

♈ **D'Arcy McGee's Irish Pub** (716-853-3600), 257 Franklin Street, Buffalo. Open 11 AM–4 AM. Downtown Buffalo's only authentic Irish pub. You can get the best corned beef sandwich in the city here, along with other Irish specialties, such as boiled Irish dinner, shepherd's pie, and Guinness beef stew. See also Nightlife.

Grill 33 (716-881-2603) 33 Gates Circle, Buffalo. Open for dinner 5–11 daily. Casual pub dining adjacent to the Park Lane Restaurant. Selections include salads, sandwiches, pizza, burgers, pasta, and more.

♿ **The Hatch** (716-851-6501), 329 Erie Street (at the Erie Basin Marina), Buffalo. Seasonal, seven days 7:30 AM–9 PM. While the food here is good—burgers, sandwiches, hot dogs, and a standard-fare breakfast menu—come here for the view. The restaurant offers a picturesque vista of the Buffalo River, Lake Erie, and the boat harbor, with most of the seating outdoors under a canopy or along the water. They also serve ice cream and have a clam bar that sells beer and wine. Special note: Don't leave your food unattended; there are many hungry seagulls nearby.

Laughlins Beef and Barrel (716-842-6700), 333 Franklin Street (at Tupper Street), Buffalo. Open 11 AM–4 AM daily. This newly opened bar/restaurant, housed in a charming turn-of-the-20th-century building, features hand-carved roast beef and prime rib as well as soups, salads, and sandwiches. Diners can enjoy a basket of pretzels with dipping mustards as an appetizer instead of the usual bread or rolls.

Pearl Street Grill & Brewery (716-856-2337; www.pearlstreetgrill.com), 76 Pearl Street, Buffalo. Monday–Thursday 11:30–9, Friday–Saturday 11:30–10, Sunday 3–9. This restored 1870 building in the old Erie Canal district features brick walls, tin ceilings, and an antique pulley fan system. A microbrewery is located on the first floor of the restaurant.

Ulrich's Tavern (716-855-8409; www.ulrichstavern.com), 674 Ellicott Street, Buffalo. Open for lunch Monday–Friday 11:30–2:45, dinner Friday and Saturday 5–9:30. Established in 1868, Ulrich's is Buffalo's oldest continuously operating tavern. The restaurant features a German-American menu, with beers from Buffalo and Germany. Lunch selections include beef on weck, burgers, and potato pancakes. Or try such German fare as bratwurst and weisswurt sausage.

Elmwood Village/Allentown

Allen Street Hardware Company (716-842-6900), 245 Allen Street, Buffalo. Open Sunday–Wednesday 3 PM–midnight, Thursday–Saturday 3 PM–2 AM. This small café and bar gets its name from the hardware store that formerly occupied this space. This neighborhood pub features wine, beer, and an assortment of soups, salads, and sandwiches, including wraps and panini.

♿ **Ambrosia** (716-881-2196), 467 Elmwood Avenue (at Hodge), Buffalo. Open 7 AM–11 PM daily. If you look up the word ambrosia in the dictionary, one of the definitions is "food of the Greek gods"—an appropriate name for this café that specializes in Greek cuisine, with menu selections like Greek meze and moussaka. Year-round patio dining is available. Valet parking is offered Friday and Saturday evenings.

Aqua (716-881-2782), 206 Allen Street, Buffalo. Open Thursday–Sunday for lunch 11–3, dinner 5–11. A newly open restaurant that focuses on contemporary cuisine with an emphasis on seafood. they also have vegetarian and meat entrées on the menu. Eat indoors or on the patio in back.

&. **Astoria** (716-884-4711), 423 Elmwood, Buffalo. Open Monday–Wednesday 11–9, Thursday 10–10, Friday 11–11 Saturday 4–11. This small intimate café, with its red walls and white-linen tablecloths, features Greek and American cuisine. Greek specialties include standard fare like gyros and souvlaki, while the American menu offers steak, grilled salmon, and pork tenderloin, among other choices. It has one of the best covered dining patios in the city.

Y **J. P. Bullfeathers** (716-886-1010; www.jpbullfeathers.com), 1010 Elmwood Avenue, Buffalo. Open 11 AM–2 AM daily. A classy restaurant by day and early evening and a popular college tavern by night. Menu selections range from chicken wings to filet mignon. Dine indoors by the fireplace or outdoor on the patio (weather permitting).

&. **Caffè Aroma** (716-884-4522), 957 Elmwood Avenue, Buffalo. Open Sunday 8 AM–10 PM, Monday–Thursday 6:30 AM–11 PM Friday 6:30 AM–1 AM, and Saturday 8 AM–1 AM. This locally owned and operated coffee shop, connected to Talking Leaves Bookstore, features gourmet coffees plus sandwiches and sweets, along with beer and wine.

&. **Café 59** (716-883-1880), 59 Allen Street, Buffalo. Open Monday–Friday 8–9, Saturday 10–5. This coffee shop and cyber café features large tables, great for spreading out your laptop and paperwork. The menu features soups, salads, pita pockets, and sandwiches.

♪ &. **Casa di Pizza** (716-883-8200; www.casadipizza.com), 477 Elmwood Avenue, Buffalo. Open Monday–Saturday 11:30 AM–12 AM, Sunday 12–12. Since 1953 folks living and working along Elmwood Avenue have come to love pizza from this establishment. Or choose from a full menu of Italian and American dishes. Take out and delivery is also available.

&. **Cecelia's** (716-883-8066), 716 Elmwood Avenue, Buffalo. Open Monday–Friday 10:30–10, Saturday 4:30–11, Sunday 3:30–10. Offering the largest open-air patio along Elmwood Avenue, this restaurant features numerous Italian entrées like manicotti and pizza along with specialty dishes like chicken or veal Cecelia. Other popular menu selections are the panini sandwiches. Also on the menu are over fifty varieties of martinis, from classic to unusual. The restaurant even has a children's menu. Live jazz is featured Thursday–Saturday.

Y &. **Coles** (716-886-1449), 1104 Elmwood Avenue, Buffalo. Open for lunch Monday–Saturday 11–3, dinner Monday–Sunday 6–11, Sunday brunch 11–3. This popular restaurant/bar has been a neighborhood fixture since 1934. Enjoy your meal in the dining room, in the wicker-furnished atrium, or on the outdoor patio. Menu selections include dishes like port wine-glazed tenderloin medallions or chicken with pesto, goat cheese, and roasted peppers, plus a large selection of seafood specials and sandwiches. Complimentary Champagne is served with the Sunday brunch, which includes omelet selections with names like Huey Louie Andouille and the Green Flash.

Y &. **Cozumel Grill & Tequila Bar** (716-884-3866), 153 Elmwood Avenue, Buffalo. Kitchen open 11 AM–midnight. This former carriage house has been converted into a popular restaurant known for Mexican fare, including fajitas, chimichangas, enchiladas, and cactus strips. Or go the steak, seafood, and pork tenderloin route. Wash dinner down with a margarita, their specialty.

& **Falafel Bar** (716-884-0444) 1009 Elmwood Avenue, Buffalo. Open Monday–Thursday 11–9, Friday and Saturday 11–10. This restaurant specializes in Mediterranean and Middle-Eastern food.

🦞 **Everything's Special** (716-883-8355), 244 Allen Street, Buffalo. Open Tuesday–Saturday 1–9. A small take-out restaurant specializing in Southern-style cooking like fried chicken and collard greens. It's recommended that you call ahead to place your order.

Fat Bob's Smokehouse (716-887-2971; www.fatbobs.com), 41 Virginia Place, Buffalo. Open Monday–Friday 11:30 AM–10 PM, Saturday 3:30 PM–1 AM, Sunday 12 PM–1 AM. Dine in or take out. Enjoy BBQ and smokehouse-style foods at the only smokehouse in Buffalo. Fat Bob's specializes in "slow and low" cooking. Meats are dry rubbed and cooked for several hours on low heat in their 24-foot, 7,000-pound smoker. Menu selections include pulled Memphis pork topped with coleslaw on a kaiser roll, St. Louis pork ribs, and sliced beef brisket. Sides include fries and potato salad, along with collard greens, hush puppies, and cornbread. There is live music on Wednesday evenings, and outdoor dining is available on their patio.

Gabriel's Gate (716-886-0602), 145 Allen Street, Buffalo. Open Sunday–Wednesday 11:30 AM–midnight, Thursday 11:30 AM–1 AM, Friday–Saturday 11:30 AM–2 AM. This high quality, casual dining establishment is located in a historic 1864 row house.

Menu selections include burgers, salads, and steaks. Their French onion soup is outstanding as well as their Friday fish fry.

& 🦞 **Indian Gate** (716-886-4000) 1116 Elmwood Avenue, Buffalo. Open daily for lunch 11:30–2:30, dinner 4:30–10. This bright and cheery restaurant features naturally healthy and high-quality Indian cuisine. It offers a mix of vegetarian and non-vegetarian dishes, including delicacies from their clay oven like chicken tikka and fish tandoori. The lunch buffet is very popular and a good value.

& 🦞 **Jim's Steakout** Several locations throughout Buffalo: 938 Elmwood (885-2900), 3094 Main (838-6666), 92 Chippewa (854-6666), and 196 Allen (886-2222). Open daily 10:30 AM–5 AM. Since 1981 Jim's Steakout has been the place to go once the bars close since they are open until 5 AM. This locally owned and operated restaurant chain is famous for their steak hoagies.

Just Pasta (716-881-1888), 307 Bryant Street, Buffalo. Open for lunch Monday–Friday 11:30–4, dinner Monday–Thursday 5–10, Friday–Saturday 5–11. In business for over 20 years, this comfortable restaurant has an extensive pasta menu as well as a fairly large selection of wines.

& **Kien Giang** (716-885-7030), 494 Elmwood Avenue, Buffalo. Open Sunday and Tuesday–Thursday 11–10:30, Friday and Saturday 11–12. Enjoy authentic Vietnamese cuisine—including hot-and-sour soup and stir-fried lemongrass beef—in a relaxing environment. Top off your meal with a Vietnamese coffee.

🍸 & **LeMetro Bakery and Bistro** (716-885-1500), 518 Elmwood

Avenue, Buffalo. Monday–Friday 7–11, Saturday 8–midnight, Sunday 9–11. This casual bistro is known for its global cuisine and Old World–style bread. Menu selections include items like pan-seared duck breast and sesame-encrusted tuna.

Ⴘ **Mother's** (716-882-2989), 33 Virginia Place, Buffalo. Restaurant open 5 PM–3 AM; bar open 4 PM–4 AM. This has been a popular pub and restaurant in Allentown for many years. Located in a former carriage house, Mother's offers fine dining in a relaxed atmosphere.

✍ **Off the Wall** (716-884-9986; www.offthewallonline.com), 534 Elmwood Avenue, Buffalo. Open Monday–Thursday 8 AM–11 PM, Friday and Saturday 8 AM–2 PM, Sunday 9 AM–4 PM. Almost everything is for sale in this unique retro eatery, including the tables and chairs! Specialties include Scotch eggs and Monte Cristo. Or try their soups, salads, pastas, and sandwiches. A children's menu is available.

Palm Tree Caribbean Restaurant (716-886-5501), 69 Allen Street, Buffalo. Open Monday–Thursday 9–11, Friday and Saturday 9–midnight. This restaurant features dishes like oxtail stew along with entrées made with curry and tofu. They also have a selection of vegetarian items.

ꗥ **Pano's** (716-886-9081), 1081 Elmwood Avenue, Buffalo. A Greek-style restaurant that's open 24 hours daily. Enjoy dining outdoors on the deck in summer. To find this restaurant, just look for the blue and white buffalo on the roof.

Quaker Bonnet Eatery (716-885-7208; www.quakerbonnet.com), 175 Allen Street, Buffalo. Open Monday–Friday 9–7, Saturday 10–5. This well-known bakery from Buffalo's west side recently opened up this Elmwood Avenue location. Sandwiches on homemade bread, soups, hot entrées, and their famous desserts are available to eat in or take out. Their frozen foods feature items you'd cook yourself—if you had the time—like chicken pot pie and lasagna. They also make their own ice cream, available by the pint and quart.

ꗥ **Sweet Tooth** (716-884-2520; www.atsweettooth.com), 478 Elmwood Avenue, Buffalo. Open Monday–Thursday 8 AM–11 PM, Friday and Saturday 8–midnight, Sunday 2–10 PM. This small café has all sorts of goodies to satisfy your sweet tooth, including muffins, cookies, brownies, breads and specialty desserts like napoleons and éclairs. They also have ice cream and coffee.

Towne Restaurant (716-884-5128), 186 Allen Street, Buffalo. Open Monday–Saturday 7 AM–5 AM, Sunday 7 AM–11 PM. This Greek restaurant, a fixture in Allentown for over 30 years, is known for its souvlaki and rice pudding. Breakfast is available all the time.

Hertel Avenue

✍ ꗥ **Bertha's Diner** (716-836-8981), 1430 Hertel Avenue, Buffalo. Open Monday–Saturday for breakfast and lunch 7 AM–2 PM, Sunday 7 AM–1 PM. This small, cozy diner will take you back to the 1950s. Enjoy a specialty sandwich, such as the Elvis, Marilyn Monroe, or James Dean, along with burgers, homemade soups, and salads. Their milk shakes, made with a Hamilton-Beach shake mixer and served in the stainless steel shake glasses, are so thick, it's like drinking ice cream. Breakfast is served anytime. Bertha's is known for their Belgian Waffles, which are served on Friday, Saturday, Sunday, and holidays.

Bob & John's La Hacienda (716-836-5411; www.bobandjohns.com), 1545 Hertel Avenue, Buffalo. Open Sunday–Thursday 11–11, Friday–Saturday 11–midnight. Bob and John's has been a fixture on Hertel Avenue for over 30 years. They specialize in Italian cuisine, along with pizza, wings, sandwiches, and salads. You can eat indoors in the dining room or outdoors on the sidewalk patio in the warmer months. Take-out is also available. Daily specials include an all-you-can-eat pizza, soup and salad bar at lunchtime, and an all-you-can-eat spaghetti dinner on Monday and Tuesday evenings. A children's menu is available.

& **Café Allegro** (716-874-3321), 1374 Hertel Avenue, Buffalo. Open Monday–Thursday 7:30 AM–10 PM, Friday 7:30 AM–11 PM, Saturday 8 AM–11 PM, Sunday 8 AM–10 PM. This upbeat little café features tables that look like checkerboards, a selection of board games and music to choose from, and a few comfy couches. The menu features gourmet coffees and teas, along with homemade soups, salads, sandwiches, and homemade pastries.

Café Garangelo's (716-875-8940), 1197 Hertel Avenue, Buffalo. Open Monday–Thursday 11–10, Friday 11–11, Saturday 4–11. Enjoy authentic Old-World Italian cuisine for lunch and dinner. Choose from many classic Italian dishes, including pasta e fagiole. Their gorgonzola garlic bread, which is served with all entrées, is very tasty.

& **Grandma Mora's** (716-837-6703), 1465 Hertel Avenue, Buffalo.

Open Tuesday–Thursday 11–10, Friday 11–11, Saturday noon–11, Sunday 2–9. Well known for the most authentic Mexican cuisine in the city. This friendly restaurant offers good food at a reasonable price.

Kostas Restaurant (716-838-5225), 1561 Hertel Avenue, Buffalo. Open Monday–Friday 6:30 AM–1 AM, Saturday 7 AM–2 AM, Sunday 8 AM–12 AM. This popular Greek restaurant has been a landmark on Hertel Avenue since 1977. Try the Greek combo platter, which is big enough for two people.

& **La Dolce Vita Caffè & Bistro** (716-446-5690), 1474 Hertel Avenue, Buffalo. Open Tuesday–Thursday 8 AM–9 PM, Friday and Saturday 8 AM–10 PM. This small café serves authentic Italian cuisine like bruschetta, panini sandwiches, pasta, and dek-oven pizzas, which are smaller and flatter than an ordinary pizza. They also offer a selection of homemade desserts, gelato, and specialty coffees.

Mastman's Kosher Delicatessen (716-876-7580), 1322 Hertel Avenue, Buffalo. Open Monday–Saturday 9–5, Sunday 9–2:30. This small deli serves Buffalo's best corned beef and pastrami sandwiches.

& **MT Pockets** (716-838-4658), 1519 Hertel Avenue, Buffalo. Open daily 11 AM–1 AM. This friendly corner bar is best known for their steak sandwich and their "Buffalo" atmosphere.

& **Romeo's Bakery Café** (873-5730), 1292 Hertel Avenue, Buffalo. Open Monday–Friday 7:30 AM–9 PM, Saturday 8:30 AM–9 PM. When you step into this small corner café, with soft Italian music playing in the background and the smells of authentic Italian cooking, you feel like you've been transported to Italy. Owners Vito and Susan Semeraro, who hail from Milan, strive to create an authentic Italian bistro. Selections include gourmet pizza, specialty sandwiches served on focaccia bread, appetizers like bruschetta, and wonderful desserts like cannoli and biscotti. Next door at **Juliet's** you can enjoy wine and cheese, along with salads and appetizers. The Semeraro's also operate a bakery where you can order cake by the slice or whole, along with specialty cookies and desserts.

The Wellington Pub (716-833-9899; www.wellingtonpub.com), 1541 Hertel Avenue, Buffalo. Open Monday–Saturday 11–12, Sunday 12–12. Traditional American cuisine is served in this casual restaurant. It's also a great place to enjoy an order of wings while watching the Bills or Sabres on TV. Be sure to try a bowl of their award-winning chili.

University District
♿ 🐾 ✈ **Lake Effect Diner** (716-833-1952), 3165 Main Street, Buffalo. Open 24 hours daily. Take a trip back to the '50s when you visit the Lake Effect Diner, an authentic 1952 diner originally erected in Wayne, Pennsylvania, and known as the Wayne Diner. In the 1990s it was moved to its present location near the Main Street campus of the University at Buffalo. Breakfast selections include eggs, bacon, and stuffed pancakes. For lunch or dinner choose from burgers, sandwiches, beef on weck, salads, souvlaki, and homestyle entrées like meatloaf, roast beef, or turkey. If you're really hungry, order the Blizzard Plate, which is piled high with meatloaf, turkey, roast beef, vegetables, and smothered in gravy.

East Side
Scharf's Schiller Park Restaurant (716-895-7249), 34 South Crossman Street, Buffalo. Open Tuesday–Sunday 11–10. This small German-American restaurant, located in a former residence in a predominantly German neighborhood, specializes in potato pancakes, roast duck, and Wiener schnitzel.

West Side
La Nova Pizzeria (716-881-3355; www.lanova.com), 371 West Ferry Street, Buffalo. Open Sunday–Thursday 10 AM–1 AM, Friday and Saturday 10 AM–2 AM. The number-one independent pizza operation in the U.S. Their food has even been served on Air Force One! Owned and operated by the Todaro family since 1957, this Buffalo institution serves pizzas, along with wings, subs, and more. A second location is located at 5151 Main Street, Williamsville (716-634-5151).

✳ Entertainment

MUSIC **Buffalo Chamber Music Society** (716-838-2383; www .bflochambermusic.org), Kleinhans

AN AUTHENTIC 1952 DINER SERVING CLASSIC DINER FOOD.

Christine A. Smyczynski

Music Hall, 71 Symphony Circle, Buffalo. For over 80 years this group of musicians has been entertaining Buffalo audiences. Performances are held Thursday evenings in the **Mary Seaton Room** at Kleinhans Music Hall.

Buffalo Philharmonic Orchestra (716-885-5000 or 800-699-3168; www .bpo.org), Kleinhans Music Hall, 71 Symphony Circle, Buffalo. The acoustically perfect Kleinhans Music Hall is the permanent home of the internationally renowned Buffalo Philharmonic Orchestra, under the direction of conductor JoAnn Falletta. The orchestra performs classical as well as pops and children's concerts. Kleinhans is also a popular venue for concerts for local and national acts. See also *Unique Architecture*.

Righteous Babe Records. Located in the former Asbury Delaware United Methodist Church, Delaware and West Tupper, Buffalo. This 130-year-old church is undergoing a $6 million restoration to become the headquarters of singer Ani DiFranco's record company. The building also houses Hallwalls Contemporary Arts Center.

NIGHTLIFE While clubs come and clubs go, the most popular nightspots in the city can be found on Chippewa Street and the theater district in downtown, and along Elmwood Avenue and Allentown.

Some of the current downtown nightspots include **The Shaker Lounge** (at the Hampton Inn, Chippewa and Delaware), known for its innovative and unusual martini flavors; **67 West** (67 West Chippewa), a neighborhood pub-style bar that's laid-back and friendly; **McMonkeez** (75 West Chippewa), which has the reputation

as one of Buffalo's best party bars; **Big Shotz** (46 West Chippewa) which has themed nights during the week; **D'Arcy McGees** (257 Franklin Street), a traditional Irish pub atmosphere on the first floor, a cigar bar on the second, and a Skybar on the top floor that features dancing under the stars. Another popular downtown nightspot is the **Sphere Entertainment Complex** (681 Main) that features a restaurant, nightclub, and entertainment venue. If your looking to dance to a Latin beat, check out **La Luna** (52 West Chippewa).

In Allentown and along Elmwood, some of the hot spots include **The Allen Street Grille** a.k.a. **The Old Pink Flamingo** (223 Allen Street), Buffalo's favorite "dive" bar that features live DJs spinning rock and roll tunes, and **Neitzche's** (248 Allen Street), Buffalo's legendary live music night spot. Buffalo's oldest original night spot is **Mulligan's Brick Bar** (229 Allen Street). Farther up Elmwood popular spots include **Mr. Goodbar** (1110 Elmwood Avenue), serving up daily drink specials and live music on Fridays; **J. P. Bullfeathers** (1010 Elmwood Avenue); and **Coles** (1104 Elmwood Avenue)— plus several of the restaurants mentioned in the *Eating Out* section.

Another popular nightspot is **The Tralf** (716-854-3068; www.newtralf .com) 622 Main Street, Buffalo. This theater-district mainstay—recently renovated and reopened under new management—features concerts, community acts, and other special events.

THEATERS African American Cultural Center/Paul Robeson Theatre (716-884-2013; www.paul robesontheatre.com), 350 Masten

Avenue, Buffalo. The African American Cultural Center, founded in 1958, was the first Black educational/cultural institution in the City of Buffalo. The facility contains the African World Studies Archive and the 110-seat Paul Robeson Theatre, the oldest African American theater in Western New York. The theater, which has cabaret-style seating, showcases the talents of African American performers. The African American Cultural Center is home of the Tas'hama Children's Peer Performance Group. The center also offers educational workshops dealing with African history, dance, drumming, theater, arts and crafts, and more.

Theatre of Youth Company (TOY) (716-884-4400; www.buffalo.com/toy), Allendale Theater, 203 Allen Street, Buffalo. The mission of the Theater of Youth (TOY), founded in 1972, is to bring quality entertainment to young audiences. Performances take place in the restored 469-seat **Allendale Theater,** built in 1913. After each show an interactive talk-back with the audience allows young theatergoers to ask questions of the actors.

Alleyway Theatre (716-852-2600; www.alleyway.com), 1 Curtain Up Alley, Buffalo. Founded in 1980 by Neal Radice, this theater is located in Buffalo's former bus terminal. Four or five productions are featured each theater season, plus their annual production of *A Christmas Carol.* The theater company also offers educational workshops.

Forbes Theatre (716-856-7495; www.thebcc.org), 500 Pearl Street (Christian Center), Buffalo. This theater offers a variety of family-oriented plays and concerts.

Irish Classical Theater (716-853-4282; www.irishclassicaltheatre.com), 625 Main Street, Buffalo. This theater in the round was founded in 1990 by Dublin natives Chris O'Neill and James Warde.

Kavinoky Theatre (716-881-7668; www.kavinokytheatre.com), 320 Porter Avenue, Buffalo. This restored 250-seat 1908 Victorian auditorium is located on the campus of D'Youville College. Since 1981 the resident professional theater company has been presenting productions from September through May. The theater is named after Edward Kavinoky, a prominent Buffalo attorney, who was the first lay person to chair the college's board of trustees.

New Phoenix Theatre (716-853-1334), 95 North Johnson Park, Buffalo. This theater, which resembles an off-Broadway theater, presents productions a bit edgier and avant-garde than most Buffalo theater groups. It started out as a gay-themed theater but has since expanded to include other themes.

& **Rockwell Hall** (716-878-3005; www.buffalostate.edu/pac), Buffalo State College, 1300 Elmwood Avenue, Buffalo. The performing arts center at Rockwell Hall hosts a variety of events each season, including dance, vocal, and musical performances.

Shakespeare in Delaware Park (716-856-4533; www.shakespearein delawarepark.org) Shakespeare Hill in Delaware Park, behind the Albright-Knox, near the Rose Garden and Casino. Late June–August. Performances Tuesday–Sunday 7:30 PM. Free admission. For over 25 years works by the Bard have been presented in this open-air theater located on a grassy knoll in Delaware Park—one of the largest free Shakespeare events in the United States. Bring lawn chairs, blankets, munchies, and even Fido for this beloved outdoor theater experience.

♿ **Shea's Performing Arts Center** (716-847-1410; www.sheas.org), 646 Main Street, Buffalo. This cultural institution, listed on the National Register of Historic Places, is one of only four theaters still in existence that were designed by Louis Comfort Tiffany. It has been fully restored in recent years to reflect its original splendor, including the painted ceiling and intricate plasterwork. Modeled after European opera houses, the theater opened in 1926 as a movie house and later hosted live stage shows. It was the most ornate of the 13 movie theaters operated by Michael Shea. It was saved from demolition in the 1970s and went through years of restoration before becoming the showplace it is today. Currently, Shea's presents a wide variety of entertainment: Broadway productions, concerts, opera, ballet, and even classic films. One of the notable fixtures in the theater is the restored custom–built 1926 Mighty Wurlitzer pipe organ, the second largest organ of its type in the state. Note the reproduction of the original 1926 sign that hangs above the marquee.

♿ **Studio Arena Theatre** (716-856-5650; www.studioarena.org), 710 Main Street, Buffalo. Studio Arena was chartered as a theater and educational institution in 1927. The theater itself opened in 1965 as Buffalo's only professional resident theater. Since then it has premiered numerous productions and showcased the acting talents of local and national artists.

Notables who have performed on Studio Arena's stage include Kathy Bates, Glenn Close, Kelsey Grammer, and John Goodman. The Studio Arena Theatre School, which has been in existence for almost eighty years, is the oldest continually run theater school connected with a professional theater in the United States

Ujima Theatre Company (716-883-0380), 545 Elmwood Avenue, Buffalo. The only professional theater company in western New York that focuses on works by African-American and other artists of color.

SPORTS College Sports **Canisius College Golden Griffins** (716-888-2970; www.gogriffs.com), 2001 Main Street, Buffalo. NCAA Division 1 basketball.

University at Buffalo Bulls (716-645-6666; www.buffalobulls.com) UB Stadium/Alumni Arena, Amherst. The University at Buffalo offers 20 Division 1 intercollegiate sport teams for both men and women that compete in the NCAA, including football, baseball, and basketball.

SHEA'S PERFORMING ARTS CENTER WAS BUILT IN 1926 IN THE STYLE OF A EUROPEAN OPERA HOUSE.
Courtesy Buffalo–Niagara Convention & Visitors Bureau and Angel Art Ltd.

Professional Sports **Buffalo Bandits Lacrosse** (716-855-4100; www
.bandits.com), HSBC Arena, One Seymour H. Knox III Plaza, Buffalo. The Bandits are a three-time world championship team.

Buffalo Bills Football (716-648-1800, tickets: 877-BB-TICKS; www
.buffalobills.com), Ralph Wilson Stadium, 1 Bills Drive, Orchard Park.

Buffalo Bisons Baseball (716-846-2003, 888-223-6000; www.bisons
.com), Dunn Tire Park, 275 Washington Street, Buffalo. The Bisons are the AAA farm team of the Cleveland Indians.

Buffalo Sabres Hockey (716-855-4110 or 888-GO-SABRES; www.sabres.com), HSBC Arena, 1 Seymour H. Knox III Plaza, Buffalo.

✳ Selective Shopping
ANTIQUES

Elmwood Village/Allentown
Antiques Allentown (716-882-9535), 138 Elmwood Avenue, Buffalo. Open Tuesday–Saturday 12–5. This shop

THE BUFFALO BISONS—AAA FARM TEAM OF THE CLEVELAND INDIANS—PLAY AT DUNN TIRE PARK.
Courtesy Buffalo–Niagara Convention & Visitors Bureau

specializes in midcentury primitives and miniatures.

Arthur's Antiques (716-885-7808), 141 Elmwood Avenue, Buffalo. Open Tuesday–Saturday 12–5. This shop, which has been in business for 40 years, is located in a vintage Allentown house.

Assets Antiques (716-882-2415), 140 Elmwood Avenue, Buffalo. Open Tuesday–Saturday 12–5. Specializes in Victorian to 1940s furniture, along with fine china, silver, Depression glass, pottery, and jewelry.

Buffalo Bungalow (716-886-4271), 739 Elmwood Avenue, Buffalo. Open Wednesday–Saturday 12:30–6. This small attractive shop carries furniture, vintage clothing, artwork, art glass, pottery, and jewelry.

Eaton Galleries Antiques (716-882-7823), 110 Elmwood Avenue, Buffalo. Open Tuesday–Saturday 11–4:30. Antique furniture, glassware, dishes, and more.

Tom Mileham Antiques (716-884-4550), 148 Elmwood Avenue, Buffalo. Open Tuesday–Saturday 11:30–5. Antiques, accessories, and furniture restoration.

The Source (716-883-2858), 119 Elmwood Avenue, Buffalo. Tuesday–Saturday 12–5. Paintings and fine art, with an emphasis on western New York artists. Other items include porcelain, silver, decor items, and jewelry.

Carl Stone (716-884-0211), 65 Elmwood Avenue, Buffalo. Open Friday and Saturday 11–5 or by appointment. Specializes in stained glass and period lighting.

Dana E. Tillou (716-854-5285), 417 Franklin Street, Buffalo. Open Wednesday–Saturday 11–5. Specializing in furniture, fine paintings, and works of art from the 18th and 19th century.

Wwwhatever (716-885-1162), 262 Bryant, Buffalo. Open Monday, Wednesday, Thursday and Saturday 10–8; Tuesday 10–7, Friday 10–4:30, Sunday 10–6. Antiques and collectibles.

Hertel Avenue

The Antique Center, 1677 Hertel Avenue, Buffalo. Two shops can be found in one location: **Webb Trading Company** (716-836-2380), Open Wednesday–Saturday 11-5. Furniture, paintings, silver, pottery, jewelry, oriental rugs, and lamps. **Treasure Hunt Antique Gallery** (716-694-5300), Open Wednesday–Saturday 11-5. Fine antiques, used furniture, and decorative home accessories.

The Antique Lamp (716-871-0508; www.antiquelampco.com), 1213 Hertel Avenue, Buffalo. Open Tuesday–Saturday 11–4 Antique and vintage lighting, including polishing, repairs, and rewiring.

Buffalo Antiques and Quality Furniture (716-832-4231), 1539 Hertel Avenue, Buffalo. Open Tuesday–Saturday 11–5 or by appointment. Features furniture, rugs, carved items, and art objects.

CooCooU (716-837-3385), 1478 Hertel Avenue, Buffalo. Open Tuesday–Saturday 12–5, Wednesday by chance. Western New York's only Modern Deco dealer. Dealing in 20th century furniture from 1920s–1960s.

Thomas Mileham Antiques (716-603-1609), 1590 Hertel Avenue, Buffalo. Open Wednesday–Saturday 11–5 or by appointment. This shop features a general line of antiques, including furniture and rugs.

The Second Reader (716-862-0001), 1419 Hertel Avenue, Buffalo. Open Tuesday–Thursday 11–5, Friday and Saturday 10–7. Used books, prints, and ephemera.

The Stock Exchange (716-838-8294), 1421 Hertel Avenue, Buffalo. Open Tuesday–Saturday 12–5. Antiques and decorative furniture. They just opened a second location at 567 Exchange Street, near Chef's restaurant.

West Side

Gothic City (716-874-4479; www.gothiccity.com), 1940 Niagara Street, Buffalo. Open Tuesday–Saturday 11–5 (Thursday–Saturday November 1–April 1) Specializes in architectural items for the home, including iron fencing, gates, garden furnishings, and more.

ART GALLERIES Benjamin's Art Gallery (716-886-0898; www.benartgallery.com), 419 Elmwood Avenue, Buffalo. Open Thursday–Saturday 11–5:30. This gallery, in business over 35 years, specializes in fine art, from antique to contemporary. Located in a historic Elmwood Avenue Victorian home, the studio also offers conservation framing, with thousands of frames to choose from.

&. **Buffalo Big Print** (716-884-1777), 78 Allen Street, Buffalo. Open Monday–Friday 9–5:30, Saturday by appointment. This gallery features prints, fine art reproductions, photo restoration, and Sally Danforth Pottery.

College Street Gallery (716-882-9727), 244 Allen Street, Buffalo. Open Thursday–Saturday 2–8, Sunday 2–5. This gallery features painting, photographs, sculptures, and other art exhibits.

&. **Cone Five Pottery Gallery** (716-332-0486), 105 Elmwood Avenue, Buffalo. Open Tuesday–Friday 11–6, Saturday 11–5. This unique gallery features pottery, blown glass, glass jewelry, paintings, and photography.

Nina Freudenheim Gallery (716-882-5777; www.ninafreudenheim gallery.com), Hotel Lenox, 140 North Street, Buffalo. Tuesday–Friday 10–5, Sunday and Monday by appointment. This gallery showcases a variety of national and international contemporary artists. Four exhibits are featured annually.

&. **El Buen Amigo** (885-6343; www.lacany.org), 114 Elmwood Avenue, Buffalo. Open Monday–Saturday 11–7, Sunday 11–4. An art and crafts gallery operated by the Latin American Cultural Association features finely crafted jewelry, pottery, clothing, masks, musical instruments, and other handmade items from South and Central America. Spanish classes are also offered.

El Museo Francisco Oller y Diego Rivera, (716-884-9693; www.elmuseobuffalo.org or www.buffalo.com/elmuseobuffalo), 91 Allen Street, Buffalo. Open Tuesday–Saturday 12–5. Displaying works of art by Latinos, African-Americans, and other artists of color. About half of the exhibits are the works of local artists; the remainder come from national and international artists. The center has ongoing children's programs.

Kepa3 Gallery, (716-883-1163; www.kepa3art.com), 204 Allen Street, Buffalo. Open Wednesday 4–8, Saturday 11–5 A working studio and art gallery that promotes western New York artists. Located upstairs from the Rust Belt Book Store.

Lexington Gallery/Wild Things, 218 Lexington Avenue, Buffalo. Open Monday–Saturday 11–6. For jewelry and pottery.

Michael Morgulis Studio-Local Color Gallery (716-885-5188; www.newbuffalographics.com), 226 Lexington Avenue, Buffalo. Open Tuesday–Saturday 12–6. Features the works of Buffalo artist Michael Morgulis.

Storehouse 22 (716-883-2221), 245 Allen Street, Buffalo. Open Tuesday, Wednesday, Friday 11–6, Thursday 11–8, Saturday 11–4. This gallery, located adjacent to the **Allen Street Hardware Café,** offers artwork along with home decor.

BOOKSTORES Old Editions Book Shop & Café (716-842-1734; www.oldeditions.com or abebooks.com/stores/nystate/oldeditions), 72 East Huron Street, Buffalo. Open Monday–Saturday 10–5:30. One of the largest antique bookstores in upstate New York, the 12,000 square-foot shop, housed in a vintage 1896 building, contains an array of old, rare, and collectible books, prints, maps, autographs, and engravings. The store's café serves breakfast, lunch, and gourmet teas and coffees.

Rust Belt Books (716-885-9535), 202 Allen Street, Buffalo. Open Tuesday–Wednesday 10–6, Thursday–Saturday 10–8, Sunday 10–5. A large collection of vintage books.

Talking Leaves Books (716-837-8554; www.tleavesbooks.com) 3158 Main Street, Buffalo. Open Monday, Tuesday, Friday, Saturday 10–6, Wednesday–Thursday 10–8. Western New York's largest independent bookstore for over 20 years. The store features the largest selection of poetry in the United States along with the latest best-sellers, local interest books, Native American studies books, and books for students at the University at Buffalo. The staff is helpful and knowledgeable. A second smaller store is located at 951 Elmwood Avenue, Buffalo (716-884-9524). A cozy coffee shop, **Caffè Aroma** (716-884-4522) is connected to the Elmwood Avenue store and offers a selection of coffees and teas, along with lunches and desserts.

FARM MARKETS Clinton-Bailey Market (716-822-2466), 1443-1517 Clinton Street, Buffalo. Open May 1–Thanksgiving Sunday–Friday 7–6, Saturday 6:30–1; remainder of year Saturdays only 6:30–1. There is no better way to spend the morning than wandering through the Clinton-Bailey Market. Since 1931 this establishment has been the largest privately owned farmer's market in New York State. During the growing season, thousands of people flock here for the best selection of locally grown produce. During the off-season, produce from other parts of the country is available.

Downtown Buffalo Country Market (716-856-3150), Main Street (between Eagle and Court Streets), Buffalo. Open mid-May–late October Tuesday and Thursday 8–2:30. For over 20 years farmers, gardeners, and florists have been bringing their goods to downtown office workers and residents. Everything sold here is locally grown on western New York farms.

Elmwood Village Farmers Market (contact Forever Elmwood, 716-881-0707), Corner of Elmwood Avenue and Bidwell Parkway, Buffalo. Open April–early November Saturday 8–1.

This market, located in the heart of the Elmwood Village, features organic fruits, vegetables, and flowers.

SPECIAL SHOPS

Downtown/Center City
Buffalo Niagara Convention and Visitors Center (716-852-0511 or 800-BUFFALO; www.buffalocvb.org), 617 Main Street, Suite 400, Buffalo. Open Monday–Friday 10–2. A large selection of Buffalo-themed items from key chains to hats and shirts. Items can also be purchased online.

Definitely Buffalo (716-856-7399), Lower Level, Main Place Mall, Main Street, downtown Buffalo. Open Monday–Saturday 9–5:30. This small shop specializes in everything Buffalo, from small souvenirs to Frank Lloyd Wright items. Choose from shirts, stuffed animals, cards designed by local artists, foods made in Buffalo, books about Buffalo and Western New York, and much more.

Pitt Petri (716-852-7876), 378 Delaware Avenue, Buffalo. A Buffalo tradition that opened its doors in 1925, this store, voted as one of the best places to buy a special gift by *Buffalo Spree* magazine, has a large selection of fine gifts, home decor, Buffalo-related items, and items that can't be found anywhere else in the city. It is western New York's number one bridal registry. A second location can be found at 5727 Main Street in the village of Williamsville (716-626-6700).

East Side
Broadway Market (716-893-2216; www.broadwaymarket.com), 999 Broadway, Buffalo. Open Monday–Friday 8–5, Saturday 7–5. This market is a regional treasure, noted for its ethnic Old World shopping atmosphere.

Many family-owned businesses, including butchers, sausage makers, bakeries, candy makers, and green-grocers, have been passed from generation to generation since the market opened in 1888. It's an especially popular place to shop before Easter or Christmas.

Hertel Avenue/North Buffalo

Conley Interiors (716-838-1000; www.conleyinteriors.com), 1425 Hertel Avenue, Buffalo. Open Monday–Friday 10–5, Saturday by appointment. This 25,000-square-foot showroom, established in 1925, offers fine furniture, unusual lighting, fine art, accessories, and antiques.

Elmwood Yarn Shop (716-834-7580; www.elmwoodyarnshop.com), 1639 Hertel Avenue. Buffalo. Open Monday, Thursday, Friday 10–5, Tuesday 10–7, Saturday 10–3. This shop carries a wide variety of yarns and knitting supplies. Lessons are available.

Homeward Bound (716-873-4764), 1297 Hertel Avenue, Buffalo. Open Tuesday, Wednesday, Saturday 10–5,

BROADWAY MARKET IS A REGIONAL TREASURE, NOTED FOR ITS OLD-WORLD CHARM AND ETHNIC CUISINE. Courtesy Buffalo–Niagara Convention & Visitors Bureau and David Gorden Photography

Thursday and Friday 10–8. This upscale shop, located in the former Hertel Station post office, features all new furniture and home decor items, including linens, books, lighting, rugs, pictures, floral, and seasonal items.

Knot by Knot Oriental Rug Exchange (716-447-3983; www.knotby knot.us), 1376 Hertel Avenue, Buffalo. Open Tuesday, Wednesday, Friday, and Saturday 10–5:30, Thursday 10–8. This shop features oriental carpeting.

Maria's Italian Gifts (716-837-1707), 1415 Hertel Avenue, Buffalo. Open Tuesday–Saturday 11–5. A selection of beautiful Italian imports and gifts. One of their specialties is handmade Italian wedding favors.

North Park Florist (716-838; 123 www.northparkflorist.com), 1514 Hertel Avenue, Buffalo. Open Monday, Tuesday, Thursday, Friday 9–5, Wednesday 9–2, Saturday 9–4. A variety of floral items and gifts are sold here.

Elmwood Village/Allentown

Blue Mountain Coffees (716-883-5983), 509 Elmwood Avenue, Buffalo. Open Monday–Friday 8–6, Saturday 8–5, Sunday 8–2. Since 1981 this has been a popular shop to buy freshly roasted coffees from all over the world, a variety of loose teas, brewing accessories, gift items, magazines, and greeting cards.

Diggin' It (716-885-7884), 801 Elmwood Avenue, Buffalo. Open Monday–Friday 11–6, Saturday 10–5. Unique garden supplies, including planters, garden tools, and lawn ornaments.

Dolci's Bakery (716-882-5956), 732 Elmwood Avenue, Buffalo. Open Tuesday–Friday 10–5:30, Saturday 10-4. Specializes in Italian cookies and biscotti.

Eminent Design (716-883-0075), 191 Allen Street, corner Elmwood, Buffalo. Open Tuesday–Saturday 10–6 Gifts, furniture, artwork, pottery, and custom framing

Everything Elmwood (716-883-0607), 740 Elmwood Avenue, Buffalo. Open Monday–Friday 10–8, Saturday 10–6, Sunday 12–5 A mix of eclectic upscale items, including glassware, home decor, jewelry, stained glass, cards, clothing, and cards.

Globe Market (716-886-5242) 762 Elmwood Avenue, Buffalo. Open Monday–Saturday 10–8, Sunday 10–6. A gourmet grocery and cookware store that also offers fresh entrées, soups, and salads to eat in or take out from their café.

Moda (716-881-MODA), 616 Elmwood Avenue, Buffalo. Open daily 11:30–5:30 and by appointment. Designer furnishings, jewelry, accessories, and antiques.

Neo Gift Studio (716-884-1119; www.neogifts.com), 55 Allen Street (at Franklin), Buffalo. Open Monday–Friday 10–6, Saturday 10–5. This 5,000-square-foot store offers a eclectic mix of gifts, jewelry, furniture, and home decor. Its renowned signature gift wrap includes handmade bows and silk flowers.

Pavlov's Togs (716-881-1401) 567 Elmwood Avenue, Tuesday, Wednesday, and Friday 11–5, Thursday 11–7, Saturday 10–5. This store features custom screen-printed and designed items, including handprinted Buffalo shirts.

Pensandote (716-883-6788), 181 Allen Street, Buffalo. Open Wednesday–Friday 1–7, Saturday 10–7, Sunday 12–5. This art gallery and shop, located in a vintage house, features

Christine A. Smyczynski

ALL SORTS OF UNUSUAL FINDS AWAIT SHOPPERS AT THUNDER BAY IN ELMWOOD VILLAGE.

artwork, chocolates, jewelry, candles, cards, and gifts.

Plum Pudding Boutique (716-881-9748), 779 Elmwood Avenue, Buffalo. Open Monday–Saturday 11–5:30, Thursday until 8, Sunday 11–4. A unique boutique featuring clothing, jewelry, masks, and musical instruments from over 30 countries. Profits from these products are returned to the Third World artisans who created them.

Positively Main Street (716-882-5858), 773 Elmwood Avenue, Buffalo. Open Monday–Friday 10–6, Saturday 10–5. This neat shop has distinctive jewelry, picture frames, gifts, cards, and home decor items.

Stravagarious (716-886-0650), 567 Elmwood Ave., Buffalo. Open Tuesday–Friday 11:30–7, Saturday 10–8. This shop specializes in gourmet products, mugs, jewelry, toys, books, and bath and body items.

Thunder Bay (716-882-8645), 734 Elmwood Avenue, Buffalo. Open Monday 10:30–6, Tuesday–Friday 10:30–7, Saturday 11–6, Sunday 12–5.

This idiosyncratic shop, owned by Newell Nussbaumer, features all sorts of unusual items that capture the spirit of the Elmwood Village. Choose from books, jewelry, home decor, gifts and more, most with a Buffalo-related theme.

The Treehouse, 754 Elmwood Avenue, Buffalo. Open Sunday 12–4, Tuesday, Wednesday, Saturday 10-6, Thursday and Friday 10–7. Choose from all sorts of educational toys, stuffed animals, and other special playthings. The vintage shop features decorative copper and tin ceilings.

✳ Special Events

February: **Olmsted Winterfest** (716-884-9660), Delaware Park. A celebration of Buffalo's winter weather, including indoor and outdoor activities, musical entertainment, and children's activities. **Mardi Gras Festival,** Downtown Buffalo and Allentown. This annual Mardi Gras Festival, held on "Fat Tuesday" and sponsored by the newspaper *Artvoice,* features over 40 parade floats and more than 30 participating bars and restaurants. Proceeds from the festival are donated to a local charity.

March: **St. Patrick's Day Parade** (716-875-0282; www.buffaloirish .com), Delaware Avenue. An annual event where everyone in Buffalo is Irish. **Dyngus Day Celebrations** (716-668-6888). Buffalo's large Polish community holds this traditional post-Lenten celebration the day after Easter in numerous locations throughout the city.

May–September: **Thursday in the Square Concert Series** (716-856-3150; www.buffaloplace.com), Lafayette Square, Main and Court Streets. Thursdays 5–8:30 PM. For almost 20 years Thursday in the Square has been a Thursday-evening tradition for many downtown office workers and residents. This free concert series features local, regional, and national musical acts.

June: **Allentown Art Festival** (716-881-4269). More than 400 artists display their works in Buffalo's historic Allentown district. **Juneteenth Festival,** MLK Jr. Park (716-857-2121; www.juneteenth.com) A celebration of African American culture, featuring ethnic foods, wares, entertainment, and family activities. **Buffalo Niagara Guitar Festival** (716-845-7156; www.guitarfestival.org). America's first and largest all-guitar music festival. This week-long event features musical entertainment at various locations throughout downtown Buffalo.

July: **Friendship Festival** (905-871-6454 or 888-333-1987; www.friend shipfestival.com), Buffalo and Fort Erie, Ontario. One of the largest international events in the Niagara region, this festival commemorates the friendship between the United States and Canada. Activities include concerts, children's rides, and an international air show over the Niagara River. **Italian Heritage Festival** (716-874-6133; www.buffaloitalian festival.com), Hertel Avenue. This five-day festival has been a Buffalo favorite since the 1930s. Enjoy musical entertainment, cultural displays, Italian foods, rides, games, and vendors. **Taste of Buffalo,** Main Street, downtown Buffalo (716-652-0628; www.tasteofbuffalo.com) This second largest "taste" festival in the country offers a weekend of food and entertainment for the entire family. **Garden Walk** (716-879-0123; www .gardenwalkbuffalo.com), Elmwood

THE NATIONAL CHICKEN WING FESTIVAL

Held on Labor Day Weekend, the National Chicken Wing Festival revolves around eating chicken wings—lots of them; over 20 tons are consumed in two days. More than two dozen restaurants from all over the United States serve up traditional, Cajun, BBQ, and other uniquely flavored wings. The festival, which began in 2002, was inspired by the movie Osmosis Jones, which featured a junk-food addict, played by actor Bill Murray, going to the National Chicken Wing Festival in Buffalo—though, in fact, no such event existed at that time. After the release of the movie, Donn Esmonde, a reporter for the Buffalo News, wrote a column asking why Buffalo didn't have a National Chicken Wing festival. Buffalo-based food promoter Drew Cerza, saw the column and decided to make this concept a reality. Besides eating, activities include musical entertainment, the Miss Chicken Wing competition, and—the climax of the festival—the chicken wing eating contest, sanctioned by the International Federation of Competitive Eating.

Village and Buffalo's West Side. More than 150 city gardens are open to the public for viewing, with many of the gardeners themselves available to offer horticultural advice.

August: **Elmwood Avenue Festival of the Arts** (716-830-2484; www .elmwoodartfest.org), Elmwood Avenue, between Lafayette and West Ferry. A family-friendly summer street festival focusing on the artists and craftspeople located on and around Elmwood Avenue. Live musical performances and foods for local restaurants are also featured.

Labor Day Weekend: **National Chicken Wing Festival** (716-565-4141, ext.10; www.buffalowing.com), Dunn Tire Park, 275 Washington Street, Buffalo. What more natural place to have the National Chicken Wing Festival than the birthplace of the buffalo wing.

September: **Curtain Up!** (716-645-6921), Theater District. The opening of Buffalo's theater season starts with

a black-tie dinner and ends with a post-theater street party.

October: **Doors Open Niagara** (888-333-1987; www.doorsopenniagara .com). Various location throughout western New York and southern

AMERICA'S FIRST AND LARGEST ALL-GUITAR FESTIVAL IS HELD ANNUALLY IN BUFFALO.
Courtesy Buffalo–Niagara Convention & Visitors Bureau and WNED

Ontario. A bi-national event that features tours of historic and cultural sites on both sides of the border.

November: **Rail Barons Model Train Exhibit,** Buffalo and Erie County Historical Society (716-873-9644), 25 Nottingham Court, Buffalo. This exhibit, which usually runs from the day after Thanksgiving until February, features period locomotives on 200 feet of track and over 80 handcrafted miniature versions of notable western New York buildings. **World's Largest Disco** (716-635-8668; www .worldslargestdisco.com), Buffalo Convention Center. This retro party features 72,000 watts of sound on the largest disco floor in New York.

December: **Victorian Christmas, Theodore Roosevelt Inaugural National Historic Site** (716-884-0095; www.nps.gov), 641 Delaware Avenue, Buffalo. This event features Victorian seasonal decorations and gifts, vintage fashion shows, entertainment, lunches, and dinners. **First Night Buffalo** (716-635-4959; www .firstnight.buffnet.net), Elmwood Avenue (Museum District). A family-oriented New Year's celebration that features music, rides, games, and fireworks.

NORTHERN ERIE COUNTY

Northern Erie County, referred to as the "Northtowns" by locals, is made up of mainly Buffalo bedroom communities and upscale suburbs, but it also has many interesting historical museums, and lots of recreational activities, including an abundance of parks and some of the area's best golf courses. The Northtowns also have many eating establishments, from fine dining to hot-dog joints, and everything in between. If you like to shop, you'll find a wide variety of stores, from the enormous Walden Galleria, the area's largest shopping mall, to quaint shops in the town of Clarence, the antiques capital of western New York. For entertainment of a different sort, the Amherst Campus of SUNY at Buffalo—aside from being one of the finest educational institutions in the area—is a performing arts venue.

GRAND ISLAND AND THE TONAWANDAS

Grand Island is one of 19 islands in the upper Niagara River. At seven and a half miles long and six miles wide, it is one of the largest freshwater islands in the world. The Seneca Indians called the island *Ga-We-Not:* the great island; French explorers referred to it as *La Grande Isle*. In 1815 the land was purchased from the Seneca Indians by the state of New York for $1,000. Grand Island was originally part of the city of Buffalo, until it became part of Tonawanda in 1836. The town of Grand Island, which became a separate entity in 1852, was known for its farms and orchards during its early days. Today, with 25 miles of shoreline, Grand Island an ideal location for fishing, boating, swimming, and other recreational activities.

Before pioneer settlers arrived in the area now known as the Tonawandas in the early 1800s, it was a forested land traveled by Native Americans. But after the construction of the Erie Canal in 1825, Tonawanda and North Tonawanda developed rapidly. Lumber shipped from the western U.S. and Canada passed through eastward here on the Erie Canal—the Tonawandas are located where the Erie Canal meets the Niagara River. By 1890 the area was the lumber capital of the world, shipping over one million board feet of lumber each year. While Tonawanda and North Tonawanda are two separate towns, located in two different counties, they always functioned as one community; in the past as a

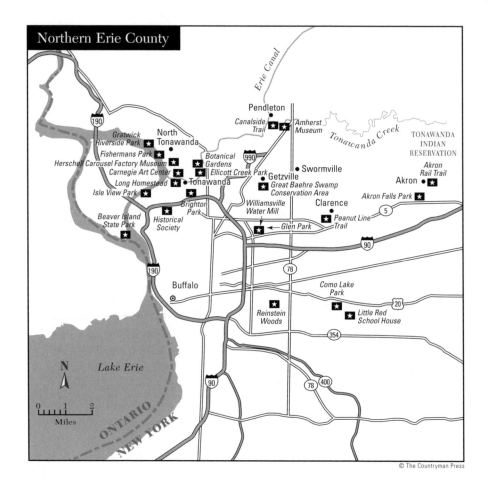

manufacturing center and today as a tourist destination. (Note: Although North Tonawanda is actually located in Niagara County, for the purposes of this book it has been included under Erie County to simplify the listings.)

Located next door to Tonawanda is Kenmore, one of the first planned bedroom communities in western New York. In the late 19th century, Louis Philip Adolph Eberhardt came up with the idea of creating a community away from the hustle and bustle of Buffalo, yet close enough for people to commute to their jobs in the city. Kenmore, which was incorporated in 1899, was the first suburb in western New York and one of the earliest in the United States. (For more about the history of Kenmore, read *Images of America: Kenmore, New York* by John Percy and Graham Millar.)

AREA CODE The area code is **716.**

GUIDANCE **Chamber of Commerce of the Tonawandas** (716-692-5120; www.the-tonawandas.com), 15 Webster Street, North Tonawanda. Open

Monday–Friday 8:30–4:30. They publish a summer guide called the *Tonawanda Tourist Tattler* in addition to brochures about area attractions.

Grand Island Chamber of Commerce (716-773-3651; www.gichamber.org), 1980 Whitehaven Road, Grand Island. Open Monday–Friday 9–4.

Kenmore-Town of Tonawanda Chamber of Commerce (716-874-1202; www.ken-ton.org), 3411 Delaware Avenue, Kenmore. Open Monday–Friday 9–5.

GETTING THERE *By bus:* The #40 NFTA bus runs between Grand Island and downtown Buffalo; buses #61 (North Tonawanda) and #79 (Tonawanda) offer express service to and from Buffalo.

By car: Grand Island is accessible from I-90 from either Buffalo or Niagara Falls. The major expressways running through the Tonawandas include the I-290 (Youngmann Memorial Highway) and NY 425 (Twin Cities Memorial Highway).

MEDICAL EMERGENCY Call 911

DeGraff Memorial Hospital (716-694-4500; kaleidahealth.org), 445 Tremont Street, North Tonawanda.

Kenmore Mercy Hospital (716-447-6100; chsbuffalo.org), 2950 Elmwood Avenue, Kenmore.

✳ To See

ART MUSEUMS **The Carnegie Art Center** (716-694-4400; www.carnegieart center.org), 240 Goundry Street, North Tonawanda. Open Wednesday–Friday 11–4 and Saturday 1–4. This building, originally a public library, was erected in 1903, one of many library buildings throughout the country built with funds donated by Andrew Carnegie. It was placed on the National Register of Historic Places in 1995. The arts center features contemporary art exhibits, with a special focus on new media and digital art as well as art education classes.

MUSEUMS AND HISTORIC HOMES ♿ ✐ **Herschell Carrousel Factory Museum** (716-693-1885; www.carouselmuseum.org), 180 Thompson Street, North Tonawanda. Open Wednesday–Sunday 1–5. Admission: $4 adults, $2 children age 2–12. On display at this National Historic Site are a collection of carousel animals, exhibits on the early carousel industry, and the growth of "kiddie rides." The Allan Herschell Company, founded in 1915, manufactured over 2,000 hand-carved carousels at this factory. Seventy-one of the remaining 148 hand-carved carousels still in existence in the U.S. were made by Allan Herschell. Watch wood carvers demonstrate how carousel horses are made, and ride on an antique 1916 hand-carved wooden carousel. Small children can also ride on a 1940s aluminum kiddie carousel. The gift shop is stocked with hundreds of unusual carousel-related items.

Historical Society of the Tonawandas (716-694-7406), 113 Main Street, Tonawanda. Open Wednesday–Friday 10–4:30. Displays inside this circa-1886 former NY Central & Hudson Valley Railroad station depict the area's early lumber days and Erie Canal history. The research center has over 6,000 indexed photos and obituaries dating back to 1877.

Long Homestead (716-694-7406), 24 East Niagara Street, Tonawanda. Open Sunday 1–4, May–October; also open the first three Sundays in December. Admission: $2, under 12 free. The restored Pennsylvania German-style 1829 home of Benjamin and Mary Long, who came to this area from Lancaster County, Pennsylvania, in 1828, is constructed of hand-hewn timber. The home has six narrow fireplaces throughout, and the decorating reflects the style of home built by a relatively well-to-do family of the era. The homestead is furnished with period furnishings from the early 1800s. Mr. Long was a farmer, businessman, and politician and was one of the organizers of the Town of Tonawanda. Docents from the Historical Society of the Tonawandas conduct guided tours of the home.

Railroad Museum of the Niagara Frontier (716-694-9588; www.nfcnrhs.com), 111 Oliver Street, North Tonawanda. Open Sunday 1–4 June through August or by appointment. Donation. This museum is housed in a 1923 Erie Railroad station. It includes indoor exhibits as well as two locomotives, two cabooses, a boxcar, and an operating hand car.

River Lea Farm House (716-773-3817, Grand Island Historical Society), 2136 Oakfield Road, Grand Island. Open for special events and a monthly open house; call for details. This historic Victorian farmhouse, constructed in 1849, was once the home of Lewis Allen, founder of the Erie County Fair and uncle of Grover Cleveland, the 22nd and 24th president of the United States. Mr. Allen provided a young Mr. Cleveland with his first job working on the farm. The museum, maintained by the Grand Island Historical Society and furnished in the Victorian style, houses a collection of books, documents, and pictures relative to Grand Island in the 1800s. Docents dressed in Victorian costume conduct tours during the monthly open house.

Town of Tonawanda-Kenmore Historical Society (716-873-5774; www.tona wanda.ny.us/history), 100 Knoche Road, Tonawanda. Open Sunday 2–5 May–October. The historical society is housed in a brick church built in 1849. Displays include a collection of stained-glass windows from the Eberhardt mansion, books, and other memorabilia from the town, including genealogy records. There is even a display dedicated to the resident ghost. Several town residents have reportedly seen the ghost of a young girl who is buried in the cemetery next to the museum. Some have even offered the girl a ride home, only to discover that she disappears on the way there.

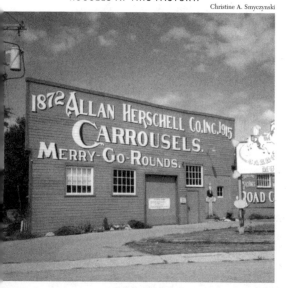

FOUNDED IN 1915, HERSCHELL MANUFAC-TURED OVER 2,000 HAND-CARVED CAR-ROUSELS AT THIS FACTORY.
Christine A. Smyczynski

HISTORIC SITES U.S. Post Office on Goundry and Oliver Streets is listed on the National Register of Historic Sites.

ARCHITECTURE Take a walk down **Goundry Street** in **North Tonawanda** to get a glimpse of the mansions built by the lumber barons during Tonawanda's early days. They are private residences and not open for tours, but reportedly many of the homes have beautiful wood carvings and wainscoting. Pay special attention to **208 Goundry Street,** known as Kent Place. Considered one of the most beautiful mansions on the block, it was designed for Alexander Kent by Stanford White, the designer of Madison Square Garden and New York Central Terminal in New York City.

✳ To Do

AMUSEMENT PARKS ♿ ✎ **Martin's Fantasy Island** (716-773-7591; www .martinsfantasyisland.com), 2400 Grand Island Boulevard, Grand Island. Open mid-May–mid-September Sunday–Friday 11:30–8:30, Saturday 11:30–9. Admission: $19.95, $14.95 under 48 inches, $9.95 seniors, under 2 free. Martin's Fantasy Island, a popular summertime destination for western New Yorkers, is a family-oriented park with rides, shows, and attractions that will please everyone from tots to teens. It's home to a classic wooden roller coaster, the Silver Comet, and the ever-popular Fantasy Island Iron Horse #1 train ride. Live shows include the Wild West Shoot-Out and the crowd-pleasing Western Musical Review. Catch a wave at the wave pool, ride the giant water slide, or cool down on the log flume ride. There is also a wading pool and mini-waterslide for small children. The "pay-one-price admission" includes the rides, shows, water park, and miniature golf. A KOA campground is located adjacent to the park.

BOAT EXCURSIONS *Grand Lady* **Cruises** (716-774-8594; www.grandlady.com), Offices located in the Holiday Inn, 100 Whitehaven Road, Grand Island. Open May–October for lunch, dinner, and specialty cruises as well as charter for private parties. Hours and dates vary according to season. This 80-foot-long, yacht-style cruise vessel holds 90 people for dining or 115 for receptions. The luxurious interior has an atrium dining salon with gleaming hardwood and sophisticated table settings and is surrounded with glass windows to view the sights along the Niagara River. Step outside on the aft deck veranda to enjoy a refreshing breeze. The dining selections are similar to what one might find at an exclusive club, including seafood salad croissant, country club sirloin filet, and stuffed sole.

CROSS-COUNTRY SKIING See **Ellicott Creek Park** and **Beaver Island State Park** in *Green Space.*

FISHING The following parks are popular for fishing: **Ellicott Creek Park, Fisherman's Park, Gratwick Riverside Park, West Canal Marina,** and **Oppenheim County Park.** Fishing licenses can be obtained at any town or county municipal clerk's office, Dick's Sporting Goods stores, Wal-Mart, and most bait and tackle shops. For more information on fishing in Erie and Niagara Counties, including a compete list of where to get a license, fishing supplies, and charter captains, see www.erie.gov/hotspot.

FAMILY FUN ✐ **Island Fun Center** (716-774-8450), 2660 Grand Island Boulevard, Grand Island. Hours and fees vary according to season and activity. The Island Fun Center offers a world of family fun. Their motto seems to be: If it's fun, it's here. There are many activities to keep the whole family busy including a racetrack, 18-hole miniature golf course, batting cages, video games, skeeball, and a snack bar.

✐ **Niagara Climbing Center** (716-695-1248; www.niagaraclimbingcenter.com), Wurlitzer Common Office Park, 1333 Strad Avenue, North Tonawanda. Open Tuesday–Friday 3–10, Saturday 12–10, Sunday 12–6. Admission: $10 for day, $2 lesson fee for first-time climbers. Folks of all ages, from preschoolers to senior citizens, can safely enjoy the sport of rock climbing, with safety lessons offered to first-time climbers. Climbers are strapped into a safety harness, so if you do slip, the only thing that's bruised is your ego. The center is a popular place for kids' birthday parties—you supply the climbers and the cake, they'll supply the rest. If you can't come to the wall, the wall can come to you. A 24-foot portable wall, "The Rolling Stone," the most realistic portable rock climbing tower in the Northeast, can be the hit of your next event.

 & ✐ ⊤ **Tonawanda Aquatic and Fitness Center** (716-876-7424; www.tonawanda.ny.us/alert.php), 1 Pool Plaza, Tonawanda. Open Monday–Friday 6 AM–10 PM, Saturday 8 AM–9 PM, Sunday 9–9. Admission: $8.75 adults, $0 children, $18 family rate. This 48,000-square-foot, state-of-the-art fitness facility offers a wide variety of aquatic and fitness activities. The fully stocked fitness center has every kind of exercise equipment imaginable, including cardio equipment like Stairmasters, Quinton treadmills, Versa climbers, Stepmills, Cybex recumbent bikes, and more, including weight-training machines. The center's aerobic room has a Gerstung shock-absorbing floor. Make a splash swimming or doing aquatic exercises in the 50-meter pool that ranges in depth from 4 feet to 13 feet. Water-fitness classes are offered along with swim lessons for tots up to seniors. The facility also has a 2-foot splash pool for kids, along with a whirlpool, steam room, and sauna.

GOLF Beaver Island State Park Golf Course (716-773-4668, pro shop 716-773-7143), 2136 West Oakfield Road, Grand Island. An 18-hole, par-72 golf course and driving range. See also *Parks.*

Brighton Park Golf Course (716-695-2580), 70 Brompton Road, Tonawanda, A public 18-hole, par-72 course with driving range.

Deerwood Golf Course (716-695-8525), 1818 Sweeney Street, North Tonawanda, A public course with 27 holes (9-hole course, plus 18-hole course). It has a restaurant, full bar and snack bar.

& ✐ ⊤ **Paddock Chevrolet Golf Dome** (716-504-3663; www.tonawanda.ny.us/parks), 175 Brompton Road, Tonawanda. Open 8–9 September 1–June 30. You can practice your swing no matter what the weather at the Paddock Chevrolet Golf Dome. Inside the 82-foot high dome are 48 tee stations on two levels plus a 3,500-square-foot putting and chipping green. Kids will enjoy the 18-hole Brighton Bay miniature golf course. The golf dome has a pro shop, Gallery Grill restaurant, and a private party room, perfect for hosting children's birthday parties.

Sheridan Park Golf Course (716-875-1811), Center Park Drive, Tonawanda. A public 18-hole, par-71 course with restaurant and snack bar.

MARINAS **Anchor Marine** (716-773-7063), 1501 Ferry Road, Grand Island. A full-service marina.

Blue Water Marina (716-773-7884), 340 East River Road, Grand Island. A full-service marina with a boat launch, boating and fishing supplies and boat storage.

River Oaks Marina (716-774-0050), 101 Whitehaven Road at East River, Grand Island.

Six Mile Creek Marine (716-773-3270), West River and Whitehaven Road, Grand Island.

SCENIC DRIVES **West River Parkway**, between Buckhorn Island State Park and Beaver Island State Park is a limited-access seasonal highway that offers spectacular views of the Niagara River and Canadian shore. There are three overlook parking areas along the route and a picnic area located near Staley Road.

SKATING *⚡* **Bikes Blades and Boards** (716-807-0434), 3355 Niagara Falls Boulevard, North Tonawanda. Open Wednesday and Friday 4–9, Saturday–Sunday 12–9, weather permitting; open daily in summer. Admission: $5/hour, $10/day. As the name implies this is the place to ride bikes, blades, boards and scooters. This family-operated facility includes a 6-foot half-pipe, 3½-foot half-pipe and a 12-foot half-pipe with a 15-foot roll in. A street course includes handrails, wedges, and pyramids. There is an observation area, picnic spot, and a retail outlet selling necessary equipment for the sport.

⚡ **Grinders Skatepark** (716-404-8888; www.grindersskatepark.com), 2088 Grand Island Boulevard, Grand Island Summer open seven days noon–10; off-season open Friday 4–9, Saturday 12–10, Sunday 12–9. Admission: $5/hour or $10/day. An outdoor skatepark that has a 12-foot vertical ramp, a vertical wall, and a fun box section. It also has a city center, bike ramps, flyboxes, and grinding rails.

⚡ 🍴 **Rainbow Rink** (716-693-1100) 101 Oliver Street, North Tonawanda. Open Wednesday 4–8, Friday 4–7:30, Saturday–Sunday 12–4:30. Admission: $4. The Rainbow Rink has been a North Tonawanda landmark for a several generations. The roller rink was originally built in 1949 by the grandfather of the current owner. This family-run facility offers traditional skating along with a small section of ramps for stunt skaters. A tiny tots skating session for young skaters is offered on Saturday mornings. Birthday skating parties can be scheduled any time during open skating sessions.

✳ Green Space

BEACHES See *Beaver Island State Park*

NATURE PRESERVES **Buckhorn Island State Park** (716-773-3271), Beaver Island State Park, 2136 West Oakfield Road, Grand Island. Open dawn to dusk.

Free admission. This 895-acre preserve consists of marsh, meadows, and woods, including wetlands that are home to great blue herons and other waterfowl. The public is invited to walk the nature trails, hike, fish, and cross-country ski in the winter. The park is currently undergoing restoration to increase the diversity of the native flora and fauna. Part of this restoration includes increasing the trail system, putting in more overlooks, and adding a bike path.

PARKS & ♂ **Beaver Island State Park** (716-773-3271), 2136 West Oakfield Road, Grand Island. Open dawn to dusk. Free admission Labor Day–Memorial Day, $7 car parking Memorial Day–Labor Day. This beautiful 950-acre park is located at the south end of Grand Island in the upper Niagara River. Playgrounds, picnic facilities, an 80-slip marina, fishing access, an 18-hole golf course and a half-mile long sandy beach make it a popular spot on summer weekends. Recreational and nature programs are offered year-round. Also located in the park is the historic River Lea Farm House, once the home of Lewis Allen, founder of the Erie County Fair and uncle of President Grover Cleveland. (See *Museums and Historic Homes*.) During the winter months, visitors to Beaver Island enjoy cross-country skiing, snowshoeing, sledding, and ice fishing.

Ellicott Creek Park (716-693-2971), Niagara Falls Boulevard at Ellicott Creek Rd, Tonawanda. Open dawn to dusk. Free admission. This park, which opened in 1926, is located along Ellicott Creek. Park activities include baseball, fishing, ice skating, picnicking, sledding, cross-country skiing, softball, and tennis.

Fisherman's Park (716-695-8520), River Road, North Tonawanda. This park, located along the Niagara River, offers two shelters, fishing, a band shell presenting Thursday-evening concerts, and a nationally recognized monument to U.S. Navy Seabees. There is also a U.S. Marine Corps Memorial.

Gateway Harbor Park (716-695-8520, North Tonawanda; 716-743-8189, Tonawanda), Main and Webster Streets, North Tonawanda. Gateway Harbor Park is a two-block park bordering the Erie Canal along Niagara Street in the City of Tonawanda and Sweeney Street in North Tonawanda. One of seven major harbors along the New York State Canal System, the park is the site of the annual Canal Fest each July. Docking facilities are equipped with electricity and water, and showers and rest rooms are available for boaters at the Harbor Master's Station on the Tonawanda side.

Gratwick-Riverside Park (716-695-8520), River Road, North Tonawanda. Open dawn to dusk. Free admission. This 53-acre park has docking facilities, picnic shelters, nature areas, bird watching, nature trails, and fishing along the Niagara River. You can see the mist of Niagara Falls from here.

Isle View Park (716-692-1890), 796 Niagara Street, Tonawanda. Open dawn to dusk. Free admission. This park, located along the Niagara River overlooking Grand Island, offers a variety of activities, including biking, hiking, and rollerblading on the Riverwalk trail, which passes through the park. Isle View is also a popular place for fishing; a boat launch is available. A pedestrian foot bridge connects Isle View with Niawanda Park.

Lincoln Park (716-831-1009), Decatur Avenue, Tonawanda. A 65-acre park that includes picnic shelters, sports fields, and a swimming and wading pool.

Niawanda Park (716-852-1921), NY 266 and River Road, Tonawanda. A long, narrow park with picnic tables and a boat launch on the Niagara River. A paved biking and walking trail connects with the Riverwalk Trail, which goes all the way to Buffalo.

North Tonawanda Botanical Gardens, Sweeney Street at Robinson Road. This canalside park features flowers, a gazebo, a boat launch, and walking paths.

West Canal Marina (716-439-7950), 4070 Tonawanda Creek Road, North Tonawanda. Find picnic shelters, fishing, a boat launch, and observation points.

WALKING, HIKING AND BIKING TRAILS Niagara River Walk and Bicycle Trail (completion pending). This 10-foot wide, 2-mile blacktop trail winds in and out of Gratwick Park, Fisherman's Park, and Gateway Harbor Park as well as the downtown business district. It connects with the **Buffalo and Erie County Riverwalk.** Bicycling is also popular along **East** and **West River Roads** in **Grand Island.**

WALK, BIKE, OR SKATE ON THIS PAVED TRAIL ALONG THE NIAGARA RIVER

Christine A. Smyczynski

✳ Lodging

INNS AND RESORTS

Holiday Inn Grand Island (716-773-1111; www.holiday-inn.com/grandislandny), 100 Whitehaven Road, Grand Island. Located along the Niagara River. Many of the 261 rooms and suites have balconies over-look-ing the river. The newly renovated hotel features tennis courts, an indoor/outdoor pool and fitness center. $75–$159.

OTHER LODGING KOA Kamping Kabins and Kampsites (716-773-7583), 2570 Grand Island Boulevard, Grand Island. Facilities include 60 cabins, almost 200 trailer sites (70 with water and electric), and 43 tent sites with electric hookups. They have two pools, two fishing ponds, canoes, and miniature golf. Sites range from $22–$41.

✳ Where to Eat

DINING OUT Frog Grill (716-694-3700), 561 Main Street, Tonawanda. Open for lunch Tuesday–Friday, dinner Tuesday–Saturday 5–9:30. The decor of this restaurant is frogs, with frog figurines everywhere and pictures of frogs on the walls. Picture the Mona Lisa as a frog, and you get the idea. The menus features upscale food, including frog legs, along with comfort foods like chicken pot pie, pot roast, and meat loaf. They also offer unique desserts like chocolate meat loaf, and peanut brittle.

Currents Holiday Inn Grand Island (716-773-1111; www.holiday-inn.com/grandislandny), 100 White-haven Road, Grand Island. Open for breakfast 7–11, lunch 11–2, dinner 5–10. A seafood bistro located on the waterfront. Menu items include planked salmon, smothered steak, boneless pork chops, chicken entrées, and grilled vegetable pesto.

River Oaks Clubhouse Restaurant (716-773-3337), 201 Whitehaven Road, Grand Island. Open for lunch and dinner. Country club dining open to the public, proper dress required. Enjoy dining indoors or on the patio overlooking the golf course.

Saigon Bangkok (716-837-2115), 512 Niagara Falls Boulevard, Tonawanda. Open Sunday–Thursday 11–10, Friday and Saturday 11–11. This upscale Thai and Vietnamese restaurant offer selections like Spicy Rainbow (a vegetarian dish), chicken satay, and pad Thai, the national dish of Thailand. They are also noted for their soups. The restaurant's ambience includes soft music and cloth napkins and tablecloths.

EATING OUT ☕ **The Beach House** (716-773-7119), 5584 East River Road, Grand Island. Open year-round, Sunday–Thursday 11–10, Friday 11–11, Saturday 3–11. A small restaurant serving reasonably priced food, located near the river with indoor and outdoor dining. Home-made soup is served daily, along with lunch and dinner specials. Fish fry served Wednesday and Friday

Café del Mare (716-694-3788), 329 Niagara Street, Tonawanda. A small seasonal take-out café, located in the 300 block of Niagara Street along the Niagara River, serving coffee, desserts, and ice cream.

JP Dwyers Irish Pub (716-692-4837), 65 Webster Street, North Tonawanda. Open Monday–Friday 4 PM–2 AM, Saturday 4 PM–3 AM, Sunday noon–2 AM. This bar and restaurant serves traditional pub-style food. They are known for their 14 different varieties of chicken wings. The restaurant, which has a cigar store Indian in the corner by the bar, is located adjacent to the Riviera Theater, about a block from the canal.

✄ ♿ 🍴 **Lou's Restaurant** (716-694-6025), 73 Webster Street, North Tonawanda. Open Monday–Friday 7–7, Saturday–Sunday 7–2. A small family-run restaurant, featuring home-style cooking, daily specials, and homemade desserts. Located right next door to the historic Riviera Theater and a short walk from the Erie Canal.

✄ **Mississippi Mudds** (716-694-0787), 313 Niagara Street, Tonawanda. Open March–October 11–7:30 daily. This two-tiered restaurant, overlooking the Niagara River, is usually packed on a hot summer day. Enjoy hot dogs, burgers, chicken, roast beef, and more. End your meal with a homemade waffle cone topped with soft-serve custard or locally made Perry's ice cream.

Nestors (716-695-3596), 102 Webster Street, North Tonawanda. Open 24 hours. This family-owned-and-operated family restaurant features Texas red hots, Greek food, and an old-fashioned ice cream parlor.

✄ **Old Man Rivers** (716-693-5558), 375 Niagara Street, Tonawanda. Open April–September 11–7:30 daily. Enjoy burgers, hot dogs, and ice cream, along with sweet potato fries, grilled carrots (better known as "bunny dogs"), and more. The rear seafood shack serves up clams, shrimp cocktails, crab legs, and chowder. This eatery is located across the street from the Niagara River, so the view is great.

The Shores Waterfront Restaurant (716-693-7971, 2 Detroit Street (Tonawanda Island) North Tonawanda. Open seasonally May–October, daily 11–9, Friday and Saturday until midnight. Casual American cuisine, everything from sandwiches and burgers to steaks and seafood, with a great view of the Niagara River and Grand Island. Live bands are featured on the weekend.

Towpath Café (716-743-8878), 11–13 Main Street, Tonawanda. Open Monday–Thursday 8:30–8, Friday and Saturday 7–2. This restaurant boasts the best fish fry in town as well as homemade lasagna and meat loaf. Other specialties include ribs, steaks, and chops.

✳ Entertainment

THEATERS New Melody Fair Theater (716-694-2760), 1 Majestic Lane, Wurlitzer Park, North Tonawanda. Summer theater and concerts in the round.

Riviera Theater and Performing Arts Center (716-692-2413; www.rivieratheatre.org), 67 Webster Street, North Tonawanda. This restored Italian Renaissance–style performing-arts venue was built in 1926 and is listed on the National Register of Historic Places. The theater's lobby boasts stained-glass windows, while a 15-foot-high French chandelier with stained-glass-light-bulbs is suspended from the dome of the auditorium. Throughout the year the Riviera features plays, musical concerts, movies, and more, including a monthly American Theatre Organ concert on the 1926 "Mighty Wurlitzer" organ. The Riviera is one of only a handful of theaters in the country that has a silver screen and vintage projectors capable of running the nitrate film used for silent movies.

Ghostlight Theatre (716-743-1614; www.mytonawandas.com/ghostlight .html), 170 Schenk Street, North Tonawanda. A year-round community theater that's housed in a 100-year-old church.

✳ Selective Shopping

ART GALLERIES Partners in Art Gallery & Studio (716-692-2141), 83 Webster Street, North Tonawanda. Open Tuesday–Wednesday 1–6, Thursday 1–5, Friday and Saturday 10–4. This gallery is located upstairs in a bright pink building, which once housed the *Evening News*. The exhibits change monthly, and most of the artwork is for sale. Classes are offered.

FARM MARKETS ⅃ North Tonawanda City Market (716-693-3746), Payne Avenue (at Robinson Street), North Tonawanda. Open year-round Tuesday, Thursday, and Saturday 7 AM–1 PM. Established in 1908, this is the oldest farmer's market in Niagara County. While it is open year-round, the most popular time to visit is in the summer and early fall, when over 70 local farmers set up shop.

SPECIAL SHOPS Hodgepodge (716-694-4715), 72 Webster Street, North Tonawanda. Open Monday–Saturday 10–5:30. This spacious and neat gift shop features a variety of items, including North Tonawanda and Tonawanda merchandise (the only store to carry these items), books on the Erie Canal, gift items, cards, candles, locally made pottery, and

antiques. A collection of vintage North Tonawanda photos sits on the counter for customers to browse through.

♪ Kelly's Country Store (716-773-0003 www.kellyscountrystore.com), 3121 Grand Island Boulevard, Grand Island. Open 10–6 daily. Kelly's Country Store has been a Grand Island landmark since 1962. Chose from old-fashioned candy, scented candles, brass and crystal giftware, and more. The "Christmas Room" features visits with Santa on weekends, after Thanksgiving along with gifts, stocking stuffers, and toys. At Easter enjoy homemade candies, along with a visit from the Easter Bunny.

Premier Gourmet (716-877-3574), 3465 Delaware Avenue, Kenmore. Open Monday–Saturday 9:30–9, Sunday 11–5. Everything that you need to prepare a gourmet meal can be found at Premier Gourmet, including flavored vinegars and oils, spices, cookware, utensils, and kitchen linens plus prepared food and baked goods, caviar, and gourmet candies. The **Premier Café,** located in the shop's foyer, serves specialty sandwiches, coffee, and juices. The **Premier Center** (716-873-6688), Western New York's wine and spirits superstore, is located in the same complex.

Teddy Bear Carpet & Linoleum (716-692-4756), 64 Webster Street, North Tonawanda, Open Monday–Friday 10–6, Saturday 10–4. This building has been a fixture on Webster Street for many years. But more than just a home improvement store, they also have a large selection of cotton fabrics and quilting supplies. Quilting classes are offered Wednesday and Thursday evenings. Another section of the store focuses on toys from the '60s, '70s, and '80s.

Udderly Country (716-692-4221), 38 Webster Street, North Tonawanda. Open Tuesday–Saturday 10–4. A unique gift shop carrying collectibles, porcelain dolls, candles, baskets, garden items, stuffed animals, and more. Art classes, including tole painting, are offered.

✳ **Special Events**

July: **Canal Fest of the Tonawandas** (716-692-3292; www.canalfest .org), This eight-day festival is the largest of its kind along the Erie Canal. Events include parades, youth activities, midway rides, musical entertainment, tours of historical sites, gaming, lots of foods, arts and crafts show, car show, and much more.

AMHERST

Amherst, population 121,000, is a 54-square-mile suburban community that includes the village of Williamsville plus the hamlets of Eggertsville, Getzville, Snyder, Swormville, and East Amherst. Home to the Amherst Campus State University of New York at Buffalo, it has been recognized by Morgan Quitno Press as the safest town of its size in the nation.

The first inhabitants of the region were Native Americans, who found the area good for hunting and fishing. Later, though western New York was considered by most Europeans to be a wilderness frontier, title to 3,300,000 acres was acquired in 1798 by the Holland Land Company, a group of Dutch financiers. Joseph Ellicott, an experienced land surveyor, was hired to oversee the task of surveying the land acquired in what is known as the Holland Land purchase.

Ellicott and his crew were responsible for improving some of the Indian trails so that settlers could come into the area in their wagons. Some of these roads include what was referred to as the Buffalo Road, now Main Street, and Transit Road, which was named after the surveyors' instrument used to help make a straight line.

Early settlers included John Thompson and Benjamin Ellicott, brother of Joseph, who in 1799 purchased 300 acres of land around the Ellicott Creek waterfall, known today as Glen Falls. By 1803 some six homes had been constructed in the vicinity. Jonas Williams, traveling through the area, realized the potential of water power in the area and decided to acquire the land. In 1811 he built a gristmill on the west side of the waterfall (still in operation today as Williamsville Water Mills), and the location became known as Williams Mills, later changed to Williamsville. It was the first and biggest settlement in the town, which was officially incorporated as the town of Amherst in 1818. At that time the town also included all of what now is Cheektowaga and part of West Seneca. Amherst may have been named for Sir Jeffrey Amherst, commander in chief of the British troops in America before the American Revolution, or it may have been named after Amherst, Massachusetts.

More settlers began arriving into the area, which was still a wilderness. Life was hard for the early pioneers—the land needed to be cleared, and much of the area was swampy, so roads were hard to build. The opening of the Erie Canal helped the town prosper since it gave farmers a means to send their crops to larger markets. It was also easier for new settlers to reach the area, many of whom were German or "Pennsylvania Dutch."

By the late 1870s Amherst's main occupation was farming, which continued up until the 1920s, when farmland was sold to make room for housing subdivisions. While only four working farms remain in Amherst, many areas of the town still maintain a rural feel.

(For more information on Amherst history, consult *Glancing Back: A Pictorial History of Amherst, New York* by Joseph A. Grande, Ph.D.)

AREA CODE The area code is 716.

GUIDANCE **Amherst Chamber of Commerce** (716-632-6905; www.amherst.org), 325 Essjay Road, Suite 200, Williamsville. Open Monday–Friday 9–5.

Amherst Town Hall (716-631-7000), 5583 Main Street, Williamsville. Open Monday–Friday 8–4:30.

Village of Williamsville (716-632-4120; www.willvill.com) 5565 Main Street Williamsville. Open Monday–Friday 8–4.

GETTING THERE *By bus:* There are several bus routes between Amherst and downtown Buffalo. Some of these routes take passengers to the Light Rail Rapid Transit station at the University at Buffalo Main Street Campus.

By car: From the I-90 take the I-290 (exit 50). The next several exits feed into various parts of Amherst.

MEDICAL EMERGENCY Dial 911

Millard Fillmore Suburban Hospital (688-3100; kaleidahealth.org), 1540 Maple Road, Williamsville.

✷ To See

MUSEUMS AND HISTORIC HOMES ♿ 🖉 **Amherst Museum** (716-689-1440; www.amherstmuseum.org), 3755 Tonawanda Creek Road, Amherst. Open November–March, Tuesday–Friday 9:30–4:30; April–October, Tuesday–Friday 9:30–4:30, Saturday and Sunday 12:30–4:30; closed municipal holidays. Admission: $5 adults, $1.50 children, $12 family, members free. Historic buildings open April 1–mid-October. The Amherst Museum is a 35-acre historical park, with 12 restored buildings decorated with period furnishings. In addition to the historic structures, a modern exhibit building focuses on local history, antique radios, decorative arts, and more. The children's Discovery Room features hands-on exhibits, including a replica Erie Canal packet boat. A research library has over 3,000 books and other records pertinent to western New York. The museum has year-round educational programs; schools and scout groups are encouraged to spend the day at the museum learning about 19th-century life. For adults there are several craft guilds that promote and teach 19th-century crafts and activities, including rug braiding, lace making, quilting, and Victorian dance. Numerous special events and festivals, reflecting 19th-century life, are held throughout the year.

HISTORIC SITES Williamsville Water Mill (716-632-1162), 56 Spring Street, Williamsville. Open Monday–Saturday 10–6, Sunday 11–6. This mill has been in operation since 1811, the oldest continuously operating business on the Niagara Frontier and the oldest building in Amherst. One of seven mills built by Jonas Williams, it is the only one still in existence. Today you can purchase fresh pressed cider in season or browse in the gift shop.

Mennonite Meeting House, Main and North Forest Streets, Williamsville. This small stone building, erected in 1834, was one of the first houses of worship in Amherst. The one-story structure, which is on the National Register of Historic Places, was built from fossilized limestone. The building was used by the Mennonites until the 1980s, when it was purchased by the Town of Amherst. It currently is used to house town records and archives and is not open to the public.

✳ To Do

FAMILY FUN ✍ ₺ ᛏ **Doc's Fun Center** (716-636-8368) 5445, Transit Road, Williamsville. Open Wednesday–Thursday 3–10, Friday 3–11, Saturday 11–11, Sunday 11–9. This is a pay-one-price video game arcade where kids never have to beg mom and dad for more coins or tokens. Whether you like car racing, shooting games, basketball, pinball, air hockey, or pool, it's all here. This is a popular place for birthdays and other parties. Party packages include unlimited games, pizza, pop, and use of the party room.

✍ ᛏ **LaserTron** (716-833-8766; www.laser-tron.com), 5101 North Bailey Avenue, Amherst. Open 10 AM–midnight daily, Friday and Saturday until 2 AM. Admission: $11 for a half-hour session. Reservations suggested. Teams enter the futuristic arena filled with wild lighting, swirling fog, pillars, and passages. Each player has a vest with sensors, vibrators, identification lights, and LED readout, and everyone is equipped with a phaser—ready to zap the enemy. Sounds like a video game; the only difference is that you are actually a player in the game. LaserTron, launched in Buffalo in 1988, was originally developed as a marketing project by LaserTron's founder and CEO, Jim Kessler, when he attended Canisius College in 1985. This original facility, which now totals 18,800 square feet, houses LaserTron and "Ground Zero," the ultimate laser shooting gallery. It is also the research and development center for the many

THE AMHERST MUSEUM IS A 35-ACRE HISTORICAL PARK FOCUSING ON 19TH-CENTURY LIFE.
Courtesy Buffalo–Niagara Convention & Visitors Bureau and Amherst Museum

locations that use the LaserTron Game System across the U.S. and Canada. In addition to the laser games, they have a wide variety of arcade games, a snack bar, and a party room.

✂ ⊤ **Monkey Around** (716-626-1626; www.monkeyaround.biz), Eastern Hills Mall, 4545 Transit Road, Williamsville. Open Tuesday–Thursday 10–2, Friday 10–3, Saturday 10–7, Sunday 12–4. This interactive play center is geared to children ages one to eight. The play areas are designed to help children develop social, physical, and intellectual skills. Some of the activities include a water table for boats, a rice box (like a sandbox. but with rice instead of sand), ball pool with slide, art center, costumes for dress-up, a reading area, climbing areas, forts, and a "flying" ride. There is also a party area since this is a great place to host a child's birthday party. Monkey-a-Round is a safe, fun place where kids and parents can learn and play together.

GOLF **Audubon Golf Course** (716-631-7139) 500, Maple Road, Williamsville. An 18-hole, par-71 public course.

Audubon Par-3 Golf Course (716-631-7124), 475 Maple Road, Williamsville. A public 9- hole, par-3 course.

Evergreen Golf Club (716-688-6204), 168 Tonawanda Creek Road, Amherst. A public 9-hole, par 35 course.

Glen Oak Golf Course (716-688-4400 or 716-688-5454; www.glenoak.com), 711 Smith Road, East Amherst. A public 18-hole, par-72 course with driving range.

Oakwood Golf Course (716-689-1421), 3575 Tonawanda Creek Road, East Amherst. A 9-hole, par-34 golf course with snack bar.

MARINAS **Amherst Marine Center** (716-691-6707), 1900 Campbell Boulevard, Amherst. A full-service marina located on the Erie Canal.

RECREATIONAL FACILITIES ⅁ ✂ ⊤ **Amherst Pepsi Center** (716-631-7555), 1615 Amherst Manor Drive, Williamsville. Call for hours as they vary from month to month. Admission: $3 Amherst residents with ID card, $6 nonresidents. This 182,000-square-foot, two-story facility is one of the largest recreational ice complexes in the country, offering four ice surfaces, a youth center, fitness center, snack bar, video arcade, and more. The arena is home to many local youth hockey teams, and the Buffalo Sabres practice here. Three of the rinks are NHL sized (200 feet by 85 feet), while the fourth rink is Olympic sized (200 feet by 100 feet). Sports-related retail stores are also located in the complex, and skate sharpening is offered in the pro shop. Skates and helmets are available for rental in a variety of sizes. The center is surrounded by 20 acres of green space that includes five softballs and two baseball diamonds, three soccer fields, and a junior football field.

SKATING ✂ ⊤ **Eastern Hills Roller Rink** (716-633-6060), 4675 Transit Road, Williamsville. Open Friday 4–11, Saturday 12–4:30 and 7–10:30, Sunday 12–4:30. Enjoy traditional roller skating and in-line skating at a clean, indoor facility with a family-oriented atmosphere. This is the perfect place for a kid's birthday party, a family outing, or a date with a special someone. Top tunes are played for your skating pleasure, along with classic favorites like the hokey pokey and the chicken dance (chicken *skate?*). A small snack bar serves kid-favorite foods such as pizza, nachos, and hot dogs.

SLEDDING Margaret Louise Park sledding hill, Hopkins Road (between Dodge and West Klein), Williamsville. A very popular spot to take the kids after a snowfall, this hill is big enough to be fun for older kids, yet small enough to be safe for younger sledders.

✳ Green Space

NATURE PRESERVES ⟁ ✿ **Great Baehre Swamp Conservation Area/ Margaret Louise Park,** Hopkins Road (between Dodge and West Klein), Williamsville. Open dawn to dusk. Free admission. Get up close to nature when you walk on the boardwalk through the Great Baehre Swamp. A variety of waterfowl, turtles, and deer and other wildlife can be observed, along with plants native to the area.

PARKS Amherst State Park, 400 Mill Street, Williamsville. Open dawn to dusk. Free admission. This 77-acre undeveloped park was the former site of the St. Mary of the Angels convent. Enjoy walking and biking trails along Ellicott Creek, bird watching, and an old orchard.

Bassett Park, Klein and Youngs Road, Williamsville. A 40-acre park with a small lake, band shell, woodlands, and rolling lawns. There is a small playground and rest room facilities. On Tuesday and Thursdays during the summer, free concerts take place in the band shell.

THE BOARDWALK AT THE GREAT BAEHRE SWAMP CONSERVATION AREA.

Christine A. Smyczynski

Garrison Park, Garrison Road and South Ellicott Street, Williamsville. This small neighborhood park has playground equipment, a wading pool, and a gazebo.

Glen Park, Between Main Street and Glen Avenue, Williamsville. Without a doubt, Glen Park is the most scenic site in the village. Ellicott Creek, cascading over the Onandoga Escarpment, forms Glen Falls. The 10-acre park and natural wildlife area is a place to enjoy picnicking, fishing, or just strolling the trails. During the warmer months it is a popular spot for wedding pictures. Back in the 1940s and '50s, Glen Park was the site of an amusement park and the Glen Casino, which attracted nationally known performers. That complex was destroyed in a spectacular fire in 1968. The property was converted into parkland in 1976.

Island Park (716-632-4120), 5565 Main Street, Williamsville. This triangle-shaped park is actually an island, formed in 1841 when Jonas Williams built a raceway to divert water to power his gristmill. The park features a large pavilion, a playground, and a wading pool. It's site of Old Home Days and the Taste of Williamsville each summer.

POOLS ✐ ♿ **Clearfield Recreation Center** (716-689-1418), 15 Plaza Drive (off Hopkins Road), Williamsville. Open daily 1–7 late June until just before Labor Day. Enjoy either a wading pool with a large splash park, with a maximum depth of 18" or a swimming pool, with a handicapped access ramp, that's 3½ to 5 feet deep. The recreation area also has tennis courts, a playground, two baseball diamonds, a basketball court, and an indoor multiuse sports court.

✐ **North Forest Park and Pool** (716-631-7275), 85 North Forest Road, Williamsville. Open daily 1–7 late June until just before Labor Day. This park has a swimming pool, a wading pool, and a recreation area.

WATERFALLS Glen Falls. Glen Park, Williamsville. A 27-foot-high falls is located in a beautiful park used by people of all ages. The viewing spot next to the falls is considered to be quite a romantic location, a popular place for both marriage proposals and wedding pictures.

WALKING, BIKING, AND HIKING TRAILS (Note for all bike trails: Pets must be on a leash not exceeding 6 feet in length, speed limit is 15 MPH, no motor vehicles, trails are closed 10 PM–6 AM.)

Bailey Campus to Amherst Campus (a.k.a. Inter-Campus Bikeway). This marked urban trail, designed with students at the University at Buffalo in mind, starts on the southwest corner of Main Street and Bailey Avenue by UB's City Campus. It follows Bailey Avenue down several side streets, to Sweet Home Road, where a 5-foot-wide restricted lane starts on the east side of the road and continues to the Amherst Campus.

Amherst Canalway Trail (a.k.a. Tonawanda Creek Bike Path). This 6-mile path starts by Tonawanda Creek Road and New Road, near the Amherst Museum, and runs along the New York State Barge Canal (Erie Canal).

Ellicott Creek Bike Path. This 5-mile-long paved trail follows Ellicott Creek from a parking lot on North Forest Road in Williamsville to Niagara Falls Boulevard near Ellicott Creek Park. It is popular with walkers, bikers, and in-line skaters, especially on the weekend. As it winds its way along the creek, it passes many scenic vantage points. The area is also abundant in waterfowl and an occasional deer. There are many secluded areas along the trail, so for safety it is strongly recommended to travel with a friend.

Lehigh Valley Railroad Path. Access it by the old Lehigh Valley Railroad depot on South Long Street in Williamsville. This paved walking and biking path in the village of Williamsville is about 1.5 miles long.

Margaret Louis Park Boardwalk. See **Great Baehre Swamp Conservation Area.**

Village of Williamsville Walking Tour (www.willvill.com). A printable version of a walking tour through historic Williamsville can be found on this Web site.

Walton Woods Bike Path. This bike and walking path, located in a wooded area behind Amherst Police headquarters, loops around Lake Audubon, a small pond that's home to native waterfowl. It has 6 acres of old-growth forest, including several 150-year-old trees.

Willow Ridge Bike Path. This short bike trail runs between Ellicott Creek Road and Sweet Home Road in Amherst with a bridge crossing over the I-990 Expressway.

✳ Lodging

INNS AND RESORTS University Inn & Conference Center (716-636-7500; www.universityinn.com), 2402 North Forest Road, Amherst. Closest accommodations to the University at Buffalo, this hotel is located on 14 wooded acres, featuring 120 well-appointed guest rooms. Amenities include a workout room and hiking trails. $79–$139.

MOTELS AND HOTELS Buffalo–Niagara Marriott (716-689-6900; www.buffaloniagaramarriott.com), 1340 Maple Road, Amherst. Convenient to both downtown Buffalo and Niagara Falls, the Marriott offers quality accommodations to business travelers as well as vacationers. It features 356 guest rooms, a fully-equipped fitness center, and an indoor/outdoor pool. $59–$189.

Hampton Inn Williamsville (716-632-0900 or 800-Hampton; www.hamptoninnwilliamsville.com), 5455 Main Street, Williamsville. The hotel, located right in the village of Williamsville, blends Old-World charm with modern amenities. Each guest room has custom-designed Thomasville furniture that includes a large desk plus high-speed Internet access. Suites include whirlpools, decorative fireplaces, and full kitchens. The hotel has a complimentary buffet breakfast, a fitness room, an indoor heated pool, and an airport shuttle. It was recently awarded the Hampton Lighthouse Award, given to hotels that offer exemplary service. $109–$199.

Holiday Motel (716-632-2140), 5801 Main Street, Williamsville. A family-owned-and-operated motel in a suburban location, with 27 guest rooms, including suites, kitchenettes, and standard rooms. The hotel, only a few blocks from Williamsville, is popular with relocating families as well as tourists. $44–$78.

Lord Amherst Motor Hotel (716-839-2200), 5000 Main Street, Amherst. This suburban motel, conveniently located next to the I-290 expressway, offers 95 large, comfortable rooms with Early American decor. Rooms have either a king, queen, or two double beds. Amenities include an exercise room and outdoor pool. A continental breakfast is served each morning. $65–$75.

✳ Where to Eat
DINING OUT

Amherst
Audubon Room Restaurant and Lounge (716-636-7500; www .universityinn.com), University Inn and Conference Center, 2402 North Forest Road, Amherst. Open 6 AM–12 AM. This elegant restaurant features New American cuisine and award-winning wine. Dinner selections include fresh salmon filet and braised lamb shank. The dining room, with decor based on the art of naturalist John James Audubon, overlooks Ellicott Creek. During the warmer months enjoy dining on the outdoor patio. It has been rated 3½ stars out of 4 by the *Buffalo News* food reviewer.

Bings (716-839-5788), 1952 Kensington Avenue, Amherst. Open Tuesday–Saturday 4:30–9:30. This small, cozy restaurant, specializing in Italian dishes and fresh seafood, has won numerous awards at the Taste of Buffalo. Start your dining experience with their signature baked artichokes. Menu selections include traditional favorites like manicotti and baked ziti

along with osso buco and chicken Francese.

Christino's (716-689-6900), Buffalo Niagara Marriott, 1340 Millersport Highway, Amherst. Open for breakfast Monday–Friday 6:30–11:30, Saturday 7–11, Sunday 7–10; Sunday brunch buffet 7–1:30; lunch Monday–Saturday 11:30–2; dinner daily 5–10. An upscale Italian restaurant with a nice atmosphere and good service with dinner entrées that feature steaks, seafood, and pasta.

Dakota Grill (716-834-6600), 4224 Maple at Sweet Home Road, Amherst. Open Monday–Thursday 11:30–10, Friday and Saturday 4–11, Sunday 4–10. This restaurant has four separate dining rooms: a casual restaurant serving contemporary American cuisine like steak and seafood; a New York City–style cigar bar (one of the few places where smoking is allowed inside in western New York); and two garden rooms that can accommodate banquets from 10 to 110 guests. Specialty items include Bourbon Street salmon and black and bleu filet of sirloin.

Fanny's Restaurant (716-834-0400; www.fannysrestaurant.com), 3500 Sheridan Drive, Amherst. Open for lunch Monday–Friday 11:30–3, dinner Monday–Saturday 5–10, Sunday 4–8. You know you're in for a special dining experience from the moment you enter Fanny's and notice the fresh flowers adorning the tables covered with crisp linen tablecloths. Perhaps you'll be seated in one of the private booths, which allow more intimate conversations. Start your dining experience with delicacies like escargot, clams casino, or shrimp soufflé. Entrées include pasta selections, rack of lamb, seafood, duck, and steaks.

Grapevine (716-691-7799; www
.grapevinerestaurant.com), 2545 Niagara Falls Boulevard, Amherst. Open
Monday–Thursday 11:30–10, Friday
and Saturday 11:30–11, Sunday 10–9.
This restaurant, which has a large
menu featuring seafood, beef,
chicken, and pasta, is decorated with
several large aquariums located
throughout the restaurant. It is usually very busy, so expect a wait.

Getzville

Byblos (716-636-3102), 270 Campbell Boulevard Getzville. Open
Monday–Friday 11–10, Saturday
2–10. Enjoy Middle Eastern delicacies such as humus, tabouli, stuffed
grape leaves, and kabobs in a bright
country setting. House specialties
include leg of lamb and baked kibbi.
A patio is open during the summer
months. The restaurant is located
right across the parking lot from the
Port of Entry Complex of shops.

Dacc's Restaurant (716-568-2130),
3175 Millersport Highway, Getzville.
Open for lunch Monday–Friday 11–4
dinner Monday–Thursday 4–10, Friday 4–11, Saturday 5–11. One of Getzville's best-kept secrets, Dacc's offers
city-style dining in a suburban location. This small, intimate restaurant
offers steaks, seafood, pasta, and
more, including an extensive wine list.

♂ **Sean Patrick's** (716-636-1709),
3480 Millersport Highway, Getzville.
Open Monday–Saturday 11–10, Sunday 11–9. This popular casual fine-
dining restaurant features an Irish
atmosphere and an extensive menu,
with items like filet mignon, fettuccini
Alfredo, and charbroiled pork chops
along with meat loaf and liver and
onions. They also have a large banquet room.

Williamsville

&. **Butterwood Gourmet Desserts**
(716-204-0939; www.cakeart.com),
5409 Main Street, Williamsville. Open
Monday–Thursday 10–11, Friday and
Saturday 1 PM–midnight, Sunday
11–10. Forget about dinner and go
straight for the desserts. This upscale
dessert restaurant, located in a
century-old house, serves world-class
desserts as the entrée, with about
eight different menu selections
offered each evening. Some of their
creations include Belgian chocolate
pâté, black bottom tiramisu, white
chocolate mousse cake, and crème
brûlée. Pastry chef Paschal Gagnon
creates desserts that are beautiful as
well as delicious. Enjoy a glass of
wine or Italian coffee along with your
meal. Dine indoors near the fireplace
or outdoors on the front porch
(weather permitting). Butterwood's
original location, on Route 240 in
West Falls, also serves up similar fare.

&. *♂* **Chang's Garden Chinese
Restaurant** (716-689-3355), 938
Maple Road, Williamsville. Open
seven days Monday–Thursday
11:30–10, Friday 11:30–11, Saturday
12–11, Sunday 12–10. This elegant,
upscale yet casual restaurant features
beautifully presented traditional Chinese dishes. All dishes are of excellent
quality, and service is attentive and
quick. The decor is as elegant as the
food presentation; you won't find any
Chinese dragons or lanterns here.
Take-out is available.

Creekview Restaurant (716-632-
9373; www.creekviewrestaurant.com),
5629 Main Street, Williamsville. Open
for lunch Monday–Saturday 11:30–4,
dinner Monday–Saturday 4–11, Sunday 1–9. Located in a historic older
home overlooking Ellicott Creek, this

restaurant features an American regional menu with dinner selections including steak, salmon, trout, lamb, and fresh haddock. A heated patio is open spring, summer, and fall for al fresco dining.

Daffodil's Restaurant (716-688-5413), 930 Maple Road, Williamsville. Open for lunch Monday–Friday 11:30–2:30, dinner Monday–Thursday 5–11, Friday 5–12, Sunday 4–10. This elegant and sophisticated restaurant serves traditional American cuisine, including its signature rack of lamb, lobster tails, and fresh seafood. Be sure to save room at the end of the meal for their famous carrot cake.

Eagle House (716-632-7669; www.eaglehouseonline.com), 5578 Main Street, Williamsville. Open Monday–Thursday 11–10, Friday and Saturday 11–11, Sunday 3–9 (closed Sunday in July and August). The Eagle House is one of the most well-known landmarks in the Village of Williamsville. This building has been in continuous service since 1827, from an inn and stagecoach stop to present-day fine dining. Menu selections include a variety of American cuisine, including fresh salmon, beef, Yankee pot roast, chicken, and low-fat specialties. A passageway leading out of the cellar to Glen Park indicates that this may have been a stop on the Underground Railroad.

McMahon's (716-689-3011), 952 Maple Road, Williamsville. Open Monday–Thursday 4–10, Friday and Saturday 4:30–11. Enjoy prime beef, seafood, chops, and lobster plus an extensive martini and wine list. Dress is business casual.

Protocol (716-632-9556; www.protocolrestaurant.com), 6766 Transit Road, Williamsville. Open for lunch Monday–Friday 11–3:30, dinner Monday–Saturday 4–11. This restaurant has their seafood flown in fresh daily from one of Boston's finest seafood markets. They are also noted for their ribs. Other menu choices include grilled meats, pasta, and poultry.

Red Mill Inn Rib and Seafood House (716-633-7878; www.redmillinn.com), 8326 Main Street, Williamsville. Open Monday–Thursday 4–9, Friday and Saturday 4–10, Sunday 11–9. Enjoy fine dining in a circa- 1858 landmark building that has lots of rustic charm. Dine on prime rib, hand-cut steaks, fresh fish, and seafood plus traditional favorites like Yankee pot roast and roast turkey.

& **Sonoma Grille** (716-204-0251; www.sonomagrille.com), 5010 Main Street, Snyder. Open daily 11–11. This large, bright, airy, California-style restaurant, named after the famous wine region in California, has five separate dining and banquet rooms. The menu features a mix of Northern California and Mediterranean cuisine, with selections such as pesto grilled swordfish and veal scaloppini as well as filet mignon and prime rib.

& **Tandoori's** (716-632-1112; www.tandooris.com), 7740 Transit Road, Williamsville. Open for lunch Monday–Friday 11–2:30, dinner daily 5–10. This restaurant serves the most authentic Indian cuisine in the area. The extensive, upscale menu includes selections like tandoori chicken, paneer makhani, and kabab reshmi.

& *⁄* **Zu Zon Bar & Grille** (716-634-6123) 5110, Main Street, Williamsville. Open Monday–Saturday 11:30–10, Sunday 4–10. Toddlers to business people will feel at ease at this casual and friendly restaurant, which has something for the whole family. Its artistic, contemporary interior, complete with animal-print fabrics and hand-painted murals, add a certain ambiance. You can find everything from upscale entrées to comfort food, along with chef Mark Warren's famous desserts like the Ultimate Snowball and pastry swans.

EATING OUT

Amherst

🐾 ✈ **Alice's Kitchen** (716-834-4182), 3122 Sheridan Drive, Amherst. Open daily 7 AM–10 PM. Look for the bright purple roof, and you've found Alice's Kitchen—a bright, busy, family restaurant featuring daily specials, freshly baked pies, and muffins.

✈ ♿ 🐾 **Duff's** (716-834-6234), 3651 Sheridan Drive, Amherst. Open Monday–Thursday 11–11, Friday and Saturday 11–midnight, Sunday 12–10. This small, casual restaurant is known for its chicken wings. It was opened in 1946 by Louise Duffney as a corner gin mill, but business took off when wings were introduced in 1969. Today over 12,000 pounds of Buffalo's favorite snack food are sold per week. Be advised: Medium is hot, medium hot is very hot, and hot is very, very hot! Besides wings, they also serve sandwiches, burgers, and salads. Beer and wine are available, as is a children's menu.

East Amherst

Grovers (716-636-1803), 9160 Transit, East Amherst. Open Monday–Saturday 11–10. This neighborhood tavern has one of the best hamburgers around.

Getzville

✈ ♿ 🐾 **Lebros** (716-688-0404; www.lebrosrestaurant.com), 330 Campbell Boulevard, Getzville. Open Monday–Thursday 11–10, Friday and Saturday 11–11, Sunday 4–9. Enjoy Italian dining in a relaxed atmosphere, from traditional favorites to unique homemade pastas. Lebros has won awards in both the Taste of Buffalo and Savor the Flavor of Williamsville several years in a row.

✈ ♿ 🐾 **Nina's Custard** (716-636-0345), 2525 Millersport Highway, Getzville. Sunday–Open Thursday 11–10, Friday and Saturday 11–11. Menu selections in this bright, casual restaurant include such fare as hot dogs, burgers, sweet potato fries, and chicken sandwiches, plus a large selection of ice cream treats. Dine indoors or outdoors on the patio (weather permitting).

Snyder

♿ 🐾 **Café in the Square** (716-839-5330), 4476 Main Street (corner of Harlem Road), Snyder. Open Monday–Friday 10:30–8, Saturday 10:30–9. A cozy café with a reputation for good food at reasonable prices. Entrées include pastas, seafood, chicken, pork, and more. Desserts are made by Carriage Trade Pastries. The café is located adjacent to the Cabaret in the Square Theatre.

Williamsville

♿ 🐾 ✈ **Anderson's Frozen Custard** (716-632-1416; www.andersons custard.com), 6075 Main Street, Williamsville (several other locations throughout western New York). Open Sunday–Thursday 11–9:30, Friday and Saturday 11–10. Specialties include beef on weck, oven-roasted turkey sandwiches, and a variety of ice cream treats.

✈ ♿ **Buffalo Brew Pub** (716-632-0552; www.buffalobrewpub.com),

6861 Main Street Williamsville. Open Sunday–Thursday 11:30–midnight, Friday and Saturday 11:30–1 AM. This popular, casual restaurant is Buffalo's original brew pub and the oldest brew pub in New York State. Enjoy a selection of in-house-brewed draft beer with your meal. Entrées include typical pub food like sandwiches, pizza, ribs, wings, and chicken dishes. They also have a kid's menu since the restaurant is popular with families—perhaps because they let you throw peanut shells on the floor.

✏ ও **Five Star Chinese Buffet** (716-633-9336), 5449 Sheridan Drive, Williamsville. Open for lunch Monday–Saturday 11–3:30, Sunday 11:30–3:30; dinner Monday–Thursday 3:30–9:30, Friday and Saturday 3:30–10:30, Sunday 3:30–9. Can't make up your mind what to order at a Chinese restaurant? Try the Five Star Chinese Buffet, where you can try a little of everything and go back for more. Enjoy traditional Chinese food like lo mein, happy family, and General Tso's chicken, along with sushi, fried squid, and even all-you-can-eat crab legs (Friday, Saturday, and Sunday).

Glen Park Tavern (716-626-9333), 5507 Main Street, Williamsville. Open Monday–Thursday 11:30 AM–midnight, Friday and Saturday 11:30 AM–2 AM, Sunday 10 AM–10 PM. Serving sandwiches, snacks, salads, pastas, and seafood in a pub atmosphere in a historic village building. Specialties include BBQ ribs, steak, and Chef Tony's hot peppers.

ও **Golden Duck** (716-639-8888), 1840 Maple Road, Williamsville. Open seven days for lunch and dinner. Open Sunday–Thursday 11:30–9:30, Friday and Saturday 11:30–10:30. A fortune cookie might say, "Don't be put off by outward appearances." Kept that in mind when you pull up to this restaurant, a simple storefront located in a tiny strip plaza. However, once inside, the decor is exquisite and the food is first class to boot. Dim sum Mongolian BBQ is available for lunch on Saturday and Sunday.

ও ✏ **La Nova** (716-634-5151; www.lanova.com), 5151 Main Street, Williamsville. Open daily 9:30 AM–12:45 AM. This restaurant, along with their original Buffalo location, is the largest seller of chicken wings in the country and the winner of the Best Wings in Buffalo award. Choose from an array of specialty pizzas and several different flavors of chicken wings, including traditional Buffalo, BBQ, honey mustard, and raspberry. They will overnight ship their pizza and wings anywhere in the U.S. (716-881-3355 or 800-652-6682).

ও ✦ **McPartlan's Corner** (716-632-9896), 669 Wehrle Drive, Williamsville. Open Sunday–Thursday 10 AM–midnight, Friday and Saturday 10 AM–1 AM. A small, casual restaurant and neighborhood corner bar that has been popular since 1955 for its Friday night fish fry. While fish and seafood dominate the menu, they also serve sandwiches, liver and onions, pork chops, and other down-home favorites. Good food at a good price.

ও **Original Pancake House** (716-634-5515; www.originalpancakehouse.com), 5479 Main Street, Williamsville. Open daily 6:45 AM–9 PM. No matter when you come here, it's always busy, especially Sunday mornings when Mass lets out at St. Peter and Paul's Church across the street. However, the food is worth the wait, so give you name to the hostess, and get your taste buds ready. While pancakes and breakfast are the most popular meal here, lunch and dinner are also served. If you're really hungry and in the mood for something sweet, order the house specialty apple pancake: a huge puffy pancake loaded with apples and topped with cinnamon glaze.

✴ Entertainment

THEATERS **Cabaret in the Square** (839-3949; www.cabaretinthesquare .com), 4476 Main Street, Snyder. O'Connell & Company is the resident theater group at Cabaret in the Square. They offer a full season of musicals, concerts, and plays along with dinner-theater packages.

& **SUNY Buffalo Center for the Arts** (716-645-2787 or 716-645-6259; www.ubcfa.org, www.arts.buffalo .edu), Mainstage Theater, 103 Center for the Arts, SUNY Buffalo Campus. This 250,000-square-foot modern building on UB's Amherst campus houses art, theater, media, and dance programs. Western New York's largest and most technically advanced performing arts venue has four theaters, three art galleries, and a screening room. Events include performances by world-renowned musicians and dance ensembles, distinguished speakers, and family entertainment.

& **Central Station Dinner Theater** (716-634-7878; www.redmillinn.com), 8316 Main Street, Williamsville. Interactive theater featuring mystery and comedy by the Mobile Theater. The evening begins with dinner, followed by a live show.

& **Katherine Cornell Theatre** (716-645-2038) on the UB Amherst campus, North Campus, Ellicott

Complex, Amherst. This theater, which seats 400 in the round, is a venue for speakers, educational programs, stage productions, and more.

MusicalFare Theatre Company (716-839-8540; www.musicalfare .com), 4380 Main Street, Suite 810, Amherst. This professional musical theater company resides at Daemen College. Performances take place year-round at the theater, located at the back of the campus. Since its inception in 1990, the company has produced over 100 shows and has won numerous *ArtVoice* Theatre Awards. MusicalFare is a significant regional theater group that presents new works as well as traditional musicals.

MUSIC **Amherst Saxophone Quartet** (716-632-2445; http://amherst saxophonequartet.buffalo.edu), SUNY Department of Music, 222 Baird Hall, Buffalo. This group presents all types of music from the 1850s through the 20th century, including classical, romance, baroque, renaissance, jazz, and ragtime.

Amherst Symphony (716-633-4606; www.amherst.ny.us/news/symphony .asp) Amherst Middle School, 55 Kings Highway, Snyder. For over 60 years the Amherst Symphony has been a community cultural asset. Four concerts, free to the public, are held in the middle school auditorium during the symphony's season (October–March).

✴ Selective Shopping

ANTIQUES **J & M Antiques** (716-636-5933 or 716-636-5874; www.east amherstantiques.com), 6407 Transit Road, East Amherst. Open daily 12–5. Victorian lighting and period furniture plus professional lamp restoration.

Josephine's Gifts and Vintage Decor (716-626-5461), 5428 Main Street, Williamsville. Open Wednesday 12–5, Thursday 1–7, Friday 11–4, Saturday 10–4. A two-floor Victorian general store featuring antiques, gifts, collectibles, candles, furniture, vintage linens, and much more.

Muleskinner Antiques (716-633-4077; www.muleskinnerantiques.com), 5548 Main Street Williamsville. Open Monday–Saturday 10–5. This shop, located in the historic village of Williamsville, is known for its high-end Americana items. They specialize in 18th- and 19th-century antiques, including folk art, weathervanes, furniture sporting originals finishes, redware, stoneware, and picture frames.

ART GALLERIES Vern Stein Fine Art (716-626-5688), 5747 Main Street, Williamsville. Open Tuesday–Friday 10–5, Saturday 10–4. A collection of art, from antique photos and paintings to contemporary works.

FARM MARKETS ✿ **Badding Brothers Farm Market** (716-636-7824), 10830 Transit Road, East Amherst. Open seven days May–December, Monday–Saturday 9–8, Sunday 9–7. This family-owned and operated farm has been a landmark on Transit Road for many years. Brothers Mike and Bob offer in-season produce, annuals, and hanging baskets. In the fall they have a Scarecrow Village, along with pumpkins and other fall produce.

Spoth's Farm Market (716-688-1110), 5757 Transit Road, East Amherst. Open May–December Monday–Friday 8:30–6, Saturday–Sunday 8:30–7. Spoth's Farm Market has grown from a simple roadside stand to one of the largest and best-known farm markets in the East Amherst/Clarence area. Brothers Dave and Ed grow most of the produce on their 75-acre farm, located in Clarence Center.

SHOPPING MALLS Boulevard Mall (716-834-8600; www.boulevard-mall.com), 730 Alberta Drive (Maple Road at Niagara Falls Boulevard) Amherst. Open Monday–Saturday 10–9, Sunday 11–6. Anchor stores include JC Penney, Kaufmann's, and Sears, along with over 100 specialty shops.

Eastern Hills Mall (716-631-5191; www.simon.com), 4545 Transit Road, Williamsville. Open Monday–Saturday 10–9, Sunday 11–6. Anchor stores include JC Penney, Kaufmann's, Bon Ton, and Sears, along with over 100 specialty shops.

SPECIAL SHOPS Ed Young's Hardware (716-632-3150; www.edyoungs.com), 5641 Main Street, Williamsville. Open Monday, Tuesday, Thursday, Friday 8–9, Wednesday and Saturday 8–6, Sunday 11–4. If you can't find a part at Ed Young's, it probably doesn't exist! This place has all sorts of tools and supplies along with a large gift shop with numerous upscale items. Before the holidays they have a large selection of lights, artificial trees, ornaments, and other seasonal decorations. This family-owned business, which has been at its present location since 1971, has been serving Williamsville since 1919.

Just a Reminder (716-633-6761), 5544 Main Street, Williamsville. Open Monday, Wednesday, Friday 10–6, Tuesday, Saturday 10–5, Thursday 10–7:30. This cozy shop specializes in handcrafted home decor and seasonal decorating items, including candles and bridal and baby gifts. The hand-painted items are really exceptional here, especially the furniture.

Karma Knitting (716-631-YARN [9276]), 5546 Main Street, Williamsville. Open Monday, Tuesday, Wednesday, Friday 10–5, Thursday 10–8, Saturday 11–5, Sunday 12–3. You will be tempted to take up knitting if you don't already know how when you walk into this store. The selection of yarn is absolutely gorgeous. Store owners and cousins Karin Kaye and Mary Ann Krause have set up an inviting area with plush chairs where customers can come in to sit, knit, and have a cup of tea. Lessons are available.

Mulberry Street Toys (716-688-7112), 9300 Transit Road, East Amherst. Open Monday, Tuesday, Friday, Saturday 10–5, Thursday 10–8. This shop, located in a restored farmhouse, features collectible dolls, stuffed animals, educational toys, and books.

Nook & Cranny (716-631-3650), 8495 Sheridan Drive Williamsville. Open Monday–Saturday 11–5, Sunday 12–4. Even though this store is located along a busy intersection, once you step inside, you feel like you're in a quaint shop out in the country. The shop has a collection of antiques, florals, linens, furniture, candles, and gifts.

Port of Entry Square (716-689-8895), 635 Dodge Road, Getzville. Open Monday–Wednesday 10–4:30, Thursday–Saturday 11–4:30, Sunday 1–4:30. At first glance the Port of Entry Square complex looks like a collection of old barns and outbuildings from Getzville's early farming days. Don't be put off by appearances.

This collection of shops, located off the beaten trail in the heart of Getzville, offers a unique shopping experience. The buildings, dating back to the 1860s, once were part of a grist-mill operation. The Port of Entry Store, housed in the former mill, features two floors of collectibles and antiques as well as Annalee dolls, Margaret Furlong angels, miniatures, tin toys, and Christmas decorations. Find more antique goodies in the new Port of Entry Annex. Other shops in the complex include **Yurhaus Decor Consignments** (716-689-4513), which carries old and new linens, glasses, dishes, and furniture; **Antiques and Junk** (716-688-0328), which offers a wide variety of knick-knacks; **Hands and Hearts** (716-688-0378), a vintage floral shop; and **Cobblecreek Antiques** (716-688-6321). Enjoy lunch or dinner at nearby Byblos restaurant.

✿ **Puddle Duck Toys and Dolls** (716-632-3277), Georgetown Plaza (Sheridan and Evans), Williamsville. Open Monday, Tuesday 10–6, Wednesday, Thursday 10–8, Friday, Saturday 10–5:30. Open Sunday 12–4 in late November and December. Children can enter the store through their own little red door if they wish. The store carries quality toys, including Brio, Playmobile, collectible dolls, doll houses, educational toys, books, infant items, and stuffed animals.

Spotted Giraffe (716-631-0153), 5454 Main Street, Williamsville. Open Monday–Saturday 10–5:30, Thursday until 8. This popular village shop carries an assortment of gifts, greeting cards, and home decor items.

Tis the Season Gift Shop (716-839-5090), 15 Lincoln (near Main and Harlem), Snyder. Open Monday,

Tuesday, Thursday, and Friday 10–5; Saturday 10–4. The items in this store change with the season. Choose from home decor, seasonal decorations, clothing, jewelry, and designer soaps.

Village Desserts (716-632-6004; www.villagedesserts.com), 5542 Main Street, Williamsville. Open Monday–Wednesday and Friday 8 AM–6 PM, Thursday–Saturday 8–6, Sunday 8–3 (December only). Special-occasion cakes, cookies, gift baskets, and party trays. They also carry gourmet cookies, muffins, brownies, muffins, éclairs, cannoli, and puffs.

Williamsville Water Mill (716-632-1162), 56 Spring Street, Williamsville. Open Monday–Saturday 10–6, Sunday 11–6. Gifts, fresh-pressed cider (seasonally), birdseed, and birdfeeders are sold in the gift shop located in a building listed on the National Register of Historic Places. The water-powered mill, built in 1811, is still operating. See *Historic Sites.*

✳ **Special Events**

July: **4th of July Fireworks,** SUNY Buffalo Amherst Campus. Music and fireworks display. **Old Home Days** Island Park (716-632-4120), A four-day festival featuring a parade, food, rides, children's activities, and nightly entertainment.

August: **Savor the Flavor** Island Park, Family activities and food samplings from local restaurants. **Scottish Festival** (716-689-1440; www.amherstmuseum.org), Amherst Museum, Highland games, dancers, and entertainment.

September: **Harvest Festival and Craft Show,** Amherst Museum (716-689-1440) Celebrate the fall harvest season with crafts, fresh produce, hayrides, entertainment, food, and more.

December: **Victorian Christmas Tours** (716-689-1440; www.amherstmuseum.org), Amherst Museum. Experience a 19th-century Amherst Christmas.

CLARENCE AND AKRON

Clarence, located about 12 miles east of Buffalo, is home to one of the largest variety of antiques-related businesses in the entire Northeast. Established in 1808, it is the oldest township in Erie County, so it's not surprising that it has managed to preserve many artifacts from the past.

Native American inhabitants referred to this area as Ta-Num-No-Ga-O, which means "place full of hickory bark." Main Street was once an Indian trail that ran along the Onondaga escarpment. In 1799 Joseph Ellicott—an agent for the Holland Land Company—offered lots for sale to any "proper man" who would build and operate taverns on them. The first settler to take advantage of this offer was Asa Ransom, a silversmith from Geneva. He erected a log house and tavern in the area now referred to as the "hollow," and later added a sawmill and a gristmill.

Today the town can be divided into six historic districts. Clarence Hollow, where Asa Ransom first settled, is now filled with antiques stores, restaurants, the historical society, and an upscale inn built on the property once owned by

Ransom. The Hollow recently underwent an extensive renovation, with the area redesigned to appear as it did in the 1920s, complete with new street lights resembling gaslights, decorative walkways, and over 200 trees and 400 shrubs. Harris Hill, about 4 miles west of the Hollow along Main Street, was a refuge for people from Buffalo displaced when their city was burned by the British during the War of 1812. The intersection of Main and Transit roads has been the town's center of commerce and travel ever since Joseph Ellicott laid out the county's main north-south "transit" line in 1800.

Wolcottsburg, which is still largely undeveloped farmland, was settled by German immigrants in the 1820s. The first movable carousel was built in Wolcottsburg for the carnival industry. These nonmechanical carousels, or whirligigs, consisted of carved horses attached to a huge wheel that were taken from place to place on the back of a wagon. Clarence Center, at Goodrich and Clarence Center Roads, was once the intersection of two Indian trails. The brick three-story building on the corner was built in 1872 by John Eshelman and operated as a dry-goods store for over 100 years. Across the street, in the building that originally housed the post office, is a popular coffee shop and restaurant.

The sixth historic area in the town, Swormville, sits on the border of Clarence and Amherst, so both towns claim it as their own. This area was originally settled by Bavarian and French immigrants in the 1830s. Adam Schworm, who emigrated to the area in the 1850s, built a store on Transit Road, and the community was dubbed Schwormville, from which its current name evolved. Rev. John Neumann, a missionary who was canonized a saint by the Catholic church in 1977, founded St. Mary's parish. The brick church, completed in 1865, was built during the Civil War. The annual St. Mary's Church picnic in July is locally famous for its chicken clam chowder.

The village of Akron, the central business district for the town of Newstead, is located in a predominately rural area. The first settlers, Asa Chapman and Peter Vandeventer, arrived in the area around 1801. Originally part of Batavia, Newstead was incorporated in 1823 as Erie. The name was changed in 1831 because mail often got misdirected to Erie, Pennsylvania. The name Newstead was suggested by the town's assemblyman at that time, Millard Fillmore. It seems that Mrs. Fillmore had been reading poetry by Lord Byron, so she suggested to her husband that the town be named after Byron's home in England, Newstead Abbey. The name Akron was suggested by a prominent local resident who had once worked near Akron, Ohio. Akron comes from the Greek word *Akros*, which means high.

The main occupation in the town's early days was farming. As the town grew, other businesses sprang up, including several retail stores, blacksmiths, mills, and cement manufacturers, which turned Akron into a boomtown. The cement was produced by crushing, firing, and mixing local limestone with water. By the 1880s Akron was considered one of the most prosperous towns in Erie County. However, by the early 1900s all the local cement plants closed as other cement manufacturers in the nation began producing better quality cement. Shortly after, gypsum was discovered in the area, and mining of the product began in 1905. By the late 1940s many of these mines closed.

Today one of the town's best known businesses is Perry's Ice Cream, founded by Morton Perry. The business began as a home delivery dairy in 1918. In the

1930s the Akron High School cafeteria staff requested ice cream, and Morton complied by making the frozen confection using a family recipe. Soon they were delivering ice cream to local stores and restaurants, and today it's one of the best-known ice cream manufacturers in the state.

Akron is a pleasant, small community of well-kept houses. One of the village's unique attractions is the circa 1849 Octagon House, listed on the National Register of Historic Places and operated as a museum by the town's historical society. Another area attraction is Akron State Park, a popular spot to picnic and hike.

AREA CODE The area code is 716.

GUIDANCE Akron Chamber of Commerce (716-542-4050), 85 Main Street, Akron. Open Tuesday, Thursday and Friday 9–12:30.

Clarence Chamber of Commerce (716-631-3888; www.clarence.org), 8975 Main Street, Clarence. Open Monday–Friday 9–4:30.

Clarence Hollow Association (716-759-2345; e-mail cha@clarencehollow.org; www.clarencehollow.org), 10490 Main Street, Clarence. They publish a brochure listing businesses, stores, and attractions in Clarence Hollow along with a walking tour of the historic buildings in the area.

GETTING THERE *By air:* **Akron Airport** (716-542-4607), small landing strip for private planes. See also *Getting There—Buffalo*.

By bus: NFTA Metro bus from Buffalo stops at Transitown Plaza (Main and Transit).

By car: Clarence and Akron are accessible from NY 5 (Main Street).

MEDICAL EMERGENCY Dial 911.

✳ To See

ART MUSEUMS Museum of European Art (716-759-6078; www.meaus.com) 10545 Main Street, Clarence. Open Tuesday–Friday 10–5, Saturday 1–4. Free admission. This museum brings the works of contemporary European artists—including Salvador Dali, Pablo Picasso, Arno Breher, and Paul Belmondo—to the American public. Works represented include sculptures, portraits, paintings, and lithographs

MUSEUMS AND HISTORIC HOMES Clarence Historical Society Museum (716-759-8575 www.clarencehistory.org), 10465 Main Street, Clarence. Open Wednesday 10–2, Sunday 1–4 PM or by appointment. Free admission, donations accepted. The building that houses the museum was built in 1843 as a church meeting house. Interesting facts about Clarence include that the first Girl Scout cookie sale was organized in the town, the first carousel horse was carved here, and the first nonmechanical merry-go-round in America was built in the town in 1879. The museum houses artifacts from area churches as well as an automotive display, Civil War, World War I, and World War II artifacts and many other items. Visitors can also see household items that were used in the early 1800s. The centerpiece of the technology wing is the original red barn where local resident Wilson Greatbatch invented the implantable heart pacemaker in the 1950s. Also located on the grounds of the museum is an early 1800s log cabin, moved here from the northern part of the town.

Rich-Twinn Octagon House (716-542-2254), 145 Main Street, Akron. Open the first and third Sundays of the month 1–3 PM or by appointment. Admission: $3 self-guided tour, $4

RICH-TWINN OCTAGON HOUSE

Christine A. Smyczynski

guided tour. Some mid-19th-century Americans believed that living in a home the shape of an octagon would allow them to live a longer and healthier life. The Rich-Twinn House, built in 1849 by Charles B. Rich, is a stunning example of Greek Revival architecture and a beautifully restored specimen of a mid-19th-century architectural fad. The first floor features a receiving room, where the family would have spent most of its time, and a kitchen complete with a beehive oven, dumbwaiter, speaking tube, and pantry. A grand foyer with a curved staircase dominates the second floor, which features etched-glass doors and ornate plaster moldings. Other rooms on this floor include a drawing room with a black-glass fireplace, a dining room with a white-marble fireplace, a morning room, sewing room, and library. Bedrooms are located on the third floor. The fourth floor cupola offers spectacular views of the village.

✳ To Do

CROSS-COUNTRY SKIING See *Green Space—Walking and Hiking Trails.*

FAMILY FUN ✐ **Great Pumpkin Farm** (716-759-2260 or 800-343-5399), 11199 Main Street, Clarence. Open seven days 10–dusk, last weekend of September through Halloween. Admission charged first two weekends for festivals. Get your Halloween pumpkins and other fall decorating needs at the Great Pumpkin Farm. The World Pumpkin Weigh Off takes place the first weekend of October, with folks from all over the northeast hauling their gigantic gourds to Clarence for this competition. Some of these pumpkins weigh over 1,000

THE GREAT PUMPKIN FARM IS THE SITE OF THE WORLD PUMPKIN WEIGH-OFF EVERY OCTOBER.

Christine A. Smyczynski

pounds! Halloween and fall activities take place each weekend, including hayrides, an amusement midway, and special events.

Kelkenberg Farm (716-542-2314), 12607 Stage Road, Akron. Open to the public the last weekend in September and every weekend in October 10–6. Open by reservation for group tours in the spring and weekdays in September and October. Parties can be scheduled year round. This small family-operated farm tucked into the back roads of Akron is a great place for kids to learn about agriculture and farm life. Sheep, goats, pigs, and horses can be found in their barns, while pumpkins, cornstalks, and other fall decorating items can be found in the farm market.

GOLF **Arrowhead Golf Course/ Bright Meadows** (716-542-2441 or 716-542-4653), 12287 Clarence Center Road, Akron. A newly redesigned 18-hole, par-72 course with very few trees.

Dande Farms Golf Course (716-542-2027), 13278 Carney Road, Akron. A semi-private, 18-hole, par-71 course.

Greenwood Golf Course (716-741-3395), 8499 Northfield Road, Clarence Center. A 9-hole, par-35 public course with full bar and snack bar.

Pine Meadows Golf (716-741-3970), 9820 Greiner Road, Clarence. A public 9-hole, par-34 course with snack bar.

Rothland Golf Course (716-542-4325; www.RothlandGolf.com), 12089 Clarence Center Road, Akron. A 27-hole (three 9-hole courses), par-72 (for 18 holes), privately owned, professionally managed golf course open to the public.

✳ Green Space

PARKS **Akron Falls Park** (716-542-2330), NY 93, Parkview Drive, Akron. Open dawn to dusk. Free admission. A 285-acre Erie County park that features walking and hiking trails, fishing, tennis courts, baseball diamonds, and picnic shelters. The park has a creek, waterfall, and lake. In winter, enjoy sledding, cross-country skiing, and ice skating on a pond. The park's creek, Murder Creek, is so named because legend has it that it is haunted by the ghosts of Ah-Weh-Gag and Gray Wolf, two Seneca lovers, and her father, Great Fire. The three were murdered by a white man named Sanders, who fell in love with Ah-Weh-Gag.

WALKING AND HIKING TRAILS **Akron Rail Trail** (716-542-4574). This 6.5-mile trail starts in Akron and continues through Newstead and Clarence. Enjoy walking, biking, and skating along with cross-country skiing and snowshoeing during the winter. Snowmobiling is allowed on the trail, except in the village of Akron.

Peanut Line Trail. This 7.5-mile trail, which runs from Main Street west to just past Shimerville Road, follows the railbed of the old Canandaigua and Niagara Falls Railroad, which was known as the "Peanut Line."

West Shore Trail. This 5.25-mile trail begins at Main and Salt Roads in Clarence Hollow, following the former railroad lines of the New York, West Shore, and Buffalo Railroad, and continues into Akron. Another Clarence trail runs 3 miles from Clarence Town Park to Wherle Drive.

✳ Lodging

INNS AND RESORTS Asa Ransom House (716-759-2315 or 800-841-2340; www.asaransom.com), 10529 Main Street, Clarence. This relaxing country inn is located on the site where Asa Ransom, a young silversmith, built the first gristmill in Erie County in 1803. The ruins of the mill can still be seen at the rear of the property. Part of this historic inn was built in 1853, with additions added in 1975 and 1993. The nine guest rooms, each with a private bath, are furnished with antiques and period reproductions. To combine the convenience of the present with the charm of the past, each room has individual heat and air conditioning and a hidden TV. Seven of the rooms have fireplaces, and most rooms have either a porch or a balcony. Operated by Robert Lenz, the inn has a fully licensed fine dining room and a charming gift shop, the Sunshine Square. Located on the property is a garden with over 70 different types of herbs. $98–$175

✳ Where to Eat

DINING OUT The Akron House (716-542-2280), 15 Main Street, Akron. Open Tuesday–Thursday 11–9, Friday 11–10, Saturday 3:30–10, Sunday 10–8. Enjoy casual dining in a cozy Victorian setting. The building dates back to 1872, when it first opened as a saloon, restaurant, and hotel. This restaurant is very popular with the locals. Lunches are casual, serving up burgers, salads, and sandwiches, while dinners are more upscale and gourmet.

Asa Ransom House (716-759-2315; www.asaransom.com), 10529 Main Street Clarence Open for dinner Sunday, Tuesday– Thursday 4–8, Friday and Saturday seating at 5:30, 7:30; prix fixe lunch Wednesday only 11:30–2:30, tea Tuesday and Thursday 1–4. The menu offers a selection of items that change seasonally, along with fresh rolls and muffins served with flavored butters. Desserts are homemade. See also *Lodging*.

Fredi (716-741-4012), 6010 Goodrich Road, Clarence Center. Open Sunday–Thursday 5–9, Friday and Saturday 5-11. This small gourmet restaurant in the heart of Clarence Center serves an array of international entrées, with emphasis on South American, Mediterranean, and Asian. Specialties include ceviche, saganaki, and bouillabaisse. Meals begin with complimentary slices of garlic toast topped with pesto, green olives, and red peppers.

Orazios Restaurant (759-8888; www.orazios.com), 9415 Main Street, Clarence. Open Monday–Saturday 11–11, Sunday 12–9. A traditional restaurant, formerly on Hertel Avenue, specializing in made-to-order pasta dishes with what has been

THE RUINS OF THE FIRST GRISTMILL IN ERIE COUNTY ARE ON THE PROPERTY OF THE ASA RANSOM HOUSE INN IN CLARENCE.

Christine A. Smyczynski

deemed the best red sauce in the Buffalo area. Chef Orazio Ippolito's specialties include seafood lasagna and stuffed lamb chops.

EATING OUT 🍴 ✍ ♿ **Berrafato's Char-Pit** (716-759-8429) 9980 Main Street, Clarence. Open Monday–Saturday 11–8, Sunday 11:30–8. This family restaurant has an extensive menu featuring sandwiches, hot dogs, and burgers along with kids' meals. They have a large selection of ice cream treats, including shakes and sundaes. They also have a catering service.

✍ ♿ 🍴 **Billy Bob's** (716-759-6881), 11661 Main Road, Newstead. Open daily year-round 11–7. This restaurant opened as Hoffman's in the late 1950s. It is a popular spot to enjoy hot dogs, hamburgers, and ice cream treats.

Clarence Center Coffee Company and Café (716-741-8573; www .clarencecentercoffee.com), 9485 Clarence Center Road, Clarence Center. Open Monday–Wednesday 7 AM–10 PM, Thursday–Saturday 7 AM–11 PM, Sunday 7:30 AM–9 PM. This unique coffee café is located in the former Clarence Center post office, which dates back to 1829. Prior to opening this café, owner, Kyleena Falzone Gracefia, a real coffee connoisseur, spent over 10 years traveling the globe to learn all she could about coffee. In addition to coffees from around the world and specialty beverages, the café offers gourmet sandwiches, wraps, salads, and desserts. In warmer weather, sip your coffee on the wraparound porch.

♿ **Finnlocks** (716-759-8917), 10250 Main Street, Clarence. Open Sunday–Thursday 11–9, Friday and Saturday 11–10. Choose from steak, ribs, seafood, sandwiches, wings, and more at this popular eatery.

♿ **Ohlson Bakery & Café** (716-626-7783; www.ohlsonbakery.com), 8500 Sheridan Drive (at Harris Hill Road), Clarence. Open Monday 7:30–6, Tuesday–Friday 6:30–6, Saturday 7:30–4. This charming turn-of-the-20th-century style bakery features a European-style café that serves fresh Danish and muffins, egg sandwiches, freshly made café sandwiches, hot panini sandwiches, and quiche. They are known for their made-from-scratch baked goods, including pastries, cookies, coffee cake, and cheesecake. They also sell award-winning special-occasion cakes for wedding, first communions, anniversaries, and graduations.

Valley Inn (716-759-6232; www .valleyinnbbq.com), 10651 Main Street, Clarence. Open Monday–Thursday 11:30–9, Friday and Saturday 11:30–10, Sunday 12–8. Take-out available. A family-style BBQ and catering restaurant specializing in ribs, pulled pork, chicken, and prime rib. All BBQ items are slow smoked over real wood and have been rated four stars by both the *Buffalo News* and *Artvoice*.

✳ **Entertainment**

THEATERS Central Station: See listing under *Town of Amherst*.

✳ **Selective Shopping**

ANTIQUES Antique Lighting (716-759-1429), 10626 Main Street, Clarence. Open Monday–Friday 10–5, Saturday 12–5. Specializing in antique lighting, including repairs and restoration. They also have some furniture and other antique items.

Antique World (716-759-8483, 800-959-0714; www.antiqueworldflea market.com), 10995 Main Street Clarence. Open Monday–Saturday 10–4 (closed Wednesday), Sunday 8–4. The largest indoor and outdoor antiques market in New York state. More than 350 indoor dealers year-round display their wares in over 25,000 square feet in three buildings, plus hundreds of outdoor dealers every Sunday during the summer. Every May and August they host a super antiques extravaganza that attracts over 800 dealers from across the U.S. and Canada.

Clarence Courtyard Antique Co-op, Inc. (716-759-7080), 11079 Main Street, Clarence. Open Monday–Saturday 10–5, Sunday 8–5. Several dealers have a variety of goods displayed here. This store is located next to the Antique World complex.

Courtyard Antique Center (716-759-1726), 10255 Main Street (corner of Shisler Road), Clarence. Open daily 10–5. A 10,000-square-foot multidealer mall with a variety of antiques and collectibles. Choose from glass, fine china, silver, linens, vintage clothing, jewelry, lamps, primitives, toys, dolls, and much more.

Kelly Schultz Antiques (716-759-2260), 11145 Main Street, Clarence. Open Thursday–Saturday 9–5, Sunday 10–4. Fine antiques and oriental rugs.

Kelly's Antique Market (716-759-2260, 800-343-5399), 11111 Main Street, Clarence. Open every Sunday. A variety of antiques and collectibles are displayed.

Nelson J. Herdic Antiques (716-759-6343), 10882 Main Street, Clarence. Open Saturday and Sunday 11–5, weekdays by appointment or chance. A general line of quality antiques displayed in three buildings.

Red Balloons (716-759-8999), 10912 Main Street, Clarence. Open Saturday and Sunday 11–4, Tuesday–Friday by chance. Antique linens, lace, and textiles.

Tschoppe Stained Glass (716-759-6010), 10830 Main Street, Clarence. Open Tuesday–Saturday 10–5, Sunday 12–5. Antiques, along with window and lamp restoration.

FARM MARKETS Clarence Hollow Farmer's Market, At the corner of Main and Strickler Road, Clarence. Saturdays 8 AM–1 PM June–October. This market features local produce, baked goods, cheese, and more. The market will eventually be held in the parking lot right in the "Hollow."

SHOPPING MALLS Eastern Hills Mall (716-631-5191; www.simon .com), 4545 Transit Road, Williamsville. Open Monday–Saturday 10–9, Sunday 11–6. Anchor stores include JC Penney, Kaufmann's, Bon Ton, and Sears, along with over 100 specialty shops.

SPECIAL SHOPS Adventures in Heat (716-759-HEAT; www .adventuresinheat.com) 10189 Main Street, Clarence. Open Tuesday–Friday 11–6, Thursday until 7, Saturday–Sunday 11–5. This gourmet store specializes in the hot and spicy. They carry grills, BBQ accessories, Southwest-style giftware, and gourmet hot sauces and other hot and spicy delicacies.

Aurora Sewing Center (716-759-8081; www.aurorasewingcenter.com), 10750 Main Street, Clarence. Open

Monday 10–8, Tuesday–Thursday 10–9, Friday 10–5:30, Saturday 10–4. Located in an old church, this shop features a large selection of cotton fabrics for quilting, plus patterns, thread, and other sewing supplies. They are also an authorized Bernina sewing machine dealer. Even if you don't sew, be sure to stop here just to look at the quilts that adorn the walls.

The Bag and Barrel Country Store (716-542-2254), 99 Main Street, Akron. Open Monday–Saturday 10–5. The Bag and Barrel Country Store, located in Akron's historic downtown, offers modern shoppers an old-fashioned shopping experience. The eight-room store is brimming with many unique items, such as Bennington and Rowe pottery, Willyrae collectibles, Lt. Moses Williraye Country lighting, folk art, candles, and other country home accessories.

The Candle Shop (716-759-1334), 10863 Main Street, Clarence. Open Tuesday–Wednesday 10-5, Thursday 12–6:30, Friday and Saturday 10–5:30, Sunday 12–5. Find unique candles from around the world, including beeswax candles, aromatherapy candles, dripless tapers, votives, candles holders, and cards.

Chochkey's (716-759-9400), 10622 Main Street, Clarence. Open Wednesday–Friday 10–5:30, Saturday 10–4, Sunday 12–4. This shop, located in a circa 1920s purple barn, offers unique items for your home, including wall hangings, table decorations, painted furniture, and hand-blown glass pieces. Owner, Michelle Peller White also offers decorative painting classes.

Clear Light Studio (716-759-6480; www.clearlightstudio.com), 10852 Main Street, Clarence. Open daily 11–5 or by appointment. Browse the backyard behind this pink-and-purple studio for handmade fountains, garden jewels, and other creations by artist Donna Ioviero.

Craftsmen of Clarence Hollow (716-759-0830), 10622 Main Street, Clarence Tuesday–Saturday 10–5:30, Thursday until 8, Sunday 10–2. This unique artisan shop, owned by Tina Tompkins Ames, features a selection of items crafted by local artisans. Choose from jewelry, accessories, home decor, paintings, and much more. The café features homemade items, including soups, sandwiches, and baked goods.

Destinys (716-759-1070), 10295 Main Street (George Courtyard), Clarence. Open Tuesday–Saturday 11–6, Sunday 12–5. A nice selection of gifts and home decor items.

Family Chocolate Shoppe (716-759-0658), 10295 Main Street, Clarence (George Courtyard). Open Monday–Friday 10–6, Saturday 10–5, Sunday 11–4. This shop has a large selection of candies, including Buffalo sponge candy and novelties like chocolate chicken wings.

Garden in the Hollow (716-759-1883), 11072 Main Street, Clarence. Open Monday–Friday 9–6, Saturday and Sunday 9–4. Located across the street from Antique World, this shop features seasonal decorations, country decorating items, soaps, and garden decorations, along with live flowers and plants in season.

Henry & Co. (716-759-2400; www .seesale.com/henry), 10678 Main Street, Clarence. Open Monday–Saturday 10–5, Sunday 12–5. This unique shop located in a former church features home furnishings, antiques, and rugs.

The Hydrangea Patch (716-984-7886), 8585 Main Street, Clarence (in the Harris Hill Plaza). Open Friday 4:30–7:30, Saturday and Sunday 10–4. A unique shop with primitive decor and homespun items, including candles, folk art, rustic ware, and greeting cards.

✧ **The Perfect Gift** (716-741-0722), 6000 Goodrich Road, Clarence Center. Open Monday–Thursday and Saturday 10–6, Friday 10–7, Sunday 11–5. This family-owned and operated store is located in the historic Eschelman Building in the heart of Clarence Center. This three-story brick building was built in 1872 as the Square Deal store, which was operated by the Eschelman family for nearly 100 years. The Perfect Gift carries quality home decor items, original artwork, handpainted glassware, hand-made jewelry, greeting cards, seasonal gifts, and old-fashioned candy. Owner Deborah Tangelder strives to operate the store with the same values she grew up with, allowing it to be a nice shopping destination for the entire family.

The Podge (716-759-2080), 10205 Main Street, Clarence. Open Monday–Saturday 10–6, Sunday 11–5. This has to be one of the most unique—and delicious—stores in town. Whether you are a gourmet cook or just like to eat, you will find this store to be just plain yummy. They have a large selection of foods from around the world, including candies, cookies, spices, coffees, and teas, along with all sorts of cookware items, copperware and cast iron among them. This shop has everything you can imagine for the gourmet kitchen.

Stargate General (716-759-8605), 10844 Main Street, Clarence. Open Tuesday–Sunday 11–6. This shop specializes in primitives, antiques, and folk art. Owner Jane Yousey likes to create unique folk art from recycled items—for example, rustic lamps from old fence posts. She builds the furniture in the shop using wood purchased from the Amish, and she makes her own candles and potpourri.

Sunshine Square Gifts (716-759-2315), 10529 Main Street, Clarence (in the Asa Ransom House). Open daily 9–9. A collection of charming gifts and unique items.

Swormville Station (716-636-1958), 9900 Transit Road, Swormville. Call first as shops are staffed by volunteers and hours vary. Several delightful shops are located in this historic post-and-beam building, which once served the community as a tavern. They include **Cranberry Hollow** (716-636-4322), featuring 18th–20th-century American primitives along with period antiques and reproductions. They also have lots of home decor accessories such as wreaths, lamps, pottery, and painted wood items. The **Craft Boutique** (716-636-1958), located in the rear of the building, features handcrafted items made by local artisans, including seasonal, floral, and baby items. The adjacent shop, **Violets and Lace**, specializes in bridal and floral items.

Town & Country Gifts (716-759-7485), 10440 Main Street, Clarence. Open Monday–Friday 9:30–8, Saturday 9:30–6. This store has a nice selection of gifts, cards, and Ty Beanie Babies. Cards are offered at a 50 percent discount.

✳ Special Events

May and August: **Antique Expo** (716-759-8483 or 800-959-0714; www
.antiqueworldfleamarket.com), Antique World and Marketplace, Clarence. Over 800 dealers display their wares at these annual open-air shows.

July: **St. Mary's Church Picnic** (716-688-9380), Transit Road, Swormville.

People come from miles around for their famous chicken clam chowder. Held third Sunday in July.

October: **World Pumpkin Weigh Off** (716-759-2260 or 800-343-5399), Great Pumpkin Farm, 11199 Main Street, Clarence. A competition for the biggest pumpkin in the country.

LANCASTER, DEPEW, AND CHEEKTOWAGA

The first settlers, Alanson Eggleston and the Woodward brothers, arrived in the Lancaster area in 1803, building homes on Ellicott Creek in what is now Bowmansville. (Lancaster was part of the town of Clarence until 1833.) Many of the earlier settlers who followed came from New England and started businesses that included woodworking, tanning, milling and slaughterhouses. In about 1830 German settlers, from both Pennsylvania and Germany, arrived in the region to set up farms.

Probably the most famous of the town's early industries was the glass factory, which produced bottles from 1849–1904. A new automated glass factory was built in 1907, which continued to operate until 1965.

The railway brought expansion and increased prosperity to the area in the 1890s. A small village grew around the shops erected by the New York Central railroad near Transit Road. This village was named Depew, after Chauncey Depew, president of the New York Central & Hudson River Railroad. Several industrial plants that produced goods needed by the railway industry were opened in Depew. Today these communities are largely bedroom communities for Buffalo.

The first inhabitants in the town now known as Cheektowaga were the Iroquois, who called the area *Ji-ik-do-wah-gah,* meaning "the land of the crab apple." The area was first settled by Appollos Hitchcock and his family in 1809. The town was officially incorporated in 1839, with Alexander Hitchcock, Appollos's son, elected the first supervisor.

Cheektowaga became a transportation center for the region, with four railroads by the end of the Civil War. In the 1920s an airport was constructed on Genesee Street, and in the 1950s the New York State Thruway cut across town.

While it remained semirural prior to World War II, Cheektowaga quickly developed after the war to become one of Buffalo's most populous suburbs as well as a retail and business center.

AREA CODE The area code is 716.

GUIDANCE Cheektowaga Chamber of Commerce (716-684-5838; www.cheektowaga.org), 2875 Union Road, Suite 50, Appletree Business Park, Cheektowaga. Open Monday–Friday 8:30–4.

Lancaster Chamber of Commerce (716-681-9755; www.laccny.org www .delchamber.org), 39 Central Avenue, Lancaster. Open Monday–Thursday 10–3.

Town of Cheektowaga (716-686-3434), Town Hall, 3301 Broadway, Cheek-towaga. Open Monday–Friday 9–4:30. Call first as some departments may have different hours than listed.

GETTING THERE *By air:* **Buffalo Niagara International Airport** (716-630-6000; www.buffaloairport.com), 4200 Genesee Street, Buffalo. Served by most major airlines. **Car rentals** at the airport include **Alamo** (631-2044), **Avis** (632-1808), **Budget** (632-4662), **Enterprise** (565-0002), **Hertz** (632-4772), **National** (634-9220), and **Thrifty** (633-8500). **Lancaster Airport** (683-7203) 6100 Transit Road Depew. Small landing strip for private planes.

By bus: **Niagara Frontier Transportation Authority** (716-855-7211; www .nfta.com), 181 Ellicott Street, Buffalo. 14203 Several routes run between these suburbs and downtown Buffalo, including two express routes.

By car: Exits 51 and 52 off I-90 will take you into this area, as will exit 49 and then take NY 78 south.

By Train: **Amtrak** (716-683-8440 or 800-872-7245; www.amtrak.com), 55 Dick Rd, Depew.

GETTING AROUND *By bus:* Several bus routes run from downtown Buffalo to these suburbs.

MEDICAL EMERGENCY Dial 911

St. Joseph Hospital (716-891-2400; www.chsbuffalo.org), 2605 Harlem Road, Cheektowaga.

✳ To See

MUSEUMS AND HISTORIC HOMES **Cheektowaga Historical Museum** (716-684-6544), 3329 Broadway, Cheektowaga. Open 2–4 the first Sunday of month.

Lancaster Historical Museum (716-681-7719) 40 Clark Street, Lancaster. Open Sunday 2–5. This elegant home contains a collection of items made at the old Lancaster Glass Factory in addition to artifacts and memorabilia pertaining to the history of Lancaster.

Little Red School House (operated by Lancaster Historical Society), William Street and Bowen Road, Lancaster. Open Sunday 2–5 May–October. This one-room schoolhouse, constructed in 1868 from locally made bricks, features a pot-belly stove, single and double desks, a teachers desk from the 1880s, and antique slates, toys, and books. The historical society welcomes school groups to plan field trips to the museum. Classes can spend the entire day here experiencing what school was like for children in the 1870s.

HISTORIC SITES **Hull House** (contact the Landmark Society 716-852-3300), 5976 Genesee Street, Lancaster. Tours are offered on select weekends by the Landmark Society. Hull House, built in 1810 by Warren and Polly Hull, is the oldest stone house in Erie County. Mr. Hull was a Revolutionary War veteran who farmed about 360 acres in Lancaster. The Federal-style home is currently being restored.

✳ To Do

AUTO RACING **Lancaster Speedway** (716-629-8531 or 716-759-6818; www .lancasterracing.com), Lancaster Motorsports Park, 57 Gunnville Road, Lancaster. Open Saturdays at 6 PM; admission $12 adults, $5 children 8–15, $1 under 8. Fridays at 7 PM; admission $8 adults, $4 children 8–15, $1 under 8. Speedsters, including modifieds, late models, and stocks, race every Saturday night May–September. Dragsters race on Friday evenings April–October.

FAMILY FUN ✍ **The "Airport Tunnel,"** Aero Drive at Youngs Road, Cheektowaga. Kids of all ages will get a kick out of driving under the runway of Buffalo Niagara International Airport. It's just a simple tunnel, but you get an almost surreal feeling if you approach the tunnel while an airliner is taxiing overhead on the runway.

✍ ⬈ **Fast Freddies Speedway** (716-686-0173), 3052 Walden Avenue, Depew. Open Wednesday–Sunday to the public, hours vary. Monday and Tuesday track rental available. If you feel the need for speed, this is the place to be. Enjoy indoor sprint car racing at this unique facility. Kids over 46 inches as well as adults can live out their fantasy of being a race-car driver.

✍ **Rick Lancellotti's Buffalo School of Baseball** (716-681-9410), 2500 Walden Avenue, Cheektowaga. Open Monday–Friday 1–8, Saturday 10–1, longer hours in fall and winter. Imagine practicing your baseball skills at Yankee Stadium, Wrigley Field, or Fenway Park. You can do this without ever having to set foot out of Cheektowaga. Buffalo School of Baseball, operated by former pro baseball player Rick Lancellotti, is an indoor baseball facility featuring batting cages, pitching mounds, and an outfield where players of all ages and abilities can perfect their hitting, pitching, catching, and fielding skills. The objective of the school is to instruct players and their coaches on the fundamentals and finer points of baseball and softball. Private, semiprivate, group, and team lessons for boys and girls are offered. In addition, clinics staffed by professional players and coaches are held throughout the year. The batting cages and facilities can be rented by the hour by teams or individuals when not in use by the school's instructional staff.

GOLF **Harris Hill Golf Center** (716-684-4653), 5360 Genesee Street, Bowmansville. A 9-hole, par-3 public course.

Walden Golf Range (716-681-1670), 4011 Walden Avenue, Lancaster. A family-owned and -operated practice range since 1960. Considered one of the best public driving ranges in western New York.

✳ Green Space

NATURE PRESERVES **Reinstein Woods Nature Preserve** (716-851-7201) 77 Honorine Drive, Depew. Public access is limited to free naturalist-led tours:

March–October, Wednesday and Saturday at 10 AM and 1 PM; November–February, Wednesday and Saturday at 10 AM. This 300-acre preserve has undisturbed ancient forests that look like they did in prehistoric time, 19 ponds, marshes, and swamps. Marks are still visible from the original Holland Land Survey in 1797. The land was purchased in 1932 by Dr. Victor Reinstein, a doctor, attorney, and conservationist, for his own private sanctuary. The preserve is home to native western New York wildlife, including deer, beaver, hawks, and woodpeckers. Educational programs and educational tours are offered.

PARKS **Cheektowaga Town Park** (716-895-7529), 2600 Harlem Road, Cheektowaga. Open dawn to dusk. This 66.5-acre park has numerous picnic shelters, playground equipment, sports fields, a swimming pool, and an open-air band shell. It is the site of many festivals throughout the summer.

Como Lake Park (716-683-5430), 2220 Como Park Boulevard, Lancaster. Open dawn to dusk. The third largest Erie County Park, Como Lake is named after a famous tourist resort in Italy. The park features a 4.5-acre man-made lake; used for ice skating in the winter, it is the largest natural ice rink in western New York. Other park features include a stone lighthouse next to the lake and a circa 1928 lodge, along with facilities for baseball, biking, fishing, hiking, picnicking, sledding, and cross-country skiing.

Stiglmeier Park, 810 Losson Rd, Cheektowaga. Open dawn to dusk. This 386-acre park is best known for its wooden boardwalk walking trails that wind through the woods.

Walden Pond Park (716-683-3949 or 716-684-3320), Walden Avenue and Ranson Road, Lancaster. Open dawn to dusk. The 70-acre park has a playground, sports fields, walking trails, and a scenic pond.

✳ Lodging

MOTELS AND HOTELS **Four Points Sheraton Buffalo Airport** (716-681-2400 or 800-323-3331; www.fourpoints .com), 2040 Walden Avenue, Buffalo. This hotel offers 292 large guest rooms—many with balconies—an indoor pool, and exercise facility. It is located adjacent to the Galleria Mall and I-90 and only 3 miles from the airport. $109–$154.

Garden Place Hotel (716-635-9000 or 800-GARDEN1; www.salvatores .net), 6615 Transit Road, Williamsville. This luxurious hotel—a subsidiary of Salvatore's Italian Gardens restaurant—has quadrupled in size since it first opened in 1995. This hotel is almost always booked, so be

NAMED AFTER THE FAMOUS ITALIAN RESORT, COMO LAKE PARK FEATURES A STONE LIGHTHOUSE NEXT TO A MAN-MADE LAKE.

Christine A. Smyczynski

sure to make reservations well in advance. Many of the 160 rooms and suites include king-sized beds and Jacuzzis. The rooms are especially clean: Maids are required to spend one hour cleaning each room, compared to maids at some major hotel chains who clean three or four rooms in that time frame. A continental breakfast is served in the beautifully decorated courtyard each morning, where owner Russ Salvatore can often be seen greeting guests. $84–$250.

Several other regional chain hotels are also located near the airport.

✴ Where to Eat

DINING OUT **Adam's Steak and Seafood Restaurant** (716-683-3784), 204 Como Park Boulevard, Cheektowaga. Open Monday–Thursday 4–10, Friday and Saturday 4–11; also open for lunch during December. This well-appointed restaurant is known for its steaks, lobster tails, king crab legs, and marinated grilled pork chops, along with many weekly specials.

& **The Friar's Table** (716-833-5554), 301 Cleveland Drive, Cheektowaga. Open for dinner daily 4–10. You would expect to find a restaurant of this caliber somewhere in a big city, not tucked away along a residential side street in a middle-class neighborhood. Don't be fooled by the location; the Friar's Table is a truly first-rate dining experience. Start out your meal in their elegant oak dining room with one of their colossal shrimp cocktails; then partake of the house specialty, prime rib, or try Alaskan king crab legs, lobster, filet mignon, or one of their daily specials. If you're really hungry and want to splurge, treat yourself to the "ultimate surf and

turf" a 3-pound lobster tail served with a 3-pound cut of prime rib.

Eddie Ryan's Restaurant (716-651-0950), 50 Central Avenue, Lancaster. Open Monday–Wednesday 11–9, Thursday–Friday 11–midnight, Saturday 7:30–midnight, Sunday 7:30–8. This casual fine-dining establishment has an Irish theme. Specialties include Irish pot roast, potato pancakes, shepherd's pie, French onion soup, and the best fish fry in Lancaster. A homemade soup bar is available Monday–Thursday for lunch.

🍲 **Fireside Inn Restaurant and Lounge** (716-683-0462), 203 Central Avenue, Lancaster. Open Monday–Saturday 8 AM–3 AM, Sunday 12 PM–3 AM. This casual yet upscale restaurant is decorated with dark colors and lots of woodwork. The menu features homemade cuisine—everything from wings and burgers to prime rib. One of their specialties is pasta fassola. They have a bar area with dining as well as a separate dining room.

& **Ripa's Restaurant** (716-684-2418; www.ripas.com), 4218 Walden Avenue, Lancaster. Open Tuesday–Thursday 11:30–2:30, Friday 11:30–10:30, Saturday 4–10, Sunday 1–7. Since 1955 Ripas has been serving high-quality food like grilled pork chops, charcoal-broiled fish, stuffed shrimp, steaks, and homemade pasta. They are known for their peanut butter cheesecake, served frozen. Other desserts are from the Butterwood Bakery.

& **Salvatore's Italian Gardens** (716-683-7990), 6461 Transit Road, Lancaster. Open Tuesday–Sunday 5–10. One of western New York's most elegant restaurants for over 35 years. Offered are such classic entrées as filet mignon and prime rib as well as Salvatore's specialty pastas, including spaghetti ala Caruso with a lobster dill sauce and pasta primavera with shrimp. Russ Salvatore and his staff have been the recipients of numerous national and international awards for excellence. The restaurant also has several banquet rooms, and they operate the nearby Garden Place Hotel. See *Lodging*.

EATING OUT AJ's Gelateria and Café (716-683-7004; www.ajsgelateria cafe.com), 36 Central Avenue, Lancaster. Open Monday–Thursday 9–9, Friday and Saturday 9–10; call for Sunday hours. This café in the heart of Lancaster features gelato, pastries, and desserts as well as salads, sandwiches, and specialty coffees.

& **Al-E-Oops** (716-681-0200), 5389 Genesee Street, Lancaster. Open daily 3–11. Enjoy authentic hickory-smoked BBQ ribs, pork, and chicken along with smoked turkey and hickory-house ham in a casual home-style atmosphere. The restaurant has been voted number one for the best BBQ for several years in a row. They also serve seafood and specialty sandwiches.

🍴 **Casa Di Bello** (716-634-2828; www.angelfire.com/ny2/casadibello/in dex.html), 442 Beach Road, Cheektowaga. Open Monday–Thursday 11–11, Friday and Saturday 11 AM–midnight, Sunday 1–10. This tiny take-out restaurant has been serving some of the area's best chicken wings, pizza, tacos, and subs for over 15 years. Their slogan proclaims that they are the serious alternative to fast food. Casa's pizzas include a variety of toppings and are made with a special homemade sauce. Subs are served on fresh toasted rolls, and a variety of salads are also offered, including their

popular antipasto salad. Daily specials include a Friday fish fry. They deliver to all airport area hotels. If you're craving authentic Buffalo-style food, give them a call.

& 🍴 **Charlie the Butchers** (716-633-8330), 1065 Wehrle Drive, Cheektowaga. Open Monday–Saturday 10–10, Sunday 11–9. When locals think of beef on weck, Charlie Roesch often comes to mind since he is considered by many to be the food ambassador of western New York. This small vintage restaurant has indoor as well as outdoor seating. Often you'll see Charlie himself—wearing his trademark white hard hat and butcher's apron—behind the counter, carving up his famous roast beef, smoked turkey, and other daily specials.

🖊 🍴 **50's Diner** (716-683-9248), 4870 Broadway, Depew. Open Monday–Friday 7 AM–8 PM, weekends 7 AM–2 PM. This genuine 1955 stainless steel Silk City diner takes you back to the 1950s. Menu selections, which are all homemade, include "Be Bop A-Lula" burgers and "Do Wop" deli sandwiches, along with "Shake, Rattle and Roll," beverages like thick shakes. Dinner entrées include comfort food like meat loaf, chicken à la king, and daily specials.

✳ Entertainment

THEATERS Lancaster Opera House (716-683-1776; www.lancopera.org), 21 Central Avenue, Lancaster. Every small town and village in the country had a theater, or "opera house," at the turn of the 20th century. Even though opera was rarely performed in them, these buildings were called opera houses rather than vaudeville theaters because it sounded more cultured to

Victorian-era art patrons. Most of these structures had village offices located on the first floor and performance space on the second. Originally opened in 1897, the Lancaster Opera House hosted dances and recitals as well as musicals and traveling shows. Over the years the building has functioned in various capacities, including a center for food distribution during the Great Depression and a Civil Defense Headquarters after World War II. After undergoing restoration during the late 1970s and early 1980s, the opera house is once again a performing-arts center. Today visitors can enjoy a variety of entertainment, including musicals, theater produc-

EVERY SMALL TOWN AND VILLAGE HAD A THEATER, OR "OPERA HOUSE," AT THE TURN OF THE 20TH CENTURY.
Christine A. Smyczynski

tions, operettas, special events, family performances, and student matinees.

✳ Selective Shopping

ANTIQUES **Sweet Briar Antiques** (716-681-7330), 87 Central Avenue, Lancaster. Open Tuesday–Saturday 10–4, Sunday 12–4. This shop, housed in a historic brick 1850s home, specializes in Early American, primitive, and Victorian furniture and accessories.

The Tattered Cat (716-400-9455), 213 Central Avenue, Lancaster. Open Tuesday–Saturday 1–5, Sunday 11–3. This unique shop features antiques, primitives, folk art, birdhouses, handpainted furniture, candles, and more.

SHOPPING MALLS **The Walden Galleria** (716-681-7600; www.walden galleria.com), 1 Walden Galleria Drive, Cheektowaga. Open Monday–Saturday 10–9, Sunday 12–5. The largest shopping mall in western New York features over 200 stores on two levels, including The Bon Ton, JC Penney, Kaufmann's, Sears, Lord & Taylor, plus an international food court and 12 movie theaters.

SPECIAL SHOPS **Niagara Hobby & Craft Mart** (716-681-1666; www .niagarahobby.com), 3366 Union Road at Walden Avenue, Cheektowaga. Open Monday–Saturday 10–9, Sunday 10–5. Billed as the "Biggest Hobby Shop in the U.S.A.," this store features all types of trains and model car supplies. Kids especially enjoy the large, interactive display of model trains and the Thomas the Tank play tables. They'll also enjoy climbing aboard the fully restored red caboose in the parking lot (weather permitting). A huge craft shop, with paints, needle art supplies, dollhouses, and more, is located in the rear of the store.

Lancaster Village Bookstore (716-685-8025), 31 Central Avenue, Lancaster. Open Monday–Wednesday 10–6, Thursday–Saturday 10–8, Sunday 12–5. This small stenciled bookstore, located just down the street from the Lancaster Opera House, features new books for adults and kids as well as gifts, reading glasses, and more.

Scarlette's (716-686-9291), 1 West Main Street, Lancaster. Open Monday and Thursday 10–8, Tuesday 10–7, Wednesday, Friday, and Saturday 10–5. This shop across the street from the historic Lancaster Opera House features Victorian gifts, collectibles, and Christmas decorations.

✳ Special Events

July: **Polish Festival** (716-686-3465), Cheektowaga Town Park. A three-day event celebrating Polish heritage

SOUTHERN ERIE COUNTY— "THE SOUTHTOWNS"

S outh of the City of Buffalo, generally referred to as the "Southtowns," is a mixture of residential areas, farmland, and rolling hills. One Southtown is historic East Aurora, once home to President Millard Fillmore, and today the headquarters of Fisher-Price Toys.

Located just south of Buffalo is Lackawanna, home of Father Nelson Baker, who is being considered for sainthood in the Catholic Church. It is also the location of the century-old Victorian glass conservatory that houses the area's botanical gardens. The largest bicycle museum in the world is located in Orchard Park, as is Ralph Wilson Stadium, home of the Buffalo Bills.

The shores of Lake Erie in Hamburg, Derby, and Angola boast several popular beaches, along with Graycliff, a historic home designed by noted architect Frank Lloyd Wright, which is open for tours.

The southernmost portion of the county is ski country. This is also a great place to view fall foliage.

TOWN OF AURORA: East Aurora, Marilla, and Elma

Aurora, located about 20 miles south of Buffalo, is a quaint town that's rich in history. The town's first settler, Jabez Warren, arrived in 1804, and soon other pioneers came from New England, eastern New York, and the settlement of Buffalo after it was burned by the British. Many of them established farms. At one point during the late 19th century the town was nationally known as a horse-breeding center and was home to the world's only 1-mile covered racetrack, built by the Jewett family. One of the town's early settlers was Millard Fillmore, who came to East Aurora in 1923 to study law and teach school. He went on to be the 13th president of the United States. The home he built in 1825 for his bride, Abigail, is now a National Historic Landmark and museum. During the early part of the 20th century, East Aurora was the home of the Roycroft Arts and Crafts Movement, established by Elbert Hubbard in 1895. East Aurora is also known as "Toy Town U.S.A" since Fisher-Price Toys was founded here and remains the international headquarters for the toy company. Today many shops, restaurants, and antiques stores are located in the historic village, including the 14-building Roycroft Campus, now a National Historic Landmark. As you walk

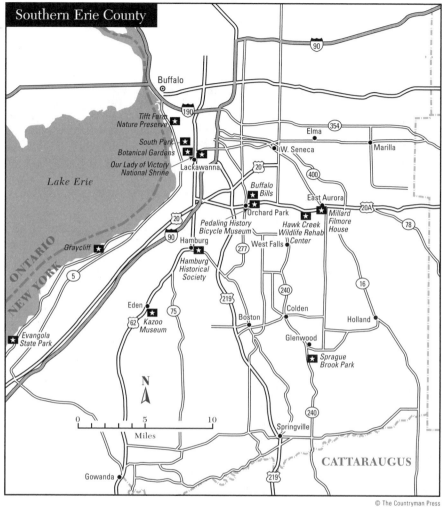

Southern Erie County

down Main Street, be sure to note the fire hydrants. Each has been individually designed and hand painted.

The nearby hamlet of Marilla, named after Marilla Rogers, the wife of an early settler, was established in 1853. Two early buildings are still standing, the Marilla General Store, built in 1851, and the Spring Hotel, now known as the Marilla Grill, also built in 1851.

The town of Elma—carved out of both Aurora and Lancaster—was officially formed by the county in 1857. It was named Elma in honor of a giant elm tree that once stood on the corner of Clinton and Bowen Roads. Elma was originally part of the Buffalo Creek Indian Reservation, which had several native villages located throughout its area. Settlers arrived shortly after the completion of the

Erie Canal, and the first lots were sold in 1828 along an Indian trail, which today is Seneca Street (NY 16). Because the area was covered with abundant forests, these early settlers built lumber mills.

AREA CODE The area code is 716.

GUIDANCE Greater East Aurora Chamber of Commerce (716-652-8444, 800-441-2881; www.eanycc.com), 431 Main Street, East Aurora. Open 8–4:30 Monday–Friday.

East Aurora Web site: www.eastaurorany.com. This site features local events and shopping information.

GETTING THERE *By bus:* The NFTA bus #70 is an express route between Buffalo and East Aurora.

By car: I-90 (New York State Thruway) to NY 400 (exit 54). East Aurora can also be reached via NY 16 or U.S. 20A.

MEDICAL EMERGENCY Call 911

✳ To See

MUSEUMS AND HISTORIC HOMES Aurora Historical Society Museum (716-652-7944), 5 South Grove Street, East Aurora. Open June–October Wednesday, Saturday, and Sunday 2–4. This historic building, which serves as the town's public meeting room, was erected in 1899 by the Roycrofters. It contains a museum that documents the complete history of the Town of Aurora, from Native American inhabitants to the present. On the walls of the museum are 15 murals, painted by Rix Jennings, son of a Roycroft artisan, that detail the town's history. In front of each mural is a glass exhibit case containing objects reflecting the times depicted in the mural. On their self-guided tour, visitors will learn about the growth of the town, how it was a popular horse-trotting area in the 1800s, about the Roycroft Arts and Crafts Movement in the early 1900s, and much more

Elbert Hubbard Museum (716-652-4735; www.roycrofters.com), 363 Oakwood Avenue, East Aurora. Open June 15-October 15, Wednesday, Saturday, and Sunday 2–4. Admission $3. In 1895 Elbert Hubbard acquired a print shop in East Aurora, and very rapidly the Roycroft Press became well-known for its beautiful books. An interesting and sometimes controversial person, Hubbard published a pocket-sized magazine, *The Philistine,* that was filled with wit, wisdom, and irreverence. He was also the first printer to make use of color, white space, and endorsements in his advertising. This museum, formerly the home of a Roycroft artisan, is filled with artifacts belonging to Hubbard and his craftsmen, including rare books, furniture, and leatherworks. One of the Roycroft artists, W. W. Denslow, was the illustrator for the book *The Wizard of Oz.*

♫ ❂ Millard Fillmore House Museum (716-652-8875), 24 Shearer Avenue, East Aurora. Open June–October Wednesday, Saturday, and Sunday 2–4. Admission: $3. Millard Fillmore, 13th president of the United States, built this home in 1825 for his new bride, Abigail, shortly after he began his law career in East

Aurora. The tour of this National Historic Landmark begins in the stenciled living room and moves to the kitchen. Children will be fascinated by the antique kitchen utensils, which they are permitted to touch. Upstairs in the children's bedroom is a collection of toys and dolls from the 1800s. Some of the furnishings were owned by the Fillmore family, and a portrait of Fillmore, done in his later years, is on display. Outside are several gardens plus a carriage barn that contains a sleigh used by the Fillmore family.

Marilla Historical Museum (716-652-7608, town historian), 1810 Two Rod Road, Marilla. Open the third Sunday of each month from 2–4. The town historian is also in his office in the town hall next to the museum Tuesday 7–9 PM. Free admission. This museum has displays pertaining to the history of the town of Marilla.

Elma Historical Museum (716-655-0046, museum; 716-652-0759, curator; 716-652-9274, town historian), 3011 Bowen Road, Elma. Open July–August the third Sunday of the month 1–4; rest of year Thursday 1–4 or by appointment. Donations accepted. This museum has information about the history of Elma.

✳ To Do

CROSS-COUNTRY SKIING See *Green Space—Parks*

FAMILY FUN ✎ ♿ ⬆ **Explore & More Children's Museum** (716-655-5131; www.exploreandmore.org), 300 Gleed Avenue, East Aurora. Open Wednesday–Saturday 10–5, Sunday 12–5; until 8 the first Friday of the month. Admission: $2 adults, $3 children. This unique museum encourages children to touch the exhibits as they experiment, discover, play, and learn. The museum's fundamental philosophy is that play is essential for learning. The museum has educational workshops, activity days, and traveling exhibits for preschoolers through sixth graders.

✎ ⬆ **Toy Town Museum** (716-687-5151; www.toytownusa.com), 636 Girard Avenue, East Aurora. Open Monday–Saturday 10–4. Free admission. This 8,000-square-foot museum features a permanent collection of Fisher-Price toys as well as changing exhibits of toys and artifacts on loan from other museums and private collectors. In "Toyworks," an interactive play area, children can lean as they play. The museum's major annual event, Toyfest, takes place in late August. It features a parade, amusement rides, a craft show, antique car show, and many other activities.

MILLARD FILLMORE, 13TH PRESIDENT OF THE U.S., BUILT THIS HOME FOR HIS BRIDE IN 1825.

Christine A. Smyczynski

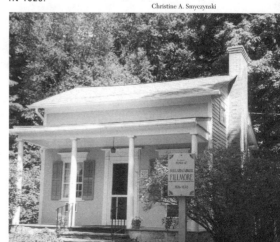

GOLF Aurora Driving Range (716-655-3894), 591 Olean Road, East Aurora.

ELBERT HUBBARD AND THE ROYCROFT ARTS AND CRAFTS MOVEMENT

In 1892 Elbert Hubbard quit his job as a soap salesman in Buffalo and traveled to England, where he became acquainted with William Morris, father of the English Arts and Crafts movement. When he returned to the United States, he acquired a print shop in East Aurora and soon became well-known for the beautiful books he produced. One published essay, *A Message to Garcia,* brought him international fame. Hubbard went on to develop a self-contained community of over 500 craftsmen, including furniture makers, metalsmiths, leathersmiths, and bookbinders. Items produced by the artisans were marked with the "Roycroft Mark," which signified that the work was of their highest qualify.

Hubbard viewed the Roycroft as not merely a place but a state of mind. In 1905 the Roycroft Inn was opened to accommodate the thousands of people who journeyed there to learn about the Arts and Crafts movement. The community flourished until 1915 when, tragically, Hubbard and his wife perished on the *Lusitania.* The community continued on, under the leadership of his son, until it closed in 1938. The 14-building **Roycroft Campus** was designated a National Historic Landmark in 1986 and began going through extensive restorations and preservations during the 1990s.

East Aurora Country Club (716-652-6800), 300 Girdle Road, Elma. An 18-hole, par-71 public course.

✿ **Elma Meadows** (716-652-5475), 1711 Girdle Road, Elma. Open April–November. An 18-hole, par-72 course and driving range. A top course with reasonable prices.

Springbrook Golf Center (716-652-0783), 6831 Seneca Street, Elma. This facility features a driving range, indoor practice range, instructions, equipment repair, and pro shop.

✳ Green Space

NATURE PRESERVES Hawk Creek Wildlife Rehabilitation Center (716-652-8646; www.hawkcreek.org), 655 Luther Road, East Aurora. Hawk Creek is a 52-acre wildlife center that specializes in birds of prey and mammals. The center's staff is committed to preserving wildlife and the environment through rehabilitation, reproduction, research, and education. Many of the creatures taken in are injured and orphaned birds. Hawk Creek is the largest educational outreach facility in the state, and its educational programs include talks on owls, rare species, and unique mammals. They even have special programs designed for preschoolers. Although the facility is only open to the public during their open house, the center operates an information booth on weekends at the Galleria Mall in Cheektowaga.

Sinking Ponds Nature Preserve, Pine Street Extension, East Aurora. Open dawn to dusk. Free admission. A 70-acre area of woods and natural ponds that features walking trails and natural ponds for bird-watching.

PARKS Aurora Town Park (716-652-8866), South Street (at Olean Road), East Aurora. This 3-acre park has a playground, picnic areas, and an outdoor pool.

Elma Meadows (716-652-5475), 1711 Girdle Road, Elma. Open dawn to dusk. Free admission. This Erie County park includes picnic facilities, athletic fields, a decorative rock garden, and an 18-hole, par-72 golf course and driving range. Winter activities include cross-country skiing, sledding, and tobogganing.

Emery Park, (716-652-1380), 2084 Emery Road (Route 200), South Wales. Open dawn to dusk. Free admission. This park was established in 1925, when the parks commission purchased 175 acres from Josiah Emery. Today the park has 489 acres. Facilities include baseball diamonds, biking and hiking trails, and picnic tables, along with cross-country ski trails and downhill skiing with a T-bar.

Hamlin Park (716-652-8866), Prospect and South Grove Street, East Aurora. A 16-acre village park, located just a few blocks from the historic Roycroft Inn. Facilities include a large picnic area, playground, baseball fields, bandstand, tennis courts, and running track.

Knox Farm State Park (716-655-7200), 437 Buffalo Road (Seneca Street), East Aurora. Open daily dawn to dusk. Admission: $6 parking fee. This 633-acre park, formerly known as Ess Kay Farm, the estate of East Aurora's socially prominent Knox family, is a mixture of grasslands, woodlands, pastures, and ponds. Park activities include hiking, biking, horseback riding (by permit), and cross-country skiing. The park also has a number of farm animals used in educational programs. The visitors center, which has exhibits on nature, agriculture, and the farm's history, is located in the "milk house" near the main parking lot. The park's Audubon center provides walking tours and educational programs on the park's birds and wildlife.

❋ Lodging

INNS AND RESORTS Hampton Inn & Oakwood Event Center (716-655-3300 or 800-875-9440; www.oakwoodevents.com), 49 Olean Road, East Aurora. This inn is the only complete hotel and event center in East Aurora. This newly built inn features 80 deluxe guest rooms, including 8 Jacuzzi suites with fireplaces. Amenities include an indoor heated pool, fitness center, and deluxe complimentary breakfast. $109–$149, winter rates lower.

❂ **The Roycroft Inn** (716-652-5552; www.roycroftinn.com), South Grove Street, East Aurora. This National Historic Landmark inn was built in 1905 to accommodate all the guests that Elbert Hubbard's Arts and Crafts movement attracted to the area. It was restored in 1995 and offers luxurious accommodations in a historic setting. The 22 unique guest suites have original and reproduction furnishings, along with modern amenities like Jacuzzi tubs, VCR TVs, and thick terry-cloth robes. Each room has the name of a notable personality carved into the door, including Ralph Waldo Emerson, Henry David Thoreau, and Susan B. Anthony. A complimentary breakfast is offered each morning to inn guests. $120–$230.

BED & BREAKFASTS Green Glen Bed & Breakfast (716-655-2828; www.green-glen.com), 898 East Main Street, East Aurora. Innkeepers Martha and Ed Collins offer four unique antique-filled guest rooms in their large restored Victorian home built in 1892. Two rooms have private baths, and the other two share a bath. The 6 acres of woodlands surrounding the B&B include a glen and a creek. A full or continental breakfast is included with the room. $70–$80.

✳ Where to Eat

DINING OUT Borealis (716-652-1640) 687 Main Street, East Aurora. Lunch Monday-Saturday 11-2:30, Dinner Monday-Thursday 5-9, Friday-Saturday 5-10. This upscale, contemporary restaurant, located in an old house in the middle of the village, features an innovative menu that includes pasta, poultry and seafood dishes, along with old favorites like rack of lamb and strip steak.

The Lodge (716-652-5004; www.thelodge.ws), 2090 Bowen Road, Elma. Open Monday–Saturday 11–11, Sunday 10 AM–11 PM. This casual yet elegant landmark restaurant—in a rustic log cabin—features home-cooked meals in a friendly atmosphere. It has served the community for six generations. Traditional favorites include roast beef, BBQ ribs, honey-dipped chicken, and fettuccine Alfredo, plus a large selection of steaks and seafood and even a kids' menu.

The Old Orchard Inn (716-652-4664; www.oldorchardny.com), 2095 Blakeley Road, East Aurora. Open for lunch and dinner. Open Monday–Sat-

urday 11:30–2:30 and 5–9, Sunday 12–7. This cozy restaurant, built in 1901 as a hunting lodge and converted to a tearoom in 1931, is located on 25 acres in the East Aurora countryside. Home-cooked entrées include everything from chicken fricassee to surf and turf.

❂ The Roycroft Inn (716-652-5552; www.roycroftinn.com), 40 South Grove Street, East Aurora. Open year-round for lunch Monday–Saturday 11:30–3; dinner Sunday–Thursday 5–9, Friday and Saturday 5–10; Sunday brunch 10–2. The restaurant in the 1905 National Historic Landmark inn has a superb and elegant menu, including rack of lamb, pan-seared salmon, and homemade desserts, as well as a "Signature Dinner Menu" that changes seasonally. They are well-known for their Sunday brunch buffet. During the warmer months guests can dine outdoors on the peristyle. Guided tours of the inn can be arranged during lunch and dinner hours.

Tantalus (716-652-0341), 634 Main Street, East Aurora. Open Monday–Thursday 11–10, Friday and Saturday 11–11, Sunday 12–8. This large, casual, contemporary restaurant is housed in the former Griggs & Ball grain elevator building. The interior still has the original concrete floor and walls and wooden elevators. The menu includes a variety of gourmet brick-oven pizzas, burgers, and sandwiches, plus salads, pasta, and quiche.

❦ Tony Rome's Globe Hotel & Restaurant (716-652-4221), 711 Main Street, East Aurora. Open Monday–Saturday 11–11, Sunday 12–10. Located in a historic 1824 hotel and stagecoach stop, this casual restaurant is East Aurora's oldest business operating in its original location

—it was frequented by Millard Fillmore and Grover Cleveland. The building's exterior has changed little from the 1860s, while the interior also reflects its heritage, including exposed-beam ceilings in the dining room, tin ceilings in the bar, and an unusual twin fireplace. The restaurant is noted for BBQ dishes, especially ribs. Other selections include steak, chicken, and fish fry seven days a week.

EATING OUT 🌹 **Bar Bill Tavern** (716-652-7959), 185 Main Street, East Aurora. Open Monday–Saturday 8–4, Sunday 12–4. A popular neighborhood tavern that's an East Aurora institution. Specialties include beef on weck in three sizes and several varieties of super-jumbo chicken wings. They also offer five different kinds of French fries.

🌹 ✿ **Charlie's** (716-655-0282), 510 Main Street, East Aurora. Open Monday–Saturday 5 AM–8 PM, Sunday 7 AM–1 PM. This popular restaurant has been at this location for nearly 60 years. Menu selections include hearty fare like omelets and French toast for breakfast, homemade soups and specialty burgers for lunch, and meat loaf and liver and onions for dinner. During the warmer months, the patio is *the* place to dine, with customers waiting an hour or more for a table.

✿ ♿ 🌹 **Iron Kettle Restaurant** (716-652-5310), 1009 Olean Road (2 miles south of the village) East Aurora. Open Monday–Saturday 7 AM–8 PM, Sunday 9 AM–7 PM (brunch served 9–3). This large family restaurant features country decor and hospitality. You can dine in their bright and cheerful dining rooms, or eat outdoors on the screened patio in the warmer

months. The menu features family favorites like sandwiches, wraps, salads, and pastas. Dinner selections include steaks, ribs, roast beef, pork chops, and a Friday fish fry.

Libbys (716-655-1630), 701 Main Street, East Aurora. Open Monday–Thursday 11–9, Friday and Saturday 11–10, Sunday 12–8. This newly open '50s-style dinner serves up burgers, shakes, and other diner foods.

Marilla Grill (716-652-3097), 11591 Bullis Road, Marilla. Open Monday–Thursday and Saturday 11–10, Friday 11–8:30, Sunday 11–9. This tavern and restaurant was originally built in 1853 as a hotel and restaurant. It was called the Spring Hotel after a natural spring located nearby. It burned and was rebuilt in 1865. Over the years it has seen various owners and has been known by many names. It has been known as the Marilla Grill since 1945. They are known for their casual fare, including specialty sandwiches, grill house favorites, wings, burgers, and the "famous" Marilla Grill steak sub. They also serve seafood dinners, including a fish fry on Friday. It is located across the

ENJOY FINE DINING ON THE PERISTYLE AT THE ROYCROFT INN IN WARMER WEATHER.

street from the Marilla Country Store, a unique place to shop.

Taste (716-655-1874), 634 Main Street, East Aurora. Open Monday–Thursday 7–10, Friday 7–11, Saturday 8–11, Sunday 8–10. Located in the former Griggs & Ball building, this cozy café with brick walls and exposed ceilings offers hearty fare for breakfast, lunch and dinner. Breakfast, which is served all day, includes selections like Belgian waffles and tiramisu French toast. All meals include fresh-baked scones, muffins, buns, or bagels. Items on the "Good Stuff" section of the menu reflect East Aurora's heritage. Try a Millard Fill-me-more, a chicken salad in a bistro blanket, or Fish-for-a-price, a real toy-town favorite. They also offer a nice selection of soups, sandwiches, and salads.

The Village Restaurant (716-652-5788), 726 Main Street, East Aurora. Open Monday–Saturday 11–10, Sunday 1–10. Featuring slow-roasted prime rib, seafood, and steaks plus a Thursday night crab legs special. Soup and salad bar are available for lunch Monday–Friday.

Wallenwein's Hotel (716-652-9801), 641 Oakwood, East Aurora. Open Monday–Thursday 10–12. Friday and Saturday 10–1, Sunday 12–12. This turn-of-the-20th-century hotel is now a tavern and restaurant noted for chicken wings and a Friday fish fry. Enjoy your meal in the dining room or outdoors on the deck.

✳ Entertainment

THEATERS **Aurora Theater** (652-1660), 673 Main Street, East Aurora. Major motion pictures along with independent and foreign films in a 600 seat circa 1925 theater.

Aurora Players (716-687-6727; www.auroraplayers.org), PO Box 206, East Aurora. This 70-year-old community theater group presents performances in the rustic Roycroft Pavilion in Hamlin Park. This historic pavilion seating 200 people was built by and for the Roycrofters and dedicated on July 4, 1903.

✳ Selective Shopping

ANTIQUES **Bonnie's Antiques** (716-652-0227 or 716-652-8316), 1241 Bowen Road (at Jamison), Elma. Open April–December Friday and Sunday 12–5. Quality antiques can be found in this unique barn with a scenic mural.

Hubbard's Cupboards (716-652-3235, 716-652-1565), 37 South Grove Street, East Aurora (Roycroft Campus). Open Monday–Saturday 10–5, Sunday 12–5. Located in the original Roycroft furniture building, this co-op features antiques, collectibles, fine linens, and original Roycroft items.

Adrian Morris Antiques (716-655-3374), 205 Main Street, East Aurora. Open Tuesday–Saturday 10–5. This shop specializes in 18th- and 19th-century American furniture, folk art, fine art, and accessories.

Punkin's Patch Antiques (716-655-6235; www.punkinspatchantiques.com), 93 Elm Street, East Aurora. Open Wednesday–Saturday 11–5. An early 1900s mill building is now an antiques shop carrying a large selection of household accessories, glassware, silver, books, linens, furniture, tools and Buffalo-related items.

Roycroft Campus Antiques (716-655-1565 or 716-652-3235), 37 South Grove Street, East Aurora (Roycroft Campus) Open Monday–Saturday

10–5, Sunday 12–5. Carries a variety of banks, furniture, Pan-Am buttons, glass, pottery, china, guns, steins, clocks, jewelry, toys, coins, dolls, and more.

& **Williston Antiques/Aurora Shooting Supplies** (716-655-7000), 19 Hamburg Street (at the traffic circle) East Aurora. Open Tuesday, Thursday, Friday 10–6, Wednesday 12–6, Saturday 10–3. This shop combines a room full of general antiques with a gun shop specializing in new and used firearms.

ART GALLERIES **Big Tree Gallery** (716-655-5200), 720 Main Street, East Aurora. Open Monday–Saturday 10–5:30. This gallery features the work of local and other American and Canadian artists. Choose from pottery, stained-glass items, T-shirts, and more.

Meibohm Fine Arts (716-652-0940; www.meibohmarts.com), 478 Main Street, East Aurora. Open Tuesday–Saturday 9:30–5:30. This family-owned and operated shop has been an East Aurora fixture since 1957. The Meibohm name has been known in western New York since 1901, when Carl Meibohm was photographer at the Pan-Am Exposition. The store features a selection of artwork for collectors and home decorators, specializing in antique and vintage prints plus works by local artists.

Norberg's Art Gallery and Custom Framing (716-652-3270), 37 South Grove Street (Roycroft Campus) East Aurora. Open Tuesday–Friday 10–5, Saturday 10–3. This gallery features original artwork by western New York and Roycroft Renaissance artisans. They also do custom framing and have handcrafted gift items.

& **West End Gallery** (716-652-5860; www.west-end-gallery.com), 48 Douglas Lane (corner U.S. 20A) East Aurora. Open Monday–Friday 10–5:30, Saturday 9–5. This unique shop features handmade contemporary gifts, distinctive and one of a kind items including glass, pottery, metal, paintings, and prints. It is located in a circa 1800 schoolhouse, the first school in East Aurora.

FARM MARKETS ✔ **Bipperts Farm Market** (716-668-4328), 5220 Clinton Street (near Transit) Elma. Hours vary seasonally, closed January and February. For over 50 years the Bippert family has been selling fresh produce grown on their 500 acre farm, along with fresh Angus beef raised on the farm. Their in-house bakery features baked goods made fresh daily, plus a variety of jams and jellies. Farm tours are available for school groups in the fall.

SPECIAL SHOPS **Amish Country Oak** (716-655-2489), 695 Main Street, East Aurora. Open Monday–Saturday 10–5. Quality Amish-made furniture in solid oak and cherry along with home decor items and accessories.

Aurora Rails and Hobbies (716-652-5718), 2268 Blakeley Road, East Aurora. Monday and Wednesday 8–6, Tuesday and Thursday 8–7:30, Friday 8–5:30. Model-railroad enthusiasts will enjoy this shop, which specializes in trains and accessories for all scales of model railroads.

Cassandra's Gift Shop (716-655-5529), 664 Main Street, East Aurora. Open Monday–Wednesday 10–5, Thursday 10–8, Friday 10–7, Saturday 10–6, Sunday 11–4. This shop features a wide variety of gift items, including handmade scarves and baby items, jewelry, garden items, and bird feeders.

Cosefini (716-655-1900), 660 Main Street, East Aurora. Open Monday–Friday 10–6, Thursday until 8, Saturday 10–5. This unique boutique carries an extensive selection of European soaps, robes and pajamas, linens, bath items, candles, jewelry, and more.

The Cottage (716-652-0292), 306 Main Street, East Aurora This shop, located in a beautifully restored home, features a nicely displayed array of furniture and home decor items, including unique glassware, dishes, and potpourri. All the furniture is sold at a 30 percent discount and can be custom ordered.

The Feather Tree (716-655-5969), 695 Main Street, East Aurora. Open Tuesday–Saturday 10–5. This cute little shop with stenciled walls specializes in gifts for the heart and home, including dried wreaths, baskets, folk art, redware, and feather trees. They also have a large selection of Christmas ornaments and decorations.

Fisher-Price Toys Store (716-687-3300), 636 Girard Avenue, East Aurora. Open Monday–Friday 10–6, Saturday 10–5. Located right in front of the Fisher-Price Toy Factory, this store has an extensive collection of Fisher-Price and Mattel items, including closeouts.

Gingerbread Cottage (716-652-5425), 280 Main Street, East Aurora. Open Tuesday–Saturday 10–5:30. The exterior of this store really does look like a gingerbread cottage! Indoors, find hand-painted walls and a large selection of adorable children's clothing and accessories.

The Legacy Bookshop & Gallery (716-652-6797), 654 Main Street, East Aurora. Open Monday–Wednesday, Saturday 11–5; Thursday and Friday 11–9. Featuring new and used books, many on the Arts and Crafts movement. They also sell art pottery and tiles, Mission-style furniture and lamps, and doormats and door-knockers.

& **Maggie's Roots** (716-655-0900), 155 Oakwood, East Aurora. Open Monday–Saturday 10–5, Thursday until 7. This shop specializes in Maine cottage furniture and other items that proprietor Bethann Geiger finds on her buying trips to Maine. Some items are antiques, while others are newly made and handcrafted.

Marilla Country Store (716-655-1031; www.marillacountrystore.com), 1673 Two Rod Road (corner of Bullis Road) Marilla. Open daily 7 AM–9 PM. This place has a little bit of everything, from hardware to gifts. Originally opened in 1851, the store still serves locals as a grocery and dry-goods store on the first floor. But climb up to the second floor to browse the area's largest selection of country decorating items. The building features the original floor, countertops, and gaslights. A museum located on the second floor has displays of inventory and store fixtures from the past as well as a Porter music box.

Peppermint Farms (716-655-5214), 7431 Seneca Street, (NY 16), Elma. Open seasonally Monday–Saturday 9–4, Sunday by chance. Pesticide-free plants and herbs grown in a homelike setting. Six greenhouses are filled with over 50 varieties of herbs. They also carry annuals, perennials, and hanging baskets along with an assortment of herb-inspired items in their gift shop.

Pink-Eclectic Home Decor (716-655-4478), 640 Main Street, East Aurora. Open Monday–Friday 10–5, Thursday until 8, Saturday 10–4, Sunday 12–4. This store specializes in imported hand-carved armoires and dining room tables, hand-painted cabinets, and handcrafted chairs and benches, plus curtains, pillows, and duvet covers.

Roycroft Shops (716-652-3333; www.roycroftshops.com), 31 South Grove Street, East Aurora. Open daily 10–5. Located in the original copper shop on the Roycroft Campus, the Roycroft Shops are your complete Arts and Crafts movement resource. Choose from books and memorabilia, some made by the original Roycrofters at the turn of the 20th century. They also have a large selection of giftware, Roycroft china, and more.

Schoolhouse Gallery and Cabinet Shop (716-655-4080), 1054 Olean Road, East Aurora. Open Monday–Friday 8–4, Saturday 10–3:30. Owners Ben Little and Tom Harris make fine furniture in the Roycroft tradition in this circa 1850 former schoolhouse. The shop also has a nice selection of handmade crafts and gifts.

Seasons with Eleanor Rose (716-655-7673), 651 Oakwood, East Aurora. Open Monday–Tuesday 11–5, Wednesday 11–6, Friday and Saturday 11–4. Folk art, candles, seasonal decor, quilts, garden statuary, birdhouses, and more.

Simple Treasures (716-652-0833) 404 Main Street, East Aurora. Open Tuesday–Saturday 10–5. Find vintage wares and fine gifts: linens, home accessories, soaps, and more. Owner Bonnie Valentine also offers custom window treatments and interior design service.

Toy Loft (716-652-3277), 700 Main Street, East Aurora. Open Monday–Wednesday 10–5:30, Thursday–Friday 10–8, Saturday 10–6. An old-fashioned toy shop, featuring books, educational toys, infant gifts, dolls, and collectibles.

The Upper Room (716-655-6272), 245 Main Street, East Aurora. Open Monday–Saturday Closed Sunday and Holy Days of Obligation. Specializing in Catholic books and treasures.

Upstairs Treasures (716-652-1146), 37 Church Street (off Main across from Aurora Theatre), East Aurora. Tuesday–Saturday 10–5. Gift items, including antiques, folk art, Mission furniture, quilts, and collectible dolls. Local crafters make many of the items, such as stained-glass lamps, folk art on wood and slate, and hand-knit sweaters.

Vidlers 5 & 10 (716-652-0481; www.vidlers5and10.com), 680-694 Main Street, East Aurora. Open Monday–Thursday, Saturday 9–5:30; Friday 9–9, Sunday 12–4. Look for the red-and-white awning on Main Street, and you'll find one of East Aurora's most beloved landmarks. Vidlers 5 & 10, housed in four connected 1890s-era buildings, has retained the atmosphere of an old-fashioned five and dime. They sell many interesting and hard-to-find items along with yarn, fabric, crafts, housewares, toys, candy, and cards. This business has been family owned since 1930, when Robert Vidler Sr. opened the store in the midst of the Great Depression.

The Woolly Lamb (716-655-1911), 712 Main Street, East Aurora. Open Monday–Wednesday and Friday 11–5, Thursday 11–8, Saturday 10–5, Sunday 12–4. Hand-knit items along with natural-fiber yarns.

✳ Special Events

January: **Millard Fillmore's Birthday** (716-652-8444), Roycroft Inn, East Aurora. A tongue-in-cheek political roast, celebrating the anniversary of the birth of Millard Fillmore. Each year "Mr. Fillmore" himself shows up to recap the year's worst political blunders and award the Millard Mallard to the politician who made the biggest faux pas.

June: **Chamber Music Festival** PO Box 281, East Aurora, NY 14052; www.roycroftchambermusic.bfn.org), St. Matthias Church in East Aurora. Musicians from all over the U.S. and Canada come to perform at this festival. **Roycroft Summer Festival** (to contact write RALA, 21 South Grove Street, Suite 110, East Aurora, NY 14052), Roycroft Campus, East Aurora. An arts, crafts, and fine art show held the last full weekend of June.

August: **Toyfest** (716-687-5151; www.toytownusa.com), Main Street, East Aurora. A family-oriented weekend featuring a giant parade, crafts, rides, and other activities, including displays focusing on Fisher-Price toys which are made in East Aurora. **Wildlife and Renaissance Festival** (716-652-8646; www.hawkcreek.org), Hawk Creek Wildlife Center. An open house at the wildlife center features up-close encounters with hawks and other birds of prey.

December: **Roycroft Winter Festival** (to contact write RALA, 21 South Grove Street, Suite 110, East Aurora, NY 14052), East Aurora Middle School. Craftsmen and artisans display their wares for holiday shopping the first weekend of December.

LACKAWANNA AND WEST SENECA

The area that is today known as West Seneca was first occupied—like the rest of the region—by Native Americans. At the end of the 18th century much of this land was purchased by the Holland Land Company, with land south of Buffalo Creek set aside for an Indian reservation. West Seneca was part of this land. The Native Americans built dwellings, mills, and gristmills similar to those built by incoming settlers to the area.

In 1842 a group of German settlers under the leadership of Christian Metz, known as the Community of True Inspiration, or Ebenezers, came to the area to escape religious persecution. They purchased reservation land from the Native Americans at $10 per acre and set up four self-sufficient communities that revolved around the Word of the Lord. Metz and his group moved into the Seneca dwellings. Each man was designated a trade to benefit the whole community, while the women worked in the kitchen and laundry. The Ebenezers led a very austere life that revolved around work and religion. They wore plain, dark-colored clothing, similar to the Amish.

In the mid-1850s the religious community needed more land. They purchased 18,000 acres in Iowa and moved west. After they moved out, the area was settled by German immigrants and was basically a farming community until about the late 1960s, when it became a commercial and residential suburb.

The city of Lackawanna was once known as the "Steel City of the Great

Lakes," taking its name from Lackawanna County, Pennsylvania, where the steel industry began. The steel industry was the major employer in the city from about 1900 until the early 1980s, when massive layoffs forced the plants to shut down. At one point Bethlehem Steel employed about 24,000 and was the largest steel plant in the world. Information on the steel industry can be found at a small museum in Lackawanna's public library. The library itself is an interesting building: One of many Carnegie-funded libraries across the country, it was built in 1922 on the site of a former pauper's cemetery (the bodies were exhumed and reburied elsewhere).

Lackawanna, which was incorporated in 1901, is a very cosmopolitan city. According to census records, over 77 different ethnic groups have settled here at one time or another, many of whom were drawn to the area by the steel industry. Today the city may be best known as the "Home of Father Baker." Our Lady of Victory, the massive basilica that dominates the cityscape, was built in 1926 by the late Fr. Nelson Baker, who currently is being considered for canonization by the Catholic church.

AREA CODE The area code is **716**.

GUIDANCE Lackawanna Area Chamber of Commerce (716-823-8841) 638 Ridge Road, Lackawanna. Open 9–4 Monday–Friday.

West Seneca Chamber of Commerce (716-674-4900; www.westseneca.org) 950 Union Road, West Seneca. Open Monday–Friday 9–5.

GETTING THERE *By bus:* NFTA bus #42 (Lackawanna) and #75 (West Seneca) travel from downtown Buffalo.

By car: Exit 55 off I-90 will get you here. From Buffalo, NY 5 will take you into Lackawanna.

MEDICAL EMERGENCY

DIAL 911 Our Lady of Victory Hospital (716-825-8000; www.chsbuffalo.org) 55 Melroy Place, Lackawanna.

✳ To See

MUSEUMS Steel Plant Museum (716-823-0630; www.buffalolib.org) Lackawanna Public Library, 560 Ridge Road, Lackawanna. Open Monday, Wednesday 1–9, Tuesday, Thursday, Saturday 10–5. Free admission. This large exhibit, located in the lower level of Lackawanna's Carnegie Library, is a tribute to Western New York's steel workers and Bethlehem Steel, the "largest steel plant in the world." The collection consists of salvaged and donated items. Many retired steelworkers have generously donated uniforms, tools, badges, and other memorabilia pertinent to the region's steel industry. On your self-guided tour through this extensive exhibit you will learn about the history of the steel industry in our area through photos and other items. The museum also has old city directories and microfilms of Lackawanna's newspapers. As a point of interest: The circa

1922 library building, a Colonial-style structure with oak woodwork throughout the interior, is one of the last Carnegie libraries ever constructed.

West Seneca Historical Society (716-674-4283), 919 Mill Road West Seneca. Open 10–4 Tuesday, 2–4 on the first Sunday of the month, and by appointment. Local history artifacts, including items from Seneca and other Native Americans and the Ebenezers, are displayed in an original 1850 Lower Ebenezer Society building.

HISTORIC SITES &. ⏳ **Our Lady of Victory National Shrine and Basilica** (716-828-9648; www.ourladyofvictory.org), 780 Ridge Road, Lackawanna. Open daily 7–7. This magnificent Italian Renaissance–style basilica, completed in 1926, was the great dream of the late Father Nelson H. Baker—being considered for canonization to Catholic sainthood—who named it Our Lady of Victory to honor the Blessed Virgin Mary. The basilica is constructed almost entirely of marble. Its most prominent feature is its 165-foot copper-topped dome. When it was built, the dome was second in size only to the U.S. Capitol. A small museum in the basilica basement has information on Father Baker's life as well as some of his personal belongings.

✳ To Do

GOLF **South Park** (716-851-5806), 3284 South Park Avenue. Open May 1–October 31, fees range from $7–$16. A well-maintained 9-hole, par-36 course, which is great for beginners since the fairways are wide open. See also **City of Buffalo** *Green Space—Parks.*

✳ Green Space

GARDENS &. ✎ 🌿 ⏳ **Buffalo and Erie County Botanical Gardens** (716-827-1584 www.buffalogardens.com), 2655 South Park Avenue, South Buffalo. Open 9–4. Free admission. This 100-year-old Victorian-style glass conservatory is listed on the New York State and National Register of Historic Places. The 11.3-acre site features plants from around the world, including cacti, fruit trees, palms, and many beautiful flowers. The conservatory is 350 feet long and boasts a 60-foot-tall central dome. Two smaller palm domes are connected to the central dome by glass growing ranges. The conservatory, designed by Lord and Burnham, is one of only two tri-domed conservatories in the United States. The Botanical Gardens, located in South Park, is part of the Buffalo Parks system designed by noted landscape artist Frederick Law

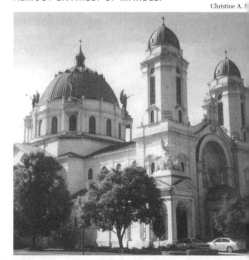

OUR LADY OF VICTORY NATIONAL SHRINE AND B. CA WAS COMPLETED IN 1926 AND IS CONSTRUCT ALMOST ENTIRELY OF MARBLE.

Christine A. S

Olmsted (1822–1903). It is America's oldest coordinated system of public parks. Educational programs, children's workshops, and special events are held throughout the year

NATURE PRESERVES ✦ **Charles E. Burchfield Nature and Art Center** (716-677-4843; www.burchfield natureandart.org), 2001 Union Road at Clinton Street, West Seneca. Visitors center open Monday–Friday 10–4, free admission; trails open daily dusk to dawn. This 29-acre nature preserve includes nature trails, gardens, children's adventure area, replicas of watercolors by Burchfield and more.

THE 100-YEAR-OLD VICTORIAN-STYLE CONSERVATORY IS THE HIGHLIGHT OF THE BUFFALO AND ERIE COUNTY BOTANICAL GARDENS.

PARKS **South Park** (716-838-1249; www.buffaloolmstedparks.com), South Park Avenue, South Buffalo The design for South Park was first proposed by Olmsted in 1892, with its central feature being a circuit drive so that visitors could enjoy the view of the park. Today the park features 155 acres of green space, including

FATHER NELSON BAKER

Born in western New York in 1841, Nelson Baker started out as a businessman. However, he heard the calling to the priesthood at age 27 and was ordained at 34. His first assignment was St. Patrick's parish, which was also responsible for two orphanages. Father Baker, known as the "Padre of the Poor," was especially concerned about young people, particularly orphans and abandoned children and founded several institutions in the early 1900s, including a home for infants and unwed mothers, a hospital, and an orphanage. He established a home for boys, where they could learn a trade. These boys were affectionately referred to as Father Baker's Boys—a few of whom are still alive today.

Father Baker died in 1936 at age 95. The funeral director preserved Father Baker's body fluids in glass vials, and these were buried with him. This was done because many people considered the priest to be a saint while he was alive; so there was the hope that he would one day be canonized.

In March 1999 his body was exhumed and reburied within the basilica. The vials of the body fluids were found to be in the same condition as when he was buried 60 years earlier. Doctors confirmed that this was impossible; Rome considered it a miracle. Father Baker is currently being considered for canonization in the Catholic Church.

a shrub garden, lake, and golf course. The focal point of the park is the circa 1900 Victorian glass conservatory, home to the Buffalo and Erie Country Botanical Gardens (see above). The roadway that circles the park is popular with walkers, joggers, and in-line skaters.

✳ Lodging

MOTELS AND HOTELS Hampton Inn (716-824-2030), 1750 Ridge Road, West Seneca. A five-story hotel with 105 guest rooms, 5 of them suites. Amenities include a small indoor pool and an exercise room. $69–$150.

✳ Where to Eat

DINING OUT Connor's (716-674-9945), 3465 Seneca Street, West Seneca. Open Monday–Thursday 11–10, Friday 11–11, Saturday 11–midnight, Sunday 12–10. Dinner specials include Tuesday all-you-can-eat crab legs and Sunday fresh turkey dinners.

Curly's Bar and Grill (716-824-9716; www.jerksauce.com), 647 Ridge Road, Lackawanna. Open for lunch Monday–Friday 11–3, dinner Tuesday–Saturday 5–10, Sunday 3–9. This popular upscale restaurant is noted for its Jamaican jerk chicken, which is marinated in chef Krista VanWagner's special Caribbean-style BBQ sauce. (Keeping with the Jamaican theme, the front dining room has been decorated with hand-painted murals that make you feel you are on the island.) Other menu selections include dishes like osso buco, seafood linguine, and rack of lamb Dijon.

Deerhead Inn (716-823-9500), 2683 Clinton Street, Gardenville. Open Monday–Saturday 11:30–2 and 3:30–9, Sunday 1–9. Serving home-style dinners for over 40 years. They are noted for their Friday fish fry.

Orchard Inn (716-825-9730), 259 Orchard Park Road, West Seneca. Open Sunday–Thursday 11–11, Friday and Saturday 11–midnight. This family restaurant has been open for 35 years. The Friday fish fry is popular.

Tony Roma's (716-675-4351), 1537 Union Road, West Seneca. Open Monday–Friday 11–10, Saturday 4–10, Sunday 2–10. This quaint, comfortable restaurant is noted for its ribs. Other menu selections include steak, chicken, pasta, and seafood.

EATING OUT ✍ ⅗ ❀ **Daisies Café** (716-824-2886), Corner South Park at Ridge, Lackawanna. Open Monday–Friday 6:30 AM–4 PM, Saturday and Sunday 6:30 AM–2 PM. Cute is the word that comes to mind when you enter Daisies. This small corner café is decorated with blue-and-white gingham tablecloths—with daisies on them, of course. There's even a white picket fence along the wall. Start your day with omelets, pancakes, and other breakfast favorites, including a Mickey Mouse pancake. Lunch selections include burgers, club sandwiches, hot sandwiches, and even some ethnic favorites like Greek spaghetti and homemade pierogi.

The Ebenezer Onion (716-674-0114), 4348 Seneca Street, West Seneca. Open Monday–Thursday 11:30–10, Friday and Saturday 11:30–11, Sunday 4–9. Start your dining experience with their signature dish, an Ebenezer onion, a homemade battered and fried onion blossom served with a spicy sauce. Other selections include Angus beef, pasta, and ribs.

✍ **Great Lakes Station** (716-675-5001), 1729 Union Road, West

Seneca. Open seasonally April–September Monday–Saturday 11–11, Sunday 12–11. This is *the* place to come for ice cream in West Seneca. Housed in a bright-red train caboose, this stand serves up all sorts of ice cream treats, from cones to malts to shakes and sundaes. Choose from hard ice cream or soft custard along with fruit slush and lemon ice.

Schwabl's Restaurant (716-674-9821), 789 Center Road, West Seneca. Open Monday–Saturday 11–10:30, Sunday 1–8:30. This restaurant has been in business since 1837 and at its present location since 1942. It's best known for its beef on weck sandwiches, but other menu selections include low-priced beef and seafood dishes along with a daily fish fry.

❦ ✆ **Steve's Ox and Pig Roast** (716-824-8601), 951 Ridge Road, Lackawanna. Open Monday–Saturday 11–9. This place may not be fancy, but it has been voted to have one of the best beef on weck sandwiches in the Buffalo area. They are equally well-known for their roast pork, lamb, and turkey sandwiches.

✆ ♿ **Victoria Square** (716-825-6627), 717 Ridge Road, Lackawanna. Open daily 24 hours. This recently renovated family restaurant—tastefully decorated in shades of light green and salmon—features daily dinner specials, club sandwiches, soups, salads, and homemade chili.

✳ Selective Shopping

Major shopping areas include **Southgate Plaza** (716-674-5050; www.southgateplaza.com), Union Road, West Seneca. Open Monday–Saturday 10–9, Sunday 12–5. Shop at **The Bon Ton** as well as numerous smaller specialty stores.

SPECIAL SHOPS **Buffalo Candle and Craft** (716-675-7393), 1900 Ridge Road (Seneca Square Plaza), West Seneca. Open Monday–Saturday 10–9, Sunday 10–5. Billed as the "country store in the city," this shop features hundreds of Christmas ornaments, plus Boyd's Bears, Yankee Candles, linens, lace curtains, collectible dolls, and other gift items.

Ebenezer Mill (716-674-7100), 1012 Union Road (in Southgate Plaza) West Seneca. Open Monday–Saturday 10–9, Sunday 10–5. If you like handmade crafts and antiques, check this place out. The store's motto is: "It's like being at a giant craft show every day of the year"—which pretty much says it all. Choose from thousands of crafts and gift items, with a few antiques mixed in. They also have a café and bakery located in the front of the store for sandwiches, salads, baked goods, and more.

Woyshner's The Christmas Shoppe (716-821-0416), 880 Ridge Road, Lackawanna. Open Monday–Wednesday 10–6, Thursday–Friday 10–8, Saturday 10–5, Sunday 10–4. It's Christmas all year long at Woyshner's, the largest Christmas store in New York. Choose from a large selection of imported glass ornaments, Santas, snowmen, custom-made wreaths and centerpieces, Irish gift items, Dept. 56 Villages, and more.

✳ Special Events

Sunday before Labor Day: **Classic Car Show** (716-674-5050; www.southgateplaza.com), Southgate Plaza, West Seneca.

October: **Halloween Parade** (716-674-5050; www.southgateplaza.com), Southgate Plaza, West Seneca.

ORCHARD PARK

Orchard Park, founded by Quakers in the early 1800s, is a community of lovely homes and many small businesses. The town of Orchard Park is about 40 square miles of rolling hills and wooded areas. The town's center is the village of Orchard Park, located at the "Four Corners" where NY 277 and U.S. 20A intersect. The light classical music you hear as you stroll the village streets is coming from the gas lamp–style streetlights. It is a town for all seasons. In spring and summer, enjoy concerts at the Quaker Arts Pavilion. Come fall, get a start on your holiday shopping at the Quaker Arts Festival or cheer on the Buffalo Bills at Ralph Wilson Stadium. In winter, head out to Chestnut Ridge Park for tobogganing, skiing, and sledding.

AREA CODE The area code is 716.

GUIDANCE Orchard Park Chamber of Commerce (716-662-3366; www.orchardparkchamber.com), 4211 North Buffalo Road (Barrington Professional Center) Orchard Park. Open Monday–Friday 9–4.

GETTING THERE *By bus:* NFTA #72, an express route, travels between downtown Buffalo and Orchard Park.

By car: U.S. 219, Orchard Park exit (U.S. 20A).

MEDICAL EMERGENCY 911

Mercy Ambulatory Care Center (716-662-0500), 3669 Southwestern Boulevard, Orchard Park.

✹ To See

MUSEUMS AND HISTORIC HOMES Orchard Park Historical Society (716-667-2301), 4287 South Buffalo Street Orchard Park. Open first and third Saturday of month and by appointment. This circa 1870 brick Italianate architecture mansion was the home of Dr. Willard Jolls, a beloved country doctor who served Orchard Park and the surrounding communities. It currently houses the collections of the Orchard Park Historical Society.

🚲 **Pedaling History Bicycle Museum** (716-662-3853; www.pedalinghistory.com), 3943 North Buffalo Road, Orchard Park. Open January 15–March 31: Monday, Friday, and Saturday 11–5, Sunday 1:30–5; April 1–January 14: Monday–Saturday 11–5, Sunday 1:30–5. Admission: $6 adults, $3.75 children. This is the largest bicycle museum in the world, with more than 300 rare and one-of-a-kind bicycles displayed. Push-button speakers located throughout the museum explain the exhibits, which depict over 180 years of bicycling history. Children of all ages will enjoy mounting the high-wheeled "ordinary" bicycle, popular in the 1870s. Since there are no other hands-on exhibits, this museum is best suited for children third grade and up. The museum offers educational programs throughout the year, mainly geared to adults and older kids.

HISTORIC SITES Quaker Meeting House (716-662-5749), 6924 East Quaker Street, Orchard Park. The Quaker Meeting House, constructed in 1820, is still a place of worship for the Quakers (Sunday service 11 AM). When it was built, a partition in the center separated the men from the women. The original hand-built wooden benches are still used today.

✳ To Do

FAMILY FUN See *Green Space—Chestnut Ridge Park*.

GOLF Bob-o-Link Golf Course (716-662-4311) 4085 Transit Road (U.S. 20A), Orchard Park. Open April–October. Driving range and 18-hole, par-3 golf course. Course is lit at night.

✳ Green Space

PARKS ✐ **Chestnut Ridge Park**, (716-662-3290), 6121 Chestnut Ridge Road, Orchard Park. Open 7 AM–dark, 7 AM–9 PM during winter sports season. Chestnut Ridge, the largest park in Erie County, is popular year-round for a variety of activities. The park, located south of the city, is one of the four original county parks. Almost every outdoor winter sport you can think of is available, including four toboggan runs. Lit slopes for towrope skiing are open from 10 AM to 9 PM; there are hills for every age and ability of skier. Other activities include cross-country skiing, sledding, saucering, snowmobiling, and ice skating. All activities are weather dependent. In the warmer months Chestnut Ridge is a haven for picnickers, runners, and tennis players.

EVERYONE ENJOYS A RIDE ON THIS HIGH-WHEELED 1870S BIKE AT THE PEDALING HISTORY BICYCLE MUSEUM.
Christine A. Smyczynski

Yates Park (716-662-6450), South Buffalo Street, Orchard Park. This 51-acre town park located along Green Lake is technically for Orchard Park residents only. It includes picnic areas, boating access, swings, and hiking trails. An outdoor skateboard park is open spring, summer, and fall. In winter it becomes an ice skating rink.

PONDS AND LAKES Green Lake See **Yates Park**

WALKING AND HIKING TRAILS Village Walk. A walking guide, with descriptions of the historic houses along East Quaker Street and South Buffalo Street, is available from the chamber of commerce.

✳ Where to Eat

DINING OUT David's Grill (716-662-4247), 4247 North Buffalo Road, Orchard Park. Open Sunday–Thursday 5–10, Friday and Saturday 5–11. This newly opened upscale restaurant features dishes like lobster pasta, cowboy steak (a rib eye topped with onion rings), and Atlantic salmon with citrus sauce. They also have an array of decadent desserts.

Jemiolo's South (716-662-3644), 4190 N. Buffalo Road, Orchard Park. Open Monday–Thursday 11–10, Friday 11–midnight, Saturday 4–midnight. This restaurant features a large selection of entrées, including New York strip steak, stuffed boneless chicken, beer battered scallops, and spaghetti and meatballs.

EATING OUT Cappelli's (716-662-2290), 3643 N. Buffalo Road, Orchard Park. Open Monday–Thursday 10:30–11, Friday and Saturday 10:30–midnight, Sunday 2–11. Since 1986 Gerard and Jodie Cappelli have been serving up pizza, subs, wings, and pasta to Orchard Park residents.

Danny's South Restaurant (716-649-1194), 4300 Abbott Road, Orchard Park. Open Monday–Thursday 11–11, Friday and Saturday 11–midnight, Sunday 10–8. A casual Irish-themed restaurant located near the stadium, serving a variety of food such as chicken, steaks, fresh seafood, and salads.

The Dove (716-823-6680), 3002 Abbott Road, Orchard Park. Open for lunch Monday–Friday 11:30–2, dinner Monday–Thursday 5–9, Friday and Saturday 5–10. This restaurant specializes in upscale Italian food, with special touches like mixing your martini tableside, and giving you a bag of fresh rolls to take home. Menu selections include veal piccata and eggplant rolletini.

◢ ♿ ☙ **Duff's** (716-674-7212), 3090 Orchard Park Road, Orchard Park. Open Monday–Thursday 11–11, Friday and Saturday 11–midnight, Sunday 11–10. Chicken wings are the specialty of the house at this popular Southtowns branch of the original Duff's in Amherst.

Eckl's Restaurant (716-662-2262), South 4936 Ellicott Road, Orchard Park. Opens daily at 4:30. Since the 1930s Eckl's has been noted for its beef on weck sandwiches—thinly sliced slow-roasted beef on a salt and caraway seed–topped roll—cooking over 800 pounds of beef each week. Try some of their authentic German potato salad along with your sandwich. Other menu selections include steaks, prime rib, and pork chops.

Eddie's Orchard Park Brewery & Grille (716-667-2314), 4244 N. Buffalo Road., Orchard Park. Open for dinner daily 4–10, limited menu on Sunday. Orchard Park's only brew pub, complete with a brewery right inside the restaurant. Eat indoors or on their sidewalk patio. Menu selections include "spag-eddie," prime rib, breaded sea scallops, and the house specialty chicken "eddie's"

Francine's Village Restaurant (716-667-9709), 4236 North Buffalo Road, Orchard Park. Open for breakfast and lunch Tuesday–Friday 7–2, Saturday 8–2, Sunday 8–1. A quaint family restaurant located right in the village of Orchard Park.

◢ **Snowflake Creamery** (716-667-2802), 6185 West Quaker Street, Orchard Park. Open April–Thanksgiving, Sunday–Thursday 12–9, Friday and Saturday 12–10. This family-owned and operated business specializes in homemade hard ice cream, which is made on site. Besides the standard flavors like vanilla and chocolate, you can also get some unique seasonal flavors, such as pumpkin pie

Two Sister's Café (716-667-6887), 4211 N. Buffalo Road (Barrington Professional Center), Orchard Park. Open Sunday 8 AM–2 PM (breakfast only) Tuesday–Wednesday 8–2, Thursday–Saturday 8–8. Kate Klinck's inviting village restaurant specializes in panini sandwiches: flat Italian bread filled with meat and veggies, then grilled and served warm. Other selections include salads, quiche, and grilled sandwiches. The café is also open for breakfast. Dine in the attractive dining room, complete with floral tablecloths, or outside on the covered deck.

✳ Entertainment

MUSIC Orchard Park Symphony Orchestra (716-643-4000), September–March. Performances take place in the Orchard Park Middle School auditorium.

PROFESSIONAL SPORTS Buffalo Bills Football (716-648-1800 or tickets 877-BB-TICKS; www.buffalo bills.com), Ralph Wilson Stadium, One Bills Drive, Orchard Park. Ralph Wilson Stadium is one of the NFL's premier stadiums. It features one of the largest Jumbotrons in the United States. Built in 1973, the facility, which can hold over 80,000 spectators, was originally named Rich stadium after a prominent western New York family. The name was later changed to Ralph Wilson Stadium to honor the current owner of the Buffalo Bills.

✳ Selective Shopping

ANTIQUES Orchard Park Antique Mall (716-677-9566; www.op antiquesmall.com), 3025 Orchard Park Road, Orchard Park. Open Monday–Thursday 10–9, Friday and Saturday 9–9, Sunday 10–5 Hundreds of antique dealers and collectors have their wares neatly displayed in row upon row of glass enclosed cabinets at this 31,000 square foot antique mall. Furniture and larger items can be found lining the perimeter of the store. Every type of antique and collectible imaginable can be found including jewelry, dolls, toys, glassware, dishes, linens, and much more.

Vintage House (716-667-3800), 4184 North Buffalo Road, Orchard Park Gifts, antiques, lamps, furniture, dishes, and home decor.

FARM MARKETS Orchard Park Farmers Market (716-662-3605), Orchard Park Railroad Depot. Open Saturday 8–1 May–October.

Special Shops **The Animal Kingdom** (716-675-1986), 2799 Southwestern Boulevard, Orchard Park. Open Monday–Thursday 10–7, Friday and Saturday 10–5; also Sunday 10–2 in December. Unique gifts for pets and pet lovers. For four-legged friends choose from basic pet supplies plus gourmet treats, unique toys, leashes, collars, beds, bowls, and mats. Two-legged animal fanciers can choose from novelty gifts, games, jewelry, cards, clothing, and much more. This is an animal-friendly shop, so feel free to bring Fido along.

Days Gone By (716-662-2570), 4164 North Buffalo Road, Orchard Park. Open Monday, Tuesday Thursday, Friday, and Saturday 10–5. A country gift shop.

Quaker Country Homes (716-667-1541), 4203 North Buffalo Road, Orchard Park. Open Monday, Tuesday, Thursday 10–6, Friday and Saturday 10–5. This century-old building, originally ordered from the Sears, Roebuck catalog, houses a showroom featuring fine Early American and Shaker furniture plus gifts and decorating accessories.

Village Cross Stitch Shoppe and Village Framer (716-662-6646), 6624 East Quaker Road, Orchard Park. Open Monday–Friday 10–5, Saturday 10–4. This shop, which was featured in *Stitchery* magazine several years ago, has over 10,000 cross-stitch patterns and books, plus yarns, frames, and other needlework accessories. The building was once the switchboard for the town of Orchard Park, then later the town library.

✳ Special Events

January: **Winter Carnival** (716-662-3366; www.orchardparkchamber.com), Chestnut Ridge Park, 6121 Chestnut Ridge Road, Orchard Park.

March: **Orchard Park Expo and Trade Show** (716-662-3366; www.orchardparkchamber.com), Orchard Park High School, 4040 Baker Road, Orchard Park. This event highlights businesses and community organizations in the town.

July: **Quaker Days** (716-662-3366; www.orchardparkchamber.com), Orchard Park. This village-wide event includes sidewalk sales and a car show.

September: **Quaker Arts Festival** (716-667-ARTS), Orchard Park. Village-wide indoor and outdoor arts and crafts festival, featuring over 400 artists and craftsmen.

December: **Santa's Park** (716-662-3366; www.orchardparkchamber.com), Chestnut Ridge Park, 6121 Chestnut Ridge Road, Orchard Park. Weekends in November and December. Take a hayride to see Santa at the North Pole.

LAKE ERIE TOWNS — Hamburg, Blasdell, Eden, Angola, and Derby

Lake Erie and Erie County were named after the Erie Indians, who made their home in this area. The Hamburg Fairgrounds, site of the Erie County Fair, the largest county fair in the United States, was once the location of a Native American village. Eighteen Mile Creek, which runs through the town of Hamburg, is internationally famous for Devonian fossils found along its banks.

Hamburg is a 45-square-mile town incorporated in 1812. In those early days a large number of wolves and panthers roamed the dense forests in the area. Prior to 1850 Hamburg included the towns of Orchard Park and West Seneca. A number of the earliest settlers to the town came from New England around 1803, followed in the 1830s by Germans, many of whom established farms.

The nearby town of Eden is best known for the Original American Kazoo Company. Established in 1916, the company is the only metal kazoo factory in the world. This working museum is still making kazoos using the same process and equipment as when the factory first opened.

The villages of Angola and Blasdell, located along Lake Erie, have several popular beaches. Farther south on Lake Erie's shores is Derby, home to the Frank Lloyd Wright–designed mansion Graycliff, which is open for tours.

AREA CODE The area code is 716.

GUIDANCE Hamburg Chamber of Commerce (716-649-7917; www.hamburg-chamber.org), 8 South Buffalo Street, Hamburg. Open Monday–Friday 9–5.

GETTING THERE *By bus:* NFTA bus #30 travels between downtown Buffalo and Hamburg.
By car: The NYS Thruway (I-90) exit 57A will bring you into the area, as will US 62.

MEDICAL EMERGENCY Dial 911

✳ To See

ART MUSEUMS Centennial Art Center of Hamburg (716-649-3592) 3185 Amsdell Road, Hamburg. Call for current hours and classes. A nonprofit community art center that offers classes, workshops, lectures, and demonstrations.

MUSEUMS AND HISTORIC HOMES Boies Lord House–Hamburg Historical Society (716-649-9232 or 716-649-6748), 5853 South Park Avenue, Hamburg. Open Saturday and Sunday 1–4 or by appointment. This 1850 Greek Revival home has been restored and furnished in 1860s period furnishings and now serves as the Hamburg Historical Society.

Dunn House (716-648-6460), 6902 Gowanda State Road, Hamburg. Open Sunday 1–4. An estate originally built as a farmhouse in 1860, it is owned and operated by the Hamburg Historical Society.

Graycliff (585-614-6195; www.graycliff.bfn.org), 6472 Old Lake Shore Road, Derby. Tours of the house and grounds are offered by reservation only Saturday 11–3, Sunday 1–4, and Wednesday at 11; tours open to children 10 and older. Admission: $10. Built in 1927, this magnificent lakeside home, set on a 70-foot cliff overlooking Lake Erie, was the summer home of Darwin D. Martin, an executive at the Larkin Soap Company in Buffalo. Mr. Martin commissioned renowned architect Frank Lloyd Wright, who also designed Martin's house on Jewett Parkway in Buffalo, to design his summer retreat. Graycliff is referred to as a see-through house: It uses the first-story windows to frame the scenery on the Lake Erie side, and when standing on the front lawn of the house, one can look straight through to see the lake. Wright incorporated shapes he found in the surrounding landscape into his design. For example, diamond shapes found in the limestone along the lakeshore is a motif repeated inside the home.

✐ ⚘ Original American Kazoo Company (716-992-3960; www.kazooco.com), 8703 South Main Street, Eden. Open Tuesday–Saturday 10–5, Sunday 12–5. The Kazoo Capital of the World, Eden is home to the only metal kazoo factory in the world. Kazoos of all shapes and sizes are on permanent display at the museum, where you can learn the history of the kazoo and view kazoos being made on the original 1907 equipment. You can even make your own kazoo using a purchased form and a special press machine. The tour is self-guided, but staff members are happy to answer your questions. Guided tours can be arranged for groups of 15 or more. The museum has a large gift shop with a variety of items.

✳ To Do

GOLF **Eden Valley Golf Course** (716-337-2190), 10401 Sisson Highway (NY 75), Eden. Open April–November An 18-hole, par-73 public course with restaurant and full bar.

Grandview Golf Course (716-549-4930), 444 Central Avenue, Angola. Open mid-February–November. A public 9-hole, par-36 course.

South Shore Country Club (716-649-6674), 5076 Southwestern Boulevard, Hamburg. A semiprivate 18-hole, par-71 course that has a restaurant, snack bar, full bar, and driving range.

Town of Hamburg Golf Course (716-648-4410; www.townofhamburgny .com), 6374 Boston State Road, Hamburg. Open April–November. A public 18-hole, par-72 course.

HORSE RACING ↑ **Fairgrounds Gaming & Raceway** (716-649-1280; www.fairgroundsgamingandraceway.com, www.the-fairgrounds.com), 5600 McKinley Parkway, Hamburg. Open seven days 10 AM–2 AM, live harness racing Wednesday, Friday, and Saturday at 7:35 PM. The raceway's half-mile track was first used in 1868 during the county fair. Pari-mutuel harness racing began here in the 1940s. The grandstand and clubhouse, owned and operated by the Erie County Agricultural Society, can hold up to 10,000 racing fans. The clubhouse also features a new 27,000-square-foot gaming facility that features close to 1,000 video lottery terminals.

RETREAT HOUSE **St. Columban Center** (716-947-4708; www.st columbancenter.org) 6892 Lakeshore Road, Derby. The St. Columban Center is a facility that offers all people the opportunity to renew themselves, to discover a closer relationship with God, and to discover ways to live in harmony. Founded by lay Catholics

GRAYCLIFF WAS BUILT BY FRANK LLOYD WRIGHT AS THE LAKESHORE SUMMER HOME FOR DARWIN D. MARTIN, WHO ALSO COMMISSIONED WRIGHT TO BUILD HIS BUFFALO HOUSE.
Courtesy Buffalo–Niagara Convention & Visitors Bureau and Angel Art Ltd.

with a mission to help people meet the present and future needs of the Church,
the center offers overnight retreats and day sessions throughout the year for
men, women, priests, nuns, families, and engaged couples. The St. Columban
Center, located along the shores of Lake Erie offers a peaceful, wooded setting
where one can come to reflect on their life and find spiritual direction.

✳ Green Space

BEACHES **Angola on the Lake,** 8934 Lake Shore Road, Angola. This long,
sandy beach boasts two popular beach bars, Mickey Rats Beach Club and Captain Kidds.

Bennett Beach, Bennett Road, off NY 5, Derby. This sand dune–lined beach is
popular with swimmers, fishermen, and birdwatchers.

Wendt Beach (716-947-5660), 7676 Old Lake Shore Road, Derby. Park open
year-round; beach open Memorial Day–Labor Day 11–dusk. Free admission.
This Erie County beach is located on Lake Erie at the mouth of Big Sister
Creek. There is a bathhouse and snack bar near the beach. The 178-acre park,
which was the site of the old Wendt Mansion, also has picnic areas, bike and
nature trails, and sports fields. It is also a popular spot to view waterfowl and to
fish.

Woodlawn Beach State Park (716-826-1930), S-3585 Lake Shore Road, Blasdell. Open dawn to dusk year-round. Beach open Memorial Day–Labor Day.
Admission: $7 parking fee, rest of year free admission. Summer swimming:
weekends only Memorial Day–July 3, daily July 4–Labor Day. This park is
known for its mile-long natural sand beach and its panoramic view of Lake Erie.
During the summer months visitors can swim, windsurf, play volleyball, and sun-
bathe. It is also a good place to bird-watch, especially during the migration seasons. The park also has a playground, hiking trails, visitors center, and nature
exhibits.

NATURE PRESERVES ✒ **Penn Dixie Paleontological and Outdoor Education Center** (716-627-4560; www.penndixie.org), North Street, Hamburg. Open
May–October, Saturday 9 AM–noon; also open Monday–Friday 9–3 during
July–August and Easter school break. Admission: $5 adults, $4 children. Once a
quarry, this 32-acre regional fossil site is owned and operated by the Hamburg
Natural History Society, founded in 1993 to protect and promote education
about our natural resources. The site contains an abundance of 380-million-year-
old fossils from the Devonian era. The public can visit the site to study and collect fossils and learn about local geology. Volunteers will help visitors collect and
identify the fossils they find. Each month, special educational programs are held,
and weekday tours are available for school groups. Weekend tours can be scheduled for scouts, families, and other interested parties.

PARKS **Woodlawn Beach State Park** (716-826-1930), S-3585 Lake Shore
Road, Blasdell. See *Beaches*

✳ Lodging

MOTELS AND HOTELS McKinley Park Inn Hotel (716-648-5700), 3950 McKinley Parkway, Blasdel. This three-diamond hotel features amenities that include a fitness room, Jacuzzi suites, and a free continental breakfast. $74–$159.

In addition, several major chain motels are just off I-90 exits 56 and 57.

BED & BREAKFASTS Quinn's West End Inn (716-649-2446), 340 Union Street, Hamburg. Innkeeper Desmond Quinn offers nine cozy guest rooms with private baths in this circa 1868 former railroad hotel. While they cater mainly to large groups who may want to rent all the rooms for reunions, etc., they also rent individual rooms. A turn-of-the-20th-century dining room is open to the public for lunch and dinner, along with an Irish pub–theme lounge and banquet facilities. (See *Where to Eat*.) $55+.

✳ Where to Eat

DINING OUT Daniel's Restaurant (716-648-6554), 174 Buffalo Street Hamburg. Open Tuesday–Friday 5–9, Saturday 5–9:30 This intimate restaurant, located in a former residence, features elegant food made from scratch by chef Daniel Johengen, using only fresh ingredients. Specialties include horseradish-crusted salmon filet with garlic mashed potatoes and leek cream, duck breast with roast-pear puree and raspberry sauce, and rack of lamb with sea scallops. Daily specials feature seasonal ingredients and local produce.

Dock at The Bay (716-823-8247; www.dockatthebay.com), 3800 Hoover Road, Blasdell. Open Sunday–Thursday 11:30–10, Friday and Saturday 11:30–11. This popular waterfront restaurant overlooks Lake Erie, with a menu featuring fresh seafood, prime rib, king crab legs, and lobster tails. The sunsets from the deck are fabulous. It is a popular nightspot during the summer, with DJs and live music featured on the outdoor patio overlooking the lake.

&. **Ilio DiPaolo's** (716-825-3675; www.iliodipaolos.com), 3785 South Park Avenue, Blasdell. Open for lunch Monday–Friday 11:30–3, dinner Monday–Friday 3–10, Saturday 2–12, Sunday 1–10. Since 1965 this upscale yet casual restaurant has specialized in Italian-American cuisine, plus steaks, chops, and seafood. The walls are adorned with photos and other memorabilia documenting the pro-wrestling career of restaurant founder, the late Ilio DiPaolo. Popular menu selections include veal parmigiana, chicken cacciatore, and linguini with clam sauce.

&. **Romanello's South** (716-649-0450), 5793 South Park Avenue, Hamburg. Open Monday–Thursday 4–10. Friday and Saturday 4–11, Sunday 3–9. This sophisticated restaurant— owned and operated by the Romanello family, who also own the legendary Roseland Restaurant on Buffalo's west side and the Old Orchard in East Aurora—has been a popular fine-dining destination for over 25 years. Try their prime rib or dinner for two specials. Banquet facilities are available.

&. **Root Five** (716-627-5551; www.rootfive.com), 4914 Lakeshore Road, Hamburg. Open daily 11:30–10. This waterfront contemporary restaurant offers an extensive menu that includes

American favorites like chicken marsala, surf and turf, and pork tenderloin plus a great view of Lake Erie and the Buffalo skyline. Signature desserts include chocolate toffee mouse with Kahlúa and apple Bavarian cheesecake.

EATING OUT ✍ ♿ 🌸 **The Block Hotel** (716-549-5280) 9050, Erie Road, Angola. Open Monday–Thursday 4–10, Friday 11–10, Saturday 4–9. This historic hotel was built in 1905 as a way station for people traveling by horse and buggy between Buffalo and Erie, Pennsylvania. It was dubbed the "block" hotel after a new building block technique that produced rectangular and square blocks from stone and concrete. It is rumored that Ted E. Behr, the 450-pound stuffed black bear in the foyer, was shot by President Woodrow Wilson in 1916 when he was in Angola on a hunting expedition. Today the hotel still offers good food (but, alas, no rooms) to travelers. Lunches include hot roast beef and hot roast turkey sandwiches plus deli sandwiches, pasta dishes, burgers, and salads. For dinner choose from chicken, seafood and steaks, along with chicken wings, subs, pizza, and more. A children's menu is available.

♿ **Buffalo Street Grille** (716-646-9080), 61 Buffalo Street, Hamburg. Open Monday 4–midnight, Tuesday–Saturday 11:30–midnight, Sunday 11:30–10. The corner dining room overlooking Buffalo and Union Streets features Tiffany-style lighting. Daily specials include selections like open-faced BBQ sandwiches and homemade roasted red pepper bisque.

✍ 🌸 ♿ **Comfort Zone Café** (716-648-5779; www.comfortzonecafé .com), 17 Main Street, Hamburg.

Open Monday–Thursday 8–11, Friday and Saturday 8–midnight, Sunday 9–10. This bright, sunny restaurant with glass-topped tables and a view of Main Street, features specialty coffees, teas, and desserts. Lunch and dinner specials—which include homemade soup, sandwiches, and entrées like spaghetti and salmon—are written on the board daily. It's family friendly, too, with crayons and coloring books available. Teapots, tea and coffee cups, candles, and even coffee beans can be found in a small gift area.

♿ **Common Ground Café & Bakery** (716-649-4967), 327 Buffalo Street, Hamburg. Open Monday–Thursday 11–9, Friday 11–3. This café and bakery is run as a cottage industry by a community of people—one of several throughout the world—known as the Twelve Tribes, who live, work and worship together. The café, which has the feel of being inside a tree house, is noted for fresh, organic foods made with no preservatives, including soups, salads, wraps, whole-wheat pizza, and sandwiches as well as daily dinner specials. Be sure to try a glass of their house iced tea, a blend of mint, honey, and lemon, or a hot cup of their signature blend Common Ground tea. They also sell bread, cookies, and muffins baked with organic ingredients plus other organically made items, like soap, jams, and candles.

♿ **Coyote Café** (716-649-1837), 36 Main Street, Hamburg. Open Monday–Thursday 11–9, Friday and Saturday 11–10. Enjoy authentic Mexican cuisine in a large dining room with southwestern decor. Specialties include tequila-lime shrimp and pork tenderloin with raspberry glaze.

American menu also available. Carlo's Cantina, which specializes in margaritas, has a happy hour Monday–Thursday evenings.

Hoak's (716-627-7988 or 716-627-4570), S-4100 Lakeshore Road, Hamburg. Open daily 11–11. A landmark Hamburg restaurant since 1949, this casual lakeside eatery, which has a great view of the Buffalo skyline, specializes in fresh seafood seven days a week. They also have a great beef on weck sandwich.

🦞 ⚅ **Linda's Promenade Family Restaurant** (716-646-5527) 32 Main Street, Hamburg. Open Monday–Thursday 7:30–3, Friday 7:30–8, Saturday and Sunday 7:30–2. Promenade down a long hallway from the street to this small restaurant. It's well worth the walk. Owner Linda Sibiga offers home-cooked, healthy meals—breakfast, lunch, and Friday dinner. Everything is made fresh; soups are made from scratch, meats are freshly roasted, and breads and biscuits are homemade. Since they have their own farm, in-season, fresh-from-the field veggies are offered during the summer. Linda freezes vegetables to be used during the winter months. According to Linda, these are the kind of meals you'd cook for yourself if you had the time.

⚅ **Quinn's West End Inn** (716-649-2446; E-mail: westend340@aol.com), 340 Union Street, Hamburg. Open Monday–Thursday 11:30–9, Friday and Saturday 11:30–10, Sunday 12–8. Enjoy delicious entrées while dining in a turn-of-the-20th-century dining room complete with a pulley fan system, pressed tin ceilings, and copper-plated walls. Lighter fare includes salads, sandwiches, and traditional pub grub like chicken wings and fingers.

Heartier meals include home cooked favorites like roast pork, pot roast country meat loaf, and roast turkey, all served with homemade mashed potatoes, homemade gravy and fresh vegetables. Other menu selections include chicken, beef, and seafood entrées, along with a kids menu.

⚅ 🦞 ✒ **Tina's Italian Kitchen** (716-648-0100), 22 Main Street, Hamburg Open Sunday 4–10, Monday–Thursday 11–10, Friday and Saturday 11–11; dine in or take out. Choose from sensational salads, home-baked Italian dinners, veal, and chicken specialties. You can also get pizza, wings or fingers, subs or chicken sandwiches, or Tina's specialties that include eppie rolls, calzones, and stromboli. Their homemade sausage is also very popular. The restaurant is located in the ornate former Hamburg Grange building.

✒ ⚅ 🦞 **Tubby's Take Out** (716-549-1666), NY 5, Angola. Open seasonally May–August, 6 AM–midnight. A small hot dog and ice cream stand serving burgers, dogs, fries, and a variety of ice cream treats. A car cruise night is held Fridays at 6 PM. The adjacent convenience store and gas station, owned by the same family, is open daily 11–11.

✒ 🦞 **Water Valley Inn** (716-649-9691), 6656 Gowanda State Road, Hamburg. Open Tuesday–Friday 11–9, Saturday 12–9, Sunday 12–8. This historic inn dates back to the 1800s, when it served as a tavern and stagecoach stop. The walls of the inn are adorned with historic area photos. It even boasts a working vintage 1930s bell system for calling a waitress to the table. While the ambiance is good, the food is even better. Menu selections include substantial entrées like steak, chops, seafood, and chicken to lighter fare, including sandwiches, burgers, and homemade soup. A kids' menu is available. They do not accept credit cards.

✳ Entertainment

NIGHTLIFE **Captain Kidds & Mickey Rats** (716-549-9828; www.mickey rats.com), Angola-on-the-Lake (I-90 exit 57A to Lake Shore Road). A popular beach nightclub, featuring a spacious patio overlooking Lake Erie, live music, and outdoor dining.

See also **Dock at the Bay** in *Dining Out*.

✳ Selective Shopping

ANTIQUES **Antiques of Hamburg** (716-648-2341), 11 Buffalo Street, Hamburg. Open Monday–Saturday 10–5. They carry a general line of antiques, including smalls, glassware, furniture, and books

FARM MARKETS **Zittels Country Market** (716-649-3010), 4415 Southwestern Boulevard (US 20) Hamburg. Hours vary seasonally, closed January–March. The Zittel family has been making their living growing crops for four generations, since 1898. The season starts out with spring flowers and plants, all grown in Zittel's Eden Valley greenhouses. Fresh produce is offered throughout the summer and early fall, along with fall decorating items. In December choose from trees, wreaths, poinsettias, and more, including custom-made gift baskets.

SHOPPING MALLS ♿ **McKinley Mall** (716-824-0462), McKinley Parkway at Milestrip Road, Blasdell. Open Monday–Saturday 10–9, Sunday 11–6. One of western New York's best-kept

secrets. A lovely mall with over 100 shops and a large food court. Anchor stores include JC Penney, Sears, and Kaufmanns.

SPECIAL SHOPS **Elizabeth's Gourmet Coffee and Tea Shoppe** (716-648-2114; www.elizabethscoffee andtea.com), 6153 South Park Avenue, Hamburg. Open Tuesday–Friday 10–9, Monday and Saturday 10–6. One of the largest selections of coffees and teas in the area, plus teapots and teabag holders, syrups, jams, and candies. Gift baskets made to order. They also have a small café for tea and coffee by the cup.

Expressions Floral & Gift Shoppe (716-648-2110), 11 Buffalo Street, Hamburg. Open Monday–Thursday 8:30–6, Friday 8:30–8, Saturday 8:30–5, Sunday 10–2. This floral shop also carries a large selection of seasonal decorations and the wooden Hamburg Village Series, which features historic homes and buildings from the Hamburg area.

Holiday Baskets and Gifts (formerly the Fruity Stand; 716-627-3780), 484 Sunset Drive (off Camp Road), Hamburg. Open 12–6 daily; November–December open 10–7 daily. This shop specializes in handmade items, candles, gift baskets, fruit baskets, and even "hands and paws" items for your favorite pooch and feline. Owners Fred and Sandy Dinkel are friendly and very knowledgeable about the Hamburg area.

Irish Angels Gift Shop (716-649-5343), 3 Buffalo Street, Hamburg. Open Tuesday–Thursday 10–6, Friday 10–7, Saturday 10–5. Even the walls and light fixtures are wearing the green in this shop specializing in Irish imports and Irish gift items.

Let's Do Wine (716-646-9979), 67 Main Street, Hamburg. Open Monday–Friday 10–7, Saturday and Sunday 10–5 This shop specializes in wine accessories, gifts, and gadgets, including wine-making supplies.

& **Ravensong** (716-337-2836), 2132 Seneca Street (1 block from U.S. 62), Lawtons. Open Tuesday–Sunday 12–6. This shop specializes in Native American crafts plus greeting cards, T-shirts, and more, all with a Native American theme.

✳ Special Events

July: **Burgerfest** (contact Gary Allen 716-649-8250), along Main Street, Hamburg. Celebrate the birth of the hamburger at this annual festival, which takes place the third Saturday of July. Although it's been hotly debated among some burger aficionados whether or not the first burger was actually created back in 1885 in this namesake town, it's a good excuse to party and chow down. Events include food vendors, a burger eating contest, live entertainment, children's activities, a craft show, and a classic car show.

August: **Eden Corn Fest** (716-992-9141), American Legion Post 880, Legion Drive (off U.S. 62), Eden. Over 500,000 ears of corn are consumed at this four-day festival that pays homage to one of the area's favorite summer delicacies. Activities include rides, entertainment, a parade and more. **Erie County Fair** (www.americas-fair.com), Hamburg. The largest county fair in the United States, the Erie County Fair celebrates the agricultural and historic legacy of Erie County. Enjoy amusement rides on the "mile-long midway," browse though barn upon barn of animal exhibits, catch some top-name musical entertainment, view historical displays, buy the latest items for your home, and, of course, consume mass quantities of delicious, and unfortunately fattening, fair food.

ERIE COUNTY'S SKI COUNTRY—Boston, Chaffee, Holland, Colden, Glenwood, and West Falls

This area well south of Buffalo is an area of natural beauty, a perfect destination when taking a drive "to the country." Holland, an area of rolling farmland along Cazenovia Creek, was settled in 1772, and many of the town's residents are descendants of those early settlers. Incorporated in 1818 when it separated from the town of Willink (today known as Aurora), Holland prospered through the middle of the 1800s, especially with the building of a plank road to Buffalo that allowed farm goods to be taken to market. After the Civil War, cheese making was one of the main industries in the area. Holland is probably best known in western New York for the annual tulip festival, heralding the coming of spring. This three-day event includes a parade, rides, and crafts, among other activities.

Formed from a portion of the town of Holland in 1827, Colden was named after Cadwallader Colden, a Scottish American who served as lieutenant governor of New York in the 1760s. The first pioneer to settle in Colden was Richard Buffum, who came from Rhode Island. His sawmill and the surrounding area was referred to as "Buffum's Mills." In the early days the village had numerous taverns as well as cheese box and barrel factories, due to the large number of dairy farms. Other early industries included charcoal works and asheries, which used the area's abundant virgin forest to make products that could be sold to distillers and soap manufacturers.

Boston, Chaffee, Glenwood, and West Falls offer travelers places to dine, shop, and enjoy various recreational activities.

AREA CODE The area code is 716.

GUIDANCE **Colden Town Hall** (716-941-5012), NY 240, Colden. Open Monday–Friday 9–5.

Town of Holland (716-537-9443), 47 Pearl Street, Holland. Open Monday–Friday 9–5 (Wednesday 4–9).

GETTING THERE *By bus:* The NFTA bus #74, an express route, travels between downtown Buffalo and Boston.

By car: These towns can be reached via US 219 or NY 240.

MEDICAL EMERGENCY Dial 911

Bertrand Chaffee Hospital (716-592-2871; www.chaffeehomeandhospital .com), 224 East Main Street, Springville.

✳ To See

MUSEUMS AND HISTORIC HOMES **Buffum Homestead** (716-992-4666), 8334 Boston-Colden Road (near NY 240), Colden. Open by appointment or chance. This home once owned by the Buffum family now houses the Colden Historical Society.

Holland Old Fire Hall (716-537-2591), Main Street, Holland. Open by appointment. Free admission. This former fire hall houses the Holland Historical Society.

✳ To Do

AUTO RACING **Holland International Speedway** (716-537-2272; www .hollandspeedway.com), 2 N. Main Street, Holland. Open Saturday nights April–September. One of the finest NASCAR sanctioned ⅜-mile short track racing facilities in the United States.

GOLF **Concord Crest Golf Course** (716-592-7636; www.concordcrest.com), 9255 Genesee Road, East Concord. An 18-hole, par-72 public golf course.

Holland Hills (716-537-2345), 10438 Holland Glenwood Road, Glenwood. An 18-hole, par-71 semiprivate course open to the public. It has a restaurant, bar, and pro shop.

Rolling Hills (716-496-5016), 10739 Olean Road (NY 16), Chaffee. A 9-hole, par-3 course with snack bar.

SKIING

Downhill Skiing

Kissing Bridge (716-592-4963; www.kissing-bridge.com or www.kbski.com), 10296 State Road (NY 240) Glenwood. This resort, which is within a one-hour drive from metro Buffalo, is located in the Colden "snowbelt."

Lifts: 10 (one mighty mite, one J-bar, two T-bars, four double chair, two quad chair).

Trails: 38 (35 percent beginner, 35 percent intermediate, 20 percent difficult, 10 percent expert).

Vertical Drop: 550 feet.

Snowmaking: 80 percent, with 182 inches of natural snowfall annually.

Facilities: Nighttime skiing and tubing, plus a terrain park.

Ski School: Ski rentals and lessons available.

For Children: Children's lessons and child care available.

Rates: $18–$40.

SNOW TUBING *❧* **Colden Tubing** (716-592-4228), adjacent to Kissing Bridge North, 10296 State Road, Glenwood. Open December–March, depending on conditions, Wednesday–Friday 5–9, Saturday and Christmas holidays 10–9, Sunday 10–6. Colden Tubing is western New York's largest downhill tubing park. Climb aboard a tube, get towed to the top, and then hold on for the slide of your life. It's fun for all ages, but participants must be at least seven years old, with only one person allowed per tube.

✳ Green Space

NATURE PRESERVES **Erie County Forest** (716-496-7410), Warner Gulf Road, East Concord. Open dawn to dusk, year-round. Free admission. Here is where Erie County's reforestation program began. There are two 1.75-mile yellow-blazed hiking trails. The easier trail, on the southern side of Genesee Road, has nature study stations along the trail, and in winter this path can be used for cross-country skiing and snowshoeing. For ambitious hikers, the more difficult trail covers rough terrain. There is also a Braille trail for the visually impaired. Wildlife in the area includes white-tailed deer, raccoon, fox, and mink. A working sawmill, which offers tours during special events, is located in the forest.

PARKS **Sprague Brook Park** (585-592-2804), 9674 Foote Road (NY 240), Glenwood. Open dusk to dawn. Activities include baseball, hiking, biking, fishing, camping (at 27 campsites), tennis, picnicking, and cross-country skiing and snowshoeing in winter.

❋ Lodging

BED & BREAKFASTS **Back of the Beyond** (716-652-0427), 7233 Lower East Hill Rd, Colden. Open year-round. Hosts Bill and Shash Georgi have created a country mini-estate that's especially convenient for skiers. The chalet includes three bedrooms, 1.5 baths, and a fully furnished kitchen. They also have a greenhouse and Herbtique gift shop (open by appointment), along with a swimming pond with three boats and 15 acres of wooded land to hike on. During the winter enjoy cross-country skiing on their trail. $51–$75.

Heath Hill Bed & Breakfast (716-941-6789), 8669 Heath Road, Colden. Open year-round. Mike and Lona But-ler have created a home away from home in the Colden hills. This lovely bed & breakfast inn, just minutes away from several ski resorts, offers one suite with a private entrance that's built for comfort. Amenities include an outdoor garden hot tub, queen-sized bed, fold-out sofa bed, and private bath. A continental breakfast is offered on weekdays, with a full breakfast served on weekends. $75–$90, $25 each extra person.

🐾 **Pipe Creek Farm Bed & Break-fast** (716-652-4868; www.bedand breakfast.com), 9303 Falls Road, West Falls. Open year-round. Kathy and Phil Crone offer four guest rooms in this vintage farmhouse, which is locat-ed on a 200-acre working equine farm. One room has a private bath, while the other three share a bath. A gourmet continental breakfast that includes homemade bread, eggs, and sausage is served each morning. The inn has an in-ground pool and is located about 6 miles from Kissing Bridge Ski Resort.

$50/room–$300/entire house.

OTHER LODGING **Colden Lakes Resort** (716-941-5530), 9504 Heath Road, Colden. Open May 1–end of October. This camping resort offers numerous leisure-time activities, including hiking trails, volleyball, horseshoes, four lakes, in-ground pool, grocery store, and snowmobile trails in winter. Camping facilities include two cabins and 100 campsites with water and electric. A full-service restaurant offers a wide variety of daily food and beverage specials. $25–$35/night. See also *Eating Out*.

❋ Where to Eat

DINING OUT **Boston Hotel** (716-941-5271), 9378 Boston State Road, Boston. Open daily 12–10. The origi-nal tavern, built in the late 1800s as a hotel and restaurant, burned and was rebuilt in 1921. While the tap room in front is popular as a local watering hole, the dining room in back serves up lunches and dinners. They are noted for their steaks and seafood, especially their Friday-night fish fry. The Boston Inn, across the street, is open Friday and Saturday evenings to handle the overflow dinner crowd.

Dog Bar (716-652-5550), NY 240, West Falls (about 6 miles south of Orchard Park). Open Wednesday–Saturday 5–10, Sunday 4–9.This circa 1845 restaurant features casual, fine fare in a unique dining room that's also a museum. The bar, dedicated to man's best friend, is best known for its lamb chops, garlic croutons, and porterhouse steak, plus chicken and seafood.

Colden Lakes Resort Restaurant (716-941-5530), 9504 Heath Road, Colden. Open year-round, hours vary according to season. This bar/restaurant offers casual dining at moderate prices. Enjoy everything from pizza and wings to pasta and prime rib. It is located at a camping resort. See *Other Lodging.*

& **Colden Mill Restaurant** (716-941-9357), 8348 Boston-Colden Road, Colden. Open Tuesday–Saturday 4:30–10, Sunday 3–9. An 1830 feed mill is now a large country restaurant serving steaks, rack of lamb, prime rib, check, pasta, and seafood specialties.

& **The Hearth Restaurant** (716-496-1088), 12249 Olean Road, Chaffee. Open Monday–Saturday 11:30–10, Sunday 11:30–8. This casual fine-dining restaurant in a country setting serves hearty food in the rustic dining room. Menu selections include prime ribs, steaks, and seafood.

✍ ❀ **Holland Hotel** (716-537-9983), NY 16 at Pearl Street, Holland. This 120 year old hotel is a popular family dining spot in the heart of Holland. Menu selections include steaks, chicken, seafood, Italian entrées, and more. They also serve burgers, salads, and sandwiches for lunch.

EATING OUT Butterwood Desserts (716-652-0131 or 800-321-CAKE), 1863 Davis Road, West Falls. Open Monday–Friday 9 AM–10 PM, Sunday 11 AM–10 PM. The desserts at Butterwood are a feast for the eyes as well as the taste buds. Carolyn and Bill Panzica founded this delicious dessert deli in 1996 in the basement of their 200-year-old home, which was once a stop on the Underground Railroad. Soon they were marketing their desserts to many of the finer restaurants and hotels in western New York. Carolyn, trained at LaVarenne in Paris, is one of the world's top wedding cake designers. Butterwood currently sells their desserts to thousands of restaurants and hotels worldwide. In addition to ordering cakes for special occasions, patrons can enjoy cake, tarts, pies, and tortes by the slice in a small dining room. They have a second location in Williamsville in Northern Erie County.

Country Breads & More (716-655-0039), 1089 Davis Road (NY 240) West Falls. Open for breakfast and lunch Tuesday–Sunday 9–3, dinner Friday until 9. This country bakery and restaurant serves up the best sweet rolls in the Southtowns, which are included with all meals. Start your day with eggs, pancakes, waffles, or quiche. If you arrive at lunch or dinner time, choose from soups, including Ray's meatball vegetable soup, salads, or hearty country style lunches, such as chicken and biscuits or roast turkey dinner. Be sure to save room for their homemade desserts. Baked good sampler gift baskets are available in all price ranges.

✍ & ❀ **Charlaps's** (716-312-0592), 7264 Boston State Road, North Boston. Monday–Saturday 10–10, Sunday 12–10. People come from miles around for Charlap's ice cream, which was started by Henry Charlap in 1961 and is now operated by his son, Nick. Charlap's has the feel of an old-fashioned '50s ice cream parlor, complete with a juke box. On an average summer day they sell over a thousand cones, along with other goodies like shakes and banana splits. You can also purchase ice cream in containers to take home. They recently started serving hamburgers and hot dogs, too. Stop by their Friday car cruise nights during the summer months.

♂ ♿ 🍴 **Earl's** (716-496-5125; www
.earlsdrivein.com), NY 16, Chaffee.
Sunday 8–8, Monday–Thursday
6–8:30, Friday and Saturday 6–9.
This unique eatery was founded in
1956 by Earl and Marilyn Northrup.
The restaurant's theme is definitely
country western—even the table legs
are decked out in their jeans and
cowboy boots, ready to dance a two-
step. A small country-western museum can be found in the back corner.
Menu selections feature "real" foods
like burgers, wings, sandwiches, and
homemade soups, along with Earl's
broasted chicken dinners, a popular
entrée since 1959. Be sure to save
room for a slice of Earl's homemade
pies, dubbed the "best pies in the
world." On selected summer weekends, live musical entertainment
takes place in the adjacent music
park.

✳ Selective Shopping

ANTIQUES Back Barn (716-649-
8291; e-mail: bckbarn@aol.com), 7098
Boston State Road (NY 391), North
Boston. Open daily April–December.
Open Memorial Day–Labor Day
11–5, call for hours rest of year. Vince
and Arlene Weiss's shop, located just
off the 219 expressway, has three
barns full of antiques and collectibles.
They specialize in mirrors made out
of antique picture frames, furniture,
and small antique items.

Colden House of Antiques (716-
480-5509), 8335 Boston Colden Road,
Colden. Open year-round Wednesday–Saturday 12–8:30, Sunday 11–5.
This shop on the first floor of the historic Buffum homestead has a general
line of antiques, including smalls, furniture, collectibles, and textiles. They
also buy and clean out entire estates.

Holland Emporium (716-537-2648),
30 North Main Street, Holland. Open
Saturday and Sunday 12–5. This shop
carries a general line of antiques and
reproductions, including furniture,
smalls, and glassware.

House of Smalls (716-649-6544),
7334 Boston State Road, North
Boston. Open Tuesday, Thursday, Friday 11–4, Saturday 3–5, Sunday 1–4.
The owner is a retired teacher who has
turned his living room into an antique
shop filled with all sorts of small items
he has collected over the years.

Idlewood Galleries (716-537-9619),
62 North Main Street, Holland. Open
by chance or appointment. Antiques,
fine art, and collectibles.

Rachael's Attic Sales (716-941-5338),
6865 Boston Cross Road, Boston.
Open Friday–Sunday 12–5. The wares
of more than 20 dealers of antiques,
collectibles, crafts, vintage toys, furniture, and art can be found in this vintage 19th-century retail building.

**SPECIAL SHOPS Boston Place Gift
Shoppe** (716-646-1150), Boston State
Road, North Boston. Open daily
10–5, Thursday until 7. This unique

THE BACK BARN IS PROOF THAT
ANTIQUES SHOPS COME IN ALL
SHAPES AND SIZES.

Christine A. Smyczynski

shop located in a castlelike building features gifts and collectibles from around the world.

Colden Country Store (716-941-5016), NY 240 and Heath Road, Colden. Open year-round; hours vary seasonally. This classic country store, complete with wooden floors and original tin ceilings, has been popular with western New Yorkers for several decades. Choose from home decor, books, cards, jewelry, kitchen gadgets, holiday decorations, and more.

The Merry Meeting Shoppe (716-496-5075), 12020 Olean Road, Chaffee. Open Monday–Thursday 9:30–6, Friday 9:30–7, Saturday 9:30–6, Sunday 9:30–5. This charming shop is located in an older home formerly known as the Butternut Inn. Recently expanded, the shop features one of the area's largest selections of Boyd's Bears and other furry plush animals, along with candles, glassware, stationery, garden items, and holiday decor.

The Quilt Farm (716 941-3140), 5623 South Feddick Road, Boston (US 219 south to Rice Road exit; turn right at stop sign, and follow signs). Open Tuesday and Thursday 11–7, Wednesday, Friday, and Saturday 11–5. The largest quilt shop in western New York is located in a large red barn in the countryside. Choose from hundreds of bolts of fabric, patterns, threads, and other supplies. Get inspired when you see all the quilts, pillows, and wall hangings displayed throughout the store. Quilting classes are offered in an upstairs room.

The Whistling Thistle (716-941-3299; www.treasuregiftbaskets.net), 9671 State Road, Glenwood. Open Wednesday, Friday, and Saturday 10–6, Thursday 10–7, Sunday 12–5. Store owner Diane Bridenbaker hand paints all the primitive and folk-art items in this shop, located in the heart of ski country. She also carries cards, candles, and other gift items.

✳ Special Events

May: **Holland Tulip Festival** (town of Holland 716-537-9443), Main Street, Holland. This three-day festival celebrates the flower that originated in the "other" Holland. The festival features craft vendors, carnival rides, kids' activities, food vendors, and more.

September: **Colden Arts Festival** (www.coldenarts.com), Colden. A visual-arts festival that has been a Colden tradition for over 30 years. It features the works of local artists, along with musical entertainment and children's activities.

NIAGARA COUNTY

While Niagara County's best-known tourist destination is, of course, Niagara Falls, there are many other interesting things to see and do here. Niagara County is home to the French Castle, the oldest building in the Great Lakes region, as well as the historic Erie Canal. You can even take a boat ride and "lock through" the double set of canal locks in Lockport. Sports fishermen will find an abundance of fish in Lake Ontario and the Niagara River as well as in creeks and streams.

Numerous parks are located throughout the county, including several along the Niagara Gorge and Lake Ontario. Our Lady of Fatima Shrine, located just north of Niagara Falls, was modeled after the shrine in Lisbon, Portugal, and attracts thousands of pilgrims each year.

Niagara County is one of the largest agricultural producers in the state, so you will see all types of farms dotting the countryside. In summer visitors can buy farm-fresh produce at roadside farm markets.

There are also many antiques stores located to be found here, plus many fine restaurants and several wineries.

CITY OF NIAGARA FALLS, NEW YORK

Approximately 900 waterfalls, both large and small, beautify western New York State, but the best known—both locally and worldwide—is, of course, Niagara Falls. One of the Seven Natural Wonders of the World, the falls draws tourists from around the globe to witness its splendor and awesome power. Niagara Falls is actually made up of three waterfalls: the Horseshoe or Canadian Falls, the American Falls, and the smaller Bridal Veil Falls. The first European to write an account of the falls was Father Louis Hennepin, a missionary who traveled to the area in 1678 with the explorer Robert de la Salle.

Shortly after the War of 1812, tourists began arriving in the area. In the early days, the falls were surrounded by factories and mills on privately owned land, with landowners often charging visitors a fee to view the falls. Fortunately, after landscape architect, Frederick Law Olmsted, architect, Henry H. Richardson, and attorney, William Dorschmier visited the area in 1869, they decided to work toward preserving the area and returning it to its natural state.

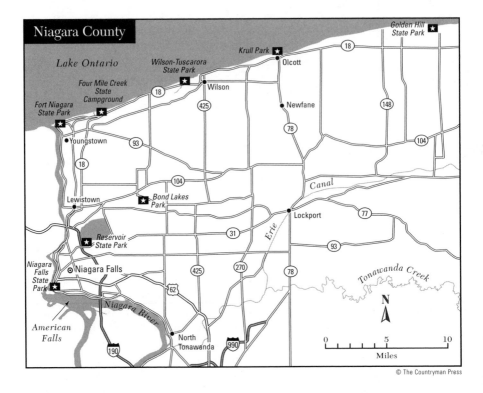

By 1885 the property surrounding the falls had been purchased by New York State and was turned into the first state park in the United States, now known as the Niagara Falls State Park. The world's first railway suspension bridge, built over the Niagara Gorge, was opened in 1855. The 825-foot bridge was a prototype for the Brooklyn Bridge.

Niagara Falls is also known as the Honeymoon Capital of the World. Local legend has it that the first newlyweds, who honeymooned here in 1802, were Joseph Alston and his wife, Theodosia Burr, daughter of Aaron Burr, vice-president of the United States. Napoleon Bonaparte's younger brother, Jerome, also honeymooned here with his wife, Elizabeth. Today the falls is still a popular spot to honeymoon or even get married.

Along with honeymooners, the falls have attracted quite a few daredevils. The Great Blondini walked across the gorge on a tightrope in 1859 and 1860. The first person to successfully go over the falls in a barrel was Annie Taylor, in 1901. Many other daredevils followed, some successful, some not. Of course, these stunts are now illegal, and attempting any type of exploit will land you in jail.

Today Niagara Falls, New York has many attractions that appeal to visitors, including the Cave of the Winds tour, the *Maid of the Mist* boat ride, and the Seneca Niagara Casino.

There are also numerous attractions across the border in Niagara Falls, Ontario, highlighted in the next chapter.

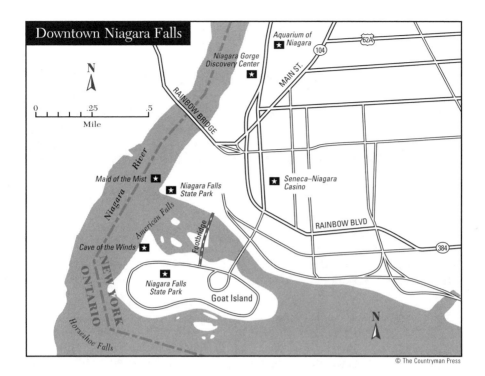

Downtown Niagara Falls

© The Countryman Press

AREA CODE The area code is 716.

GUIDANCE Niagara Co. Tourism (800-338-7890; www.niagara-usa.com) 345 3rd St., Suite 605, Niagara Falls, NY 14303. Open Monday–Friday 8:30–5.

ぐ **Niagara Falls State Park Visitors Center** (716-278-1796), 333 Prospect Street, Niagara Falls. The visitors center opens daily at 7 AM; closing times vary according to season. Information on the falls and the surrounding area, a gift shop, a small café.

GETTING THERE *By air:* See *Getting There Buffalo*. Charter and private flights also fly out of the **Niagara Falls International Airport** (716-297-4494), on Porter Road off Niagara Falls Boulevard.

By bus: The **Niagara Falls Transportation Center** (716-285-9319), is located at the corner of Fourth and Niagara Streets

By car: From the east, take I-90 to I-290 to I-190; cross over Grand Island, and follow the Niagara Falls exit (Robert Moses Parkway). From the south and west, take I-90 north to I-190, and follow above directions. From the north, take I-190 south or the Robert Moses Parkway. From Canada the main route into Niagara Falls, New York is via the Rainbow Bridge.

By train: An **Amtrak** (716-285-4224) station is located at 27th Street and Lockport Road near Hyde Park Boulevard.

GETTING AROUND *By car:* City streets are laid out in a grid pattern, with the main roads being Rainbow Boulevard, Main Street, and Niagara Street.

By bus: The **NFTA** operates routes within the city as well as connecting routes to Buffalo and Lockport. The **Niagara Falls Transportation Center** (716-285-9319) is located at the corner of Fourth and Niagara Streets. **Rural Niagara Transportation** (716-731-3540). Transportation is provided from the rural communities of Niagara County to the cities of Niagara Falls, Lockport, and North Tonawanda.

By taxi: Taxicab companies include **LaSalle Cab** (716-284-8833) and **United Cab** (716-285-9331).

By scenic trolley: This tram, which operates seasonally, stops at all points of interest in Niagara Falls State Park.

MEDICAL EMERGENCY Dial 911

Niagara Falls Memorial Medical Center (716-278-4000; www.nfmmc.org), 621 10th Street, Niagara Falls.

✳ To See

ART MUSEUMS Niagara Arts and Cultural Center (716-282-7530; www .thenacc.org), 1201 Pine Avenue, Niagara Falls. Open Tuesday–Sunday 12–5. This historic 1924 Classic Revival building, formerly Niagara Falls High School, is located less than a mile from the falls. This four-story 200,000-square-foot landmark is home to over 70 visual and performing artists studios along with two theaters and two art galleries. There are more artists under one roof in the arts center than any other place in the state except for New York City.

NIGHTLY FROM DUSK TILL MIDNIGHT NIAGARA FALLS IS ILLUMINATED, MAKING IT EVEN MORE SPECTACULAR.
Courtesy Buffalo–Niagara Convention & Visitors Bureau and Angel Art Ltd.

EVENT Nightly Illumination of Niagara Falls. Hours vary according to season, generally from dusk until midnight (until 10 PM January–March, 11 PM April). A visit to Niagara Falls is not complete unless you've experienced the nightly illumination of the falls. Huge spotlights aimed at the falls light them in shades of blue, red, and green. Be sure to arrive well before dusk to get a prime viewing spot along the railings.

MUSEUMS AND HISTORIC HOMES ⚓ **Niagara Aerospace Museum** (716-278-0060; www.niagaramuseum .org), 345 Third Street, Niagara Falls.

Open Memorial Day–mid-September 10–6 daily, call for hours rest of year. Admission: $7 adults, $6 seniors and college students, $4 children. For a time, the center of aviation in the United States was Buffalo, New York, where the world's largest aircraft plant was built in 1917. This museum is dedicated to the thousands of western New Yorkers who contributed to the aviation and aerospace industry. Among the large collection is a Bell X-22A research aircraft, one of only two ever built, and a Bell Model 47 Helicopter, which was granted the world's first commercial helicopter license. Also on display are model planes and products made for the aviation industry in Buffalo. View a vintage aviation video in the 140-seat theater with full surround sound.

& **Daredevil Museum** (716-282-4046; www.niagarafallsalive.com), 303 Rainbow Boulevard, Niagara Falls. Open 9 AM–11 PM. Free admission. Located in a convenience/souvenir shop. OK, so going over Niagara Falls is illegal and really, really dangerous—but did that stop these brave and foolhardy souls? No. Over the years there have been many attempts to "conquer" Niagara by going over the falls. Some attempts were successful, others . . . well, not so successful. Some of the items on display include the two-person barrel used by Steve Trotter and Lori Martin in 1995 and the Jet Ski used by Robert "Firecracker" Overcracker in his attempt to ski over the falls. The complete history of the falls' daredevils is displayed here.

& **Niagara Wax Museum of History** (716-285-9495), 363 Prospect Street, Niagara Falls. Open May–September daily 9:30 AM–10:30 PM, April and October–December daily 11–9, rest of year 11–5 daily. Admision: $4.95 adults, $3.95 children. Exhibits include displays of daredevils' barrels as well as street scenes of Niagara's past, Native American villages, and more, all depicted in life-sized wax figures.

HISTORIC SITES✪ **Adams Power Plant Transformer House,** Buffalo Avenue (near 15th Avenue and Portage Road), Niagara Falls. This little-known National Historic Landmark was the largest hydroelectric plant in the world when it was constructed in 1895. It is considered the birthplace of the modern power generating station.

✳ To Do

BALLOONING **Flight of Angels** (716-278-0824), Great American Balloon Company, 310 Rainbow Boulevard South, Niagara Falls. Open April–May daily 10–10, June–September daily 9 AM–midnight. Fee: $18 adult, $9 children under 15, $60 family rate (up to 5 people). Enjoy a 15-minute tethered flight over Niagara Falls in a permanently inflated helium-filled balloon that soars 400 feet into the air. This ride affords a spectacular view of Niagara Falls and the surrounding area.

BUFFALO WAS ONCE THE CENTER OF AVIATION, TO WHICH THE NIAGARA AEROSPACE MUSEUM PAYS TRIBUTE.

Christine A. Smyczynski

BOAT EXCURSIONS ♿ *Maid of the Mist* **Tours** (716-284-8897; www.maid ofthemist.com), 151 Buffalo Avenue, Niagara Falls. Memorial Day Weekend and mid-June–Labor Day, rides start at 9:15; April–mid-June and Labor Day–October, rides start at 10. Admission: $11.50 adult, $6.75 children 6–12. Since 1846 visitors, including movie stars, presidents, and kings, have been enjoying the *Maid of the Mist* boat tours, one of the oldest tourist attractions in North America. The ride originally started out as a ferry service across the Niagara Gorge between the United States and Canada. However, in 1848, after a new bridge across the gorge caused business to decline, the owner turned the operation into a sightseeing venture, which continues to this day. On this tour, visitors can see the falls from another perspective. Hooded raincoats are provided for the 30-minute cruise to the base of the American and Horseshoe (Canadian) Falls. You can hear the water thundering and feel the mist. Teddy Roosevelt commented, "The ride was the only way to fully realize the grandeur of the great falls of Niagara." See also *Boat Excursions, Niagara Falls, Ontario.*

CASINO GAMING **Seneca Niagara Casino** (716-299-1100 or 877-8-SENECA; www.snfgc.com) 310 Fourth Street, Niagara Falls. Open 24 hours. Gaming enthusiasts can enjoy 2,900 reel-spinning slot machines and 100 table games along with fine dining and live entertainment at this casino operated by the Seneca Nation of Indians. Smoking is allowed in the casino; they also have a non-smoking section. High-stakes gamers will enjoy the opulent Blue Heron Room. Live entertainment is featured in the Bear's Den Showroom. See also *Dining Out* (Western Door Steak House). Note: You must be at least 21 to enter the casino.

CROSS-COUNTRY SKIING See *Green Space—Parks*

FAMILY FUN ✈ **Aquarium of Niagara** (716-285-3575; www.aquarium ofniagara.org), 701 Whirlpool Street, Niagara Falls. Open daily 9–5. Admission: $7.50 adults, $5.50 children 4–12. During your self-guided tour you'll explore the undersea world from the Great Lakes to coral reefs. The facility has over 1,500 species of aquatic animals including sharks, piranha, moray eels, California sea lions, and even penguins. The two-floor sea-lion tank allows for viewing above as well as below the water. Make sure you catch the sea lion show; it's guaranteed to make a real splash.

♿ ✈ **Niagara Gorge Discovery Center** (formerly Schoelkopt Geological Museum) (716-278-1780 or 716-278-1796), Off Robert Moses Parkway

THE *MAID OF THE MIST* TAKES PASSENGERS UP CLOSE TO SPECTACULAR NIAGARA FALLS.
Courtesy Buffalo Niagara Convention & Visitors Bureau and Angel Art Ltd.

near Main Street, Niagara Falls. Open Memorial Day–Labor Day daily 9–7, April–Memorial Day and Labor Day–October 31 daily 9–5. Admission: $5 adults, $3 children 6–12. Virtual-reality exhibits, including the Gorge Cam, explore the history and geology of the Niagara Gorge. The Cataract Theater, with its 32-foot-diameter circular screen, presents a multimedia presentation of the Niagara Gorge. The building's exterior features a 26-foot climbing wall.

GOLF & **Hyde Park Golf Course** (716-286-4956), 4343 Porter Road (NY 62 and Robbins Drive; enter via Porter Road) Niagara Falls. This 18-hole, par-72 course features a restaurant, pro shop, and indoor driving range.

Niagara Golf Wonderland (716-731-5155; www.mywonderdome.com), 2609 Niagara Falls Boulevard, Niagara Falls. A public 9-hole, par-27 course with restaurant.

GUIDED TOURS **Bedore Tours, Inc.** (716-285-7550 or 800-538-8433; www .bedoretours.com), 454 Main Street, Niagara Falls. Tours of the Niagara Falls area, including both sides of the border and the *Maid of the Mist*.

Cave of the Winds (716-278-1730), Goat Island, First Street and Buffalo Avenue, Niagara Falls. Open seasonally. The Cave of the Winds tours offers a unique view of the American Falls. Don a hooded raincoat before descending the elevator down to the cave. When you emerge from the cave, you'll be able to walk along the catwalk that has been constructed near the base of the Bridal Veil Falls. Be prepared to get soaking wet; you'll only be an arm's length away from the thundering water.

Gray Line of Niagara Falls (716-694-3600 or 800-695-1603; www.grayline .com), 3466 Niagara Falls Boulevard, North Tonawanda. This well-known tour company offers several tour packages of the Niagara Falls area, covering one or both sides of the border. You will experience scenic vistas as well as learn about the region's rich history.

Helicopter Rides by Rainbow Air (716-284-2800), 454 Main Street, Niagara Falls. If you are a real thrill seeker, why not view Niagara Falls from a different perspective. Rainbow Air's quiet turbine engine helicopters provide guests with a unique experience of their visit to Niagara Falls. Get a bird's-eye view as you enjoy the beauty of the falls from the air. Make sure you bring you camera or camcorder; this is a once-in-a-lifetime experience.

Motherland Connextions (716-282-1028; www.motherlandconnextions.com), Bridge Street Station, Niagara Falls. The western New York area played a major role in the Underground Railroad—not an actual railway but paths and roads followed by slaves seeking freedom during the 1850s. Motherland Connextions provides an educational and enlightening experience. "Conductors" in period clothing take your group to stops along the Underground Railroad in both western New York and southern Ontario. The tours are designed to be emotional as well as educational and encourage participants to "stop and feel" the experience of those who risked their lives for freedom. This tour is not only about the slaves, but also about the Native Americans and European settlers who helped the slaves on their journey to freedom. Motorcoach tours, which are up to four hours long, start in downtown Buffalo and travel to the Niagara Falls/Lewiston area.

Niagara Majestic Tours (716-285-2133 or 877-285-2113; www.niagaramajestic .com), Niagara Falls. Day and night tours of the attractions on both sides of the border.

Over the Falls Tours, Inc. (716-283-8900 or 877-783-8900; www.overthefalls tours.com), Tours of attractions in both Niagara Falls, U.S.A and Canada. They will pick up guests at local hotels.

WEDDING CHAPELS ⚭ **The Falls Wedding Chapel** (716-285-5570 or 888-311-8697; www.fallswedding.com), 240 Rainbow Boulevard, Niagara Falls. Open by appointment. Weddings and vow renewals can be arranged in several locations, including at the brink of the falls, in a helicopter, or a balloon over the falls, in a local cathedral, or in their chapel at the Quality Hotel & Suites. Rev. Gerald Fedell and Rev. Barry Lillis, pastors of an interdenominational Christian church, and their staff are dedicated to helping couples celebrate their love. Wedding packages start at $195 and include minister's services, music, witness, bottle of champagne, and a keepsake wedding certificate. Wedding photographer, cake, and bouquet available as additional options. See also *Lodging*.

⚭ **Rainbow House Bed & Breakfast and Wedding Chapel** (800-724-3536; www.rainbowchapel.com), 423 Rainbow Boulevard South, Niagara Falls. This Victorian bed & breakfast is a romantic setting for small weddings. Outdoor weddings by the falls can also be arranged. See *Lodging*.

✳ Green Space

PARKS **De Veaux Woods State Park** (716-284-5778), 3180 DeVeaux Woods Drive, Niagara Falls. Open daily dawn to dusk. Free admission. This park which connects to the Robert Moses Trail and Whirlpool State Park, includes two baseball diamonds and old-growth forest.

& **Devil's Hole State Park** (716-278-1796), Robert Moses Parkway North, Niagara Falls. Open daily dawn to dusk. Free admission. This ominous-sounding park overlooking the lower whirlpool rapids was the scene of a 1763 massacre, in which British

GETTING MARRIED IN NEW YORK STATE

To get married in New York, a couple must obtain a marriage license at any city or town clerk's office. The Niagara Falls city clerk's office is located at 745 Main Street. Licenses are issued Monday–Friday 9 AM–3:30 PM, except legal holidays. Both parties must appear before the clerk and present one form of photo ID, such as a driver's license or passport. If either party is divorced, they must present a certified copy of their divorce decree. There is no blood test required, but there is a 24-hour waiting period between the issuing of the license and the wedding ceremony. The license is good for 60 days after issue. See also *Wedding Chapels, Niagara Falls, Ontario*.

soldiers were pushed into the gorge by a group of warring Seneca Indians. The upper portion of this park has several picnic areas. A hiking trail leads down the embankment about 300 feet into the gorge, where visitors can get an up-close view of the rapids. It is a popular spot for fishermen. While you're down in the gorge, look for a wide-mouthed, 50-foot long cave near the bottom. Legend has it that this is the home of an evil spirit, hence the name of the park. If the devil doesn't get you, return to the rim of the gorge by continuing on the main hiking trail, which will lead you to the rim about 1 mile south of where you began.

& **Hyde Park** (716-286-4956), U.S. 62 and Robbins Drive, Niagara Falls. Open daily dawn to dusk. Free admission. This park offers picnicking, swimming, bocce courts, volleyball, baseball, indoor ice skating, hiking and nature trails, tennis, fishing, and a golf course.

& ✪ **Niagara Falls State Park** (716-278-1770 or 716-278-1796; www.niagara fallsstatepark.com), Prospect Street, Niagara Falls. Open daily dawn to nightly illumination of falls. Free admission; however, there is a $7 parking fee if you park in their lot. America's oldest state park, established in 1885 and designed by noted landscape architect Frederick Law Olmsted, is made up of several small islands plus Prospect Point, which offers a great view of the falls. The park, a designated National Historic Landmark, includes access to the American Falls, Bridal Veil Falls, and Goat Island. Facilities include hiking and nature trails, fishing, picnic tables, and a restaurant. The visitor's center offers information on park history as well as New York State information. Elevators in the observation deck take visitors to the *Maid of the Mist* boat ride. The Cave of the Wind Tour, located on Goat Island, takes visitors on a close-up tour of the falls.

Oppenheim County Park (716-439-7950), 2713 Niagara Falls Boulevard, Niagara Falls. Open daily dawn to dusk. Free admission. Facilities include picnic shelters, fishing, and playgrounds.

Reservoir State Park (716-297-4484), Witmer Road and Military, Niagara Falls (near Lewiston) Open daily dawn to dusk. Free admission. One of this popular park's most interesting and scenic aspects is that it overlooks the Robert Moses Power Plant Reservoir—a great spot for fishing. Facilities in the park include four tennis courts, eight baseball diamonds, and a basketball court. The park also has picnic amenities and a playground besides nature trails for hiking and biking. Winter visitors can enjoy sledding and cross-country skiing.

Whirlpool State Park (716-285-7740) Niagara Rapids Boulevard (off the Robert Moses Parkway), Niagara Falls. Open daily dawn to dusk. Free admission. This two-level park, located along a 90 degree turn in the Niagara River Gorge, overlooks the whirlpool that forms 3.5 miles downstream from the falls. From street level there are many spectacular overlooks to view the swirling rapids and the whirlpool. During the winter months many people also enjoy cross-country skiing here. Picnic areas and a playground are on this level. The lower level, located along the river, is accessible by walking down 300 feet of trails and steps. Here you will find nature trails and fishing access.

WALKING AND HIKING TRAILS See *Parks*.

NIAGARA REGIONAL PARK INTERPRETIVE PROGRAMS
The New York State Office of Parks, Recreation, and Historic Preservation offers a selection of public programs throughout the year to educate the public about our natural resources and regional history. Included are tours, hikes, walks, lectures, and outreach programs. Over a dozen state parks in both Erie and Niagara Counties are used for these programs. Some of the programs offered in the past included snowshoe and cross-country skiing hikes, birding adventures, fishing experiences, and nature photography lessons. In addition to these special programs, Niagara River Gorge Adventure hikes are offered May–October. School outreach programs are available November–March, and adult and community education programs are available on request. A Niagara Gorge Trail System Hiking Patch can be earned by hiking several of the trails along the Niagara Gorge. For more information, contact **Niagara Regional Park Interpretive Programs Office** (716-278-1728 or 716-745-7848), PO Box 1132, Niagara Falls State Park, Niagara Falls, NY.

❋ Lodging

INNS AND RESORTS Red Coach Inn (716-282-1459 or 800-282-1459; www.redcoach.com), 2 Buffalo Avenue, Niagara Falls. The Red Coach Inn, modeled after the Old Bell Inn in Finedon, England, overlooks the upper rapids, and at only 1,500 feet from the falls, it's the closest lodging: Guests can hear the thundering rapids from their rooms. It's the only AAA three diamond bed & breakfast in the city of Niagara Falls. Accommodations include two-bedroom guest suites elegantly decorated with period antiques and reproductions. All suites have private baths, whirlpool tubs, a small kitchen, living room/dining room overlooking the rapids, fireplaces, and cable television. Several one-bedroom suites are also available, along with two standard guest rooms. A continental breakfast is served daily. The inn's main dining room is open for lunch and dinner for guests as well as the public. $129–$339.

GUESTS CAN HEAR THE THUNDERING RAPIDS FROM THEIR ROOMS AT THE RED COACH INN, ONLY 1,500 FEET FROM THE FALLS.

Christine A. Smyczynski

MOTELS AND HOTELS Hundreds of small, nondescript motels line Niagara Falls Boulevard (NY 62) from Amherst to Niagara Falls. Numerous larger motor inns and chain hotels can be found in the Niagara Falls area. All of them provide clean, comfortable accommodations at fairly reasonable prices. There are also hundreds of nondescript motels located along Niagara Falls Boulevard between Amherst and Niagara Falls. My personal recommendation is to stay at a hotel that's within walking distance of the falls. Below are just a few.

Four Points Sheraton Hotel-Niagara Falls (716-285-2521), 114 Buffalo Avenue, Niagara Falls. This hotel with a family atmosphere offers 189 rooms, a children's indoor playground, indoor pool and sauna, and on-site restaurant and lounge. It's also close to the falls. $109–$209.

Hampton Inn (716-285-6666), 501 Rainbow Boulevard, Niagara Falls. This hotel offers 100 rooms, including several deluxe king whirlpool rooms. Amenities include an indoor heated pool, fitness room, and a free continental breakfast buffet. It's close to the falls, and sightseeing tours leave from the lobby. $79–159.

Howard Johnson Inn (716-285-5261), 454 Main Street, Niagara Falls. This inn is located close to the falls and attractions. Amenities include a free continental breakfast, indoor pool and sauna, and a really nice on-site gift shop. $69–$175.

🐾 ⓒⓓ **Quality Hotel and Suites** (716-282-1212; www.qualityinn niagarafalls.com), 240 Rainbow Boulevard, Niagara Falls. The hotel offers 199 spacious rooms, including two-room family suites and Jacuzzi suites. Walk to the falls and the Seneca Niagara Casino. $99–$299 The on-site **Falls Wedding Chapel** is available for wedding ceremonies and vow renewals. (See *Wedding Chapels*.)

BED & BREAKFASTS Butler House Bed & Breakfast (716-284-9846 or 800-706-5004; www.butlerhousebb .com), 751 Park Place, Niagara Falls. Built in 1928, this B&B is located on a quiet street in the heart of the city of Niagara Falls. Hosts Mike and Marcia Yoder offer four bright and airy guest rooms, each with a private bath. The enclosed front porch offers privacy for guests. A homemade breakfast can be enjoyed in the dining room or outdoors on the covered veranda. $65–$135.

Hanover House Bed & Breakfast (716-278-1170 or 877-848-0543; www .hanoverhousebb.com), 610 Buffalo Avenue, Niagara Falls. This Italianate-style mansion, within walking distance of the falls, was built in 1922 and retains many of the original features. Innkeeper Barbara Leoncavallo offers three antiques-furnished rooms, each with a private bath. The house is decorated with numerous photos and paintings of Niagara Falls along with beautiful furniture hand-painted by Barbara. She also painted the murals in the nearby Rainbow House Bed & Breakfast. This property is within walking distance of the falls. $105–$125.

Manchester House Bed & Breakfast (716-285-5717 or 800-489-3009; www.manchesterhouse.com), 653 Main Street, Niagara Falls. Innkeepers Carl and Lis Slenk offer three beautifully decorated guest rooms with private baths in this inn, which is within walking distance of the falls. Several of the rooms feature hand stenciling and hand-painted furniture by Lis. A full breakfast, which includes baked goods, fruit cup, and a hot entrée, is served each morning. $60–$110.

Park Place Bed & Breakfast (716-282-4626 or 800-510-4626; www.park placebb.com), 740 Park Place, Niagara Falls. Innkeepers Louise and Tom Yots have restored this 1913 Arts and Crafts Prairie-style home, which is on the National Register of Historic Places. Tom, who is the Niagara Falls city historian, will be able to fill you in on the history of the city as well as tell you about the house. This historic home features oak paneling, open spaces, and Steuben glass chandeliers in the den. Four antiques-furnished rooms, each with a private bath, are located on the second floor. The Master Bedroom features a 50-gallon bathtub, and the Mantle Room features a 1910 brass bed and a 1930s German dental cabinet converted into an armoire. $65–$110.

⊙ **Rainbow House Bed & Breakfast** (716-282-1135 or 800-724-3536; www.rainbowhousebb.com), 423 Rainbow Boulevard, Niagara Falls. This Victorian home, built in 1895, has original woodwork and stained glass throughout. The walls are adorned with stencils and vintage Niagara Falls photos. Innkeeper Laura Lee Morgan offers four unique guest rooms, beautifully decorated with stenciling and hand-painting done by Laura Lee's friend and fellow innkeeper Barbara Leoncavallo, who operates the nearby Hanover House Bed & Breakfast. Each room has a private bath, air-conditioning, and a ceiling fan. The Bridal Suite features a king-sized bed and a private porch with swing, while the Seaway Room has a nautical theme. The Garden Room has a hand-painted country mural, and the Country Room features a whimsical hand-painted mural in the bathroom. Awake in the morning to the aroma of

Laura Lee's famous cinnamon buns, part of a hearty country breakfast. Ms. Morgan, an expert wedding coordinator, plans close to 300 small, intimate weddings and vow renewals each year, many which take place either in the Rainbow House's Victorian wedding chapel or outdoors near the falls, which is within walking distance of the inn. $60–$150.

✳ Where to Eat

DINING OUT Como Restaurant (716-285-9341), 2220 Pine Avenue (NY 62A), Niagara Falls. Open Sunday–Thursday 11:30–10, Friday and Saturday 11:30–11. This warm and inviting restaurant, located in Niagara Falls's "Little Italy," features pasta and other Italian specialties.

Fortunas Restaurant (716-282-2252), 827 19th Street, Niagara Falls. Open Monday–Thursday 4–9:30, Friday 11:30–10, Saturday 4–10:30, Sunday 12–8:30. One of the finest Italian restaurants in Niagara Falls, Fortunas has been family owned since 1945. Choose from homemade pasta entrées, specialty sauces, veal, seafood, and chicken plus steak and pork entrées.

John's Flaming Hearth Restaurant (716-297-1414), 1965 Military Road, Niagara Falls. Open for lunch Tuesday–Saturday 11:30–3, dinner Tuesday–Thursday 4–10, Friday and Saturday 4–11, Sunday 12–9. This popular restaurant has been a landmark in Niagara Falls for over four decades. Dining can be described as casual yet elegant. The menu features classic American fare, including New York strip steak dinners and seafood, and daily specials. They are best known for their signature pumpkin ice cream pie, one of the best known desserts in western New York, and have sold an average of 50 pies per week for over 50 years.

Red Coach Inn (716-282-1459, 800-282-1459; www.redcoach.com), 2 Buffalo Avenue, Niagara Falls. Open Monday–Saturday 11:30–10 (Friday and Saturday until 11), Sunday 12–10. The Red Coach Inn is Niagara Fall's only AAA three diamond restaurant. The menu changes daily and features Black Angus beef, pasta, and seafood, along with chicken and pork dishes. Warm yourself by the inn's natural stone fireplace during the winter months, or enjoy fine dining during warmer weather on their outdoor patio, which overlooks the rapids. The glass-walled Rapids Room also offers a spectacular view of the rapids. See also *Lodging*.

Shadows Martini Bar (716-205-0808 or 205-0757), 441 Third Street, Niagara Falls. Open Tuesday–Thursday 5–10, Friday and Saturday 5–11. Bar stays open until 2 AM. This attractive, sophisticated restaurant and lounge is located close to the Seneca Niagara Casino. They are noted for their extensive martini menu, including daily specials, as well as its good ambiance and original creative food.

& **Top of the Falls Restaurant** (716-278-0348), Goat Island, Niagara Falls. Open late May–October 1, daily 11–7, Friday and Saturday until 10. This upscale restaurant offers a magnificent view of Horseshoe Falls. It has outdoor seating as well as indoor tiered seating, so everyone gets a view of the falls. The menu features classic American fare, plus a kids' menu.

& **The Western Door** at the Seneca Niagara Casino (716-299-1100, 877-8-SENECA; www.snfgc.com), 310 Fourth Street, Niagara Falls, Open

daily 5–11. This nicely decorated, opulent, five-star steakhouse overlooking the casino's gaming floor features aged beef, including a 48-ounce porterhouse. They also have a selection of seafood as well as New York State wines and beers to go with your meal. Your dining experience begins with their signature jalapeño and cheddar scones, served with a variety of other gourmet breads. When ordering, keep in mind that entrée accompaniments, such as salad, potato and vegetable, are sold à la carte. However, the sides are quite large and will easily serve two people. Desserts are huge, too. See also *Casino Gaming*.

EATING OUT **Macri's** (716-282-4707), 755 West Market Street (City Market), Niagara Falls. Open Sunday–Thursday 11–10, Friday and Saturday 11–11. When Mama D'Avolio first started this Italian restaurant, it was best known for her "pizza frites," a fried bread to die for. Today they serve Italian and American cuisine in a relaxed atmosphere.

& **Marketside Café** (716-282-0644), 7112 East Market Street (City Market), Niagara Falls. Open Monday–Friday 7:30 AM–1:30 PM, Saturday 7:30 AM–noon. This is the place to go if you want the scoop on what's happening in town. You'll find early risers, politicians, farmers, and locals dining here. The food is very good, including homemade soup, desserts, and sandwiches.

& 🐾 ✿ **Michael's Italian Restaurant** (716-282-4043), 3011 Pine Avenue, Niagara Falls. Open for breakfast, lunch, and dinner. Open Sunday–Thursday 11–11, Friday and Saturday 11 AM–12 AM. You'll find this small, cozy restaurant right under the "Little Italy" sign that hangs over Pine Avenue. All entrées come in enormous portions, so be prepared to take home leftovers. Their extensive menu include Michael's famous calzones, deep-fried Italian turnovers stuffed with ricotta and mozzarella, and the city's best eggplant parms, along with a selection of Italian and American fare, including pizza, wings, and a kids' menu.

Orchard Grill (716-282-0879), 1217 Main Street, Niagara Falls. Open daily 11–3, and 5:30–9. Enjoy homemade food in a relaxed and casual publike atmosphere. This restaurant is very popular with locals. It is about a 1 mile walk from the falls. In addition to standard pub fare, the restaurant also offers a selection of heart-smart healthy dishes.

& ✍ 🐾 **Page's Restaurant—Home of the Whistle Pig** (716-297-0131), 7001 Packard Road, Niagara Falls. Open year-round 7 AM–10 PM daily. Since 1939 this hot dog joint has been famous for the "Whistle Pig," a skinless red or white hot dog wrapped in bacon and covered in a creamy cheese sauce. Other menu items include beef on weck, chicken wings, and complete dinners. They are also open for breakfast. During the summer months, children can ride on five small kiddie rides outside next to the restaurant.

🐾 ✍ & **Twist o' the Mist** (716-285-0702), Rainbow Boulevard and Niagara Street (across from the Rainbow Bridge) Niagara Falls. Open seasonally. This casual eatery features hot dogs, burgers, and fries, plus hard ice cream and soft custard served from an ice cream cone-shaped building.

✳ Entertainment

THEATERS **Niagara Festival Theater,** 333 Prospect Street, Niagara Falls (located in the Niagara Falls State Park Visitors Center). Open daily 9–5; movie shown on the hour. Admission: $2 adults, $1 children 6–12, under 6 free. A 50-seat interactive theater that uses 2-D and 3-D technology to allow guests to experience the beauty and power of Niagara Falls. Learn the history of the Falls, from the first European sighting in 1697 to modern times.

Niagara Arts and Cultural Center, (716-282-7530; www.naccarts.net, www.thenacc.org), 1201 Pine Avenue, Niagara Falls. The arts center features a 900-seat Grand Theatre and the smaller Woodbox Theater. See *Art Museums.*

✳ Selective Shopping

ANTIQUES **McMullen's Antiques** (716-283-2900), 7724 Buffalo Avenue, Niagara Falls. Open Monday–Friday 9–5, Saturday 9–4. A former garage, this shop features 9,500 square feet of antiques and collectibles.

ART GALLERIES **Artisans Alley** (716-282-0196 or 800-635-1457), 10 Rainbow Boulevard, Niagara Falls. This shop, located within walking distance of the falls, offers contemporary and traditional works of over 600 American artists, with works in fiber, wood, leather, and glass, plus furniture, wall hangings, jewelry, sculpture, paintings, and much more.

Niagara Arts and Cultural Center See *Art Museums.*

SPECIAL STORES **Dicamillo Bakery** Four locations: 811 Linwood (716-282-2341), 7927 Niagara Falls Boulevard (716-236-0111), 1700 Pine Avenue (716-284-8131), and 535 Center Street in Lewiston (716-754-2218). Open 7 AM–9 PM. Dicamillo's has been a local institution for over 80 years. Stop by to sample some of their crusty bread, pizzas, and cookies. They are nationally known for their line of biscotti, crisp bread, and focaccia, sold in Nieman Marcus, Macy's, and Bloomingdales.

Harris & Lever Florist (800-729-4401; www.harrisandleverflorist.com), 1225 Main Street, Niagara Falls. Open Monday–Saturday 9–5. Harris & Lever, established in 1916, was the first florist established in the city. The shop has the original fixtures and shelves. This family-owned and operated store offers fine floral arrangements, gourmet baskets, and other gift items.

Niagara Falls City Market, Pine Avenue at Market Street, Niagara Falls. Located in the heart of Niagara's "Little Italy," a farmer's market takes place here during the summer months.

Niagara Falls Public Library Gift Shop (716-286-4911; www.niagara fallspubliclibrary.org), 1425 Main Street, Niagara Falls. Open Monday–Friday 11:30–3:30. Find a variety of creative handmade gifts for adults and children, along with a selection of books on Niagara Falls and photography by local artists.

Prime Outlets (800-414-0475; www .primeoutlets.com), Military Road off Rt. 62, Niagara Falls. Monday–Saturday 10–9, Sunday 11–6. Bargains galore at hundreds of factory outlet stores.

Souvenirs (716-285-6117), 16 Rainbow Boulevard, Niagara Falls. Open Sunday–Thursday 8 AM–10 PM, Friday and Saturday 8 AM–11 PM. If you've traveled all the way to Niagara Falls, you'll probably want to bring back a little something to remember your trip. This store offers the city's largest selection of souvenirs and gifts related to Niagara Falls.

Three Sisters Trading Post (716-284-3689; www.threesisterstrading post.com), 454 Main Street, Niagara Falls. This family-owned rustic shop features a unique collection of home-decor items, handcrafted jewelry, and Native American art. They also have really cute stuffed animals, Niagara Falls souvenirs, country and primitive items, and nautical-themed gifts. The shop has a tiny coffee café, with a few seats by the counter and a small outdoor patio. Niagara Falls tours can be booked here.

✳ Special Events

March: **SEAsonings—A Taste of Niagara,** Aquarium of Niagara, Niagara Falls An evening of food from Niagara's finest restaurants to benefit the aquarium.

July: **Polka Festival** (716-285-3604), St. Stanislaus Kostka Church, 2437 Niagara Street, Niagara Falls. Western New York's biggest and best polka festival. Enjoy dancing to live music and authentic Polish cuisine.

LEWISTON AND YOUNGSTOWN

Established in 1798, Lewiston was named to honor Morgan Lewis, the third governor of New York. The village was on a key portage route around the falls until the early 1800s, when the Erie Canal was built. Lewiston was then burned to the ground by the British in 1813, during the War of 1812. However, the town was rebuilt right after the war and many of the homes constructed during this period are still standing. The village also played an important role in the Underground Railroad during the mid-1800s. During America's Bicentennial in 1976, Lewiston was proclaimed by President Jimmy Carter to be the most historic square mile in America.

Today Center Street has numerous boutiques and restaurants, all within easy walking distance of each other. The village is also home to Artpark, a state park that offers an array of art and cultural events throughout the summer. Our Lady of Fatima Shrine, the second largest tourist attraction in Niagara County, attracts visitors from all over the world.

Youngstown, at the mouth of the Niagara River, is one of the most scenic spots in Niagara County. Some of the most spectacular sunsets in the region can be seen over the river and the lake. Located only 12 miles from Niagara Falls, Youngstown is a popular spot to stay since it is relaxing yet not far from area attractions. This section of the lower Niagara River is popular with bird-watchers, who come from all over the country. Every type of seagull that you can think of can be found here. It's also a popular spot for sports fishing, with anglers from as far away as Ohio and New Jersey coming for the salmon, trout, walleye, and steelhead. Recreational boaters and sailors appreciate Youngstown as well, with the largest freshwater regatta in North America taking place every July.

Of course, history is key in Youngstown. Fort Niagara, which has the oldest structure in the Great Lakes region, played an important role in many military battles, especially during the French and Indian War and the War of 1812. Youngstown was one of the first settlements to grow outside Fort Niagara in the late 1700s.

AREA CODE The area code is 716.

GUIDANCE Lewiston Visitors Information (716-754-9500; www.northofthefalls.com), 476 Center Street, Lewiston. Visitors info can be found inside this circa 1816 house.

Youngstown (www.youngstownnewyork.com). Be sure to check out the Web cam on the site. For additional Youngstown information, contact Sue MacNaughton at the **Dory Shop** (716-745-3335), 435 Main Street, Youngstown. Open Monday–Saturday 9–6, Sunday 9–2.

Lewiston Council on the Arts (716-754-0166; www.artcouncil.org), PO Box 1, Lewiston, NY 14092. Many arts and cultural events take place in Lewiston throughout the year.

GETTING THERE *By car:* From Niagara Falls take the Robert Moses Parkway. This area can also be reached from NY 104.

Mount St. Mary's Hospital (716-297-4800; www.msmh.org), 5300 Military Road, Lewiston.

✳ To See

ART MUSEUMS & **Castellani Art Museum** (716-286-8200; www.niagara.edu /~cam), Niagara University Campus, NY 104, Lewiston. Open Tuesday–Saturday 11–5, Sunday 1–5; closed holidays. Free admission. This museum on the beautiful campus of Niagara University has something for everyone, including works by Picasso and Dali, pieces depicting Niagara Falls, and regional folk arts. A small café is located in the sculpture court.

MUSEUMS AND HISTORIC HOMES **Lewiston Historical Museum** (754-4214), 469 Plain Street, Lewiston. Open Wednesday 1–4. Displays on the history of Lewiston and the Niagara Frontier.

Town of Porter Historical Society (716-745-1271), 240 Lockport Street, 2nd Floor, Youngstown. Open Wednesday–Thursday 2–4, Saturday 10–2. This museum focuses on the history of Youngstown and the Town of Porter.

HISTORIC SITES ✔ **Frontier House** (716-754-2663), 460 Center Street, Lewiston. This Federal-style building built between 1820 and 1824 with stone from the old Lewiston Stone Quarry, is listed on the National Register of Historic Places. In its day the Frontier House was a well-known stagecoach stop and considered to be the finest hotel west of Albany. Many prominent people spent the night here, including James Fenimore Cooper, Charles Dickens, President Abraham Lincoln, and Thomas Edison.

✪ **Lewiston Portage Landing Site** at Artpark, 450 South 4th Street, Lewiston. This National Historic Landmark site along the Niagara River marks the spot where Native Americans and fur traders would land their vessels to portage the boats and goods to the upper landing above Niagara Falls, avoiding the lower rapids and the falls. An ancient Native American burial site is located just above the landing.

✔ ✪ **Old Fort Niagara** (716-745-7611; www.oldfortniagara.org), Fort Niagara State Park, NY 18F at the north end of the Robert Moses Parkway, Youngstown. Admission: $7 adults, $4 children, under 6 free. Take a step back in time at Old Fort Niagara. Preserved as they stood in the 1700s, the fort's structures include

THE "FRENCH CASTLE" AT OLD FORT NIAGARA IS THE OLDEST BUILDING IN THE GREAT LAKES REGION.

Christine A. Smyczynski

the French Castle—the oldest building in the Great Lakes region. This National Historic Landmark fort, just minutes from Niagara Falls, was the site of many historic battles. The fort's costumed staff demonstrate 18th-century military life, including drills and musket and cannon firings. Re-enactments are held several times a year, and educational programs are offered to youth groups. Visitors can explore original buildings and discover the region's fascinating history. Fort Niagara is a year-round destination where history comes alive.

LIGHTHOUSES Old Fort Niagara Lighthouse (716-745-7611; www.oldfortniagara.org), Fort Niagara State Park, Youngstown. Open weekends in June, daily July 1–Labor Day. Free admission. Built in 1871 to mark the mouth of the Niagara River, the original tower was an octagon 50 feet high. Over the years it has gone through many renovations, including making it shorter and changing the roof of the work room to resemble a medieval castle. In 1900 alterations were made to make it more visible to passing ships. The lighthouse was in use until 1993. The base of the lighthouse serves as a museum, gift shop, and information center.

RELIGIOUS SITES & **Our Lady of Fatima Shrine** (716-754-7489; www .fatimashrine.com), 1023 Swann Road, Lewiston. Open daily 9–5. During the Festival of the Lights November–January open 9–9. Free admission. This shrine, operated by the Barnabite Fathers, is a place of natural beauty, art, prayer, and renewal to the thousands who visit it each year. Constructed in 1954, the shrine was modeled after the Fatima Shrine in Lisbon, Portugal. The focal point of the shrine is the basilica, which was completed in 1965. This dome-shaped church, 100 feet in diameter and 55 feet high, depicts the Northern Hemisphere. A 13-foot statue of Our Lady of Fatima rests on the dome. The heart-shaped pond in front of the basilica is surrounded by a giant rosary. On the grounds of the 20-acre shrine are over 100 life-sized marble statues representing saints from every race and walk of life.

✳ To Do

BOATING AND SAILING With the abundance of water in the area, boating and sailing are very popular pastimes. One can launch a boat in Lewiston at the public ramp by **Lewiston Landing Waterfront Park** on South Water Street. In Youngstown there are two ramps located in **Fort Niagara State Park** as well as a public ramp located next to the **Youngstown Yacht Club** on Water Street. Youngstown is also the site of the annual **Level Regatta,** attracting some 350 boats from all over the East Coast and southern Ontario. (See *Special Events.*)

MARINAS Village of Lewiston Marina (716-754-8271), 145 North 4th Street, Lewiston.

Williams Marine, Inc. (716-745-7000), 555 Water Street, Youngstown.

BOAT EXCURSIONS Whirlpool Jet Boat Tours (888-438-4444; www.whirlpool jet.com) 115 South Water Street, Lewiston. Open May 1–end of October. Take a

jet boat ride to the whirlpool through the world-famous Lower Niagara rapids
for some great scenery and an exciting whitewater adventure. Choose either the
wet-jet option (rain suits, ponchos, and life jackets are provided, but bring a
change of clothes since you will get soaked during your adventure) or the jet
dome ride (same exciting whitewater ride in a fully enclosed boat).

CROSS-COUNTRY SKIING See **Bond Lake, Joseph Davis State Park, Reservoir State Park, Fort Niagara State Park** in *Green Space—Parks.*

GUIDED TOURS **Historic Walking Tours-Seaway Trail Walks** (716-754-0166
or 800-732-9298; www.seawaytrail.com), Lewiston Visitors Information Center,
476 Center Street, Lewiston. June–October Tuesdays at 5 PM. Step back to discover Lewiston's colorful past when you join a walking tour led by costumed historical characters. You will journey past historic homes on Plain Street, the
village cemetery, and the Lewiston Historical Museum.

FISHING The **Lower Niagara River** is a prime year-round fishing spot. From
November through May steelhead are plentiful here, while lake trout are the
catch of the day January through May. Brown trout can also be found in abundance during early winter and spring, and in spring the salmon fishing is phenomenal. Fishing licenses can be obtained at any town or county municipal
clerk's office, Dick's Sporting Goods stores, Wal-Mart, and most bait and tackle
shops. For more information on fishing in Erie and Niagara Counties, including
a compete list of where to get a license, fishing supplies, and charter captains,
see www.erie.gov/hotspot. Fish-cleaning stations are located at Fort Niagara
State Park and in Lewiston. For more information, contact the Niagara River
Anglers Association (www.niagarariveranglers.com), PO Box 203, Niagara Falls,
NY 14304.

FISHING ACCESS The Lower Niagara River offers many spots where anglers
can fish from shore, including the following state parks: **Artpark, Devil's Hole,
Fort Niagara, Joseph Davis,** and **Whirlpool.** Other fishing access sites
include **Niagara Power Project Visitors Center Fishing Platform** (access
road into the gorge near Niagara University), and the **New York Power
Authority Upper Reservoir** at **Reservoir State Park.**

FISHING CHARTERS **Riverside Sport Fishing** (716-754-4101; www.niagara
fish.com), Lewiston. Captain Bruce Blakelock will be your guide to fishing on
the Niagara River and Lake Ontario. See also *Riverside Motel.*

FAMILY FUN & ✿ **Power Vista-Niagara Power Project Visitors Center** (716-286-6661 or 800-NYPA-FUN; www.nypa.gov), 5777 Lewiston Road, Lewiston.
Open 9–5 year-round. Free admission. Exhibits on energy, electricity, and local
history generate fun for the entire family. The "Power Vista," which overlooks
the Niagara Gorge, attracts thousands of visitors yearly. Hands-on activities let
visitors learn about electricity and more. Get some helpful hints on energy efficiency, learn about hydropower in western New York history, and even send an

electronic postcard over the Internet. Enjoy a "hair-raising" experience courtesy of the Van der Graff generator, or create some electricity of your own on a bicycle generator. The visitors center has displays explaining the Power Authority's mission of providing electricity to the public plus a giant map of the entire New York Power Authority System. If you're an angler, a fishing platform, which includes a fish cleaning station and public rest rooms, is located just upstream from the power project. An annual hands-on wildlife festival takes place on the grounds in the fall.

SCENIC DRIVES **Seaway Trail** (800-SEAWAYT). Follows Lake Road (NY 18) through Porter and Youngstown, River Road (NY18 F) in Lewiston, and NY 104 and Main Street in Niagara Falls. The drive between Youngstown and Lewiston is very scenic, with the Niagara River on one side and large well-kept homes on the other.

SLEDDING See **Bond Lake County Park** in *Green Space—Parks.*

✳ Green Space

NATURE PRESERVES **Walleye Ponds and Nature Preserve,** Balmer Road, Porter. This 61-acre nature preserve was created to raise walleye to be transferred to the Niagara River. There are areas for camping, hiking, fishing, picnicking, and bird-watching. The preserve is maintained by the Niagara River Anglers association for use by their members. Anyone interested in fishing here can become a member for a nominal fee. Contact Niagara River Anglers Association PO Box 203, Niagara Falls, NY 14304; www.niagarariveranglers.com.

PARKS

Lewiston
Academy Park (716-754-8272), Ninth and Center Streets, Lewiston. This village green has a picnic area, recreational areas, and a baseball diamond.

Artpark State Park See *Theatres.*

Bond Lake County Park (716-731-3256), 2531 Lower Mountain Road, Lewiston. This park offers picnicking, boating, hiking trails, fishing, a nature center (open Sunday 12–4), and a 100-foot sledding hill in winter.

Hennepin Park (716-754-8271), 14th and Center Streets, Lewiston. This small park has a gazebo and several sitting areas.

Joseph Davis State Park (716-754-4596), 4143 Lower River Road, Lewiston. Open dawn to dusk. Free admission. The terrain in this park along the lower Niagara River is flat, with fields, woodlands, and ponds. Facilities include a playground, a nature trail, and a 27-hole Frisbee disc golf course. Fishermen can either fish in the pond for largemouth bass or head down to the river for a variety of freshwater fish. During the winter months, park visitors enjoy cross-county skiing, snowshoeing, and snowmobiling. Plans are underway for a "Birds of Prey" bird sanctuary in the park. Along the river, across the street from the park, is the "Spirit of Victory" sculpture by Tom Mullany. It was originally installed at

Artpark in 1989 and restored by the Lewiston Arts Council in 1998. Several picnic tables are located nearby.

Lewiston Landing Waterfront Park (716-754-8271), Water Street, Lewiston.
Overlooking the Niagara River, this park is one of the most scenic spots in
Lewiston. There's also a public boat launch.

Reservoir State Park (716-284-5778), Routes 265 and 31, Lewiston. Open
dawn to dusk. Free admission. Overlooking the Robert Moses Power Plant Reservoir, this park is one of the most used in Niagara County. Facilities include four
tennis courts, eight baseball diamonds, a softball complex, picnic facilities, and
open spaces for flying kites or model planes. It's a popular place to sled and cross-
country ski during winter and has excellent fishing in the reservoir during the
summer.

Youngstown

Constitution Park (716-745-7721), Main Street, Youngstown. This small park
with a gazebo overlooks the Niagara River (steps lead down to boat docks), with
a great view of Fort George in Niagara-on-the-Lake, Ontario. It was the site of a
salt battery—so named because salt bags were used in its construction—an
important factor in defense of the Niagara Frontier in the War of 1812. This
area was also the location of the Battle of LaBelle Famille, July 24, 1759.

Falkner Park (716-745-7721), 355 Second Street, Youngstown. This large park
has a playground, walkways, benches, and a picnic gazebo.

Fort Niagara State Park (716-745-7273), NY 18F, Youngstown. Open dawn to
dusk. Admission: $7 car parking. Fort Niagara State Park offers breathtaking
views of Lake Ontario; on a clear day you can see the skyline of Toronto, 24
miles across the lake. Some of the oak trees located in the 708-acre park are over
200 years old. Picnicking is popular here; over 500 picnic tables and five reserv-
able shelters are located within the park. There are also playgrounds, tennis
courts, a wading pool, and an Olympic-sized swimming pool. If fishing is what
interests you, two boat launches provide access to the lower Niagara River and
Lake Ontario. Trout, salmon, bass, muskellunge, and walleye are abundant in the
area. The park's 18 soccer fields are often used for regional and national competitions. In winter, visitors can cross-country ski, snowshoe, and sled. Historic Old
Fort Niagara, located at the mouth of the Niagara River, offers visitors a glimpse
of 18th-century military life (see *Historic Sites*). Fort Niagara State Park has
something for everyone. One of the area's best sunset vistas can be found at this
park on the hill overlooking Lake Ontario. If you come late in the day, you
usually are not charged for parking. See also *Lighthouses*.

Four Mile Creek State Campgrounds (716-745-3802 or 800-456-CAMP),
Lake Road, Youngstown. Open for camping mid-April–mid-October. This park
on the southern shores of Lake Ontario is used mainly for fishing, picnicking,
and camping. There are 266 campsites, many with beautiful river views. Facilities include central shelters with flush toilets, showers, and laundry. Hiking trails
follow densely wooded bluffs overlooking the lake. For a variety of the area's
fauna and flora, head to the marsh at the mouth of Four Mile Creek, where you
may see great blue herons or white trillium and greenbrier.

Veteran's Park (716-745-3061), Third Street, Youngstown. Facilities include baseball diamonds, tennis court and basketball courts, and picnic facilities.

WALKING AND HIKING TRAILS More information on the following trails can be obtained by calling the **New York State Office of Parks, Recreation and Historic Preservation** (716-278-1770).

Lewiston Branch Gorge Trail (in Artpark State Park). Starting at the edge of the Niagara Escarpment in Lewiston, this round-trip hike of under 2 miles offers upper and lower trail options, with the lower trail closer to the Niagara River. The trail ends under the Lewiston-Queenston Bridge.

Ongiara Trail (in Devil's Hole State Park), This 2.5-mile round-trip trail goes from the parking lot, down stairs into the gorge near the Whirlpool and Devil's Hole Rapids.

Whirlpool Rapids Trail (Whirlpool State Park), A 3.25-mile round-trip trail that spans Whirlpool State Park and leads into the Niagara River Gorge. There is the option of two paths, one at the river level and one at midgorge.

Whirlpool Rim Trail (Whirlpool State Park), A 2.5-mile round-trip trail along the rim of the Niagara Gorge.

Upper Great Gorge Trail, This easy 2-mile round-trip trail starts at the Gorge Discovery Center and takes you into the gorge to the head of the rapids. The **Upper Great Gorge Rim Trail**, which also starts at the Gorge Discovery Center, is another easy 2-mile, round-trip hike, this one leading to the American Falls, Goat Island, and the Horseshoe Falls.

Lewiston River Walk, Along NY 18F between Lewiston and Youngstown. This paved, 6-foot-wide path offers scenic vistas of the Niagara River and the historic homes that line the parkway.

✳ Lodging

INNS AND RESORTS The Fyfe and Drum Inn (716-745-1295; www.fyfe-and-drum.com), 500 Main Street, Youngstown. Open year-round. Innkeeper Quain Weber operates a smoke-free circa 1850 Victorian inn offering five rooms with private baths and air conditioning. The Toy Room and Lighthouse Room feature queen-sized beds, while the Regatta Room has both a king and a single. The Youngstown Room has two queen beds and the Step Down Room features a queen and a single. Breakfast is not included, but a kitchen is available for guest use, and several restaurants are within walking distance. $60–$125.

Riverview Inn (716-745-3335), 445 Main Street, Youngstown. Open year-round. This inn offers a handicapped-accessible suite on the first floor that includes twin beds, a couch that opens to a queen, dining room, and kitchenette. It also has a spectacular view of the Niagara River and over-looks Canada. Upstairs are four more guest rooms, all with private baths and two with river views. A fitness center is located in the basement. $85–$120.

BED AND BREAKFASTS Cameo Manor North (716-745-3034; www.cameoinn.com), 3881 Lower River

Road, Youngstown. Open year-round. For over 17 years innkeepers Greg and Carolyn Fisher have offered a tranquil getaway in this circa 1860 English manor house situated on three secluded acres. It is private and quiet, yet close to area attractions. The manor's great room has a fireplace at either end, along with a piano, assorted board games, and puzzles. Two of the four guest rooms are suites with private sunrooms, cable TV, and private baths. The two smaller rooms share a bath. A full breakfast is served each morning. $75–$175.

The Country Club Inn (716-285-4869; www.countryclubinn.com), 5170 Lewiston Road, Lewiston. Open year-round. Innkeepers Barbara Ann and Norman Oliver offer travelers a respite in an elegant, nonsmoking bed & breakfast with three guest rooms, each with queen bed and private bath. The inn's sitting room features a pool table, TV, and wood-burning fireplace. Breakfast is served in either the elegant dining room or on the deck that overlooks the golf course. $80–$115

✿ **Joanne's Bed & Breakfast** (716-754-7052 or 800-484-6449), 1380 Swann Road, Lewiston. Open year-round. Joanne and Larry Brennen offer a touch of Ireland in this country Victorian home located in the countryside just 20 minutes from Niagara Falls. The inn is decorated with antiques throughout, including the stove Joanne cooks on. Music is emphasized here; the parlor features a player piano with over 100 music rolls, and Larry himself is known for his Irish music. Four guest rooms share two full baths. Children are welcome. The inn is located on a half-

acre of land, just a mile from the Fatima Shrine. $55–$75

Sunny's Roost Bed & Breakfast (716-754-1161; www.sunnysroost.com) 421 Plain Street, Lewiston. Open year-round. Four sunny and comfy nonsmoking rooms are offered in this 100-year-old brick home, right in the heart of Lewiston. The Bantam and Rhode Island Red rooms share a bath, while the Ancona and Leghorn rooms each have private baths. A full breakfast, which includes fresh scones, home-baked breads, fresh fruits, and hot entrée, is served each morning in their large dining room. $70–$80

MOTELS Riverside Motel (716-754-4101; www.niagarafish.com), 160 South Water Street, Lewiston. Open February–December. Hosts Bruce and Andrea Blakelock offer 10 cozy, cottagelike rooms with a large front yard with outdoor seating and a view of the lower Niagara River. All rooms are decorated with a country decor and include air conditioning, HBO, and refrigerators. According to Andrea, her guests, many of them repeat customers, say that staying at the motel is like staying at a bed and breakfast, minus the breakfast. Guided fishing trips are available, as Bruce is a fishing charter captain. A boat launch is located nearby. $65–$75

Youngstown Motel (716-745-9906), 365 Second Street, Youngstown. Open seasonally April–November. Nine spacious and clean modern motel rooms with reasonable rates are available in this newly built motel centrally located in Youngstown. Fresh coffee and pastries are available each morning. $60–$70

OTHER LODGING **Four Mile Creek State Campground.** See *Green Space—Parks*.

✳ Where to Eat

DINING OUT ♿ **Brennans Irish Pub** (716-745-9938), 418 Main Street, Youngstown. Open Sunday–Thursday 11–10, Friday and Saturday 11–11. The building housing this relaxing restaurant dates back to 1840, and its brick and green walls are decorated with vintage Youngstown pictures. Dinner selections include steak, shrimp, chicken, roast beef, and seafood, plus lighter fare like sandwiches, pitas, wraps, subs, and pizza. The adjacent Main Street Station is a favorite Youngstown watering hole.

♿ **Carmelo's Coat of Arm's** (716-754-2311; www.carmeloscoatof arms.com), 425 Center Street, Lewiston. Open Monday–Thursday 4:30–9, Friday and Saturday 4:30–10. Contemporary cuisine is served in this 1838 building in the heart of the historic district. Chefs Carmelo Raimondi and Matthew Ott design food that's as pleasing to the eye as it is to the palate. Entrées served in this elegant upscale restaurant include dishes like seafood risotto, chicken fantasia, and grilled filet mignon with garlic-smashed potatoes.

The Clarkson House (716-754-4544), 810 Center Street, Lewiston. Open for lunch Monday–Friday 11:30–2; dinner Monday–Saturday 5–10, Sunday 4–9. This institution, which has recently been remodeled, features fine dining, including steaks and chicken dishes. This popular restaurant is well-known for their desserts that include cherries jubilee, and baked Alaska.

♿ **The Fyfe and Drum Restaurant** (716-745-3133; www.fyfe-and-drum.com), 440 Main Street, Youngstown. Open Sunday–Thursday 11–9, Friday and Saturday 11–10. Casual dining in an 1840s pub that has a central fieldstone fireplace and colonial atmosphere. Entrées include steaks, lamb chops, shepherd's pie, pastas, and vegetarian dishes, plus burgers, sandwiches, and a children's menu. Specialty drinks from the bar include Hot Brick Toddy, Colonial Rummer, and a Fyfe Manhattan.

Olde Fort Inn (716-745-7141), 110 Main Street, Youngstown. Open Tuesday–Saturday 4–10, Sunday 2–9. Enjoy casual fine dining in a Colonial atmosphere with Old-World prices. Start out your dining experience with a shrimp cocktail, steamed mussels, or onion soup. Entrée selections include ribs, pork tenderloin, pasta, lobster tails, surf and turf, and salmon.

♿ **Steelhead Irish Pub** (716-754-8181), 453 Center Street, Lewiston. Open Sunday–Thursday 11–9, Friday and Saturday 11–10. One of Lewiston's newer restaurants, specializing in traditional Irish and Irish American foods. Fresh fish is offered on the menu every night.

Villa Fortunata's (716-754-4904) 490 Center Street, Lewiston. Open Saturday–Wednesday 5–11, Thursday–Friday 12–11. Fine Italian cuisine, along with seafood and brick-oven pizza, is offered in this large white house with a dining room overlooking Center Street. Start your dining experience with appetizers like mozzarella in carozza, or calamar succhini fritti. Italian specialties include filetto di bue, petto di pollo rollato, veal Sorrentino, and lobster ravioli.

Water Street Landing (716-754-9200), 115 S. Water Street, Lewiston.

Open daily for lunch 11:30–3, dinner 4:30–10. This riverside restaurant, located in the former Riverside Inn, overlooks the Niagara River and the lower gorge and features a varied menu that includes steaks, chops, chicken, and seafood. In warmer weather dine outdoors on the patio overlooking the river and the Canadian shore. They have an extensive wine list, and desserts are made by the Village Bakery just down the street.

EATING OUT ✍ ᖴ **Apple Granny** (716-754-2028), 433 Center Street, Lewiston. Open Tuesday–Thursday 11–11, Friday and Saturday 11–12 and Sunday 11–10. Enjoy casual dining at its finest in this circa 1830 building. This popular family restaurant serves perennial favorites like sandwiches and burgers, plus their specialty Granny's Awesome Blossom blooming onion. Dinner selections include prime rib, filet mignon, chicken, veal, Italian specialties, seafood, and Granny's famous beer-battered fish fry on Friday.

✍ ᖴ 🍷 **Clark's Burger House** (716-754-1950), 869 Cayuga Street (behind Academy Park), Lewiston. Open Monday–Thursday 6 AM–8 PM, Friday 6 AM– 9 PM, Saturday and Sunday 6 AM–3 PM. This family diner with a 1950s theme was recently renovated following a fire. It has been serving the Lewiston area for over 50 years. The car-themed back room has framed vintage car ads and a shelf of model antique cars and hot rods. The menu features a variety of items, from all-day breakfast to sandwiches and burgers to homemade soups and dinner entrées. They also have ice cream cones, floats, sundaes, and milkshakes.

A Wednesday evening "car cruise" takes place March–September.

Dicamillo Bakery (716-754-2218), 535 Center Street, Lewiston. Open daily 7 AM–9 PM. They've been serving quality baked goods since 1920. Take out bread, rolls, donuts, bagels, pastries, and pizza. Two small tables are located in the front of the shop to eat in.

✍ **Lewiston Silo** (716-754-9680), North Water Street, Lewiston. Open 11 AM–10 PM daily April 15–October 1. Enjoy casual dining, including 30 flavors of hand-dipped ice cream, in a circular restaurant on the water's edge.

ᖴ **Main Street Gas and Grill** (716-745-1130), 311 Main Street, Youngstown. Open Sunday–Thursday 11–9, Friday and Saturday 11–10, Sunday 12–9. A cute spot to stop for a quick bite to eat. It has a small, casual restaurant and shop with groceries and other essentials that boaters may need, plus public rest rooms and a gas station.

The Village Bake Shoppe (716-754-2300; www.villagebakeshoppe.com), 419 Center Street, Lewiston. Open Monday–Saturday 7:30–5:30, Sunday 7:30–3:30; summer till 9 PM daily. A quaint, small shop featuring award-winning, from-scratch desserts, including pies, cookies, scones, coffee cakes, breads, and authentic Italian gelato. A few small tables are located in the front of the shop.

ᖴ **Youngstown Coffee Co.** (716-745-1000), 400 Main Street, Youngstown. Open Monday–Friday 8–3, Saturday and Sunday 9–2. A cozy coffee shop with a nice sitting area. Serving coffee and teas along with sandwiches, cakes, and pies.

⌀ & ⚘ **Youngstown Village Diner** (716-745-9858), 425 Main Street, Youngstown. Open Monday–Thursday 6 AM–9:30 PM, Friday and Saturday 6 AM–3 PM, Sunday 6 AM–2 PM. Dine at the counter or at tables in this neat and clean restaurant overlooking the Niagara River. Enjoy salads, sandwiches, burgers, and wraps, plus breakfast and dinner specials that are posted on the blackboard.

✳ Entertainment

THEATERS & **Artpark** (716-754-9000; www.artpark.net), 450 South Fourth Street, Lewiston. Park open daily dawn to dusk; theater performances July and August. Call or see Web site for schedule. Parking $7. Artpark is a 200-acre state park designed to bring the arts to the general public. Here, one can experience natural beauty as well as visual and performing arts during the summer season. Enjoy professional musical theater along with concerts and hands-on art activities. Visitors can also picnic along the gorge or enjoy a hike on the scenic trails. Geologists believe that 10,000 years ago Niagara Falls was located at this site, before the turbulent waters etched away at the gorge. Nowadays the falls is about 7 miles south of Artpark.

The Marble Orchard (716-754-0166; www.artcouncil.org), This unique theatrical performance, which started as a tour of the village cemetery, features costumed actors portraying notable people from the area's past. Performance location and schedule varies.

MUSIC **Blue Mondays,** Hennepin Park Gazebo, Lewiston. A summer outdoor concert event held each Monday.

Lewiston Jazz Project, Hennepin Park Gazebo, Lewiston. Wednesdays, July and August.

SPORTS **Niagara University Purple Eagles** (www.niagara.edu), Niagara University, Lewiston. NCAA Division 1 Basketball.

✳ Selective Shopping

Note: Some of the buildings the shops are housed in date back to the early 1800s and have several different levels, making wheelchair and stroller accessibility difficult.

ANTIQUES **The Country Doctor Antiques and Gifts** (716-754-0775), 500 Center Street, Lewiston. Open Monday–Saturday 10:30–5:30, Sunday 11–5. This building houses several small shops that specialize in gifts, antique furniture, glassware, and jewelry.

Mimi Pyne's Antiques (716-754-8560), 175 Niagara Street (corner of Cayuga Street), Lewiston. Open Thursday–Saturday 12–6. Mimi and Jim Pyne have an assortment of antiques, furniture, glass, jewelry, and collectibles displayed in a tiny two-story carriage house.

Rita's Memory Lane (716-754-9081), 536 Center Street, Lewiston. Open 11–5 daily. A general line of antiques and collectibles.

Stimson's Antiques & Gifts (716-754-7815), 1727 Ridge Road (NY 104) Lewiston. Open 1–5 daily; winter, Friday and Saturday only. Located in a farmhouse basement, this shop has a nice selection of antiques and collectibles.

SPECIAL SHOPS **Blooms & Company** (716-754-2212), 703 Center

Street, Lewsiton. Open Monday–Saturday 10–8, Sunday 10–6. Owner Sandie Zientara has created a wonderful shop inside a circa 1820 building that features reasonably priced designer clothing and lingerie plus home decor items like hand-painted glassware and custom-order, hand-painted furniture as well as handmade children's clothing, Crabtree & Evelyn items, and a garden accessories room.

Canterbury Place (716-754-4818), 547 Center Street, Lewiston. Open Tuesday–Saturday 10–5. A New England–style gift shop with a mix of romantic, traditional, and folk art accessories for the home, including Yankee Candles, Cats Village, and Williraye Studios.

Cheri Amour (716-754-8675), 522 Center Street, Lewiston. Open Monday 11–5, Tuesday–Friday 11–6, Saturday 11–5. Specializing in unique gifts, including hand-painted bottles, Votivo candles, and Nomination Italian charms.

The Dory Shop (716-745-3335), 435 Main Street, Youngstown. Open Monday–Saturday 9–6, Sunday 9–2. This shop, located in a vintage building with exposed brick walls carries T-shirts, Harbour Lights lighthouses, carved wooden santas, and Carhartt outdoor clothing. It is also a drop-off/pick-up location for Capitol Cleaners. An art studio overlooking the Niagara River at the rear of the store, features prints, photos, and artwork depicting Youngstown and Niagara region scenes.

Josette's Fashion and Gift Boutique (716-754-7709), 400 Plain Street, Lewiston. Open Monday–Wednesday 10–5:30, Thursday and Friday 10–7, Saturday 10–5. Special-

izing in mother-of-the-wedding and formal clothing, accessories, and gifts.

Lewiston Gift Shoppe (716-754-7010), 480 Center Street, Lewiston. Open Monday 12–5:30, Tuesday–Saturday 10–5:30, Sunday 12–4. This shop specializes in Irish imports and general giftware.

Lewiston Harbor Sweet Shoppe (716-754-4494), 449 Center Street, Lewiston. Open Monday–Thursday 11–4, Friday and Saturday 11–5. A sweet place to shop, they are the only retailer on the East Coast that carries Moonstruck Chocolates, artisan candies handmade in Oregon from French and Belgian chocolate. (Moonstruck Chocolates are served at

SOME OF LEWISTON'S INVITING CENTER STREET SHOPS.

Christine A. Smyczynski

the Emmy Awards.) The shop also carries seven flavors of fudge, sugar-free candy, and specialties made by Harbor Sweets of Salem, Massachusetts.

Lewiston Hollow Mercantile Co. (716-754-2970), 335 Center Street, Lewiston. Open Tuesday–Saturday, hours vary. Unique country home decor, antiques, gifts, and even a sock monkey or two are housed in a vintage 1910 building that originally was an ice cream parlor. It has the original pressed-tin ceiling and walls, and the original mirrors line the wall in the front of the shop.

Quote & Quill (716-754-8582), 469 Center Street, Lewiston. Open Monday–Thursday 10–6, Friday 10–7, Saturday 10–4, Sunday 12–4. Choose from candy like fudge truffles as well as cards, gifts, seasonal decor, and candles.

Spotted Leopard Boutique (716-754-1900), 736 Center Street, Lewiston. Open Tuesday, Thursday, and Saturday 12–5 and by appointment. Located in the historic 1840 Lewiston Opera Hall, Karen Olin's shop features vintage hats, jewelry, and accessories along with sterling and artist-designed jewelry and gifts. The **Couture Fifth Avenue** shop (716-998-6381), in the same building and open seasonally, features women's and children's fashions, accessories, gifts, silver jewelry, and Egyptian items.

Village Vendor (716-754-8458), 467 Center Street, Lewiston. Open Tuesday–Friday 10–5, Saturday 10–6, Sunday 12–4. This shop carries quilts, clothing, and seasonal decorating items along with gifts and art from the Niagara region, including Lewiston wine glasses, mugs, and other memorabilia.

✳ Special Events

June: **Strawberry Festival** (716-745-3337), St. John's Episcopal Church, Main and Chestnut Streets, Youngstown. This annual festival held in late June features strawberry shortcake, crafts, a Chinese auction, and a flea market.

July: **French and Indian War Encampment** (716-745-7611), Old Fort Niagara. This is Old Fort Niagara's largest yearly special event, the longest-running French and Indian War event in the world, with hundreds of reenactors gathering at the fort to depict the war. **Tuscarora Nation Picnic,** Tuscarora Nation (Lewiston). This event, which is the oldest field day in Niagara County, showcases Native American culture. **Level Regatta** (716-745-7230; www.yyc.org), Youngstown Yacht Club, 491 Water Street, Youngstown. This competition first started in 1974 with 20 boats. Now it's the largest freshwater regatta in North America, with over 300 sailboats participating. The best view of the event is from Fort Niagara State Park.

August: **Lewiston Outdoor Fine Arts Festival and Chalkwalk Competition** (716-754-0166; www.artcouncil.org), A two-day event, ranked one of the top 100 attractions along the Seaway Trail, that showcases more than 150 artists from the United States and Canada. The festival's Chalkwalk is a popular art competition among area high schools. **Lewiston Jazz Festival** (716-754-9500; www.lewistonjazz.com/hompage.php), Music, antiques and culinary samplings throughout the village.

September: **Niagara County Peach Festival** (716-754-9500). Lewiston Festivities include amusement rides, games of chance, Peach Queen Pageant, and, of course, peach-related food. **New York Power Authority's Wildlife Festival** Power Vista (716-286-6661; www.nypa.gov). A day of free family fun, featuring live animals, music, art workshops, and more. **Youngstown Volunteer Field Days** (716-745-3335), Veteran's Park, Youngstown. Family fun celebrating the end of summer. Activities include a parade, car show, fireworks, and lawn mower racing.

October: **Frontier Fur Traders Weekend** (716-745-7611), Old Fort Niagara. Fort Niagara becomes a wilderness trading post once again as trappers and traders depict the early history of the fort. Reenactors recreate the era when fur trade dominated the region. **The Haunted Fortress** (716-745-7611), Old Fort Niagara. Get up close and personal with some

of the ghosts of the fort. **The Marble Orchard** (716-754-0166), Lewiston Village Cemetery. This annual event features stories about Lewiston's past and the Underground Railroad.

November–January: **Festival of Lights** (716-754-7489), Our Lady of Fatima Shrine. Enjoy 15 acres of religious-themed light displays.

December: **Castle by Candlelight** (716-745-7611), Old Fort Niagara. An annual holiday fund-raiser for the fort. **Christmas in the Village** (716-745-3061), Youngstown. Festivities include a Christmas play, musical entertainment, wagon rides, and Santa Claus. **Historic Lewiston Christmas Walk** (716-754-9500), Lewiston. This annual event offers visitors old-fashioned fun, including caroling, roasting chestnuts, sleigh rides, crafts shows, and a parade down Center Street.

LAKE ONTARIO SHORE—Wilson, Olcott, Burt, Newfane, and Barker

The first settler in Wilson, on the shores of Lake Ontario, was Henry Lockwood, who arrived in 1808. Most of the area's growth, though, can be attributed to Reuben Wilson and his family, who came here from Canada in 1810. Reuben's son, Luther, developed the hamlet of Wilson in 1827, adding numer-ous buildings and additions to the village, including a cobblestone home built in 1844 that now houses the Wilson House Inn and Restaurant. Wilson was incorporated in 1858. The surrounding area is known as the fruit-growing region of Niagara County (a top area employer is Pfeiffer Foods, which makes salad dressings). Wilson is also known as a good fishing area, especially for trout, bass, and salmon. Popular with recreational boaters and fishermen, it has a small, protected boat harbor with a marina and docking facilities.

Visitors to Olcott find a quaint lakeside village consisting of a huge park, small beach, good fishing, and many small shops and restaurants. However, most visitors are unaware of the town's "golden era" from 1900 to 1937, when thousands of people flocked to the village each summer by steamship or trolley to stay in the 100-room hotel with a grand ballroom that featured acts such as Guy Lombardo, Louis Armstrong, and the Dorsey Brothers.

The communities of Newfane, Burt, and Barker are primarily agricultural.

AREA CODE The area code is 716.

GUIDANCE Newfane Town Hall/Newfane Tourism (716-778-8531; www
.olcott-newfane.com), 2896 Transit Road, Newfane. Open Monday–Friday
8:30–4:30. Maps, brochures, and other area information are also available at the
Red Caboose, corner of NY 18 and 78 in Olcott Beach. The Red Caboose is
open daily 9–5, end of April–beginning of November.

Village of Wilson (716-751-6764), 375 Lake Avenue, Wilson.

GETTING THERE *By car:* Take exit 49 off I-90, and head north on NY 78 (Transit
Road) to Newfane and Olcott. Wilson, Burt, and Somerset are accessed from
NY 18.

MEDICAL EMERGENCY Dial 911

Inter-Community Memorial Hospital (716-778-5111), 2600 William Street,
Newfane.

✳ To See

MUSEUMS AND HISTORIC HOMES Babcock Cobblestone House Museum
(716-795-9948), 7449 Lake Road, Barker. Open Saturday and Sunday 1–4, last
Saturday in June through second Sunday of October. Donation. This two-story
Greek Revival–style cobblestone house built in 1848 by farmer Jeptha Babcock
represents the mid--to-late period of the Cobblestone era. Cobblestone construction is unique to the western
New York region. One of the more
interesting features of the home is the
brick bread oven that was reconstructed in the restored kitchen. The rest of
the house has been carefully restored
to reflect 19th-century life. The property is currently owned by New York
State Electric and Gas Corporation,
and the house is maintained and furnished by the Town of Somerset Historical Society.

THIS 1848 GREEK REVIVAL–STYLE HOME,
NOW BABCOCK COBBLESTONE HOUSE
MUSEUM, IS A CLASSIC EXAMPLE FROM
THE COBBLESTONE ERA.
Christine A. Smyczynski

**Newfane Historical Society
Grounds** (716-778-6151), West
Creek Road, Newfane. The grounds
have eleven historical buildings that
are open to the public during festivals
and by appointment.

Van Horn Mansion (716-778-7197),
2165 Lockport-Olcott Road, Burt.
Open Sunday 2–4, summer only.
Donation. This lovely brick mansion

was built in 1823 by James Van Horn, who built the first gristmill in Newfane in 1811. Maintained by the Newfane Historical Society since 1987, this home has been restored to its former grandeur. On your walking tour of the house and gardens, your guide will tell you many interesting tales about the home, such as it's rumored to have been a stop on the Underground Railroad. Many people also believe that the ghost of Malinda Van Horn, the young wife of James Jr., who died in childbirth, roamed the grounds. In the late 1920s the remains of the Van Horn family were all moved from the family plot on the grounds to a local cemetery—except for Malinda because they could not locate her grave. From that time until her remains were finally located in 1992, ghostly sightings and noises were observed in the mansion. No one has seen or heard the ghost since her grave was marked, and it's believed that Malinda is finally at rest.

Wilson Historical Society (716-751-9883 or 716-751-9827, 716-751-9886; www.wilsonnewyork.com), 645 Lake Street, Wilson. Open Sunday 2–4 April– December. A 1912 railroad station houses vintage cars and trucks. Local historical information is available.

Christine A. Smyczynski

FOG SHROUDS THIRTY-MILE POINT LIGHTHOUSE IN BARKER.

LIGHTHOUSES **Olcott Lighthouse.** Located at the end of NY 78 at Lake Ontario. This full-size replica of an 1873 lighthouse was dedicated in 2003.

Thirty Mile Point Lighthouse (716-795-3885 or 716-795-3117), Golden Hill State Park, Lower Lake Road, Barker. Tours Saturday and Sunday 2–4, Memorial Day–Labor Day. Admission: $7 for parking. Climb to the top of this 1875 lighthouse built of hand-carved stone to enjoy a spectacular view of Lake Ontario. The 60-foot lighthouse was built to warn ships of the rocky shoal and shifting sandbar in Lake Ontario, the site of at least five major shipwrecks prior to the construction of the lighthouse. The original navigational light, purchased from France, produced 600,000 candlepower and was the most powerful light on Lake Ontario. A rental suite is available in the lighthouse year-round. See *Other Lodging*.

WINERIES **Marjim Manor** (716-778-7001), 7171 East Lake Road, Appleton. Open weekends. This newly opened winery, which produces fruit wines, is operated by Margo and Jim Bittner, is located in an 1853 mansion known as Appleton Hall.

See additional wineries listed under *Lockport.*

✳ To Do

BOAT LAUNCHES AND MARINAS **Wilson Harborfront** (716-751-9202) 57 Harbor Street, Wilson. Several years ago this harbor underwent an extensive face-lift. The harbor has a boat-launching facility and is a good spot to fish for trout, bass, and salmon. Other improvements have been made to the docks, harbor-front shops have been added as well as a harbor-front pool, and major

---

FISHING **ANGLING IN NIAGARA AND ERIE COUNTIES**

With its abundance of waterways, including Great Lakes Erie and Ontario, the Niagara River, and the Erie Canal, the Greater Niagara Region has a reputation for excellence among sports fishermen. Anglers can reel in trophy trout plus salmon, bass, walleye and muskellunge, and other fish species. The Newfane/Olcott area is especially noted as a popular destination for fishing year-round. It's the ideal location for lake fishing from April to October, with its close proximity to the Niagara Bar and the ports of Wilson and Point Breeze. In September and October salmon can be caught right from the Olcott Pier as they first enter Eighteen Mile Creek. From October to April, a popular fishing spot for a wide variety of fish is just north of the Burt Dam on Eighteen Mile Creek and a few miles south of Olcott. For more info on sport-fishing in the Greater Niagara Region and to obtain a "hot spot" fishing map, contact the **Erie County Dept. of Environmental Planning**, 866-345-FISH. For information on New York State Fishing Regulations, a booklet can be requested from the **New York State Department of Environmental Conservation Bureau of Fisheries**, 625 Broadway, Albany, NY 12233; www.dec.state.ny.us Other resources include **The Niagara County Sport Fishing Program** (Niagara U.S.A Tourism, 800-338-7890; www.niagara-usa.com) **Olcott Fishing** (www .olcottfishing.com), **Niagara River Anglers** (www.niagarariveranglers.com), **Lake Ontario Counties (LOC) Fishing Derbies** (1-888-REEL-2-IN; www.loc.org), which sponsors fishing derbies in the spring and fall, and **Niagara County Fishing Hotline** (716-433-5606). Fishing licenses can be obtained at any town or county municipal clerks office, Dick's Sporting Goods stores, Wal-Mart, and most bait and tackle shops. For more information on fishing in Erie and Niagara counties, including a compete list of where to get a license, fishing supplies, and charter captains, see www.erie.gov/hotspot.

renovations have been made to the Wilson Boathouse Restaurant (see *Dining Out*).

FAMILY FUN ♪ **Olcott Carousel Park** (716-778-7066), Main Street, Olcott. Open May–October, Saturday and Sunday 12–6. Summer months open Thursday–Sunday 12–7. Enjoy a ride on a restored, historic 1928 Allen Herschel carousel, and reminisce about a bygone era. Plans are underway to include more vintage rides, including a 1940s auto/fire truck kiddy ride, which originally operated at a former Olcott amusement park, as well as a 1940s kiddie skyfighter ride.

FISHING CHARTERS Numerous fishing charters run out of Olcott. For a complete list, consult the visitors guide published by Niagara USA Tourism. Here are just a few:

Cinelli's Sportfishing Service (716-433-5210), PO Box 773, Olcott.

Muddy Rudder Charters (716-778-5233), 2219 West Creek Road, Burt.

Phillips Charter Service (716-778-7860), 2481 Lockport-Olcott Road, Newfane.

Pursuer Charter Service (716-778-7310), 6025 McKee Road, Newfane.

GOLF Newfane Pro-Am Par 3 (716-778-8302), 2501 North Main Street (NY 78), Newfane. Open May–September. A 9-hole, par-27 course. Niagara County's only course lit for nighttime play. Fine food and legal beverages are served at Duffer's Restaurant and Tavern.

✳ Green Space

BEACHES Olcott Beach. See **Krull Park**. There is also a swimming beach at **Wilson-Tuscarora State Park**.

Wilson Pool Club (716-751-3682). At Wilson Harbor. While the club is mainly for members, visitors can pay a day-use fee, approximately $10, to use the pool, which overlooks Wilson Harbor.

PARKS Golden Hill State Park, (800-456-CAMP), 9691 Lower Lake Road, Barker. Open dawn to dusk. Admission: $7/car. Popular with campers for its scenic location and fishermen because of the excellent fishing on Lake Ontario, the park offers a variety of activities, including biking, picnicking, Frisbee golf, nature trails, playgrounds, and hiking. Recreational programs are offered during the summer months. During the winter, visitors enjoy cross-country skiing, snowmobiling, and snowshoeing. Thirty Mile Point Lighthouse, built in 1875 of hand-carved stone, is located in the park. The lighthouse, which was recognized on a postage stamp in 1995, is open for tours Saturday and Sunday 2– 4, Memorial Day—Labor Day. Make sure you climb to the top for a great view of the lake. See also *Lighthouses, Lodging*.

Keg Creek Rest Area, NY 18, between Olcott and Appleton. This roadside rest area has a few parking places and several picnic tables overlooking Keg Creek.

Krull Park/Olcott Beach (716-778-7711), NY18, Olcott. Open dawn to dusk. Free admission. Krull Park is one of Niagara County's most beautiful parks. The 323-acre park, located along the southern shore of Lake Ontario, has 10 acres of wooded areas, 50 acres of semiwoods, and 100 acres of brush, as well as ample space for family and sporting activities. Looking toward Lake Ontario, one can observe sea ducks, diving ducks, and gulls. The spruce and pine portion of the park is a habitat for winter finches. Krull Park offers a wide variety of family activities, including fishing, boating, baseball fields, basketball courts, tennis courts, and soccer fields. There are also hiking trails, picnic facilities, a model plane airfield, and Olcott Beach, a small swimming beach. Krull Park/Olcott Beach is the site of the annual polar bear swim in March and the site of many summer fairs and festivals.

Wilson-Tuscarora State Park (716-751-6361), 3371 Lake Road, Wilson. Open dawn to dusk. Admission: $7/car. Wilson-Tuscarora State Park has 395 acres of mature woods, open meadows, and marshland. Its 4 miles of hiking trails can also be used for snowshoeing and cross-country skiing in the winter months. The park has a boat launch located on a narrow strip of land referred to as "the island." Fishing, from either boats or shore, is very popular here. Other facilities include picnic areas, playgrounds, and a swimming beach.

✳ Lodging

MOTEL AND HOTELS Rooms at the Pool (716-751-9202), Wilson. Harbor innkeeper Peter Doyle offers four guest rooms next to the Wilson Pool Club, three of which have a spectacular view of Wilson Harbor. The back room, Wawbeek Lodge, is a fishing-themed room with two single beds. The Caneel Bay room has a Caribbean motif and two single beds, while the Oriental Room has a queen bed. The Casa del Mar is a two-room suite with two singles, a double futon, and a queen bed. All four rooms share one bath. A coffee shop is nearby. $89–$159.

Wilson House Inn and Restaurant (716-751-9888), 300 Lake Street, Wilson. Owner Chuck Mercurio offers six neat and clean standard rooms with two double beds and private baths on the second floor of the 1844 cobblestone inn and restaurant that was once home to Luther Wilson. Chuck says that some guests have claimed the inn is haunted, citing unexplained noises, areas of coldness, and ghostly pushes. $50.

BED & BREAKFASTS Hendricks House Bed & Breakfast (716-778-7342), 2666 Lockport-Olcott Road, Newfane. Innkeeper Jeffrey Hendricks offers guests two rooms to choose from in an "in-law" apartment separate from the main house, one with a double bed, or one with two twins. He rents to only one party at a time, so you won't have to share the one bath with strangers. This B&B, which is right in Newfane, is popular with grandparents visiting from out of town. $20.

OTHER LODGING Fisherman's Choice (716-751-9481), 4793 East Lake Road, Wilson. Choose from a log cabin, two other cabins, and an efficiency apartment. $110–$135.

Lighthouse Cottage Golden Hill State Park (716-795-3885 or 800-456-2267), 9691 Lower Lake Road Barker.

The original lighthouse keepers' quarters in Thirty Mile Point lighthouse is a second-floor, three-bedroom apartment that sleeps up to six people, has a fully equipped kitchen, and a beautiful view of Lake Ontario. Minimum one week rental during the summer season, two-day minimum stay during the nonpeak season. Note: The lighthouse is not handicapped accessible, and no smoking or pets are allowed. Late June–late August: weekly rentals only, $600/week. Rest of year: $150/night, minimum two night rental or $600/week.

✳ Where to Eat

DINING OUT **Mariner's Landing** (716-778-5535), 1540 Franklin Street, Olcott. Monday–Saturday 4–10, Sunday 2–9. A cozy seafood restaurant near Lake Ontario across the street from Krull Park. Entrées include broiled scallops, grilled salmon, filet mignon, chicken cordon bleu, and pasta dishes.

The Rib House (716-778-7910), 2990 Lockport-Olcott Road, Newfane. Open for dinner Tuesday–Thursday 4–9, Friday and Saturday 4–10, Sunday 12–8. This casual restaurant features fine dining selections such as filet mignon, chicken cordon bleu, and jumbo shrimp. They are famous for their prime rib and Canadian pork baby-back ribs. The Rainbow Luncheon Theater, a senior citizen entertainment event, takes place at the Rib House on select afternoons April–November. Contact the Newfane Town Hall (716-778-5098) for details.

Wilson Boat House Restaurant (716-751-6060; www.wilsonboat house.com), 57 Harbor Street, Wilson. Open for lunch Wednesday–

Sunday 11:30–3, dinner Wednesday–Thursday 4–10, Friday and Saturday 4–11, Sunday 4–9. This historic circa 1907 restaurant, located directly on the water, has one of the best views in town and the largest covered outdoor patio in the area. Menu selections include north coast sea scallops, Niagara vineyards chicken chardonnay, grilled pork tenderloin, steak, pasta, and a Friday fish fry. The Five Coconut, a Jamaican-themed bar, is located in the lower level of the restaurant.

Wilson House Inn and Restaurant (716-751-9888) 300 Lake Street, Wilson. Open Sunday–Thursday 11–9, Friday and Saturday 11–11. This popular restaurant is located in a charming 1844 cobblestone inn, the former home of Luther Wilson, who laid out the hamlet in 1827. House specialties include strip steak, steak Neptune, chicken pinot, and Cajun chicken. They also have a large selection of Italian specialties and serve locally made Pfeiffer dressings with their salads. The lunch menu includes deli sandwiches, burgers, and salads. The house specialty dessert is a caramel apple blossom served with vanilla ice cream. See *Lodging*.

EATING OUT 🐾 ♿ 🍦 **Baehr's Ice Cream Cottage** (716-778-9602), 7080 Lake Road (NY 18), Appleton. Open seasonally April–Labor Day, daily 12–9. Choose from ice-cream treats like cones and milkshakes, as well as sundaes topped with fresh in-season fruit.

🐾 ♿ 🍦 **Barbara Ann's Carousel Concessions and Images of the Past** (716-735-7489), 5976 Ontario Street, Olcott Beach (next to the Olcott Beach Carousel Park). Spring and fall, weekends only 12–6; June–August, open seven days 12–6. This take-out stand serves hot dogs, hamburgers, fries, and ice cream. Or get a "picnic in the park," complete with picnic basket, that includes fried chicken, potato or macaroni salad, beverage, dessert, tablecloth, cutlery, and even three Olcott Beach plastic ants!

✍ ♿ ☕ **Boardwalk Sandwich Shoppe** (716-778-8343), 5953 Ontario Street (Lakeview Village Fair) Olcott Beach. Open seasonally, weekdays 11–6, weekends 8–8. This small takeout restaurant has all sorts of finger foods, including sandwiches, subs, hot dogs, and more. Their specialty is the Big Olcott burger made with a half pound of ground beef and topped with all the "fixins." They also have a breakfast menu.

✍ ♿ ☕ **Cameron's Lakeside Ice Cream Shoppe,** Ontario Street, Olcott Beach. A seasonal take-out shop in Lakeview Village Fair.

The Coffee Emporium (716-778-9050). 2691 Maple Avenue, Newfane. Open Monday–Friday 6 AM–9 PM, Saturday 8 AM–9 PM. A charming coffee shop located in the old brick Patterson Grocery building in the heart of Newfane. Enjoy tea, coffee, baked goods, and gourmet sandwiches.

Creekside Country Café (716-778-5512), 3039 Lockport-Olcott Road, Newfane. Open Saturday–Thursday 6 AM–2 PM, Friday 6 AM–8 PM. A family restaurant.

✍ ♿ ☕ **Gordie Harpers Bazaar** (716-778-8048), 3333 Lockport-Olcott Road, Newfane. Open Sunday–Thursday 8–8, Friday and Saturday 8–9. A large, popular, rustic, country-style restaurant that features home-cooked favorites like pot roast, steaks, seafood, and chicken. See also *Specialty Shops*.

✍ **Snack Shack at the Wilson Pool Club** (716-751-3682), A seasonal take-out restaurant next to the pool club by Wilson Harbor. Choose from hot dogs, burgers, chicken fingers, meatball subs, and Philly cheesesteak sandwiches.

Time Out Sports Bar (716-778-5890), 5852 East Main Street, Olcott. This restaurant and bar, overlooking Eighteen Mile Creek and the Olcott Harbor, has reasonably priced sandwiches and wings, as well as pasta and seafood entrées.

✳ Selective Shopping

ANTIQUES ♿ **Barbara Ann's Carousel Concessions and Images of the Past** (716-735-7489), 5976 Ontario Street, Olcott (next to the Olcott Beach Carousel Park). Spring and fall, weekends only 12–6; June–August, open seven days 12–6. Barbara Colley's shop features furniture, glassware, gifts, and collectibles, along with a museum. A food concession serving ice cream, hot dogs, and hamburgers is located at the rear of the building.

Barn Place Antiques (716-778-5555), 2421 Lockport-Olcott Road (NY 78), Newfane. Open April–October Wednesday–Saturday 11–3. A variety of eclectic, smalls, and other unique items can be found inside this rustic 1937 log cabin that was once home to the Newfane Conservation Club. The two moose heads hanging over the stone fireplace are original to the building. The shop has a $1 bargain room in the back. Owner Christine Irr also has Girl Scout Museum in one corner, featuring scout memorabilia from 1912 to the 1960s.

FARM MARKETS **Murphy Orchards** (716-778-7926; www.murphyorchards .com), 2402 McClew Road, Burt. Open seven days 8:30–6 May–November; Orchard Tea Room open Tuesday–Sunday 11–4 year-round. Take a drive out to rural Niagara County to pick your own fresh fruit and vegetables at this 65-acre farm that has been in continuous operation since the mid-1800s. (It was once a stop on the Underground Railroad, so be sure to check out the secret room beneath the barn where slaves were once hidden.) The farm's Country Barn Store is stocked with jams, jellies, syrups, and vinegars along with handcrafted items. See their Web site for various guided group tours—including Underground Railroad Heritage Tours and Wildlife Habitat/ Environmental Conservation Tours—which must be booked in advance.

SPECIAL SHOPS & **Abe's Gift Shop** (716-778-5259), 2384 Lockport-Olcott Road, Newfane. Open Thursday–Saturday 11–5. Find handmade, painted, and quilted items along with garden furniture here.

& **Captured Memories Mercantile** (716-778-7171), 2019 Lockport-Olcott Road (NY 78), Burt. Open Tuesday–Saturday 10–6, Sunday 12–6. A cute little shop featuring a collection of antiques and new gift items, including baskets, candles, clocks, pottery, wreaths, and stoneware. Owner Jenny Adams tries to buy merchandise made in the U.S.A. Kids will like the retro gumball machine, where they can get a gumball for just a penny. You can also pick up area tourism brochures here.

The Garden Gate (716-751-6402), 257 Young Street, Wilson. Open Monday–Friday 9–5, Saturday 9–4.

This shop has unique gifts and floral designs.

& ✿ **Gordie Harpers Bazaar** (716-778-8048), 3333 Lockport-Olcott Road, Newfane. Open Sunday–Thursday 8–8, Friday and Saturday 8–9. This large complex of over 60 unique shops just seems to go on and on. Find everything from collectibles, antiques, books, garden ornaments, candies, florals, and more, including a large selection of handcrafted items. Their bakery specializes in pies, pastries, cakes, and other goodies. Breakfast, lunch, and dinner are served in their country dining room. See *Where to Eat*.

& ✿ **Lakeview Village Fair** (716-778-8531), NY 78 and Ontario Street, Olcott Open seasonally May–October (weekends only September–December). A charming village of retail specialty shops located on the south shore of Lake Ontario. There's a delightful view of the lake from the back walkway, and it's only a short stroll to Krull Park, the beach, and the Newfane Town Marina. Some of the shops include: **Cabana Gift Shop** (716-778-8343), which has a general selection of gift items; **It's My Turn** (716-633-6282), which has accessories, home decor, florals, and wildlife watercolors; **Vintage Cottage**, specializing in floral items and vintage linens; **Antiques of Olcott** (716-778-5657), a small general line of antiques; **Water's Edge** (716-778-0501), for a large selection of nautical-themed and lighthouse items; **Everything Cats** (716-778-7767), which has all sorts of gift items for your favorite feline, including fresh catnip, as well as home decor items with a cat theme; and **Nature's Child** (716-282-3695), for unique jewelry, scented oils, incense, recycled items, wind chimes, and unusual gifts.

& **Lighthouse Gift Gallery** (716-778-5886), 5971 Main Street, Olcott. Open Memorial Day–Labor day, Tuesday–Sunday 11–6; rest of year Thursday–Sunday 11–6. This shop has all sorts of nautical and lighthouse-related items, including books about Great Lakes lighthouses.

Olcott Beach Trading Company and Bookstore Ontario Street, Olcott. Open seasonally Saturday 10–8, Sunday 11–6. A little bit of everything, from T-shirts and gift items, to candy, soda, and snacks. A small bookstore is located in a separate building.

& **Wilson Harborfront Shops,** Wilson. Most are open seven days from the end of June–Labor Day and weekends only May–end of June, Labor Day–October. The several seasonal shops located along the harborfront include **Jayne & Co**, specializing in women's clothing and accessories; **Pier House Gifts**, which carries toys, candles, candy, gifts, and more; **The Coffee Emporium**, for gourmet coffee, baked goods, and ice cream; **A Whole New World**, also accessible from 128 Ontario Street, specializes in shabby chic, art, vintage jewelry, and other unique items; **Uncle Sam's Antiques,** located near the pool club at the harbor.

❋ Special Events

March: **Polar Bear Swim** (716-778-5930), Olcott Beach. Watch brave souls venture into the frigid waters of Lake Ontario at this annual event, one of the oldest and largest polar bear swims in the country.

May: **Apple Blossom Festival** (716-778-6151), Newfane Historical Society Grounds. An annual festival featuring displays of local history and farm equipment, a flea market, and a Civil War encampment. **Somerset Old Fashioned Farm Festival** (716-795-9948), Babcock Cobblestone Museum, Barker. A festival featuring antique vehicles, period demonstrations, and horse-drawn wagon rides.

July: **Niagara Pirate Festival** (716-778-8531; www.olcott-newfane.com), Olcott Beach. Shiver me timbers, this is Olcott's largest event of the year. Events include a pirate water war, Civil War encampment, Scottish strongman competition, live music, fireworks, and a classic car show. **Old Olcott Days** (716-778-8531; www .olcott-newfane.com), Olcott Beach. Relive Olcott's "glory days" through historical exhibits and narrated trolley rides.

August: **Labor Day Car Show** (716-778-8531; www.olcott-newfane.com), Olcott Beach. One of the area's largest classic car shows.

October: **Apple Harvest Festival** (716-778-6151), Newfane Historical Society Grounds. Attractions include eleven historic buildings, apple-butter-making demonstrations, antique car show, petting zoo, and a Civil War encampment.

December: **Victorian Christmas** (716-795-9948), Babcock Cobblestone Museum, Barker. This historic building and surrounding grounds are decorated for the holidays on the second Sunday of December.

Settlement began in the Lockport area around 1802, after the Holland Land Company improved roads to the region, but settlers didn't flock in great numbers until Erie Canal construction began in 1817. Given the tools of the day, building the canal was truly an achievement. Since Lockport is located on the Niagara Escarpment—the same massive ridge of solid rock that Niagara Falls flows over—it was quite an engineering feat to figure out how to build the canal so that boats could surmount the 59-foot-high escarpment. Lockport's claim to fame, the twin set of locks—referred to as the "flight of five"—was created after the rock was blasted through and removed. More than 1,200 laborers were needed to construct the Lockport portion of the canal. Many of these workers were Irish immigrants and, after completion of the canal, they choose to settle here. Although one set of the original locks was removed when the canal was modernized between 1908 and 1918, one set still remains today as a landmark. In fact, Lockport got its name from this impressive set of locks. Today the focal point of Lockport is still the canal, which serves as a recreational waterway from May through October. (The canal is drained in the winter months.) Another interesting bit of Lockport history: It was the first American city to have a fire hydrant system—designed by local inventor Birdsill Holly in 1863. Though far from a household name, Mr. Holly held more patents than anyone except Thomas Edison.

Middleport, located midway between Albion and Lockport, was a busy trade center during the canal's heyday. The town is the birthplace of Belva Lockwood (1830–1917), the first woman to practice law before the Supreme Court. Today it's a favorite docking spot for recreational boaters, offering electric and water hookups as well as shower and bathroom facilities. Several restaurants and shops are within walking distance of the canal.

The tiny village of Gasport got its name from a gas spring that was discovered in the area shortly after the canal opened.

AREA CODE The area code is 716.

GUIDANCE **Lockport Municipal Building** at the Big Bridge.

Hamilton House, Church and Ontario Streets. This new visitors center is set to open in 2005. A temporary facility is set up at The Art and Soul Gift Shop, 247 Market Street.

GETTING THERE *By car:* Lockport is at the crossroads of NY 78 and NY 31. Gasport and Middleport are found on NY 31.

By bus: The **NFTA** has routes between Lockport, Buffalo, and Niagara Falls.

MEDICAL EMERGENCY Dial 911

Lockport Memorial Hospital (716-514-5700), 521 East Avenue, Lockport.

✳ **To See**

ART MUSEUMS Kenan Center (716-433-2617; www.kenancenter.org), 433 Locust Street, Lockport. Gallery open daily 2–5. Free admission. This arts, education, and recreation center is located on 25 landscaped acres. The focal point of the campus is the 1800s brick Victorian Kenan House, home of philanthropist William Rand Kenan. Other buildings on the grounds include the carriage house, which now houses the 153-seat Taylor Theater, the Kenan Arena, site of special events and recreational programs, and the education building, which has an extensive art studio and classrooms on the second floor. Activities on the campus include art exhibits, educational classes, festivals, tours, craft shows, and theater.

MUSEUMS AND HISTORIC HOMES Niagara County Historical Society (716-434-7433; www.niagaracounty.org/historical-society-welcome.htm), 215 Niagara Street, Lockport. Open January–May Wednesday–Sunday 1–5, June–August Monday–Saturday 10–5, Sunday 1–5, September–December Thursday–Sunday 1–5. Admission: $1. Visitors to Niagara County can learn about the region's history by visiting the six buildings in this museum complex. The 1864 Outwater Memorial Building features a Victorian parlor, toys, a Civil War room, changing exhibits, and a unique gift shop. Displayed in the 1835 Washington Hunt Building are surveying instruments used to lay out the villages of Lockport and Niagara Falls. The Pioneer and Transportation Building includes Native American artifacts and a replica pioneer cabin, as well as Erie Canal artifacts and early automotive transportation displays. Tools of many 19th-century trades are displayed in the Yates Farm Barn. Hille House contains an old-fashioned doctor's office, a business and industry exhibit, and more.

Col. William Bond House (716-434-7433), 143 Ontario Street, Lockport. Open April–December Thursday, Saturday, Sunday 1–5. Admission: $2. This circa-1824 house is listed on the New York State and National Registers of Historic Places. Part of the Niagara County Historical Society complex, this was the first brick house built in Lockport. Colonel Bond, a land speculator, came to Lockport to purchase land where he anticipated the Erie Canal locks would be built. The house, with 12 furnished rooms, is restored to reflect the period from 1820–60. The kitchen and children's garret are especially interesting. Docents are on hand to answer your questions on this bygone era.

Canal Museum (716-434-3140), Richmond Avenue (by the locks), Lockport. Open daily 9–5 May–October. Free admission. This small, one-room museum is located in a former powerhouse that served the Erie Canal's double locks at Lockport from its construction in 1918 until the mid-1950s. Displays include tools used in canal construction, photographs, and other canal memorabilia. It is located at the site of the world-famous "Flight of Five" locks. Remnants of the flight, which now appear as five waterfalls, are located to the north of the present-day locks. The Flight of Five is best observed from an observation point on the Pine Street Bridge or from local canal tour boats. A note of caution: This museum is located well below street level and is accessible only by means of several flights of stairs. Railings are minimal, so it is not recommended to visit this site with small children or if you have trouble negotiating stairs.

Erie Canal Heritage Center (716-433-6155), 228 Market Street, Lockport. Only open for group tours and to customers of Lockport Locks & Erie Canal Cruises. May and June, September and October 9–5, June–September 9–7. Donation. This four-story stone building built in the 1840s once housed a flour mill that harnessed waterpower from the Erie Canal. The structure has been kept in its original condition and now houses the Erie Canal Heritage Center, which features hands-on, canal-related exhibits and artifacts along with a small theater. See *Lockport Locks and Canal Cruises.*

HISTORIC SITES Belva Lockwood Memorial, Griswold Street (3 miles south of NY 31), Middleport. This monument is dedicated to Middleport native Belva Lockwood, the first woman to practice law before the Supreme Court.

The Big Bridge, Lockport. Located by Locks 34 and 35, the "Big Bridge" built in 1914, is the widest bridge in the world, measuring 129 feet long and a whopping 399 feet wide. (By comparison, the George Washington Bridge is a mere 120 feet wide.)

Cold Spring Cemetery (716-434-3450), 4849 Cold Spring Road, Lockport. This historic 68-acre cemetery, incorporated in 1841, was the original burial grounds of area Revolutionary War soldiers. There are many unique monuments throughout the cemetery, of all shapes, sizes, and materials. Cold Spring is the final resting place of several notable Niagara County residents, including inventor Birdsall Holley and Jessie Hawley, proponent of the Erie Canal System.

WINERIES Niagara County Wine Trail (www.Niagarawinetrail.org). This Web site describes the wineries of Niagara County. There are currently six wineries on the trail, with several others in the planning stages. The soil and climate of this area along the Niagara Escarpment are ideal for growing grapes to produce world-class wines.

Chiappone Cellars Winery Inc. (716-433-9463), 3401 Murphy Road (off NY 104), Newfane. Open 12–5 Monday–Friday, 10–5 Saturday, Sunday 12–5. (November 1–April 1 open Friday–Sunday 12–5). Three tastings free, $2 to sample all varietals. This small family-owned and operated farm winery, specializing in French-American hybrids, produces 14 varietals of wine on site. Niagara is their most popular wine.

Eveningside Vineyards (716-867-2415; www.eveningside.com), 4794 Lower Mountain Road, Cambria. See *Wineries—Cambria.*

Marjim Manor (716-778-7001), 7171 East Lake Road, Appleton. See *Wineries—Olcott/Wilson.*

REMNANTS OF THE WORLD-FAMOUS "FLIGHT OF FIVE" LOCKS NOW APPEAR AS FIVE WATERFALLS.

Christine A. Smyczynski

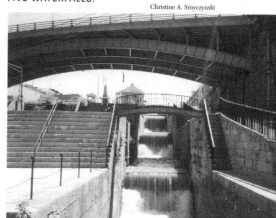

Niagara Landing Wine Cellars (716-433-8405; www.niagaralanding.com), 4434 Van Dusen Road, Lockport. Open Monday–Friday 2–6, Saturday 10–6, Sunday 12–6. (January 1–Easter, Friday–Sunday 12–6). Free samplings. This family-owned and operated winery, located off the beaten path amid vineyards dating back to the 1800s, features fine wines and original art in their tasting room and gift shop. Owners Jackie and Mike Connelly specialize in wines made from native Labrusca grapes and European vinifera varieties. Be sure to sample their best seller, Boxer Blush, a semisweet blush wine with a touch of green apple, with a picture of their bulldog on the label. Tours are offered any time to any size group.

Vizcarra Vineyards at Becker Farms (716-772-7815; www.beckerfarms.com), 3760 Quaker Road, Gasport. Open May–December 12–5 daily. This farm and farm market, operated by Oscar and Melinda Vizcarra, has been run by Melinda's family since 1894. In 2004, the Vizcarras introduced wines made from their own fruits as well as from grapes purchased from other farms in Western New York. See also *Family Fun*.

Warm Lake Estate Vineyard and Winery (716-731-5900; www.warmlake estate.com), 3868 Lower Mountain Road, Lockport. Open Monday–Saturday 10–5, 12–5 Sunday. Closed Thanksgiving, Christmas, and New Year. The $2 per tasting fee includes five varieties. Warm Lake Estate produces world-class pinot noir grown on the Niagara Escarpment, using environmental friendly and Old-World techniques. This wine is so popular, it sells out completely and is sold as futures two years in advance. Visitors can sample and purchase wines from Finger Lakes, and Long Island wineries. The gift shop carries local produce, gift items including wine jewelry, and wine publications. The winery's large deck overlooks the vineyards and Niagara County's wine country.

✳ To Do

BOAT EXCURSIONS **Lockport Locks & Erie Canal Cruises** (800-378-0352; www.lockportlocks.com) 210 Market Street, Lockport. Open daily late June–early September; Open weekends only May–late June and early September–October. Cruises at 10, 12:30, 3, and 5:30. Admission: $12.50 adult, $11.50 seniors, $8 children 4–10. Take a unique two-hour narrated trip down the historic Erie Canal. Your journey includes "locking through" the 50-foot locks 34 and 35, the only double set of locks on the entire canal. You will also have the opportunity to see the remnants of one set of the original "Flight of Five" locks, located north of the present-day locks. When the canal was built in 1825, the original locks allowed simultaneous travel in either direction; the modern locks have replaced one flight. The 363-mile-long canal was hand-dug to connect the Hudson River with the Niagara River. Your cruise captain will explain the sights and folklore of the canal. After you disembark, stop by the adjacent Erie Canal Heritage Center to learn more about the canal, have a snack in the café (open seasonally May–October), or browse in the gift shop, which features Erie Canal–related merchandise.

FAMILY FUN ✎ **Becker Farms** (716-772-2211; www.beckerfarms.com), 3760 Quaker Road, Gasport. Open May–December. Becker Farms, a popular destination for local families, offers locally grown fruit and vegetables, homemade baked goods, and craft items. Children can pet and feed farm animals. Numerous festivals take place on weekends throughout the year. Fall is the most popular time to visit, when visitors can pick their own apples and pumpkins, get lost in a corn maze, and enjoy other family-oriented activities during their Pumpkin Fiesta. In the summer of 2004 they introduced Vizcarra Vineyards products, featuring wines made from their own apples, strawberries, raspberries, and more, along with grape wines. A wine-tasting room has been added to the apple barn. See *Wineries*.

✎ **Speedway Park** (716-438-7223; www.speedwayparkfuncenter.com), 400 Corinthia Street, Lockport. Open Thursday 6–10, Friday 3–11, Saturday 12–11, Sunday 12–6. Admission: $5 for 5 minutes of racing. Must be 54 inches tall to race alone. Indoor go-cart track, featuring 21 Nascar-style cars. Video games and refreshments are available

FISHING **Nelson Goehle Marina** (Widewaters) is a popular spot to fish. See *Marinas*.

GOLF **Eagle Crest Golf Center** (716-625-9400), 6730 South Transit Road, Pendelton. A driving range to practice your shot.

Niagara County Golf Course (716-439-7954), 314 Davison Road, Lockport. A public 18-hole, par-72 course with full bar, snack bar, and restaurant.

Niagara Orleans Golf Club (716-735-9000), Telegraph Road off NY 31, Middleport. A semiprivate 18-hole, par-71 course.

Oak Run Golf Club (716-434-8851), 4185 Lake Avenue, Lockport. A semiprivate 18-hole, par-72 course.

Willowbrook Golf Course & Restaurant (716-434-0111), 4200 Lake Avenue (NY 78) Lockport. An 18-hole, par-72 semiprivate course and driving range with a full bar, snack bar, and restaurant.

GUIDED TOURS **Lockport Cave Tours and Underground Boat Ride** (716-438-0174; www.lockportcave.com), 21 Main Street, Lockport. Open daily 11–5. Admission: $8.25 adults, $5.50 children. This 75-minute guided tour starts with viewing the Lockport locks, both the modern locks 34 and 35 and the remnants of the "Flight of Five," part of the canal in 1825. As you walk along the canal toward the "cave," you'll learn a little about Lockport's industrial heritage and also have the opportunity to see the famous "upside-down bridge." The cave was originally a 2,400-foot water power tunnel used in the 1860s. Visitors take a walking tour through the cave, then the longest underground boat ride in the United States (round-trip takes 30 minutes). You not only learn about Lockport's history but also view the start of geologic cave formations.

Tow Path Trolley (716-628-6095; www.towpathtrolley.com), Departs from 210 Market Street at 12:30 and 2 PM, July 4–Labor Day. Admission: $6 adults, $3

children 5–12. A tour bus in the guise of an old-fashioned trolley takes visitors on a one-hour narrated tour of Lockport.

MARINAS The Nelson Goehle Marina at Widewaters, Market Street, Lockport. This marina on the Erie Canal, named after a former superintendent of parks, is one of the most popular boating and fishing spots in town. It is located along the canal just east of Lockport.

SCENIC OVERLOOK An **observation deck** overlooking the Erie Canal is adjacent to the parking ramp on Main Street near Pine.

SKATING ✍ **Skateland Family Fun Center** (716-433-5605), 1109 Lincoln Avenue, Lockport. Laser tag open daily 11–9; $4/one game, $6/two games. Skating Monday 6–9, Wednesday 6–8:30, Thursday 8–10:30, Friday 5–7:30 and 8–11, Saturday 12:30–5 and 8–11, Sunday 12:30–5; $4. There's much more than just skating at Skateland. While skating on the large, modern, climate-controlled rink is, of course, the main attraction, there's plenty to do here for nonskaters, too, including an interactive laser tag game. They also have a video-game arcade and Paradise Palm Adventure Golf (weather permitting).

✳ Green Space

NATURE PRESERVES Gulf Wilderness Park (716-433-1267), south side of West Jackson Street, near the 5900 block, Lockport. Open dawn to dusk. Free admission. The only full nature preserve on the Niagara Escarpment, this area is a true unspoiled wilderness. Four hiking trails traverse the amenity-free wooded ravine. It is a great place to look for fossils and study rock formations as well as observe different wildflowers and plants. Indian Falls, which runs off the west branch of Eighteen Mile Creek, is located in the park.

PARKS Niagara County Park (716-439-7950), 314 Davison Road, Lockport. This park has picnic facilities, a golf course, and model airplane field.

Outwater Park (716-433-1267), Outwater Drive, Lockport. Open dawn to dusk. Free admission. Visitors to this 48-acre park—named for Dr. Samuel Outwater, a successful Lockport physician who donated the land to the city—can enjoy picnicking, cross-country skiing, swimming, baseball, football, soccer, horseshoes, bocce, playgrounds, and hiking and nature trails. Located near the top of the Niagara Escarpment, the park also has a lovely rose garden. From the famous Outwater Park overview, one can see Lake Ontario and, on a clear day, the outline of the Toronto skyline.

Royalton Ravine (716-439-7950), Gasport Road, Gasport. Open dawn to dusk. Free admission. Facilities include picnic shelters, baseball diamonds, and a nature trail with a suspension bridge and waterfalls.

Josephine Carveth Packet Park, Opposite the Market Street Art Center, 247 Market Street, Lockport. This small park overlooks the Erie Canal.

WALKING AND HIKING TRAILS Erie Canal Heritage Trail. You could walk or bike all the way from downtown Lockport to Rochester and beyond along this paved trail along the north side of the Erie Canal. The trail, which will eventually go all the way to Albany, follows the former towpath along the Erie Canal.

City of Lockport Walking and Biking Tour (canal towpath). For those who prefer a short trail, you can walk or bike the loop trail that runs on both sides of the canal from Locks 34 and 35 to Widewaters (at Goehle Widewaters Marina) and back. The 4-mile trail takes you on the north side of the canal past the modern locks, the historic "Flight of Five" locks, through Upson Park, up to Widewaters Marina, where you'll cross over the canal and return to downtown Lockport on the south side of the waterway.

✳ Lodging

MOTELS AND HOTELS ⟨ **Holiday Inn Lockport** (716-434-6151, 800-HOLIDAY), 515 South Transit Road, Lockport. Ninety-five rooms are available at this suburban hotel. Amenities include an indoor heated pool and sauna. It is located just 2 miles from the Erie Canal. $49–$109.

⟨ **Comfort Inn Lockport** (716-434-4411, 800-228-5150), 551 South Transit Road, Lockport. This hotel, in a quiet location just south of Lockport, has 50 rooms, some with whirlpool tubs. $59–$99.

⟨ **Lockport Motel & Suites** (716-434-5595; www.lockportmotel.com), 315 S. Transit Road, Lockport. Open

year-round. This hotel has 65 modern rooms, including some Jacuzzi suites with fireplaces. Amenities include a swimming pool and in-room refrigerators and microwaves in all rooms, as well as hair dryers and coffee makers. $66–$160.

BED & BREAKFASTS Canal Country Inn Bed & Breakfast (716-735-7572; www.canalcountryinnbb.com), 4021 Peet Street, Middleport. Open year-round. This secluded 1831 home, located right beside the Erie Canal, features four large guest rooms with shared baths. One room has a fireplace. Boaters can moor at the inn's

TAKE THE CANAL TOWPATH UP ONE SIDE AND DOWN THE OTHER FROM LOCKS 34 AND 35 TO WIDEWATERS.

Christine A. Smyczynski

private dock. Innkeepers Wendell and Joan Smith serve a continental breakfast each morning that includes homemade baked goods. $38–$52.

Country Cottage Bed & Breakfast (716-772-2251; www.countrycottage bandb.com), 7745 Rochester Road (NY 31), Gasport. Open year-round. Innkeeper Susan Pearson offers two quaint guest rooms with a shared bath in a charming, intimate, air-conditioned 1940s Cape Cod home, located in the countryside of Niagara County. The inn is a 10-minute walk or 3-minute drive to the Erie Canal. Ms. Pearson offers complimentary pick-up for boaters from marinas in Gasport, Middleport, and Lockport. A pool is available for guest use. Country Cottage is a member of the western New York Bed and Breakfast Association; inns belonging to this association are held to high standards and inspected regularly. A full country breakfast is served, including Susan's famous blueberry muffins. $60+.

DeFlippo's Bed & Breakfast (716-433-2913 or 888-826-0488; www .deflippos.com), 326 West Avenue (NY 31 W), Lockport. Open year-round. Innkeepers Jerry and Joan De Flippo offer four recently remodeled and uniquely decorated rooms. The Elvis Room is decorated with 1950s Elvis memorabilia, while the Lillian Bronson Room has its namesake's memorabilia. (Ms. Bronson was a character actress from the 1940s–1960s who hailed from Lockport. Her childhood home is located next door and owned by Jerry and Joan.) The Garden Room features a queen-sized bed, while the antiques-decorated DeFlippo Room has a double bed and a pull-out sofa. The four rooms share two full baths. Rates include a

continental breakfast. Dinner packages to their restaurant are also available. See *Dining Out*. $65–$95.

Hambleton House Bed & Breakfast (716-439-9507; www.niagara bedandbreakfast.com), 130 Pine Street, Lockport. Open year-round. Three guest rooms with private baths and air-conditioning are available in this circa 1850 large yellow house within walking distance to the Erie Canal. The inn features wraparound porches, hardwood floors, crystal chandeliers, claw-foot bathtubs, and artwork by innkeeper Joan Hambelton. A continental breakfast of fruits, sweet breads, and cereal is served each morning. $60–$105.

OTHER LODGING Niagara County Camping Resort (716-434-3991; www.niagaracamping.com), 7369 Wheeler Road, Lockport. Open May 15–October 15. A comfortable, clean, family-oriented RV park and campground located 2.5 miles from the canal. There are 64 sites plus cabin rentals. The campground has a lifeguard-staffed beach and two ponds for fishing along with a playground, petting zoo, miniature golf, and weekly activities. $19/night tents, $23/night trailers plus $2 electric hookup, $139/week, $369/week cabin rentals.

✳ Where to Eat

DINING OUT Danny Sheehan's Steak House (716-433-4666), 491 West Avenue (NY 31). Open Tuesday–Thursday 4–10, Friday and Saturday 4–11, Sunday 3–9. This restaurant has been popular for steaks for over four decades. The comfortable dining room features a mural of old downtown Lockport, while a deck and patio for outdoor dining is open during the warmer months.

DeFlippo's (716-433-2913), 326 West Avenue (NY 31 West) Lockport. Open Tuesday–Saturday 4:30–11. The building housing this popular Italian restaurant was built in 1870 by carriage makers Brown and Bronson. Dominick and Barbara DeFlippo acquired the property in the early 1940s and opened a restaurant business in 1946; since 1977 their son Jerry and his wife, Joan, have continued the family tradition. They offer an extensive selection of Italian specialties, such as chicken parmigiana, baked lasagna, and a long list of pasta dishes, served amid a decor of Lockport and sports memorabilia. Other selections include surf and turf, strip steak, smoked chicken, and several low-fat choices. The Friday-night fish fry is popular, so arrive early. A children's menu is available. See also *Lodging—Bed & Breakfasts.*

The Fieldstone Country Inn (716-625-6193), 5986 S. Transit Road, Lockport. Open Monday–Thursday 11–9, Friday 11–10, Saturday 4–10, Sunday 12–8. Specialties at this cozy country restaurant, constructed out of fieldstone, include prime rib and BBQ ribs.

Garlock's (716-433-5595), 35 S. Transit Road, Lockport. Open Monday–Thursday 4:30–11:30, Friday 4:30–12, Saturday 5–12, Sunday 3:30–10. This vintage restaurant, reminiscent of a 1950s-style lodge, has been the premier steak house in Lockport for over 60 years. The casual restaurant is filled with lots of unusual decorations, including a collection of model cars. While steak dominates the menu, other selections include chicken, pork, lamb, and an assortment of seafood.

Middleport Basket Factory (716-735-9260; www.thebasketfactory.com), 2 Watson Avenue, Middleport. Open Tuesday–Thursday 11–9, Friday and Saturday 11–10, Sunday 10–8. This canalside restaurant was a manufacturing facility for bushel baskets from the late 1800s to 1930. Menu selections include steaks and pasta along with daily specials and a children's menu. A marina is located outside the restaurant for patrons who arrive by boat.

The Shamus (716-433-9809), 98 West Avenue, Lockport. Open for lunch Monday–Saturday 11–4, dinner Monday–Thursday 4–9, Friday and Saturday 4–10. Shamus, which is located in a 150-year-old building, has the reputation as one of the finest restaurants in Lockport, for both food and decor. Menu selections include fresh seafood, Angus beef, chicken, pork, and pasta. Choose from soups, salads, and sandwiches for lunch. An outdoor patio is open during the warmer months.

&. **Thaxton's Dinner House** (716-434-6020; www.thaxtons.com), 5959 Campbell Boulevard, Lockport. Open Tuesday–Thursday 5–9, Friday 4–10, Saturday 5–10, Sunday 4–9. Menu selections include their house specialty, Ozark BBQ ribs, plus prime rib, steak, and homemade soups. The small, intimate bar area is a good place to meet with friends before or after dinner.

EATING OUT &. **One-Eyed Jack's Smokehouse Grill** (716-438-5414), 5983 S. Transit Road (at Robinson Road), Lockport. Open Monday–Thursday 11–9, Friday–Saturday 11–10, Sunday 12–8. The place to go for BBQ in Niagara County. Enjoy chicken, ribs, and pork, washed down with a variety of beers. Eat outside during the summer months. Take-out is available.

✍ ♿ 🍴 **Reid's Ice Cream** (716-433-2488), Lake Avenue (at Clinton Street), Lockport. Open seasonally. A long-standing Lockport institution, serving take-out hot dogs, ice-cream, shakes, and more.

✍ ♿ 🍴 **Salonika Family Restaurant** (716-433-6335), 5925 South Transit Road, Lockport. Open Sunday–Thursday 7 AM–11 PM, Friday and Saturday 7 AM–midnight. This busy family restaurant is open for breakfast, lunch, and dinner. Choose from traditional Greek dishes like souvlaki and gyros as well as American favorites like steaks, burgers, and sandwiches.

Talk of the Town II (716-735-3366), 12 Main Street, Middleport. Open Monday–Wednesday 6–2, Thursday and Friday 6–8, Saturday 6–2, Sunday 7–2. This small canalside café is very popular with recreational boaters. Eat inside or sit outdoors at one of the picnic tables along the historic Erie Canal. Menu selections include eggs, omelets, and pancakes for breakfast, plus salads, soups, pizza, subs, sandwiches, and dinner specials.

✍ **Udder Delight** (716-772-7120), 7694 Rochester Road, Gasport. Open seasonally May–October. This popular ice cream stand has won numerous awards, including best ice cream in the Taste of Buffalo.

Wagners (716-433-1200), 246 Park Avenue, Lockport. Open Monday–Saturday 11–11. A Lockport institution for over 50 years, noted for its beef on weck. Chicken wings are another specialty.

✍ ♿ 🍴 **Widewaters Drive-In Restaurant** (716-433-9605), 767 Market Street (at Widewaters), Lockport. Open seasonally. Enjoy hot dogs and more with a great view of the canal.

✳ Entertainment

THEATERS Palace Theatre (716-438-1130; www.lockportpalace theatre.com), 2 East Avenue, Lockport. This historic theater in the heart of downtown Lockport is a beautiful example of a pre–World War II grand movie theater, now restored to its original splendor. The Palace, which opened in 1925, was once part of the Schine chain of theaters. John Philip Sousa and his band performed here the year it opened. While first-run movies at reasonable prices are the daily fare, live performances are also held here.

Taylor Theater See **Kenan Center**.

✳ Selective Shopping

ANTIQUES Clotilda Antiques and Collectibles (716-998-0323), 39 East Avenue, Lockport. Open Tuesday–Friday 10–5, Saturday and Sunday 12–5. A collection of vintage items, gifts, and candy.

Mack's This 'N That, 73 Locust Street, Lockport. Open Thursday–Saturday 10–6, Sunday 12–4. You'll find a little bit of this and a little bit of that at this unique shop that carries antiques, artwork, gifts, and more.

Olde Main Street (716-434-4495) 2 East Avenue (adjacent to the Palace Theater), Lockport. Open Wednesday–Sunday 12–5. Specializing in antique furniture and other 19th- and 20th-century decorative and utilitarian items, including Mission, Art Nouveau, and country pieces.

Tattered Tulip (716-438-5257), 4090 Lake Avenue (NY 78 north of Lockport, about 0.25 mile south of NY 104), Lockport. Open Tuesday–Saturday 10–5, Sunday 12–5; January–March Friday–Sunday only. Browse through 2,000 square feet of antique furniture, glassware, pottery, quilts, folk art, woven rugs, candles, garden decor, and more, displayed in a two-story, century-old barn.

ART GALLERIES Market Street Art Center (716-478-0083; marketstreet studios.com), 247 Market Street, Lockport. Open Monday–Friday 8–4, Saturday and Sunday 10–4. This unique art center—in the historic Western Block and Tackle building on the banks of the Erie Canal—features several art galleries showcasing the work of Niagara County artists, plus 20 working artists studios and an art-supply store.

FARM MARKETS Becker Farm See *Family Fun*

Niagara County Produce (716-639-0755), Transit Road (at Millersport), East Amherst. Open daily year-round 8 AM–9 PM. This open-air market on the border of Erie and Niagara Counties has been in operation for over 70 years. In season, choose from Niagara County crops—including apples, berries, and grapes—picked fresh daily. In the off-season enjoy apples and potatoes from cold storage as well as produce shipped in from other parts of the country. The market is also known for its full-service deli counter, featuring quality meats and freshly made sausage.

Schwab's Farm Market (716-735-7570), NY 31, Gasport. Open year-round Monday–Friday 8–8, Saturday

8–6, Sunday 10–5. Choose from home-grown produce in-season, baked goods, deli meats, gift baskets, and locally made handcrafted items

SPECIAL SHOPS Artsong Gallery (716-735-3471; www.artsonggallery .com), 24 State Street, Middleport. Located just a few steps from the banks of the Erie Canal, this shop features metal sculptures created by owner Chazz Elstone. Several larger pieces are on display in the gallery's outdoor sculpture garden. The store also carries new and used musical instruments and offers music lessons.

Crafts and Creations (716-434-2816), 1149 Lincoln Avenue, Lockport. Open Monday–Friday 10–9, Saturday 10–7, Sunday 12–4. This large store carries a sizeable selection of crafting supplies, giftware, collectibles, and porcelain dolls.

Every Nook-N-Cranny Country Gift Market (716-438-1988), 151 East Avenue (across from the post office), Lockport. Open Tuesday–

SCULPTURES IN ARTSONG GALLERY'S SCULPTURE GARDEN.

Joanne Michaels

Friday 11–5, Saturday 10–5, Sunday by chance. Every little nook and cranny of this vintage Lockport home is filled with primitive and country-home decor, candles, country crafts, cards, cookbooks, and more.

Grimble's Hardware Store (716-434-1790), 18-20 West Main Street, Lockport. Open Monday–Friday 8–5:30, Saturday 8:30–5, Sunday 9–3. An old-fashioned hardware store, complete with wooden floors and a popcorn machine up front—the place to go in Lockport for those hard-to-find gadgets. This store is one of Lockport's oldest businesses, established in 1920 and owned by the third generation of the same family.

Just Lookin' (716-438-5712), 38 Main Street, Lockport. Open Monday 10–8, Tuesday–Saturday 10–5, Sunday 12–4. Choose from a wide variety of antiques and general merchandise in this antiques and crafts co-op, including country decorations, bird feeders, candles, wooden items, and painted glassware. All items are neatly displayed in wooden booths.

Lockport Canalside (716-433-6155, 800-378-0352; www.llecc), 210 Market Street, Lockport. Open May–September 9:30–7:30 daily, October–April Monday–Friday 9:30–5, weekends by chance. This gift shop located along the historic Erie Canal offers a large selection of Erie Canal and Lockport memorabilia, plus nautical gifts.

Outwater Emporium at the Niagara County Historical Society (716-434-7433), 215 Niagara Street, Lockport. Open January–May Wednesday–Sunday 1–5; June–August Monday–Saturday 10–5, Sunday 1–5; September–

December Thursday–Sunday 1–5. Find a selection of books and items related to Lockport and Erie Canal history.

✳ Special Events

May/June: **100 American Craftsmen Festival** (www.kenancenter.org/arts/craftsmen), Kenan Center, Lockport. A juried arts-and-crafts show featuring artisans from all over the country.

July: **Niagara County Fair** (716-433-8839), Niagara County Fairgrounds, 4487 Lake Avenue (NY 78), Lockport. The Niagara County Fair is known as the "best little county fair in western New York." The fair originated in downtown Lockport in the late 1800s and was held sporadically until 1945, when it was moved to its present location. The fair's primary focus is on the achievements of youth involved in 4-H and other activities. Attractions include animal shows, crafts, live entertainment, midway rides, and vendors. The fair also features an antique tractor display and a car show.

September: **Johnny Appleseed Fest** (716-772-2211; www.beckerfarms .com), Becker Farms, Gasport. Celebrate the beginning of the apple harvest season with family-oriented activities such as apple picking, pony rides, musical entertainment, and more.

October: **Pumpkin Fiesta** (716-772-2211; www.beckerfarms.com), Becker Farms, Gasport. Old-fashioned fun for the entire family includes hayrides, corn maze, farm animals, pumpkin picking, and live entertainment.

The village of Sanborn was named after the Reverend E. C. Sanborn, a Methodist clergyman who arrived in this area in 1846. In the early days the town had a sawmill, a gristmill, and one of the largest cheese manufacturing facilities in the state. Today the village, now part of Lewiston, is home to several unique antique shops. The nearby towns of Cambria, Wheatfield, and Ransomville are agricultural in nature.

Note: While nearby North Tonawanda is located in Niagara County, information for that area is listed under Grand Island and the Tonawandas in Erie County.

AREA CODE The area code is 716.

GUIDANCE Sanborn Historical Museum (716-731-4708) 2822 Niagara Street. Sanborn. Open Sunday 2–4 (January and February, open the first Sunday of month).

GETTING THERE *By car:* The area can be reached via NY 31, NY 104, NY 425, and NY 429.

MEDICAL EMERGENCY Dial 911

✳ To See

MUSEUMS AND HISTORIC HOMES Das Haus (716-731-9905 or 716-731-9642), 2549 Niagara Road, Bergholz. Open seasonally, Sunday 2–4. This 1843 log home and replica barn serves as the museum of the Historical Society of North German Settlements in western New York.

Ransomville Historical Museum (716-791-4073), 3733 Ransomville Road, Ransomville. Open Saturdays 2–4 or by appointment. This museum has historical artifacts pertaining to the Ransomville area.

& **Sanborn Historical Museum** (716-731-4708), 2822 Niagara Street, Sanborn. Open Sunday 2–4 (January and February only open the first Sunday of month). This former schoolhouse houses artifacts from Sanborn's past, including numerous photos, a potbelly stove, a collection of German dolls, antique sewing items, and Tuscarora Indian Reservation history. The Historical Society has plans to develop a farm museum on a 56-acre farm they recently acquired. This museum will introduce visitors to the importance of agriculture in society and have hands-on programs about farming life.

& **Joseph Jacobs Native American Museum** (716-297-0251), Smokin' Joe's Complex, 2293 Sanders Settlement Road, Sanborn. Open Monday–Saturday 10–5, Sunday 12–5. Free Admission. View artwork by internationally famous Native American sculptor Joseph Jacobs while learning about the history and culture of the Tuscarora Nation. The museum shop features Native American art, crafts, and books, along with gold jewelry.

WINERIES Eveningside Vineyards (716-867-2415; www.eveningside.com) 4794 Lower Mountain Road, Cambria. Open Weekends July and August 12–5. One of Niagara County's newest wineries.

See also *Wineries—Lockport.*

✳ To Do

AUTO RACING Ransomville Speedway, (716-791-3602; www.ransomville speedway.com), 2315 Braley Road (off Ransomville Road), Ransomville. Open Friday nights May–September. A regional motorsport track.

GOLF Shawnee Country Club (716-731-5177), 6020 Townline Road, Sanborn. A public 9-hole, par-36 course with some memberships. Amenities include electric carts, a full bar, a restaurant, and banquet facilities.

✳ Where to Eat

DINING OUT Schimschack's Restaurant (716-731-4111; www.schim schacks.com), 2943 Upper Mountain Road, Sanborn. Open for dinner Tuesday–Sunday 4–9, Saturday until 10. Reservations recommended. This four-star restaurant on the Niagara Escarpment is known equally for its excellent food as the spectacular view. On a clear day you can see the Toronto skyline on the horizon. Schimschacks, which was recently named one of the Top Ten Most Romantic Restaurants, has been featured on the Food Channel. The restaurant is built in four tiers so that each table has a perfect view of Lake Ontario and surrounding countryside through the wall of floor-to-ceiling windows. Its American-style menu features selections like filet mignon, Alaskan king crab legs, prime rib, and BBQ ribs as well as numerous chicken and seafood dishes. Desserts include peanut butter slide, coconut cream pie, and flaming bananas Foster. Schimschack's was also named one of New York's most romantic restaurants by New York State's First Lady, Libby Pataki.

Suzanne's Fine Dining (716-694-6562; www.suzannesfinedining.com), 2843 Niagara Falls Boulevard, Wheatfield. Open Tuesday–Saturday 3–10. This fine-dining establishment is noted for its award-winning bacon-wrapped crab-stuffed shrimp, which can be ordered as an appetizer or dinner. Other dinner selections include French-cut pork chops, chicken and artichokes, and shrimp scampi, plus fresh pasta, seafood, and steaks.

EATING OUT Annie's Attic Café (716-698-4326), 6608 Shawnee Road (NY 425, in the Shawnee Country Barns Antique Co-op), Wheatfield. Open Tuesday–Sunday 10–4. This cozy little café, perched under the rafters of a 1912 restored barn, features gourmet sandwiches and salads along with breakfast specialties. Save room for the cake or pie of the day or other brownies, muffins, and ice cream treats. Shop while you wait for your food. See *Antiques.*

Johnston's Family Restaurant (716-791-3511), 2575 Academy Street, Ransomville. Open Sunday–Tuesday 6 AM–9 PM, Wednesday–Friday 6 AM–10 PM, Saturday 7 AM–10 PM. This restaurant has been family-owned and operated since Prohibition. The extensive menu features old-fashioned home cooking made with locally grown produce. Selections include homemade soups, salads served in an edible taco bowl, sandwich platters, steaks, seafood, ribs, and chicken.

✳ Selective Shopping

ANTIQUES **Asti Antiques** (716-731-4669), 6608 Shawnee Road, Wheatfield. Open Monday, Tuesday, Thursday, and Saturday 10–5, Sunday and Friday 12–5. Located in a small outbuilding next to the Shawnee Country Barns Antique Co-op, this shop specializes in Victorian items plus fine collectibles and antiques.

Jacobs Ladder Antiques (716-694-6305) 5835 Buffalo Street (NY 429), Sanborn. Open Thursday–Monday 11–5. A small shop specializing in vintage dolls, glass, china, and collectibles.

Lauffers Antiques & Collectibles (716-693-2818), **Oldies & Goodies** (716-695-7612), 3039 Niagara Falls Boulevard, Wheatfield. Open Thursday–Monday 11–5. Two shops in one feature antique furniture, glass, pottery, and Christmas items as well as collectibles from the '40s and '50s.

& **Old Sanborn Milling Company Antiques & Collectibles** (716-731-2150), 5890 Ward Road (NY 429), Sanborn. Open Wednesday–Sunday 10–6, Monday–Tuesday 10–4. An antiques co-op and marketplace, located in a restored 1860 flour mill, features over 40 shops dealing in antiques, collectibles, primitives, jewelry, gifts, glassware, military, coins, and more.

Ransomville Antique Co-op (716-791-3930), 3596 Ransomville Road, Ransomville. Open Wednesday–

Sunday 12–5; January–April, Saturday and Sunday only. Three floors of antiques and collectibles are located in an 1877 church.

Sanborn Old General Store (716-731-4578), 5837 and 5856 Buffalo Street (at Ward Road), Sanborn. Open Wednesday–Saturday 10–5, Sunday 11–4. This multidealer antiques and collectibles co-op is located in the former LeVan Grocery & Hardware store, built in 1910. Choose from furniture, primitives, glassware, candles, and gifts.

Shawnee Country Barns Antique Co-op (716-731-1430), 6608 Shawnee Road (NY 425), Wheatfield. Open daily 10–5. Over 70 dealers are housed in this restored 1912 barn. Browse through two floors of glassware, furniture, jewelry, toys, and country and primitive items. Be sure to stop by Annie's Attic Café on the barn's second floor for breakfast or lunch. See *Where to Eat.*

FARM MARKETS **Wagners Farm Market** (716-731-4440), 2672 Lockport Road, Sanborn. Open daily 9–6. Since 1967 the Wagner family has been offering a full range of produce from apples to zucchini as well as fresh baked goods, fresh and frozen meats, and gift baskets. The market's café restaurant features hot dogs, hamburgers, beef on weck, and more.

SPECIALTY SHOPS **Kissel Country Tin** (716-692-0052), 7296 Schultz Road at Niagara Falls Boulevard, Wheatfield. Open Monday–Saturday 10–5, Sunday 12–4. This rustic country store features painted items, country gifts, Americana, pottery, seasonal decorations, and candles, along with weaving supplies. Knitting, weaving, and felting classes are taught in the fiber studio at the rear of the store.

& **Smokin' Joe's** (716-297-0251; www.smokinjoe.com), 2293 Sanders Settlement Road, Sanborn Monday–Saturday 9 AM–10 PM. Shopping at Smokin' Joe's is a unique experience. Since it's located on the Tuscarora Indian Reservation, which does not collect New York sales tax, it's best known for tax-free gas and cigarettes. But there's a whole lot more here. You can get groceries, gifts, jewelry, and even cigars, and a large café open 7 AM–8 PM. Be sure to stop by the Joseph Jacobs Museum of Native American Art to see the work of Tuscarora's best known sculptor, Joseph Jacobs.

✳ Special Events

October: **Fall into Country** (716-731-1430), Shawnee Country Barns Antique Co-Op, 6608 Shawnee Road, Wheatfield. Enjoy antique shopping amid the fall countryside of Niagara County. Refreshments served.

November: **Country Christmas Open House** (716-731-1430), Shawnee Country Barns Antique Co-Op, 6608 Shawnee Road, Wheatfield. Have an old-fashioned Christmas-shopping experience, complete with festive trimmings and antique ornaments.

SOUTHERN ONTARIO

A book about western New York would not be complete without a chapter focusing on our neighbors to the north in Canada. Southern Ontario is a vast area, though, with lots to see and do—a whole book could be written on the Niagara region alone! This chapter will highlight just the towns immediately across the border—Fort Erie, Niagara Falls, Queenston, and Niagara-on-the-Lake—that visitors to western New York may want to include on their itinerary.

Crossing the Border. United States citizens are not required to have passports to enter Canada, but bring yours along if you have one. You must have proof of citizenship, such as a birth certificate, and a photo ID. Noncitizens must have their resident alien card. If you are traveling with children, have a copy of their birth certificates and photo IDs if available. If both parents aren't traveling with the children, it's recommended that you have a note from the absent parent granting permission to bring the children across the border.

Due to increased security at border crossings since 9/11, expect delays. Be sure to stop your vehicle where instructed by the signs. Be prepared to answer the customs inspectors' questions with straight, no-nonsense answers; they take their jobs seriously, and joking around will delay your crossing. Questions they might ask include: Where were you born? Where are you going? What is the purpose of your visit? What are you bringing into Canada? *Do not attempt to cross the border with guns or weapons, radar detectors, alcoholic beverages, illegal drugs, or more than a few packs of cigarettes.* Certain produce and plants are also not permitted into Canada.

There are four border crossings from western New York to Canada: The Peace Bridge, from Buffalo, New York to Fort Erie, Ontario; the Rainbow Bridge from Niagara Falls, New York to Niagara Falls, Ontario; the Whirlpool Bridge, a NEXUS-only crossing (see below), also goes between the two cities; and the Lewiston–Queenston Bridge, which crosses the border between Lewiston, New York and Queenston, Ontario. For up-to-date information on border traffic conditions call the **Bridge Information Hotline** at 800-715-6722.

Frequent travelers to Canada can apply for the NEXUS program, designed to simplify border crossings for low-risk, preapproved travelers. As stated above, the Whirlpool Bridge, located north of the falls tourist area, is a NEXUS-only crossing. The cards can also be used at the Rainbow and Peace Bridges.

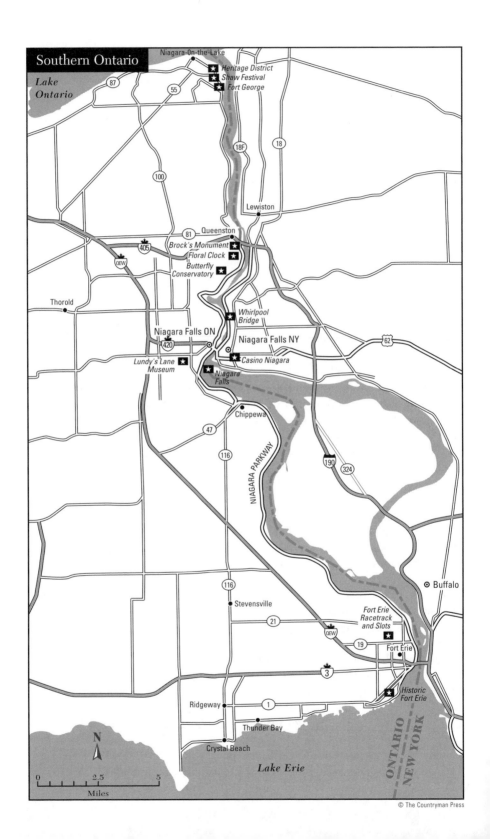

Southern Ontario

Lake Ontario

Niagara-On-the-Lake

Heritage District
Shaw Festival
Fort George

87

55

18F

18

100

Lewiston

81 Queenston

405 Brock's Monument
Floral Clock
Butterfly Conservatory

QEW

Thorold

Whirlpool Bridge

62

Niagara Falls ON

420

Niagara Falls NY

Lundy's Lane Museum

Casino Niagara

Niagara Falls

Chippewa

47

116

NIAGARA PARKWAY

190 324

Buffalo

116

Stevensville

21

QEW

Fort Erie Racetrack and Slots

19 Fort Erie

3

Ridgeway

1

Historic Fort Erie

Thunder Bay

Crystal Beach

N

Lake Erie

ONTARIO
NEW YORK

0   2.5   5
Miles

© The Countryman Press

Participants in this program carry an electronic pass, eliminating the long wait at customs and immigration. For more information call toll free 866-NEXUS26 (866-639-8726) or go online to www.ccra.gc.ca.

When traveling to Canada by boat: Four hours prior to your arrival call 888-226-7277 to request permission to enter the country. You will be asked your destination, time of arrival, length of stay, and the name, date of birth, and citizenship of each person on board. On arrival, call again to receive a reporting number.

Many U.S. citizens take advantage of the favorable exchange rate of American dollars and shop in Canada. Americans are allowed to bring back up to $200 of merchandise per day, duty free; after 48 hours in Canada, visitors can bring back $800 of duty-free goods. Note that any dollar amounts mentioned in this section are in Canadian funds.

FORT ERIE

The area known today as the town of Fort Erie is made up of numerous communities, each with its own interesting history. While space doesn't permit discussing each one in depth, here is an overview of the area's rich past.

Archeologists suspect that the Fort Erie shore of the Niagara River near the Peace Bridge was home to an aboriginal flint manufacturing site over 9,000 years ago. Nearly a million artifacts have been discovered in the area in the past 10 years.

The area was first inhabited by the Chippewa and Mississauga tribes. European settlement began after the American Revolution in 1776, when Americans who remained loyal to Britain emigrated to Canada. One of the first settlers was William Dunbar, who built a gristmill along the Niagara River in 1792. The area was named Bertie Township in 1793, honoring Willoughby Bertie, Fourth Earl of Abingdon. During the 1800s the township was divided into several different villages, including Crystal Beach and Fort Erie, named after the circa 1764 historic fort that dates back to the French and Indian War. Several major battles of the War of 1812 were also fought in this region, along with the Irish Fenian Raid after the U.S. Civil War.

Around the time of the U.S. Civil War, over a million people of Irish birth were living in the United States. A large number of them belonged to the Fenian Brotherhood, a revolutionary group fighting for Irish independence. One wing of this group had the view that an invasion of Canada could achieve Irish independence because this would put the U.S. and Great Britain in a war, diverting the British military from Ireland. In June of 1866 the forces under General John O'Neill moved into the Fort Erie area, but the expected larger supporting forces never materialized, and the campaign was a strategic failure.

The village of Crystal Beach was first settled in the late 1700s and remained a farming community until 1888, when John Rebstock started a religious assembly there. This assembly grew into Crystal Beach Amusement Park—at one point Canada's largest and most popular park—drawing summer visitors by steamship and trolley from both Buffalo and Toronto. The park closed in 1989, but many people from both sides of the border still have fond memories of the popular summertime destination. Today Crystal Beach is mainly residential, with a sprinkling of retail stores.

The entire area saw economic growth when the railroad came to town in the mid-1800s and again in 1927, when the Peace Bridge opened. Today the Greater Fort Erie area is best known for its numerous Asian restaurants, duty-free shopping, the historic old fort, high-stakes bingo, and a Thoroughbred racetrack. In addition, the area has several historical museums and beautiful sandy beaches.

AREA CODE The area code is 905.

GUIDANCE & **Economic Development & Tourism Corporation** (905-871-1332 or 888-270-9151; www.forteriecanada.com), 660 Garrison Road, Fort Erie, Ontario. You'll find local tourism information and brochures here.

& **Greater Fort Erie Chamber of Commerce** (905-871-3803; www.forteriechamber.com), 660 Garrison Road, Fort Erie, Ontario.

& **Ontario Information Center at "The Crossroads"** (905-871-3505), 350 Bertie Street, Fort Erie. Open daily 8:30–5. This large information center is located just off the Queen Elizabeth Way, a busy expressway known locally as the QEW. In addition to tourism information, the Crossroads has several fast-food restaurants, retail shops, and a currency exchange.

GETTING THERE *By air:* See *Getting There—Buffalo*

By bus: **Greyhound** offers three trips to Buffalo daily and **Coach Trentway** offers four trips daily to Buffalo. For information on both, contact **Robo Mart** (905-871-3738), 21 Princess Street, Fort Erie.

By car: The Peace Bridge is the main route from the United States into the Fort Erie area. Take the I-90 to I-190 and get off at the Peace Bridge/Porter Avenue exit. From other points in Canada (Niagara Falls, Niagara-on-the-Lake) take the Queen Elizabeth Way (QEW) to Fort Erie.

MEDICAL EMERGENCY Dial 911

Douglas Memorial Hospital (905-871-6600), 230 Bertie Street, Fort Erie, Ontario.

VILLAGES Several villages are part of the town of Fort Erie, including Bridgeburg, Fort Erie's original downtown; Crystal Beach, once the site of a popular amusement park that is developing into an artist's community; Ridgeway, an old-fashioned small town that has numerous boutique-type shops; and Stevensville, a rural community.

✳ To See

MUSEUMS Historic Fort Erie (905-871-0540), 350 Lakeshore Road, Fort Erie. Open 10-5 May–September, 10–6 June–August. Admission $7.50 adults, $4.50 children 6–12. Originally built in 1812 and reconstructed in the 1930s, this stone fort features period rooms and artifacts from the British Garrison of the War of

1812. Costumed interpreters bring the fully restored fort to life. Guided and self-guided tours are available.

Fort Erie Historical Museum (905-894-5322), 402 Ridge Road, Ridgeway. Open summer 9–5 daily, Monday–Friday 9–5 rest of year. Admission $1.50 adults, 50¢ children. Located in the former Bertie Township Hall built in 1874, this museum features exhibits on the history and archeology of the region. The main exhibit highlights 4,000 years of the region's archaeology, with pottery and flint points dating back to 2000 B.C. Other exhibits include the Fenian Raids of the 1860s and Crystal Beach Amusement Park.

Fort Erie LaFrance Association Museum (905-871-1271), 1118 Concession Road, Fort Erie. Open by appointment only. Donation. This museum has some of the oldest working fire-fighting equipment in southern Ontario, including a 1904 Steamer, a 1917 Model T, a 1924 LaFrance, and a 1947 LaFrance. The collection also includes two hand pumpers from the 1800s and a variety of other fire-fighting apparatus.

Fort Erie Railroad Museum (905-894-5322), 400 Central Avenue, Fort Erie. Open summer, 9–5 daily; Labor Day–Thanksgiving, Saturday and Sunday 9–5. Admission $2 adults, 50¢ children. The railroad played an important role in the development of Fort Erie. This museum showcasing numerous railroad exhibits is housed in the circa 1873 Ridgeway station. This station served that nearby community until 1975, when it was relocated to the museum grounds. Among the displays on the museum grounds are the cab of CN No. 6218. Built in 1942, it was the last steam engine to carry rail passengers in Canada. Also exhibited are a 1944 caboose, a 1943 Porter fireless locomotive, and a handcar.

Mahoneys Dolls' House Gallery–Bertie Hall (905-871-5833), 657 Niagara Boulevard (2 miles north of the Peace Bridge), Fort Erie. Open daily 10–4. May–December. Admission $5 adults, $4 seniors, $3 children 6–16. The Mildred Mahoney 140-plus dollhouse collection is the largest of its type in the world, with some dollhouses dating back to 1780. The most striking in the collection is Marygate House, a five-story English manor house built in 1810, which is furnished with German Beidermeier dollhouse furniture. Bertie Hall, the stately structure that houses the dollhouse collection, was named in honor of Sir Perefine Bertie III, the Duke of Ancaster and 19th baron of Willoughby. The National Historic Site brick home, constructed in the 1830s, was an important stop on the Underground Railroad. A tunnel went from the riverbank into the house's basement, allowing escaping slaves from the United States, who had crossed the Niagara River on a ferry, to seek refuge in Canada. An authentic restoration of 1800s slave quarters,

HISTORIC FORT ERIE WAS BUILT FOR THE BRITISH GARRISON DURING THE WAR OF 1812.

Christine A. Smyczynski

where escaping slaves hid while on the road to freedom, is located in the basement.

HISTORIC SITES **Ridgeway Battlefield Site** (905-894-5322), Highway #3 (Garrison Road) and Battlefield Park, east of Ridge Road, Ridgeway. This historic site commemorates the beginnings of the Battle of Ridgeway. A log house containing a small museum is on the site of the Fenian Raids of June 2, 1866.

"The Crossing." A commemorative plaque can be seen along the Niagara River near Historic Fort Erie. This marks the major entry point for escaped slaves from the southern United States seeking freedom in Canada. Nearby Bertie Hall was a "safe house" to these freedom seekers once they crossed the river.

LIGHTHOUSES **Point Abino Lighthouse** (905-994-7825, Town of Fort Erie Parks and Leisure Department). Access by scheduled tour only. Tours take place on the second and fourth Saturdays of the month June–September at 10, 11:15, 12:30, and 1:45. Admission: $10 adults, $5 children. (Tours include a trolley ride to the lighthouse as well as a guided tour.) This Classic Revival–style lighthouse was erected in 1917 due to navigational difficulties around Point Abino. The remains of many shipwrecks are below the waters off the point. It is the fifth oldest-remaining lighthouse on the Great Lakes and was dedicated a National Historic Site in 1998.

✳ To Do

BOATING **Black Creek** feeds into the Niagara River near 4301 Niagara River Parkway, and is popular with canoeists and kayakers. Many have described the tranquil creek surrounded by weeping willows as "dreamy."

There are several private boat clubs in the area, including the **Buffalo Canoe Club** (905-894-2750; www.buffalocc.on.ca), 4474 Erie Road (RR1), Ridgeway Ontario; the **Buffalo Yacht Club** (905-894-6111; www.buffaloyachtclub.org), 1007 Point Abino Road, Ridgeway, Ontario; and the **Bertie Boating Club** (905-894-3223), 1010 Point Abino Road, Ridgeway, Ontario.

BOAT LAUNCHES AND MARINAS

Crystal Beach Waterfront Park and Boat Launch Ramp (905-994-7825; www.forterie.on.ca), 3875 Terrace Lane (end of Ridgeway Road), Crystal Beach. Open from May until mid-September. This waterfront park and boat launch offers a scenic view of Lake Erie, with Buffalo on the horizon. Park facilities include a picnic pavilion, washrooms, and plenty of parking.

Niagara Parks Commission Marina (905-871-4428), 2400 Niagara Parkway (about 5 miles north of the Peace Bridge), Fort Erie. The only public marina on the Canadian side of the Niagara River. Facilities include 135 seasonal docks, washrooms, showers, snack bar, and gift shop.

FAMILY FUN ✿ **Zooz Nature Park** (905-382-9669 or 866-FOR-ZOOZ; www.zooz.ca), 2821 Stevensville Road, Stevensville (Fort Erie). Open May–June daily 10–5, July–August daily 9–6, early September daily 10–4, mid-September–

mid-October weekends only 10–4. Admission $18 adults, $13 children, under 2 free. A 109-acre wildlife park that features interactive exhibits, art, playgrounds, picnic areas, and over 400 exotic and domestic animals. Complimentary tram system and guided educational tours.

GOLF **Fort Erie Golf Club** (905-991-8883), 1640 Garrison Road, Fort Erie. A public, 18-hole, par-71 course with restaurant, pro shop, lessons, and driving range.

International Country Club of Niagara (905-382-2000), 2900 College Road, Stevensville A semiprivate, 27-hole (three nines; par-36 for each nine) course with restaurant and full bar.

Ridgeway Shores Golf Club (905-894-1887) 3570, Thunder Bay Road, Ridgeway. A semiprivate 9-hole, par-3 course, with two par 5s and four par-4s.

Rio Vista Golf Club (905-871-0921; www.riovista.ca), Crooks Street and Bowen Road, Fort Erie. A semiprivate 18-hole, par-72 course.

GAMING: BINGO. Fort Erie is known for its three high-stakes Bingo halls that regularly attract visitors from both sides of the border.

Delta Bingo Center (905-871-6440; www.deltabingo.com/forterie/erie.crm), 549 Garrison Road, Fort Erie. Open seven days at 10 AM; call for game times. There are no taxes charged on their prices or prizes.

Golden Nugget Bingo (905-871-1277 or 888-739-6149; www.goldennugget.ca), 655 Garrison Road, Fort Erie. Opens daily at 10 AM; call for game times.

Uncle Sam's Bingo (905-871-3377), 427 Garrison Road, Fort Erie. Open seven days at 10 AM; call for game times. with the biggest prizes in Canada.

HORSE RACING AND GAMING & **Fort Erie Racetrack and Slots** (905-871-3200 or 800-295-3770; www.forterieracing.com), 230 Catherine Street, Fort Erie. Slots open Monday–Thursday 9 AM–3 AM. Friday–Sunday 24 hours. Live Thoroughbred racing from April–mid-November. This 1897 track—host to one of the racing season's premier events, the Prince of Wales Stakes, the second leg of Canada's Triple Crown—is regarded as North America's most picturesque live Thoroughbred racetrack. The track also has 1,200 slot machines with a carousel theme that range in price from a nickel to $5. The track's Prince of Wales Dining Room is known for its all-you-can-eat buffet.

SCENIC VISTAS For a great view of Buffalo, stop at the small parking area along **Lakeshore Drive between the Peace Bridge and Old Fort Erie.** Another scenic locale is the **Crystal Beach Waterfront Park,** which has views of both Buffalo and Point Abino.

✳ Green Space

BEACHES ♪ **Crystal Beach** (905-871-7825; www.forterie.om.ca), 4155 Erie Road, Crystal Beach. Open dawn to dusk. Free admission. Enjoy over 1,000 feet of well-maintained sand beach, which can get quite crowded on the weekends. It has a snack bar and washrooms but no lifeguards.

⚓ **Crescent Beach,** on the Friendship Trail at the end of Crescent Road. Open dawn to dusk. Free admission. A small beach with 65 feet of beachfront. A popular spot for families.

Thunder Bay Beach, end of Bernard Avenue. Open dawn to dusk. Free admission. Sixty-five feet of beachfront.

Waverly Beach, end of Helena Street at Edgemenore Road along the Friendship Trail. Open dawn to dusk. Free admission. A groomed white-sand beach next to the site of the old Erie Amusement Park, which was a popular destination at the turn of the 20th century.

NATURE PRESERVES Shagbark Trail, Corner of Dominion Road and Burleigh Road. Open dawn to dusk. This 64-acre wooded and meadowy park is popular with nature lovers. The wooded area is especially noted for owls.

Stevensville Conservation Area (905-788-3135), Ott Road, Fort Erie. Open dawn to dusk. This 121-acre passive recreation area, under the auspices of the Niagara Conservation Authority, features Carolina forest, wetlands, a fishing pond, and picnic area.

PARKS Lions Sugar Bowl Park, Gilmore Avenue at Central, Fort Erie. Open dawn to dusk. The park features a central fountain, playground, and municipal swimming pool. The park's bowl-like shape resembles a giant sugar bowl when it's filled with snow.

♿ **Mather Arch** (905-356-2241), 11 Niagara Parkway at the base of the Peace Bridge, Fort Erie. This structure was built in 1940 as a gateway for travelers arriving into Canada via the Peace Bridge. It was named after American inventor and manufacturer Alonzo Mather, who donated the land on which the arch is constructed. The park surrounding it consists of manicured lawns and two 165-foot-long flower beds.

Niagara River Parkway. Fort Erie is the southern terminus of the 38-mile Niagara River Parkway, one of the most scenic drives in the world. The Fort Erie portion overlooks the Niagara River, the Peace Bridge, and Riverwalk Park.

Riverwalk, located just below the Peace Bridge at the intersection of Queen Street and Niagara Boulevard This riverfront park features a sculpture commemorating the Underground Railroad, patios, outdoor cafés, and public seating. The park connects the Friendship Trail and the Niagara River Recreational Trail.

Windmill Point Park (905-894-2809), 2409 Dominion Road Ridgeway. Open dawn to dusk. Swimming, fishing, and scuba diving in a 12-acre quarry. Camping is available.

Crystal Beach Waterfront Park. See *To Do—Marinas and Boat Launches.*

WALKING AND HIKING TRAILS Friendship Trail. The Fort Erie portion of the Niagara River Recreational Trail is popular for walking, jogging, cycling, and rollerblading as well as cross-country skiing and snowshoeing in winter. The trail passes many area attractions, including Historic Fort Erie, Fort Erie Historical Museum, and Ridgeway Battlefield Museum.

Niagara River Recreational Trail See *Niagara River Parkway.*

Riverwalk see *Parks.*

✳ Lodging

INNS AND RESORTS ♿ **Holiday Inn Fort Erie Convention Centre** (905-871-8333 or 888-269-5550; www .holidayinn.com), 1485 Garrison Road, Fort Erie. One hundred seven quality guest rooms, some including fireplaces and whirlpools, are available in this hotel located in the Fort Erie Civic Centre. $99–$299.

MOTELS AND HOTELS Crystal Beach Motel (905-894-1750; www.crystalbeachmotel.com), 122 Ridgeway Road, Crystal Beach. Open year-round. Joyce Heuvelmans offers 17 comfortable, air-conditioned, non-smoking motel rooms that include refrigerators and TVs. Amenities include an outdoor pool, BBQ grill, and play area. The motel is located near Lake Ontario beaches and a short drive from Niagara Falls. $79–$89.

BED & BREAKFASTS Split Rock Farms Bed & Breakfast (905-382-7777; e-mail: splitrockfarmsbb@ aol.com), 1652 Ridge Road North, Ridgeway. Open year-round. Glen and Lynda Finbow offer three guest rooms in their 60-acre country retreat. Each guest room in their Cape Cod–style home is decorated with a collection of Canadian antiques and adorned with fresh flowers and hand-sewn quilts. All rooms have private baths and air conditioning. A brunch-style breakfast is served in the dining room each morning. $85–$125.

OTHER LODGING Hide-Away Park (905-894-1911; www.knightsfamily camping.com), 1154 Gorham Road, Ridgeway. Open May 1–October 15. One hundred seventy-five tent and trailer sites are located on 28 scenic acres. Facilities include flush toilets, hot showers, a camp store, playground, swimming pool, and game room.

✳ Where to Eat

DINING OUT *Fort Erie (Note: Fort Erie is noted for its many Asian restaurants.)*

Happy Jacks (905-871-3970), 98 Niagara Boulevard, Fort Erie. Open Monday–Thursday 11 AM–12:30 AM, Friday and Saturday 11 AM–3:15 AM, Sunday 11 AM–11:15 PM. Happy Jack's has been *the* place to go for Chinese food in the Fort Erie area since 1967. This large family-owned restaurant, with a covered patio overlooking the Niagara River and the Peace Bridge, specializes in Cantonese- and Peking-style food. American/Canadian specialties include steak, lobster, and Alaskan king crab.

May Wah (905-871-2422), 90 Niagara Boulevard, Fort Erie. Open 11–11 daily. Enjoy authentic Chinese cuisine in a beautiful setting overlooking the Niagara River. House specials include phoenix nest and sesame chicken.

Ming Teh (905-871-7971), 126 Niagara Boulevard, Fort Erie. Open Tuesday–Sunday 11–10. This restaurant with exquisite Chinese decor is known for Peking duck and escargot plus an extensive Mandarin and Szechwan menu.

Ridgeway

Ridgeway Restaurant (905-894-4229), 335 Ridge Road, Ridgeway. Open daily 8–9. This upscale café features specials like chicken Oscar and prime rib. Dine indoors or outside in the courtyard. Live music is featured in the Other Side Lounge.

EATING OUT

Crystal Beach

Crystal Chandelier Café, Etc. (905-894-9996), 3878 Erie Road, Crystal Beach. Open Sunday–Thursday 1–10, Friday and Saturday 10–midnight. A shop and restaurant in one. The store offers a line of natural foods, cosmetics, vitamins, essential oils, and more. The restaurant, which has an outdoor patio, features specialty coffees, teas, and wines plus an array of decadent desserts and light treats.

🍴 ♿ 🐾 **Dagwood's Lakeview Restaurant** (905-894-7037), 423 Derby Road, Crystal Beach. Open seasonally June–September. This casual family restaurant features specialty dishes—including "Dagwood" sandwiches, just like in the comics—plus pizza, burgers, hot dogs, chicken wings, ribs, and seafood specials. Homemade desserts on weekends include a deep-fried cheesecake.

🍴 ♿ 🐾 **Tropical Hut** (905-894-0667), Derby Rd, Crystal Beach. Open seasonally June–September. This take-out hot dog and hamburger stand is located in the former "hot dog alley," a popular spot to grab a bite to eat when the amusement park was still in existence. Owners Shelley and Bobby Bland also operate the small year-round café next door and Bland's Boxing Club in the rear of the building. Bobby Bland is a New York State Golden Gloves champ and a five-time Canadian champ.

Sugar Waffle Trailer Municipal parking lot off Erie Road. The well-known Crystal Beach sugar waffles are available from this trailer, weekends in summer.

Fort Erie

Artemis Restaurant (905-871-5344), 199 Garrison Road, Fort Erie. Open Monday–Saturday 7 AM–9 PM, Sunday 7 AM–3 PM. This restaurant is noted for souvlaki and other Greek specialties.

🍴 ♿ 🐾 **Green Acres Family Restaurant** (905-871-1212), 1554 Garrison Road, Fort Erie. Open Wednesday–Sunday noon–9 PM. This family-owned and operated establishment has been a Fort Erie landmark for over 40 years. They specialize in fish and chips, plus other affordable family favorites.

Ridgeway

🍴 ♿ 🐾 **Doreens Family Restaurant** (905-894-5000), 301 Ridge Road, Ridgeway. Open seven days for breakfast, lunch, and dinner. Open Monday–Saturday 7 AM–3 PM, Sunday 7–7. Get home-cooked meals here, plus pasta, pizza, wings, subs, and burgers. Kids' and senior menus are available.

🍴 **Sweet Dreams Ice Creamery** (905-894-9573), 356 Ridge Road, Ridgeway. Open seasonally June–September. Enjoy take-out ice cream treats.

❋ Entertainment

THEATERS **Gypsy Theater** (905-871-4407, 877-990-PLAY; www.gypsy theatre.com), 465 Central Avenue, Fort Erie. Theater productions May–December.

✳ Selective Shopping

ANTIQUES **Anthony T. Antiques** (905-894-0939), 395 Derby Road, Crystal Beach. Open seasonally June–September. This shop has a general line of antiques as well as knick-knacks, collectibles, and paintings.

Antiques on Erie (905-894-6397, www.erieantiques.com), 3896 Erie Road, Crystal Beach (Fort Erie). Open summer, Wednesday–Sunday 10–5; winter, Friday–Sunday 10–5. Closed Christmas–mid-April. This 8,000-square-foot multidealer antiques and collectibles mall, located in a former roller rink, carries articles from Victorian to retro. They are also the Canadian headquarters for Lorna Bailey Art Ware.

Bridgeburg Antique Village (905-871-0132), 40 Courtwright Street (off Central Avenue), Fort Erie. Open Wednesday–Sunday 10–5. More than 50 dealers of fine antiques and collectibles have their wares displayed at this, the region's largest antique mall. The two-floor, 10,000-square-foot warehouse was built as a factory in the late 1800s by Dr. Ray Vaughn Pierce, known for his medicinal tonics, including Dr. Pierce's Golden Medical Discovery.

George's Antiques and Junk (905-894-6586 or 905-894-5012), Erie and Derby Roads, Crystal Beach. Open Tuesday–Thursday 11–4:30, Friday–Sunday 10–5; call first during winter. They have a general line of antiques and furniture.

HRM Crows Nest, 34 Queens Circle, Crystal Beach. Open seasonally by chance. Antiques, collectibles, and memorabilia.

Mia's Antiques and Upholstery (905-894-2127), 421 Derby Road, Crystal Beach. Open year-round 12–5 daily. This shop deals in antiques, but their biggest business is reupholstery, custom slipcovers, and custom furniture painting done by owner Mia Russell.

SPECIAL SHOPS

Crystal Beach (Note: Most stores in Crystal Beach are open seasonally.)
✍ ♿ **Crystal Beach Trading Post** (905-894-1893), 3950 Erie Road, Crystal Beach. Open 12–5 off-season, 8 AM–9 PM in summer. This shop carries an array of useful items, including T-shirts and beachwear, as well as handmade crafts, handcrafted and silver jewelry, gift items, candy, and more.

Maple Rock Farm Soap Company (905-894-8867), 394 Derby Road, Crystal Beach. Open seasonally June–September. This shop has fine hand-milled all-natural soaps and bath products, including African shea butter, which is good for soothing and healing. Owner Sharri Clark also custom makes gift baskets.

Paint Life Grand (905-894-2020), 3948 Erie Road, Crystal Beach. Open seasonally June–September. Retail shop open seasonally, custom work done year-round. Iris Bernardi's shop features hand-painted new and recycled items. She is known for her floor mats and nautical-theme items.

Woodland Wonders (905-894-9150 or 905-991-8467), 393 Derby Road, Crystal Beach. Open Tuesday–Saturday 10–5, Sunday 11–5. Artist Stacey Thomas offers painted items for sale as well as painting and craft classes. She also does custom artwork.

Ridgeway

Beyond Stress (905-894-5663; www .beyondstressglobal.com), 3653 Dominion Road, Ridgeway. Open Thursday 11–6, Friday–Saturday 10–6. This beautiful shop specializes in items designed to help you reduce stress in your life. Choose from home decor, aromatheraphy, bath and body, organic skin care, music, books, and more.

✍ ♿ **Brodie's Guardian Drug Store and Village Shoppes** (905-894-2520), 315 Ridge Road, Ridgeway. Open Monday, Tuesday, Thursday, Friday 9–8, Wednesday and Saturday 9–6. Since 1902 Brodie's has been *the* place to shop in Ridgeway. The store is huge and just goes on and on. In addition to a full pharmacy and drugstore, you can find toys, shoes, household items, greeting cards, crafts, and much more.

Country Bunny Gifts (905-894-1864), 411 Ridge Road, Ridgeway. Open Tuesday–Saturday 10–5. A cute little shop that carries folk art, bunnies, Beanies, giftware, and home decor.

Crystal Beach Candy Company (www.crystalbeachcandy.com orders through internet only), PO Box 935, Ridgeway. For those of you who still remember crossing the boarder to visit Crystal Beach amusement park, this is your mail-order source for the original Halls suckers and Crystal Beach sugar waffles you've been craving. They also sell a one-hour video, *One Last Ride*, which was filmed on the last day the park was open in 1989.

Gifts on the Ridge (905-894-0433; www.villagecraftworks.com), 341 Ridge Road, Ridgeway. Open Monday–Saturday 10–5. This shop features a large selection of unique gifts, including crystal, nautical-themed items, craft supplies, and rubber stamping supplies.

Heritage Cheese and Specialty Shop (905-894-6874), 401 Ridge Road, Ridgeway. Open Monday–Saturday 10–5, Sunday 12–4. This shop features specialty cheese, gourmet foods, and custom gift baskets.

Mrs. Murphy's Chocolate Outlet and Pantry (905-894-9542), 311 Ridge Road, Ridgeway. Open Monday–Saturday 10–5. Choose from bulk chocolates, dried fruits and nuts, gourmet food, and more.

Of Cabbages and Kings (905-894-8588) 329 Ridge Road, Ridgeway. Open Monday–Saturday 10–5; also open Sunday 11–3 in November and December. This shop features folk art, wood crafts, paintings. and items crafted by Canadian artists.

Somewhere in Time (905-894-9580), 283 Ridge Road, Ridgeway. Open Tuesday–Saturday 11–5. This shop specializes in imported brass items, jewelry, and furniture. You can order custom handcrafted furniture that's carved and inlaid with brass.

Zat Bead Store (905-894-0557), 304 Ridge Road, Ridgeway, Open seven days in summer 10–5; winter, Tuesday–Saturday 10–5. Pat Beiner's shop has all sorts of unique beads to choose from.

Fort Erie

Peace Bridge Duty Free Shop (800-361-1302; www.dutyfree.ca). Located at the Peace Bridge on the Fort Erie side. Open 24 hours, seven days a week. Americans can spend up to $200 duty free on every trip to Canada. The largest duty-free store in North America features exceptional prices on designer clothing, fragrances, china, and crystal, plus beer, alcoholic beverages, and cigarettes. Another **duty-free shop** is located at the **Queenston-Lewiston Bridge** (905-262-5363; www.dutytaxfree.com).

✳ Special Events

January: **Winterfest** (905-994-1771; www.winterfestniagara.com). This festival established in 1994 is held in various locations throughout the Greater Fort Erie area. Events throughout the month including a polar bear dip, chili cook-off, kids' activities, and more.

July: **Friendship Festival** (905-871-6454; www.friendshipfestival.com), Mather Arch in Fort Erie and LaSalle Park in Buffalo. A multiday event that includes concerts, amusement rides, crafts, children's activities, and fireworks celebrating the friendship between Canada and the United

States. **Ridgeway Summer Festival** (905-894-1720; www.vaxxine.com/ridgeway), Ridgeway. An outdoor festival for the entire family that features food, crafts, and entertainment. **Crystal Beach Festival** (905-871-5449; www.crystalbeachcandy.com), Crystal Beach. Enjoy antiques, family activities, and crafts as well as artifacts and memorabilia at the former Crystal Beach Amusement Park.

October: **Doors Open Niagara** (905-704-3942; www.doorsopenniagara .com) Various locations throughout western New York and southern Ontario. See Web site for specifics. A binational event that features tours of historic and cultural sites on both sides of the border.

December: **Spirit of Christmas and Dickens Style Open House** (905-894-1720), Ridgeway. Do your holiday shopping while sipping cider and listening to carols.

NIAGARA FALLS, ONTARIO

Niagara Falls, Ontario is probably one of the most unique cities in the world. It has seen massive commercial and tourism growth in the last several years while being the site of one of the Seven Natural Wonders of the World. The Niagara Falls area is definitely a study in contrasts. On the one hand, you have the thundering falls and the wild, scenic beauty of the lower gorge, yet just a few hundred feet away you have a bustling city that, in some aspects, rivals Las Vegas in its glitz. The city, which has about 80,000 permanent residents, attracts some 14 million visitors annually from around the world.

The history of the entire Niagara Peninsula goes back over 12,000 years, when native aboriginal people used the area as hunting and burial grounds. The name *Niagara* is a derivation of the aboriginal word Onighiara, meaning "thundering waters." Many of the early European settlers in the region were British United Empire Loyalists, who left the United States after the Revolutionary War.

The city of Niagara Falls is actually a conglomeration of a number of different villages that eventually merged. These villages include Drummondville (named

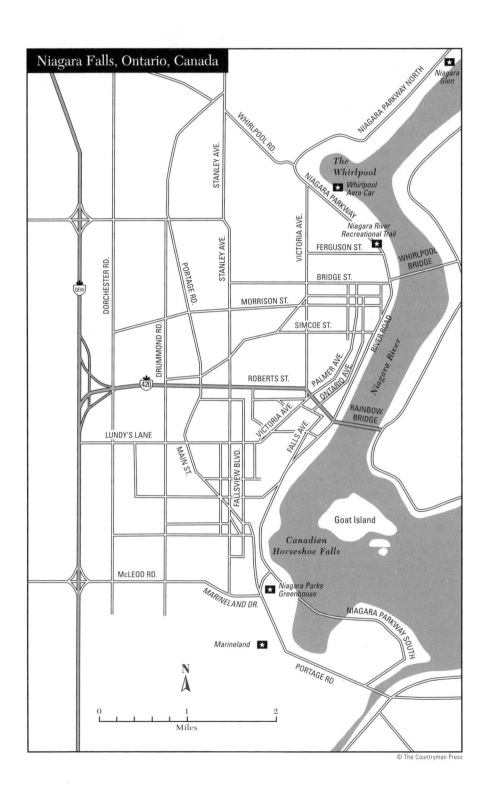

Niagara Falls, Ontario, Canada

NIAGARA PARKWAY NORTH

Niagara Glen

WHIRLPOOL RD.

The Whirlpool

Whirlpool Aero Car

NIAGARA PARKWAY

Niagara River Recreational Trail

STANLEY AVE.

STANLEY AVE.

VICTORIA AVE.

FERGUSON ST.

WHIRLPOOL BRIDGE

DORCHESTER RD.

PORTAGE RD.

DRUMMOND RD.

BRIDGE ST.

MORRISON ST.

SIMCOE ST.

RIVER ROAD

Niagara River

QEW

420

ROBERTS ST.

PALMER AVE.

ONTARIO AVE.

RAINBOW BRIDGE

LUNDY'S LANE

VICTORIA AVE.

FALLS AVE.

MAIN ST.

FALLSVIEW BLVD.

Goat Island

Canadian Horseshoe Falls

McLEOD RD.

Niagara Parks Greenhouse

MARINELAND DR.

NIAGARA PARKWAY SOUTH

Marineland

PORTAGE RD.

N

0   1   2
Miles

© The Countryman Press

after Lt. General Gordon Drummond, who fought in the battle of Lundy's Lane, a decisive battle in the War of 1812), near present-day Portage Road and Lundy's Lane; Clifton, which was located in the vicinity of today's Skylon Tower; and Elgin, which was located near the Whirlpool Bridge. Clifton and Elgin merged in 1856, and the name was changed to the town of Niagara Falls in 1881. The same year Drummondville changed its name to the village of Niagara Falls. Town and village later combined to make the city in 1904.

There are many attractions in the Niagara Falls area. Of course, you have the Falls and attractions connected to it, like the *Maid of the Mist* and Journey Behind the Falls. Gardeners enjoy the dazzling Niagara Parks Botanical Gardens and Niagara Parks Butterfly Conservatory as well as the Floral Clock. If you have children in tow, be sure to visit Marineland and the Niagara Falls Bird Aviary, and take a walk along Clifton Hill. Golfers can enjoy over a half-dozen challenging courses in the Niagara Falls area.

The Niagara Falls, Ontario area is an ever-changing one. As this book went to press, millions of dollars of planned and developing attractions were in the works, including an expansion to Marineland that will make it the largest theme park in North America and the largest aquarium in the world. A huge resort complex and waterpark is also being planned by Ripley Entertainment, along with several other projects in the planning stages. For up-to-date information on developing attractions, consult www.discoverniagara.com.

AREA CODE The area code is 905.

GUIDANCE Niagara Falls Tourism Association (905-356-6061 or 800-563-2557; www.discoverniagara.com), 5515 Stanley Avenue, Niagara Falls, Ontario. Open daily 9–5. The official tourism site of Niagara Falls. Be sure to pick up their publication, *Discover Niagara,* for comprehensive information and maps of the area.

Ontario Travel Information (905-358-3221), 5355 Stanley Avenue, Niagara Falls, Ontario. Open daily 8:30–5. This information center has Niagara region information as well as for the rest of Ontario.

Lundy's Lane Tourist Area (905-356-1161 or 866-551-LANE; www.lundyslane .com), PO Box 26008, Niagara Falls, Ontario. Contact them for information on the Lundy's Lane business district, a 2-mile area of lodgings, restaurants, shops, and entertainment just west of the falls.

GETTING THERE *By air:* See *Getting There: City of Buffalo.*

By bus: **City of Niagara Falls Bus Terminal** (905-356-1179), Corner of Bridge and Erie Streets, Niagara Falls, Ontario.

By car: The main entrance point from the United States is via the Rainbow Bridge. The Whirlpool Bridge is a NEXUS-only crossing.

GETTING AROUND *By car:* Traffic in the tourist area can be very congested, especially during the summer. It's best to park and walk, or take the People Mover bus. The main roads include Niagara Parkway/River Road, which runs along the gorge and river; Clifton Hill, Falls Boulevard, and Victoria Avenue, which are the main streets in the Clifton Hill area; while Fallsview Boulevard goes past most of the major hotels and the new casino. Lundy's Lane has national chain hotels and restaurants located along it.

By bus: **Niagara Parks "People Mover Transportation"** (905-371-0254 or 877-642-7275; www.niagaraparks.com), Upper Rapids Drive off the Niagara Parkway, Niagara Falls. Operates mid-May–mid-October. Park your car and ride all day around the falls tourist area in an air-conditioned People Mover Bus.

5-0 Transportation Shuttle (905-685-5463 or 800-330-5050), This shuttle-bus service has daily runs between Niagara Falls and Niagara-on-the-Lake.

MEDICAL EMERGENCY Dial 911

Greater Niagara General Hospital (905-358-0171), 5546 Portage Road, Niagara Falls, Ontario.

✴ To See

Nightly Illumination of the Falls. Hours vary according to season, generally from dusk until midnight (10 PM January–March, 11 PM in April). A visit to Niagara Falls is not complete unless you've experienced the nightly illumination of the Falls. Huge spotlights light the falls in shades of blue, red, and green. Be sure to arrive well before dusk to get a prime viewing spot along the railings.

MUSEUMS AND HISTORIC HOMES **Lundy's Lane Museum** (905-358-5082; www.lundyslanemuseum.org), 5810 Ferry Street, Niagara Falls. Open daily 9–4, May 1–November 30; 12–4 Monday–Friday, December 1–April 30. Admission $3/adults, $2/children. This museum is housed in an 1874 building originally constructed as a town hall. On display are War of 1812 artifacts, information on the founding and development of Niagara Falls, and historical photos of the city. It is located on the site of the battle of Lundy's Lane, July 25, 1814.

VIEW ARTIFACTS AND LEARN THE SEVEN BASIC PRINCIPLES OF BUDDHISM AT THE CHAM SHAN TEMPLE.

Christine A. Smyczynski

Willoughby Museum (905-295-4036; www.niagara.people.org/~willomus), 9935 Niagara Parkway, Niagara Falls. Open May–September daily 12–5, by appointment rest of year. Donation. This museum, housed in a 1916 one-room schoolhouse, has historical treasures and artifacts from the towns of Willoughby and Chippewa.

ARCHITECTURE **Cham Shan Temple** (905-371-2678), 4303 River Road (across from the White Water

Boardwalk, just north of the Whirlpool Bridge), Niagara Falls. Open daily 11–5 June–September. Visitors can learn the basic principles of Buddhism and view artifacts on a 45-minute guided tour of this seven-level temple.

✴ To Do

BOAT EXCURSIONS ♿ *Maid of the Mist* (905-358-0311; www.maidofthemist .com), 5920 River Road, Niagara Falls. Open seasonally mid-April–Labor Day, 9:45 to dusk, starting at 9 after Memorial Day. For over 150 years this boat excursion has been taking visitors on a journey close to the thundering waters of the Falls. This is considered a "must-do" when you visit the area. See also *Boat Excursions, Niagara Falls, New York*

FAMILY FUN ✎ **Falls Incline Railway** (905-371-0254; www.niagaraparks.com), Between Portage Road and the Niagara Parkway across from Horseshoe Falls, Niagara Falls. Operates late March–late October, daily schedule varies. Admission: $2.50 one-way fare. Visitors can descend or ascend the escarpment to the falls area in an open-air car.

✎ ♿ **Marineland** (905-356-2142; www.marinelandofcanada.com), 7657 Portage Road, Niagara Falls. Open mid-May–late June and Labor Day–October 31 10–5 daily, late June–Labor Day open 9–6 daily. Admission: $32.95 adults, $27.95 ages 5–9 and over age 59. This attraction features a marine mammal

---

CLIFTON HILL

Clifton Hill (905-358-3676; www.cliftonhill.com) is a unique area in the heart of Niagara Falls. Part Las Vegas, part carnival midway, part Halloween, Clifton Hill's glitziness is in direct contrast with the natural wonder just a block away. While some visitors may find it chaotic and commercial—it's adjacent to Casino Niagara—it does offer a refuge on a rainy day or a place to appease bored teenagers. The area is jam-packed with fast-food restaurants, amusements, shops, and other diversions. Here is a sampling of Clifton Hill attractions:

Louis Tussaud's Waxworks (905-374-6601), 4915 Clifton Hill.

♿ **Ripley's Believe-It-Or-Not! Museum** (905-356-2238; www.ripleysniagara .com), 4960 Clifton Hill.

Screamers House of Horrors (905-357-7656), 5930 Victoria Avenue.

The Fun House (905-357-2200), 4943 Clifton Hill.

House of Frankenstein (905-357-9660), 4967 Clifton Hill.

Great Canadian Midway (905-358-3673), Clifton Hill 70,000 square feet of family entertainment.

♿ **Moviland Wax Museum of Stars** (905-358-3061), 4960 Clifton Hill

Dinosaur Park Miniature Golf (905-357-5911), 4960 Clifton Hill

Guinness World of Records Museum (905-356-2299), 4943 Clifton Hill.

show, with whales, dolphins, and seals, and interactive animal displays. Visitors can actually touch the whales at the interactive whale habitats, Friendship Cove and Arctic Cove. The park also has thrilling amusement rides, including Dragon Mountain, the world's largest steel roller coaster. One of the newest rides is the Sky Screamer, a 450-foot tower that propels riders skyward for a view of the falls. Marineland is in the middle of an expansion project that will make it the largest theme park in North America.

✐ ♿ **Niagara Falls Aviary: Birds of the Lost Kingdom** (905-356-8888 or 866-994-0090; www.niagarafallsaviary.com), 5651 River Road, Niagara Falls. Open 9–9 May–September, 9–5 October–April. Get up close with exotic and tropical birds and other creatures. Kids will enjoy seeing in person the colorful critters normally seen only on TV or in books, including poison dart frogs, toucans, and macaws. Visitors are permitted inside the lorikeet cage to mingle with and feed nectar to these tiny, friendly birds. A large gift shop offers a huge selection of bird-related items.

FISHING **Niagara Fishing Adventures** (800-332-6865; www.niagarafishing adventures.com), A variety of locations along the Niagara River. Fishing adventures along the Niagara Gorge. You will be provided with a fishing license, fishing tackle and lunch after the excursion. Trout, salmon, and bass are the more popular catches.

GAMING (Note: No one under 19 is permitted in the casinos.)

♿ **Casino Niagara** (905-374-3598 or 888-946-3255; www.casinoniagara.com), 5705 Falls Avenue, Niagara Falls. Open 24/7/365 This well-known destination features 200,000 square feet of gaming area, including 150 table games and 2,700 slot and video poker machines, plus dining and entertainment.

♿ **Niagara Fallsview Casino Resort** (905-358-3255, 888-FALLSVUE or 888-325-5788; www.discoverniagara.com), 6380 Fallsview Boulevard (corner Murray Hill and Buchanan Avenue), Niagara Falls. This large, new casino features 3,000 slot machines and 150 gaming tables. The casino's Avalon Ballroom features top entertainers, including some Las Vegas headliners. A 30-story, 368-room hotel is at the center of the property, along with a retail complex and meeting center. The parking garage has space for 3,000 vehicles.

GOLF **Beechwood Golf & Country Club** (905-680-4653; www.beechwood golf.com), 4680 Thorold Towline Road, Niagara Falls. A semiprivate 18-hole, par-71 course with restaurant and full bar.

Eagle Valley Golf Club (905-374-2110; www.golfeaglevalley.com), Niagara Falls. A public 18-hole, par-63 course. Amenities include restaurant, full bar, club making, lessons, driving range, and health pro shop.

Legends of the Niagara Golf Complex (905-295-9595 or 866-830-4478; www.niagaraparksgolftrail.com or www.niagaralegends.com), 9233 Niagara Parkway, Niagara Falls. Two championship 18-hole courses plus a 9-hole putting course. Owned and operated by the Niagara Parks Commission, this course borders the historic grounds of the 1814 Battle of Chippewa site.

The Links of Niagara at Willodell (905-295-GOLF or 800-790-0912; www
.thelinksofniagara.com), 10325 Willodell Road, Niagara Falls. A semiprivate 18-
hole, par-72 course with a restaurant, full bar, banquet facilities, lessons, pro
shop, and practice facilities.

Niagara Falls Golf Club (905-358-5846 or 888-5GOLF40; www.niagarafalls
golf.com), 6169 Garner Road, Niagara Falls. A semiprivate 18-hole, par-72
course with restaurant and full bar. This challenging course is designed for all
levels of golfers.

Oak Hill Par 3 Golf Course (905-358-6418; www.niagaraparkgolftrail.com),
7516 Portage Road, Niagara Falls. A semiprivate 9-hole, par-35 course with a
snack bar.

Oaklands Golf Course (905-295-6643), 8970 Stanley Street, Niagara Falls. A
public 18-hole, par-72 course with restaurant and full bar.

Rolling Meadows Golf & Country Club (905-384-9894; www.rolling
meadows.ca), Montrose Road, Niagara Falls. A semiprivate 18-hole, par-72
course with restaurant.

Whirlpool Public Golf Course (905-356-1140; www.niagaraparksgolftrail.com),
3351 Niagara Parkway, Niagara Falls. This 18-hole, par-72 course has been
ranked one of the top public golf courses in Canada.

GUIDED TOURS **Double Deck Tours** (905-374-7423; www.doubledeck
tours.com), 3957 Bossert Road, Niagara Falls. April–October. Tours start every
30 minutes beginning at 9:30 during July and August, schedule varies rest of season. This fully guided tour company, which has been in business for over 40
years, offers tours of the Niagara Falls area on double-decker sightseeing buses.
Three major attractions—*Maid of the Mist,* Journey Behind the Falls, and
Whirlpool Aero Car—are included.

Niagara Adventure Tours (905-356-5487 or 888-640-8687; www.niagara
express.com). They pick up at all hotels in Niagara Falls Ontario. All-inclusive
day and night tours are offered, including complete tours of Niagara Falls and
the upper river, the lower river, gorge, and whirlpool, Niagara-on-the-Lake, and
many more local attractions. $75–$325.

Niagara Falls Scenic Tours (905-354-6099 or 888-325-5786; www.fallstour.com),
Pickup from all Niagara Falls Ontario hotels. Niagara Falls. April–October. They
offer a variety of packages with both daytime and evening tours of Niagara Falls
by bus. Prices range from $95–$130 U.S.

& **Table Rock Complex–Journey Behind the Falls** (877-642-7275), 6650
Niagara Parkway, Niagara Falls. Open year-round. Tours begin at 9; closing
times vary throughout the year. Admission $10/adult, $6/children. This tour takes
visitors down 100 feet through century-old tunnels to an observation platform
near the base of the Horseshoe Falls. Raincoats are supplied.

See also **Grayline Tours** (716-695-1603 or 800-695-1603), listed under Niagara
Falls, New York.

HERITAGE WALKING TOURS Several **self-guided walking tours brochures** that highlight historical buildings in various sections of the city are available at Niagara Falls Tourism. These include the **downtown area** (near the Whirlpool Bridge), the **Drummondville area** (off Main Street and Lundy's Lane), and the **village of Chippewa** (just south of the falls near Marineland). See *Guidance*.

SCENIC DRIVES Niagara Parkway. Winston Churchill called the Niagara Parkway "the prettiest Sunday afternoon drive in the world" when he visited Canada in 1943, and it's still true today. The 38-mile parkway, stretching from Fort Erie to Niagara-on-the-Lake, follows the curves of the Niagara River past stately mansions and well-manicured properties. To fully enjoy this scenic parkway, pick up a copy of the booklet "The Drivers Guide to the Niagara Parkway," by Colin Duquemin (Norman Enterprises, Street Catharines, ON 1997), which highlights the historic sites, attractions and scenic vistas along the way.

SCENIC VIEWS Falls Tower (905-358-3676), 4912 Clifton Hill, Niagara Falls. Open seasonally. This Clifton Hill attraction has a spectacular view of both the Falls and the Clifton Hill area.

& **Minolta Tower Centre** (866-325-5785), 6732 Oakes Drive, Niagara Falls. When it opened in 1962, it was the first tower built in the Falls area. It was renovated in 2001 and now includes the 42-room Ramada Plaza Hotel Fallsview, the Pinnacle Restaurant, and an observation deck.

& **Niagara Helicopters Limited** (905-357-5672; www.niagara-helicopers.com), 3731 Victoria Ave, Niagara Falls. Daily 9–dusk year-round, weather permitting. Fee: $100/ adult, $55/child 2–11, $190 couple. They've been offering a bird's-eye view of Niagara Falls since 1961.

& **Skylon Tower** (905-356-2651; www.skylon.com), 5200 Robinson Street, Niagara Falls. One of three yellow bug elevators will whisk you up to the top of the tower in 52 seconds. From the observation deck 775 feet above the Falls you can see almost 80 miles. You can even dine in one of two restaurants located in the tower, the Revolving Dining Room or the Summit Suite. When you come back to earth, shop in one of the many stores located at the base of the tower.

Skyway Helicopters (905-641-2222 or 800-491-3117; www.skywayhelicopters .com), Open year-round, 9–sunset by reservation, weather permitting. Basic rate: 20-minute tour $124/adult, $70/child; group rates available. A unique and comprehensive tour by helicopter.

Whirlpool Aero Car (905-371-0254) 3850, Niagara Parkway (3 miles downriver from the falls) Niagara Falls. Open daily 9–5, March–November, weather dependent; longer hours in summer. Admission: $10 adults, $6 children 6–12. An open-air gondola ride across the gorge, suspended 250 feet over the Niagara Whirlpool. The car, which was built in 1913, was designed by Spanish engineer Leonardo Torres Quevedo and has been in operation since 1916. It is often referred to as the Spanish Aero Car.

Christine A. Smyczynski

THE WHIRLPOOL AERO CAR,
AN OPEN-AIR GONDOLA RIDE SUSPENDED
250 FEET OVER THE NIAGARA WHIRLPOOL,
HAS BEEN IN OPERATION SINCE 1916.

∞ **WEDDING CHAPELS** While there are numerous wedding chapels in the Niagara Falls area, most don't offer Las Vegas–style "quickie" weddings. Reservations must be made in advance, so be sure to call ahead. American citizens who have been previously married must obtain a Canadian lawyer to fill out the necessary paperwork with the Canadian government before a new marriage can take place. It costs about $150 and takes two to four weeks. See also *Wedding Chapels—Niagara Falls, New York.*

Little Wedding Chapel (905-357-0260 or 800-463-0884; www.niagara fallsweddingchapel.ca), 7701 Lundy's Lane, Niagara Falls. Open by appointment. This chapel offer non-denominational services.

Niagara Fallsview Weddings (905-356-1944; www.niagara-fallsview-weddings.com), 6732 Fallsview Boulevard, Niagara Falls. Open by appointment. Niagara Falls's premier wedding and honeymoon service provider. Get married while overlooking the falls from atop the 525-foot Minolta Tower.

Niagara Weddings (905-374-3957; www.niagaraweddingscanada.com), 5669 Main Street, Niagara Falls. Open by appointment. They offer services seven days a week. Their specialty is elopements.

Occasions in Niagara (905-357-7756 or 877-286-9436; www.occasionsinniagara .com), 5368 Menzie Street, Niagara Falls. Open by appointment. A wedding-planning service.

Peninsula Inn Wedding Services (905-354-8812), 7373 Niagara Square Drive, Niagara Falls. Open by appointment. A resort hotel and spa that offers weddings in either their chapel or garden gazebo.

Two Hearts Wedding Chapel (905-371-3204), 5127 Victoria Avenue, Niagara Falls. Open by appointment. A small, dignified chapel that holds up to 60 guests.

Wedding Company of Niagara (905-371-3695 or 877-6451-3111; www.wedding companyniagara.com), 6053 Franklin Avenue, Niagara Falls. Open by appointment. A full range of services for all denominations.

✳ Green Space

NATURE PRESERVES Dufferin Island Nature Area (905-371-0254; www .niagaraparks.com), Open dawn to dusk. Located just south of the Falls, this area has trails that wind over 11 small islands connected by numerous bridges. A good place for picnicking, birding, and fishing.

Niagara Glen Nature Area See *Walking and Hiking Trails.*

GARDENS & **Niagara Parks Botanical Gardens** (905-358-8633 or 877-NIA-PARKS; www.niagaraparks.com), 2565 Niagara Parkway, Niagara Falls. Open dawn to dusk. Free admission. The 100-acre manicured gardens are maintained by students from the Niagara Parks School of Horticulture. The gardens are noted for their roses, along with their large collection of formal and informal gardens

🖉 & **Butterfly Conservatory** (905-371-0254; www.niagaraparks.com), 2565 Niagara Parkway (in the Niagara Parks Botanical Gardens), Niagara Falls. Open daily 9–5. Admission: $10 adult, $6 children 6–12, under 6 free. Get up close and personal with 2,000 tropical butterflies in this 11,000-square-foot, climate-controlled butterfly conservatory, the largest of its type in North America. Stroll along the 600-foot path that winds through the conservatory, and observe more than 50 varieties of butterflies in all four stages of their life cycle.

& **Floral Clock,** Along the Niagara Parkway, just south of the Lewiston-Queenston Bridge. One of the world's largest working floral clocks, this horticultural attraction, built in 1950, is 40 feet in diameter and formed by 15,000 plants. It is designed, planted, and maintained by the Niagara Parks Commission.

& **Niagara Parks Greenhouse** (905-371-0254), 7145 Niagara River Parkway, Niagara Falls. Open daily 9–5. Free admission. The displays in this popular greenhouse change about eight times a year to celebrate the seasons or holidays. Plants from all over the world are featured, along with waterfalls, pools, tropical song birds, turtles, and fish.

Oakes Garden Theatre (905-371-0254), River Road, Niagara Falls. Located at the base of Clifton Hill across from the American falls. Open dawn to dusk. Free admission. This park, built in 1937 as an outdoor stage, is a blend of formal gardens and architecture, based on Greek amphitheaters.

PARKS **Kings Bridge Park** (905-877-642-7275; www.niagaraparks.com), Niagara River Parkway. A great spot to picnic on the upper river.

Queen Victoria Park (905-358-5935 or 877-642-7272), Niagara Parkway across from the American falls. Open dawn to dusk. This 154-acre park, created in 1887, has manicured lawns and a variety of gardens. A popular restaurant in the park overlooks the falls.

WEAR BRIGHT COLORS TO ATTRACT BUTTERFLIES AT THE BUTTERFLY CONSERVATORY IN THE NIAGARA PARKS BOTANICAL GARDENS, NIAGARA FALLS, ONTARIO.
Christine A. Smyczynski

WALKING AND HIKING TRAILS
Bruce Trail (905-529-6821 or 800-665-HIKE; www.brucetrail.org), Mailing address: PO Box 857, Hamilton, ON. Trailhead is located near Brock's Monument in Queenston Park, Queenston. The Bruce Trail is Canada's oldest and longest footpath and provides the only public access to the Niagara Escarpment. This well-known Canadian trail goes from the Niagara

Falls area to Tobermory in northern Ontario, near Georgian Bay and Lake Huron.

Niagara Glen Nature Area. Open dawn to dusk. Free Admission. Niagara Parkway, across from the Whirlpool Golf Course between Queenston and Niagara Falls. This nature area features hiking trails along the gorge. Many rare species of flora exist in this area, which is also an important birding area. Hikes through the area involve a change in elevation of over 200 feet. Niagara Glen has a large parking area, picnic tables, rest rooms, and a gift shop. Guided rim tours are provided seasonally.

Niagara River Recreational Trail (905-371-0254 or 877-NIA-PARK; www .niagaraparks.com), This trail is located alongside the Niagara Parkway and the Niagara River from Fort Erie to Niagara-on-the-Lake.

& **White Water Boardwalk** (905-371-0254; www.niagaraparks.com), Niagara Parkway, Niagara Falls. Open daily 9–5 mid-March–mid-November, with limited access in winter. Admission: $7.50 adults, $4.50 children 6–12. About a mile and a half past the Whirlpool Bridge along the Niagara Parkway is the parking lot for the trail down into the gorge. This 1,000-foot boardwalk along the river's edge passes some of the strongest Class VI rapids in the world, past the swirling whirlpool. Be sure to wear sturdy shoes or hiking boots.

✳ Lodging

Author's note: If you are planning to stay in the area, my advice is to splurge and stay at one of the hotels overlooking the falls. These hotels—primarily operated by major hotel chains—offer spectacular views of both the American and Canadian Falls. There are hundreds of accommodations in and around the Falls, which has the third most hotel rooms in Canada. Space allows for just a small number of these accommodations to be highlighted in this book. For a complete list contact the **Niagara Falls Tourism Association** (905-356-6061 or 800-563-2557; www.discoverniagara.com). All rates are listed in Canadian funds.

HOTELS, INNS, AND RESORTS

Overlooking the Falls
Brock Plaza Hotel (905-374-4444 or 800-263-7135; www.niagarafalls hotels.com) 5685 Falls Avenue, Niagara Falls. This elegant 233-room

hotel is connected to Casino Niagara by an indoor walkway. It offers spectacular Falls-view rooms and suites, some with terraces overlooking the falls. Amenities include an indoor pool, whirlpool, and sauna, along with a five-star gourmet restaurant. $99–$699.

Doubletree Resort Lodge & Spa (905-358-3817 or 800-730-8609), 6039 Fallsview Boulevard, Niagara Falls. This newly constructed hotel, which opened in early 2004, features 224 large guest rooms—including family and whirlpool suites—many with a spectacular view of the Falls. Amenities include indoor pools and fitness room, year-round outdoor hot tub and sun deck, full-service spa, and on-site parking. $99–$349.

Embassy Suites (905-356-3600 or 800- 420-6980; www.embassysuites niagara.com), 6700 Fallsview Boulevard, Niagara Falls. This 42-story luxury hotel features 512 two-room suites, many overlooking the Falls. Amenities include an indoor pool, fitness center, two restaurants, complimentary breakfast, and shuttle to attractions and the casino. $89–$599

& **Hilton Niagara Falls** (905-354-7887 or 888-370-0700; www.niagara falls.hilton.com), 6361 Fallsview Boulevard, Niagara Falls. This four-diamond, 516-room hotel features standard rooms as well as Jacuzzis suites, many with a fabulous view of the falls. The hotel's 10,000-square-foot indoor pool has the area's only spiraling three-story waterslide. Guest can enjoy fine dining in the water-themed rooftop restaurant, the Water-mark. $99–$499.

Michael's Inn by the Falls on the River (905-354-2727 or 800-263-9390; www.michaelsinn.com), 5599 River Road, Niagara Falls. Luxurious rooms and suites, many with balcony views of the Falls and Niagara River. Choose from standard rooms, family units, or one of their themed suites, including the Scarlett O'Hara, Midnight at the Oasis, or Romance by the Falls Suite. Amenities include an indoor pool and state-of-the-art fitness center. $48–$288.

& **Niagara Falls Marriott Fallsview** (905-357-7300; www .niagarafallsmarriott.com), 6740 Fallsview Boulevard, Niagara Falls. A four-diamond property located just 100 yards from the brink of the Falls, this 23-story, 427-room hotel features standard rooms plus Jacuzzi, loft, family, and fireplace suites. Many rooms have a falls view. Amenities include a 3,000-square-foot, full-service spa, indoor pool, fitness room, and arcade. $129–$599.

& **The Oakes Hotel** (905-356-4514 or 877-THE-OAKES; www.niagara hospitalityhotels.com), 6546 Fallsview Boulevard, Niagara Falls. This new 167-room hotel offers first-class accommodations overlooking the Horseshoe Falls. Many of the suites have fireplaces, Jacuzzis, and/or terraces. Hotel amenities include an indoor pool, exercise facilities, and room service. It is adjacent to the Niagara Fallsview Casino Resort. $79–$569.

& **Radisson Hotel & Suites Fallsview** (905-356-1944 or 877-325-5784; www.niagarafallsview.com), 6733 Fallsview Boulevard, Niagara Falls. This hotel offers 227 rooms, many with a view of the Falls, Jacuzzi tubs, microwaves, and mini-fridges. They also have an indoor pool and fitness center plus four restaurants. $89–$249.

Ramada Plaza Hotel Fallsview (866-325-5784; www.niagarafallsview .com), 6732 Fallsview Drive, Niagara Falls. This landmark boutique hotel located in the Minolta Tower offers 42 spacious suites, including some with Jacuzzis. $99–$349.

& **Renaissance Fallsview Hotel** (905-357-5200 or 800-363-3255; www.renaissancefallsview.com), 6455 Fallsview Boulevard, Niagara Falls. Within walking distance of the Falls, this hotel features 262 guest rooms, 60 of them with Falls views. Amenities include an indoor waterfall pool, state-of-the-art exercise room, and squash and racquetball courts. $99–$349.

Sheraton Fallsview (905-374-1077 or 800-781-6782; www.fallsview.com), 6755 Fallsview Boulevard, Niagara Falls. Over 400 luxury guest rooms and suites are available at this 32-story hotel, voted Niagara's best four-diamond hotel. Amenities include an indoor pool, sauna, and exercise facility. $99–$349.

Sheraton on the Falls (905-374-4445 or 800-263-7135; www.niagara fallshotels.com), 5875 Falls Avenue, Niagara Falls. This hotel—adjacent to Casino Niagara and directly across from the American falls—offers 670 luxury rooms, suites, and bi-level suites, many with a great view of the Falls. Amenities include a spa and fitness center. $99–$599+.

Other Areas

よ **Old Stone Inn** (800-263-6208; www.oldstoneinn.on.ca), 5425 Robinson Road, Niagara Falls. Just a block from the falls is this unique English-style country inn located in a former 1904 stone flour mill. The inn features 114 recently renovated cozy guest rooms, some with Jacuzzis and fireplaces. Amenities include an indoor/outdoor pool, hot tub, and poolside patio bar. $99–$400. See also *Dining Out.*

よ **Americana Conference Resort and Spa** (905-356-8444 or 800-263-3508; www.americananiagara.com), 8444 Lundy's Lane, Niagara Falls. This 160-room hotel is the only full-service resort in Niagara Falls. Along with standard rooms, they offer family and two-room suites, Jacuzzi suites, and rooms with balconies. The Americana has a luxurious spa that provides massages, facials, body wraps, and more. Recreational facilities include indoor and outdoor pools—one of which is a 25,000-square-foot water park—fitness center, video arcade, and indoor and outdoor playgrounds. Their signature restaurant, Jack Tanner's, serves up steaks, burgers, and chicken. $99–$249.

MOTELS Many nondescript national chain and family-owned motels are located throughout the city. While most don't offer a Falls view, many are within walking distance to the cataracts, and in most cases these accommodations are moderately priced. There are also numerous hotels in the Lundy's Lane section of town, a short drive from the falls tourist area. **Lundy's Lane Tourism Information**: 866-551-LANE. One such accommodation:

Ramada Inn (905-356-6119), 7389 Lundy's Lane, Niagara Falls. This 73-room hotel adjacent to the Canada One Factory Outlet Mall features heated indoor and outdoor pools and an exercise room. $90–$230.

BED & BREAKFASTS Close to 50 bed & breakfast inns can be found in Niagara Falls, many in the area between the Whirlpool and Rainbow Bridges, about a 10-minute walk to the Falls. The B&Bs located on River Road, many of them in Victorian-era homes, offer views of the gorge. For a complete list of bed & breakfast inns, contact **Niagara Falls Tourism** (see *Guidance*), or visit discoverniagara .com. Here is a sampling:

Absolute Elegance Bed & Breakfast (905-353-8522; www.aebedand breakfast.com), 6023 Culp Street, Niagara Falls. Doddy Sardjito and David Tetrault offer two elegant antiques-furnished guest rooms in this circa 1855 Queen Anne-style Victorian home. $100–$170.

Ambiance by the Falls Bed & Breakfast (905-374-4314; www .ambiancebythefalls.com), Niagara Falls. This turn-of-the-20th-century home is a three-minute walk from the falls. Host Rebecca Cooper offers three colorful guest rooms with queen-sized beds and en suite baths. $120.

Angel's Hideaway Bed & Breakfast (905-354-1119; www.angels hideaway.net), 4360 Simcoe Street, Niagara Falls. This romantic inn is located on a quiet tree-lined street, a perfect spot for a relaxing getaway. Hosts Gordon and Sue Weston offer two air-conditioned rooms with queen beds and private baths. The Angel Suite includes a Jacuzzi tub and fireplace, while the Aztec room has a South American theme. A full English breakfast is served, including in-season fruit, homemade muffins, hash browns, toast, and jam. Aztec Room $95 ($65 off-season), Angel's Suite $125 ($115 off-season).

Cairngorm Bed & Breakfast (905-354-4237; www.cairngorm–niagara .com), 5395 River Road, Niagara Falls. Innkeeper Mary Cable offers five guest rooms in this elegant Greek Revival–style home overlooking the Niagara Gorge. Each room has an en suite bath with Jacuzzi tub. Three of the five rooms overlook the gorge. $110–$150.

Chestnut Inn Bed & Breakfast (905-374-7623), 4835 River Road, Niagara Falls. Karen and Luciano Canali offer four air-conditioned guest rooms with private baths in this 1800s home that overlooks the Niagara River Gorge. The inn has hardwood floors and antique furnishings. All rooms have fireplaces and sun decks overlooking the river. A breakfast that includes fruits, cereals, and a hot entrée is served each morning. Summer $115, off-season (October 31–May 31). $95.

Cosy Inn (Coopers) Bed & Breakfast (905-354-1832), 5725 Robinson Street, Niagara Falls. Innkeepers

Marie and Walter Wyse offer three large rooms with queen beds and private baths in this lovely renovated home. A full country breakfast is served each morning. Summer $80–$120, winter $65–$75.

Danner House Bed & Breakfast (905-295-1753 or 866-295-1805), 12549 Niagara River Parkway, Niagara Falls. This historic stone home was built in 1805. Each of the three guest rooms offered by hosts Mary and Keith McGough has a private bath and waterfront view. An in-ground pool is available for guest use. $115–$125.

Eastwood Lodge Bed & Breakfast (905-354-8686; www.theeastwood .com), 5359 River Road, Niagara Falls. Eastwood Lodge, which opened in 1960, is the oldest established bed & breakfast of its kind in the region. Joanne Van Kleef's 1891 Eastlake Victorian home sits on an acre overlooking the Niagara River, just a five minute walk from the Falls. The home has fine oak trim and the original leaded beveled-glass windows. Rooms feature king-sized beds, balconies, refrigerators, TVs, and a view of the gorge. A full breakfast is served each morning. $107–$175.

Strathaird Bed & Breakfast (905-358-3421; www.strathairdinn.com), 4372 Simcoe Street, Niagara Falls. Tom and Val Jackson offer Scottish hospitality in this newly renovated inn on a tree-lined street. Each of the three guest rooms has a private bath. A full Scottish-style breakfast is served each morning. $65–$105.

Victorian Charm Bed & Breakfast (905-357-4221; www.victorian charmbb.com), 6028 Culp Street, Niagara Falls. Host Anne Marie Dubois offers four guest rooms with en suite baths in this 1889 Victorian home. Breakfast is served in a conservatory overlooking the gardens or in a screened gazebo. The inn is about a 15-minute walk to the Falls. $150+.

✳ Where to Eat

DINING OUT *Overlooking the Falls*

Most of the hotels overlooking the Falls have fine dining rooms located on their top floors—great food *and* a great view.

Fallsview Dining Room (905-374-1077, ext. 2261), Located in the Sheraton Fallsview Hotel, 6755 Fallsview Boulevard, Niagara Falls. Lunch and dinner buffets are served daily, plus Sunday brunch. Open 7 AM–10 PM. Dine overlooking Niagara Falls and the upper rapids. Menu selections include roasted salmon fettuccini, grilled raspberry chicken cordon bleu, and slow-roasted prime rib.

Penthouse Fallsview Dining Room (905-374-4445, ext. 4092), Sheraton on the Falls, 5875 Falls Avenue, Niagara Falls. Open for breakfast 7–10, lunch 11:30–2, dinner 5–9:30. This penthouse restaurant features an 80-foot-long buffet, world-class cuisine, and a breathtaking view of the falls.

The Pinnacle Restaurant (905-356-1501 or 800-461-2492), 6732 Fallsview Boulevard, Niagara Falls. Open daily 7 AM–midnight, for breakfast, lunch, and dinner. All tables overlook the Falls at this unique, elegant restaurant, located in the Minolta Tower. Specialties include surf and turf Minolta style, grilled seafood platter, charbroiled Black Angus steak, prime rib, rack of lamb, and pasta primavera.

Rooftop Fallsview Dining Room (905-357-5200, ext. 6272; www .renaissancefallsview.com), Renaissance Fallsview Hotel, 6455 Fallsview Boulevard, Niagara Falls. Open daily 5–10 PM, open until 11 PM May 1–October 31. Enjoy elegant, yet casual dining with a spectacular view of Niagara Falls from the 18th floor. Entrées include tricolor tortellini, pan-seared Ontario walleye, and grilled rib-eye steak. Their signature desert is chocolate-drizzled strawberry cheese shortcake.

Rainbow Room (905-374-4444, ext. 4134), 10th Floor, Brock Plaza Hotel, Niagara Falls. Open daily for breakfast 7–10, lunch 11–2, dinner 5–10. A five-star, fine-dining experience with a great view of the Falls.

Skylon Tower Revolving Dining Room (905-356-2651 or 877-840-0314; www.skylon.com), 5200 Robinson Road, Niagara Falls. Open for lunch 11:30–3:30, dinner 4:30–10. Without a doubt, this 280-seat restaurant is one of the most romantic dining spots in the city. The award-winning continental cuisine, combined with the spectacular view from 775 feet above the Falls, makes for a memorable evening. While romance is in the air in the evening, the restaurant, which makes a complete rotation each hour, is more family-oriented for lunch, complete with a children's menu. The **Summit Suite Dining Room**, also located in the Skylon Tower, is known for its buffet-style dining for breakfast, lunch, dinner, and Sunday brunch.

Terrapin Grille Fallsview Dining (905-357-7300), Niagara Falls Marriott Fallsview, 6740 Fallsview Boulevard Niagara Falls. Open 6 AM–11 PM. This restaurant with a view of the Falls specializes in steak and seafood.

Watermark Restaurant at the Hilton Niagara Falls (905-354-7787 or 888-370-0700; www.niagarahilton.com), 6361 Fallsview Boulevard, Niagara Falls. Open daily 7 AM–10:30 PM. Reservations required for dinner. This restaurant on the 33rd floor of the Hilton Niagara Falls, 555 feet above the falls, has a great view along with delicious, wonderfully presented food. The water-themed decor is a perfect backdrop to a romantic evening.

Other Niagara Falls restaurants:
Beef Baron (905-356-6110; www.niagarafallsrestaurants.com), 5019 Center Street, Niagara Falls. Open daily 4–midnight. This restaurant is well known for their steaks, especially their giant T-bone and porterhouses steaks for bigger appetites.

Casa Mia (905-356-5410), 3518 Portage Road, Niagara Falls. Open for lunch Monday–Friday 11:30–2:30; dinner Monday–Friday until 10, Saturday and Sunday 5 PM–1 AM. Voted one of the best upscale Italian restaurants in the Niagara region and the prettiest dining room to boot, this family-owned and operated eatery is known for its veal parmigiana, along with daily pasta specials and catch of the day.

Casa d' Oro (905-356-5646 or 888-296-1178; www.thecasadoro.com), 5875 Victoria Avenue, Niagara Falls. Open Sunday–Friday 12–10:30, Saturday 4–11. This elegant restaurant features Italian specialties, steaks, seafood, prime rib, and an extensive wine cellar of fine and rare vintages. Enjoy patio dining in-season.

Happy Wanderer (905-354-9825), 6405 Stanley Street, Niagara Falls. Open 8 AM–11 PM. Enjoy some of the best German fare this side of the Atlantic. Start your dining experience

with the house specialty appetizer, potato pancakes. Entrées include wiener wurstchen, bratwurst, and breast of chicken schnitzel. They also serve traditional fare like steak, ham steak, roast beef, and pork chops.

The Love Boat Steak & Seafood (905-357-4500), 5845 Victoria Avenue, Niagara Falls. Open Sunday 11:30–8, Monday–Friday 11:30–9, Saturday 3–9. An authentic seafood house with nautical décor, featuring live lobsters, fresh clams, oysters, and more, along with steaks, chicken, pasta, and a kids' menu.

Monticello Grille House and Wine Bar (905-357-4888 or 800-843-5251; www.monticello.ca) 5645 Victoria Avenue, Niagara Falls. Open daily 12–10:30. This traditional grille house serves up dinner with a southern flare, with recipes inspired by Louisiana cuisine. Enjoy veal Monticello, pecan pork loin with apples and jalapenos, or breast of bayou chicken, along with traditional dishes like surf and turf, prime rib, and pasta.

Old Stone Inn Millery (905-357-12234 or 800-263-6208; www.old stoneinn.on.ca), 5425 Robinson Road, Niagara Falls. Open daily 7–3 and 4:30–10. Fine dining is offered in a circa 1904 structure that once housed a flour mill. The dining room features stone walls, cathedral ceiling, and a wood-burning fireplace. Classic and regional cuisine using fresh ingredients is featured on their extensive menu. Choose from prime rib, chateaubriand, filet mignon, salmon, pasta, and more. House desserts include bread pudding, crème caramel, tiramisu, and even flambé desserts for two, served tableside. Overnight accommodations are available; see *Lodging*.

Twenty-One Club (905-374-3598, ext. 1250), in Casino Niagara, 5705 Falls Avenue, Niagara Falls. Open Sunday–Thursday 11:30–11, Friday and Saturday 11:30–midnight. This restaurant inside Casino Niagara has received the AAA/CAA four-diamond award several years in a row. Specialties include classic French onion soup, Caesar salad, prime rib, steak, and lobster. The wine cellar features vintages from Niagara's wineries as well as wines from around the globe.

EATING OUT Visitors will find hundreds of casual eateries in the Niagara Falls area, especially along Clifton Hill and Victoria Avenue. There are also many restaurants, both local and national chain establishments, along Lundy's Lane, a short drive from the tourist area. Below is just a sampling of what's available:

&. **Mick and Angelo's** (905-357-6543), 7600 Lundy's Lane, Niagara Falls. Open 11 AM–12:30 AM daily. A popular restaurant and bar noted for homemade pasta, chicken, ribs, and steak.

&. ℰ **Rainforest Café** (905-374-CAFÉ), 5875 Falls Avenue, Niagara Falls. Open daily 11–11, Friday and Saturday until midnight. A unique dining experience, featuring an 80-foot-tall erupting volcano, live shark exhibit, animatronic elephants and gorillas, and daily live animal encounters.

ℰ **Secret Garden Restaurant** (905-358-4588; www.secretgarden restaurant.net), 5827 River Road, Niagara Falls. Open daily 8–8; closed January. This affordable restaurant's dining room overlooks the American falls. Outdoor patio dining is available in the summer, adjacent to Oakes Garden Theatre.

&. ℰ **Table Rock Restaurant** (905-354-3631), Niagara Parkway (at the brink of the Canadian falls), Niagara Falls. Open May–October daily 11:30–9. This casual family-dining establishment has a bird's-eye view of the Canadian Horseshoe Falls.

ℰ &. ℰ **Victoria Park Restaurant** (905-536-2217), Across from the American falls on Niagara Parkway, Niagara Falls. Open seasonally May–October 11:30–9. This full-service restaurant, located in Queen Victoria Park and operated by the Niagara Parks Commission, offers an excellent view of the American and Canadian Falls. Dine indoors or on the outdoor terrace. Reasonably price meals are offered, including a children's menu.

&. **Whirlpool Restaurant** (905-356-7221), 3351 Niagara Parkway (at the Whirlpool Golf Course), Niagara Falls. Open April 1–November 1 daily 6 AM–9 PM. Pub fare and wholesome casual meals, along with Niagara region wines, are offered at this restaurant,. Children's menu available. The dining room as well as the outdoor patio have a great view of the golf course.

✳ Entertainment

THEATERS ℰ **Oh Canada Eh? Dinner Show** (905-374-1617 or 800-467-2071; www.ohcanadaeh.com), 8585 Lundy's Lane, Niagara Falls. May–October, nightly at 6:30 PM; schedule varies rest of year. Tickets: $49 adult, $39 ages 13–16, $24.50 under 13. A musical celebration of Canadian heritage, plus a family-style meal.

✳ Selective Shopping

ANTIQUES **Olde Country** Antiques (905-356-5523; www.oldecountry antiques.com), 4604 Erie Avenue,

Niagara Falls. Open Thursday–Sunday 10–5. Browse through 5,000 square feet of furniture, dolls, collectibles, primitives, and other nostalgic items.

SPECIAL SHOPS There are hundreds of stores in Niagara Falls, from inexpensive souvenir shops to exclusive boutiques with upscale items. You'll find numerous retailers on Falls Avenue, including the **Coca Cola Shop** and **Hershey's** (905-374-4444, ext. 4561). Be sure to try one of Hershey's chocolate shakes. Even more shops are located along Victoria Avenue, Clifton Hill, Fallsview Boulevard, and on Lundy's Lane. Numerous small retail shops are also located at the **Maid of the Mist Plaza** and at the base of the **Skylon Tower**. The new **Fallsview Casino Resort** includes 45 upscale retail shops.

YOU CAN'T LEAVE NIAGARA FALLS WITHOUT A VISIT TO SOUVENIR CITY.

Christine A. Smyczynski

Major shopping centers include the **Canada One Factory Outlet Mall,** on Lundy's Lane near the QEW Expressway. (905-356-8989 or 866-2844-5781; www.canadaoneoutlets .com), which has 40 brand-name outlet stores, and the **Pen Centre**, located in nearby St. Catharines (905-687-6622 or 800-582-8202), which has 170 stores.

The **Mount Carmel Gift Shop** (905-356-0047; www.carmelniagara.com; 7021 Stanley Avenue, Niagara Falls) is a religious gift shop specializing in European imports, statues, gold jewelry, rosaries, and crucifixes. They also have a retreat center for groups and individuals. **Souvenir City Headquarters** (905-357-1133 or 866-344-0985; www.souvenircityheadquarters .com, 4199 River Road, Niagara Falls), offers the largest selections of souvenirs in the Niagara Falls area. The complex is comprised of four distinct stores: **Souvenir City**, which has a complete line of items carrying the Niagara Falls name; **First Nations Craft Store**, carrying Native Canadian crafts, including Eskimo carvings, totem poles, and more; **Market Place**, for unique gift items and a food court, serving items like pizza and nachos; and **Christmas Treasures**, a year-round Christmas store.

✳ Special Events

May: **Spring Festival Art Show** (905-356-2241; www.niagara parks.com), Niagara Parks Botanical Gardens. This show features well-known artists from the Parkway Artists Guild.

October: **Doors Open Niagara** (905-704-3942; www.doorsopenniagara .com). Various locations throughout western New York and Southern Ontario. A binational event featuring tours of historic and cultural sites on both sides of the border.

November –January: **Winter Festival of Lights** (905-356-6061 or 800-563-2537). For over 20 years the Niagara Falls area has been transforming into a winter wonderland of lights and color. Hundreds of displays light up the area along the Niagara Parkway and the falls. There are also weekly events, including live performances, parades, and fireworks.

NIAGARA-ON-THE-LAKE AND QUEENSTON

Both Niagara-on-the-Lake and Queenston were major battlefields during the War of 1812, when U.S. forces invaded Canada. The towns were destroyed at the end of that war, but they were quickly rebuilt, and many of these 18th- and 19th-century structures have been preserved. Niagara-on-the-Lake, originally called Onigahara, was Upper Canada's first capital, the site of the first sitting of the provincial legislature and where the first newspaper was published in Ontario.

Niagara-on-the-Lake has been judged the prettiest town in Canada. With its beautifully manicured gardens and historic Victorian properties, it is charming and picture-postcard perfect. Visitors can enjoy museums, boutique shopping, fine dining, winery tours, and scenic vistas. The Old Town section along Queen Street features numerous specialty shops and restaurants. The cool nights and mild days September and October make this region perfect for grape production and wine making.

The town is probably best known for the Shaw Festival, an internationally acclaimed theater season that features the works of George Bernard Shaw and his contemporaries.

If you are visiting during the summer, plan on arriving by 9 AM if you want to avoid crowds and get a decent place to park. It is very peaceful walking around the town before all the shops open.

A special note on accessibility: Since this is a town of historic structures, many of the stores and restaurants are not accessible to wheelchairs and strollers or have limited accessibility.

AREA CODE The area code is 905.

GUIDANCE **Niagara-on-the-Lake Chamber of Commerce** (905-468-1950; www.niagaraonthelake.com), 26 Queen Street (lower level). Open seven days 10 AM–7:30 PM. Located in the lower level of a historic 1847 courthouse, they have a large selection of brochures on attractions, accommodations, shopping, and dining.

GETTING THERE *By car:* Take I-190 to the Lewiston/Queenston Bridge. After passing through customs and toll, take an immediate right turn, then a left at the stop sign. Turn right at the next street, and follow the Niagara Parkway to Niagara-on-the-Lake, about 8 miles. Alternately, cross the Peace Bridge from Buffalo or the Rainbow Bridge in Niagara Falls, and follow the scenic Niagara Parkway along the river.

By bus: **5-0 Transportation Shuttle** (905-685-5463 or 800-330-5050), This shuttle bus has daily runs between Niagara Falls and Niagara-on-the-Lake.

MEDICAL EMERGENCY Dial 911

✷ To See

ART MUSEUMS Riverbrink (905-262-4477; www.riverbrink.org), 116 Queenston Street, Queenston. Open Victoria Day weekend–Canadian Thanksgiving, 10–5 Wednesday–Sunday. Admission $5 adults, $4 seniors, children under 12 free. This gallery houses the collection of paintings, drawings, prints, sculpture, and decorative arts amassed by the late art collector Samuel E. Weir. The collection reflects Mr. Weir's interest in Canadian art and the history of the Niagara region.

Niagara Pumphouse Visual Arts Center (905-468-5455; www.niagarapump house.on.ca), 247 Ricardo Street, Niagara-on-the-Lake. Open 1–4 Friday–Sunday off-season, daily during summer. This arts center offers, classes, exhibits, workshops, and lectures in a restored 1891 water-pumping station.

MUSEUMS AND HISTORIC HOMES Laura Secord Homestead (905-262-5676), 29 Queenston Street, Queenston. Open June–August 10–4 daily. Admission $3.50, under 6 free. This restored homestead was the home of War of 1812 heroine Laura Secord, who journeyed 20 miles through the wilderness and the American lines to warn her husband and the British forces of an impending attack.

McFarland House (905-468-7405 or 877-NIA-PARK), 15927 Niagara Parkway, Niagara-on-the-Lake. Open June–August Monday–Friday 10–5, Saturday 10–8. Admission $3.50, under 6 free. This 1800s Georgian home is decorated in the gracious style of the 1840s.

Mackenzie Heritage Printery Museum (905-262-3676 or 877-NIA-PARK), 1 Queenston Street, Queenston. Open June–August daily 10–5. Admission $3.50, under 6 free. This museum is located in the restored home of William Lyon Mackenzie, who published *The Colonial Advocate*.

Niagara Apothecary Museum (905-468-3845), 5 Queen Street, Niagara-on-the-Lake. Open mid-May–Labor Day daily 12–6. Free admission. Staffed by volunteers from the Ontario College of Pharmacists, this working museum takes you back in time to see how pharmacists worked over 100 years ago. The apothecary first opened its doors in the late 1860s.

&. **Niagara Historical Society and Museum** (905-468-3912; www.niagara .com/~nhs), 43 Castlereagh Street, Niagara-on-the-Lake. Open May–October 10–5, rest of year 1–5. Admission $5 adults, $3 seniors, $2 students, $1 ages 5–12. The first building in Ontario designed and built to be a museum, this 1906 building has one of the finest collections of early Canadian artifacts in the country. The museum's interactive computer digitization program stores thousands of images from their archives.

William Stewart Homestead (for information contact the Niagara Foundation: 905-468-7932), 507 Butler Street, Niagara-on-the-Lake. Open by appointment. This 1835 Neo-Classical home constructed for William Stewart, a black teamster, is one of the few surviving homes built by black settlers. It is owned by the Niagara Foundation and serves as an interpretive center for Niagara's black history.

HISTORIC SITES **Brock Monument,** located in Queenston Heights Park. Open daily 10–5. Admission: $2 adults, $1 children 6–16. This 185-foot statue honors Sir Isaac Brock, a British general killed at the Battle of Queenston Heights during the War of 1812. The memorial, a National Historic Site, was constructed between 1853–1856. Visitors can climb the 235 stairs to the top, visit the museum in the base of the monument, and take a guided tour of the battlefield.

Cenotaph Clock Tower, Queen Street and King Streets. Probably the best known landmark of Niagara-on-the Lake, this clock tower was erected in 1922 as a memorial to fallen World War I townsmen.

Fort Mississauga Ruins (905-468-6602), Niagara-on-the-Lake Golf Course, Niagara-on-the-Lake. Open dawn to dusk. To reach this site, you take a walking trail through the Niagara-on-the-Lake Golf Course, so watch for stray balls. The tour of the remains of this fort is self-guided, with historical markers explaining the significance of the structure.

& **Fort George National Historic Park** (905-468-4257), Picton Street, Niagara-on-the-Lake. Open daily 10–5 April 1–October 31, November 1–March 31 by appointment. Admission: $10 adults, $8.50 seniors, $5 children 6–16. This 1796 British fort played a key role in the Niagara Frontier during the War of 1812. Costumed interpreters recreate the period leading up to the war.

✳ To Do

BOAT EXCURSIONS & **Whirlpool Jet Boat Tours** (905-468-4800 or 888-438-4444; www.whirlpooljet.com), Boats depart from King George III Inn, 61 Melvill Street, Niagara-on-the-Lake, Ontario, and 115 South Water Street, Lewiston, New York. Journey into the whirlpool on specially designed jet boats and learn about the history, scenery, and white water of the Niagara River Gorge. If you opt for the open-boat tour, you will get wet despite wearing the full-length splash suit and wet boots provided, so bring a change of clothing. (See also *To Do—Boat Excursions*, Niagara County, Lewiston and Youngstown.)

BE PREPARED TO GET WET ON A WHIRLPOOL JET BOAT TOUR OF THE NIAGARA RIVER GORGE.

Charles Lyle

GOLF Heritage Woods Golf Course (905-685-9204), 1140 Airport Road, Niagara-on-the-Lake. A semiprivate 11-hole course.

Niagara-on-the-Lake Golf Club (905-468-3271), 143 Front Street, Niagara-on-the-Lake. A semiprivate, 9-hole, par-35 course, with a restaurant overlooking the Niagara River. The oldest golf course in North America, it overlooks Lake Ontario. The Fort Mississauga ruins are located adjacent to the course.

Peach Trees Golf Club (905-468-1811), 221 Niven Road (off Hwy 55 and Lakeshore Road), Niagara-on-the-Lake. Nine challenging holes for golfers of all abilities.

Queenston Golf Club (905-262-4528), 269 Progressive Avenue (off Regional Road #81) Queenston. A public 9-hole, par-34 course with snack bar and full bar.

Royal Niagara Golf Club (905-685-9501 or 866-ROYAL-18; www.royalniagara .com), 1 Niagara-on-the-Lake Boulevard, Niagara-on-the-Lake. Three 9-hole courses built to championship standards. The courses feature sculpted fairways and an abundance of water.

GUIDED TOURS Niagara College Canada's Niagara Learning Vacations (905-641-2252; www.NiagaraLearningVacations.com), 135 Taylor Road, Niagara-on-the-Lake. Some of their tours include "Wine from Vineyard to Table," "War of 1812," and "Gardening in Niagara."

Niagara Wine Tours International (905-468-1300 or 800-680-7006; www .niagarawinetours.com), 92 Picton Street, Niagara-on-the-Lake. Bicycle tours and passenger van and coach tours through the Niagara wine region.

Niagara-on-the-Lake Trolley Wine Country Tours (905-468-2195; www .vintageinns.com), 48 John Street, Niagara-on-the-Lake. Tours depart at 10 AM and 1:30 PM. This three- to four-hour completely guided tour includes a minimum of two tastings at selected area wineries, along with history and information about the region.

Queens Royal Tours (905-468-1008; www.queensroyaltours.com), 128 Anne Street, Niagara-on-the-Lake. Tours offered daily 10 AM–11 PM. Reservations recommended. Historic horse-drawn or vintage car tours through historic Old Town Niagara-on-the-Lake.

Winery Tours with Niagara Airbus (905-374-8111; www.niagaraairbus.com), Mailing address 8626 Lundy's Lane, Niagara Falls. Tours depart from the Gate House at Niagara-on-the-Lake. Experience the Niagara region's wineries without having to drive.

Zoom Leisure Bicycle Tours and Rentals (905-468-2366), 275 Mary Street, Niagara-on-the-Lake. Tours at 10 AM and 1:30 PM. Cycle through Niagara's winery region while learning about the region's past and present. Rental bicycles are also available for you to explore the area on your own.

WINERIES The Wineries of Niagara-on-the-Lake (www.wineriesofniagara onthelake.com), is a group of 16 wineries—all within a 10-minute drive of each other in the Niagara-on-the Lake area—that welcome visitors to enjoy tours and tastings. Three even have full-service restaurants. The wineries sponsor many events throughout the year, including the Niagara Icewine festival in January.

& **Hillebrand Estate Winery** (905-468-7123; www.hillebrand.com), 1249 Niagara Stone Road, Niagara-on-the-Lake. Open daily 10–6; extended hours in summer. Tours are given on the hour. Hillebrand Estates, established in 1982, is Niagara-on-the-Lake's most recognized winery, winning over 300 awards in international competitions. Tour the underground barrel cellar and vineyards. If you have the time, dine in their acclaimed café overlooking the vineyards. Specialties include dishes cooked with local produce and wines.

& **Inniskillin Winery** (905-468-3554; www.inniskillin.com), Niagara Parkway at Line 3, Niagara-on-the-Lake. Guided 45-minute tours at 10:30 and 2:30 daily May–October, weekends only November–April. This winery is named after the famous Inniskilling Fusiliers, an Irish regiment that served in the War of 1812. The visitors center is housed in the historic Brae Burn barn, which was built in the 1920s of a design influenced by the work of Frank Lloyd Wright. Inniskillin was granted a winery license in 1997, the first wine producer in Ontario to be given a license since 1929. The winery offers many premium wines, including merlot, pinot noir, chardonnay, and icewine.

& **Jackson-Triggs Niagara Estate Winery** (1-866-589-4637; jacksontriggs winery.com), 2145 Niagara Stone Road, Niagara-on-the-Lake. Open summer 10:30–6:30, rest of year 10:30–5; tours every half hour. This state-of-the-art winery is a blend of modern winemaking technology and traditional skills. Be sure to visit their tasting gallery, where wines are skillfully paired with food. They also have a 500-seat open-air amphitheater used for summer musical entertainment.

TAKE A TOUR OF THE AWARD-WINNING PELLER ESTATES WINERY LOCATED ON 40 PICTURESQUE ACRES.

Christine A. Smyczynski

Joseph's Estate Wines (905-468-1259; www.josephsestatewines.com), 1811 Niagara Stone Road, Niagara-on-the-Lake. Open daily June–October 10–7, November–May 10–6. Winery and vineyard tours at 11, 1, and 3 May–October. Owner Joseph Pohorly, who founded this winery in 1992, offers unique wines like pinot gris, a white wine with fruit aromas. Pohorly also founded Newark Wines, which later became Hillebrand Estates.

& **Konzelmann Estate Winery** (905-935-2866; www.konzelmannwines.com) 1096 Lakeshore Road, Niagara-on-the-Lake. Open May–September Monday–Saturday 10–6, Sunday 12–6; November–April Monday–Saturday 10–5, Sunday 12–5; tours offered May–September at 2. This winery—the only one on the shores of Lake Ontario—offers breathtaking views. Owner Herbert Konzelmann, a native of Germany, introduced German winemaking and vineyard techniques to the Niagara region. Winemaking is definitely in his blood: The craft has been practiced on his mother's side of the family since 1521. The winery has won many national and international awards, including the Winemaker of the Year Award.

Lailey Vineyard (905-468-0503; www.laileyvineyard.com), 15940 Niagara Parkway, Niagara-on-the-Lake. Open May 1–October 31 daily 10–6, November 1–April 30 daily 11–5; tours by appointment. The Lailey family has been growing premium wine grapes since 1970 and are known for producing wines with fruit characteristics. Their wines include chardonnay, Riesling, sauvignon blanc, and icewines.

& **Marynissen Estates** (905-468-7270; www.marynissen.com), 1208 Concession Road, Niagara-on-the-Lake. Open May–October daily 10–6, November–April daily 10–5; tours by appointment. This winery produces small-volume, high-quality red wines.

& **Peller Estate Winery** (905-468-4829 or 888-609-4442; www.peller.com), 290 John Street East, Niagara-on-the-Lake. Open daily 10–6; tours hourly on the half hour. Explore the vineyards as well as their underground barrel aging cellar when you take a tour of this award-wining winery located on 40 picturesque acres.

& **Pillitteri Estates Winery** (905-468-3147; www.pillitteri.com), 1696 Niagara Stone Road, Niagara-on-the-Lake. Open May 15–October 15 daily 10–8, October 16–May 14 daily 10–6; tours at 12 and 2. The grapes used to make their wines are grown on the family's 53-acre farm. Their philosophy is to produce the finest wines possible from the highest quality Niagara Peninsula grapes. The Italian *carretto,* or cart, depicted on their label, reflects their Italian heritage. This family heirloom, which was brought from Sicily, is displayed in the winery's tasting room.

Reif Estate Winery (905-468-7738; www.reifwinery.com), 15608 Niagara Parkway, Niagara-on-the-Lake. Open April–October daily 10–6, November–March daily 10–5; tours May–September at 1:30. This winery and wine boutique, surrounded by 135 acres of vineyards, is located on the scenic Niagara Parkway overlooking the Niagara River. Reif Estate winery produces outstanding wines using winemaking techniques passed down over 13 generations. Guided tours are offered daily at 1:30, May-Sept. Wine tasting includes their world-famous icewine.

&. **Strewn Estate Winery** (905-468-1229; www.stewnwinery.com), 1339 Lakeshore Road, Niagara-on-the-Lake. Open daily 10–6; tours at 1 PM. Customized tours and tastings are offered at this winery housed in a unique building that once was a canning factory. It is home to Canada's only winery cooking school. Lunches and dinners are served in their restaurant.

Sunnybrook Farm Estate Winery (905-468-1122), 1425 Lakeshore Road, Niagara-on-the-Lake. Open May–October daily 10–6; November, December, March, April daily 10–5; January and February Thursday–Monday 10–5. This winery specializes in wines made from fruits other than grapes, including peaches and strawberries.

✳ Green Space

PARKS **Queenston Heights Park** (905-356-2241), Niagara Parkway (just north of the Lewiston-Queenston Bridge), Queenston. Open daily dawn to dusk. This park includes a picnic area, formal gardens, tennis court, wading pool, and hiking trails. Brock Monument is located in the park, along with an upscale restaurant. See also *Historic Sites* and *Where to Eat*.

Queens Royal Park (905-468-4362), Front and King Streets, Niagara-on-the-Lake. This park on the banks of the Niagara River has a panoramic view of the river, Lake Ontario, and Old Fort Niagara across the river in Youngstown, New York. The park's gazebo was built for the Stephen King movie *The Dead Zone* and was donated to the town by the film company.

Simcoe Park (905-468-4362), Picton and King Streets, Niagara-on-the-Lake. Open daily dawn to dusk. A small picturesque public park with a playground, wading pool, and outdoor stage.

✳ Lodging

Over three hundred accommodation properties are in and around Niagara-on-the-Lake, from five-star resorts to bed & breakfast inns to small cottages. Though it would obviously be impossible for one person to visit and describe them all for this book, I would like to note that Niagara-on-the-Lake has a reputation for quality accommodations, so you won't find a bad room here. The **Niagara-on-the-Lake Chamber of Commerce** (905-468-1950; www.niagaraonthelake.com) offers an accommodations booking service as well as brochures on the properties. Reservations should be made well in advance, especially during the theater season, April– November. I recommend the booklet published by the **Shaw Festival** (800-511-SHAW; www.shawfest.com), which lists all lodging, with brief descriptions and prices. Below are a few of Niagara-on-the-Lake's accommodations.

INNS AND RESORTS **Moffat Inn** (905-468-4116; www.moffatinn.com) 60 Picton Street, Niagara-on-the-Lake. This charming inn, located in Old Town, offers 22 unique rooms plus a luxury suite. All have private baths, some have fireplaces. It is a historic building without elevators. Rooms $95–169, suite $400+.

Oban Inn (905-468-2165, 888-669-5566; www.vintageinns.com), 160 Front Street, Niagara-on-the-Lake. This four-diamond, full-service inn was built in 1824 as the home of a Captain Duncan Milloy of Oban, Scotland. The original structure was destroyed by fire in 1992 and rebuilt the following year. Surrounded by beautiful English-style gardens, the inn has 26 luxurious guest rooms, many with a view of the lake. $150–$455.

Pillar and Post (905-468-2123 or 888-669-5566; www.vintageinns.com), 48 John Street, Niagara-on-the-Lake. This two-story, 123-room luxury brick hotel was built in 1862 as a canning factory and converted into an inn and restaurant in 1969. It was named the Top Country Inn in Canada in 1999. Amenities include indoor and outdoor pools, fitness center, European spa, world-class dining, and a theatre shuttle. $150–225+.

Prince of Wales Hotel (905-468-3246 or 888-669-5566; www.vintage inns.com), 6 Picton Street, Niagara-on-the-Lake. One of the finest heritage hotels in the world, the Prince of Wales offers personalized service, award-wining cuisine, and an exclusive European spa. Built in 1864, the hotel offers 114 individually appointed guest rooms. $225–$295+.

& **Queens Landing** (905-468-2195, 888-669-5566; www.vintageinns.com), 155 Byron Street, Niagara-on-the-Lake. This four-diamond Georgian-style mansion offering 144 luxurious guest rooms—some with fireplaces and whirlpool baths—is situated close to the Niagara River. Amenities include an indoor pool, sauna, outdoor gardens and patio, and fine dining. $150–$510.

South Landing Inn (905-262-4634; www.southlandinginn.com), corner of Kent and Front Streets. South, Queenston. This historic 1800s country inn overlooking the Niagara River was built by Thomas Dickson to accommodate the many travelers passing through Queenston, which was the terminus of the portage route around Niagara Falls. Of the 13 inns that once stood in this area, South Landing is the only one still in existence. Innkeepers Kathy and Tony Szabo offer six guest rooms with private baths in the original inn. The South Landing Annex, built in 1987, offers 18 additional rooms, including four with balconies. Breakfast is available in the inn's café for a nominal charge. Summer rates (April 30–Oct. 31): inn $95–$125, annex $125. In winter all rooms are $75.

& **White Oaks Royal Niagara Spa Resort and Conference Center** (905-688-2550 or 800-263-5766; www.whiteoaksresort.com), 253 Taylor Road, Niagara-on-the-Lake. Niagara's only four-diamond, five-star resort has 220 elegant, oversized guest rooms. Amenities include a private fitness and racquet club, preferred rates at the Royal Niagara Golf Course, and a luxurious spa. Fine dining is available at the four-diamond Liv restaurant. $350+.

BED & BREAKFASTS With so many properties to choose from, it would be impossible to visit and rate each one. Here are some associations that can be of assistance:

The Niagara-on-the-Lake Bed & Breakfast Association (905-468-0123 or 866-855-0123; www.bba.notl .on.ca). Members maintain high standards and follow a strict code of ethics. Over 150 properties are listed on this site. Reservations can be made online.

About Historic Bed and Breakfasts in Old Town Centre (contact through Web site only: www.historic bb.com). Accommodations in private homes built before 1850. See the Web site for details All inns are open year-round, air-conditioned, have private baths, parking, and full breakfasts.

Hallmark Properties of Historic Niagara-on-the Lake (905-468-9668 or 866-469-9668; www.hallmark properties.net). A group of bed & breakfasts that provide distinguished accommodations and amenities.

✳ Where to Eat

DINING OUT Escabeche (905-468-3246), 6 Picton Street, (in the Prince of Wales Hotel), Niagara-on-the-Lake. Open for breakfast 7:30–11, lunch Saturday and Sunday 12–2, dinner Sunday–Thursday 6–9, Friday and Saturday 6–10. Five-diamond service is offered in this exquisite dining room, which features contemporary Canadian cuisine on the menu.

Hillebrand Vineyards Café (905-468-7123; www.hillebrand.com), 1249 Niagara Stone Road (Hwy. 55), Niagara-on-the-Lake. Open daily 11:30–2:30 and 5–9. Their café overlooks vineyards and the Niagara Escarpment. Specialties include dishes cooked with local produce and wines.

Liv (905-688-2032, ext. 5248 or 800-263-5766; www.whiteoaksresort.com), 253 Taylor Road, Niagara-on-the-Lake. Open daily for breakfast and lunch 7–2, dinner 5–10. This chic four-diamond restaurant is Niagara's only concept restaurant, mixing a variety of world flavors and cooking styles. Dinner selections include oven-roasted rack of lamb, grilled prime tenderloins, and grilled sea scallops. All desserts are baked on-site by their own pastry chef.

♿ **The Oban Inn** (1-888-669-5566), 160 Front Street, Niagara-on-the-Lake. Dining room hours: lunch 11:30–2, dinner 5:39–8:30; pub hours: 11:30–10. Both the dining room and the pub serve meals reminiscent of traditional English cuisine, including salmon and lamb dishes. The dining room features large windows overlooking English-style gardens.

♿ **Peller Estates Winery Restaurant** (1-888-673-5537), 290 John Street East, Niagara-on-the-Lake. Open daily for lunch 12–3, dinner 5–9. This upscale restaurant offers elegant regional wine-country cuisine, paired with Peller's award-winning wines. Dine indoors or out, weather permitting.

Ristorante Giardino (905-468-3263; www.gatehouse-niagara.com), 142 Queen Street, Niagara-on-the-Lake. Authentic metropolitan Italian cuisine and an extensive wine list.

Queenston
♿ **Queenston Heights Restaurant** (905-262-4274), Queenston Heights Park, Niagara Parkway, Queenston. Open April 1–June 30 and September 1–September 30 for lunch 12–3, dinner 5–9; July 1–August 31 daily for lunch and dinner 11:30–9:30; October 1–December 31 dinner only 5–9; closed January 1–March 31. This elegant restaurant offers a breathtaking view of the Niagara Gorge. Dine on unique Niagara cuisine selections either indoors or out on the patio.

EATING OUT ✐ ☙ **The Anchorage** (905-468-2141; www.theanchorage .ca), 186 Ricardo Street, Niagara-on-the-Lake. Open year-round Monday–Thursday 11:30–9, Friday–Saturday 11:30–11, Sunday 11:30–9:30. Ensconced in a building that once was a motor plant and later a basket warehouse, this casual restaurant is Niagara-on-the Lake's premier steak and seafood house. The menu features fresh produce and gourmet pizzas, as well. Dine inside or on the patio during summer. Overnight accommodations are available in the adjacent motel.

The Buttery (905-468-2564), 19 Queen Street, Niagara-on-the-Lake. Open Sunday–Thursday 11–8, Friday–Saturday 11–10. This casual eatery is known for its fun Henry VIII Feast, a medieval interactive dinner theater.

The Clubhouse Restaurant (905-468-3424), 43 Front Street, Niagara-on-the-Lake. Open Sunday–Thursday 7–8, Friday–Saturday 7–9. This restaurant overlooks the Niagara-on the-Lake golf course, the oldest golf course in North America, circa 1875. Reservations required.

The Grill at the Epicurean (905-468-0288; www.epicurean.ca), 84 Queen Street, Niagara-on-the-Lake. Open daily 5:30–9; also open for lunch in summer. A cafeteria-style gourmet deli by day and a trendy French bistro with full table service at night. All food is made on premises. Dine indoors in the Provence-inspired dining room or outdoors on the garden patio. The lunch menu includes gourmet sandwiches, salads, quiche, and meat pies, while the dinner menu features grilled salmon, braised lamb shank, and roast chicken. Good food at a reasonable price with fast pre-theater service.

The Olde Angel Inn (905-468-3411; www.angel-inn.com), 224 Regent Street, Niagara-on-the-Lake. Open 11:30 AM–1 AM daily. The oldest inn in town, circa 1816, features a lively English pub along with a fine-dining restaurant. The restaurant includes a prix-fixe menu as well as entrées like prime rib, rack of lamb, and strip steak, while the pub features traditional English and Irish pub fare and more than 16 draft beers.

✷ Entertainment

THEATERS Shaw Festival (905-468-2172 or 800-511-7429; www.shawfest .sympatico.ca), 10 Queen's Parade, Box 774, Niagara-on-the-Lake. Niagara-on-the-Lake is probably best known for the Shaw Festival, the only theater company specializing exclusively in plays either by George Bernard Shaw or those written about his era. For over 40 years the Shaw Festival has been North America's foremost theater organization. The season runs April–early November, usually with 12 plays per season performed in three different theaters, which are:

Court House Theatre, 26 Queen Street, Niagara-on-the-Lake. This 1840 National Historic site is where the Shaw Festival began in 1962. It has a 327-seat auditorium with a thrust stage.

Festival Theatre, 10 Queen's Parade, Niagara-on-the-Lake. This 869-seat venue, the flagship theatre of the festival, recently underwent a $50 million expansion and renovation.

Royal George Theatre, 83 Queen Street, Niagara-on-the-Lake. This

328-seat theater was built in 1913 as the Kitchener and used to entertain troops stationed in the area during World War I, then later used as a silent film house. In the 1980s it was purchased by the Shaw Festival and renovated to resemble an Edwardian opera house.

✳ Selective Shopping

A high concentration of shops and boutiques can be found along Queen Street, between Wellington and Gates.

ANTIQUES **Forum Galleries Antiques & Collectibles** (905-468-2777; www.forumgalleries.com), 2017 Niagara Stone Road (Hwy 55), Niagara-on-the-Lake. Open 10–6 daily. Browse through 8,000 square feet of fine antiques, Canadian furniture, toys, artwork, jewelry, silver, glass, and more. This is the largest antique center in the Niagara region.

Lakeshore Antique Treasures (905-646-1965), 855 Lakeshore Road, Niagara-on-the-Lake. Open year-round 10–5 daily. A 6,000-square-foot multidealer shop, carrying everything from pre-Victorian to retro to country, located just west of historic Niagara-on-the-Lake.

Nana's Antiques & Treasures (905-468-1515), 188 Victoria Street, Niagara-on-the-Lake. Open daily 11–6. A collection of charming antiques from Victorian to retro, plus home decor items and giftware.

ART GALLERIES **Angie Strauss** (905-468-2570; www.angiestrauss.com), 125 Queen Street, Niagara-on-the-Lake. Open 10–6 daily. Displayed in this gallery are Angie's paintings that portray country cottages, gardens, and popular Niagara scenes. The shop also features Canadian-made women's clothing, handmade scarves, and jewelry.

Doug Forsythe Gallery (905-468-3659; www.dougforsythegallery.com), 92 Picton Street, Niagara-on-the-Lake. Open 10–5:30 daily. This, the oldest art gallery in Niagara-on-the-Lake, features the works of Canadian artists/printmakers Doug and Marsha Forsythe. Choose from art cards, posters, original paintings, and prints, wooden-boat serving trays, and their world-famous Dory planters.

The Preservation Fine Art Gallery (905-468-4431 or 800-667-8525; www.preservationgallery.com), 177 King Street, Niagara-on-the-Lake. Open Tuesday–Saturday 10–6, Sunday 1–6; until 5 November–April. This gallery, housed in a Victorian building, features a fine collection of art, including works by Trisha Romance, Philip Craig, and Alex Colville.

FARM MARKETS ✿ ⅙ **Kurtz Orchards Country Market and Orchard Tours** (905-448-2937; www.kurtzorchards.com), 16006 Niagara Parkway, Niagara-on-the-Lake. Open seasonally. This large farm market has a bounty of in-season produce along with jams and preserves, maple syrup, honey, fresh baked goods, Canadian crafts, and more. Visitors can tour the orchard in a tractor-drawn tram ride. Country-style lunches are available, including salads, soups, and ice cream.

SPECIAL SHOPS **Bernard's: The Shaw Festival Shop** (800-511-7429, ext. 286). Two locations: next to the Festival Theatre and 79 Queen Street. Open daily 10–5:30, until 8 on performance evenings. This shop has a mix of books, music, toys, pottery, home accessories, and handcrafted items. They also stock scripts for the current season's plays, posters, books about theater and art, and Shaw Festival clothing.

La Crème Decor (905-468-0652 or 866-868-0652; www.lacremedecor .com), 233 King Street, Niagara-on-the-Lake. Monday–Saturday 10–6, Sunday 11–5:30. This store specializes in fashion and home decor in shades of ivory, white, and gold. Owner Nancy Boudreau has created an elegant shopping atmosphere, where one can shop for special-occasion apparel, accessories, gifts, and more. A second location can be found in Street Jacobs, Ontario (877-664-3275).

J. W. North (905-468-1815), 11 Queen Street, Niagara-on-the-Lake. Open daily 9:30–7. Specializing in Canadian-made clothing, gifts, and souvenirs, including Native Canadian art, such as Inuit soapstone carvings and local Canadian crafts.

✐ **Maple Leaf Fudge** (905-468-2211; www.mapleleaffudge.com), 114 Queen Street, Niagara-on-the-Lake. Open Monday and Tuesday 9:30–6, Wednesday–Friday 9:30–7, Saturday 9:30–8, Sunday 9:30–7. Watch fudge being made daily on marble tables. Since 1967, they have been offering 25 varieties of quality fudge, old-fashioned candies, brittles, maple products, and other candies and gift items.

The Nutty Chocolatier (905-468-0788; www.nuttychocolatier.com), 233 King Street, Niagara-on-the-Lake. Open Sunday–Thursday 9–8, Friday–Saturday 9–9. An old-fashioned candy store that features fine Belgian chocolates, truffles, and handcrafted chocolate specialties. They also have homemade fudge and frozen yogurt.

✐ **The Owl and the Pussycat** (905-468-3081), 16 Queen Street, Niagara-on-the-Lake. Open 10–6 daily. This store has a selection of toys and gift items for children and adults.

✳ Special Events

January: **Niagara Icewine Festival** (905-688-0212; www.niagaraicewine festival.com), This event takes place at wineries throughout Niagara-on-the-Lake and the Greater Niagara region. This 10-day festival celebrates Ontario icewine, which has earned gold medals in competitions around the world. Icewine is produced during December, January, and February at temperatures of at least -8 degrees Celsius. The grapes are pressed while frozen, which produces the sweet concentrated juice used to make icewine. The festival features gourmet dinners, tours, tastings, and other special events.

July: **War of 1812 Reenactment** (905-468-4257), Fort George, Picton Street, Niagara-on-the-Lake. Battle re-enactments, camp life demonstrations, artisans, and children's activities.

September: **Niagara Grape & Wine Festival** (905-688-0212; www.grape andwine.com), From Niagara-on-the Lake to St. Catharine's. For over 50 years this internationally acclaimed wine festival has taken place the last 10 days of September. Events include dinners, live entertainment, wine tastings and seminars, and artisan shows.

Bed & Breakfast House Tour (Contact Niagara-on-the-Lake Chamber of Commerce 905-468-1950 for details.) A self-guided tour of some of Niagara-on-the-Lake's unique bed & breakfast homes, sponsored by the Chamber of Commerce.

October: **Doors Open Niagara** (905-704-3942; www.doorsopenniagara.com). Various locations throughout western New York and southern Ontario. See Web site for specifics. A binational event featuring tours of historic and cultural sites on both sides of the border. **Ghost Tours** (905-468-6621; www.friendsoffortgeorge.ca), Fort George, Niagara-on-the-Lake. Explore Fort George by candlelight as your learn about its history and hear accounts of real-life encounters at the fort with the spirits and phantoms that lurk there. This is a very popular tour; tickets must be purchased in advance because they do sell out.

December: **Candlelight Stroll** (Contact Niagara-on-the-Lake Chamber of Commerce 905-468-1950 for details). A guided stroll through the historic town of Niagara-on-the-Lake.

GENESEE COUNTY

Genesee County, established in 1802, is located in the center of western New York, midway between Buffalo and Rochester. Batavia is the county seat, and it was from the Holland Land Office in Batavia that early settlers bought three million acres of western New York land in the early 1800s. The name Genesee comes from the Seneca word *Gen-nis-he-yo,* which translates to "beautiful valley" or "pleasant banks."

Today the county is agricultural in nature, a couple of the main crops being onions and potatoes. There are many unique places to visit in Genesee County, no matter what your interests. History buffs won't want to miss the Jell-O Museum in LeRoy, while nature lovers will enjoy the pristine beauty of the Bergen Swamp, a National Natural History Landmark, in the northern part of the county. Of course, families and thrill seekers alike will enjoy Six Flags Darien Lake amusement park, Genesee County's best known attraction.

ALONG ROUTE 5—Batavia, Stafford, LeRoy, and Pembroke

Batavia is considered the birthplace of western New York. The town was named by Joseph Ellicott in honor of the Dutch investors in Batavia's Holland Land Company since, at the time, Holland was known as the Republic of Batavia. Aside from being the county seat and the center of county services, Batavia is the center of the county's arts and culture. Batavia has a very low crime rate, which rates it as one of the best places to live in western New York.

Stafford, located between Batavia and LeRoy, was the site of the first settlement on the Holland Land Purchase in 1798 and was formed as a town in 1820. In its early days it was known as a business and trade center.

LeRoy, a historic village with many Victorian homes, was first settled in the late 1790s. The first women's university in the United States, Ingham University, was founded in LeRoy in 1837 and remained there until 1892. The town was the birthplace of the stringless green bean, cultivated by Calvin Keeney, which proved to be a big development in the vegetable canning industry. However, LeRoy's most notable claim to fame was the 1897 invention of a new gelatin dessert, dubbed Jell-O. America's most famous dessert was manufactured in the

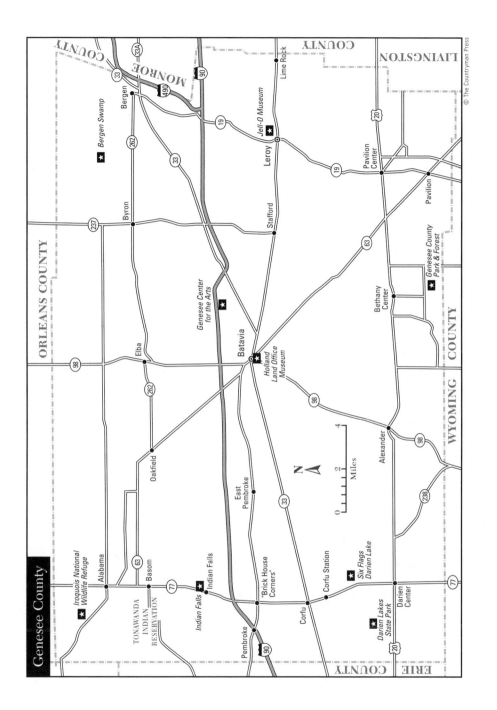

© The Countryman Press

town until 1964. Today the town is home to the Jell-O Museum as well as numerous restaurants and antiques shops.

The town of Pembroke, which includes the villages of Corfu, East Pembroke, and Indian Falls, was named after Pembroke in Wales. Called *O-a-geh* ("on the road") by Native Americans, the town, first called Richville, was incorporated in

1812. Pembroke can be divided into several sections. Brick House Corners, now the intersection of NY 5 and NY 77, was the crossroads of two Indian trails and for many years the site of a tavern and stagecoach stop (located in a brick house). Corfu—originally Longs Corners—was incorporated in 1868 and named after the island of Corfu in Greece. At the intersection of NY 33 and NY 77, Corfu is the business center of the town. In the late 1800s and early 1900s the town's leading industry was raising flowers, to be shipped by railroad all over the United States. The area known as Indian Falls, located near a 30-foot waterfall on Tonawanda Creek, was the site of an Indian village until 1857. By the turn of the 20th century, it was a thriving village, with the waterfall providing businesses with power. In the 1940s and '50s the Boulder Amusement Park, which was located here, was a popular destination. Today this area is primarily residential and farmland.

The area's most famous citizen was Ely Samuel Parker (1828–1895) a Native American, also known as Do-Ne-Ho-Ga-Wa, who was born near Indian Falls on the **Tonawanda Indian Reservation**. He joined the army and eventually became General Ulysses S. Grant's military secretary. Parker was instrumental in drafting the final terms of the Confederate surrender at Appomattox Court House at the end of the Civil War. He was commissioned as Brigadier General in the army and was appointed the first Commissioner of Indian Affairs by President Grant in 1869. The **Holland Land Office** features an exhibit on Parker's life.

AREA CODE The area code is 585.

GUIDANCE Genesee County Chamber of Commerce (1-800-622-2686; www.geneseeny.com), 210 East Main Street, Batavia. Open year-round Monday–Friday 8:30–5. A tourism information booth is open Memorial Day–Labor Day daily 9–7 next to the Holland Land Office Museum, 131 West Main Street, Batavia.

Village of Corfu (585-599-3327), 116 East Main Street, Corfu. Open Tuesday–Friday 9–5, Saturday 9–12.

Village of LeRoy (585-768-2527), 3 West Main Street, LeRoy. Open Monday–Friday 8–4:30.

Genesee County History Dept. (585-344-2550, ext. 2613 or www.co.genesee.ny.us), 3 West Main Street (NY 5), Batavia. Open Monday, Tuesday, Wednesday 9–4:30.

GETTING THERE *By air:* See *Getting There: Buffalo*. Private and small charter planes can land at **Genesee County Airport** and **LeRoy Airport** 8267 East Main, LeRoy.

By car: NYS Thruway (I-90) exits 47 (LeRoy) and 48 (Batavia). NY 5, Main Street, passes through the center of the county.

GETTING AROUND *By bus:* **B-Line** (585-343-3079; www.rgrta.com), 153 Cedar Street, Batavia. Batavia Bus Service, a subsidiary of the Rochester Genesee

Regional Transportation Authority, offers public transportation throughout Genesee County. Three bus loops are operated within the city of Batavia Monday–Friday There are also four trips daily between Batavia and LeRoy.

MEDICAL EMERGENCY Dial 911

United Memorial Medical Center (585-343-6030; www.ummctr.org), 127 North Street and 16 Bank Street, Batavia.

Batavia VA Medical Center (585-343-7500), Redfield Parkway, Batavia.

✳ To See

ARCHITECTURE A booklet "Batavia Walking Tour" by Susan Conklin, describes a self-guided walking tour of the architecturally significant buildings in downtown Batavia. It is available for a nominal fee from the **Holland Land Office Museum.**

ART MUSEUMS GO ART! Cultural Facility (585-343-9313 or 800-774-7372; www.goart.org), Genesee Orleans Council on the Arts, 201 East Main Street (at Bank Street), Batavia. Open 9–4 Monday–Friday and by appointment. Located in a circa 1831 Federal-style brick mansion on the National Register of Historic Places, this facility houses the Genesee–Orleans Regional Art Council, the offices of the Genesee Symphony Orchestra, and several other cultural programs. Satellite galleries are located in the **Genesee County Senior Center,** 2 Bank Street, Batavia; the **Orleans Chamber of Commerce,** 433 Main Street, Medina; and at **Kafana Gourmet Coffee,** 10 East Bank Street, Albion.

MUSEUMS AND HISTORIC HOMES ✪ ♿ Holland Land Office (585-343-4727; www.hollandlandoffice.com), 131 West Main Street, Batavia. Open Tuesday–Saturday 10–4; also open Mondays Memorial Day–Labor Day. Free Admission. This 1815 Federal-style stone building with 20-inch-thick walls served as the fireproof office for the business transactions of the Holland Land Company, an association of six Dutch banking firms. This was the third structure to be used by the company, which purchased 3.5-million acres of land in western New York. In 1800 they surveyed the land and began selling it for $2 an acre, but in 1830 the Holland Land Company closed its books, and the office fell into disuse. In 1894 the structure was saved from demolition and restored to be maintained as a museum; it was designated a National Historic Landmark in 1961 because of the Holland Land Company's role in the development of western New York. Currently the museum has

THE 1815 HOLLAND LAND OFFICE MUSEUM HAS 20-INCH-THICK WALLS.

Christine A. Smyczynski

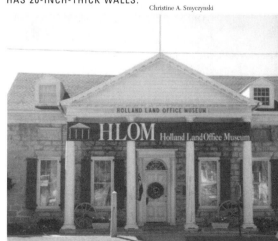

exhibits focusing mainly on Genesee County's history, people, and culture. It has several permanent exhibits of Seneca Indian history, Civil War memorabilia, and pioneer items as well as early 20th-century business items. Rotating exhibits are changed three to four times a year. Tours, classes, and lectures are offered for students and history buffs.

✐ **The Jell-O Museum/LeRoy Historical Museum** (585-768-7433; www .jellomuseum.com), 23 East Main Street, LeRoy. Open May–October Monday–Saturday 10–4, Sunday 1–4. Open November–March Monday–Friday 10–4. Admission: $3. The adjacent LeRoy House is open daily during the summer; call for hours. The quaint little village of LeRoy is the birthplace of Jell-O, "America's favorite dessert." LeRoy native Peter Cooper, looking to invent a soothing cough remedy, created Jell-O, but it was entrepreneur O. T. Woodward (who bought Cooper's patent in 1899 for $450) who successfully marketed it. The Jell-O Museum has exhibits explaining the history of the jiggly concoction as well as Jell-O memorabilia, several hands-on exhibits for children, and a video about Jell-O. There are also examples of some failed Jell-O flavors, including coffee. The adjacent LeRoy House, operated by the LeRoy Historical Society, has displays on the history of the village.

Pembroke Historical Museum (585-762-8246), 1145 Main Road, Corfu. Open by appointment Monday–Friday. Located on the second floor of the Pembroke Town Hall, this small museum has maps, clothing, tools, and information on local history.

HISTORIC SITES Genesee County Courthouse Historic District. Five architecturally significant buildings are in this district, including the **Genesee County Courthouse** (Main and Ellicott Streets), **Batavia City Hall** (10 West Main Street), **United States Post Office** (2 West Main Street), **Genesee County Jail** (14 West Main Street), and **Genesee County Building No.1** (Main and Court Street). The district was created in 1983 to preserve this section of Main Street, which reflects mid-19th- and early 20th-century architectural styles.

✳ To Do

AUTO RACING Batavia International Motorsports Park (585-345-9680), 3490 Harloff Road, Batavia. Open April–October.

Genesee Speedway (585-345-9090), County Fair Grounds, NY 5, Batavia. Featuring modified sportsman, late-model super stocks, DIRT pro stock, street stock, and mini stockcar racing.

CROSS-COUNTRY SKIING See *Greenspace—The Northern Mucklands*; **Iroquois National Wildlife Refuge**; *Greenspace—Alexander, Bethany*; **Genesee County Park.**

FAMILY FUN ✐ **The Gravel Pit Family Entertainment Center** (716-343-4445; www.5a.com/gravelpit) 5158 East Main Road (NY 5), Batavia. Enjoy activities fun for the entire family, including a picnic area, playground, video arcade, and hayrides. In addition, they have go-karts, a lit driving range with 16 stalls, batting cages, two regulation volleyball pits, an 18-hole miniature golf course, and a paintball course.

⚓ **Holiday Hollow Village** (585-762-8160; www.holidayhollow.com), NY 5 (just east of NY 77), Pembroke. Open 11–5 Saturday and Sunday during October. Also open Columbus Day. Looking for nonscary Halloween fun for young children? Take a scenic drive down Main Street to Holiday Hollow. This family-run business, which has been entertaining youngsters since 1993, is the only complete village in western New York built exclusively for Halloween family entertainment. This hidden Old English-style village on 7.3 acres of wooded hills offers a day of shows and attractions. Family entertainment includes a live outdoor comedy stage show with Captain Hook & Mr. Smee, a hilarious haunted forest walk, a talking pumpkin show with wooden puppets, and a haunted hotel with special effects. There are also games of skill, a gift shop, refreshments, and more. Kids as well as their parents will enjoy this delightful place that emphasizes special effects rather than blood and gore for Halloween.

FISHING **Oatka Creek**, which runs through the center of the village of LeRoy, is very popular for trout fishing. Fishing licenses can be obtained at any Genesee County K-Mart; Barretts Hunting Supplies, Main Street, Batavia; and at Fin, Feather and Fur, NY 63, Oakfield (next to WalMart).

GOLF **Batavia Country Club Public Golf Course** (585-343-7600; www .bataviacc.com), 7909 Batavia-Byron Road, Batavia. An 18-hole, par-72 semiprivate championship course with pro shop and restaurant.

LeRoy Country Club (585-768-7330; www.leroycc.com), 7759 East Main Street, LeRoy. An 18-hole, par-71 semiprivate course.

Meadowbrook Golf Course (585-343-0837), 6 Woodland Drive, Batavia. A 9-hole, par-33 course.

Sweetland Pines (585-343-7059; www.iinc.com/sweetlandpines), 5795 Sweetland Road, Stafford. This public 9-hole, par-33, quiet country course is easy to walk.

Terry Hills Golf Course (585-343-8060; www.terryhills.com), 5122 Clinton Street (NY 33), Batavia. Voted the best golf course in Genesee and Wyoming Counties and rated one of the top five courses in western New York by *Golf Digest* readers. Offers 27 holes, par 36 each 9. Facility also includes miniature golf and batting cages.

HORSE RACING AND VIDEO GAMING
Batavia Downs Racetrack (585-343-3750; www.batavia-downs.com), 8315 Park Road, Batavia. Open

PICTURESQUE OATKA CREEK IN LEROY IS POPULAR FOR TROUT FISHING.

Christine A. Smyczynski

July–January. Live harness racing is featured at this most modern racetrack in New York and America's oldest lit track. Modern amenities include over 250 video walls and TVs located throughout the facility, so you can keep track of the racing action. Bets can be placed at betting windows, self-betting terminals, or via hand-held computers. Over 750 video gaming machines were installed at the raceway in 2004. Dining is available in the clubhouse restaurant, with banquet facilities for up to 300.

SNOWTUBING ✍ **Polarwave Snowtubing** (888-727-2794; www.polarwavesnow tubing.com), 3500 Harloff Road, Batavia. Polarwave Snowtubing is one of the coolest winter destinations in western New York. If you're unfamiliar with this winter pastime, it involves riding down snow-topped hills on specially designed air-filled tubes. The tubing hill at Polarwave offers six different runs with various terrains for slow, medium, and fast riders. After zipping down the hill, you don't have to trudge back up—just catch a ride back to the top on one of the three tube tows. The park features lights for night tubing and state-of-the-art snow-making equipment to keep the hill covered even when Mother Nature doesn't cooperate. Since snowtubing operations are subject to cancellation due to inclement weather, call ahead for current conditions.

UNDERGROUND RAILROAD A driving tour guide of Underground Railroad sites in the LeRoy area is available from the LeRoy Historical Museum (585-768-7433), 23 East Main Street, LeRoy. Call for hours.

✳ Green Space

PARKS **Austin Park,** Jefferson Avenue Batavia. A downtown city park that was once part of a large estate.

Centennial Park, Richmond Avenue and Ellicott Avenue, Batavia The oldest park in the City of Batavia. It is the site of the annual July 4th picnic, concerts and sledding during the winter.

✳ Lodging

MOTELS AND HOTELS There are numerous chain motels at the Batavia exit (#48) off the NYS Thruway (I-90). Some of these include:

Comfort Inn (585-344-9999), 4371 Federal Drive, Batavia. This hotel has 60 standard rooms, an outdoor pool, and a free continental breakfast. $69–$189.

Ramada Limited (585-343-1000), 8204 Park Road, Batavia. This hotel has 74 rooms, and outdoor heated pool, and a free continental breakfast. $69–$119.

Microtel Inn & suites (585-344-8882), 8210 Park Road, Batavia. The hotel has 53 rooms, an indoor pool, exercise room, and free continental breakfast. $75–$125.

BED & BREAKFASTS **Edson House Bed and Breakfast** (585-768-8579; www.bbwny.com/edsonhouse), 7856 Griswold Circle, LeRoy. Open year-round. Innkeeper Dave Graham offers four unique air-conditioned rooms with either king- or full-sized beds. In summer enjoy lounging on the open front porch. This inn is conveniently located near I-90 and I-490 and a short drive from Genesee Country Village. A continental breakfast is included with lodging. $79–$109.

OTHER LODGING Lei-Ti Campground (585-343-8600 or 800-HI-LEI-TI; www.leiti.com), 9979 Francis Road, Batavia. Open April–November. This family fun and leisure resort features campsites and primitive cabins, with a 5-acre lake for swimming, boating, and fishing plus mini-golf, tennis, picnic pavilion, and planned activities. $27/night including electric and water, $29/night including electric, water, and sewer.

Lei-Ti II Campground (585-343-8600 or 800-HI LEI-TI; www.leiti .com), Conlon Road, LeRoy. Formerly known as Frost Ridge, this campground near Oatka Creek is open year-round. It has 150 campsites, a lodge, planned activities, and a camp store. $21.50–$23.50.

✳ Where to Eat

DINING OUT Alex's Place (585-344-2999), 9332 Park Road, Batavia. Open Monday–Thursday 11–11, Friday and Saturday 11–12, Sunday 12–9. Located near Batavia Downs, Alex's offers a variety of delicious selections, including Italian specialties, BBQ ribs, steak, and seafood. Watch dinner being cooked on a charcoal pit in their open kitchen.

Bel Gustos Restaurant (585-344-2100), 8250 Park Road, Batavia. Open for breakfast and lunch Monday–Saturday 6:30 AM–2 PM, Sunday 8 AM–1:30 PM, dinner daily 5–9. Located in the Holiday Inn, Bel Gustos serves up great Italian-American cuisine and daily specials, including steak and seafood, and low-carb brekfast choices, in an upscale atmosphere.

Bohn's Restaurant (585-344-1543;www.bohnsrestaurant.com) 5256 Clinton St. (NY 33) Batavia. Open Monday-Thursday 11-9, Friday 11-10, Saturday 4-10, Sunday 12-9. This restaurant offers casual, fine dining in a warm and comfortable atmosphere. Menu selections include traditional dishes like beef wellington, shrimp scampi, surf 'n turf, steaks and prime rib. End your meal with homemade desserts including creme brulee and chocolate orange Grand Manier cake.

Center Street Smokehouse (585-343-7470; www.restaurant.com/centerstreet), 20 Center Street, Batavia. Open Monday–Thursday 4–10, Friday and Saturday 4–12, Sunday 4–9; lunch buffet Wednesdays 11–3. The best BBQ place in Batavia, serving up authentic southern barbecue along with live entertainment. Located in the historic Times Publishing Building, the restaurant features a 1940s theme. Choose from entrées like smoked ribs and pork, with smokehouse sides like dirty rice and hush puppies. Live blues and jazz is featured Wednesday–Saturday evenings.

L. B. Grand Steak & Spaghetti House (585-768-6707), 37–39 Main Street, LeRoy. Open Monday–Thursday 11–9, Friday and Saturday 11–10. Brick walls and stained glass are prominent in the decor of this elegant yet casual restaurant located in an 1800s-era building. Specialties include strip steak, filet mignon, and porterhouse, or go for pasta, soups, salads, and sandwiches. They are well-known locally for their Saturday evening prime rib special.

The Red Osier Landmark (585-343-6972 or 888-343-6972; www.red osier.com), 6492 Main Road (NY 5), Stafford. Open Tuesday–Thursday

4–8:30, Friday and Saturday 4–10, Sunday 1–8:30. This is the ultimate beef-lovers' restaurant, well-known throughout western New York for its prime ribs of beef carved tableside. They also serve a variety of other foods, including steaks, seafood, and poultry.

EATING OUT ✏ 🍴 **D & R Depot Restaurant** (585-768-6270; www .dandrdepot.com), 63 Lake Street (NY 19), LeRoy. Open Monday–Saturday 7–9, Sunday 11:30–9. Step back in time when you dine on home-cooked meals served in a former B & O train depot. Their specialty is the "conductor's special," a chicken pot pie with large chunks of chicken, peas, and carrots topped with a flaky crust. Other menu selections include petite filet mignon, homemade soups, seafood entrées, and even ostrich filet.

✏ ♿ 🍴 **Miss Batavia Family Restaurant** (585-343-9786), 566 East Main Street, Batavia. Open daily 6–9. Established in 1933, this family restaurant offers affordable home-cooked food for breakfast, lunch, and dinner.

✏ 🍴 **Pontillo's** (585-768-6660), 49 Main Street, LeRoy. Open Sunday–Thursday 11–11, Friday and Saturday 11–midnight. Since 1947 Pontillo's has been serving up pizza, pasta, and other Italian specialties. This inviting restaurant features a daily lunch buffet plus dinner and take-out.

✏ 🍴 **Settlers Family Restaurant** (585-343-7443), 353 West Main Street (NY 5), Batavia. Open daily 5 am–10 PM. A comfortable family restaurant; their specialty is Greek chicken salad.

✏ 🍴 ♿ **Tyler's Family Restaurant** (585-768-7160), 15 Main Street, LeRoy. Open Monday–Saturday 6–8, Friday 6–9, Sunday 6–3. A large,

bright restaurant with cozy booths and a lunch counter. Breakfast selections include Belgian waffles, frittatas, and omelets, while lunch includes a large variety of hot and cold sandwiches, burgers, and salads. At dinner choose from traditional home-style meals like ham steak, chicken cutlet, and liver and onions.

✳ Entertainment

THEATERS **Genesee Center for the Arts** (585-345-6814; www.genesee .edu/finearts), 1 College Road, Batavia. Season September–April; hours and days vary. Located on the campus of Genesee Community College, the Genesee Center for the Arts is home to many community cultural and entertainment events. The center's focal point is the 328-seat Stuart Steiner Theater, offering theatrical productions, concerts, lectures, and more.

MUSIC **Genesee Symphony Orchestra** (585-343-9313; www .geneseesymphony.com), Mailing address: 201 East Main Street, Batavia. Concerts held at Genesee Community College's Stuart Steiner Theater. The symphony, which is affiliated with Genesee Community College, performs two concerts per semester and one summer pops event. Call or see Web site for concert schedule.

Jackson Square Concert Series, Jackson Square (between Center and Jefferson Streets, next to Center Street Smokehouse), Batavia. Concerts take place every Friday night in summer in Jackson Square Alley, which is painted with numerous interesting murals.

PROFESSIONAL SPORTS **Batavia Muckdogs Minor League Baseball** (585-343-5454; www.muckdogs.com), Dwyer Stadium, 299 Bank Street, Batavia. Season May and June. The Muckdogs, who compete in the New York Penn League, are the farm team of the Philadelphia Phillies. Dwyer Stadium was opened in 1996, with a seating capacity of 2,600.

✳ Selective Shopping

ANTIQUES **Lone Gable Emporium** (585-768-4569), 7991 East Main Road, LeRoy. Open 10–5 Tuesday–Sunday. Bill and Lois Lambert have been operating this 5,000-square-foot shop, the largest one-dealer shop in the area, since 1979. The store features antique furniture and collectibles, along with custom refinishing, reproduction brass hardware, and furniture stripping and refinishing supplies.

Magnolia Antiques and Collectibles (585-768-6310), 7895 East Main Street, LeRoy. Open Friday and Saturday 11–5, Sunday 12–5. A collection of yesterdays wares located in a 1890s carriage house.

Peters Treasures (585-343-4808), 310 West Main Street, Batavia. Open Tuesday–Saturday 10–5. Collectibles, antiques, and used tools.

Red House Antiques, formerly Paris Flea Market (585-344-3111), 314 East Main Street, Batavia. Open Monday–Saturday 10–5. Come inside this beautiful Victorian home to find a full line of quality antiques from smalls to large pieces and furniture.

Stafford Old Town Hall Antiques and Collectibles (585-345-1080 www.oldtownhallantiques.com), 6178 NY 5 at NY 237, Stafford. Open Wednesday–Sunday 10–5. A general line of antiques is housed in this vintage former town hall building.

ART GALLERIES **John Hodgins Art Gallery and Studio** (585-343-3613), 3817 West Main Road, Batavia. Open Monday–Friday 10–5. John Hodgins was in the printing and sign business for over 45 years. Since his retirement he devotes his time to painting.

FARM MARKETS **Genesee Country Farmer's Market** (585-343-9491), corner of Lewiston & Park Roads, Batavia. Open Tuesday and Friday 8–5 mid-June–November. Farm-fresh produce grown on Genesee County farms, plus plants, maple syrup, honey, and baked goods.

SHOPPING MALLS The only major shopping mall in the county is the **Genesee County Mall** (585-344-2518), Main Street, Batavia. The anchor store, JC Penney, is open 10–9. Several smaller stores, including a shoe store, florist, and candy store, are open 10–6.

SPECIAL SHOPS ✐ **Adam Miller Wheel Goods, Inc.** (585-343-0548), 8 Center Street, Batavia. Open Monday–Thursday 8–5:30, Friday 8–7, Saturday 8–4. This neat old building, tucked away on a side street in downtown Batavia, started out as a bicycle shop in 1918. It still has many of the original fixtures, including wooden shelves and oak molding. Owned and operated by John Roche, the shop specializes in old-fashioned, hands-on educational toys, including dolls, wagons, building toys, and bicycles.

The Barn Country Marketplace (585-599-4480 or 585-599-4611),

9093 Allegheny Road, Corfu. Open Friday and Saturday 10–6, Sunday 12–6. Country crafts and painted items, jewelry, baskets, antiques, Amish gifts, furniture, fudge, cookies, and Christmas items.

Daffodils Floral Boutique (585-768-2205), 24 Main Street, LeRoy. Open Monday–Friday 6:30–5, Saturday 6:30–1. Owner Christina DeBiase has a selection of fresh flowers plus gifts for all occasions. Stop by the rear of the store to enjoy a cup of coffee and a snack in the Daisy Café.

Dolly's Candle Shop (585-344-0880), 1 School Street, Batavia. Open Tuesday–Wednesday 10–5, Thursday–Friday 10–6, Saturday 10–4. A large selection of candles, baskets, and gift items can be found in this shop.

1874 House (585-599-3774), 9202 Allegheny Road, Corfu. Open Tuesday–Saturday 10–5. This store specializes in New England primitive items, including wooden furniture, birdhouses, and scenery boards.

Forget-me-not Mercantile (585-343-3455), 419 East Main Street, Batavia. Open Wednesday–Friday 11–5, Saturday 11–3:30; call for winter hours. Three large rooms in a Victorian-style home are filled with dolls, plush animals, table linens and curtains, jewelry, collectibles, and home decor.

The Hobby Horse (585-768-8130), 54–56 Main Street, LeRoy. Open Monday–Wednesday 12-5, Thursday and Friday 10:30–6, Saturday 9:30–3. There's something for everyone at this store, including handmade crafts, candles, country-decor items, garden items, craft, and hobby supplies.

Just Browsing (585-599-3985), 1270 Main Road, Corfu. Open Tuesday–Saturday 10–5, Sunday 12–4. Closed January– March. The first thing you notice when you get out of your car is the wonderful aroma of Just Browsing's homemade potpourri and candles. Inside the rustic wooden store you'll also find seasonal decorations, country decor items, and garden accessories. Between Thanksgiving and Christmas, the entire second floor is filled with Christmas decorating needs.

Kutter's Cheese Factory (585-599-3693; www.kuttercheese.com), 857 Main Road, Corfu. Open Monday–Saturday 9–8, Sunday 12–8. This cheese factory and retail outlet, offering homemade and imported cheeses, was opened in 1947 by Leo Kutter, who emigrated to the United States from Germany. Along with numerous varieties of cheese, Kutter's is also an outlet for Hunt Country wines from the Keuka Lake region of Western New York.

✐ ♿ **Oliver's Candies** (585-343-5888 or 800-924-3879; www.olivers candies.com), 211 West Main Street, Batavia. Open daily 9–9. This well-known area candy shop was established in 1932 by Joseph Boyd Oliver. He started out by selling homemade blanched peanuts door-to-door and went on to create his signature Cashew Glaze and Hostess Squares. Oliver's carries over 350 varieties of candy and has the largest selection of locally made chocolates in western New York. The candies are made in small batches using tried-and-true recipes. Mail order is available. The store also has a small ice cream parlor.

Phelps Furniture (585-344-5742), 35 Jackson Street, Batavia. Open Monday–Friday 10–8, Saturday 10–6. Quality Amish-made and hand-crafted oak furniture.

RLR Railroad (585-344-8874; www .rlrrailroad.com), 15 Jackson Street, Batavia. Open Tuesday–Saturday 10–5, Sunday 11–4. This hobby shop specializes in model railroading supplies and accessories. They carry HO, N, O/O-27, S, and G scale, plus Thomas the Tank Engine, Playmobile, and die-cast, antique-reproduction toys and trucks.

South Main Country Gifts (585-345-1616), 3356 South Main Street Road (near Wortendyke Road) Batavia Open December–September, Thursday–Sunday 11–6; October–December, Monday–Friday 11–7, Saturday and Sunday 11–6. This 2,500-square-foot rural country store carries a variety of items, including Amish oak and pine furniture, pottery, candles, dolls, plush animals, gourmet foods, and candles. Check out their sale room in the basement.

✳ Special Events

July: **Oatka Festival** (www.oatka festival.com). Held on the banks of Oatka Creek by NY 5 and Wolcott Street, LeRoy. This festival features arts, crafts, music, and games. **Genesee County Fair** (585-344-2424; www.gcfair.com), Genesee County Fairgrounds, 5031 East Main Street, Batavia. **July 4th Picnic in the Park** (sponsored by GOART 585-343-9313), Centennial Park, Batavia.

August: **Wing Ding Weekend** (sponsored by Batavia Improvement District, 585-344-0900), Batavia. A summer block party and street dance.

September: **Brick House Corners Fair** (village of Pembroke 585-762-8246), Pembroke Town Hall, NY 5 and 77. An old-fashioned fair, featuring craft vendors, demonstrations of old-time pursuits, and kids' activities.

October: **Halloween Festival** (585-762-8160; www.holidayhollow.com), Holiday Hollow, Pembroke. See *To Do: Family Fun.*

November: **The Great Batavia Train Show** (585-343-3750), Batavia Downs Racetrack. The largest train show in western New York.

THE NORTHERN MUCKLANDS—Alabama, Oakfield, Elba, Byron, Bergen, and Basom

Northern Genesee County is home to farms and nature preserves. The Elba area, a mainly agricultural region, was first settled in 1801 and is noted for its onion production—it was once proclaimed the Onion Capital of the World. The rich, black, "muck" soil, revealed when developers drained parts of Tonawanda and Oak Orchard Swamps in 1915, proved to be perfect for growing onions and potatoes.

The town of Bergen in the northeast corner of the county, not too far from Rochester, is known for the National Natural Landmark Bergen Swamp—a botanist's paradise. And the Iroquois National Wildlife Refuge, known locally as the Alabama Swamps (it's located in the town of Alabama) is the largest wildlife refuge in New York State.

GUIDANCE **Town of Bergen** (585-494-1121), 13 South Lake, Bergen. Open Monday, Tuesday, Wednesday, Friday 9–12 and 1–5, Saturday 9–12.

Village of Bergen (585-494-1513), 11 Buffalo Street, Bergen. Open Monday–Friday 8:30–4.

Town of Elba (585-757-2762), 7 Maple Avenue. Open Monday–Friday 9–12 and 1–4.

Village of Elba (585-757-6889), 4 South Main Street, Elba. Monday–Friday 9–12 and 1–4.

Village of Oakfield (585-948-5862; http://vi.oakfield.ny.us or www.oakfield.gov office.com), 37 Main Street, Oakfield. Open Monday–Friday 9–5.

GETTING THERE *By car:* Alabama and Basom can be reached by NY 77N from exit 48A off I-90. Take exit 48 to reach Elba via NY 98 or Oakfield via NY 63. Bergen is accessible from I-90 exit 47; then take NY 19 north. It is also accessible from I-490.

MEDICAL EMERGENCY Dial 911

✳ To See

MUSEUMS AND HISTORIC HOMES **Bergen Museum of Local History** (585-494-1121), 7547 South Lake Road (NY 19, south of NY 33), Bergen. Open Sunday 2–5 during summer, by appointment rest of year.

Historical Society of Elba (585-757-6609), Maple Avenue Extension, Elba. Open Sunday 2–4, Memorial Day–Labor Day.

✳ To Do

FISHING See **Iroquois National Wildlife Refuge** in *Green Space.*

✳ Green Space

NATURE PRESERVES **Bergen Swamp** (585-548-7304; www.bergenswamp.org) 6646 Hessenthaler Road, Byron. By appointment only. The Bergen Swamp, one of the United State's seven National Natural History Landmarks, is one of the most unique locations in Genesee County. Owned and operated by the Bergen Swamp Preservation Society, the swamp is actually a marl bog and supports many plants that can't grow in acidic bogs. For over a century naturalists have come to study rare plants and animals in an unchanged habitat going back 125,000 years. This 1,900-acre swamp is home to the Eastern Massasauga (pygmy) rattlesnake, a rarity in western New York, plus over 2,500 species of plants.

Iroquois National Wildlife Refuge (585-948-5445; http://iroquoisnwr.fws .gov/), 1101 Casey Road, Basom. Visitors center open year-round Monday–Friday 7:30–4, trails open daily. Free admission. This nearly 11,000-acre site, known locally as the Alabama Swamps because it's located in the town of Alabama, is the largest wildlife refuge in New York. Situated in both Genesee and Orleans Counties, the refuge consists of wooded swamps, marshlands, wet meadows, pastures, and cropland. It is a habitat for migratory waterfowl and other birds, including 10 different species of ducks. Over 20,000 people attend the annual hatching of the endangered bald eagle. Look for resident wildlife such as deer and fox. There are four overlooks and three nature trails, which can be used for cross-country skiing in winter. If you enjoy fishing, the refuge has northern pike, bluegill, pumpkinseed, yellow perch, white perch, brown bullhead, and carp.

Oak Orchard Wildlife Management Area (716-226-2466), Albion Road, 3.5 miles north of Oakfield. Open dawn to dusk. Free admission. This 2,500-acre area is located in the wetland known as Oak Orchard Swamp, which was created by a natural barrier across Oak Orchard Creek. In spring, a high concentration of waterfowl converge here, as does a large deer herd in winter. There are many public use areas where hiking, wildlife observation, and photography can be enjoyed. Some areas also allow hunting and fishing, with the proper permits. Four nature trails are located near the Oak Orchard education center on Knowlesville Road. An observation tower is located off Albion Road.

Tonawanda Wildlife Management Area (716-226-2466), NY 77, between Lockport and Batavia. Open dawn to dusk. Free admission. This 5,600-acre area is located in the Tonawanda Creek flood plain, southwest of the Oak Orchard Swamp. It is an outstanding waterfowl viewing area from March to May.

WALKING AND HIKING TRAILS See **Iroquois National Wildlife Refuge.**

WATERFALLS Indian Falls A 30-foot waterfall on the Tonawanda Creek, located along Allegheny Road (NY 77) near the Tonawanda Indian Reservation. *Tonawanda* is the Iroquois word for "swift water."

✳ Lodging

OTHER LODGING Southwood RV Resort (585-548-9002; www.south woodsrvresort.com), 6749 Town Line Road (NY 262), Byron. Facilities include showers, rest rooms, a game room, playground, swimming pool, basketball and volleyball, and more. Water/electricity $23.50, with sewer $25.

✳ Selective Shopping

FARM MARKETS Ole Barn Country Market (585-757-6815), 98 S. Main Street (NY 262 & 98), Elba. Open daily July–December. Farm market—including world-famous Elba onions and potatoes—antiques, and gifts.

SPECIAL SHOPS Clarissa's Country Cupboard (585-548-2344), 5839 Merrill Road, Byron. Open Saturday

11–4, Sunday 12–4. Two barns filled with country treasures, including candles, country foods, baskets, antiques, specialty items, and gifts.

Cute as a Button Country Gift Shop (585-948-5920), 1638 Ham Road (off NY 63), Basom. Open April–December Thursday–Saturday 10–5, Sunday 12–4. A country gift shop filled with candles, baskets, bears, pottery, primitives, crafts, and more.

Becky's Treasures & Crafts (585-948-8873), 116 North Main Street, Oakfield. Open Monday–Saturday 8-6, Sunday 10-3. This shop carries everything, from a full line of hardware, garden supplies and lumber to antiques and collectibles, used furniture, and new gifts. Local people come here to save a trip into Batavia.

Pine Hill Mercantile (585-757-2025), 4397 Drake Street, Elba (NY 262 near NY 98), Elba. Open Thursday–Saturday 12–5. This shop carries country decor items and more.

Warner's Gift Shop (585-948-5500), 21 Main Street, Oakfield. Open Monday–Friday 9–5, Saturday 9–12. This family-owned and operated florist in business since 1944 also has a nice selection of candles, framed prints, gift baskets, garden accents, bird houses, and gift items.

Wonder of Wood Gift Barn (585-494-2146), 7451 Lake Road (2 miles from I-490), Bergen. Open Tuesday–Friday 10–6, Saturday and Sunday 10–5. This old barn goes on and on. Its multitude of rooms are filled with wood crafts, candles, folk art, jams, seasonal decorations, dried wreaths, oak furniture, and kitchen linens.

"SMOKE SHOPS" It's popular to travel to the many smoke shops located along Bloomindale Road (off NY 77) on the Tonawanda Reservation for low-price cigarettes and gas.

✳ Special Events
August: **Elba Onion Festival** (village of Elba 585-757-6889), Village Park, NY 98, Elba. A summer festival celebrating the onion.

SOUTHERN GENESEE COUNTY—Darien, Alexander, Pavilion, and Bethany

The southern part of Genesee County is mainly an agricultural region with gently rolling hills. Most folks traveling this way are likely to be heading to Six Flags Darien Lake, the largest theme park and family entertainment resort in New York. However, the area has other points of interest such as Darien Lakes State Park, a 1,846-acre site, that's popular with campers, hikers, and hunters.

The town of Darien was founded in 1832 along an old trail, now Route 77, used by the Seneca tribe. Farmers later used this route to transport their goods to the Erie Canal.

The small farming community of Alexander—named after the first settler, Alexander Rea, a surveyor for the Holland Land Company—was organized as a town in 1812. It is has the only three-story cobblestone town hall in America.

The village of Pavilion is located next to picturesque Oatka Creek, between two of the highest hills in Genesee County. The Seneca called it *Chi-nose-heh-geh,* which means "on the far side of the valley." Isaac Kyon, one of the first settlers, arrived in 1805. The Sprague family, who arrived in 1812, built one of the first water-powered mills in the town on Oatka Creek and helped develop farmland. The name Pavilion was thought up by a settler who hailed from Saratoga, New York, and recalled the name of a grand hotel located in that city.

Bethany is surrounded by a mix of rolling hills, farmland, and forested areas. The Genesee County Park and Forest is located here.

AREA CODE The area code is 585.

GUIDANCE **Town of Alexander** (585-591-0908), 3350 Church Street, Off U.S. 20 near NY 98, Alexander. Open Monday, Tuesday Friday 9–4:30, Thursday 9–12:30 and 5–9.

GETTING THERE *By car:* U.S. 20 is the major route through southern Genesee County.

MEDICAL EMERGENCY Dial 911

✳ To See

MUSEUMS AND HISTORIC HOMES **Alexander Town Museum** (585-591-0908 or 585-591-1204), 3350 Church Street, Third floor of Alexander Town Hall, off US 20 near NY 98, Alexander. Open by appointment. Built as a private school in 1837, this is the only three-story cobblestone hall in the United States. The building was listed on the National Register of Historic Places in 1973.

✳ To Do

AMUSEMENT PARKS ✍ ♿ **Six Flags Darien Lake** (585-599-4641; www.sixflags .com/darienlake) 9993 Allegheny Road, Darien Center. Open May–October; weekends only May, September, and October; July–August daily 10:30–10; call or see Web site for hours rest of season. Admission: $31.99 over 49 inches tall, $19.99 under 49 inches, under 3 free. A 1,500-acre family vacation destination theme park with hundreds of rides and attractions, including a huge water park complex. Special events are held throughout the season, such as a Father's Day car show, Kingdom Bound Christian Festival, and Frightfest in October. Overnight accommodations are available in an adjacent campsite and in a modern hotel complex. See *Lodging*.

GOLF **Bethany Hills Golf Course** (585-591-2763), 11191 Molasses Hill Road, East Bethany. An 18-hole, par-61 semiprivate course.

Chestnut Hill Country Club (585-547-9699; www.chestnuthill.com), 1330 Broadway (NY 20), Darien Center. A semiprivate 18-hole, par-72 course with a restaurant, full bar, pro shop, and driving range.

Davis Countryside Meadows (585-584-8390; www.dcmeadows.com), 11070 Perry Road, Pavilion. An 18-hole, par-72 course.

SIX FLAGS DARIEN LAKE OFFERS HUNDREDS OF RIDES AND ATTRACTIONS.

Christine A. Smyczynski

FAMILY FUN ✏ **Conquest Golf, Pizza, and Ice Cream** (585-547-9894 www.conquestgolf.com), NY 77 just south of Six Flags Darien Lake, Darien. Open Monday, Tuesday, Thursday 4–midnight, Friday–Sunday 12–12. June–Labor Day. An interactive outdoor café and miniature golf course. Ice cream is brought to customers by a model train, and pizza is served from the mouth of a talking Tiki idol.

✷ Green Space

PARKS Darien Lake State Park (585-547-9242), 10289 Harlow Road, Darien Center. Open year-round, dawn to dusk. Admission: Memorial Day–Labor Day $7/car, after 6 pm free; Labor Day–Memorial Day $6/car, after 4 pm free. Darien Lake State Park is a 1,846-acre forested and fairly underdeveloped park. The hilly terrain includes ravines, streams, and a 12-acre lake. There are 158 campsites (45 with electric hookups) located near heated comfort stations and showers. Campsites are available weekends year-round and daily June–October. In summer swim from the sandy beach, fish for largemouth black bass, picnic, and enjoy the playgrounds. There are also 19 miles of trails for hiking, horseback riding, and biking. Workshops on arts, crafts, and nature are offered in summer. In winter trails are open for hiking, cross-country skiing, and snowmobiling. There is also an outdoor ice-skating rink.

Genesee County Park and Forest (585-344-1122; www.co.genesee.ny.us), 11095 Bethany Center Road, East Bethany. Open May–September 9–9, October–April 9–5; interpretive center open Saturday–Sunday 12–4, weekdays by appointment. Free admission. The first and oldest county forest in New York, the park has gently rolling hills and five small ponds. There is a self-guided trail system, including a Braille and large-print nature trail, and the interpretive center offers an array of hands-on exhibits for children of all ages. Park facilities include picnic tables, grills, horseshoe pits, volleyball nets, sandboxes, playgrounds, and baseball fields. During the winter months the trails can be used for cross-county skiing.

Pavilion Park, Intersection NY 19 and 63, Pavilion. A small park with benches, a gazebo, and picnic table.

✷ Lodging

INNS AND RESORTS ✏ ♿ **Lodge on the Lake** (585-599-2211), 9993 Allegheny Road (NY 77 adjacent to Six Flags Darien Lake Amusement Park), Darien Center. Open seasonally May–October. This wilderness-themed lodge has 163 family-sized guest rooms that sleep up to six people. Amenities include a heated outdoor swimming pool plus a wading pool. If you prefer camping, Six Flags has a campground with 2,000 camp-sites and 395 rental RVs. All accommodation packages include admission to the amusement park. $145–$210.

MOTELS AND HOTELS ✏ ♿ **Darien Lakes Econo Lodge** (585-599-4681), 8493 NY 77, Corfu. This recently renovated hotel is located just off the NYS Thruway exit 48A, just five minutes from Six Flags Darien Lake. $65–$90.

BED & BREAKFASTS **Top of the World Gardens** (585-584-3794), 7284 Cobb Road, Pavilion. Open May–late September. Deb and John Slusser offer one antique-furnished room with a private bath overlooking their beautiful gardens at this quiet country retreat located on top a gently rolling hill. Since it's located far from the city lights, it is a perfect place to watch the stars at night. Guests are treated to a full country breakfast in a casual country atmosphere, plus full use of the decks and gardens. $85–$90 (no credit cards). See also *Selective Shopping—Special Shops*.

OTHER LODGING **Six Flags Darien Lake Camping Resort** (585-599-4651; www.sixflags.com/darienlake), 9993 Allegheny Road NY 77 (adjacent to Six Flags Darien Lake Amusement Park), Darien Center. Open May–October. Chose from either on-site RV campers, or bring your own RV or tent to the campsite. Their RVs have room for six and include a table, refrigerator, stove, and bath with shower. Guests must bring their own bedding, dishes, cutlery, and cooking utensils. Campsites have water and electric hookups, with an additional charge for sewer hookup. RV rates range from $175–$195 for four people, $25 each additional person. Campsites rates range from $100–$125 for four people, $25 each additional person. Reduced rates are available in spring and fall and to season-pass holders. Theme-park admission is included with all accommodations.

Skyline Camping Resort (585-591-2021), 10933 Townline Road, Darien Center. Open May–Columbus Day. Facilities include two swimming pools, a 6-acre stocked lake, recreational facilities, 18-hole miniature golf, and planned activities. $26/daily, $156/weekly; holiday weekend three-night minimum stay $93.

✷ Where to Eat

EATING OUT 🍴 🏌️ **Beachy's** (585-547-9339), 1415 Broadway (US 20 near NY 77), Darien. Open 8 AM–10 PM, call for winter hours. This casual restaurant features hot dogs, hamburgers, ice cream treats, and more.

🏌️ **Conquest Golf** See *To Do—Family Fun*

🍴 **Remission Café** (585-584-8010), 11116 West Park Street (near NY 19 and 63), Pavilion. Open Tuesday–Sunday 7 AM–2 PM. This quaint, tiny café is decorated with baskets and birdhouses. The menu features breakfast fare as well as sandwiches and salads for lunch.

✷ Entertainment

THEATERS ♿ **Six Flags Darien Lake Performing Arts Center** (585-599-4641; www.sixflags.com/darienlake), 9993 Allegheny Road (NY 77), Darien Center. Some of the summer's hottest acts perform at this seasonal 20,000-plus-seat amphitheater.

✷ Selective Shopping

SPECIAL SHOPS **Country Cottage** (585-547-9591), 10448 Harper Road, Darien Center. Open daily 11–6 year-round. This country gift shop has a collection of useful and decorative items for the home, including lots of country decorating items, candles, garden accessories, and even penny candy for the kids. Owners Peggy and Bruce Tyrrell also open a small café on weekends, serving hot cinnamon buns, scones, cookies, coffee, and tea.

During the warmer months you can walk among their gardens to the back cottage.

Country Hill Home Accessories & Gifts (585-584-3540), 11119 West Park Street (NY 19 & 63), Pavilion. Open Tuesday, Thursday, Friday 10–6, Wednesday 12–6, Saturday 10–4. This cute little shop in the heart of Pavilion carries lots of wonderful home-decor and country decorating wares. Choose from items by Lang, including cards, candles, and calendars, along with gifts, tinware, pottery, primitives, flags, and wallpaper. The shop has a selection of Lang's August Moon collection and Byer's Choice carolers. Owner Cathie Carlsen also carries items made by local artisans, such as Al Strobel's wooden clocks, Ginna Westacott's quilted items, and Cheryl Dreyer's "woolies" figurines.

Country Tyme (585-584-3588), 10490 Linwood Road (off U.S. 20 near the Genesee/Livingston County line), Linwood. Open Thursday–Saturday 10–5 and by appointment; extended hours before Christmas. This two-story rustic shop features antiques, Shaker furniture, Ty products, candles, and country accessories. They have a big craft show before Christmas.

East Bethany General Store (585-813-0239), 5769 Ellicott Street Road (NY 63), East Bethany. An old-time working general store built in 1835 that has the original walnut counter and oak floor. It operates as a convenience store and take-out restaurant.

Rolling Hills Country Mall (585-344-2888), 11001 Bethany Center Road (next to Genesee County Park), Bethany. Open Saturday and Sunday 10–5. About two-dozen craft, antiques, and flea market vendors have shops in this massive circa 1828 building, which once housed the insane and destitute in Genesee County. The building served the county until the mid-1970s, then remained vacant until the early 1990s, when it was converted into a craft co-op. It has been operated by current owners Jeff and Lori Carlson for the last several years. The Hilltop Café serves up breakfast and lunch, including burgers, sandwiches, and hot lunch specials.

Top of the World Gardens (585-584-3794) 7284 Cobb Road, Pavilion. Open daily 8–6 May–late September. A small, high-quality nursery with over 4 acres of gardens that offer inspiration to their customers. A nice quiet place to come and relax, sit on the benches or read a book. It's a popular destination for garden club tours. The gardens can be rented for weddings and/or wedding pictures. See also *Lodging—Bed & Breakfasts.*

✳ Special Events

August: **Kingdom Bound** (716-633-1117; www.kingdombound.org), Six Flags Darien Lake, 9993 Allegheny Road, Darien Center. A Christian religious festival amid the fun of Six Flags Darien Lake amusement park. Events include speakers, musical entertainment, seminars, and worship services.

September: **WNY Gas and Steam Engine Association Rally** (800-622-2686), 10400 Gillate Road, Alexander. Western New York's largest display and demonstration of steam- and gas-powered engines, farm equipment, and construction equipment.

ORLEANS COUNTY

Whether you're interested in history, rural charm, agricultural products, recreational boating, or sportfishing, Orleans County is a popular destination. Orleans County was incorporated in 1825, the same year as the completion of the Erie Canal. During that time, numerous small villages sprang up along and near the canal. Still thriving today are Medina, Albion, and Holley.

History buffs will enjoy the railroad museum in Medina and the world's only museum for cobblestones, located just north of Albion. Agriculture is the number-one industry in the county, so visitors can stop at numerous roadside stands and farm markets to get fresh-picked produce in-season. Recreational boating is popular on the Erie Canal, Oak Orchard River, and Lake Ontario. If sportfishing is your thing, Lake Ontario is noted for its giant salmon, along with brown and steelhead trout.

Orleans is a rather small county, only 23 miles across, permitting visitors to cover a lot of territory in one day.

MEDINA

Medina developed during the construction of the Erie Canal in 1825 and was incorporated in 1832. The first dwellings were built to house the laborers working on the canal. Many of the buildings are made of what is known as "Medina sandstone," which was discovered during the construction of the Erie Canal. This durable sandstone—ranging in color from deep reddish-brown to light gray—was quarried and used not just locally but nationally and even internationally. Medina sandstone can be found on the state capitol in Albany, in Rochester, in Cleveland, and even in Havana, Cuba. Medina Sandstone was also used in the construction of Buckingham Palace. For about 80 years, 48 quarries from Medina to Holley were in operation.

The village has seen few changes over the years. As you stroll along the downtown business district, look up at the tops of the buildings; some have their construction dates inscribed on them, with many dating back to the 1860s. The oldest public building still in use in Medina is Saint John's Episcopal Church on East Center Street, built in the 1830s. It is referred to as the "Church in the

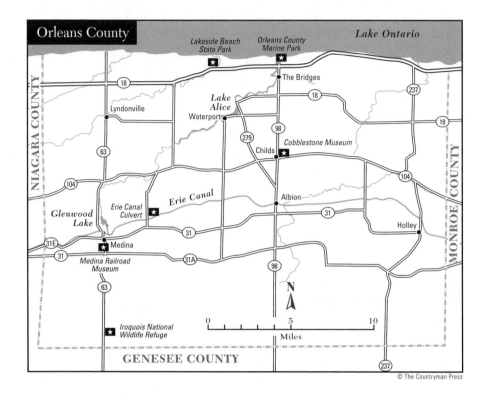

Middle of the Street" and was mentioned in *Ripley's Believe It or Not* because it is literally in the middle of an intersection.

Visitors to Medina, a village of 7,000, will find tree-lined streets, fertile farmland, 19th-century architecture and recreational activities that focus on the Erie Canal. Some of the interesting canal-related attractions in the area include the largest man-made turning basin, the only aqueduct on the Erie Canal, and the Culvert, which is the only place where a road crosses *under* the Erie Canal.

AREA CODE The area code is 585.

GUIDANCE Orleans County Tourism (800-724-0314; www.orleansny.com/tourism), 14016 NY 31, Albion. This office is a division of the government of Orleans County. Information on the county can be obtained through their 800 number or through their Web site.

Medina Chamber of Commerce Information Center (585-798-4287), 433 Main Street, Medina. Open Monday–Friday 9–4:30, closed for lunch 1–2.

GETTING THERE *By car:* From the west or east: NY 31 from Lockport or Albion. From the south: New York State Thruway exit 48A, and follow NY 63 north.

MEDICAL EMERGENCY Call 911

Medina Memorial Hospital (585-798-2000), 200 Ohio Street, Medina.

MUSEUMS AND HISTORIC HOMES **Medina Historical Society Museum** (585-798-3006), 406 West Avenue, Medina. Open Sunday 2–4 June–September or by appointment. A collection that offers visitors a glimpse of what life was like in the community's early days. The 1841 home, decorated in turn-of-the-20th-century style, was built for a prominent mill owner.

✐ **Medina Railroad Museum** (585-798-6106; www.railroadmuseum.net), 530 West Avenue, Medina. Open Tuesday–Sunday 11–5. Admission $5 adults, $4 seniors, $3 children, under 3 free. This unique museum is in a circa 1905 wooden freight house that's 300 feet long and 34 feet wide, one of the largest surviving such structures in the United States. Displayed are all sorts of railroad artifacts and memorabilia, including the original 16-foot-long steel logo of the Heinz pickle. Heinz had a large manufacturing plant in Medina, and they shipped most of their products by rail. When the plant closed, Heinz donated this logo to the local historical society, but since they did not have the space to display it, it was given to the rail museum. There is also a large display of scale-model trains and toys. The museum is in the process of developing educational programs and has a growing number of interactive exhibits. They are currently constructing one of the largest prototypical HO-scale layouts in the country that when finished will measure 204 feet long and 14 feet wide. Rail excursions are offered from the museum on a limited basis.

HISTORIC SITES ✐ **The Erie Canal Culvert,** Culvert Road, Medina. There are many places motorists can drive over the 363-mile-long Erie Canal, but there is only one place that allows motorists to drive under the historic canal. The Culvert Road aqueduct, a unique engineering feat in 1825, was built to avoid the expense and time needed to construct a bridge over the canal. The culvert was featured in *Ripley's Believe it or Not.*

✳ To Do

BOAT LAUNCHES **Route 31E,** 2 miles west of Medina on south side of canal.

Bates Road, Medina, on the north side of the canal.

Glenwood Lake Boat Launch (800-724-0314), NY 63, north of Medina.

FAMILY FUN ✐ **Medina Stone Farm Corn Maze** (585-798-9238; www.medinastonefarm.com), 255 North Gravel Road (NY 63), Medina. Saturday and Sunday 11:30–6 Labor Day–mid-October. Kids of all ages will enjoy getting lost in the cornfield

THIS CULVERT OUTSIDE THE TOWN OF MEDINA IS THE ONLY PLACE WHERE YOU CAN DRIVE *UNDER* THE ERIE CANAL.

Christine A. Smyczynski

maze. Other activities include mule-drawn hayrides and a pumpkin patch. It's simply frightful the week before Halloween when ghost and goblins roam the maze.

✳ Green Space

NATURE PRESERVES Iroquois National Wildlife Refuge. See *Genesee County.*

PARKS Erie Basin Marine Park, Access from North Main Street or East Center Street, Medina. This area was enlarged in 1913, and the aqueduct was built over Oak Orchard Creek upstream from the Medina Falls. There is a boat docking area, picnic tables, a gazebo, and a paved path to stroll along the Erie Canal.

John E. Butts Memorial Park, NY 63, south of Medina along Oak Orchard Creek. A municipal park for the village of Medina.

State Street Park, State Street and NY 31, Medina. A small, picturesque park located along Oak Orchard Creek and the Erie Canal.

PONDS AND LAKES Glenwood Lake, NY 63, about 1 mile north of Medina. A popular spot for boating and canoeing.

WALKING AND HIKING TRAILS Erie Canal Heritage Trail (Towpath Hike and Bike Trail). A very scenic paved path that follows the old towpath along the north side of the Erie Canal. The towpath was used by mules to pull the canal boats. This trail follows the canal from Lockport to past Rochester and eventually will go all the way to Albany.

FALL IN ORLEANS COUNTY OFFERS SPECTACULAR FOLIAGE AND GREAT FISHING.
Courtesy Buffalo–Niagara Convention & Visitors Bureau

WATERFALLS Medina Falls, a 40-foot waterfall on Oak Orchard Creek that can be viewed from the towpath walkway just beyond the Horan Road Bridge, near where Oak Orchard Creek emerges from beneath the Erie Canal aqueduct.

✳ Lodging

BED & BREAKFASTS Garden View Bed & Breakfast (585-798-1087; www.gardenviewbandb.com), 11091 West Center Street Extension, Medina. Open year-round, reservations required. No children under 14 or pets. This 1910 home features Revival pillars on the porch and leaded-glass windows throughout the house. Guests can stroll through the garden, meet the llamas in the barn, or sit in the gazebo to enjoy a view of the Erie Canal, which borders the property. Accommodations include three guest rooms with a shared bath. Innkeeper Pat Mufford serves a continental breakfast in the country kitchen or outside in the gazebo. $50–$60.

Medina Stone Farm Bed & Breakfast & Parlor Theater (585-798-9238; www.medinastonefarm.com), 255 North Gravel Road (NY 63), Medina. Open year-round. Three large guest rooms with private baths, two with claw-foot "soaking tubs," can be found in this 1860s brick farmhouse situated on 90 acres along the Erie Canal. Each room is furnished in antiques and has a beautiful handmade quilt on the bed. The downstairs guest room is fully handicapped accessible. Hosts Ron and Nancy OneSong can often be found entertaining guests in the Parlor Theater. Ron and Nancy have performed traditional American music in Canada, Europe, and at the Ryman Auditorium in Nashville. Special events take place at the farm throughout the year, including square dances and musical entertainment. Afternoon entertainment can be arranged for bus tours. The farm features a corn maze in the fall. $89–$109

OTHER LODGING Wildwood Lake Campground (585-735-3310), 2711 County Line Road (NY 269), Medina. Facilities at this 300-site camping resort include a 12-acre stocked lake, planned activities, musical entertainment on holiday weekends, boat rentals, and a small beach.

✳ Where to Eat

DINING OUT Apple Orchard Inn (585-798-2323; www.apple-orchard inn.com), 11004 West Center Street Extension (NY 31E), Medina. Open Monday–Thursday 11–9, Friday and Saturday 11–10, Sunday 12–8; Sunday brunch 9–2. For over 60 years this large, cheery restaurant serving high-quality fine food has been a popular landmark destination. Originally built in 1927 as a hot dog stand, it has grown to be the most beautiful restaurant and banquet facility in Orleans County. Lunch features salads, sandwiches, and daily specials. Diner entrées include hometown favorites like baked ham and liver and onions along with steaks, chicken, and seafood dishes. Be sure to save room for their signature dessert, the Blooming Apple: ice cream topped with sliced deep-fried apple and whipped cream. Beginning in the spring of 2005 they will offer mule-drawn Erie Canal dinner tours on a replica packet boat.

EATING OUT Cafora's Pizza & Restaurant (585-798-1902), 408 Main Street, Medina. Open Monday–Wednesday 11–8, Thursday 11–9, Friday and Saturday 11–10, Sunday 4–9. Italian specialties in a casual, relaxed atmosphere, just a short walk from the Erie Canal.

Country Club Restaurant (585-798-4072), 535 Main Street, Medina. This family-style restaurant is the only 24-hour restaurant in Medina.

Rudy's Restaurant (585-798-5166), 118 West Center Street, Medina. A 1950s soda fountain-style restaurant featuring hot dogs, hamburger, and ice cream treats.

✳ Selective Shopping

ANTIQUES Another Time, Another Place (585-798-0501), 12338 Maple

Ridge Road (NY 31A), Millville (4 miles east of Medina). Open year-round; call for hours. Antiques, candles, greeting cards, crafts by local artisans, jewelry, candles, lamps, and more are displayed in a historic 1870 church. The second floor features A Knitters Corner (yarn shop) and Morgans Toy Box (educational toys.) After shopping, enjoy a bite to eat in the tea parlor, for soups and sandwiches served in an elegant atmosphere. Be sure to note the "windows" on the front of the building painted by artist Ninandre Bogue.

Jeddo Mills (585-735-3535), 10267 Ridge Road (NY 104), Jeddo (just west of Medina). Open Thursday–Sunday 11–4. This 1858 gristmill houses a wide variety of antiques, including furniture, dishes, 19th-century Americana, and architectural items.

Karen's Kollectables (585-798-5430), 3422 North Gravel Road (NY 63 north of Medina), Medina. Open Monday–Saturday 10–5. Antiques, china, pottery, furniture, collectibles, and gifts are featured in this shop.

Vande's Antiques (585-798-9755), 484 East Center Street, Medina. Open Monday–Saturday 9–5, Sunday 11–5 in summer; shorter hours in winter. A large antiques shop featuring glassware, artwork, primitives, furniture, and other memorabilia.

CRAFTS **Canal Country Artisans** (585-798-4760), 135 East Center Street, Medina. Open Tuesday–Saturday 10–5. A craft and gift consignment shop where shoppers can choose from a large selection of quality handcrafted items, including painted-wood items, florals, and fabric crafts.

FARM MARKETS **Bashford's Fruit Farm Market** (585-798-0235), 11074 Ridge Road (NY 104), Medina. Open 11–9 May–October. Vegetables, fruits, flowers, and ice cream.

Flyway Farms (585-798-0751), 10888 West Shelby Road, Medina. Open year-round; call for hours, as they vary. Choose from maple syrup and other maple products produced from over 800 tree taps. Flyway Farms, located next to the Iroquois National Wildlife Refuge, recently won international awards for their maple products. At the North American Syrup Judging they came in third place for their dark syrup and second place for their molded sugar products.

Jantzi's Bushel 'n Peck (585-798-2927), 10858 Ridge Road, Medina. Open weekends January–April 30, daily May 1–mid-December. Open Monday–Saturday 10–6, Sunday 12–5. Step back in time when you visit Bushel and Peck, an old-time general store and farm market. Choose from locally grown, in-season produce, Amish baked goods, country-themed gifts and handcrafted items, and canned goods. During the summer visitors can enjoy an ice cream cone while sitting on the porch.

Smith Family Farm Market (585-798-2656), 4362 South Gravel Road, Medina. Open 10–6 daily May 1–October 31, closed Sunday in July and August. The owners pride themselves on the freshness of their produce, grown on their own farm and by other local growers. Anything not sold by the end of the day is discarded. In autumn they carry a huge selection of fall decorating items.

SPECIAL SHOPS **Apple Junction Hobby Shop** (585-798-9861), 513

Main Street, Medina. Open Monday, Tuesday, Thursday 10–5, Wednesday 12–5, Friday 10–7, Saturday 10–5. Trains and train accessories, paints, doll houses, and miniatures are available for sale in a historic building that once housed a mercantile store.

The Book Shoppe (585-798-3642) 519 Main Street, Medina. Open Monday–Thursday 10–5, Friday 10–8, Saturday 10–5. The front of the store features a selection of best-sellers and books by the latest authors. Head toward the back of the store to find educational books and toys. They also carry gourmet coffee and hot cocoa gift baskets.

Case-nic Cookies (585-798-1676; www.caseniccookies.com) 439 Main Street, Medina. Open Monday–Friday 10–5, Saturday 9–1. Old-fashioned cookies, cakes, and other baked goods. Gifts baskets are available.

Rosenkrans Pharmacy and Gift Shop (585-798-1650) 526 Main Street, Medina. Open Monday–Friday 8:30–9, Saturday 9–5, Sunday 10–1. A nice selection of gifts, candles, and toys is located in the front of this small neighborhood drugstore.

✳ Special Events

Early June–late August: **Cruise Nights by the Canal**. A classic car show every Friday evening, also featuring live entertainment and other activities.

COBBLESTONE COUNTRY—Albion, Childs, and Holley

Albion, the county seat of Orleans County, was incorporated in 1826, just a year after the completion of the Erie Canal. Prosperity came to the town with the canal, especially through the exporting of sandstone and fruit. Today the centerpiece of downtown Albion is the Court House Square Historic District, which is on the National Register of Historic Places. Thirty-four historical and architecturally significant buildings make up this district, including seven churches that surround the courthouse square.

Nearby, in the village of Childs, visitors can learn about cobblestone construction, a building method unique to the region, at the world's only Cobblestone Museum. Cobblestone masonry, where stones were laid in horizontal rows, was developed by rural masons outside Rochester shortly after the building of the Erie Canal. About 800 of these buildings, many private residences, are still in existence in this area of western New York, referred to as "Cobblestone Country."

Holley was first settled in 1812, and when it was incorporated in 1850, it was named after Mayor Myron Holley, who was canal commissioner from 1816–1824. The town has a boardwalk, gazebo, and nature trails along the canal. Docking facilities with electric hookups and a comfort station with showers are available for recreational boaters.

AREA CODE The area code is 585.

GUIDANCE Orleans Chamber of Commerce (585-589-7727; www.orleans chamber.com), 121 North Main Street, Albion. Open Monday–Friday 9–4:30, closed for lunch 1–2.

Orleans County Tourism (800-724-0314; www.orleansny.com/tourism), 14016 NY 31, Albion. This office is a division of the government of Orleans County. Information on the county can be obtained through their 800 number or through their Web site.

Village of Holley (585-638-6367), 72 Public Square, Holley. Open Monday–Friday 8:30–4:30.

GETTING THERE *By air:* **Pine Hill Airport** is a small landing strip for private planes. See also *Getting There—Buffalo* and *Rochester.*

By car: Exit 48, New York State Thruway (I-90) to NY 98; NY 31 leads into Holley. For a more scenic route, take NY 104 from either Niagara Falls or Rochester.

MEDICAL EMERGENCY Dial 911

✳ To See

MUSEUMS AND HISTORIC HOMES ✪ **The Cobblestone Museum Complex** (585-589-9013), NY 104 & 98, Childs. Open end of June–Labor Day Tuesday–Saturday 11-5, Sunday 1–5. September and October Sunday 1–5. Group tours by appointment April–October. Admission $3.50 adults, $3 seniors over 54, $2 children 5–17. Between 1825 and 1860 approximately 1,000 buildings made out of smooth, rounded cobblestones were built in North America. About 800 are still in existence, and 90 percent of these structures are within 75 miles of Rochester. (Route 104 has more cobblestone houses along it than any other highway in America.) The Cobblestone Museum Complex consists of seven historic buildings. Three of the museum's buildings, of cobblestone construction, are designated National Historic Landmarks. These include the oldest cobblestone church in North America (1834), a parsonage (1840), and a schoolhouse (1849). Four wood-frame buildings include a blacksmith shop, harness maker, print shop, and a farmer's hall, which contains close to 300 farming artifacts.

THE COBBLESTONE MUSEUM COMPLEX CONSISTS OF SEVEN HISTORIC BUILDINGS.

Christine A. Smyczynski

Holley Depot Museum (585-638-6333 or 585-638-8188), Geddes Street Extension (off Public Square), Holley.

> **COBBLESTONE CONSTRUCTION**
>
> Cobblestone masonry, a construction method where stones were laid in horizontal rows, was developed in this area by rural masons shortly after the completion of the Erie Canal. Two types of cobblestones were used: "lake-washed stones," found on the southern shores of Lake Ontario, and "field-stones," found in fields.
>
> Settlers had to remove the stones to farm the land, a job often designated to the children. It was considered a status symbol when a farmer was able to have a cobblestone house constructed.

By appointment only. Free admission. This former 1907 New York Central depot houses artifacts relating to the Erie Canal and the railroad era along with local genealogical records.

HISTORIC SITES **Courthouse Square Historic District** (716-589-9510), Courthouse Square, Albion. The focal point of the historic district, which is on the National Register of Historic Places, is the 1858 Greek Revival–style domed county courthouse. The large dome, topped with a cupola, serves as an area landmark. Located near the courthouse is the 1882 County Clerk's Building. These two buildings are surrounded by 34 architecturally significant structures, including seven churches. The most interesting of these is the Pullman Memorial Universalist Church, built in 1894 by millionaire railway car manufacturer George M. Pullman as a memorial to his parents. The church, designed in Old English Gothic style, is constructed of Medina sandstone and has many windows created by the Tiffany Glass Company. The other structures, while not built by a millionaire, are each interesting architecturally. A walking guide to the district, describing many buildings in detail, is available from the chamber of commerce.

Mount Albion Cemetery (585-589-5416), 14925 NY 31 East, Albion. Grounds open daily 6 AM–8 PM. Designated a National Historic Place, Mount Albion Cemetery has 25 miles of paths winding through the many burial terraces and garden areas. This 100-acre cemetery set on a hill opened in 1843 and has many outstanding monuments and mausoleums, the best known being the Soldiers and Sailors Civil War Memorial Tower. Be sure to pick up a map at the main gate (or in town at the chamber of commerce) because it is easy to get lost on the cemetery's narrow, winding roads.

✳ To Do

AIR SHOWS **Vintage Aircraft Group** (585-589-7758; www.vintageaircraft group.org), Pine Hill Airport, 4906 Pine Hill Road (off NY 31A), Albion. The mission of the Vintage Aircraft Group is to educate the public about all aircraft, with an emphasis on the unusual or unique. If you stop by on the weekends you can see members of this group restoring vintage aircraft. Call for hours.

GOLF Hickory Ridge Golf and Country Club (585-638-4653 or 888-346-5458; www.hickoryridgegolfandcountryclub.com) 15816 Lynch Road, Holley. A championship 18-hole, par-72 course only 35 minutes from downtown Rochester. The club has a pro shop, driving range, and snack shop. The course is open to the public, and club memberships are also available.

Pap Pap's Par 3 (585-589-4004), 3431 Gaines Basin Road, Albion. A public 9-hole, par-3 course.

Ricci Meadows Golf Course (585-682-3280), 1939 Oak Orchard Road, Albion A public 18-hole, par-71 course.

✳ Green Space

PARKS Bullard Park, NY 31, Albion. This large town park has picnic facilities, playgrounds, and a skateboard park.

Canalside Park, Albion. Located along the canal near the lift bridge, this park offers boat docking and a landscaped vantage point to watch the lift bridge in operation.

WALKING AND HIKING TRAILS Erie Canal Heritage Trail (Towpath Hike and Bike Trail). This trail follows the towpath once use by mules towing packet boats on the Erie Canal. This trail follows the canal from Lockport to past Rochester and eventually will go all the way to Albany.

WATERFALLS Holley Falls, end of Frisbie Terrace, off Village Square. This beautiful waterfall is located in a small park accessed by a service road next to the Department of Public Works garage. The waterfall flows from the Erie Canal into the east branch of Sandy Creek, a popular area for fishing. The park, which has a picnic shelter and a nature trail, is a peaceful spot to sit and look at the falls.

✳ Lodging

INNS AND RESORTS Fair Haven Inn (585-589-9151; www.tillmans villageinn.com), 14369 Ridge Road (NY 104 at NY 98), Childs. Open year-round. Hosts Mark and Tom Tillman offer four unique, antique-furnished rooms, with modern amenities, in this historic 1837 house, located within walking distance to the world's only cobblestone museum complex. Four modern motel rooms are also available in an adjacent unit. $60.

BED & BREAKFASTS Friendship Manor Bed & Breakfast (585-589-7973; www.friendshipmanorbnb.com), 349 South Main Street, Albion. Open year-round. Hosts Jack and Marylin Baker offer four spacious guest rooms, furnished in Victorian style, in this historic late 1870s Italianate-style brick home. Two guest rooms have private baths while the other two share a bath. Guest can enjoy a lovely rose garden along with a traditional herb garden. A breakfast of muffins, bread, fruit, and beverages is served buffet-style. $55–$65.

LaMont's Orchard View Bed & Breakfast (585-589-7702; www .orchardviewbb.com), 3027 Densmore Road, Albion. Open year-round.

Located in a rural setting, this turn-of-the-20th-century farmhouse has original furnishings, mahogany and oak woodwork, and a wraparound porch to relax on. Decorating also reflects a touch of Sweden. Three spacious bedrooms, named after the three children who grew up in this home originally, each has a private bath. Hosts Ingrid and Roger LaMont, see to it that their guests start the day with a full breakfast—including baked goods, fruit, and Swedish pancakes—served on fine china in the dining room. The inn is operated by the sixth generation of the LaMont family to live on the land since it was purchased in 1815 by Josiah LaMont. $80–$95.

Rosewood Bed & Breakfast (585-638-6186; www.rosewdbnb.com), 68 Geddes Street, Holley. Open year-round. Hosts Karen Cook and Roy Nichols offer five luxurious guest rooms in an 1891 Victorian home furnished with antiques, vintage linens, and Victorian silver. Four rooms have queen-sized beds, and the fifth has two singles. Unwind on the huge wraparound porch with plenty of comfortable chairs. A four-course gourmet breakfast, featuring fresh local produce in-season, is served daily. $69–$89.

✴ Where to Eat

DINING OUT ✎ ⅛ **Tillman's Historic Village Inn** (585-589-9151; www.tillmansvillageinn.com), 14369 Ridge Road (NY 104 at NY 98), Childs. Open Sunday–Friday 12–9, Saturday 11:30–10. This fine restaurant in the Cobblestone Historic District first opened in 1824 as a stagecoach stop and has been open almost continuously since. The restaurant is known for its steaks, seafood, and home-style

"comfort food" like real roast turkey with stuffing.

✎ ⅛ 🍴 **Village House Restaurant** (585-589-5012), 16 East Avenue, Albion. Open Monday–Saturday 5:30 AM–10 PM, Sunday 6:30 AM–9 PM. Quality food for a reasonable price. Selections include breakfast specials until 11 AM, a daily fish fry, seafood, steaks, prime rib, chops, and pasta, along with diner-type foods.

EATING OUT ⅛ ✎ **Apple Country Quilt Shop & Café** (585-638-5262 or 866-340-6100; www.applecountryquilts.com), 51 State Street, Holley. Café Hours Tuesday–Saturday 11–3. This cute café, adjacent to the Apple Country Quilt Shop, has walls adorned with an array of quilts, from historical heirlooms to contemporary designs. Noted for their Baltimore Star crab cakes topped with dill sauce, they also serve homemade soups, sandwiches, and quiches as well as homemade desserts like crème brûlée and bread pudding. See also *Specialty Shops.*

Kafana Café & Ice Cream (585-589-0197), 10 East Bank Street Albion. Open Monday–Saturday 7 AM–8 PM. Enjoy coffee, light meals, and ice cream in this small café, which serves as a satellite art gallery for the Genesee Orleans Arts Council. Canal Antiques and Collectibles can be accessed via the café.

🍷 ⅛ ✎ **Wiggly & Jiggly's English Pub** (585-589-6327), 172 South Main Street, Albion. Open Monday–Saturday 11 AM–2 PM, Sunday noon–2 AM. One of Albion's newer establishments, specializing in baby-back ribs smoked in Jack Daniels oak-wood chips. Or try Big Ben's strip steak, Sir Francis Warthog pulled-pork sandwich, fish and chips, and Red Osier roast beef sandwiches, among others. The restaurant even has an outdoor volleyball court and a patio. It's a family-friendly restaurant by day and a popular club by night.

✳ Selective Shopping

FARM MARKETS *Special note:* A complete list of Orleans County farm markets is available from the **Orleans County Cooperative Extension** (585-589-5561; www.cce.cornell .edu/orleans/orleans.html), 20 South Main Street, Albion, NY 14411.

🐾 ♿ **Watt Farms Country Market** (585-589-800 or 800-274-5897), 3121 Oak Orchard Road, Albion. Open May–December Monday–Friday 9–6, Saturday 9–7, Sunday 9:30–6; shorter hours November and December, longer hours in summer. This family-owned business operates six fruit orchards in the Albion area. The season begins with strawberries in late June, followed by cherries, raspberries, apricots, nectarines, peaches, and plums and, in the fall, apples. Twenty-five flavors of homemade fudge are available in their country gift shop, plus they have an ice cream parlor. On weekends, take a ride through the orchards on their 70-foot-long, 90-passenger train.

🐾 ♿ **Hurd Orchards** (585-638-8838; www.hurdorchards.com) NY 104 and Monroe/Orleans County Line Road, Holley. Open 9–6 daily May–December. The Hurd family has been in the farming business for seven generations, so they know how to do things right. Hurd Orchards, one of the earliest farms in western New York, offers a large variety of in-season produce, flowers, herbs, specialty foods, and gift baskets. Their gourmet jams and jellies

are sold in specialty stores throughout the country. Special "tastings" and teas are offered, by reservation only, throughout the season, as are school tours and nature craft classes.

SPECIAL SHOPS Apple Country Quilt Shop & Café (585-638-5262 or 866-340-6100; www.applecountry quilts.com), 51 State Street, Holley. Open Tuesday–Saturday 10–4. Hundreds of bolts of designer quilting fabrics, notions, books, and patterns fill this 3,000-square-foot shop. Quilting classes are given on a regular basis. They also offer Long Arm Machine Quilting service, so you can get your quilt done in no time, and they are a dealer for Gammill Quilting Machines. The adjacent Apple Country Café serves delicious lunches. See *Eating Out.*

Clarendon Cheesecakes (585-638-0008 or 866-74C-CAKE; www .clarendoncheesecakes.com), 101 Cadbury Way, Holley (located in Holley Industrial Park, off NY 31 near Holley Cold Storage). Open Tuesday–Friday 11–6, Saturday 9–2. Many people consider Clarendon Cheesecake the world's best, and I think they're right. The store is a bit hard to find, but it's worth it. Owner Debbie Patt started making cheesecakes in her basement just a few years ago; today she has a state-of-the-art facility that makes more than 50 varieties of cheesecake, including sugar free and reduced carb. Her cheesecakes have even been featured on the *Today Show* and the Food Channel. They also make wedding cakes, pastries, cream puffs, éclairs, cannoli, cookies, and pies. Pastries, cheesecake, and coffee are served during business hours.

Fair Haven Gift Shop (585-589-9151; www.tillmansvillageinn.com), 14369 Ridge Rd. (NY 104 at NY 98), Childs. Open daily 5–9. A quaint country gift shop featuring local crafts and art, adjacent to the Fair Haven Inn and Tillman's Historic Village Inn. See *Where to Eat* and *Lodging*.

Primitive Garden (585-589-9636), 13996 Ridge Road, Albion. This cute little shop has unique birdhouses and primitive dolls along with handmade cupboards, benches, and other items.

✂ ♿ **Ridge Road Station and Christmas Shop** (585-638-6000, 877-447-2253; www.rrstation.com), 16131 Ridge Road West (NY 104), Holley. Open Monday–Friday 10–8, Saturday–Sunday 10–6. Ridge Road Station is the largest independent toy store in New York, featuring 30,000 square feet of toys and trains plus Christmas decorations and ornaments. The train room has the finest G-gauge train layout east of the Rio Grande. Five trains run on 3,300 feet of track on four levels, including 14 tunnels and 11 bridges. They carry all scales of trains, including the largest inventory of G-gauge engines between New York City and Los Angeles. They also carry Brio trains, Playmobile, Legos, hobby models, slot cars, and many other fun and educational toys. A large selection of gift items is also available.

✳ Special Events

June: **Albion Strawberry Festival** (585-589-7727), Albion. This festival, which celebrates one of summer's favorite fruits, includes a parade, Strawberry Festival Queen pageant, arts and craft show, classic car display, and, of course, lots of strawberry desserts.

July: **Orleans County 4-H Fair** (585-589-5561; www.orleans4-Hfair.com), Knowlesville. The Orleans County Fair features agricultural exhibits, hands-on activities, free entertainment, midway rides, and farm animals. The fair allows 4-H youth to exhibit the results of all the hard work they've done throughout the year.

August: **Cobblestone Antique Fair** (585-589-9013), Cobblestone Museum, Childs. This antiques and collectibles show is set amid the National Historic Landmark Cobblestone Museum. **Orleans County Trout and Salmon Fishing Derby** (585-589-5605 or 585-589-3220). Anglers compete for prizes while fishing for salmon and trout in Lake Ontario.

September: **Old Timer's Day** (585-589-9013), Cobblestone Museum, Childs. Demonstrations of such old-time crafts and skills as weaving and blacksmithing, along with musical entertainment and storytelling. **Hands on Day** (585-638-8838), Hurd Orchards, Holley. This special event is designed to educate families about life on the American farm, including demonstrations of apple-butter making and cider pressing.

LAKE ONTARIO SHORE — Waterport, Point Breeze, and Lyndonville

Lake Ontario is known as one of the most spectacular trout and salmon fisheries in the country. Many serious anglers find that the best fishing can be experienced by chartering a guide. In spring, brown trout are the catch of the day, while in summer and fall deep-water trolling will net you giant Chinook salmon. It's also an excellent fly-fishing area. Some of the towns and villages in this area, which have campgrounds, fishermen's accommodations, and other angler-related businesses, include Waterport, Point Breeze, and Lyndonville.

Oak Orchard Harbor, near the mouth of the Oak Orchard River at Lake Ontario, about 8 miles north of Albion, is one of the more pleasant harbors on the south shore of Lake Ontario. The harbor channel has two piers and is protected by a break wall, so calm, safe waters greet boaters at the port entrance. Centuries ago this area was a Native American settlement known as the Black North for the dense forest that was as dark as night even during the day.

AREA CODE The area code is 585.

GUIDANCE Orleans County Tourism (800-724-0314; www.orleansny.com/tourism), 14016 NY 31, Albion. This office is a division of the government of Orleans County. Information on the county can be obtained through their 800 number or through their Web site.

Orleans County Chamber of Commerce (585-589-7727; www.orleans chamber.com), 121 North Main Street, Albion.

GETTING THERE *By car:* Lake Ontario State Parkway from Rochester or NY 98 north from the New York State Thruway (I-90), exit 48.

MEDICAL EMERGENCY Dial 911

✳ To Do

FISHING CHARTERS For information on fishing charters, including an extensive list of charter captains, request the "Oak Orchard Harbor Fishing and Port Services Guide" from the **Orleans County Tourism Office** (585-589-7727; www .orleanschamber.com). Fishing licenses can be purchased at Narby's Bait & Tackle (585-682-4624), 1292 Oak Orchard Road, Kent.

GOLF Harbour Pointe Country Club (585-682-3922), 1380 Oak Orchard Road, Waterport. A public 18-hole, par-70 (men) or par-72 (women) course.

White Birch Golf Course (585-765-2630), 1515 Lyndonville Road, Lyndonville. A 9-hole, par-3 public course with pro shop, bar, and restaurant.

MARINAS ♿ **Four C's Marina** (585-682-4224), 988 Point Breeze Road, Kent. This marina features docking facilities, storage, repairs, gas. See also *Lodging*.

♿ **Lake Breeze Marina** (585-682-3995), 990 Point Breeze Road, Kent.

SPORTFISHING ON LAKE ONTARIO

"World-class" is a term often used to describe Lake Ontario fishing. In Orleans County anglers can find colossal Chinook salmon, steelhead, and brown trout all concentrated in one area. During spring and summer, trophy catches are abundant offshore in the cool, deep waters of western Lake Ontario. Small- and largemouth bass can be found in the Oak Orchard River and its tributaries, Marsh Creek, and Johnson Creek. Come fall, Chinook salmon, some weighing up to 30 pounds, and brown trout weighing between four and 17 pounds can be found in great numbers. Steelheads are the catch of the day when winter sets in.

The popular Lake Ontario Counties (LOC) Spring and Fall Fishing Derby offers anglers a chance to win cash and other prizes while enjoying world-class fishing. Proceeds from the derby are used to improve fishing on Lake Ontario and its tributaries. For more information on Lake Ontario Fishing and the fishing derby, contact: LOC at 315-539-3991 or 888-REEL-2-IN; www.loc.org; or write PO Box 49, Waterloo, NY 13165.

For information on fishing in Orleans County, contact the Orleans County Tourism Office (585-589-7727 or 800-724-0314; www.orleansny.com/tourism) and ask for an Orleans County fishing guide and county fishing map.

Wiley's Riverside Marina (585-682-4552), 1180 Point Breeze Road, Kent. Find additional marinas under *Lodging*.

✳ Green Space

LAKES ♿ **Lake Alice Boat Launch** (800-724-0314; www.orleansny.com/tourism/waterway.htm), NY 279, Waterport. Access Lake Alice and enjoy fishing, waterskiing, and canoeing.

PARKS **Orleans County Marine Park** (585-682-3641), Point Breeze Road (NY 98), Carlton. Open dawn to dusk. Free admission. A 12-acre public park on the east side of Oak Orchard River. Boat launching and trailer parking is located at Point Breeze at the mouth of the river, while docking, picnic tables, and shower facilities are located near the Lake Ontario Parkway interchange.

Lakeside Beach State Park (585-682-4888), NY 18, Waterport. Open year-round dawn to dusk. Admission: $6/car. This 743-acre park on the shores of Lake Ontario offers a panoramic view of the lake. There are 274 campsites, all with electric hookups, located in this scenic park, which once was an area of farmlands, orchards, and lakefront cottages. Facilities include picnic areas, playground, hot showers, camp store, and Laundromat plus recreation programs (summer only). The park is open for camping late April–late October and in winter for hiking, cross-country skiing, and snowmobiling.

✳ Lodging

Most accommodations in this area are geared toward sport fishers. The following places provide clean rooms with plenty of space for fishing gear.

♿ **Captain's Cove Resort** (585-682-3316; www.fishcaptainscove.com), 14339 NY 18, Waterport. Open April 1–November 15. Located on Oak Orchard River, offering full-service tackle shop, marina, boat rental, and bait. Standard rooms (2 people) $49.95, efficiencies (4 people) $72.95.

Cedar Valley Lodging (585-682-3253), 13893 Park Avenue, Waterport (on the banks of Oak Orchard River). Open March–December. Irene and Glenn Woolston offer three rooms, each with a private entrance, private shower, and in-room TV. Coffee, juice, and donuts are available in the morning. $35/person, up to four people per room.

♿ **Four C's Marina** (585-682-4224 or 877-301-1778 www.4csmarina-lodging.com), 988 Point Breeze Road, Waterport. Open first weekend in April to last weekend of October. Choose from cottages, houses, and a lodge. All units are within walking distance of the marina and Lake Ontario. $60–120.

♿ **Green Harbor Campground & Marina** (585-682-9780; http://members.aol.com/ghcampmar2), 12813 Lakeshore Road, Lyndonville. Open April–October. This campground features a 700-foot beach on Lake Ontario, tent and trailer sites, boat launch, fishing access, family activities, and more. According to owner Anne Marie Holland, it is well known for its magnificent sunsets over the beach. Campsites $23–$26, cabins $50, trailers $55.

Orleans Outdoors (585-682-4546; www.orleansoutdoor.com), 1764 Oak Orchard Road (NY 98), Albion. Open year-round. Three units with private baths are available at the Licorice Lounge. Each unit sleeps two to four people with enough room for fishing tackle. $50–$90.

Redbreeze Campsite (585-682-3156; www.redbreeze.com), 13645 Waterport-Carlton Road, Waterport. Open May 1–November 1. A private waterfront campsite located on Lake Alice. This site can accommodate up to three or four trailers and several tents, making it a perfect spot for family reunions and scout groups. Weekend rate $100 per trailer.

Riverview Campground and Marina (585-682-4213), 13987 Park Avenue, Waterport. Open April 1–October 31. This campground, located on Oak Orchard River, has 72 trailer sites and 24 tent sites. $24 full hookup, $18 water and electric.

✳ Where to Eat

EATING OUT 🍴 ✎ **Black North Inn** (585-682-4441), NY 98N on Lake Ontario, Point Breeze (mailing address: 14352 Ontario Street, Kent, NY 14477). Open Sunday–Thursday 11–9, Friday and Saturday 11–10. Where the Oak Orchard River meets Lake Ontario, you can enjoy outdoor dining on the patio or inside in the dining room at this restaurant and bar. For a good view of the river and lake, sit at one of the small tables in the front of the barroom.

✎ ♿ 🍴 **Brown's Berry Patch** (585-682-5569; www.brownsberrypatch.com), 14264 Roosevelt Highway (NY 18), Waterport. Open April–November Monday–Friday 8–6, Saturday and Sunday 8–7. Sandwiches and salads are available in the deli at this popular farm market and gift shop. Eat in the large wood-paneled dining room or outside on picnic tables. On weekends an outdoor grill, serving burgers and hot dogs, is open.

✳ Selective Shopping

FARM MARKETS ✐ **Brown's Berry Patch** (585-682-5569; www.browns berrypatch.com), 14264 Roosevelt Highway (NY 18), Waterport. Open April–November Monday–Friday 8–6, Saturday–Sunday 8–7. This large farm market offers farm-fresh fruit in-season, either already picked or pick-your-own. There is a large country gift shop with handcrafted items, jewelry, and more. Grab a bite to eat at their deli, or enjoy ice cream in one of their famous homemade waffle cones while relaxing on the antique benches on the porch. There is a play area for kids. Several festivals take place weekends in fall.

SPECIAL SHOPS **Oak Orchard Canoe and Kayak Experts** (716-682-4849; www.oakorchardcanoe .com), 2133 Waterport Road, Waterport. Open Monday, Wednesday, Thursday, Friday 10–6, Saturday 10–5, Sunday 12–4. Need a canoe or kayak? This is the place to come. Oak Orchard offers the biggest and best selection in the United States, carrying over 800 major brands. Not sure which boat is right for you? Take a test drive on Oak Orchard Creek, right outside the store. It's easier to make a decision when you can try the boat on for size. Bring your lunch, and make a day of it at their parklike facility. Canoe/kayak float trips can be arranged year-round.

Provisions (585-765-2492), 11 South Main Street, Lyndonville. Open Monday–Friday 8–8, Saturday 9–5, Sunday 9–1. An old-fashioned pharmacy and gift shop, including an upstairs Christmas shop. Choose from Boyd's collectibles, Beanie Babies, candles, books, cards, and gifts.

✳ Special Events

May and August: **Lake Ontario Fishing Derby** (585-467-9802, fishing hotline 585-589-3220; www.loc .org), Lake Ontario in Niagara, Orleans, and Monroe Counties. Fishing derbies run by the Empire State Lake Ontario Promotions are held each spring and fall. Prizes are awarded for the top catches in each category of trout and salmon. **Orleans County Wooden Boat Festival and Taste of Orleans** (585-682-3641) Orleans County Marine Park, Carlton. This festival features a display of antique wooden boats plus food vendors offering cuisine from Orleans County restaurants.

WYOMING COUNTY

W yoming County has a little bit of everything for the traveler. If you're looking for a place of scenic beauty, Wyoming County is bordered on the east by Letchworth State Park, the "Grand Canyon of the East" with its 600-foot-deep gorge. Nature lovers will also enjoy the pristine beauty of Beaver Meadow Audubon Center.

History buffs will enjoy taking a ride on the vintage steam engine Arcade & Attica Railroad, visiting the historic village of Wyoming—still lit by the original gaslights—or touring some of the areas many museums.

If you're a cowboy or cowgirl at heart, you won't want to miss the Attica Rodeo, which takes place each August. Speaking of cows, Wyoming County has some of the largest dairy farms in New York and is one of the state's most important agricultural regions.

The county—formed from Genesee County in 1841—was originally called Marshall in honor of Chief Justice John Marshall. However, at the insistence of Wyoming village Judge, John B. Skinner, the name was later changed to *Wyoming*, an Indian word meaning "broad, open, and flat lands," to reflect the area's Native American roots.

Prior to pioneer settlement in 1802, the area was used by the Seneca Nation as hunting and fishing ground. The first settlers came from New England, while later settlers were European immigrants attracted to various industries. Irish and German settlers arrived in the 1830s to farm the land. Then in the late 1880s, the salt, stone cutting, and railroad industries employed Italian immigrants while the textile mills attracted many Polish émigrés.

AREA CODE The county area code is 585.

GUIDANCE Wyoming County Tourist Promotion Agency, (585-493-3190 or 800-839-3919; www.wyomingcountyny.com), 30 North Main, Castile. Open Monday–Friday 9–5.Get information on attractions, accommodations, agritourism, biking, dining, fishing, and museums.

Wyoming County Chamber of Commerce (585-237-0230; www.wyco chamber.org), 6470 US 20A, Suite 2, Perry. Open Monday–Friday 9–5, closed 12–1 for lunch.

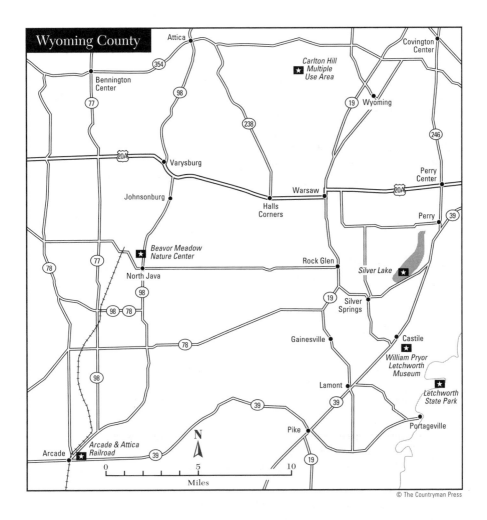

Wyoming County

Attica
Covington Center
Carlton Hill Multiple Use Area
354
Bennington Center
98
19 Wyoming
77
238
246
20A
Varysburg
Perry Center
Johnsonburg
Warsaw
20A
Halls Corners
Perry
39
Beavor Meadow Nature Center
Rock Glen
78
77
Silver Lake
North Java
98
19 Silver Springs
Castile
98 78
William Pryor Letchworth Museum
78
Gainesville
Lamont
Letchworth State Park
98
39
39
Pike
Portageville
N
Arcade & Attica Railroad
Arcade
39
0   5   10
Miles
19

© The Countryman Press

Arts Council for Wyoming County (585-237-3517; www.artswyco.org), 31 South Main Street, PO Box 249, Perry, NY 14530. This organization provides services to artists in Wyoming County and promotes the arts through arts and cultural programs.

ATTICA AND VICINITY

Attica, nestled in the foothills of the Allegany Mountains, was called *Gwete-ta-a-nete-car-do-oh*—"the red village"—by Native Americans. It is located on what was once an Indian trail known as Red Man's broad highway. The first settler, Zerah Phelps, arrived around 1802, and the area became known as Phelps Settlement. The name was later changed to Attica after a district in Greece. It was incorporated in 1811 and was a booming area by the mid-1800s, with many stores and businesses. Many of the original downtown buildings were destroyed in a terrible fire in 1907. Today Attica is a small, quaint village surrounded by farms in an area known for the production of maple products.

Attica is also known for its maximum-security prison, which was constructed outside the village in the 1930s. National attention was thrust on this small town in 1971 during the prison riot in which 43 guards and inmates died.

GUIDANCE Attica Chamber of Commerce (585-591-1385; www.geocities .com/chamberofcommerce2000), PO Box 152, Attica, NY 14011. The listed phone number is a chamber member who can point visitors in the right direction when seeking information, or see their Web site.

Town of Attica (585-591-2920), 285 Main Street, Attica 14011. Open Monday and Tuesday 5:15–6:45, Wednesday 9–4:30, Thursday 8–1.

GETTING THERE *By car:* US 20 or 20A to either NY 98 or 238 will get you to Attica.

MEDICAL EMERGENCY Dial 911

✳ To See

MUSEUMS AND HISTORIC HOMES Attica Historical Society (585-591-2161), 130 Main Street, Attica. Open Wednesday and Saturday 1–4. This museum contains a collection of local history and genealogy information, including a complete Victorian parlor, prison history, and war memorabilia

Bennington Historical Society (585-937-9718), 211 Clinton Street (NY 354), Cowlesville. Open the third Sunday of month June–October 2–4 PM. A collection of covered-bridge memorabilia, 19th-century clothing, photographs, and farm tools.

TAKE A 90-MINUTE JOURNEY INTO RAIL-ROAD HISTORY ON THE ARCADE & ATTICA RAILROAD.

Christine A. Smyczynski

✳ To Do

FISHING The best fishing in this part of the county can be found in **Tonawanda Creek**. A brochure and fishing map can be obtained by calling **Wyoming County Tourist Promotion Agency,** 585-493-3190 or 800-839-3919. Fishing licenses can be obtained at any town hall or at Wal-Mart in Warsaw.

GOLF Ironwood Golf Course (716-432-1097), 1964 Folsomdale Road, Cowlesville. A 9-hole, par-36 course.

Quiet Times Golf Course (716-591-1747), 220 Stedman Road, Attica. A public 18-hole, par-71 course.

❋ Green Space

PARKS **Attica Village Park** (585-591-0898) Exchange Street, Attica. A 6-acre developed park, including illuminated basketball and tennis courts.

❋ Lodging

MOTELS **Attican Motel** (585-591-0407 or 866-867-3007; www.attican motel.com), 11180 Alexander Road (NY 98), Attica. Open year-round. Twenty-eight clean, affordable rooms with a hilltop scenic view. A continental breakfast is offered on weekends. The motel is just 8 miles from Six Flags Darien Lake.

❋ Selective Shopping

ANTIQUES **Ancient Future** (585-591-2908), 972 Clinton Street (NY 354), Bennington. Open Saturday and Sunday 10–5. Antiques, collectibles, and gifts.

Country Treasures (585-591-0802), NY 98, Attica. Wednesday 1-5, Thursday 1-8, Friday 1-5, Saturday 10-5. A two-story barn and loft full of country gifts, primitives, antiques, and collectibles.

FARM MARKETS **Merle Maple Farm** (585-535-7136; www.merle maple.com), 1884 NY 98, Attica. Open year-round Monday–Saturday 9–5. Producing maple products has been the livelihood of the Merle family for five generations, since they arrived in this country in the early 1800s. They specialize in all sorts of maple products, including syrup, sugars, candy, and gourmet specialties. Items can be purchased at the farm or ordered online.

SPECIAL SHOPS **Pride & Joy Gifts** (585-591-1155; www.prideandjoy gifts.com), 8 Market Street, Attica. Monday–Saturday 10:30–7 (Thursday and Friday until 5 PM). This is one of the largest Colonial Candle dealers in the state. They also carry Lennox Crystal, Byers' Choice carolers, Steinbeck nutcrackers from Germany, pewter, Blue Mountain cards, Disney figures, and more.

The Homespun Shoppe (585-547-9281), 929 Friedman Road (off NY 77 between US 20 and 20A), Bennington. Open April–December, Friday and Saturday 11–5, Sunday by chance. This country shop in an old barn features everyday homespun items, cross-stitch, candles, tin items, dried florals, and handmade treasures.

❋ Special Events

March: **Maple Sunday** (585-591-1190; www.mapleweekend.com), Various locations throughout the county. See Web site for map. Maple sugar producers from all over western New York and Wyoming County open their sugar houses for tours, demonstrations, and sampling.

August: **Attica Rodeo** (www.attica rodeo.com; e-mail: tickets@attica rodeo.com), Exchange Street arena just south of the village, Attica. Voted the number-one rodeo in the American Pro Rodeo Association in the Eastern States. This event, which includes cattle penning, barrel racing, horse shows, and team roping, has been an annual event in Attica for close to 50 years. **Attica Historical Society Peach Festival** (585-591-2161), Attica Historical Society, 130 Main Street, Attica. A fund raiser to benefit the Attica Historical Society.

ARCADE AND NORTH JAVA

This area was first settled by Silas Meech in 1807 and called China until 1866, when the name was changed to Arcade—possibly after the Reynold's Arcade Building in Rochester. Today the town is best known locally for the Arcade & Attica Railroad, one of the few steam train excursions in the state.

GUIDANCE Arcade Area Chamber of Commerce (585-492-2114; www.arcade chamber.org, www.arcadeny.org), 278 Main Street, Arcade. Open Monday, Tuesday, Thursday, and Friday 9–noon.

GETTING THERE *By car:* NY 16 from the Buffalo area or NY 98 from Attica to NY 39

MEDICAL EMERGENCY Dial 911

✳ To See

MUSEUMS AND HISTORIC HOMES The Gibby House-Arcade Historical Society (585-492-4466), 331 West Main Street, Arcade. Open Tuesday and Wednesday 10–4. This 1903 Victorian home is furnished to reflect the 1930s and 1940s. It houses exhibits and artifacts pertaining to the Arcade area.

Java Historical Society (585-457-9537), 4441 NY 78, Java. Open third Sunday of month 1–4 PM. Exhibits focus on local history and artifacts.

Sheldon Historical Society (585-457-9509), School House Museum, NY 78, Strykersville. Open Tuesday 1–4 July and August. A two-room, restored Queen Anne–style schoolhouse now features exhibits on local history.

✳ To Do

CROSS-COUNTRY SKIING See *Green Space—Nature Preserves:* **Beaver Meadow Nature Center.**

FISHING Both **Clear Creek** and **Cattaraugus Creek** are popular fishing spots for brown and rainbow trout in the Arcade area. Access to Clear Creek is off NY 39 at Church Street in downtown Arcade, behind the stores, and off Bray Road off NY 98 south. Fishing access on Cattaraugus Creek is off Hurdville Road north of NY 39, on East Arcade Road (CR 11) or Sullivan Road. Fishing licenses can be obtained at any town hall or at WalMart in Warsaw.

FAMILY FUN ✐ **Arcade & Attica Railroad** (585-492-3100 or 585-496-9877; www.anarr.com), 278 Main Street, Arcade. Excursions on Saturday–Sunday at 12:30 and 3; during July–August excursions on Wednesday, Friday, Saturday, Sunday 12:30 and 3. Admission $12 adults, $7 children 3–11, under 3 free. Take a 90-minute journey into railroad history on an authentic steam train. The rail line, which opened in the 1880s as a narrow-gauge railroad, was converted to standard gauge in 1895. Regular passenger service ceased in 1951; the excursion service started in 1962. On weekdays the line is still a working one, used to haul agricultural products. On weekends the excursions take place. Passengers enjoy a 14-mile ride from Arcade to Curriers and back on restored 1920s-era passenger cars, including an open gondola. The vintage Alco/Cooke 2-8-0 steam locomotive was built in 1920.

GOLF Owens Hills Golf Course (585-492-1800), 2304 Genesee Road, Arcade. A scenic 9-hole, par-36 course.

Turkey Run Golf Course (585-496-8888; www.turkeyrungolfcourse.com), 11836 Bixby Hill Road, Arcade. Nine holes—each hole par 3 to 5—amid the beautiful scenery of Arcade.

✳ Green Space

NATURE PRESERVES ✐ **Beaver Meadow Nature Center** (585-457-3228; www.buffaloaudubon.org), 1610 Welch Road, North Java. Open year-round, nature center Tuesday–Saturday 10–5, Sunday 1–5. Trails are always open. Suggested donation $3 individual, $5 family. This beautiful 324-acre sanctuary, sponsored by the Buffalo Audubon Society, offers year-round activities, including several seasonal festivals. There are 7 miles of marked walking/hiking trails as well as a boardwalk with handrails for the physically challenged. Lectures and demonstrations are offered year-round at the visitors center, which also houses exhibits and a discovery room for children and where a naturalist is on duty to answer questions. Picnic facilities are available. On the grounds you can view many types of animals as well as migrating birds and a variety of flora. Enjoy cross-country skiing and snowshoeing during the winter months. The nature center also has an observatory with a 20-inch-diameter astronomical telescope. The observatory is open to the public the first and third Saturday of the month, from April–December (observatory, 585-457-3104).

PARKS Fireman's Park (585-492-1111), North Street (NY 39), Arcade. This 11.75-acre park includes a playground, picnic tables, and a baseball diamond.

WALKING AND HIKING TRAILS See *Green Space—Nature Preserves:* **Beaver Meadow Nature Center**.

✳ Lodging

OTHER LODGING Beaver Meadow Family Campground (585-457-3101), 1455 Beaver Meadow Road, Java Center. Open May 1–Columbus Day. This family-oriented campground features 300 sites on 100 acres. Choose from rustic sites, along with water and electric sites with either 30 or 50 amps. Enjoy hiking on their acreage and fishing and swimming in their pond. Planned activities take place on weekends. $20/night rustic sites, $25 water and electric sites (20–30 amps), $28 water and electric sites (50 amps).

Yogi Bear's Jellystone Park of Western New York Camp Resort (585-457-9644 or 800-232-4039; www.wnyjellystone.com), 5204 Youngers Road, North Java. Open May–mid-October. This family-oriented camping resort features 200 campsites with both full and partial hookups, along with 11 chalets, 9 trailers, and 5 cabins. Facilities include two pools, a beach, mini golf, fishing lakes, bike rentals, a game room, camp store, live entertainment, and special theme weekends of activities. Campsites $20–$45, cabins and trailers $90–$135.

✴ Where to Eat

EATING OUT ✦ **Delightfulls** (585-492-0586), 496 West Main Street, Arcade. Open Monday–Thursday 6:30 AM–9 PM, Friday 6:30 AM–10 PM, Saturday 8 AM–10 PM, Sunday 8:30 AM–9 PM. This place is absolutely delightful—a coffee shop and gift shop rolled into one. Choose from gourmet coffees, ice cream, fresh baked goods, salads, homemade soup, and sandwiches. Before or after your meal, browse through their Victorian gift shop that features antiques, handcrafted and collectible items, plus gift items, country decor, children's clothing, and candles. During the warmer months dine on the outdoor patio.

The Gray Fox Tavern (585-492-1483), 246 Main Street (NY 39), Arcade. Open Monday–Friday 9 AM–2 AM, Saturday 10 AM–2 AM. Enjoy casual dining in a pub atmosphere. Specialties include homemade soups, Angus beef, prime rib, and seafood.

🐾 ✦ **Jenny Lee Diner** (585-496-5253), 563 West Main Street (NY 39) Arcade. Open daily 8 AM–9 PM. Step back in time to when bobby sox, poodle skirts, and jukeboxes were the rage, when you dine at this 1950s-style diner. Burgers and combo meals, along with daily specials can be found on the menu, along with ice cream selections. All kids meals include a free ice cream cone.

Lori's Bakery & Café (585-457-

3642), 3978 Main Street, Strykersville. Open Monday 8 AM–4 PM, Wednesday 6 AM–5 PM, Thursday 6 AM–6 PM, Friday and Saturday 6 AM–8 PM, and Sunday 8 AM–1 PM. A country bake shop with a small café that serves donuts, pastries, and other baked delights, plus specials for lunch and dinner.

✦ **The Village Café** (585-492-4608), 223 Liberty, Arcade. Open Monday 6 AM–4 PM, Tuesday–Saturday 6 AM–8:30 PM, Sunday 7 AM–8:30 PM. Enjoy home cooking at one of Arcade's finest casual restaurants. Stop in at this small diner for just a cup of coffee, or stay for a complete meal.

Village Pub Restaurant (585-457-9545), 3974 Main Street, Strykersville. Open daily 11–11. This casual, cozy tavern features steaks, seafood, pasta, and chicken served in a publike atmosphere. Daily specials include all-you-can-eat ribs on Sunday and all-you-can-eat crab legs on Monday. Homemade desserts also available.

✴ Selective Shopping

ANTIQUES **Needful Things** (585-457-3424), 3929 NY 78, Strykersville. Open Thursday–Saturday 11–5. Proprietor Judie Coffey has filled this small barn with all sorts of primitive and small antiques plus a selection of antique furniture.

SPECIAL SHOPS **At Wit's End** (585-457-9747), 383 Factory Road, Strykersville. Open Thursday–Sat 10-5, Thanksgiving–Christmas open daily. Antiques, primitives, seasonal decorations, Christmas ornaments, and other country goods can be found in this cute red cottage. The hand-stenciled walls add to the shop's country charm.

Cottrill's Pharmacy & Gift Shop (585-492-2310), 255 Main Street,

Arcade. Open Monday–Friday 9–8, Saturday 9–5. This store carries a wide selection, from health and beauty items to cards, gifts, frames, collectibles, candy, and seasonal items.

The Country Oven (585-492-1050), 277 Main Street, Arcade. Wednesday–Saturday 7–4. Choose from freshly made baked goods, including apple fritters, pies, cookies, and salt-rising bread.

Domes Gift Shop & Collectibles (585-492-1931), 397 NY 39 (Hurdville Road), Arcade. Gifts and collectibles abound in this barnlike structure. Choose from candles, flags, scrapbooking supplies, seasonal decorations, cards, country decor, wind chimes, and more.

1882 Mercantile (585-492-2188), 281 Main Street, Arcade. Browse through 8,000 square feet of antiques, collectibles, and fine crafts in a historic Main Street building.

Sign of the Pineapple (585-492-1500 or 877-424-1107), 285 Main Street, Arcade. Open Monday–Wednesday 10–5, Thursday 10–7, Friday 10–6, Saturday 9–5. Inside this 1854 building is a store featuring primitive country wares, collectibles, and furniture.

✴ **Special Events**

February: **Arcade's Winterfest** (585-492-2114), This event features a parade, snow sports, chili cook-off, rides, games, a craft show, and fun in the snow.

July: **Fabulous '50s Festival** Arcade (585-492-5534; www.fab50sfest.org), Downtown Arcade. Step back to the 1950s and enjoy live music, kids' activities, a huge car show, and even a sock hop.

September: **Homestead Festival,** Beaver Meadow Audubon Center. Learn about early American life through demonstrations.

WYOMING, WARSAW, AND VARYSBURG

One of the most unique places in western New York is the village of Wyoming, which has over 70 buildings on the National Historic Register and streets still lit with the original gas streetlights. Many of the historic structures are Federal and Greek Revival architectural styles. One of the more notable structures is the 1817 Middlebury Academy, the first institution of higher learning west of the Genesee River. It now houses the area's historical society. Wyoming was first settled by Silas Newell from Rensselaer County in 1809, and was originally called Newell's Settlement.

Warsaw, established in 1803, is the county seat and has a history of manufacturing, especially the salt industry. The town's earliest settlers arrived in 1803, and several of them constructed gristmills and sawmills along Oatka Creek. During the early to mid-1800s, many Warsaw citizens were actively involved in the abolitionist movement and the Underground Railroad.

Several theories abound as to how Warsaw got its name. Some suggest it came from the Native American word *wawarsing,* meaning "winding road," referring to Oatka Creek. Another theory suggests that the town was named after Warsaw, Poland, since it was not unusual to name American communities after foreign cities. A third conjecture is that the name comes from a popular book at the time of the Wyoming County's town founding: *Thaddeus of Warsaw*, by the Scottish novelist Jane Porter.

The Victorian architecture of the homes in the village reflects the prosperity the area saw at the turn of the 20th century. Today it is primarily an agricultural region, with dairy farms, apple orchards, and maple syrup producers dotting the countryside.

GUIDANCE Warsaw Chamber of Commerce (585-786-3730), PO Box 221, Warsaw 14569.

Town of Warsaw (585-786-2800), 5454 Kenney Road, Warsaw.

Village of Warsaw (585-786-2120), 15 South Main, Warsaw.

Wyoming County Historian (585-786-8818), 26 Linwood Avenue, Warsaw. Open Monday–Friday 10–5.

GETTING THERE *By car:* Varysburg and Warsaw are along U.S. 20A, Wyoming is on NY 19 between U.S. 20 and 20A.

MEDICAL EMERGENCY Dial 911

Wyoming County Community Healthcare System (585-786-8940 or 2233), 400 North Main Street, Warsaw.

✳ To See

MUSEUMS AND HISTORIC HOMES Middlebury Academy Museum (585-495-6582), South Academy Street, just south of Gulf Road (NY 19) Wyoming. Open Tuesday and Sunday 2–5 April–October. The Middlebury Academy, which now houses the Middlebury Historical Society, was the first school of higher learning west of the Genesee River when it opened in 1817. During its prime in the 1850s and 1860s the co-educational, nondenominational institution had about 200 students. The building now houses a collection of items depicting the early history of the town and surrounding communities.

MIDDLEBURY ACADEMY WAS THE FIRST SCHOOL OF HIGHER LEARNING WEST OF THE GENESEE RIVER WHEN IT OPENED IN 1817.

Christine A. Smyczynski

Warsaw Historical Society—The Seth M. Gates House (585-786-5240; www.warsawhistory.org), 15 Perry Avenue, Warsaw. Open Monday–Friday 10 AM–12 PM. A collection of exhibits on local history is housed in this 1824 home, which is on the Historic Register.

Warsaw Public Library (585-786-5650; www.warsaw.pls-net.org), 130 North Main Street, Warsaw. Open Monday–Tuesday 10–9, Wednesday–Thursday 2–5 and 7–9, Friday 1–6, Saturday 2–5. Constructed in 1904 with a grant from the Carnegie Foundation, this library has one of the only signed copies of the History of Woman Suffrage by Susan B. Anthony.

UNIQUE SITE **Wind Turbines,** Wethersfield Rd between North Java and Rock Glen. Ten gigantic wind turbines, one of only two "wind farms" in New York State, are located here, providing an environmentally friendly alternative-energy source.

✳ To Do

CROSS-COUNTRY SKIING **Byrncliff Resort** (585-535-7300; www.byrncliff .com), U.S. 20A, Varysburg. Enjoy cross-country skiing on 20 km of well-marked, groomed trails, with 7 km lit for night skiing. Ski rentals are available. There are also snowshoe trails on the 400-acre property.

See also **Beaver Meadow Audubon Center** and **Letchworth State Park.**

FISHING **Oatka Creek** is a popular place to fish for trout in this section of the county. Fishing licenses can be obtained at any town hall or at WalMart in Warsaw.

GOLF **Arrowhead Golf Course** (585-786-2221), 6022 Bauer Road, Warsaw. A public 9-hole, par-36 course.

Byrncliff Resort & Conference Center (585-535-7300; www.byrncliff.com), US 20A, Varysburg. Play 18 holes at Wyoming County's premier course. See also *Lodging.*

Hidden Acres Executive Golf (585-237-2190), 6269 US 20A, Warsaw. This picturesque course offers either 9 holes (par 28) or 18 holes (par 58).

HORSEBACK RIDING **Wolcott Farms** (585-786-3504; www.wolcottfarms.com or www.letchworthadventure.com), 3820 Hermitage Road, Warsaw. Horseback riding, pony rides, and wagon and carriage rides are offered at Trailside Lodge in Letchworth State Park Friday–Sunday and holidays, Memorial Day weekend through Columbus Day weekend. Horseback riding is also available on their farm, along with horse-drawn sleigh and wagon rides. A corn maze is open late summer and autumn.

✳ Green Space

NATURE PRESERVES **Carlton Hill Multiple Use Area** and **Sulphur Spring Hill Cooperative Hunting Area** Three miles north of Warsaw, off Dale Road or West Middlebury Road (For more information, call the NYS Department of Environmental Conservation 716-372-8678). Open dawn to dusk. Carton Hill is a 2,700-acre tract of mainly abandoned farmland owned by the state. The area is popular for hunting fishing, trapping, bird-watching, and cross-country skiing.

The adjacent 2,000 acre Sulphur Spring Hill supports a variety of small game as well as white-tailed deer.

PARKS Warsaw Village Park (585-786-2120), Liberty Street, Warsaw. Open dawn to dusk. A 32-acre park featuring nature trails, sports fields, a pool, and picnic facilities.

✳ Lodging

INNS AND RESORTS Byrncliff Resort (585-535-7300 www.byrn cliff.com), U.S. 20A, Varysburg. This year-round golf/cross-country skiing resort is located midway between Buffalo and Rochester, in the rolling hills of Wyoming County. Twenty-five comfortable motel rooms and one suite are available. Amenities include a miniature golf course, tennis courts, a heated outdoor pool, and hot tub. Ski or golf packages are available, and their restaurant serves steaks, seafood, and prime rib, as well as a Friday fish fry and Sunday brunch. $50/single, $60/double, $125/suite. See also *Golf* and *Winter Activities.*

The Hillside Inn (585-495-6800 or 800-544-2249; www.hillsideinn.com), 890 Bethany Road, Wyoming. Open year-round. Innkeepers Nancy and Bill Squier have created a paradise

among the hills of Wyoming County. Built as a health spa in 1851 and later converted to a private residence, the Hillside Inn offers 14 luxurious and elegant guest rooms, many with fireplaces, four-poster beds, balconies, and whirlpools. The mansion, set on 48 acres, has been fully restored to its original beauty. $81–$200. See also *Dining Out.*

Wyoming Inn (585-495-6470), 1 South Academy Street (NY 19), Wyoming. Open year-round. Built in 1838, this inn served as a stagecoach stop between Buffalo and Rochester. The inn, owned and operated by Nancy Swearinger, features seven comfortable rooms, each decorated with a different theme and three with Jacuzzi tubs. Breakfast is served to inn guests in the restaurant, which is open to the public. See also *Dining Out.* $70–$125.

✳ Where to Eat

DINING OUT Gaslight Village Café (585-495-6695), 1 North Academy (NY 19), Wyoming. Open for lunch Tuesday–Friday 11–2:30, Saturday 11–3, dinner Thursday–Saturday 5–9, Sunday 11–7. This fine-dining restaurant in the center of town recently reopened under new management. The menu features pasta, seafood, steaks, and more.

Hillside Inn (585-495-6800; www .hillsideinn.com), 890 East Bethany Road, Wyoming. Dining room open daily year-round, by reservation only, for breakfast (8:30–9:30 AM) and dinner (5–8 PM). Fine dining is offered in this elegant 1851 mansion. See also *Lodging: Inns and Resorts*.

The Valley Inn Restaurant (585-786-3820), 71 East Buffalo Street (US 20A), Warsaw. Open Monday–Saturday, lunch 11–2, dinner 4:30–8; Sunday open for brunch and dinner. Enjoy fine, upscale dining in an 1861 historic home. The menu features full four-course meals as well as à la carte selections.

✏ ❧ **Wyoming Inn** (585-495-6470) 1 South Academy Street (NY 19), Wyoming. Open Sunday 8–2, Thursday 8–8, Friday and Saturday 8–9; call for hours Tuesday and Wednesday. Built in 1838, this inn served as a stagecoach stop between Buffalo and Rochester. The inn offers two dining rooms where you can enjoy casual fine dining in a relaxed atmosphere. Choose from specialty sandwiches, subs, salads, and homemade soups for lunch, and steak and seafood entrées for dinner. Homemade pies are available for dessert. Overnight accommodations are also available; see *Lodging*.

EATING OUT **Felice** (585-495-6939), 40 North Academy (NY 19), Wyoming. Open Tuesday–Saturday 10–5. This small, intimate café, located in a beautifully renovated former auto repair garage, has gourmet coffee, lattes, chai, and cappuccino as well as panini sandwiches, wraps, salads, and gelato.

✳ Selective Shopping

ANTIQUES **Parkside Antiques** (585-786-3200), 8 West Buffalo Street (US 20A), Warsaw. Open Sunday 10–5. Located in a well-preserved downtown building, this shop features books, linens, kitchen items, toys, glassware, dishes, jewelry, tinware, postcards, and other vintage items.

SPECIAL SHOPS **Bea's Dolls & Collectibles** (585-786-5031), 11 Main Street (upstairs), Wyoming. Open Saturday 10–5, Sunday 12–4. A small shop with dolls, stuffed animals, and more.

The Curiosity Shoppe (585-786-3338), 243 Liberty Street, Warsaw. Open Saturday 10–4 or by appointment. Country home decor is featured in this shop.

Excentriciti Jewelry and Gifts (585-495-6522), 11 Main Street, Wyoming. Open Monday–Saturday 10–5, Sunday 12–4. Closed Thursday. This shop carries new and vintage jewelry, antiques, gift items, and more.

Gaslight Christmas Shop (585-495-6330), Tower Street (just off NY 19), Wyoming. Open Tuesday–Saturday 11–5, Sunday 12–5. Lit by gaslights, this shop—originally a fire hall—is stocked to its historic rafters with Christmas items from around the world. While they carry mainly Christmas items, there is also a selection of Thanksgiving and Halloween paraphernalia, garden items, jewelry, and candles. The building was a gift to the village by Lydia Avery Coonly Ward, a noted Chicago socialite, who summered here in her nearby estate. It is rumored that the building's 80-foot brick bell tower was once climbed by President Theodore Roosevelt, who visited Mrs. Ward here on several occasions.

The New Farm (585-786-5380), NY19 between Wyoming and Warsaw. Open Saturday and Sunday 10–5,

April–December. Over 50 artisans display their goods in two farm buildings. Choose from handmade crafts, antiques, fresh in-season produce, and food items.

Pine Creek Country Collectibles (585-495-6070), 7 South Academy (NY 19), Wyoming. Open Wednesday–Saturday 11–5. Primitive and early-American home decor items in a circa 1842 shop.

Silas Newell's Provisions (585-495-6650), 5 Gulf Road, Wyoming. Open Tuesday–Saturday 11–5, Sunday 12–5. In fall they are open seven days 10–5, Friday and Saturday until 8. Closed January–April. Named after the founder of Wyoming, the shop has the feel of a 19th-century country store. Choose from specialty gourmet items, candy, candles, and unique gifts.

Sinclair Pharmacy (585-786-2330) 75 N. Main Street, Warsaw. Open Monday–Friday 9–9, Saturday 9–5, Sunday 9–1. A drugstore with a nice gift shop.

Sugarbuzz (585-786-3560), 4 North Main, Warsaw. Open Monday, Tuesday, Thursday, Friday 9–7, Wednesday and Saturday 9–3. This shop carries fine chocolates, along with coffee, sweets, and treats.

✳ Special Events

September: **Apple Umpkin Festival** (585-495-9940; www.appleumpkin .com), Gaslight Village, Wyoming. Popular harvest festival the last weekend in September, featuring over 300 craft vendors, musical entertainment, antiques, food, and more.

SILVER LAKE AREA—Silver Springs, Perry, and Castile

The name "Silver Springs" is a combination of Silver Lake and the seven springs that run through it. In the late 1800s a "sea serpent" was discovered in Silver Lake, attracting people from all over for a glimpse of the creature. Actually, it was an elaborate hoax created by one A. B. Walker, proprietor of the Walker Hotel. Business was slow and Mr. Walker decided to capitalize on an Indian legend that told of a monster living below the surface of Silver Lake. Walker and a group of friends crafted a "monster" from canvas and wire and sunk it into the lake. One evening they spotted a fishing boat and, operating bellows and pulleys, made the monster rise from the lake. Terrified, the fishermen ran to town to tell everyone about their experience. Business in town boomed. The mystery of the monster was solved years later, when a fire broke out in the Walker Hotel, and the remnants of the creature were discovered. Aside from monster sightings, recreational activities are plentiful in the area along Silver Lake and at nearby Letchworth State Park.

The village of Silver Springs has been home to Morton Salt for over 100 years. New York always played an important role in salt production. In the early 1800s the concept of crystallizing salt in enclosed vacuum pans was developed in the Silver Springs salt mine. When the Erie Canal opened in 1825, salt was one of the principal cargoes transported. Today the state ranks third nationally in salt production, with five western and central New York counties—Genesee, Wyoming, Livingston, Steuben, and Schuyler—producing 2.4 million metric tons each year.

The first settler to the Perry area was John Woodward, although legend has it that he only stayed two years and left. The first permanent settler, Samuel Gates, arrived in the area in 1809. The town was originally called by several different names, until the name Perry, after General Oliver Hazzard Perry, a War of 1812 hero, was decided on. In its early days, the Perry area was a thriving mill community, with many mills located along Silver Lake. Today the town, located on a scenic plateau overlooking the Genesee and Oatka Valleys, is home to some of the largest dairy farms in New York. According to census records, there are actually more cows in Perry than people! Other farms in the area produce grain, corn, soybeans, and alfalfa. Perry is also a thriving arts and cultural community, home to the Wyoming County Council of the Arts as well as a 1914 Carnegie Library that also houses an art gallery.

Castile, named after Castile in Spain, was first settled in 1808 and incorporated as a town in 1821. The surrounding area is mainly rural agricultural, with some of the largest dairy farms in New York located here. Apples and potatoes are the main crops grown in the area. The region is also popular for outdoor recreation, with Letchworth State Park and Silver Lake nearby.

GUIDANCE **Town of Castile** (585-493-5130) 53 North Main Street, Castile.

Perry Area Chamber of Commerce (585-237-5040; www.perrychamber.com), PO Box 35, Perry 14530. No regular hours; contact by phone or through Web site.

Town of Perry (585-237-2241), 22 South Main Street, Perry.

GETTING THERE *By air:* See Getting There—Buffalo and Rochester

Perry Warsaw Airport (585-237-9938), 6522 US 20A, Perry. This airport has a paved, lit 3,500-foot runway and a 1,830-feet by 60-feet grass strip.

By car: These towns are accessible from US 20A and NY 39.

MEDICAL EMERGENCY Dial 911

✳ To See

ART MUSEUMS **Arts Council for Wyoming County** (585-237-3517; www.artswyco.org), 31 South Main Street, Perry. Open Monday–Friday 9–5. Rotating exhibits are featured here.

Stowell-Wiles Art Gallery (585-237-2243), Perry Public Library, 70 North Main Street, Perry. Open Monday, Wednesday, and Friday 1–8, Tuesday and Thursday 10–8, Saturday 9–1. The collection features the works of renowned 19th-century artists Lemuel and Irving Wiles, attracting people from all over the country.

MUSEUMS AND HISTORIC HOMES Castile Historical Society (585-493-5370), 17 Park Road East, Castile. Open Tuesday 9–noon and 1–3.

William Pryor Letchworth Museum, (585-493-2760), 1 Letchworth State Park, Castile. Open mid-May–October 10–5. Free admission. The circa 1912 museum was planned by William Pryor Letchworth as an expansion to his original Genesee Valley Museum, built in 1898. Located near the Middle Falls area of the park and the Glen Iris Inn, the museum houses a collection relating to the Native American and pioneer history of the Genesee Valley, including archeological and natural history displays. The Seneca council house, Nancy Jemison cabin, and the Mary Jemison statue and gravesite are located behind the museum. See also **Letchworth State Park.**

Wyoming Historical Pioneer Association Log Cabin Museum & School House (585-237-3001), Walker Road, Silver Lake. Open June–August, Saturday and Sunday 12–5. This log cabin, built to commemorate the pioneer days, contains several hundred artifacts from Wyoming County's early settlers.

✳ To Do

AUTO RACING Wyoming County International Speedway (585-237-2510, track; 585-237-2580, shop; www.wyomingcountyinternationalspeedway.com), 35 Adrian Road, Perry. Racing takes place Sundays at 2:30 May–September. Admission: $8–$16. This track features an asphalt oval and stock-car racing.

BALLOONING Balloons Over Letchworth (585-493-3340; www.balloonsover letchworth.com), 6645 Denton Corners Road, Castile. Open April–October. $200/person, group rates available. Balloons Over Letchworth offers a view guaranteed to be breathtaking. The balloons are launched in and around the park at either sunrise or two hours before sunset, when the winds are calm. The 1.5-hour flight will take you about 2,000 feet above the scenic park, so be sure to bring your camera or camcorder. At the ride's end, the chase crew will pick you

> **MARY JEMISON, "THE WHITE WOMAN OF THE GENESEE"**
> One of the more interesting historic figures associated with the Genesee Valley region is Mary Jemison, known as "the White Woman of the Genesee." Mary was born onboard ship about 1742, while her family was en route from Ireland to America. When she was 15 her family was captured and killed, but Mary's life was spared, and she spent the rest of her life living with Native people. Given the name Deh-ge-wa-nus, or Two Falling Voices, Mary had two Native American husbands. Her first was Delaware Chief Sheninjee, with whom she had two children. She traveled to the Genesee Valley before the Revolutionary War with her second husband, Seneca Chief Hio-ka-too and their children. She was given her own reservation in the Big Tree Treaty of 1797. Her life story, *A Narrative of the Life of Mary Jemison*, by James E. Seaver, M.D., was first published in 1824.

up at the landing site (you never know exactly where you'll land due to wind direction), and after a customary champagne toast, they'll drive you back to your vehicle.

CROSS-COUNTRY SKIING See Letchworth State Park and Silver Lake State Park in *Green Space—Parks.*

FAMILY FUN **Silverland Park Roller Rink and Fun Center** (585-237-5171; www.silverlandpark.com), Walker Road, Perry. Open September–April Friday 6–9 family skate, Saturday–Sunday 11–5 general skate $4, They also have a Saturday evening skate $4 6–9 PM, $5 admission and a teen dance from 9 PM–12 AM $5 admission ($8 for both). Check voice mail message for hours May–August. This popular roller rink and fun center has been family owned since 1887.

FISHING **Wiscoy** and **East Koy Creeks** are popular fishing spots—Wiscoy is one of the state's premier streams for wild brown trout—along with year-round fishing for bass and northern pike at Silver Lake. The trout pond at Letchworth State Park is another popular fishing hole. Some of the access points on East Koy Creek include near the bridge at NY 78 at Hermitage Road, the bridge on Hardy's Road (CR 10), Green Bay Road, and Shearing Road. Fishing access on the Wiscoy Creek include Beardsley Park rest area (NY 39 near Pike), Water Street (CR 50), Main Street (NY 19 by Pike Library), and East Koy Road (CR 24). Fishing licenses can be obtained at any town hall or at WalMart in Warsaw.

GOLF **Murph's Driving Range** (585-237-2200), 204 South Main Street (NY 39) Perry.

Rolling Acres Recreational Resort (585-567-8557), 7795 Dewitt Road, Pike. This place is a dream come true for golfers who truly like roughing it. Along with a scenic 18-hole, par-71 course there are 100 wooded campsites. See *Other Lodging: Camping.*

MARINAS **Silver Lake Marine** (585-237-5185; www.silverlakemarine.com), 4213 West Lake Road, Silver Springs.

MOTORCROSS RACING **Silver Springs Motorcross Racing** (585-786-2087; www.ssmxracing.com), 5666 Fuller Road, Rock Glen. Racing takes place on select Saturdays and Sundays June–August. This family-run facility features a professionally groomed track, bike wash station, modern bathrooms and showers, food concessions, a picnic pavilion, and a camping area.

WHITE-WATER RAFTING *☞* **Adventure Calls Outfitters** (585-343-4710 or 888-270-2410; www.adventure-calls.com), Letchworth State Park. Open April–early November Saturday, Sunday, and holidays; late June–August 30 Tuesday–Friday 10:30 AM. Fee: April–May and October $27, June–September $25. Wetsuits will be required in early spring and late fall and can be rented for a nominal fee. Take a 5.5-mile-long whitewater ride on the Genesee River through the "Grand

Canyon of the East," Letchworth State Park. This is a fairly calm ride, so it's perfect for novices or families with children. Enjoy spectacular scenery while cooling off on a warm day. If the water level is too low for whitewater rafting in the summer months, you can take a trip through the gorge on canoes or "funyaks."

✳ Green Space

PARKS Castile Village Park (585-493-5340), Liberty Street, Castile. Open dawn to dusk. This 16-acre park features a playground, picnic tables, tennis and basketball courts, a baseball diamond, and horseshoe pits.

Letchworth State Park (585-493-3600), 1 Letchworth State Park, Castile. Open dawn to dusk. Admission: $7/car parking. Letchworth State Park is known as the "Grand Canyon of the East." There are many scenic overlooks along the 600-foot deep gorge, and the Genesee River—one of the few rivers in the Northern Hemisphere that flows north—goes over 20 different waterfalls, including 3 major ones, as it snakes through the gorge. The 14,350-acre, 17-mile-long park has 66 miles of hiking trails as well as trails for horseback riding, biking, snowmobiling, and cross-country skiing. Campers also love this park: 270 campsites and 80 cabins are available. Naturalists and guides are on hand for lectures and workshops on the history, geology, flora, and fauna in the area. In summer the park has picnic areas, playgrounds, and two swimming pools. Winter visitors enjoy ice skating, snowmobiling, cross-country skiing, snow tubing, and horse-drawn sleigh rides. Deer and spring turkey hunting are permitted in-season. The park also offers "step-on" guide service for bus tour groups who visit the park. A staff member will board the bus and guide the group through the park on a two-hour tour, including information on the history and nature of Letchworth. The park is named for William Pryor Letchworth, a Buffalo businessman who donated the park's original 1,000 acres to the state in1859. Located within the park is Letchworth's former country home, the Glen Iris Inn.

KNOWN AS THE GRAND CANYON OF THE EAST FOR ITS 600-FOOT-DEEP GORGE, LETCHWORTH STATE PARK IS ESPECIALLY SPECTACULAR IN FALL.
Christine A. Smyczynski

Barney Kalisz Park (585-584-3565), Park Avenue, Perry. Park facilities include picnic tables, playground, sports field, and a beach on the eastern shore of Silver Lake.

Silver Lake State Park (585-237-6310), West Lake Road off NY 19A, Silver Springs. This park features fishing, hunting, picnic areas, a boat launch, and cross-country skiing.

PONDS AND LAKES Silver Lake is a popular year-round recreational destination. During the warmer months enjoy canoeing, kayaking, jet skiing, wake boarding, sailing, swimming, waterskiing, wind surfing, and fishing on the 836-acre lake. When the lake freezes over in the winter, ice fishing is a favorite pastime.

WALKING AND HIKING TRAILS See **Letchworth State Park** in *Green Space—Parks.*

✳ Lodging

INNS AND RESORTS Glen Iris Inn (585-493-2622; www.glenirisinn.com), 7 Letchworth State Park, Castile. Open seasonally from Good Friday to the last Sunday in October. This beautiful inn, once the home of William Pryor Letchworth, has been welcoming guests since 1914 with luxurious accommodations and a wonderful view of the park's Middle Falls. The inn's restaurant, Caroline's Dining Room, is open to the public for breakfast, lunch, and dinner. The Victorian gift shop on the first floor of the inn has a selection of unique gifts and Letchworth State Park souvenirs. Efficiency rooms are also available at the nearby Pinewood Lodge. Inn $70–$135, lodge $60. See **Letchworth State Park** in *Green Space—Parks.*

MOTELS Colonial Motel (585-493-5700), 6544 NY 19A, Portageville. Open year-round. Brian and Giuliana Walton offer 14 newly remodeled rooms in this country-setting motel just 1 mile from Letchworth State Park. Each air-conditioned room has cable TV and two double beds. $60–$70.

Park Lake Motel (585-237-3654), 55 North Main Street, Perry. Open year-round. Located in the heart of the village, this motel features 12 clean, spacious rooms, all with refrigerators and microwaves along with the standard telephones, cable TV, and air conditioning. Three of the rooms have king-sized beds and full kitchens. $49–$79.

BED & BREAKFASTS Little Bit of Heaven Bed & Breakfast (585-493-2434; www.littlebitofheaven.net), 21 South Main Street, Silver Springs. Open year-round. Innkeeper Donald Kemp offers four unique antiques-furnished rooms with private baths in an elegant 1895 Victorian house built by the first mayor of Silver Springs. The inn, situated on beautifully landscaped grounds, has two enclosed porches plus a large living room and front parlor. $65–$95.

CAMPING Four Winds Campground (585-493-2794; E-mail: 4winds@wycol.com) 7350 Tenefly Road, Portageville. Open May–October. Just 3 miles from Letchworth State Park, this 235-acre campground has full hookups, modern rest rooms, and picnic areas. $27.50–$29.50.

Letchworth State Park (800-456-2267, cabin and campsite reservations). Open year-round. The park has 270 electrified campsites and 82 cabins. See *Green Space—Parks.*

Rolling Acres Recreational Resort (585-567-8557), 7795 Dewitt Road, Pike. Open May 1–October 15. One hundred wooded campsites are available here. $6.75/night plus metered electric. See *Golf.*

Zintel & Norris Campground (585-237-3080 or 237-6629), 156 Lakeshore Drive, Castile. Open May 1–October 15. Located on beautiful Silver Lake, this 32-site, family-run campground is a great spot for anglers. Facilities include hot water showers, playground, boat launch, and dock space. $12/night tents, $25/campers, $17/sites with sewer hookups.

COTTAGE RENTALS & **Meadow Wood Acres Guest House** (585-786-8312 or 800-724-1932), 6628 Denton Corners Road, Castile. This two-bedroom cottage on 10 acres near Letchworth State Park is available for rental year-round on a weekly basis. $500/week.

✳ Where to Eat

DINING OUT **Caroline's** (585-493-2622), 7 Letchworth State Park (at the Glen Iris Inn), Castile. Open Good Friday–last weekend of October, daily for breakfast, lunch, and dinner; hours vary according to season. Reservations are suggested. Enjoy American regional cuisine for breakfast, lunch, or dinner at Caroline's, which was named in tribute to Caroline Bishop, Mr. Letchworth's secretary and executive assistant. See *Lodging.*

The Lumberyard Restaurant and Lounge (585-237-3160), 18 South Federal Street, Perry. Open for lunch Tuesday–Friday 11–3; dinner Tuesday and Thursday 4:30–9, Friday 4:30–10, Saturday 3–10, Sunday 12–9; Sunday brunch 10–2. Enjoy fine dining in an authentic lumberyard converted into an inviting restaurant. The Hawley Lumber Company was founded in 1901, and the dining hall is located in what was the lumberyard's main shed, built in 1923. Its sizeable doorways allowed for wagons, and later trucks, to be driven in from one end, loaded up, and driven out the other. Menu selections include veal cordon bleu,

prime rib, and seafood, plus such lighter fare as burger, sandwiches, and wings. A children's menu is also available.

EATING OUT & ♂ ❦ **Charcoal Corral Restaurant** (585-237-3372; www.charcoalcorral.com), 7109 Chapman Road (NY 39), Perry. Open seasonally March–October. Enjoy family dining, plus soft and hard ice cream served in the ice cream parlor at this large, popular restaurant with an Old West theme. Choose from burgers, hot dogs, wings, sandwiches, subs, and pizza. Facilities include an 18-hole miniature golf course, video-game arcade, and the Silver Lake Twin Drive-In Theater.

❦ **Country Kitchen** (585-237-5640), 1 South Main Street (NY 39) Perry. Open Monday–Saturday 5:30 AM–9 PM, Sunday 5:30 AM–8 PM. Dine in a family-style restaurant with country decor that features homemade cooking and daily specials.

❦ ♂ & **The Hole in the Wall** (585-237-3003), 7056 Standpipe Road (off NY 39, south of town near the Family Dollar Plaza), Perry. Open Wednesday and Thursday 7–8, Friday and Saturday 7–9, Sunday 7–8; closed Monday and Tuesday. This restaurant, established in 1932, got its name from World War II servicemen, who would ask for direction to that little "hole in the wall" in Perry, formerly located on Main Street. During wartime, owner George Dovolous decided to provide free meals to servicemen since he himself had two sons serving in the military. After the war the name was officially adopted for the restaurant. The tradition continues, and any serviceman or -woman who comes to the restaurant in full uniform is given one free meal. Menu selections include perennial favorites like roast beef and roast pork dinners, honey-dipped fried chicken, and grilled haddock, along with stir fries, pastas, Greek entrées, salads, and sandwiches. They also have a full bar and banquet rooms available.

❧ **J & C Luncheonette,** 13 North Main Street, Perry. Open for breakfast and lunch. This tiny diner, operated by Carol and Joe Lanzone, is a place where regulars come for coffee every morning to catch up on the news in town. They serve breakfast anytime, along with hot dogs, sandwiches, and fountain treats.

♫ ♿ ❧ **Silver Lake Family Restaurant** (585-237-5840), 34 South Main Street (NY 39), Perry. Open 8 AM– 9 PM seven days. Enjoy casual dining in a large, modern, comfortable family atmosphere. Selections from their extensive menu include burgers, sandwiches, Italian and Greek dishes, daily specials, and twenty flavors of hard ice cream for dessert.

❧ **Susan's Family Restaurant** (585-493-9410), 6240 NY 19A, Castile. Open Tuesday–Thursday 11–7:30, Friday 11–8:30, Saturday 8–7:30, Sunday 8–5. Enjoy fresh homemade selections, from appetizers to desserts, in this small family diner. They are especially noted for their salads.

✳ Selective Shopping

ANTIQUES The Farmer's Wife Craft and Antique Co-op (585-237-3311), 49 South Federal Street, Perry. Open April–July, Monday–Saturday 9–5, Sunday 11–4; August–December Tuesday–Saturday 9–5, Sunday 11–4; January–March Wednesday–Saturday 9–5, Sunday 11–3. More than 60 ven-

dors sell their wares in this 6,000-square-foot former feed mill. Antiques, vintage collectibles, primitives, handmade gifts, candles, plants, and hanging baskets are among the many choices.

Light Year Behind & Friends at the Hall (585-237-6540), 2817 NY 246 (At U.S. 20A), Perry Center. Open Thursday–Sunday 11–5. This shop in the former Perry Grange Hall features antique lighting and repairs plus an assortment of antiques and collectibles. They even have a bargain basement.

Silver Lake Sampler (585-237-3965), 35-37 Main Street, Perry. Open Wednesday–Saturday 11–4, Sunday 1–4. Antiques, crafts, linens, books, glassware, pottery, quilts, silver, furniture, paintings, and primitives fill this store, located in a vintage Main Street building.

FARM MARKETS Perry Farmers Market (www.villageofperry.com), NY 39, downtown Perry. Open Saturday 8:30 AM–12:30 PM July–October. Featuring local produce, jellies, honey, maple products, baked goods, and more. The market also features live music, children's activities, and displays and demonstrations by local artisans.

SPECIAL SHOPS Bush Hill Florist and Gift Shoppe (585-237-2550), 2 North Main Street, Perry. Open Monday–Saturday 10–5, Thursday until 6. Choose from a large selection of gift items, flags, cards, and birdhouses—and, of course, fresh floral arrangements and cut flowers.

Stonewall Craftique (585-237-5835), 4286 NY 39, Castile. Open Wednesday–Sunday 10–5 April–December. Visit this classic barn filled with all sorts of gift items, including Park Design textiles, River Hill and Salmon Forest pottery, Crazy Mountain imports, and Silver Forest Jewelry.

✳ Special Events

May: **Fire on the Genesee** (585-493-3600), Highbanks Recreation area, Letchworth State Park. Civil War encampment and battle re-enactments.

July: **Ring of Fire** (585-237-5040) Silver Lake. Area residents light flares on their property along Silver Lake, followed by a fireworks display. **Highbanks Celtic Gathering** (585-493-3600), Letchworth State Park. Highland Games, bagpipe competition, Celtic crafts, and more. **Sea Serpent Balloon Festival** (585-237-5040; www.perrychamber.com), Perry. A fun-filled family-oriented festival, featuring hot-air balloon rides, live entertainment, children's activities, arts and crafts, and more.

August: **Stone Tool Technology Show** (585-493-3600), Letchworth State Park. Flint-knapping and tool-making demonstrations, along with a 19th-century mountain-man encampment. **Wyoming County Fair** (585-493-5626), Town of Pike, NY 19. This fair highlights livestock, antique farm equipment, and Wyoming County history.

October: **Letchworth Arts and Crafts Show and Sale** (Arts Council for Wyoming County, 585-237-3517), Highbanks Recreation Area, Letchworth State Park. This annual craft show takes place on Columbus Day weekend and offers more than 300 arts and craft vendors, food, and live entertainment.

CHAUTAUQUA COUNTY

When you hear the word "Chautauqua," what comes to mind? The lake with its waterfront activities? The entire county with its many attractions? Or the Chautauqua Institution, which has offered a summer program in art, culture, and recreation for well over 100 years. Chautauqua is all of this plus a whole lot more.

If you enjoy the great outdoors, Chautauqua County has a total of five lakes in the county—Erie, Chautauqua, Findley, Bear, and Cassadaga—which are popular with fishermen, recreational boaters, and swimmers. Tour Chautauqua Lake by boat, enjoy nature at the Jamestown Audubon Nature Center, or explore ancient rock formations at Panama Rocks. The county boasts over 150 parks as well as dozens of golf courses. Winter-sports enthusiasts can enjoy skiing at Peek'n Peak and Cockaigne, or explore the county's 400 miles of snowmobile trails.

Chautauqua is rich in history, with many museums and historical sites to explore, including the McClurg Museum, the 1891 Fredonia Opera House, and the Dunkirk Lighthouse. The county, founded in 1808, was named after Lake Chautauqua, which comes from the Native American word *Jad-da'gwah*, which loosely translated means "bag tied in the middle," referring to the shape of the lake. The county is noted for its many bed & breakfast inns plus a large concentration of antiques shops.

If you want intellectual stimulation, spend some time at the Chautauqua Institution, which offers theater, entertainment, lectures, seminars, and more during its nine-week summer season.

ALONG LAKE ERIE—Silver Creek, Irving, Forestville, Dunkirk, Fredonia, Westfield, and Ripley

Some of Dunkirk's earliest settlers arrived by lake over the frozen ice, many earning their living as fishermen or sailors, as Dunkirk was considered one of the finest harbors on Lake Erie. Today's visitors still enjoy fishing, boating, and other water-related recreational activities, including tours of a historic lighthouse. Dunkirk was later designated the western terminus of the New York & Erie Railway, and by the early 1900s, six railroads served the city.

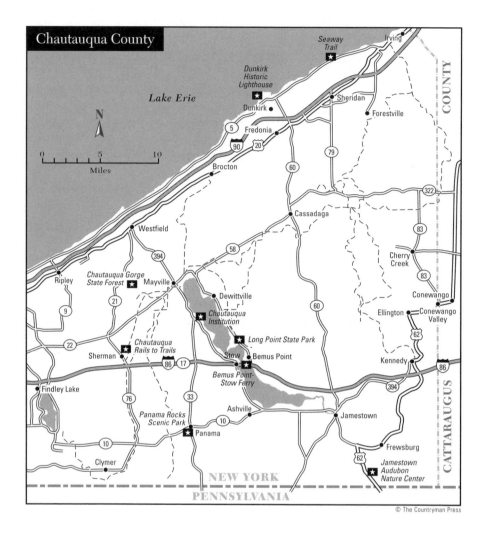

Chautauqua County

Lake Erie

N

0   5   10
Miles

Seaway Trail ⭐

Irving

Dunkirk Historic Lighthouse ⭐

Sheridan

Forestville

Dunkirk

Fredonia   5

90   20

79

Brocton   60

Cassadaga   322

83

Westfield   58

394

Cherry Creek

83

Chautauqua Gorge State Forest ⭐   Mayville

Ripley

21

Dewittville   Conewango

9   Chautauqua Institution ⭐   60   Ellington   Conewango Valley

22   Chautauqua Rails to Trails ⭐   Long Point State Park ⭐   62

Sherman   86   17   Stow   Bemus Point   Kennedy   86

Bemus Point-Stow Ferry ⭐   394

Findley Lake   76

33   Ashville   Jamestown

Panama Rocks Scenic Park ⭐   10

10   Panama   Frewsburg

Clymer   62   Jamestown Audubon Nature Center ⭐

NEW YORK

PENNSYLVANIA

ERIE COUNTY

CATTARAUGUS

© The Countryman Press

During the early part of the 19th century, much of the area now known as Fredonia was a wilderness. Settlers came to the area and began setting up homesteads along Canadaway Creek, where pioneer children delighted in discovering that if they touched fire to the strange bubbles that formed in the creek, flames would result. The "bubbles" were, of course, natural gas. In 1821 a gas well was sunk along the creek, and natural gas was used to illuminate Fredonia—the first village to do so in the nation. Fredonia was also home to the first farmer's grange in the country; Grange #1 is located on West Main Street. The village was also the birthplace of the Women's Christian Temperance Union. Today Fredonia is home to SUNY Fredonia, ranked one of the top 10 public universities in the North. The college has a nationally known School of Music as well as several other professional courses of study.

Westfield, a town filled with many Victorian homes from the early 1800s, is a great place to hunt for antiques, stop for a meal, or shop for fresh produce and crafts. It is also an area rich in history. It was the first European settlement in Chautauqua County, and it is here that young Grace Bedell advised Abraham Lincoln to grow a beard. President Lincoln's secretary of state, William Seward, built his mansion here, which is now a luxurious inn. Agriculturally, this section of New York is a large grape-producing region. Welch's was founded in nearby Westfield, and many small wineries have established themselves here. Dr. Thomas Welch, founder of Welch's Foods, built his first grape juice factory in Westfield, since this region is second only to California in grape production.

A small Amish community is located between Westfield and Stockton. Many Amish sell furniture, breads, and quilted items from their homes. Look for signs by homes on Thayer, Burdick, Finley, and Dean Roads.

Silver Creek, which is located in the Town of Hanover, was a large Native American settlement prior to the arrival of the Europeans in 1796. The first permanent settler was Amos Sottle, a surveyor for the Holland Land Company. Early industries included shipping, lumber, grain-cleaning machinery, and grape farming.

AREA CODE The area code is 716.

GUIDANCE よ **Chautauqua County Tourism** (716-357-4569 or 800-242-4569; www.tourchautauqua.com), PO Box 1441, Chautauqua Institution Main Gate, 1 Massey Avenue (off NY 394), Chautauqua, NY 14722. Open Daily 9–5, year-round.

よ **Chautauqua County Chamber of Commerce** (716-366-6200; www .chautauquachamber.org), 212 Lake Shore Drive West, Dunkirk, NY 14048. Open Monday–Friday 8–4:30.

Forestville Chamber of Commerce (716-965-2914), PO Box 415, Forestville, NY 14062. You can get information by calling or writing them.

Fredonia Chamber of Commerce (716-679-1565; www.fredoniachamber.org), 5 East Main Street, Fredonia, NY 14063. Open Tuesday and Thursday 9–1. They also have a information booth in Barker Commons during the summer months.

SUNY Fredonia (716-673-3251, 800-252-1212; www.fredonia.edu), 280 Central Avenue, Fredonia, NY 14063.

Silver Creek-Irving Chamber of Commerce (716-934-7748; www.townof hanover.org), PO Box, 434 Silver Creek, NY 14136. Inquiries by phone or through Web site.

よ **Westfield & Barcelona Chamber of Commerce** (716-326-4000; www .westfieldny.com), PO Box 25, Westfield, NY 14757. Information is available by phone year-round. Between Memorial Day and Labor Day, a large tourist information booth is open daily 9–6 at Barcelona Harbor, NY 5.

GETTING THERE *By car:* New York State Thruway (I-90) exits 58–61 access this region.

By bus: While bus transportation is available in and out of the region, there are no actual bus stations. If you need bus service, you can call one of the following to arrange transportation to or from a mutually agreed on location. **Greyhound**

Bus Lines (716-855-7531 or 800-231-222; www.greyhound.com), **Empire Bus** (Buffalo to Jamestown 716-665-3076) **NY Trailways** (716-852-1750).

GETTING AROUND *By car:* NY 5 and NY 20 are the main roads along the Lake Erie Shore.

By bus: Chautauqua Area Regional Transit (800-556-8553) Dunkirk.

MEDICAL EMERGENCY Dial 911.

Brooks Memorial Hospital (716-366-1111; www.brookshospital.com) 529 Central Avenue, Dunkirk.

Lakeshore Hospital (716-934-2654), NY 5 and 20, Irving.

Westfield Memorial Hospital (716-326-4921; www.wmhinc.org), 189 East Main Street, Westfield.

✳ To See

ART MUSEUMS **Adams Art Gallery** (716-366-7450; www.adamsart.org), 600 Central Avenue, Dunkirk. Open Wednesday–Thursday 11–4, Friday 11–5, Saturday and Sunday 1–4. A community arts center with a variety of media on display, including sculpture, paintings, prints, photography, and watercolors. The gallery also features educational programs, community events, and concerts.

Patterson Library (716-326-2154), 40 South Portage Street, Westfield. Open Monday, Tuesday, Thursday 9–8, Wednesday, Friday, Saturday 9–5. The Patterson Gallery presents about eight exhibits each year that highlight the visual and performing arts. The main exhibit area is located in an octagonal room on the lower level of the library.

Rockefeller Arts Center Gallery (716-673-3537), SUNY Fredonia. Open during the academic school year Wednesday–Sunday 2–8 pm. Exhibits feature the works of SUNY art students as well as other regional artists.

MUSEUMS AND HISTORIC HOMES **ALCO-Brooks Railroad Display**, (716-366-3797; www.railroad.net/dkny/display.html), 1089 Central Avenue (Chautauqua County Fairgrounds), Dunkirk. Open by Appointment or during the fair in July. Features a 1916 locomotive constructed at the American Locomotive Company's Brooks Works in Dunkirk, a Delaware & Hudson wood-sided boxcar, a New York Central wooden caboose, and other railroad artifacts.

Dunkirk Historical Museum (716-366-3797), 513 Washington Avenue, Dunkirk. Open Monday–Friday 12–4. A collection of memorabilia and artifacts related to Dunkirk's early days.

Fredonia Historical Museum (716-672-2114), 20 East Main Street, Fredonia. Open Tuesday–Saturday 1–5, Tuesday and Thursday until 7. The museum, housed in the original 1821 Leverett Barker Home, features exhibits and artifacts relating to the history of Fredonia and surrounding areas.

McClurg Museum (Chautauqua County Historical Society) (716-326-2977), Village Park, NY 20 and 394, Westfield. Open Tuesday–Saturday 10–4 or by appointment. This 16-room mansion, listed on the National Register of Historic Places, is filled with furnishings and artifacts from the Chautauqua County Historical Society's collection. The home was built between 1818–1820 by James McClurg, a wealthy man from Pittsburgh. Unlike most settlers who built simple log homes, he wanted to provide his family with stately living quarters. When the last of McClurg's descendants died, the home was left to the village of Westfield to be used as a public building.

HISTORIC SITES Lincoln Bedell Statue, Moore Park, Westfield. These statues, sculpted by Westfield native Don Sottile, depict the meeting between 12-year old Grace Bedell and Abraham Lincoln at the Westfield train station on February 16, 1861. Miss Bedell wrote President-elect Lincoln a letter, suggesting that he should grow a beard to improve his appearance. At the meeting, Lincoln shook her hand, kissed her, and asked how she liked the whiskers.

The Fantastic Sea Lion Ship (www.madbbs.com/users/iflyhigh747/thefantastic sealion; E-mail: sealionbarcelonany@madbbs.com), Barcelona Harbor, Westfield. This ship, which was a multiperson effort in the 1960s and 1970s, is a replica of a 16th-century sailing vessel and built in the same manner as ships in that century. Commissioned in 1985, the ship sailed on Chautauqua Lake for several years, until the group who built it sold it to the Buffalo Maritime Society. It was then towed across Lake Erie to Buffalo, where it sank in 1999. A year later volunteers from the Westfield area raised the ship and towed it back to Barcelona Harbor, where it's currently undergoing restoration.

ARCHITECTURE Fredonia's downtown historic district has numerous buildings of architectural distinction. A walking tour guide, *Downtown Historic Fredonia,* can be obtained from the chamber of commerce (716-679-1565; www.fredoniachamber.org). Some notable buildings include the **Fredonia Grange** (1915), 58 West Main Street, **Tower Gifts** (1878), 44 Temple Street; and **Fredonia Village Hall** (1891); now known as the **1891 Fredonia Opera House,** 9–11 Church Street.

Lana's The Little House (716-965-2798; www.lanasthelittlehouse.com), PO Box 267, Forestville. Open year-round by appointment. This hand-crafted storybook English cottage is set on 21 acres of rolling meadows and rambling gardens. Though built in the early 1980s, the look is centuries-old English countryside. Owner Lana Lewis, who purchased the house in 2001, decided that a home this unique should be shared with the public, so she opened it up for tours, retreats, and teas. It is also an ideal

THESE CHARMING STATUES DEPICT THE MEETING BETWEEN 12-YEAR-OLD GRACE BEDELL AND ABRAHAM LINCOLN
Christine A. Smyczynski

backdrop for photos. The house has been featured in many articles in newspapers and magazines, including *House Beautiful Weekend Homes*.

LIGHTHOUSES **Barcelona Lighthouse,** East Lake Road (NY 5), Barcelona. This privately owned 40-foot-high stone lighthouse in Barcelona Harbor was commissioned in 1829. It was first lit with oil, but when natural gas was discovered nearby two years later, the lighthouse became the first public building in the United States to be illuminated by natural gas. It was decommissioned in 1859 and auctioned off to private owners in 1872. Visitors to the area can view the lighthouse from along the road or adjacent **Daniel Reed Memorial Pier.**

Dunkirk Historical Lighthouse and Veteran's Park Museum (716-366-5050; www.netsync,net/users/skipper), Point Drive North, Dunkirk. Open May,

CHAUTAUQUA–LAKE ERIE WINE TRAIL

The area of western New York between Silver Creek and the Pennsylvania state line is the largest grape growing region in the East. The 20-mile-long Chautauqua–Lake Erie Wine Trail is home to eight wineries in New York plus four additional wineries just across the Pennsylvania border. Due to glacial ridges and rich gravel loam soil along Lake Erie's shore, left behind after the ice age, this region is perfect for grape growing.

The first vineyard was planted in Chautauqua County by Elijah Fay in 1818, and the first winery was opened by his son in 1859. But wine production was short lived, due to the Woman's Temperance Movement, which was established in nearby Fredonia. It was during this time that Dr. Charles Welch arrived in Westfield, a town with a large concentration of Concord grapes. Like his father, Welch was a teetotaler, and back in Vineland, New Jersey, the family had experimented in creating a nonalcoholic grape beverage, which they called Dr. Welch's Unfermented Wine. The younger Welch changed the name to Welch's Grape Juice, introduced it at the Columbian Exposition in Chicago, then moved his grape pasteurizing equipment to Westfield and founded the Welch's Juice Company. Welch's still produces juices, jellies, and syrups from Chautauqua County grapes.

In the 1970s winemaking made a comeback in the county due to the passage of the Farm Winery Act of 1976, which allowed grape farmers to produce up to 50,000 gallons of wine per year. Several small wineries were established, and new varieties of grapes were introduced into the region.

The Chautauqua–Lake Erie Wine Trail hosts numerous theme weekends throughout the year, such as Wine and Chocolates in February, Wine and Strawberries in June, and Wine, Wreaths, and Ornaments in November. For tickets or more information, see www.chautauquawinetrail.org, or call the Fredonia Opera House, 716-679-1891.

June, September, and October Thursday–Saturday and Monday and Tuesday 10–2 (last tour at 1). Open July–August Thursday–Saturday and Monday and Tuesday 10–4 (last tour at 2:30). Admission: $5 adults, $2 children 4–12 for tours; $1 per person to tour grounds only. A lighthouse was first established on Point Gratiot in 1827 to ensure the safety of Dunkirk Harbor. The present lighthouse, a 61-foot stone tower with an attached-brick keepers dwelling, was constructed in 1876. Visitors to the lighthouse will learn about what life was like for 19th-century lighthouse keeper's and also have the opportunity to climb the 55-step spiral staircase to the top of the tower. It is rumored that the ghost of a lighthouse keeper, who drowned while trying to save some children, roams the tower. A display of veterans' memorabilia honors those who served in the armed forces.

WINERIES **Blueberry Sky Farm Winery** (716-252-6535; www.blueberrysky farm.com), 10243 Northeast Sherman Road, South Ripley. Open Monday–Saturday 10–6, Sunday 12–5. A small family-owned winery located on a 70-acre blueberry farm, specializing in over two-dozen award-winning sweet and dry fruit wines. Flavors include blueberry, dandelion, and even honey. Fruit is carefully picked and processed by hand in the winery kitchen.

Johnson Estate Winery (716-326-2191; www.johnsonwinery.com), 8419 West Main Road, Westfield. Open seven days 10–6 year-round. The 200-acre Johnson Estate, which has been growing grapes for over a century, overlooks Lake Erie and is in one of the finest wine-growing climates in the state. Established in 1961, the winery is the oldest exclusively estate winery in New York. Like fine European wines, the wines of Johnson Estate are grown, vinified, and bottled in the château tradition. This means that the entire process is done at the winery rather than being shipped out to other locations, so the quality is under the Johnson family's direct control, which makes for a superb quality wine. Be sure to sample their signature wine, *Liebeströpfchen* ("Little Love Drops"), first produced in 1961.

Merritt Estate Winery (716-965-4800 or 888-965-4800; www.merrittestate winery.com), 2265 King Road, Forestville. Free tours and tastings year-round daily 10–5, Sunday 1–5. Local grapes are harvested, crushed, and fermented under the direction of William and Jason Merritt to produce fine wines. This winery features a large tasting room and a gift shop featuring a selection of wine and wine-related items. Some of their wines include Chautauqua White, Bella Rosa, and Late Harvest Delaware.

Roberian Winery (716-634-9382), 2614 King Road, Sheridan. Open September–October 12–5 daily, May–August and November, December, Saturday–Sunday 12–5; closed January–April. This vinifera plantation was first planted by Bob Roach in the 1970s. Currently Bob is producing *Gewürztraminer*, cabernet franc, merlot, and chardonnay. The winery features a small tasting room plus an outdoor picnic pavilion.

Schloss Dopken Winery (716-326-3636), 9177 Old Route 20, Ripley. Open daily year-round 12–5 for tasting and sales. J. Simon Watso and his wife, Roxann, acquired the property in 1972 and soon began producing world-class wines. *Schloss* is the German word for "castle" or "house of" and Doepken is Roxann Watso's maiden name. This farm winery features a small gift shop and tasting room tucked away in a 100-year-old farmhouse. Consider yourself lucky if Mr. Watso is conducting the tasting; he adds a little drama when describing his wines, which are of the highest quality.

Vetter Vineyards (716-326-3100), 8005 Prospect Station Road (off NY 20), Westfield. Open year-round 11–5 daily. Vetter's wines are made from vinifera grapes grown in the classic estate tradition. This small family-owned and operated winery is located on a hill overlooking the vineyards.

Willow Creek Winery (716-934-9463; willowcreekwines.com), 2627 Chapin Road, Sheridan. Open Monday–Friday 10-5, Saturday and Sunday 11-6. This family-owned and operated winery features a beautiful picnic grove, complete with pond and a gazebo. Each year Holly Metzger and her husband try to add more features to their winery. In addition to their tasting room and gift shop, they have recently added a catering facility which holds up to 400 people for weddings or receptions. A small restaurant on the grounds is open for lunch and dinner. They are one of the few small wineries that have the facilities to freeze their wine during the process to remove the skins and yeast. Some of their wines include Concord, Rambo Red, and Cayuga White.

Woodbury Vineyards (716-679-9463 or 888-697-9463; www.woodburyvine yards.com), 3230 South Roberts Road, Fredonia. Open year-round Monday–Saturday 10–5, Sunday 12–5. Woodbury winery features a well-stocked gift shop along with a tasting area to sample some of their vintages, including White Renard, Seaport Blush, and a delightfully sweet cranberry dessert wine.

✳ To Do

CASINO GAMING **Seneca Gaming and Entertainment** (716-549-4389 or 800-421-BINGO), 11099 NY 5, Irving. Open Sunday–Thursday 9:30 AM–4:30 AM, Friday–Saturday 9:30 AM–6:30 AM. Located on the Cattaraugus Reservation, visitors to this establishment can enjoy video gaming machines along with high-stakes bingo.

DIVING **Osprey Dive Charters** (716-326-2773; www.osprey-dive.com), 7233 East Lake Road, Westfield. Open by appointment. Captains Jim Herbert and Sam Genco take you to explore some of Lake Erie's best kept secrets: ship wrecks. There are approximately 19 wrecks beneath the waters of Lake Erie off the shores of western New York and southern Ontario.

FISHING Many spots along **Lake Erie** offer fishing access, including **Dunkirk City Pier** and **Daniel Reed Memorial Pier** (716-326-6633; NY 5 near NY 394, Barcelona). Besides ample parking for fishermen and boaters as well as docking facilities, this pier has a great view of Lake Erie. Picnic table are located near the Barcelona Lighthouse. A visitor's information center is open by the pier during the summer. Fishing licenses are available at many locations throughout Chautauqua County, including town, county, and village clerk offices. Licenses also available at **Uncle Sam's Unlimited** (716-934-4280; 278 Central Avenue, Silver Creek) and **The Clever Store** (716-595-3900; Bear Lake Road, Stockton). Licenses can be obtained by mail from the **NYSDEC License Sale Office,** 625 Broadway, Room 151, Albany, NY 12233.

FISHING CHARTERS Over two dozen fishing charters run out of eastern Lake Erie. For a complete listing, contact **Eastern Lake Erie Charter Boat Association** (E-mail: fisheasternbasin@hotmail.com), PO Box 363, Silver Creek, NY 14136.

GOLF Hillview Golf Course (716-679-4571), 4717 Berry Road, Fredonia. An 18-hole, par-70 public course.

Pinehurst Golf Course (716-326-4424), East Main Road, Westfield. A family-oriented, alcohol-free, 9-hole course open to the public.

Rosebrook Golf Course (716934-2825; www.rosebrookgolf.com), 12486 Beebe Road, Silver Creek. An 18-hole, par-72 course located among the vineyards of northern Chautauqua County.

Sugar Hill Golf Course (716-326-4653), 7060 Lake Road, Westfield. A challenging par-35, 9-hole course overlooking Lake Erie. It has a pro shop, lessons, restaurant, and patio.

MARINAS AND BOAT LAUNCHES City of Dunkirk Boat Launch (716-366-9879; www.dunkirkny.com), At Dunkirk Harbor on NY 5, Dunkirk.

Chadwick Bay Marina (716-366-1774), Lake Shore Drive and Central Avenue, Dunkirk.

Daniel Reed Memorial Pier, NY 5, Barcelona.

Stefans Marina (716-366-3388), 24 Lake Shore Drive, Dunkirk.

✳ Green Space

BEACHES ✍ ♿ **Evangola State Park** (716-549-1802), 110191 Old Lake Shore Road, Irving. See *Parks.*

Lake Erie State Park (716-792-9214), NY 5, Brocton. See *Parks.*

Point Gratiot Park (716-366-3262), NY 5 (near Point Drive), Dunkirk. See *Parks.*

Silver Creek Beach (716-934-3240), Front Street, Silver Creek. Facilities include a beach and picnic areas.

✍ ♿ **Sunset Bay Beach** (716-934-9953; www.sunsetbayusa.com), Iola and Shady Drive, Irving. Open Memorial Day–Labor Day. Sunset Bay is one of the most popular beaches on Lake Erie's shores. This beautiful, clean, sandy beach has lifeguards every day from 10–5, so it's the perfect spot to bring the entire family. The beach has rest rooms and changing rooms. Surfers, a restaurant located directly on the beach, features good, affordable food. Families rule the beach during the day, but at night the young-adult crowd takes over to party the night away at Surfers and at the adjacent Sunset Bay Beach Bar.

✒ **Wright Park** (716-366-3262), NY 5 (north of the harbor), Dunkirk. See *Parks*.

PARKS & **Barker Common,** Main and Water Streets, Fredonia. A beautifully landscaped park in the center of town adorned with trees, flowers, and benches. In 1901 the son of an early pioneer donated two unique fountains. This park is the perfect spot to sit and relax when visiting Fredonia. During the summer, concerts take place every Wednesday evening.

Evangola State Park (716-549-1802), 110191 Old Lake Shore Road, Irving. Open dawn to dusk. Admission: Memorial Day–Labor Day $6 weekdays, $7 weekends; free rest of year. This 733-acre park on the shores of Lake Erie has a natural sand beach as well as picnic areas, a concession stand, and 80 campsites. One of this park's attractive features is its beautiful arc-shaped shoreline; low cliffs of Angola shale line the edge of the beach.

Forest Place Park (Washington Sanctuary), Along Canadaway Creek near Risley Street, Fredonia. This park was established in 1931 by the Fredonia Garden and Bird Club as a quiet place to watch birds. Coming to this spot also gives visitors an idea what early 19th-century Fredonia looked like when the area was still heavily wooded.

Houghton Common, West Main Street, Fredonia. A small park landscaped with trees, shrubs, and flowers.

✒ & **Lake Erie State Park** (716-792-9214), NY 5, Brocton. Open dawn to dusk. Admission: $7 car parking fee late June–Labor Day, $6 car weekends only May– late June and Labor Day–October; free other times. Lake Erie State Park, a few miles south of Dunkirk, features almost a mile of shoreline along Lake Erie. High

SUNSET BAY BEACH IS ONE OF THE MOST POPULAR BEACHES ON LAKE ERIE.

Christine A. Smyczynski

bluffs overlooking the lake offer a great view. The park has 97 campsites and 10 cabins for overnight camping, along with a camper recreation program, swimming, picnicking, playgrounds, and nature and hiking trails. This is also a great location for birding, as migrating birds often stop to rest here before flying across Lake Erie.

Moore Park NY 20 and 394, Westfield. This park surrounding the McClurg Mansion, located in the center of town, is a peaceful place to sit and relax.

Point Gratiot Park (716-366-3262), NY 5, near Point Drive, Dunkirk. Open dawn to dusk. A 60-acre park with a playground, picnic facilities, and a 1,500-foot beach on Lake Erie.

Russell Joy Park, Howard and Spring Streets, Fredonia. The largest park in the village, it has nature trails, picnic pavilions, playground equipment, basketball and tennis courts, and a baseball diamond.

Wright Park (716-366-3262), NY 5 (north of the harbor), Dunkirk. Open dawn to dusk. A 70-acre park located along Lake Erie. Facilities include a 1,500-foot beach, picnic tables, and a playground.

WALKING AND HIKING TRAILS **Chautauqua Gorge State Forest** (716-851-7200), Access from Hannum Road, Mayville or Gale Street, Westfield. Eight miles of hiking trails in a 538-acre, state-owned forest and gorge.

✳ Lodging

INNS AND RESORTS **Glenroth Inn and Well Being Center** (716-326-6462 or 888-523-5885; www.glenroth .com and www.iwpcenter.com), 6534 South Portage Road (NY 394), Westfield. Open year-round. Located on 104 acres of natural woods and meadows, Glenroth is a center for self-empowerment and self-renewal. Kathleen Bittner Roth, an internationally recognized leader in the human potential movement, has created a sanctuary where people can come to relax, renew, and regenerate in a tranquil setting. Guests can attend classes, seminars, and retreats, or just relax. They can indulge in sound and scent therapy, Reiki treatments, or have a massage. $65–$270.

The White Inn (716-672-2103; www.whiteinn.com), 52 East Main Street, Fredonia. The beautifully restored White Inn, located in the heart of Fredonia, has 23 guest rooms, including 11 suites. Spend the night in a four-poster or brass bed surrounded by Victorian-style furnishings. Full breakfasts are included. Stay and enjoy lunch or dinner in the dining room, featuring American and Continental cuisine. The property first came into the hands of Dr. Squire White, Chautauqua County's first medical doctor, in the early 1800s. The first brick structure was built on the property in 1868; several sections of the current inn are part of that original structure. The property remained in the White family until 1918, when it was sold and opened as a hotel. In the 1930s the White Inn was part of Duncan Hines's "Family of Fine Restaurants." The inn then went into a period of neglect at the hands of several owners. Fortunately in 1980 it was purchased by two professors from SUNY Fredonia, who renovated the inn to its present grandeur. $99–$159 See *Dining Out*.

The William Seward Inn (716-326-4151; www.williamsewardinn.com), 6645 South Portage Road (NY 394), Westfield. Open year-round. Journey back to the 19th century when you visit Jim and Debbie Dahlberg's tranquil retreat, which combines modern amenities with Colonial charm. The back part of the inn, which was constructed in 1821, was once the home of William Seward, an agent for the Holland Land Office who later went into politics and is probably best known for what was then termed Seward's Folly: the purchase of Alaska from Russia. Additions were made to the home in 1837, and the inn's main building, which has eight guest rooms with private baths, is a Greek Revival structure with Palladian windows.

The home originally stood 3 miles away in the village of Westfield, at the present site of the Welch's plant. In 1966 the Seward home was badly in need of repair and facing demolition. Instead, it was dismantled, brought on a flatbed truck to its present location, and reassembled. It opened as a bed & breakfast in 1983. The adjoining carriage house, built in 1991, has four luxury suites that include four-poster beds and double Jacuzzi tubs. The Dahlbergs offer fine dining on a small scale to guests and the public by reservation only. $70–$185.

BED & BREAKFASTS Brookside Manor Bed & Breakfast (716-672-7721 or 800-929-7599; www.bbonline.com/ny/brookside), 3728 NY 83, Fredonia. Open year-round. Innkeepers Andrea Andrews and Dale Mirth offer four beautiful guest rooms with air conditioning and private baths in this brick home, which was originally built in 1875 by a local businessman. The inn is entered through a massive wooden front door that still has the original doorbell. Once inside, the curved staircase with original walnut banister leads to the guest rooms on the second floor. A full breakfast, including fresh fruit, baked goods, and Belgian waffles, is served each morning. $79–$85

Candlelight Lodge Bed and Breakfast (716-326-2830; www.landmarkacres.com), 143 East Main Street (NY 20),Westfield. Open year-round. This restored Victorian Italianate brick mansion built in 1851 is listed on the National Register of Historic homes. Innkeepers Edward and Wilma Benjamin offer guest seven spacious suites and two rooms, all with private baths and modern amenities. Rooms have 14-foot ceilings, fireplaces, and museum-quality antique furnishings. The adjacent Captain Storm House offers four additional suites in a brick Queen Anne–style home. Children over 12 welcome. $75–$165.

Lakeside B & B (716-326-3757 or 800-454-8237; www.lakesidebb.com), 8223 East Lake Road, Westfield. Open year-round. Afternoon tea and dessert can be enjoyed when you stay at this circa 1830 Colonial Revival–style home with a view of Lake Erie and the Barcelona Lighthouse. Each of innkeepers' Rodger and Lesley Hazen's four guest rooms is furnished in 18th- and 19th-century antiques and has a private bath. Two rooms have lakefront views. Enjoy spectacular Lake Erie sunsets from the verandah. Breakfast features inn-made jams and local fruits. $59–$120.

Pinewoods Cottage Bed and Breakfast (716-934-4173; www .crinopinewoodscottage.com), 11634 York Road, Silver Creek. Open year-round. Hostess Estelle Crino offers three antiques-furnished guest rooms, each with a private bath, at this secluded and eclectic cottage surrounded by 20 acres of woodlands. The house has a large front porch, a gazebo, and a sun room; or tickle the keys of an antique Steinway console piano and a small Wurlitzer organ in the family room. Breakfast includes fresh-baked muffins, in-season fruit, and cereals. $65–$85.

Westfield House B & B (716-326-6262 or 1-877-299-7496; www .westfieldhousebnb.com), 7573 East Main Road, Westfield. Open year-round. Innkeepers Kathleen Grant and Marianne Heck operate this circa 1840 Gothic Victorian inn, which features seven guest rooms furnished with antiques and reproductions. All have private baths and air conditioning. Guests can relax on the patio, enjoy a game of billiards on the antique pool table, or browse the antique shops in historic Westfield. The large, sunny living room—a great place to relax—always has a puzzle going. Enjoy a full homemade, home-style breakfast in the dining room, which can seat 24 people. $75–$125.

MOTELS AND HOTELS Best Western (716-366-7100; www.travelweb.com), 3912 Vineyard Drive, Dunkirk. This 61-room hotel features an indoor pool, free continental breakfast, and a 24-hour hot/cold beverage bar. $59–$139.

Comfort Inn (866-386-2663; www .choicehotels.com), 3925 Vineyard Drive, Dunkirk. This 61-room hotel features a deluxe continental breakfast and a 24-hour juice bar. $69–$139.

Days Inn of Dunkirk-Fredonia (716-673-1351), 10455 Bennett Road (NY 60), Fredonia. This 135-room hotel offers an indoor pool and spa and free continental breakfast. $48–$125.

Ramada Inn (800-526-8350; www .wny-dining.com/ramada), 30 Lakeshore Drive East, Dunkirk. Located on the shores of Lake Erie, this hotel features 132 guest rooms with harbor views, some with whirlpool suites. The glass-enclosed Windjammers restaurant overlooks Chadwick Bay. $59–$159.

OTHER LODGING Blue Water Beach Campground (716-326-3540), 7364 Lake Road, Westfield. Open May 1–October 15. This campground on Lake Erie has the motto: We pamper the camper. They offer 175 open-grassy or shady, wooded sites along with a variety of recreational activities. Amenities include a private beach, game room, and beautiful sunsets every night. $22/night includes electricity and water. Sites can be also rented for the entire season for $1050.

Vinewood Acres Sugar Shack Vacation Rentals (716-326-3351 or 888-563-4324; www.sugarshack1 .com), 7904 NY 5, Westfield. Gail Black offers two year-round lakeside vacation homes on 30 acres with a private beach. One home has three bedrooms, and the other has two. Amenities include a stocked pond, Jacuzzi, and picnic area. The sunsets over the beach are beautiful. The adjacent gift shop (open 1–5 daily) has a variety of syrups and other products available for purchase. Pancake breakfasts are served from 7 AM–2 PM Sundays year-round and also on Saturdays from 8–12 during June, July, and August. Farm tours are offered, weather and time permitting. $800/week, summer; call for off-season rates.

Westfield/Lake Erie KOA (716-326-3573), 8001 NY 5, Westfield. Open April 15–October 15. This 117-site campground has Lake Erie views, two pools, hot showers, and a stocked pond. They have both tent and camper sites, with about 70 sites with hookups for cable TV. $22–$37.

✳ Where to Eat

Barcelona Harbor House (716-326-2017), 8254 First Street (NY 5 on Lake Erie), Westfield. Open Monday–Saturday 4–9. Enjoy fresh seafood specialties including lake perch, walleye, and pike while overlooking a spectacular view of Lake Erie. Other dinner selections include salmon, shrimp, lobster, prime rib, and steaks.

Bark Grill (716-326-2112), 14 East Pearl Street, Westfield. Tuesday–Saturday 4:30–9, Sunday 3–8, closed Mondays. Hosts James Blanchard and Lisa Schults offer diners steaks, seafood, fish, chicken, pasta, and more, including a Friday fish fry and such daily specials as lobster and prime rib. The restaurant features a turn-of-the-20th-century mahogany bar, where you can enjoy wine from local wineries. The decor features an antique eight-foot-tall, beer bottle-shaped cooler.

Demetri's (716-366-4187), 6–8 Lakeshore Drive, Dunkirk. Open 7–10 daily. Dine inside or on the patio overlooking Chadwick Bay and Lake Erie. Greek and American cuisine for breakfast, lunch, and dinner. For casual fine dining, head upstairs to **Katerina's** (open 7–10 daily), and choose from seafood, steaks, pasta, and chicken.

Hideaway Bay Restaurant and Lounge (716-934-4442; www.hideawaybay.net), 42 Lake Avenue, Silver Creek. Open Monday–Friday 11:30–9, Saturday 3–9, Sunday 4–9. Munch on pasta dishes, seafood, or beef while enjoying a view of Lake Erie. There is a patio bar and boat dock.

The White Inn (716-672-2103; www.whiteinn.com), 52 East Main Street, Fredonia. Open Monday–Saturday 7-10 for breakfast, 11:30–2 for lunch and 5–8:30 for dinner. Sunday open 8–11 for breakfast and 12:30–8 for dinner. This elegant inn and restaurant offers one of the finest dining experiences in Chautauqua County. Start your day out with eggs Benedict, omelets, or Belgian waffles. For lunch partake in one of the inn's specialties, including chicken pot pie, lamplighter chicken, or crab-stuffed sole. Sandwiches and salads are also available. Enjoy one of the White Inn's signature dishes for dinner, such as lamb à la Madeline, filet mignon with Gouda and bacon, or Dijon grilled salmon. See also *Lodging*.

William Seward Inn (716-326-4151 www.williamsewardinn.com), 6645 South Portage Road (NY 394), Westfield. Open by appointment. Fine dining on a small scale is offered on select evenings to inn guests and the public by reservation only. Seating for the four-course, prix-fixe dinner is at 7 PM. See *Lodging*.

Windjammer Restaurant (716-366-8350), 30 Lake Shore Drive East (at the Ramada Inn), Dunkirk. Open

Monday–Saturday 6:30–11 for breakfast, 11:30–2 for lunch, and 5–9 for dinner. Sunday open 6:30–10 for breakfast, 10–2 for lunch, and 5–9 for dinner. Enjoy lakeside dining in a glass-enclosed restaurant with a spectacular view of Lake Erie. A focal point of the nautical-themed restaurant is a replica ship's mast in the center of the dining room. Serving classic American cuisine with a twist, including steaks and fresh seafood. An outdoor patio is open during the summer.

EATING OUT ✐ & 🍴 **Aldrich's Beef and Ice Cream Parlor** (716-672-5133), NY 60, Pomfret (just outside Fredonia). Open Monday–Thursday 7–8, Friday–Sunday 7–9. Serving burgers, soup, salads, wings, beef specials, and fish. Their claim to fame is their ice cream: more specifically, their April Fool's Day ice cream flavor. The tradition, started by owner Scott Aldrich in the 1980s, has people lining up early on the morning of April 1st to get a taste of the yearly creation. Past flavors include beef gravy, sauerkraut, bacon and eggs, nachos and cheese, and unheavenly hash.

✐ & 🍴 **Aunt Millie's Kitchen** (716-934-2525), Routes 5 and 20, Irving. Open 6–11 daily. The first thing you notice when you walk into Aunt Millie's is a huge dessert cooler. This reminds you to save room for a slice of their delicious pies or cakes. They have an extensive menu featuring home-cooked meals.

The Brown Bean Coffee House (716-672-8823), 12 Park Place, Fredonia. Open Monday–Saturday 8–11, Sunday 9–11. This unique coffeehouse features soups, bagels, panini sandwiches, desserts, and ice cream. Specialties include their award-winning California roll salad and eggplant and goat cheese panini.

Caddyshack Restaurant (716-326-4653), 7060 East Lake Road (NY 5), Westfield. Open April–October Tuesday–Saturday 11–9, Sunday 12–9. Casual dining with a view of Sugar Hill Golf Course and Lake Erie. Specialty sandwiches include the Eagle, a Buffalo-style chicken breast; the Driver, known in some circles as beef on weck; and a Hole-in-One, a hot hogie sandwich piled high with ham, salami, cheese, lettuce, tomato, onions, and peppers. Other selections include homemade soups, salads, pizza, and a Friday-night fish fry.

Cafe Barista (716-326-7707), 7 East Main Street, Westfield. Open Monday–Saturday 7 AM–3 PM. Casual bistro-style dining in a renovated historic building that features pressed-tin ceilings, ceiling fans, exposed-brick walls, and lots of books to peruse. Enjoy specialty coffees, espresso, baked goods, light lunches, desserts, and wines.

Calarco's (716-326-3415), 15 Market Street, Westfield. Open Monday and Wednesday–Friday 11–2 and 5–9, Saturday and Sunday 4:30–8. Closed Tuesday. Italian cuisine—including homemade lasagna, soups, and sauces—is served in this small bar/restaurant located on a short one-way street just off NY 20, right in the village. They are also known for their Friday fish fry. Prime rib is served on weekends. Leave room for their homemade desserts.

Jack's Barcelona Drive-in (716-326-2277), First Street, Barcelona. Open Monday–Saturday 7–9, Sunday 7-3. Open year-round. This small restaurant, serving up breakfast, lunch, and dinner, always has lots of cars in the parking lot, so you know the food has to be good!

✄ & **Kiki's Pierside Grill**, Dunkirk City Pier. Open Memorial Day–Labor Day. Featuring homemade fast food, including burgers, fries, chicken wraps, and ice cream.

✄ & ✿ **Starlight Diner** (716-326-8500), 7592 East Main Road, Westfield. Open daily 7-9. This recently expanded and renovated diner serves traditional breakfasts, burgers, sandwiches, home-style dinners, basket specials, and more in a family-friendly atmosphere.

✄ & ✿ **Surfer's** (716-934-9953; www.sunsetbayusa.com), Iola and South Shore Drive, Sunset Bay. A seasonal restaurant open daily Memorial Day through Labor Day for lunch and happy hour. Enjoy casual waterfront dining at this popular beach bar and grill. The restaurant features good, affordable food and usually runs daily specials. Choose from sandwiches, burgers, chicken fingers, wings, and more, including a fabulous Friday fish fry. You can even order your food to take out for a picnic on the beach. Next door, at the **Sunset Bay Beach Club** (716-934-4847), enjoy nightly entertainment and Happy Hour. It is the site of the New York State Miss Hawaiian Tropic Swimsuit Competition.

The Upper Crust (716-672-2253), 25 East Main Street, Fredonia. Open Monday–Friday 7–7, Saturday and Sunday 7–4. The aroma of fresh baked goods is almost intoxicating when you walk into the Upper Crust. Enjoy from-scratch baked goods and original-recipe soups and sandwiches. Be sure to try one of their famous potato rolls.

✄ & ✿ **Vine City** (716-326-3728; www.testmilk.com/vinecity), Holt and Main Streets, Westfield. Open 6–9 daily. Casual, home-style family dining is offered in this former dairy. Enjoy a traditional breakfast, sandwiches, and basket specials for lunch or down-home dinners like pork chops, liver and onions, and strip steak.

Vinewood Acres Sugar Shack (716-326-3351; www.sugarshack1.com) 7904 NY 5, Westfield. Pancake breakfasts are served year-round on Sunday from 7–2 and on Saturday 8–12 during June, July, and August. Twenty-one varieties of syrups are available in the gift shop, open 1–5 daily. See also *Other Lodging.*

✄ & ✿ **Westfield Main Diner** (716-326-4351), 40 East Main Street, Westfield. Open Monday–Wednesday 6–3, Thursday and Friday 6–8, Saturday 6–3, Sunday 7–3. Classic American food, like burgers and deli sandwiches, are served in a 1929 Ward & Dickinson Diner, decorated with antiques and Westfield memorabilia. Enjoy made-from-scratch chili, soup, and their famous homemade pies.

✳ Entertainment

THEATERS **The 1891 Fredonia Opera House** (716-679-1891; www.fredopera.org), 9–11 Church Street, Fredonia. When the Fredonia Opera House first opened in April 1891, it attracted many of the best late 19th-century and early 20th-century entertainers and hosted local talent and community events. In the 1920s it was converted to a movie house. By 1981 it had closed in disrepair and was awaiting demolition when the Fredonia Preservation Society stepped in and saved it from the wrecker's ball. The Opera House was restored to its original grandeur and today it is a family-oriented entertainment venue open year-round for concerts, films, plays, and professional theater.

& **Michael C. Rockefeller Arts Center** (716-673-3501 or 866-4441-4928; www.fredonia.edu/rac), State University of New York at Fredonia, 280 Central Avenue, Fredonia. Considered one of the best performing arts centers in the SUNY system, this facility consists of two theaters, a 1,200-seat concert hall, two galleries, and numerous classrooms.

MUSIC **Western New York Chamber Orchestra** (716-673-3501 or 866-4441-4928; www.fredonia.edu/rac), State University of New York at Fredonia, 280 Central Avenue, Fredonia. A professional ensemble in residence at SUNY Fredonia. Performances take place at **King Concert Hall** on the university campus.

✻ Selective Shopping

ANTIQUES **Antiques By The Lake** (716-326-7966), 13 East Main Street Westfield. Open June–September 10–5 daily (closed Tuesday and Wednesday April–May and October–December). Specializing in period lighting and lamp repair, plus jewelry, glassware, and postcards.

Antique Marketplace (716-326-2861), 25 East Main, Westfield. Open April–December 10–5 daily, Sunday 1–5; January–March, Friday and Saturday 10–5, Sunday 1–5. A group of dealers offering linens, quilts, collectibles, political memorabilia, and more.

Chautauqua Rare Books and Antiques (716-672-8988), 10 Park Place, Fredonia. Open Tuesday and Thursday 12–5, Friday and Saturday 12–7. Quality antiques and books.

Landmark Acres Antiques (716-326-4185; www.landmarkacres.com), 232 West Main Street (NY 20), Westfield. Open daily year-round 10–5. The largest and oldest antiques shop in this part of the county, Landmark Antiques is located in a two-story barn on the grounds of the first farm settled in Chautauqua County in 1802. Owners Edward and Wilma Benjamin offer a large selection of 18th- and 19th-century furniture, glass, china, porcelain, jewelry, rugs, books, decorative items, and more.

Militello Antiques (716-326-2587), 31 Jefferson Street (one block from NY 394), Westfield. Open all year 10–4 daily. This shop established in 1922 specializes in 19th-century antiques.

Prisilla B. Nixon Antiques (716-326-3511), 119 West Main Street, Westfield. By appointment only. Furniture, folk art, textiles.

Randy's Antiques (716-679-9587), 41 East Main Street, Fredonia. Open daily 11-5. A selection of collectibles and antiques, including furniture, glassware, porcelain, frames, prints, and more.

Saraf's Emporium (716-326-3590; www2.cecomet.net/antiques), 58 East Main Street, Westfield. Open 10–5 Monday–Saturday, Sunday 1–5. Several dealers exhibit their wares in this 12,000-square-foot shop. Choose from period furniture, fine art, early lighting, china, glass, jewelry, toys, and Oriental carpets

Stockton Sales (716-595-3516), 6 Mill Street (off CR 58), Stockton. Open daily 10–5. This unique antiques store, located in five buildings of the former Rownd Basket Factory, has been a popular destination for over 35 years. The 100,000-square-foot complex features unique things for the home, garden, and automobile. Many of the items are from entire estates that have been acquired. Auctions are held on Wednesday evenings, with a special furniture auction once a month.

Vilardo Antiques (716-326-2714), 7303 Walker Road, Westfield. Open May 1–October 31, Thursday–Saturday 11–5. Quality wood and wicker furniture and accessories.

The Workbench Antiques (716-366-0406), 166 Lakeshore Drive East, Dunkirk. Open all year, Monday–Saturday 11–5 and by appointment. This shop features a full line of antiques, American art pottery, and kitchen items.

ART GALLERIES **Portage Hill Gallery** (716-326-4478), NY 394, Westfield. Open January–May, 10–5 Saturday and Sunday; June–August, daily 10–5; September–December, Tuesday–Friday 12–4, Thursday 12–8, Saturday and Sunday 10–5. Located in a 1830s Greek Revival home, this gallery features top-quality paintings, sculpture, ceramics, glass, jewelry, wooden items, and photography created by regional and national artists. The gallery features the clay studio and gallery of Audrey Kay Dowling and a custom framing studio.

Surroundings (716-326-7373), 73 East Main Street, Westfield. Open daily 10–6 Memorial Day–Labor Day, Monday–Saturday 11–6 the rest of the year. This gallery is located in an early-1900s brick building with hardwood floors and pressed tin ceilings. Over 175 regional and national artists display their works here. Items for sale include stained glass, paintings, furniture, jewelry, textiles, and decorative accessories. Custom framing is also available.

SPECIAL SHOPS **The Block House** (716-792-4640; www.glassblowing4u.com), 5390 Blockhouse Road, Fredonia. Open 10–5 daily; call ahead if coming for a demonstration. Watch molten glass fashioned into decorative objects—then buy them in the gift shop. Artists take the time to answer your questions, and you are able to see everything close up. You can even sign up for a class in glassblowing.

& **Cross Roads** (716-326-6278 or 1-877-512-7307; www.thecrossroadsmarket.com), Sherman-Westfield Road (CR 21), Westfield. Open May–December 9–5 Saturday only; closed rest of year. A visit to the Cross Roads is a unique experience. Over 40 vendors in two buildings offer fine arts, crafts, collectibles, farm produce, baked goods, and more.

Ernie's General Store and Antiques (716-679-9619; www.assisttech.com/ernie's), 56 East Main Street, Fredonia. Open Monday 12–5, Tuesday–Saturday 10–5. Located in the carriage house behind the White Inn, this shop features fun and functional "gotta-haves" from A to Z. Choose from Amish furniture, baskets, candles, maple products, decorating items, toys, and more.

The Luweibdeh Shop (716-673-1915), 4587 West Main Road (NY 20), Fredonia. Open Tuesday–Saturday 10-5. This unique gift shop, located in a circa 1800 tenant farmer's cottage behind a big brick house, has handcrafted items from around the world. Selections include Vera Bradley handbags, brass and pewter items, jewelry, pottery, birdhouses, Christmas decorations, plus a whole lot more.

Time Pieces (1-888-414-4818; www
.time-piece.com), 23 White Street,
Fredonia. Open Sunday and Monday
12–5, Tuesday–Saturday 9–6. This
1870 farmhouse just down the street
from the White Inn carries traditional
and unique gifts, including handblown glassware, garden accessories,
gourmet coffee, candles, candy, and
items made by local artists.

**Treasured Dolls and Gifts from
the Tower** (716-679-9870; www
.netsync.net/towergift), 44 Temple
Street, Fredonia. Open Monday–
Saturday 10–5. Dolls, home decor,
jewelry, and baby clothes displayed in
an elegant Victorian home.

Vinewood Acres Sugar Shack (716-
326-3351 or 1-888-563-4324; www
.sugarshack1.com), 7904 NY 5, Westfield. Open daily 1–5. Farm-made
maple products, 21 varieties of fruit
syrups, butters, and jellies are available here. Sunday pancakes are
served year-round in the Pancake
Room with a view of Lake Erie; pancakes also served Saturday morning
during June, July, and August. See
also *Lodging*.

The Wool Works (716-326-2848),
7265 Martin Wright Road, Westfield.
Open Monday–Saturday 10–5. If you
value natural fibers, be sure to stop by
the Wool Works. At this unique shop
you'll find textile products from all
over the world, including wool from
proprietors Stephen and Patricia San-
dle's sheep that's been custom processed into skeins of knitting yarn and
quality blankets.

❋ **Special Events**
May: **Antique Open House** (716-
326-2714), An annual open house at
all the antique shops throughout
Westfield. **Lincoln Festival** (716-

326-4000 or 877-299-7496; www
.westfieldny.com), Westfield. A family
event held on Memorial Day weekend, featuring exhibits, entertainment, reenactors, demonstrations,
food and more.

June: **Twenty Mile Garage Sale**
(716-679-1565; festivalsfredonia.com),
Throughout northern Chautauqua
County, including Dunkirk, Fredonia,
and Westfield. A community event
where you can pick up garage sale
treasures at a good price.

July: **Victorian Dazzle** (716-679-
1565; www.festivalsfredonia.com),
Barker Commons, Fredonia. Revisit
Fredonia as it was in 1900. This event
features horse-drawn trolley rides,
music in the park, Victorian teas, and
tours. **Chautauqua County Fair**
(716-366-4752), 1089 Central Avenue,
Dunkirk. This fair, which has taken
place for over 150 years, features agricultural displays, rides, and grandstand entertainment, including
demolition derbies and auto thrill
shows. **Westfield Arts & Craft
Show** (716-326-4000), Moore Park
NY 20 and 394, Westfield. An annual
arts-and-crafts show.

August: **Antique Show** (716-326-
4000), Eason Hall, Elm Street, one
block from Main Street, Westfield.
For almost 70 years dealers from
around the area have displayed their
wares at this annual show. **Lighthouse Festival** (716-366-5050;
www.dunkirklighthouse.com),
Dunkirk. Tours of the lighthouse,
food, and more. **Barcelona Harbor-
fest** (716-326-4000), Barcelona Harbor, NY 5, Westfield. This one-day
festival features craft and food vendors, water games, exhibits, and
demonstrations.

September: **Red, White, and Blues** (716-679-1565; www.festivalsfredonia .com), Barker Commons and Fredonia Opera House, Fredonia. Celebrating red and white wine, brews, and blues music, along with a "taste of Fredonia." **Festival of Grapes** (716-549-8239), Village Square Park, NY 20, Silver Creek. Family activities along with information on the grape industry, grape stomping contest, grape desserts, and more.

October: **Harvest Moon Cemetery Tour** (716-679-1565; www.festivals fredonia.com), Fredonia. horse-drawn ghost tours through the town's historic cemetery

November: **Victorian Christmas in the Village** (716-326-4997), Westfield. Christmas shopping and family events.

December: **Miracle on Main Street** (716-679-1565; www.festivalsfredonia .com), Fredonia. Santa comes to town.

CHAUTAUQUA LAKE REGION—Mayville, Maple Springs, Bemus Point, Jamestown, and vicinity, Including Central Chautauqua County (Cassadaga, Sinclairville, and Gerry)

With its lakes and streams, the area is a noted vacation destination for its waterfront activities. People come from all over the country to fish for muskellunge (muskie), bass, pike, trout, perch, and more. Recreational events in the winter include ice skating, ice fishing, snowmobiling, sledding, and cross-country and downhill skiing. Of course, the best-known destination in the region is the Chautauqua Institution, which draws people from all over the country to a nine-week summer program of arts, lectures, and concerts—and in January and February for its horse-drawn sleigh rides.

Incorporated in 1830, Mayville is the Chautauqua County seat. The town grew rapidly with the arrival of the railroad in the 1860s. Past industries included cider making and malted-milk production. Now the area is known for business form printing and furniture manufacturing.

Native Americans were the first inhabitants in the area now known as Jamestown. Historians think they may have been from the Erie or Wanro tribes. Later, tribes from the Six Nations hunted and fished in the region.

James Prendergast, the founder of Jamestown, first arrived in the area in 1806 and built a log house and sawmill several years later. Swedish immigrants arrived in Jamestown starting in 1849, giving the region a rich Swedish heritage. Some of their contributions included woodcarving, weaving, and lace making. Today the area surrounding Jamestown is popular for both recreational and cultural activities. The Roger Tory Peterson Institute and the Jamestown Audubon Nature Center will be of interest to nature lovers, while those who enjoy cultural pursuits will want to check out the offerings at the Lucille Ball Little Theater and the Reg Lenna Civic Center. History buffs won't want to miss the Fenton History Center, which focuses on local history, or the Robert Jackson Center, which honors the life of the famed Nuremberg trial lawyer, who grew up near Jamestown. If you love Lucy, be sure to include the Lucy-Desi Museum on your agenda. Those seeking more active pursuits might want to check out some of the area's golf courses. Jamestown was named the "Best Little Golf Town in America" by *Golf Digest* magazine in 2002.

Celoron, just west of Jamestown, was named after Pierre Joseph Celoron, a military captain, who was sent to the area in 1749 to take possession of the territory for France during the French and English struggle for American territory. Today the town is probably best known as the birthplace of Lucille Ball.

AREA CODE The area code is 716.

GUIDANCE **Chautauqua County Chamber of Commerce** (716-484-1101; www.jamestownchamber.org), 101 West Fifth Street, Jamestown. Open Monday–Friday 8–4:30.

Chautauqua County Visitors Bureau (716-357-4569; www.tourchautauqua .com), PO Box 1441, Chautauqua Institution Main Gate Welcome Center, 1 Massey Avenue (off NY 394), Chautauqua. Open 9–5 daily year-round.

Downtown Jamestown Development Corporation (716-664-2477; www .discoverjamestown.com), 19 West Third Street, Jamestown. Involved in the revitalization and redevelopment of downtown Jamestown, this group has brochures on Jamestown as well as other regional attractions.

Lakewood Area Chamber of Commerce (716-763-8557), 20 West Summit Avenue, PO Box 51, Lakewood. Located in the village hall. Open Monday–Friday 8–5.

Mayville/Chautauqua Chamber of Commerce (716-753-3113), PO Box 22, Mayville. Information can be obtained by phone.

Bemus Point (www.bemuspt.com). A good Web site with lots of information on Bemus Point.

GETTING THERE *By air:* **Chautauqua County Airport** (716-484-0204 or 800-428-4322), Airport Drive, off NY 60, Jamestown. See *Getting There: Buffalo.*

By car: Accessible from exit 60 off the New York State Thruway (I-90) and I-86.

Getting Around *By car:* NY 430 runs north of Chautauqua Lake, while NY 394 runs along the south shore.

By bus: **Chautauqua Area Regional Transit** (800-388-6534), Jamestown.

MEDICAL EMERGENCY Dial 911.

WCA Hospital (716-487-0141; www.wcahospital.org), 207 Foote Avenue, Jamestown.

✳ To See

ART MUSEUMS **Arts Council for Chautauqua County** (716-664-2465), 116 East Third Street, Jamestown. Open Tuesday–Friday 8:30–5. This county-wide organization was formed in 1979 to service art organizations and artists. They support art in education, organize community events, and assist cultural organizations.

Chautauqua Center for the Visual Arts (716-357-2771), Wythe Avenue, Chautauqua. Open daily during the nine-week summer season at the Chautauqua Institution. This art center features a central gallery and three additional galleries showing a variety of exhibits.

James Prendergast Library Association (716-484-7135; www.cclslib.org/prendergast), 509 Cherry Street, Jamestown. Open Monday–Friday 9–8:30, Saturday 9–5, Sunday 1–3:30. This gallery is a showcase for regional artists, including paintings, needlework, photography, and handblown glass. The library also has a permanent collection of late 19th- and early 20th-century American and European oil paintings.

MUSEUMS AND HISTORIC HOMES **Bemus Point Historical Society** (716-386-2274), 11 Albertus Avenue, Bemus Point. Open Sunday 1–4, Thursday 5–7. This museum is located in the original village hall.

Busti Historical Society (716-483-3670), 3443 Lawson Road, Jamestown. Open during special events and by appointment.

Chautauqua Sports Hall of Fame (716-484-2272), 15 West Third Street, Jamestown. Open Monday–Friday 12–3. Free admission. This small storefront museum, formed in 1980, celebrates the history of professional, semiprofessional, and amateur sports in Chautauqua County. Each year a local sports celebrity is inducted into the Hall of Fame. The museum also has sports memorabilia from past to present on display.

Chautauqua Township Historical Museum (716-753-7535 or 716-753-7469), 15 Water Street (NY 394), Mayville. Open Memorial Day–Labor Day Friday–Sunday 1–5. Located in a former Pennsylvania Railroad station, this museum's exhibits focus on ice harvesting, furniture manufacturing, and steamboating in the Chautauqua Lake region.

Dart Airport (716-753-2160), 6167 Plank Road (NY 430), Mayville. Open year-round Tuesday–Sunday. Free admission. Antique airplanes, engines, and other memorabilia are displayed at the aviation museum. The airport also offers glider rides, flight instruction, and sightseeing rides, weather permitting. A flea market takes place on the grounds every Saturday and Sunday during the summer.

Fenton History Center (716-664-6256; www.fentonhistorycenter.org), 67 Washington Street (off NY 60 just south of downtown), Jamestown. Open Monday–Saturday 10–4; also Sundays 1–4 Thanksgiving–January 6. Admission: $5 adults, $4 children 4–12, $20 family rate. This mansion was the home of Reuben Fenton, governor of New York from 1865 to 1869. The 1863 Italian villa–style mansion was placed on the National Register of Historic Places in 1972. Period rooms and exhibits depict local history. The annual Christmas exhibit highlights observances and celebrations that mark the holiday season. A 5,000-volume reference library focuses on Jamestown and southern Chautauqua County. Group and school educational tours by appointment.

Lucy-Desi Museum (716-484-0800; www.lucy-desi.com), 212 Pine Street, Jamestown. Open Monday–Saturday 10–5:30, Sunday 1–5. Admission: $5 adults, $3.50 senior citizens (55+) and children 6–18. If you truly love Lucy, this

Jamestown shrine to Lucille Ball and Desi Arnaz should be on your itinerary. On entering, visitors are greeted with an Arnaz family portrait that once hung in the couple's Beverly Hills home. The museum contains photos, costumes, and other artifacts documenting the careers of these stellar performers as well as audio and video clips from *I Love Lucy* and *Life with Lucy*. Of course, a visit to the Lucy-Desi Museum wouldn't be complete without a peek at the gift shop, which carries hundreds of items related to everyone's favorite redhead.

Robert H. Jackson Center (716-483-6646; www.roberthjackson.org), 305 East Fourth Street, Jamestown. Open year-round Monday–Friday 8:30–1:30 and by appointment. Free admission, donations accepted. Robert Jackson was the chief American prosecutor at the Nuremberg trials of Nazi war criminals. Jackson was raised in nearby Frewsburg and practiced law in Jamestown, and this exhibit focuses on the history of this self-described country lawyer who became known worldwide during the trials.

LIGHTHOUSES Three lighthouses are located along Chautauqua Lake, which you can view from the outside. The **Mayville Lighthouse**, next to the historical society museum on Water Street, was originally going to be built in Bemus Point, but the town didn't want it there, so it was built in Mayville instead. The **Stow Lighthouse**, at the entrance to the Bemus Point–Stow Ferry, is the twin to the Mayville Lighthouse. The **Celoron Lighthouse**, adjacent to Lucille Ball Memorial Park in Celoron, was originally at Molly World Amusement Park in Lakewood.

RELIGIOUS SITES **Lily Dale Assembly** (716-595-8712; www.lilydale-assembly.org), 5 Melrose Park, Lily Dale (near Cassadaga). Open dawn–dusk daily June–August. Admission to grounds. Lily Dale is the world's largest center for the religion of Spiritualism, which began in 1879 as an Association of Free Thinkers. During the season, visitors can hear nationally known speakers, observe clairvoyant demonstrations, and seek spiritual enlightenment. The community has two hotels plus several guest homes, a cafeteria, and a few small gift shops.

✳ To Do

BALLOONING **Balloons Over Chautauqua** (716-484-9961 or 888-2BFLY-IN; www.usaonthenet.balloons.com). Open May 1–mid-September. 780

LOVE LUCY? DON'T MISS THIS SHRINE TO JAMESTOWN'S FAVORITE DAUGHTER.

Christine A. Smyczynski

✪ **Chautauqua Institution** (716-357-6200; www.ciweb.org), NY 394, Chautauqua. The Chautauqua Institution is a well-known center for performing arts, education, religion, and recreation. Its fame is so widespread, in fact, that the Chautauqua Institution has come to be synonymous with Chautauqua County. Founded in 1874 by Lewis Miller and John Vincent as a summer vacation learning experiment for Sunday-school teachers, it quickly grew to include other academic subjects, music, art, and physical education. The 856-acre grounds were designated a National Historic District because of the numerous buildings of interest. The National Historic Landmark **Lewis Miller Cottage** at 28 Miller Park (at the intersection of Vincent and Asbury Avenues) was the first permanent cottage built at Chautauqua. The Swiss chalet–style cottage was precut in Akron, Ohio, Miller's hometown, and shipped to Chautauqua for assembly. Miller's daughter, Mina, was married to Thomas Edison, so the inventor was a frequent visitor to Chautauqua.

Today over 150,000 people attend events during the institution's nine-week season from June to August. A gate fee is charged to enter the village during the summer season, except for Sunday, when admission is free. The grounds can be entered for free the rest of the year. More than a hundred lecturers speak each summer, and the 5,000-seat amphitheater features popular entertainers as well as performances by the Chautauqua Symphony, the Chautauqua Conservatory Theater, and the Chautauqua Opera.

This charming Victorian village is full of quaint cottages, charming shops, and restaurants. Chautauqua offers visitors a respite from the hustle and bustle of modern life, whether they attend lecturers, rent a bicycle, play golf, sit on the beach, or just enjoy the picturesque beauty of Chautauqua Lake. Guests can stay for an afternoon, a week, or the entire season. For more information call 800-836-ARTS, or go to www.chautauqua-inst.org or www.ciweb.org.

THE CHAUTAUQUA INSTITUTION, RENOWNED AS A CENTER FOR PERFORMING ARTS AND EDUCATION, WAS FOUNDED IN 1874.

Christine A. Smyczynski

Fairmont Avenue, Jamestown. One-hour flights over the Chautauqua Lake Region launch from either Bemus Point, Lakewood, or Fluvanna, depending on wind direction. Fee: $195/person.

Sky Sail Balloons (716-782-2280 or 716-326-7245; www.skysail.org), 2805 Carpenter-Pringle Road, Ashville. Scenic balloon rides year-round by appointment. Founded in 1989, this is Chautauqua County's first hot-air balloon company.

BOAT EXCURSIONS Bemus Point–Stow Ferry (716-753-2403), Lakeside Drive, Bemus Point. Operates seasonally on a sporadic basis. This motor-driven cable ferry, in operation since 1811, takes cars across Chautauqua Lake in six minutes. Before bridges were built, it was the only way to cross the lake. It is operated by the Chautauqua Lake Historic Vessels Company.

Chautauqua Belle (716-753-2403; www.chatauquabelle.com), 15 Water Street, Mayville. Open seven days a week, Memorial Day–Labor Day. Take a relaxing ride on an authentic stern-wheel steamboat, one of only such steamers east of the Mississippi. Note: The ship did not run during the 2004 season due to needed repairs. Call first to make sure it is back in operation in 2005.

Summer Wind **Cruises**, (716-763-7447; www.thesummerwind.com), Lucille Ball Memorial Park, Celoron. May–October. The finest way to cruise Chautauqua Lake is on the *Summer Wind,* which has an open-air upper deck and a climate-controlled interior salon. Choose from sightseeing, breakfast, lunch, or dinner cruises.

BOATING Marden E. Cobb Waterway Trail. A recreational waterway trail along the Cassadaga and Conewango Creeks. These "flatwater" creeks—tributaries of the Allegany River—are popular with canoers and fishermen alike. A map is available from Chautauqua County Tourism (see *Guidance*).

CANOE AND KAYAK TOURS See **Evergreen Outfitters** under *Special Shops*.

FISHING Sportfishing is popular both on Lake Erie and Chautauqua Lake as well as on the smaller lakes, ponds, and streams throughout the county. Fishing licenses are available at many locations throughout Chautauqua County, including town, county, and village clerk offices. Licenses also available at **Uncle Sam's Unlimited** (716-934-4280; 278 Central Avenue, Silver Creek) and **The Clever Store** (716-595-3900; Bear Lake Road, Stockton). Licenses can be obtained by mail from the **NYSDEC License Sale Office,** 625 Broadway, Room 151, Albany, NY 12233.

Here are some resources for more information.

Chautauqua Lake Fishing Hotline, 716-763-9471 or 716-386-4275.

Lake Erie Fishing Hotline, 716-679-3743.

Chautauqua Lake Fishing Reports www.chautauqualakesfishingreports.com.

Chautauqua Lake *Hot Spots Fishin' Map* available from the Chautauqua County Visitors Bureau, 716-357-4569; www.tourchautauqua.com.

FAMILY FUN Midway Park, (716-386-3165; www.midway-park.com), NY 430, Maple Springs. Open weekends only Memorial Day–mid-June; late June–early September, open Wednesday–Sunday 1–7 (grounds open at 11); closed Monday and Tuesday except holidays. Admission to the grounds is free; purchase wristband ($14) or tickets (16 for $12) for rides. Season pass is $60/adult and $52/child. Midway Park is the 16th oldest continually operating amusement park in the nation and the only remaining "Trolley and Steamboat" park in western New York. When the park opened in 1898, people flocked to it by steamboat, train, and trolley car. Today visitors come by car or speedboat, but they still visit for the same reason: family fun and entertainment. Among the many rides to choose from are a restored 1946 Alan Herschell carousel made in North Tonawanda. The rounding boards of the carousel are painted with scenes from the Chautauqua Lake Region. Other Herschell rides include Roadway cars, Helicopter, Skyfighter, and the Little Dipper Roller Coaster. Park visitors can enjoy old-time favorites such as the Tubs-O-Fun, Tilt-A-Whirl, Roto-Whip, and more. Midway Park also includes an open-air roller rink, picnic area, park museum, mini golf, and go-kart rides.

RODEOS ♂ **Gerry Rodeo** (716-985-4847 or 716-985-5754; www.gerryrodeo.org), Gerry Volunteer Fire Department Grounds (8 miles north of Jamestown on NY 60), Gerry. Started in 1945 as a fundraiser for the Gerry Volunteer Fire Department, this event has grown to be the oldest consecutive rodeo east of the Mississippi. Competitive rodeo events include bareback bronc riding, calf roping, bull riding, steer wrestling, saddle bronc riding, and barrel racing. Of course, it wouldn't be a rodeo without rodeo clowns. A western beef BBQ dinner is served before the show

GOLF Jamestown and the surrounding communities were honored with the "Best Little Golf Town in America" award in 2002 by *Golf Digest* magazine. Experts who rated the area cited accessibility, value, and the weather. The area has top-quality courses at affordable rates with package deals available. The spectacular scenery, along with the mild weather and long playing season, add to the area's golf appeal.

Bemus Point Golf Club (716-386-2893), 72 Main Street, Bemus Point. A nine-hole, par-36 public golf course complete with pro shop and lessons.

Breezewood Links (716-287-2138), 4335 Dean School Road, Falconer. A challenging 9-hole, par-36 course open to the public. The rustic clubhouse features a snack area, pro shop, and eco-friendly electric golf carts.

Cassadaga Lakes Country Club (716-595-3003), 55 Frisbee Road, Cassadaga. A 9-hole, par-35 course with lounge and dining facility.

Chautauqua Golf Club at the Chautauqua Institution (716-357-6211; www.ciweb.org), NY 394, Chautauqua. Thirty-six holes (par 72 for 18 holes) of golf on rolling countryside with lake views. This course has been regarded as one of the finest in America since it was founded in 1913.

Chautauqua Point Golf Course (716 386-GOLF), NY 430, Dewittville. This 9-hole, par-35 course is the oldest golf course in Chautauqua County.

Lakewood Golf Center (716-763-0224; www.lakewoodgolfcenter.com), 4341 West Fairmount Avenue, Lakewood. This family-oriented facility features a driving range, miniature golf lit for nighttime play, a pro shop, and a repair center.

Maplehurst Country Club (716-763-1225 or 716-763-9058), 1508 Big Tree Road, Lakewood. An 18-hole, par-70 public golf course overlooking Chautauqua Lake.

South Hills Country Club (716-487-1471), 3108 Busti-Stillwater Road, Jamestown. The least expensive semiprivate 18-hole, par-72 course in the county.

Timber Creek Golf Course (716-782-4550), 1607 Blockville Road (CR 35), Ashville. A 9-hole, par-35 course.

Woodcrest Golf Course (716-789-4653 www.woodcrestgolf.com), 3583 Wall Street, Mayville. An 18-hole, par-71 regulation-length golf course set on rolling hillsides. Facilities include a driving range and pro shop.

MARINAS AND BOAT LAUNCHES Chautauqua Marina (716-753-3913; www.chautauquamarina.com), 104 West Lake Road (NY 394), Mayville. A full-service marina that also offers boat and jet ski rental.

Holiday Harbor (716-484-7175; www.holidayharbor.com), Avon Avenue, Celoron. A full-service marina with over 400 slips, inside storage, repairs, showers, Laundromat, and swimming pool.

WALKING TOURS Old Northside Walking Tour. Take a self-guided tour through downtown Jamestown past many historic homes and businesses. A map and descriptions of the buildings is available from the Fenton History Center (see *To See—Museums and Historic Homes*).

South Side Walking Tour. Another self-guided tour, this one of homes and places of businesses owned by prominent citizens over 100 years ago. A map and descriptions of the buildings is available from the Fenton History Center (see *To See—Museums and Historic Homes*).

✳ Green Space

BEACHES Cassadaga Beach (716-595-3007), Park Avenue, Cassadaga. Open July 1–third week in August, Monday–Friday 1–8, Saturday 12–8, Sunday 12–6. Admission: $1. A 1-acre beach with lifeguards located on Cassadaga Lake. Facilities include rest rooms and changing stalls.

Chautauqua Institution See *To Do*.

Lakeside Park See *Parks*.

Long Point State Park See *Parks*.

NATURE PRESERVES ✐ Jamestown Audubon Nature Center (716-569-2345; www.jasny.org), 1600 Riverside Road, Jamestown. Grounds open daily year-round dawn to dusk; Roger Tory Peterson Nature Interpretive Building open Monday–Saturday 10–4:30, Sunday 1–4:30. Nonmember fee $4. This preserve, once a farm, has 600 acres of fields, woods, wetlands, several streams, and ponds, including Big Pond, a sanctuary for migratory birds. There are 5 miles of walking/

hiking trails, including a boardwalk by the swamplands. Deer as well as fox and other small mammals make their home here, as do at least 431 species of plants. The Roger Tory Peterson Nature Interpretive Building contains living and non-living exhibits, including over 200 mounted birds—some now extinct. Hands-on exhibits for kids are located in the Discovery Room.

✒ **Roger Tory Peterson Institute of Natural History** (716-665-2473; www.rtpi .org), 311 Curtis Street, Jamestown. Open Tuesday–Saturday 10-4, Sunday 1–5. The mission of the Roger Tory Peterson Institute is to create passion for and knowledge of the natural world in the hearts and minds of children by inspiring and guiding the study of nature in schools and in the community. The 27-acre center has nature trails, a butterfly garden, and more. Roger Tory Peterson, a Jamestown native, was considered one of the greatest naturalists of the 20th century and used his skills in painting, photography, and writing to bring nature to everyone. Displayed inside the institute is Dr. Peterson's life work, which reflects his belief that people who develop an awareness of the natural world will be committed to its preservation.

PARKS **Lucille Ball Memorial Park** (716-487-4175), Boulevard at Dunham, Celoron. This 7-acre village park on the shores of Lake Chautauqua is on the former site of the Celoron Amusement Park, where Lucy spent her youthful summers.

Richard O. Hartley Park, Foot of Chautauqua Avenue, Lakeville. A small lakeside park.

Lakeside Park (716-753-2125), NY 394, Mayville. Open dawn to dusk. Free admission. Located on Chautauqua Lake, this park has nature trails, fishing, picnic areas, sports fields, a boat launch, and a beach. It is the site of the annual Mayville Ice Castle Extravaganza in February. Blocks of ice are taken from Chautauqua Lake to build the ice castle, the southernmost ice castle in the U.S.

Lakeside Village Park, Lakeside Drive, Bemus Point. A village park with a playground and small swimming area on Lake Chautauqua.

Long Point State Park (716-386-2722), 4459 NY 430 (on Lake Chautauqua), Bemus Point. Open year-round, dawn to dusk. Admission: $7/car Memorial Day–Labor Day. Hike a nature trail that passes through thickly wooded stands of beech, maple, poplar, and oak. Or enjoy the playground and picnic facilities. The boat launch, located at the park's marina, is one of the most modern on Lake Chautauqua. The most popular fish caught are muskellunge, or muskie, which are native to the lake. Anglers like these fish for their size—they often grow to more than 30 inches—and their "fight." During the winter months visitors can enjoy cross-country skiing, snowmobiling, and ice-fishing.

SNOWMOBILE TRAILS With over 400 miles of trails, snowmobiling is one of the most popular winter pastimes in Chautauqua County. Snowmobiling in New York requires state registration. For information about registration and a "NYS Snowmobile Guide," contact one of the following: **Department of Motor Vehicle: Dunkirk** (716-366-0210), **Jamestown** (716-661-8220), or **Mayville**

(716-753-4229), or write **NYSDMV Snowmobile Unit**, Suite 204, 150 Broadway, Menands, NY 12204. Snowmobiling enthusiasts may want to subscribe to *On the Trail* (315-437-9296, 800-332-9202; PO Box 456, East Syracuse, NY 13057. This publication focuses on snowmobiling in New York and has listings for all the snowmobiling clubs in the state. For information on snowmobiling in the Mayville area, contact the **Chautauqua Lake Snowmobile Club** (716-753-2924; www.chautauquasnow.com) 7239 Hannum Road, PO Box 134, Mayville 14757.

WALKING AND HIKING TRAILS **Chautauqua Rails to Trails** (716-269-3666; www2.cecomet.net/crtt, www.traillinks.com), Mayville Train Depot (NY 394), Mayville Thirty miles of abandoned railway corridors have been converted into off-road trails for walking, hiking, bicycling, cross-country skiing, and horseback riding. The trail runs from Sherman to Brocton, with numerous access points along the way. (Map available from Chautauqua County Tourism; see *Guidance*.)

Earl Cardot Eastside Overland Trail. This 18-mile hiking trail, which passes through New York State reforestation areas, the Canadaway Creek Wildlife Management area, and private lands, runs from just east of Cassadaga to east of Gerry. (A detailed map is available from Chautauqua County Tourism; see *Guidance*.)

Fred J. Cusimano Westside Overland Trail (716-763-8928), Hannum Road, Mayville to the Pennsylvania state line. A 25-mile trail that crosses through New York State reforestation areas, Chautauqua County lands, and private property. The trail is named after Fred J. Cusimano, known as the father of the Chautauqua County Parks System. (Map available from Chautauqua County Tourism; see *Guidance*.)

Jamestown Riverwalk Park (716-483-7547), Main and Institute Streets. A city walking path and park.

✳ Lodging

CHAUTAUQUA INSTITUTION Hundreds of small cottages, guest houses, apartments, and condos are available for rent on and around the grounds of the Chautauqua Institution during the summer season. All of them couldn't possibly be reviewed for this book, but Chautauqua is a lovely area, so almost all of the accommodations are top-notch. All lodging, except for the Athenaeum Hotel, which is operated by the institution, is privately owned and operated. A good source of rental information is **Vacation Properties** (800-344-2198; www.vactionpro.com), NY 394, Chautauqua. An accommo-

dations directory of properties on the grounds of the Chautauqua Institution is available at the visitors center, or log on to www.ciweb.org. Some of the larger properties on the grounds are:

Athenaeum Hotel (716-357-4444 or 800-821-1881; www.athenaeumhotel .com) PO Box 66, Chautauqua. The Athenaeum, built in 1881, is listed on the National Register of Historic Places. It was the first hotel in the world to have electric lights, and many notable people—including Ulysses S. Grant, Teddy Roosevelt, Thomas Edison, and Susan B. Anthony—have stayed here. This elegant, Victorian-era "grande dame" full-service hotel overlooking Chautauqua Lake offers modern amenities with the charm of yesterday. Room rates are based on the American Plan, which includes three meals daily. Casual attire is acceptable in the dining room for breakfast and lunch; for dinner, gentlemen are requested to wear a jacket and tie and ladies to dress in their finest. $178–$400.

Carey Cottage Inn (716-357-2245; www.careycottageinn.com), 9 Bowman Avenue, Chautauqua. Open late May–mid-September. This 1883 Victorian inn, just steps from the Amphitheater and Bestor Plaza, has antiques-decorated rooms. $100–$150.

The Spencer (716-357-3785; www.thespencer.com), 25 Palestine Avenue, Chautauqua. Open year-round. Enjoy Victorian charm with 21st-century comforts like whirlpool tubs and king-sized beds. This 100-year old four-story hotel features 26 luxurious guest rooms, each with its own literary fantasy theme. Take a trip to Africa with Isak Dinesen, a balloon ride with Jules Verne, or experience *The Lion, the Witch and the Wardrobe* in the C. S. Lewis room. Continental breakfast served daily in the parlor or on the porches. $185–$280/night in-season, lower rates in the off-season. Weekly rates also available.

Webb's Lake Resort (716-753-2161; www.webbsworld.com), 115 West Lake Road, (NY 394), Mayville. Open year-round. Fine accommodations include 52 spacious, modern hotel rooms, some with Jacuzzi tubs and private balconies. The resort is within walking distance to the lake and close to the Chautauqua Institution. Amenities include an outdoor swimming pool, exercise room, 18-hole miniature golf course, specialty candies, and a gift shop. They also have a restaurant; see *Dining Out*. Rates: winter $69–$139, spring/fall $89–$159, summer $109–$199.

INNS AND RESORTS Hotel Lenhart (716-386-2715; www.hotellenhart .com), 20 Lakeshore Drive, Bemus

THE HISTORIC ATHENAEUM HOTEL ON THE GROUNDS OF THE CHAUTAUQUA INSTITUTION WAS THE FIRST HOTEL IN THE WORLD TO HAVE ELECTRIC LIGHTS.

Christine A. Smyczynski

Point. Open Memorial Day–September 15. This charming Victorian hotel, with a large veranda and lawn facing Chautauqua Lake, has been owned and operated by the Lenhart family since 1881. The hotel has a total of 54 guest rooms, from large parlor rooms with private baths, to small single rooms with shared baths. It is within walking distance to the beach, shops, and restaurants. The hotel's elegant dining room is open to the public. Lodging includes a full breakfast and a multi-course evening dinner (modified American plan). $60-160.

BED & BREAKFASTS Brasted House Bed & Breakfast (716-753-5500 or 888-753-6205; www.brastedhouse .com), 4833 West Lake Road, Mayville. Joyce and Scott Brasted offer year-round accommodations in their 1860s farmhouse. All seven rooms feature the original white-pine floors, ceiling fans, quilts, and lace curtains. Towels and linens are line dried and freshly ironed. Each room is furnished in antiques and period reproductions, and all have private baths. The Aunt Mippy room is fully handicapped accessible. Children 10 and older. $80–$200.

Chestnut Hill on the Lake (716-789-5371), 3736 Victoria Road, Stow. Innkeeper Barbara Schuckler's Southern Colonial mansion is located on 7.5 acres on Chautauqua Lake. It features three guest rooms with private baths; two of these rooms are located lakeside. Two additional rooms can be added to create a suite for a larger group. A full breakfast is served each morning. $85–$125.

Country House B & B (716-386-3182; www.countryhousebb.com), 4836 Hale Road, Bemus Point.

Innkeepers Dave and Misty Sack offer six individually inspired theme rooms in this 1847 country home on 314 acres of farmland. Choose from the Gone with the Wind Room, with its movie memorabilia, or the opulent Victorian Room, with its claw-foot tub. Perhaps the Little House Room is more to your liking, with its framed letter from Laura Ingalls Wilder as a centerpiece. Or view the great outdoors from the king-sized bed of the Room with a View. Start your day with a wholesome country breakfast. $79–$129.

The Farmington Inn Bed & Breakfast (716-753-7989 or 800-421-0082; www.chautauqua-inn.com), 6642 East Lake Road (NY 430), Mayville. Open year-round. Craig and Jill Colburn's 1820s farmhouse inn, surrounded by ancient shade trees, features seven country furnished guest rooms, each with a private bath. The inn is close to Chautauqua Lake and hiking trails. A full country breakfast is served. $89–$159.

Lilly Pad B & B (716-386-7675; www.madbbs.com/solopah), 4961 Ellery-Centralia Road, Bemus Point. Open year-round. Innkeeper Mike Greiner built this genuine log home from scratch. It features three guest rooms, decorated with various themes: jazz, symphony, and country. The rooms share a bath and a half. The inn is located on lots of acreage with a pond and hiking trails and is close to cross-country skiing and snowmobile trails. A full breakfast is served. $50–$70.

Maple Springs Lake Side Inn (716-386-2500; www.mslsi.com), 4696 Chautauqua Avenue, Maple Springs. Open year-round. This lakefront Dutch Colonial mansion with seven guest rooms with private baths is set on 11 acres of landscaped grounds. The inn also has a private beach and dock. Innkeeper Rosemary Stage serves a country breakfast, in-season, in the main house. They also offer breakfast on their boat, weather permitting. Rates: summer $139–$195, winter $85-195.

Morning Glory Bed & Breakfast Country Inn (716-386-5938 or 800-287-0503; www.morningglorybb countryinn.com), 4766 Maple Springs–Ellery Road, Bemus Point. Open April–October. This restored old farmhouse features four uniquely decorated rooms with private baths and king-sized beds and includes a full gourmet breakfast. The inn—owned by Pauline Trindel and operated by innkeepers Dee and Howard Smith—has a private golf practice range as well as a pottery barn and coffee shop (716-386-3285). At the pottery barn, which is open to the public, customers can try their hands at decorating bisque pottery. See *Special Shops*. $89–$129.

The Stuart Manor Bed & Breakfast (716-789-9902), 4351 West Lake Road, Mayville. Open year-round. Gladys Stuart offers six rooms, each with a private bath, in an expanded farmhouse on 3 acres. Gladys is known for her wonderful breakfasts; she has lots of specialties and never serves the same thing twice in a week—unless, of course, a guest requests it. $50–$100.

The Village Inn Bed & Breakfast (716-753-3583; www.bbonline.com/ny/villageinn), 111 South Erie Street (NY 394), Mayville. Open year-round. Innkeeper Dean Hanby offers antiques-furnished rooms in an 1899 English Victorian home near Chau-

tauqua Lake. One room has a private bath, while the other two share a bath. A complimentary continental breakfast features home-made waffles, nut kuchen, and in-season fruit. Rates $80–$95 in summer, lower in winter.

MOTELS AND HOTELS & **Best Western** (716-484-8400 or 888-321-3321; www.bestwestern.com/downtown-jamestown), 200 West Third Street (across from Jamestown Savings Bank Ice Arena), Jamestown. This newly built downtown hotel has 61 rooms, including seven Jacuzzi suites and an indoor pool. It is within walking distance to downtown attractions, including the Lucy-Desi Museum and the Reg Lenna Civic Center. A complimentary deluxe continental breakfast is served each morning. $89–$189.

& **Comfort Inn** (716-664-5920; www.comfortinn.com/hotel/ny403), 2800 North Main Street, Jamestown. This inn has 101 guest rooms available. A free continental breakfast is included. $59–$169.

& **Holiday Inn** (716-664-3400), 150 West 4th Street, Jamestown. This hotel features 148 rooms, a full-service restaurant, and a heated indoor pool. $80–$120.

Snow Ridge Motel (716-753-2712), NY 394, Mayville. Owner Cathy Notaro offers 11 standard, comfortable motel rooms plus a new luxury suite featuring a fireplace and red heart-shaped Jacuzzi tub. Located right on the snowmobile trail, the motel is a popular spot year-round. An apartment is also available year-round, and a full cottage is available during the winter months only. Standard rooms off-season $55, summer $85 (two-night minimum), suite $149 weekdays, $159 weekend.

CAMPING RESORTS Numerous camping resorts are located throughout Chautauqua County. Consult Chautauqua County Tourism (www.tourchautauqa.com) for a complete list. Here are a few:

Chautauqua Heights Camping Resort (716-386-3804; www.chautauquahgts.com), 5652 Thumb Road, Dewittville. Open May 1–October 15. Located about a half mile from Chautauqua Lake, this campground has over 200 campsites on 180 acres of wooded and open land. They also have cottages and rustic cabins available for daily, weekly, or monthly rental. Call for rates.

Camp Chautauqua (716-789-3435 or 800-578-4849; www.campchautauqua.com), West Lake Road, Stow. Open year-round. A luxury RV resort with 250 campsites on the shores of Chautauqua Lake. Amenities include a boat launch, fishing, full hookups, teen center, picnic pavilion, heated pool, beach swimming, and even an animal petting farm. Rates range from $27.50 for no hookups to $50 full hookups.

Camp Prendergast (716-789-3485), 6238 Davis Road, Mayville. A quiet, secluded, wooded family-owned and operated campground only minutes from Chautauqua Lake. Call for rates.

COTTAGES Many cottages are available for rental during the summer months. One of the larger sources of rentals is **Vacation Properties** (800-344-2198; www.vactionpro.com), NY 394, Chautauqua. Many others are listed in the "Chautauqua County Travel Guide." available at **Chautauqua County Tourism** (716-3574569 or 800-242-4569; www.tourchautauqua.com), PO Box 1441, Chautauqua Institution Main Gate, NY 394, Chautauqua, NY 14722. Open daily 9–5, year-round.

Pine Hill Cottages and Motel (716-789-3543; www.pinehillresort.com), 3884 Park Way, Ashville. Marlea, Jerome, and Dan Brown offer clean, well-kept motel rooms, efficiencies, cottages, and chalets in a wooded, private waterfront area on Chautauqua Lake just 3 miles from the Chautauqua Institution. Amenities include a fishing and boat dock, playground, and picnic tables. Motel/efficiencies $54–$134, cottages $610–$1,500 weekly in-season.

We Wan Chu Cottages (716-789-3383; www.wewanchu.com), 4445 West Lake Road (NY 394), Chautauqua. Open April–end of October. This 8.5-acre cottage resort on Chautauqua Lake features 31 fully furnished modern cabins, most with a large wooden deck. The resort has a boat dock with over 70 boat slips, a fishing dock, boat rentals, recreation room, playground, and volleyball and basketball courts. Minimum two-night stay April–late June and late August–October 30. From late June–late August rentals are available by the week only. Rates range from $190 for two nights off-peak–$3,000 weekly during peak season, depending on the size of cottage. Call or see Web site for details.

✳ Where to Eat

DINING OUT Giambrone's Seafood House (716-753-2525), NY 394, Mayville. Open daily year-round 4–9. Chuck and Mary Giambrone have made this historic lakeside seafood house one of Chautauqua Lake's most popular establishments. Giambrone's is known for its seafood entrées, including shrimp, lobster, scallops, clams, and fresh fish, but you can also order steaks, prime rib, and pasta.

& **La Fleur** (716-753-3512), 5031 West Lake Road, Mayville. Open daily June–September for lunch 11–2, dinner 5–9; rest of year banquets only. Enjoy fine French country cuisine inspired by the finest restaurants in Paris. This upscale restaurant is located in a brick farmhouse at the Red Brick Farm retail complex.

& **La Scala** (716-664-7534), NY 430, Jamestown. Open Tuesday–Saturday at 5 pm, Sunday open at noon. Only the finest and freshest ingredients are used at LaScala, family owned since 1977. Over 60 different entrées are offered each evening. Choose from such specialties as veal and crab à la Lascals, seafood platter, or seafood fettuccini.

MacDuff's (716-664-9414; www.macduffsrestaurant.com), 317 Pine Street, Jamestown. Open Monday–Saturday 5:30–9. An award-winning, chef-owned intimate restaurant with a sophisticated menu that includes signature dishes like filet mignon with port and Stilton sauce, and veal with blackberry sauce. Opened in 1980, the restaurant, housed in an 1873 townhouse, was named after owners Donna and Gary Templin's West Highland terrier, MacDuff. The restaurant, which has the largest selection of single-malt scotches in western New York, is a destination where one can enjoy European-style gourmet dining

& **Olives** (716-753-2331), Erie Street (NY 394), Mayville. Open Monday–Saturday 11:30–2:30 and 5–9. Experience the taste and feel of Northern Italy at this upscale restaurant in the heart of historic Mayville.

& **The Surf Club** (716-386-5088), Main Street and Lakeside Drive, Bemus Point. Open seasonally for lunch and dinner. A Bemus Point institution for over 40 years, featuring live music, culinary creations, and a great view of Chautauqua Lake. Enjoy casual fine dining and sushi in the tropically decorated dining room or outdoors on the patio.

& **Vullos** (716-487-9568), 2953 East Lake Road (NY 430), Jamestown. Open Monday–Thursday 5–9, Friday and Saturday 5–10. This fine-dining establishment features the best veal on the lake, along with seafood, steak, chicken, and pasta.

& **The Watermark Restaurant** (716-753-2900), 188 South Erie Street, Mayville. Open April–September daily 11:30–9, October–March Thursday–Sunday 11:30–9. This restaurant is located on the shores of Chautauqua Lake, so enjoy the view while you feast on seafood, steak, and other house specialties. Come by car or boat; docking facilities are available. Sunsets are complimentary from their three lakeside decks.

& & **Webb's Captain's Table** (716-753-3960; www.webbsworld.com), 115 West Lake Road (NY 394), Mayville. Open Sunday–Thursday 11:30–9, Friday and Saturday 11:30–10. This three-star restaurant overlooking Chautauqua Lake features five dining rooms and an open deck. The menu offers American cuisine like baked chicken, prime rib, and fresh seafood, including broiled salmon filet and walleye. A children's menu is available.

& **White Horse Inn** (716-595-3523 or 866-898-0194), NY 60. Open Tuesday–Saturday from 5 pm, Sunday 4–8 pm; June–August, Monday–Saturday from 5 pm, Sunday 12–8 pm. Enjoy upscale fine dining in a charming setting, with plants along the windows, lots of stained glass, and a collection of local artwork. Start your dining experience with baked French sweet onion soup or a jumbo shrimp cocktail. Entrées include White Horse clam chowder with special seasonings, filet mignon, grilled salmon, shrimp scampi, and a special seafood supreme dish. Top off your dining experience with a slice of White Horse peanut butter pie.

&. **Ye Hare 'n Hounds Inn** (716-386-2181; www.harenhounds.com), 64 Lakeside Drive, Bemus Point. Open Labor Day–Memorial Day Monday–Thursday 5–9, Friday and Saturday 5–10, Sunday 4–9; Memorial Day–Labor Day Monday–Saturday 5–10, Sunday 4–10. Enjoy fine dining overlooking Chautauqua Lake in the atmosphere of an old English country inn that was built in 1915 as a private retreat and established as a restaurant in 1921. The menu features traditional American cuisine, with an emphasis on seafood. Specialties include seafood julienne, rack of lamb, and Italian chicken. All desserts are homemade.

EATING OUT Andriaccio's (716-753-5200 or 716-789-4320; www.andriaccios.com), NY 394, Mayville. Open Tuesday–Saturday 11–10, Sunday 10–9; all-you-can-eat lunch buffet Tuesday–Friday 11–2; Sunday brunch buffet 10–2. If you have a craving for pizza, this is the place to come. Choose from nine styles of gourmet pizza as well as Old World Italian specialties, wings, calzones, specialty salads, subs, and steaks, served in a charming dining room.

&. **Bemus Bay Coffee Café** (716-386-4374), 8 Albertus Avenue (in the Musky Mall), Bemus Point. Open seasonally May–September. This café, in the former Bemus Bay Hardware store, features fresh-roasted coffee, cappuccino, lattes, smoothies, and ice cream. They also serve gourmet sandwiches as well as classic sandwiches for lunch. Breakfast specials include quiche, bagel sandwiches, breakfast wraps, and made-from-scratch baked goods. The café has Wi-Fi hotspot Internet access.

Cherry Lounge (716-664-4359), 326 Cherry Street, Jamestown. Open 11 AM–2 AM daily year-round. This popular bar and restaurant is noted for chicken wings and other "pub grub," including their famous pocket sandwiches.

&. ❧ **Golden Gate Deli** (716-664-7272), 20 West Third Street, Jamestown. Open Monday–Friday 8–3. This casual deli is known for its specialty sandwiches on fresh bread, wraps, vegetarian dishes, salads, soups, and fresh-baked cookies and brownies. The menu has a definite San Francisco theme, including sandwiches with names like Alcatraz, Fisherman's Wharf, and Coit Tower.

&. ❧ **Gracie's on Main Street,** Bemus Point. Open seasonally May–September. Charbroiled foods and ice cream are served in this small café.

&. ❧ **Guppy's** (716-386-4422), 4663 Lake Road (NY 430), Maple Springs. Open year-round seven days at 3:30 PM (Sunday at noon). This family restaurant and bar has been a popular Chautauqua Lake eatery for over 20 years. Their signature dish is baked fish topped with cheese, peppers, onions, mushrooms, and tomatoes; they're also known for their stromboli, pizza, wings, and sandwiches.

& **Italian Fisherman** (716-386-7000; www.italianfisherman.com), 61 Lakeside Drive, Bemus Point. Open daily 11:30–9. Not merely a restaurant but a lakeside entertainment experience, the Italian Fisherman features fresh seafood, steaks, and pastas. Patrons can come by car or boat. It has a floating stage, movies for boaters to watch, and a cool floating clam bar.

& **Kaldis Coffeehouse** (716-484-8904), 106 East Third Street, Jamestown. Open Monday–Friday 8 am–3 pm, Saturday 9–2. One of Jamestown's best-kept secrets, this very small and casual coffee shop serves excellent panini sandwiches as well as other sandwiches, soups, salads, and desserts.

& **Taco Hut Restaurant** (716-488-0226), 203 East Third Street, Jamestown. Open Monday–Thursday 11–10, Friday and Saturday 11–11. When you're craving a little something from south of the border, head to Taco Hut, Jamestown's locally owned and operated Mexican restaurant serving the community since 1972.

& **The Village Casino** (716-386-2333; www.bemuspointcasino.com), 1 Lakeside Drive (on the lake), Bemus Point. Open daily 11 AM–2 AM, first weekend in May–last weekend in September. This building opened its doors in 1930, with its second floor used for big band concerts and vaudeville acts. Tommy Dorsey, Glenn Miller, Cab Calloway, and Al Jolson all appeared on the casino's stage. The present-day restaurant was established in the early 1980s. The Village Casino is known for wings, Maryland crab cakes, sandwiches, burgers, soups, dinner specials, and ice cream. In 1985 the casino broke the Guinness Book of World Records for the most chicken wings served in a 24-hour period. Guests can come by car or boat, as they have docking facilities. The casino also has a video-arcade room and a small gift shop. Enjoy live music Monday, Thursday, Friday, and Saturday.

✳ Entertainment

THEATERS AND PERFORMING ARTS CENTERS **Chautauqua Institution**, (716-357-6200; www.ciweb.com, www.chautauqua-inst.org), 1 Ames Avenue, Chautauqua. See *To Do*.

& **Jamestown Savings Bank Ice Arena** (716-484-2624; www.jamestownsavingsbankicearena.com), 319 West Third Street, Jamestown. This new state-of-the-art facility is the anchor of downtown Jamestown's redevelopment. It serves the community as an ice arena as well as a venue for concerts and other special events.

Lucille Ball Little Theatre (716-483-1095), 18 East Second Street, Jamestown. This high-Victorian Gothic–style building was built as the Allen's Opera House in 1881 and later known as Samuel's Opera House and Shea's Theater. Today the Lucille Ball Little Theatre is one of New York's largest and most active amateur theater groups.

Reg Lenna Civic Center (716-484-7070; www.reglenna.com), 116 East Third Street, Jamestown. This historic theater opened in 1923 as the Palace Theatre for vaudeville shows and later films. Over the years the building deteriorated. A large donation from the Reginald and Elizabeth Lenna Foundation was made in the 1980s to begin renovations. The 1,269-seat theater and performing arts center reopened in 1990. Features include a 35-foot movie screen, state-of-the-art sound equipment and projector, plus a Steinway concert grand piano.

MUSIC **Bemus Bay Pops** (716-386-7000; www.bemusbaypops.com), Floating Stage, next to the Italian Fisherman Restaurant, 61 Lakeside Drive, Bemus Point. Season runs June–August. Come by car, bike, foot, or boat to hear world-class musicians perform on the Chautauqua Lake Floating Stage. Enjoy free performances from your boat in the bay or your blanket on the shore.

Chautauqua Opera (716-357-6250 http://opera.ciweb.org), PO Box 672, Norton Hall on the grounds of the Chautauqua Institution. Past productions have included *Stiffelio, Faust, Fiddler on the Roof,* and *Susannah.* They put on four or five productions during the nine-week Chautauqua summer season.

Chautauqua Symphony Orchestra (716-357-6250), PO Box 28, the amphitheater at the Chautauqua Institution, Chautauqua. They perform during the nine-week Chautauqua Institution season.

PROFESSIONAL SPORTS **Jamestown Jammers Baseball** (716-664-0915; www.jamestownjammers.com), Russell E. Diethrick Jr. Park, 485 Falconer Street, Jamestown. A Single-A affiliate of the Florida Marlins. Season runs June–September.

✳ Selective Shopping

ANTIQUES **Countryside Antiques** (716-763-1835), 3013 West Lake Road (NY 394), Ashville. Open daily 10–5. A collection of quality antiques and collectibles.

The Store and the Apartment, 53 Dunham Avenue, Celoron. Open Wednesday–Saturday 1–4. Antiques and folk art, featuring restored trunks, furniture, vintage linens, and folk-art gifts.

What in the World (716-753-3045), 32 South Erie Street, Mayville. Open Wednesday–Friday 10–5, Saturday and Sunday 10–4; closed Sunday October 1–April 1. This small shop features a variety of antiques and collectibles.

ART GALLERIES **Dave Poulin Studios** (716-487-1553; www.davepoulin studios.com), 201 East First Street, Jamestown. Office 9–5; studio tours by appointment to learn about the bronzing process. Artist Dave Poulin creates figurative sculptures and life-sized bronze figures. He offers a variety of classes for all ages, including ceramics, pottery, painting, and drawing, in a newly constructed arts center behind his studio.

FARM MARKETS **Busti Cider Mill & Farm Market** (716-487-0177), 1135 Southwestern Drive (CR 45), Jamestown. Open mid-May–November Monday–Saturday 10–6, Sunday 12–5. Choose from farm-fresh, in-season produce, country gifts, jams and jellies, baked goods, and more. Fresh-pressed apple cider available mid-September–November. Tours of the working cider mill can be arranged by appointment.

Chautauqua Farm Market (716-357-6200), at the Chautauqua Institution. Open daily 7 AM–11 AM late June–late August. Located in the old powerhouse just inside the main gate of the institution, this market offers in-season locally grown produce, baked goods, cheese, and other specialty items.

SHOPPING MALLS **Chautauqua Mall** (716-763-1823), 318 East Fairmount Avenue, Lakewood. Open Monday–Saturday 9–9, Sunday 11–5. More than 65 specialty shops, including BonTon, JC Penney, and Sears.

✳ Special Shops

BEMUS POINT ♿ **Bemus Point Pottery** (716-386-3537), 8 Albertus Avenue (Musky Mall), Bemus Point. Open daily Memorial Day–Labor Day 10–5, weekends only in fall. Handcrafted pottery and Amish-made goods are featured in this shop.

🖊 ♿ **Morning Glory Pottery and Gift Shop** (716-386-5938 or 800-286-0503; www.morningglorybbcountry inn.com), 4766 Maple Springs–Ellery Road, Bemus Point. Open April–October Monday–Saturday 10–5, Sunday 1–5. This family-friendly place let's you get creative. Choose a piece of bisque pottery, and have fun painting it. The folks at Morning Glory will glaze it and fire it in their kiln, and you can pick up your masterpiece in a few days (or have it shipped to your home). They also have stuff-you-own critters and a café serving coffee and desserts. Overnight accommodations are available in the adjacent bed and breakfast inn. See *Lodging*.

♿ 🖊 🐾 **Nanny's of Bemus Point Children's Shop** (716-386-6122), 8 Alburtus Avenue (Musky Mall), Bemus Point. Open daily Memorial Day–Labor Day 10–5, weekends only in fall. This shop features children's clothing and reasonably priced toys.

♿ 🖊 🐾 **Six Main Gifts** (716-386-5624), 6 Main Street, Bemus Point. Open Monday–Saturday 11–5:30 (Friday until 8), Sunday 11–5. Closed January–April. This store features collectibles, cards, wind chimes, and gift items.

Skillmans (716-386-3000), 9 Main Street, Bemus Point. Open daily 10–5, except Thursday 12–5. Located in the original Skillman Brothers General Store building, Skillmans has been a household name in Bemus Point since 1908. Choose from fine apparel for men, women, and children, along with gourmet foods, handmade jewelry, home decor, toys, and more.

♿ **Viking Trader Gift Shop** (716-386-6043; www.vikingtradergifts.com), 3434 NY 430 (2 miles south of Chautauqua Lake Bridge), Bemus Point. Open year-round Monday–Saturday 10–5, Sunday 1–5. In business for over 25 years, this shop features Scandinavian imports and giftware, including Chautauqua Lake merchandise. They also carry cards, candleholders, books, casual clothing, and Christmas decor. A second location is open seasonally at the Chautauqua Institution in the Colonnade Building on Bestor Plaza (716-357-3217).

White Picket Fence (716-386-2655), 15 Main Street, Bemus Point. Open daily May–December 10–8. This cute little cottage shop features jewelry, gifts, home décor, and artwork.

CHAUTAUQUA INSTITUTION
♿ **Chautauqua Bookstore** (716-357-2151), Bestor Plaza. Open daily 9–5:30 year-round. The best of the Chautauqua Institution in a store, this shop carries books dealing with Chautauqua's programs, magazines, cards, tapes of Chautauqua lectures, and Chautauqua merchandise. Merchandise can also be ordered online or through mail order.

DEWITTVILLE & **Cadwell's Cheese House and Gift Shop** (716-753-7280), East Lake Road, Dewittville. Open 10–6 daily. This store, which first opened in 1927, has domestic and imported cheeses, maple syrup, and unique gifts.

& **The Farm Bell Basket Barn** (716-386-4033), 5252 NY 430, Dewittville. Open daily 10–5 May–November; call ahead in cold weather. Since 1967 visitors to the Chautauqua Lake region have found this a resource for wicker items and baskets, along with an assortment of gift items.

Jamestown and Vicinity

& **The Basket Company** (716-487-0088), 17 West Third Street, Jamestown. Open Monday–Friday 9–5, Saturday 9–12. This unique store in downtown Jamestown features all sorts of gift baskets, nuts and candy, and more. Their specialties include "California" trays—a custom assortment of nuts, dried fruits, and candies—and specialty baskets, including the Taste of Chautauqua basket.

& **Barbara Berry's Bookshop** (716-789-5757; www.berrybks.com), 3943 NY 394, Stow. Open Tuesday–Sunday 10–5. Over 155,000 books are housed in this 8,000-square-foot store, including hardcovers, paperbacks, old and rare, out of print, and classics. Unlike other "barnsfull of books," the books here are all organized on shelves.

& **Evergreen Outfitters** (716-763-2266; www.evergreen-outfitters.com), 4845 NY 474, Ashville. Open Monday 10–2, Tuesday, Thursday, and Friday 10–6, Saturday 10–4. An outdoor gear store that has 6,000 square feet of canoes, kayaks, climbing and camping equipment, outdoor clothing, footwear, and accessories. Paddling lessons and rentals are available, along with guided paddling tours of the outlet of Chautauqua Lake, Conewango Creek, and the bluffs along Lake Erie.

Jeepers: It's a Toy Store (716-763-1220), 385 East Fairmount Avenue, Lakewood. Open Monday–Tuesday 10–5, Wednesday–Friday 10–5:30, Saturday 10–4, Sunday 12–4. A locally owned and operated toy store with a large selection of fun and educational toys.

& **Jones Tasty Baking Co., Inc.** (716-484-1988; E-mail: jrbread man@aol.com), 209 Pine Street, Jamestown. Open Monday–Friday 5 AM–3:30 PM, Saturday 5:30 AM–2 PM. The Jones family has operated a bakery in the Jamestown area since 1909. Currently operated by the third generation, Jones is known for its breads, cookies, and rolls, all made fresh with no added preservatives. Lucille Ball really enjoyed their Limpa rye bread. After she moved out to the West Coast, she would have it shipped to her. They also make Tom and Jerry batter for the traditional holiday and cold-weather drink served in taverns and restaurants. The batter can't be shipped, but a dry mix is available through mail order.

Wellman Brothers & Green Farm Gifts (716-664-4006), 130 South Main Street, Jamestown. Open Monday–Friday 9–5, Wednesday 9–12, Saturday 9–4. Fine furnishings, accessories, and gifts can be found in a historic mansion.

MAYVILLE & **The Red Brick Farm Marketplace** (716-753-7969), 5031 West Lake Road, Mayville. Open daily 10–5, until 8 Memorial Day–

Labor Day; January closed Monday. This former dairy farm is now a collection of fine specialty shops and restaurants, including The Marketplace, Henry & Co., The Gardens, and La Fleur for fine dining.

& ✐ **Webb's Candies and Gift Shop** (716753-2161; www.webbscandies .com), 115 West Lake Road (NY 394), Mayville. Open Sunday and Monday 10–5, Tuesday–Saturday 10–6. In business since 1942, Webb's is famous for chocolates, including their trademark goat-milk fudge. All their candies are made by hand using the old-fashioned copper kettle method. The gift shop has many lovely items, including Chautauqua souvenirs.

SINCLAIRVILLE & ✐ 🐾 **Kabob Bear Country** (716-962-4647; www .kabobbear.com), 6359 South Stockton–Cassadaga Road, Mayville. Open May 1–November 1, Tuesday–Saturday 10–4; November 1–December 21, Thursday–Saturday 11–3. Watch teddy bears being sewn together at this unique shop run by Rose and Connie, a mother-daughter team. The business was started by the pair 20 years ago and features hundreds of handmade bears, bear clothing, and bear-related items. You can buy ready-made bears, or stuff your own bear. Each critter comes with its own "bearth" certificate. The name Kabob—what the area the store is located in is referred to—came from the sound wagons used to make going over the plank road (now Moon Road) leading into the village.

✳ Special Events

February: **Currier & Ives Sleigh Rally** (716-569-3842, **Chautauqua County Horseman's Association**),

Chautauqua Institution. Feel like you're part of a Currier & Ives painting at one of the few continuously held sleigh rallies in the country. Races feature several different classes of sleighs and animals. After the rally, the sleighs—with drivers in Victorian costumes—parade through the grounds of the Chautauqua institution. **Mayville I.C.E. Festival** (716-753-3113), Lakeside Park, Mayville. Blocks of ice are cut from Chautauqua Lake to build this, the southernmost ice castle in the United States. It's held on Presidents Day Weekend—though, of course, all is dependent on Mother Nature. Other activities include sleigh rides, ice carving, and snow sculptures.

May: **Lucy-Desi Days** (716-484-0800; www.lucy-desi.com), Jamestown. Celebrate the life of western New York native Lucille Ball at this annual event. Includes tours, films, guest speakers, contests, and exhibits.

June: **Mayville Bluegrass Festival** (716-753-7464 www.mayvilleblue grassfestival.com), Lakeside Park, Mayville. Two days of bluegrass music on Chautauqua Lake.

July: **Nature Art Festival** (716-569-2345; www.jasny.org), Jamestown. Nature-related art is displayed and demonstrated at several locations in Jamestown, including the Audubon Nature Center, Roger Tory Peterson Institute, and the Jamestown Savings Bank Ice Arena. The show features the best nature artists from the United States and Canada.

August: **Gerry Rodeo** (716-985-4847 www.gerryrodeo.com), Gerry Volunteer Fire Department grounds. The oldest consecutively running rodeo east of the Mississippi is an annual fund-raiser for the Gerry Volunteer Fire Department. **Lucille Ball's Birthday Celebration** (716-484-0800; www.lucy-desi.com), Jamestown. Celebrate the birth of Jamestown's favorite redhead, Lucille Ball. Events include book signings by authors of Lucy books, seminars, exhibits, tours, and musical entertainment.

September: **Busti Historical Society Apple Harvest Festival** (716-483-3670), 3443 Lawson Road, Jamestown. This annual festival—which takes place the last Saturday in September—began in 1972 and was one of the first outdoor festivals of this type in western New York. Enjoy demonstrations of pioneer skills, Civil War reenactments, music, tours of the gristmill and historic buildings, a farmers market, craft vendors, and, the most popular part of the event—plenty of apple-related food to eat and take home. *October:* **Pumpkin Hurling Festival,** (716-484-8341) Busti Fire Department Grounds, Busti (about 5 miles SW of Jamestown). People come from all over the country to compete in this annual pumpkin hurling competition, a fundraiser for the Busti Fire Department. Pumpkins are hurled out of cannons, catapults, and other contraptions. The event also features family-oriented activities, including pumpkin carving, craft and food vendors.

EVERY YEAR BLOCKS OF ICE ARE CUT FROM LAKE CHAUTAUQUA TO BUILD AN ICE CASTLE FOR THE ICE CASTLE FESTIVAL IN MAYVILLE.

Christine A. Smyczynski

SOUTHERN CHAUTAUQUA COUNTY—Clymer, Findley Lake, Panama, and Sherman

In 1811 Alexander Findley settled in this southwestern New York locale near a small pond. By 1816 he had built a dam, sawmill, and gristmill. The area grew, and by the 1890s "Findley's Lake" was a prosperous community. Between 1895 and 1915 people in from all over New York and Pennsylvania, who came by steamship, were drawn to Findley Lakes Lakeside Assembly for its inspirational and entertaining programs that rivaled the nearby Chautauqua Institution. After the invention of the automobile, Findley Lake saw a decline in business; in the last 15 years or so, however, the town has seen a rebirth and is home to many shops and several bed & breakfasts. It is a village for all seasons, offering summer festivals, fall foliage, and skiing as well as a 300-acre, 3-mile-long lake popular with boaters and anglers, with plentiful bass, walleye, muskie, and panfish. There's even a candle-making factory.

The nearby towns of Clymer, Panama, and Sherman are small and rural, yet they all have attractions and events that make them popular with visitors. In Clymer, enjoy golf in the warmer months and skiing in winter at the popular Peek 'n Peak resort. Panama Rocks in Panama is a privately owned and operated park that has the world's most extensive outcropping of glacier-sculpted, ocean-quartz-conglomerated rock. If you like music, be sure to visit Sherman in July, when the great Blue Heron Music Festival takes place.

AREA CODE The area code is 716.

GUIDANCE Findley Lake Area Chamber of Commerce (716-769-7609 or 888-769-7609; www.findleylakeinfo.org), PO Box 211, Findley Lake. Obtain information by phone or through their Web site.

Water Wheel Overlook (716-769-7610 for information, hours), 10400 Main Street, Findley Lake. Open 365 days a year. This building, operated by the Findley Lake Nature Center, is in a parklike setting right across from the north end of Findley Lake. There are displays of natural and local history as well as tourism information and public rest rooms. The waterwheel is built on the same location where Alexander Findley built his waterwheel upon settling here.

GETTING THERE *By car:* Exit 4 off the Southern Tier Expressway (I-86).

MEDICAL EMERGENCY 911

✳ To See

MUSEUMS AND HISTORIC HOMES Findley Lake/Mina Historical Society (716-769-7688), Findley Lake Community Center, 2883 North Road, (one block north of Main Street), Findley Lake. Open Saturday 10–noon in winter, 9–1 in summer. This museum has displays and photos pertaining to the history of Findley Lake.

Yorker Museum (716-761-6896), Park and Church Streets, Sherman. Open June 1–Labor Day Monday–Friday 11–4. A reconstructed village, featuring buildings and memorabilia depicting rural life in the mid-1800s.

✳ To Do

GOLF Peek'n Peak Resort (716-355-4141; www.pknpk.com), 1405 Olde Road, Clymer. Chautauqua County's finest golfing facility offers two 18-hole, par-72 golf courses: a 6,900-yard upper course and a 6,300-yard lower course. Facilities include a pro shop, public driving range, and a restaurant overlooking three fountains and the fairway. Lessons available at the Roland Stafford Golf School. The PGA Nationwide Tour is held at the four-and-a-half-star rated upper course each June. See also *Skiing, Lodging.*

FISHING Boat launch and fishing access to Findley Lake along NY 430, near the big anchor. Fishing licenses are available at many locations throughout Chautauqua County including town, county, and village clerk offices. Licenses can be obtained by mail from the **NYSDEC License Sale Office,** 625 Broadway, Room 151, Albany, NY 12233.

SKIING Peek'n Peak Resort and Conference Center (716-355-4141; www.pknpk.com), 1405 Olde Road, Clymer. Since 1964 tourists have enjoyed vacationing at this European-style village that offers a wide variety of winter amenities. Enjoy tubing, alpine and night skiing, and snowboarding. See also *Golf and Lodging.*

Lifts: 10 (two magic carpets, two double chairs, six triple chairs).

Trails: 27 (20 percent beginner, 70 percent intermediate, 10 percent difficult).

Vertical drop: 400 feet.

Snowmaking: 85 percent. Modern snowmaking equipment is located throughout the trail system.

Facilities: Accommodations range from standard hotel rooms to five-room houses. Six restaurants, from elegant to casual, are located on the grounds.

Ski School: Ski and snowboarding lessons,

For Children: Children's programs as well as child care.

Rates: $25–$41, season passes also available.

SNOWMOBILING "Snowmobiling Chautauqua" map of trails available from **Chautauqua County Tourism** (716-357-4569 or 800-242-4569; www.tour chautauqua.com), PO Box 1441, Chautauqua, NY 14722.

✳ Green Space

NATURE CENTERS Findley Lake Nature Center (716-769-7610), 2882 North Road, Findley Lake. Open Saturday morning and by appointment. The nature center, located in the Findley Lake Community Center, offers a variety of programs, lectures, and exhibits, along with several short nature trails.

WALKING AND HIKING TRAILS Panama Rocks (716-782-2845; www.pamama rocks.com), 11 Rock Hill Road, Panama. Open daily May–October 10–5. This privately owned and operated park has the world's most extensive outcropping of glacier-sculpted, ocean-quartz-conglomerate rock. The rocks are believed to have originated as sand and gravel sea islands over 300 million years ago. Over time the rocks were compressed, fractured, and uplifted. During the Ice Age a glacier cut into the rocks and unearthed them. The 1-mile hiking trail that circles the formation can be easily hiked in 20 minutes, but plan on spending several hours going off the trail to explore the rocks, caves, and crevices. A snack bar and picnic grove is open daily during the summer months.

✳ Lodging

INNS AND RESORTS Peek'n Peak Resort and Conference Center 716-355-4141; www.pknpk.com), 1405 Olde Road, Clymer. This year-round resort offers family fun, no matter what the season. Enjoy skiing in the winter months and golf in the spring, summer, and fall. Accommodations range from standard and luxury hotel rooms to fairway suites located on the golf course, to condominiums to luxurious five bedroom clubhouses. Several dining rooms are located in the complex, serving full-course meals and lighter fare. Features include, indoor and outdoor pools, sauna, hot tub, fitness center, indoor and outdoor tennis courts, bicycles, lawn games, miniature golf, and a gift shop $135-375

Findley Lake Inn (716-769-7764; www.findleylakeinn.com), Shadyside Road, Findley Lake. Open seasonally May–October. Innkeepers Lynn and Cyndy Nelson offer five guest rooms with two shared baths in this inn overlooking Findley Lake. They deal mainly in group rentals for this fully furnished inn with a complete kitchen and great room, but they'll also rent out individual rooms when available. A continental breakfast is provided for individual room rentals. $80/night for a single room, $1,200/week for entire 5-bedroom inn.

MOTELS AND HOTELS Holiday Inn Express (716-769-7900; www .hiexpress.com/findleylkny/), 3030 NY 426, Findley Lake. This hotel, located convenient to I-86 and local golf and ski centers, features 87 rooms and suites. Amenities include an indoor pool and fitness room and free continental breakfast. $79–$129.

BED & BREAKFASTS Blair House Bed & Breakfast (716-769-7329; www.blairhousefl.com), 2737 Shadyside Road, Findley Lake. Open seasonally. Ruth Blair greets you at the door with her famous chocolate chip cookies on your arrival at Blair House. The circa 1890 farmhouse, overlooking Findley Lake, features four antiques-furnished guest rooms with private baths. Each room is named for a family member or friend. Sarah's Honeymoon Suite, with a view of the lake, features a hand-painted ceiling and a queen-sized bed. Ruth's Romantic Retreat has apple-green walls and imported Swedish curtains, along with a brass queen-sized bed. Les's Hideaway, named after a local hero, has a claw-foot bathtub, and Geneva's Anniversary Suite is painted in soft ivory and has a queen-sized bed. The inn is wired with DSL and cable TV access. $89–$149.

Blue Heron Inn Bed & Breakfast (716-769-7852; www.theblueheron inn.com), 10412 Main Street, Findley Lake. Open year-round. This bed & breakfast overlooking Findley Lake is located in the heart of the shopping district. Innkeepers Bruce and Tobi Ahlquist offer an atmosphere of relaxation in their three antiques-filled guest rooms with air conditioning and private baths. A full breakfast is served. $99–$125. The dining room is open to the public for breakfast and lunch. See *Dining Out*.

✳ Where to Eat

DINING OUT **Blue Heron Inn** (716-769-7852; www.theblueheroninn.com), 10412 Main Street, Findley Lake. Open Wednesday–Sunday 9 AM–2:30 PM for breakfast and lunch. Enjoy made-to-order meals in a lovely room overlooking the lake, complete with hardwood floors, deep-green walls, beautifully finished woodwork, and lace curtains. Their specialties include homemade quiche, beef burrito, Middle Eastern plate, and Meshuga, a dish consisting of a potato pancake topped with corned beef, coleslaw, and Russian dressing. Sounds weird but tastes good. See also *Bed & Breakfasts*.

The Royal Court Dining Peek'n Peak Resort and Conference Center, (716-355-4141; www.pknpk.com), 1405 Olde Road, Clymer. Open daily for lunch 11–2, dinner 5–9. Fine dining in a casual yet refined atmosphere. Start your meal with a crock of the Peek's famous seafood bisque topped with a puff pastry dome, sour cream, and caviar or a shrimp cocktail. Entrées include veal scaloppini, braised lamb shank, filet mignon, and prime rib, as well as numerous seafood dishes.

EATING OUT **Curly Maple Restaurant** (716-769-7633), 2825 NY 426, Findley Lake. Open Wednesday–Saturday lunch 11–4, dinner 5–9, Sunday Buffet 9:30–6. Hours may be shorter during winter, so call ahead. This 1884 country Victorian home turned restaurant has curly maple woodwork

throughout, hence the name. Owner Leslie Oster serves only homemade, made-from-scratch foods on her eclectic and diverse menu. Desserts are one of their specialties as Ms. Oster previously baked desserts for restaurants in New York City. They have been voted to have the best desserts in the area by the *Erie* (Pennsylvania) *Times* (Erie is only about 15 miles away). It is rumored that the restaurant has a resident ghost, the home's original builder Ora Pitt.

Thelma Lynn's Country Kitchen (716-769-6800), Main Street, Findley Lake. Open Monday–Wednesday 7–3, Thursday 7–8, Friday and Saturday 7–9, Sunday 7–8. Family-style dining in a small restaurant with large windows overlooking Findley Lake. An outdoor deck is open in season.

✳ Selective Shopping

SPECIAL SHOPS **Candle-Escents Candle House & Factory** (716-769-7874; www.candle-escents.com), Main Street, Findley Lake. Open daily 10–5 year-round. Experience the scent of Findley Lake. Watch votive candles being hand poured in the candle factory. A large gift shop in front of the factory features the largest selection of candles in the region along with other country home decor items. Orders can be placed on-line and shipped.

Country Coop (716-769-6514), 10404 School Street, Findley Lake. Open Memorial Day–Labor Day daily 11–5, rest of year Saturday–Sunday 11–5; closed January–March. An old barn filled to the rafters with a variety of antiques and collectibles.

Findley Lake Trading Co. (716-769-6690; www.findleylaketrading.com), 2762 North Road, Findley Lake. Open 9–5 daily year-round.

This shop carries rustic Adirondack-style furniture and accessories. A military museum, focusing on World War II to the Vietnam War, is located inside the store.

Gifts by Dander/Gloria's Home Accents (716-769-7177), 10371 Main Street, Findley Lake. Open 10–5 daily in summer, shorter hours in winter. Two shops in one, featuring home decor, jewelry, and holiday decorations.

Ladybugz Landing (716-769-7189; www.ladybugz-landing.com), 2782 North Road, Findley Lake. Open Monday–Friday 9–3, Saturday and Sunday 9–5; closed December–May. A coffee bar and a gift shop crawling with ladybugs, bees, dragonflies, and butterflies. Their outdoor deck is open seasonally.

Legacy Design and the Bird's Nest (716-769-7775), 10378 Main Street, Findley Lake. Open Tuesday–Saturday 11–5, Sunday 1–5 These two shops in one offer home decor items, gifts, and furniture plus wild-bird supplies, including birdhouses, feeders, and seeds.

Matters of the Hearth (716-769-7550), 10412 Main Street, Findley Lake. Showroom open daily 8–7; open for sales Saturday 10–4 or by appointment. Specializing in cast-iron parlor stoves, gas and wood buck stoves, and fireplace accessories.

Morgen & Co. (716-769-7700), 10386 Main Street, Findley Lake. Open Monday–Friday 11–5, Saturday and Sunday 10–5. The most unique products in this store are the decorative glycerin soaps, which are cut in bars off of the larger bricks. They also carry bath items and lotions.

Nostalgia at the Blue Heron Inn Country (716-769-7852; www.the blueheroninn.com), Located upstairs in the red barn next to the Blue Heron Inn, Findley Lake. Open Tuesday–Sunday 11–5; January–April, Wednesday–Sunday 11–5. This unique shop features handcrafted jewelry, suncatchers, New-Age and feng shui accessories, old-time candy, toys, and games.

Wonderments–A Victorian Shop (716-769-7190), 10365 Main Street, Findley Lake. Open Wednesday–Sunday 11–5 in fall, open seven days in spring and summer; call for winter hours. Step back into the Victorian era when you visit this distinctive store. Choose from home decor, bath and body items, plus a large selection of holiday decorations.

Yankee Bush Books & Gifts (716-769-7455), 10412 Main Street, Findley Lake. Open Wednesday–Sunday 11–5 year-round. New and used books. The new books focus mainly on children's, women's interests, nature, gardening, fishing, and golf. They also carry Lang's cards and gifts.

✳ Special Events

July: **Great Blue Heron Music Festival** (716-487-1781 www.greatblue heron.com), Sherman. A three-day music festival featuring new and established musicians playing a variety of musical styles, including folk, bluegrass, roots rock, zydeco, and old time.

October: **Peek'n Peak Fall Festival** (716-355-4141 www.pknpk.com), Findley Lake. Enjoy fall foliage in New York's Southern Tier.

November: **Christmas in the Village** (716-769-7609 or 888-769-7609; www.findleylakeinfo.org), Findley Lake. Do your Christmas shopping in Findley Lake's fine boutiques.

AMISH COUNTRY — Eastern Chautauqua and Western Cattaraugus Counties (Cherry Creek, Conawango, Leon, and Randolph)

The first Amish families arrived in Cattaraugus County in 1948, with farming as their main means of support. Old Order Amish feel that owning and using modern tools and appliances is a sin, so they live without electricity, plow the fields with work horses instead of tractors, and depend on horse and buggy for transportation. The men and boys dress in overalls and wear boots and large broadbrimmed hats, while the women and girls dress in blue or black dresses and a large bonnet. They hold church services in their own homes. The Amish community has its own school, and children are educated up to the eighth grade.

The Amish are peaceful, friendly people who tend to their own affairs. They are not interested in politics unless it involves the town in which they live. The men rarely vote in any county, state, or federal elections, and the women never vote.

About 80 percent of the population of the town of Leon is Amish. In addition to farming, these families support themselves through woodworking, leather crafts, iron crafts, and rug making, along with quilting and baking. There are also smaller Amish communities located between Sherman and Clymer in the southwestern part of Chautauqua County and west of Westfield.

Note: When visiting an Amish community, do not take photographs—the Amish have religious beliefs against making images of themselves. (This is why Amish dolls don't have faces.)

AREA CODE The area code is 716.

GUIDANCE Village of Cherry Creek (716-296-5681), 6845 Main Street, Cherry Creek 14723. Open Monday, Tuesday, Thursday, Friday 9–2, Wednesday 4:30–7, Saturday 9:30–11:30.

A map of shops in Amish Country can be obtained from the **Chautauqua County Chamber of Commerce** (716-366-6200; www.chautauquachamber .org), **Cattaraugus County Visitors Bureau** (800-331-0543; www.enchanted mountains.info), or the **Gowanda Area Chamber of Commerce** (716-532-2834; www.gowandachamber.org).

GETTING THERE *By car:* Accessible from US 62 or off of I-86.

MEDICAL EMERGENCY Dial 911.

✳ To Do

FISHING Randolph Fish Hatchery (716-358-4755), 10943 Hatchery Road, Randolph. Open daily 8–4. Many of the rivers, streams, and ponds in the county are stocked with fish bred at this facility.

GOLF Cardinal Hills Golf Course (716-358-5409), 78 Conewango Road (NY 241), Randolph. An 18-hole, par-72 course in the scenic Conewango Valley.

SKIING Cockaigne (716-287-3223; www.cockaigne.com), 1493 Thornton Road (CR. 66), Cherry Creek.

Lifts: Four (one T-Bar and three double chairs).

Trails: 10 (five slopes, 25 percent beginner, 60 percent intermediate, 15 percent difficult).

Vertical Drop: 430 feet.

Snowmaking: 70 percent.

Facilities: Alpine skiing and snowboarding are available. Slopes are illuminated at night.

Ski School: Private and group lessons.

For Children: Kids' ski programs for ages 5–8 and 9–15. No child care available.

Rates: $16–$32.

✳ Lodging

BED & BREAKFASTS Cherry Creek Inn (716-296-5105; www.cherry creekinn.net), 1022 West Road, Cherry Creek. Innkeepers Michael Fields and Mark Jones have created a relaxing retreat on 30 acres in the heart of Amish Country. The Cherry Creek Inn, an Italian villa originally built in 1860 by one of Cherry Creek's founding fathers, features four antiques-furnished guest rooms plus a two-room loft suite that's perfect for families. Each room's bed is topped with a beautiful quilt, and all rooms have private baths. The gameroom features an extensive movie library along with video and board games. A full breakfast is served. The inn is conveniently located only five minutes away from Cockaigne ski area. $65–$150.

🐾 **Foxe Farmhouse Bed and Breakfast** (716-962-3412 or 877-468-5523; www.foxefarmhouse.com), 1880 Thorton Road, Cherry Creek. Carol Lorenc's lodging especially suits the outdoor enthusiast. The century-old farmhouse is located 2 miles from Cockaigne Ski Center and near hundreds of miles of snowmobile trails.

The inn has three bedrooms that share two baths. Guest rooms can be rented individually, or the whole house can be rented (sleeps nine). Stables are available for housing horses. A self-serve, hot-and-cold cereal bar is included. Guests are also welcome to use the kitchen, appliances, and dishes to prepare their own meals. $60/room, $200/whole house.

✳ Where to Eat

DINING OUT The Trillium Lodge (716-296-8100), 6830 Main Street (NY 83), Cherry Creek. Open Tuesday–Wednesday 4–10, Thursday–Saturday 11–10, Sunday 12–8. This restaurant, which resembles a cozy Adirondack-style lodge, offers daily specials, including a Friday fish fry and prime rib on Saturdays. Dine by the fireplace in winter or on the garden patio in warmer months. Musical entertainment is featured weekly in their lounge.

✳ Selective Shopping

AMISH SHOPS Many Amish shops are located in the area surrounding **Leon**

and **Conewango,** often in the family's own home or barn, so the best way to shop is to look for a sign advertising their goods. Often they will have an open sign. Items for sale include quilts, rugs, furniture, baked goods, and maple syrup. The Amish do not conduct business on Sunday. Again, do not photograph the Amish.

Valley View Cheese Company (716-296-5821), 6028 US 62, Conewango. Open Monday–Saturday 8:30–5; closes at 4 in winter. This is one of the larger shops in the area. Goods available include Amish cheese and other Amish-made goods, including quilts, wooden items, and furniture.

SPECIAL SHOPS **The Depot** (716-296-5697), Depot Street (off Railroad Street), Cherry Creek. Open Monday–Saturday 8:30–4. In winter, closes at noon on Saturday. This gift shop in an 1896 Victorian railroad depot features Amish goods, handmade crafts, jewelry, seasonal items, and antiques.

Rustic Creations (716-296-5827), 6776 Main Street, Cherry Creek. Monday–Saturday 10–5 year-round. A cozy store with the feel of an Adirondack-style lodge features rustic and unique accessories, including nature-themed gifts, home décor, and a year-round Christmas loft. Enjoy a hot cup of their special orange-spiced tea while you shop.

CATTARAUGUS COUNTY

Cattaraugus County offers visitors vacation variety. Known as the Enchanted Mountains, Cattaraugus County is the heart of western New York's ski country, and Ellicottville in the central part of the county—home to the largest private ski resort in North America as well as one of the most popular ski resorts in western New York—has been proclaimed the "Aspen of the East." The Zoar Valley in the northern part of the county has some of the largest old-growth forests in the United States and is a popular spot for wilderness hiking and whitewater rafting. Salamanca, in the southern portion of the county, is the only city in the United States located entirely on a tribal reservation, and while in Salamanca visitors can partake in casino gambling at the Seneca Allegany Casino. Allegany State Park, at 65,000 acres, is New York's largest state park, yet nearby Olean was once one of the largest oil producers in the world.

Cattaraugus County was formed in 1808, and the first country seat was the village of Ellicottville, due to its geographic location at the center of the county. In 1868 the county seat was moved to its present location, the town of Little Valley.

Cattaraugus County is the number one county in New York State for turkey hunting and in the top three for deer hunting. Since the waterways of Cattaraugus County are stocked with fish raised at the Randolph Fish Hatchery, anglers, too, find this place a great place to visit.

AREA CODE The area code is 716.

COUNTYWIDE GUIDANCE **Cattaraugus County Department of Economic Development, Planning, and Tourism** (800-331-0543; www.enchanted mountains.info), 303 Court Street, Little Valley 14755. Open Monday–Friday 8–5.

ZOAR VALLEY AND NORTHERN CATTARAUGUS —Gowanda, Ashford, Yorkshire, Delevan, and East Otto

The Zoar Valley, near Gowanda, contains some of the largest old-growth forest trees in the eastern United States, including the world's tallest basswood (128.2 feet) and the second tallest American sycamore at 155 feet. Altogether, 12 species of trees in this area are either the biggest in the world or the biggest in

the Northeast. These trees are located in a rather remote section of the Zoar Valley Gorge known as the Gallery of the Giants. The gorge is also popular in early spring and summer for whitewater rafting.

Gowanda is divided by Cattaraugus Creek; part of the city is in Erie County and part in Cattaraugus County. Before the American Revolution the area now known as Gowanda was occupied by various Native tribes, who referred to it as *Juc Gowanda,* which means "beautiful valley among the hills." The first white settler, Turner Aldrich, a Quaker from Connecticut, came to the area in 1810 with his family. After he built a sawmill, the town was referred to as Aldrich Mills. When the village was incorporated in 1848, the name Gowanda was chosen to reflect its Native American beginnings. The village itself features Victorian architecture.

The areas surrounding Ashford, Yorkshire, and Delevan are primarily agricultural, especially for livestock and dairy farming. In the late 19th century, Delevan was a busy commercial and industrial center because of the Western

New York & Pennsylvania Railroad. In the past, cheese making was an important industry in the area. Today camping attracts people to the wooded areas. Nearby Otto and East Otto are known for the craftspeople who live and work in the area.

GUIDANCE Town of Ashford (716-942-6016), 9377 Route 240, West Valley. Open Monday–Friday 8–12, Saturday 9–12.

Town of Delevan (716-492-0281), 85 South Main Street, Delevan. Open Monday, Thursday, Friday 9–3:30; Tuesday 9–1 and 4–6.

East Otto Country Associates (716-257-9549; www.eastotto.com), PO Box 41 8420 Otto-Maples Road, East Otto 14729. Contact by phone or through website.

Gowanda Area Chamber of Commerce (716-532-2834 www.gowanda chamber.org), 28 Jamestown Street, PO Box 45, Gowanda 14070. Open Monday and Wednesday 10–2:30.

Town of Yorkshire (716-492-1640), 82 South Main Street, Delevan. Open Monday–Friday 9–2, except Wednesday 5–7 PM.

THE 400-ACRE GRIFFIS SCULPTURE PARK IN EAST OTTO DISPLAYS OVER 200 SCULPTURES AMONG PONDS, FORESTS, AND MEADOWS.
Christine A. Smyczynski

GETTING THERE *By car:* From the Buffalo area, take US 62 south to Gowanda. From the west, exit 59 off the New York State Thruway (I-90) to NY 39. Ashford is accessible from US 219, while Delevan and Yorkshire can be reached via NY 16.

GETTING AROUND *By taxi:* **Gowanda Cab Company** (716-532-5720).

MEDICAL EMERGENCY Dial 911
Tri-County Memorial Hospital (716-532-3377), 100 Memorial Drive, Gowanda.

✳ To See

ARCHITECTURE More than 200 architecturally significant properties are located in Gowanda. A self-guided walking tour brochure, featuring 35 of these properties, is available from the **Gowanda Chamber of Commerce** (see *Guidance*).

ART MUSEUMS ✐ **Griffis Sculpture Park** (716-257-9344 or 667-2808; www.griffispark.org), 6902 Mill Valley Road, East Otto (US 219 to Ahrens

Road, follow signs). Open dawn to dusk May 1–October 31; $5 admission. This 400-acre park founded in 1966 by the late artist Larry Griffis Jr. contains over 200 sculptures created by local and national artists, displayed among ponds, forests, and meadows, giving visitors the opportunity to commune with art and nature simultaneously. Visitors to the park are encouraged to interact with the sculptures, to touch and climb on or even in. You must park your car at the admission booth and hike to the various sculptures. If you don't have the time or ability to hike the park, take a drive past the sculpture park's Rohr Park site, located along Rohr Hill Road, which gives you a taste of what's located within the park.

HISTORIC SITES **Hollywood Theater** (716-532-6103; http://hollywoodtheater .org), 39 West Main Street, Gowanda. This historic theater first opened in 1926, hosting big bands, famous vaudeville performers, first-run motion pictures, and live performances. It was abandoned in 1992 and exposed to the elements until named as a landmark on the New York State and National Historic Registry. The interior of the 900-seat theater consists of wood-and-brass entry doors, a white Vermont marble lobby floor, ornate plaster trim, and painted murals. A $3 million restoration project began in 1997, and when completed, the theater will be used as a regional performing arts center.

✳ To Do

AUTO RACING **Freedom Raceway** (716-492-1564; www.freedomraceway.com), Bixby Hill Road, Delevan. Stock-car and dirt-track racing Friday nights at 7:30, April–October. Racing also takes places on several Sundays during the season. Snowmobile racing in the winter months.

CANOEING **Zoar Valley Paddling Club** (716-257-9750; www.zoarvalley.com), 9457 Harvey Road, Cattaraugus. Most creeks in the county are navigable by canoe. For a complete list of area creeks and rivers along with cautions and hints, see the map inserted into the Cattaraugus County Visitors Guide available from the Cattaraugus County Department of Economic Development, Planning, and Tourism (800-331-0543; www.enchantedmountains.info).

FISHING Salmon and steelhead can be found in great number in **Cattaraugus Creek,** a major trout and salmon tributary. Many anglers refer to Cattaraugus Creek as "fly- and spinfishing heaven." Fishing access to **Mansfield Creek** in East Otto can be found off Otto-Maples Road. Fishing licenses can be obtained at any county, town, or village clerk's office.

WHITE-WATER RAFTING **Cattaraugus Creek** in the Zoar Valley is a prime whitewater rafting area. The rapids are often unpredictable and challenging, ranging from gentle ripples to Class IV during high-water levels. The Zoar Valley has some of the most spectacular scenery in western New York, but most of it can only be viewed from the river, hence the popularity of whitewater rafting. Two companies in Gowanda offer whitewater rafting March–late May and

September–December: **Adventure Calls** (585-343-4710 or 888-270-2410) offers trips on the Genesee River in Letchworth State Park and on Cattaraugus Creek in the Zoar Valley as well as the Salmon River near Pulaski. The **Zoar Valley Canoe and Rafting Company** (716-532-2221 or 800-724-0696) runs trips through the Zoar Valley. River trips are run mainly on weekends and holidays, although weekday trips can be arranged for groups of ten or more. Zoar Valley Canoe and Rafting offers an Introduction to White Water Rafting trip that takes place along a 6-mile section of Cattaraugus Creek with I and II class rapids, which makes this trip perfect for beginners and children.

✳ Green Space

BIKE TRAILS Part of the **New York State Bicycle Tour Trail** runs through the northern section of Cattaraugus County. The Erie Mohawk route, which enters New York at the Massachusetts border, passes through the town of Perrysburg, near CR 42. The trail proceeds about 4 miles before continuing into Chautauqua County.

NATURE PRESERVES **Deer Lick Sanctuary,** Point Peter Road, Gowanda. Access by permit only (for info contact 585-546-8030, ext.29; www.nature.org/centralwestern). Many endangered species of flora and fauna can be found in this 398-acre nature preserve as well as numerous hiking trails.

Gooseneck Hill Waterfowl Farm (585-942-6835; www.gooseneckhillwater fowlfarm.com), 5067 Townline Road, Ashford. Open Sunday 2–5 June–September. This not-for-profit bird sanctuary, which opened in 1983, is the second largest waterfowl park in the world. The 4-acre farm, owned and operated by Rosemary and Milt Miner, features close to 400 geese, ducks, and swans, and 19 species of birds from all over the world.

Wild Spirit Rehab and Release Center (716-492-3223; www.wildspirit.org), 11511 Bixby Hill Road, Delevan. Open Sunday 2–5 June 1–early September. Wild Spirit was established in 1996 as a nonprofit organization dedicated to rehabilitating and releasing orphaned and injured wildlife.

WALKING AND HIKING TRAILS Hiking access to the **Zoar Valley** can be found off the following roads: Button Road, North Otto Road by the bridge, Valentine Flats Road, Forty Road (one of the more accessible paths), and Point Peter Road. Visitors are cautioned that the Zoar Valley is not a state park but a wilderness area, so few trails are marked, and the terrain is very rugged. (The **Gallery of the Giants,** old-growth trees, is accessible by narrow steep footpaths. Park at the end of Valentine Flats Road in the town of Persia, descend into the canyon, wade through the stream, then hike along the stream for about a mile.) Maps of the area can be obtained from the Gowanda Chamber of Commerce.

Deer Lick Sanctuary See *Nature Preserves*.

✳ Lodging

OTHER LODGING Campgrounds **Allegany Mountain Resort** (716-699-2352 or 699-2351), 6994 Plato Road, East Otto. Open May 15–October 15. Some 250 campsites with electric hookups, a pond, two pools, and a boat launch are offered at this 225-acre resort with a 66-acre spring-fed lake. Call for rates.

Arrowhead Campground (716-492-3715; www.arrowheadcamping.com), 10487 NY 16, Delevan. Open May 15–October 15. Two hundred campsites are available at this campground as well as activities like paddleboats, rowboats, swimming, fishing, hiking, horseshoes, volleyball, and a playground. Call for rates.

DUDE RANCHES **R & R Dude Ranch** (716-257-5663; www.recreationranch.com), 8940 Lange Road, Otto. Open year-round. The Ferguson family has two guest rooms in their 100-year-old farmhouse on a working horse farm. One room can accommodate 4 people, the other up to 6. Both rooms have private baths. They also have a loft apartment that can sleep up to 11 and a log cabin that sleeps 3 comfortably and 6 squeezing. Enjoy horseback riding, swimming, hiking, volleyball, horseshoes, fishing, cross-country skiing, and more. $40+.

✳ Where to Eat

EATING OUT **Carson's Ashford House** (716-942-3840), 9219 US 219, Ashford Hollow. Open 11–7 daily. Casual dining inside near the fireplace or outside in the garden. Menu selections include ribs, chicken, steak, Italian dishes, fish fry, and daily specials.

Moore's Sugar Shack (716-492-3067), Galen Hill Road, Freedom.

Open January and February, Sunday only 8 AM–2 PM; March 1–mid-April, Tuesday–Friday 9–6, Saturday and Sunday 8–6. Enjoy all-you-can-eat pancakes served with Moore's maple syrup. Syrup and other maple products can be purchased at the pancake house or ordered year-round by mail.

✳ Selective Shopping

Note: Some shops are located in extremely rural areas and don't have public rest rooms or restaurants nearby.

CRAFTS **Hog Shed Studio Pottery** (716-257-9549; www.eastotto.com/hogshed/hogshed01.html), 8240 Otto-Maples Road (CR 13), Otto. Open Wednesday–Sunday 10–5, May 1–December 24. Michael and Elliott Hutten have been producing pottery since 1982 in their studio in the hills. Choose from functional pieces—including plates, bowls, mugs, and bird feeders—along with wall decorations, sculptures, and porcelain jewelry.

SPECIAL SHOPS **Gowanda Harley-Davidson Inc.** (716-532-4584), 2535 Gowanda-Zoar Road, Gowanda. Open Tuesday–Wednesday 8:30–5, Thursday and Friday 8–8, Saturday 8–3. One of America's top Harley-Davidson dealers. Gift shop features a large selection of Harley memorabilia, shirts, jackets, infant wear, Christmas ornaments, and more.

Maple Glen Sugar House (716-532-5483 or 888-4R-SYRUP; www.mapleglensyrup.com), 2266 Gowanda-Zoar Road, Gowanda. Open year-round. Maple Glen features the largest variety of maple products in western New York. They also carry gift baskets and pancake mixes. Tours are offered during the annual Maple Weekend Open House in March.

Of Seasons Past Farm Shop (716-699-4471), 6578 Hencoop Road, Otto. Open Saturday and Sunday 10–6. Visit a small working sheep farm, and see spinning and weaving done in the shop. A collection of wool yarns, hand-woven rugs, scarves, gifts, natural soaps, candles, jewelry, and more can be found in this cozy shop heated by a woodburning stove. The shop is located about 2 miles from Ellicottville.

On the Rocks (716-257-9501), 9403 Utley Road, Otto. Open April 1–December 31 Wednesday–Sunday 10–5. This shop carries thousands of perennials, vines, shrubs, and more.

Their Country Garden Gift Shop is packed with garden, nature, and country decor items, plus seasonal decorations and herbal dip mixes.

✳ Special Events

June: **Hollywood Theater Harley Happening** (716-532-6103), Gowanda. An annual motorcycle rally to raise money to renovate the Hollywood Theater, sponsored by Gowanda Harley-Davidson.

November: **Holiday Open House** (716-257-9549; www.eastotto.com), East Otto. The stores in this area host an annual open house just before the holiday season.

CENTRAL CATTARAUGUS—Ellicottville, Franklinville, Little Valley, and Great Valley

Incorporated in 1837, the village of Ellicottville has been called the "Aspen of the East" since it is home to Holiday Valley, New York's largest ski resort, and Holimont, the largest private ski area in the United States. Nonskiers will enjoy the beautifully restored 19th-century buildings in Ellicottville's Historic District, which was placed on the National Register of Historic Places in 1991.

The first settler, Grove Hurlburt, arrived in 1815. The village—the county seat from 1817–1968—was named to honor the Holland Land Company's chief surveyor, Joseph Ellicott. Since the late 1880s the town's main economic force has been the logging and wood products industry. In recent years, the skiing and tourism industry have also become a large part of the economy, drawing over 650,000 visitors annually. The town is a shopper's paradise with a wide variety of specialty retail shops, along with many restaurants and bed and breakfast inns.

Franklinville, about 15 miles east of Ellicottville, is a small residential community with a history dating back to 1806, when the first settlers made their Holland Land Company claims. Many of these pioneers in what was originally called McCluer's Settlement were dairy and cattle farmers. One of the earlier farmers, Peter Ten Broeck, built an 8,000-acre cattle empire and was instrumental in providing the funds to offer free education to the youth of the area. The advent of the railroads brought a population boom to the community. In 1824 Franklinville was incorporated and named in honor of Benjamin Franklin. Today the area is popular with hunters, hikers, cyclists, cross-country skiers, and campers. It is also the hometown of 1999 Miss USA, Kim Pressler.

Little Valley, a small rural village of Victorian homes, is the county seat and the home to the Cattaraugus County fair, one of the nation's oldest county fairs. Nearby Great Valley has several large antiques stores as well as the popular fall destination Pumpkinville.

AREA CODE The area code is 716.

GUIDANCE Cattaraugus County Department of Economic Development, Planning, and Tourism, (800-331-0543; www.co.cattaraugus.ny.us or www .enchantedmountains.info), 303 Court Street, Little Valley 14755. Open Monday–Friday 8–5.

Ellicottville Chamber of Commerce (716-699-5046 or 800-349-9099; www .ellicottvilleny.com), 9 Washington Street, PO Box 46, Ellicottville 14731. Open Monday–Friday 8–5, Saturday 10–2.

Franklinville Area Chamber of Commerce (716-676-2452 or 716-676-3010), PO Box 22, Franklinville 14737. For information, contact by phone or by mail.

GETTING THERE *By car:* US 219 and NY 16 are the major roads into the central part of the county.

MEDICAL EMERGENCY Dial 911

☀ To See

MUSEUMS AND HISTORIC HOMES Cattaraugus County Historical Museum and Research Center (716-938-9111; www.co.cattaraugus.ny.us), 302 Court Street, Little Valley. Open Monday and Friday 10–4, Tuesday, Wednesday, and Thursday 8:30–1:30. The museum contains early pioneer artifacts, Civil War mementos, and farm tools, plus newspapers, census books, and many other objects relating to Cattaraugus County history.

Simeon Robbins House-Miner's Cabin (716-676-3010 or 716-676-5651), 9 Pine Street, Franklinville. Open Sundays during the summer. Tours by appointment. This restored three-story Queen Anne–style home was built in 1895 by Simeon Robbins, a successful gold miner, after Robbins returned to Franklinville from the California Gold Rush. The house, which is owned by the Ischua Valley Historical Society, was recently placed on the State and National Register of Historic Places.

Ellicottville Historical Society (716-699-8415), 2 Washington Street, Ellicottville. Open June–September Saturday and Sunday 1–4. This small structure, which houses the collections of the Ellicottville Historical Society, has served the town in the past as a county office, bank, church, millinery shop, firehouse, and library.

☀ To Do

AUTO RACING Chapel Hill Raceway (716-677-5221; www.chapelhillraceway .com), CR 51, Chapel Hill Road, Humphrey. Open mid-April–mid-October. An eighth-mile oval go-cart racetrack that features weekly racing.

Little Valley Speedway (716-938-9146; www.littlevalleyspeedway.com), NY 353, Little Valley. Open May–late September. The area's only half-mile dirt track.

FAMILY FUN ✿ **Pumpkinville** (716-699-2205; www.pumpkinville.com), 4844 Sugartown Road, Great Valley. Open 9–7 mid-September–October 31. Free admission. This popular western New York fall destination, started out as a simple roadside farm stand in the 1960s. In addition to pumpkins by the thousands, there are homemade pumpkin goodies to eat, handmade crafts, hayrides, a corn maze, petting zoo, children's activities, and refreshments.

Ellicottville Rodeo (716-699-4839; www.ellicottvillerodeo.com), Sommerville Valley Road, Ellicottville. Held each summer, the Ellicottville Rodeo is the third largest APRA sanctioned rodeo in the Northeast. In the fall the rodeo grounds are converted to the Nightmare Hayrides.

FISHING In the Franklinville area, **Ischua Creek** is known for its trout fishing. The **Great Valley Creek,** in the town of Great Valley, is well-stocked and a popular spot to fish. **Lime Lake** is noted for its large population of panfish and bass. Fishing licenses can be obtained at any county, town, or village clerk's office.

GOLF Holiday Valley Resort (716-699-2345; www.holidayvalley.com), US 219, Ellicottville. An 18-hole, par-72 course that offers challenging approaches as well as beautiful scenery. Lessons—which include on-course play, video analysis, and professional instruction—are offered through the Holiday Valley Golf School. See *Skiing.*

Ischua Valley Country Club (716-676-3630), NY 16, Franklinville. A 9-hole, par-36, semiprivate course that's open to the public. Memberships are available.

SKIING Holiday Valley (716-699-2345; www.holidayvalley.com), US 219, Ellicottville. This well-known resort offers a great skiing experience, including many improvements recently made in a $4.6 million expansion. Accommodations are available on-site. Golf is available during no-snow seasons.

Lifts: 12 (one magic carpet, one surface lift, two double chairs, one triple chair, six quad chair, one high speed quad).

Trails: 52 (33 percent beginner, 33 percent intermediate, 34 percent expert; 36 trails lit for night skiing; cross-country trails).

Vertical Drop: 750 feet.

Snowmaking: Average season snowfall is 180 inches, with snowmaking capacity of 95 percent.

Facilities: Overnight accommodations available on-site and in nearby Ellicottville.

Ski School: Ski rentals and lessons available for adults, children, and persons visually, mentally, or physically challenged.

For Children: Ski and snowboard programs as well as child care and kids' activities.

Rates: $16–$42.

Holimont (716-699-2330; www.holimont.com), 6921 NY 242, Ellicottville. The largest private ski resort in North America, with 50 slopes and trails, a terrain park, and a half pipe. Nonmembers can ski on weekdays.

Lifts: 8 (one T-bar, three double chair, two triple chair, two quad chairs).

Trails: 50 (20 percent beginner, 30 percent intermediate, 50 percent expert; plus 3.5 miles of scenic trails to hike, snowshoe, or cross-country ski).

Vertical Drop: 725 feet.

Snowmaking: 100 percent top to bottom snowmaking in addition to an average 180 of natural snow per season.

Facilities: Half pipe and terrain park; A-frame chalet; Dina's at the Mont is a fully staffed café and gourmet catering service.

Ski School: Certified instructors offer a wide range of child and adult programs.

For Children: Baby-sitting is offered on weekends for children ages six months-six years.

Rates: $22–$40.

SLEIGH RIDES **Mansfield Coach & Cutter** (716-938-6315; www.coach andcutter.com), 6864 Sodum Road, Little Valley. By reservation. Take a journey through a winter wonderland in an old-fashioned horse-drawn sleigh. In spring, rides include a trip to the sugar shack, where visitors learn about maple syrup making. Fall foliage wagon rides are also available. During the summer, their coaches and wagons can be booked for weddings or other special occasions.

❋ Green Space

BIKE TRAILS Part of the **New York State Bicycle Tour Trail** meanders through this section of the county. The **Southern Tier Route** enters the county on NY 446, and passes through 10 towns before exiting the county near the intersection of US 62 and 83. The **Bikecentennial Route** enters Cattaraugus County near NY

HOLIDAY VALLEY RESORT IN ELLICOTT-VILLE OFFERS A GREAT SKIING EXPERIENCE.

Courtesy Holiday Valley

46 and travels 55 miles before exiting near the New York/Pennsylvania border on Onoville Road.

NATURE PRESERVES Nannen Arboretum (716-699-2377 or 716-945-5200, 800-897-9189), 28 Parkside Drive, Ellicottville. Open dawn to dusk. Free admission Open since 1976, this 8-acre site of nature appreciation and environmental awareness has over 400 trees and shrubs, a Japanese stone meditation garden, an herb garden, and Lake Naponica, a fishing pond.

PARKS Rock City State Forest (For information contact the DEC Allegany suboffice 716-372-0645; www.dec.state.ny.us). Located at the end of Rock City Road, Little Valley. Open dawn to dusk. Free admission This 6,015-acre state forest is located in both Great Valley and Little Valley. Much of the land, acquired by the state for reforestation during the early 1900s, was abandoned farmland. Many projects in this area were carried out in the 1930s by the Civilian Conservation Corps (CCC), established by President Franklin D. Roosevelt to provide employment for young men during the Great Depression. One of the more scenic sites in the forest is Little Rock City, a natural outcrop of conglomerate rock on an unglaciated plateau. This site, at the end of Rock City Road, has hiking trails that take you through and around gigantic rock formations. (To reach the trailhead, take NY 353 south of Little Valley to Whig Street to Hungry Road to Rock City Road.)

PONDS AND LAKES Case Lake, Abbotts Road, Franklinville. Located 1 mile from the village, Case Lake offers swimming, fishing, and boating.

Harwood Lake, NY 98, Franklinville. Located about 6 miles east of the village of Franklinville, this lake is popular for fishing and boating.

Lime Lake, NY 16, Franklinville. A unique lake fed by underground springs, Lime Lake is the only lake with no inlets yet two outlets, each flowing to the Atlantic by different waterways. It is listed in *Ripley's Believe it or Not.* Close to 400 summer cottages are located in the Lime Lake area. It was first developed as a resort area in the 1920s, when an amusement park was built at the north end of the lake. Although the amusement park is long gone, Lime Lake is still popular for fishing and swimming.

WALKING AND HIKING TRAILS A portion of the **Finger Lakes Trail** makes it way through Cattaraugus County. For a map, contact **Finger Lakes Trail Conference** (585-658-9320; www.fingerlakes.net/trailsystem), 6111 Visitor Center Road, Mount Morris, NY 14510.

✳ Lodging

INNS AND RESORTS Edelweiss Lodge (716-699-2734; www .edelweissskilodge.com), 27 Jefferson Street, Ellicottville. This quaint lodge, located in the heart of Elli-

cottville, offers year-round fun and activities. During the winter ski season, enjoy a dip in their heated pool after a day on the slopes. During spring and summer, enjoy tennis on one of their four courts. Of course, fall is a popular season, when Mother Nature turns the surrounding hills into a blaze of color. Choose from a variety of accommodations, from standard rooms with private baths, TVs, and refrigerators to housekeeping cottages that sleep 6 to 10 people, each with fully equipped kitchens and some with fireplaces. A complimentary continental breakfast is offered to all guests. $60–$350.

Ellicottville Inn (716-699-2373, 1-888-856-9298; www.ellicottvilleinn .com), 8 Washington Street, Ellicottville. This 23-room inn, originally opened in 1890, has been completely restored and updated. Each room features its own white tile bath and luxurious bedding. Some rooms have fireplaces. $119–$159.

The Inn at Holiday Valley (716-699-2345; www.holidayvalley.com), US 219, Ellicottville. Open year-round. Guests begin to relax and unwind the minute they enter the inn's elegant lobby with its two-story fieldstone fireplace. In most of the 102 guest rooms, French doors open to a mountain view. Some suites have whirlpools and fireplaces. Other amenities include a heated indoor/outdoor pool, sauna, fitness center, and massage therapy. Golf and lodging packages available during the summer months; ski packages during the winter. The Inn at Holiday Valley has been named one of the top-rated hotels by *Mountain Sports & Living* magazine. $59–$135/person, depending on season.

The Manor House at Mansfield Coach & Cutter (716-938-6315; www.manorhousemcc.com), 6864 Sodum Road, Little Valley. This 1850s house is located on 130 secluded acres, making it a perfect spot for a romantic getaway year-round. Innkeeper Carolyn Tocha offers two large guest rooms with private baths and sitting areas. Guests can enjoy a pool in the summer and a hot tub in the winter. Other amenities include acres of hiking and biking trails, a fairway and green for golf practice, and horse-drawn carriage or sleigh rides. It is located close to Salamanca and Ellicottville. $65–$99.

BED & BREAKFASTS For a complete list of area B&Bs, go to the **Enchanted Mountain Association of Bed & Breakfasts** Website: www.enchantedmountainsbba.com. The following are personally recommended:

Black Dog Lodge (716-699-6900; www.blackdoglodge.com), 7975 US 219, Ellicottville. Innkeepers Rick and Linda Meister have created a peaceful retreat on 66 secluded, wooded acres just five minutes north of the village. They offer four rooms in the main house that have private baths with Jacuzzi tubs and fireplaces. A full country breakfast is served in the rustic dining room or, weather permitting, outdoors on the patio. They also have a pet- and kid-friendly efficiency unit, dubbed The Dog House, which can accommodate up to five people. Summer rates $110–$150, winter rates $160–$250. Reduced weekday rates available.

Bush Bed & Breakfast (716-938-6106; www.bushbedandbreakfast .com), NY 353, Little Valley. Innkeepers Ted and Marge Kochan have furnished this beautifully restored turn-of-the-20th-century country home with antiques and reproductions. The inn, which is located 1 mile from Little Valley and is midway between Ellicottville and Salamanca, has five guest rooms. Two of the five rooms have private baths, while two share a bath. The fifth room is used for additional family members for the rooms with private baths. A hearty breakfast is served each morning. Ski season $90–$130, other seasons $60–$80.

Ilex Inn Bed & Breakfast (716-699-2002 or 800-496-6307; www.ilexinn.com), 6416 East Washington Street (US 219), Ellicottville. Garry and Margaret Kinn offer six luxurious guest rooms in a turn-of-the-20th-century country farmhouse with a wraparound veranda plus a separate cottage. Each room, named after a president, has an en suite private bath and cable TV and is furnished in antiques and period reproductions. The main living room features a fireplace and TV/VCR as well as a video library. A full gourmet breakfast is served daily in the formal dining room. Summer rates $80–$125, winter $125–$195; cottage: summer $110–$155, winter $155–$125.

Jefferson Inn Bed & Breakfast (716-699-5869 or 800-577-8451; www.thejeffersoninn.com), 3 Jefferson Street, Ellicottville. This elegant 1835 inn offers vintage accommodations with modern amenities, including private baths, air conditioning, and use of an outdoor hot tub. Innkeepers Donna Gushue and Jim Buchanan offer five tastefully decorated bedrooms, one a two-room suite, for two people. A full breakfast, served on china plates on a linen tablecloth, is included. They also have two kid- and pet-friendly efficiency units that can accommodate three people, each with its own kitchen. The inn is in a quiet location

behind Ellicottville's town hall, within walking distance to many of the town's fine shops and restaurants. Ski season $109–$199, other seasons $79–$139.

Sugar Pine Lodge (716-699-4855; www.sugarpinelodge.com), 6158 Jefferson Street, Ellicottville. Art and Marilynn Chubb's Bavarian-style upscale bed & breakfast lodge has five uniquely decorated suites with fireplaces and private entrances. Most have Jacuzzi tubs. One of the units can accommodate families. The inn, which is within walking distance to the village and Holiday Valley, also has a heated pool. A deluxe breakfast is included. Off season $89–$148, ski season $135–$235

MOTELS AND HOTELS **Peace Creek Inn** (716-945-4021 or 877-945-4021), 4317 NY 219, Great Valley. Innkeeper James Bailey offers standard rooms, with either one or two beds, at this motel located midway between Ellicottville and Salamanca. Rooms include either one or two full baths, cable TV, refrigerators, microwaves, and coffee makers. $53-$87

Telemark Motel (716-699-4193 or 877-699-4193; www.telemarkmotel.com), US 219 and Holiday Valley Road, Ellicottville. Located just 129 steps from the Sunrise chairlift at the entrance to Holiday Valley, the Telemark offers comfortable, convenient rooms at reasonable prices. $59–$199.

OTHER LODGING **Shamrock Pines Campground** (716-676-2776; www.shamrockpines.com), 3900 Jarecki Road, Franklinville. Open May–October. This family-friendly campground has 73 sites with electric hookups located among 400 acres of pine trees.

$20/night no hookups, $25/night full hookups, $150/week.

Triple R Camping Resort (716-676-3856; www.triplercamp.com), 3491 Bryant Hill Road, Franklinville. Open late April–late October. One hundred thirty sites with electric, water, sewer, and cable hookups. $28/night, $156/week. Monthly and season rates available.

VACATION RENTALS Some visitors prefer to rent ski condos and homes by the week, month, or season. Below are places to contact regarding rentals.

Century 21 Town & Country (716-699-4800; www.century21town country.com), 34 Washington Street, Ellicottville.

Holiday Valley Realty Company Inc. (716-699-2000), US 219, Ellicottville.

Ellicottville Real Estate (716-699-6748 or 866-699-6748), 6162 Jefferson Street, Ellicottville.

Ellicottville Rentals (716-699-5600 or 800-263-7368; www.huntrealestate.com), 28 Washington Street, Ellicottville.

Weed Ross Agency (716-699-2388), 22 Monroe Street, Ellicottville.

✳ Where to Eat

DINING OUT Barn Restaurant (716-699-4600), 7 Monroe Street, Ellicottville. Open Monday–Saturday 5–10, Sunday 3–9. Dine in an authentic 100-year-old barn complete with stone fireplace. Specialties include lobster night on Wednesday and steak festival night on Thursday, along with daily specials.

The Fieldstone (716-945-9854), 4920 US 219, Great Valley. Open

Tuesday–Sunday noon–10. This relaxed country restaurant, with a Celtic theme, serves a variety of dishes in their full service dining room, from steak, shrimp, and pasta to burgers, sandwiches, and pizza. Their dessert menu includes cheesecake, carrot cake, and more. The gift shop features fine hand-woven articles, Celtic music, jewelry, and Irish imports.

The Hearth Restaurant (716-699-2010; www.holidayvalley.com), at **Holiday Valley Ski Resort,** Route 219, Ellicottville. Open spring-fall: lunch Monday–Saturday 11–2:30, dinner Friday–Saturday 5-9:30; winter: 11:30–9:30 daily, Friday and Saturday until 10PM. Enjoy the best view in Ellicottville while dining on specialties like vegetable spring roll, black pepper seared tuna, or California Reuben on asiago bread.

♈ **Fosters Pub** (716-699-5806 www.fosterspub.com), 8 Washington Street (in the Ellicottville Inn), Ellicottville. Open Tuesday–Thursday 5–9, Friday–Saturday 5–10. This popular Ellicottville restaurant, now in a new location, features good food in an Irish pub atmosphere. Menu selections include soups, pub grub, sandwiches, and salads along with daily specials. They also have a kids' menu. Since it is an Irish pub they, of course, have Guinness on tap.

Silver Fox (716-699-4672; www.silverfoxrestaurant.com), 23 Hughey Alley, Ellicottville. Open Wednesday–Saturday 5–10. This popular restaurant, which has a martini and cigar bar, is located in an antique fur barn where trappers traded their pelts. Dinner selections include fish, veal, lamb, and steaks, hand cut to order. Houses specialties include bouillabaisse, paella, and fresh fish. An extensive wine list is available.

Stone Creek Tavern & Grill (716-699-2051; stonecreektavern.com), 7734 US 219, Ellicottville. Fine dining Wednesday–Thursday 3–9, Friday 3–10, Saturday 11:30–11, Sunday 11:30–9 (bar open later daily). The Stone Creek Tavern & Grill, located in a beautiful country setting, specializes in European and American fare. Their upscale pub menu includes salads, sandwiches, and comfort foods while their Mélange dining room features fine European cuisine such as duck ravioli with a port wine reduction, toasted almonds, sautéed leeks, and pears. There are over 40 beer varieties as well as micro brews on tap, and a full wine list.

EATING OUT ♈ **Balloons Restaurant** (716-699-4162; www.balloons restaurant.com), 20 Monroe Street, Ellicottville. Open daily 11:30–10. Enjoy casual dining, including vegetarian specialties. Open late-night for musical entertainment.

The Bird Walk (716-699-2749), 5816 NY 242 East, Ellicottville. Open seven days 4–10. Since 1970 Ellicottville residents and visitors have enjoyed such house specialties as steak, rack of lamb, and seafood while dining amid antiques. If you like a particular display item, make an offer; all antiques are available for purchase.

Cadillac Jack's (716-699-5161), US 219 and Holiday Valley Road (at the Telemark Motel), Ellicottville. Open mid-December–March 11 AM–2 AM daily. Enjoy casual dining with a good view of the slopes in a restaurant decorated with vintage Cadillac ads and auto memorabilia. The menu includes prime rib, roast beef, salads, burgers,

and wings.

Cooling's Ice Cream Café (716-699-8860; www.coolingsicecream cafe.com), 10A Washington Street, Ellicottville. Open Sunday–Thursday 7–8, Friday and Saturday 7–9. Serving up ice cream treats and more, including baked goods, sandwiches, and homemade soup.

♈ **Dinas** (716-699-5330; www.dinas .com), 15 Washington Street, Ellicottville. Open seven days, 7–9. This restaurant features bistro-style food as well as a wine and cappuccino bar.

♈ **Double Diamond Bar and Grill** (716-699-8990), 26 Monroe Street, Ellicottville. Open Monday and Tuesday 4 PM–12 AM, Wednesday–Sunday 12–12. The menu of this newly established eatery and nightspot includes finger foods, wings, soups, salads, and sandwiches, plus dinner entrées.

Ellicottville Brewing Company (716-699-2537; www.ellicottville brewing.com), 28 Monroe Street, Ellicottville. Open Tuesday–Sunday 11:30-10. This 10-barrel, whole-grain brewery, established in 1995, features beer brewed without preservatives, making it fresher tasting than imports. Entrées include original Swiss fondue, steaks, sandwiches, wraps, chicken fingers, soups, and salads.

♪ ♣ **The Flavor Haus** (716-938-9292), 5353 Kilborn Corner Road (corner NY 242 and NY 353), Little Valley. Enjoy a changing, casual menu and a spectacular view in a custom-built European-style, timber-frame restaurant. The restaurant has a large selection of foot-long hot dogs (plus the world's largest foot-long hot dog on display). They also serve premium hard and soft-serve ice cream. Outside is a big grassy area where kids can play.

Little Berchtesgaden (716-676-9935), 8338 NY 16, Franklinville. Open Wednesday–Friday 4–9, Saturday 12–9, Sunday 12–7. Reservations required. Enjoy authentic German cuisine, including schnitzels, sauerbraten steak, German chicken, homemade apple strudel, and Black Forest cheesecake.

Maple Haven Restaurant and Bakery (716-676-9910), 103 North Main Street, Franklinville. Open 6–8 daily. A full-service restaurant, bakery, and retail outlet for Maple Haven's maple sugar products. An all-you-can-eat pancake breakfast is available daily.

Tip's-Up Café (716-699-2136), 32 Washington Street, Ellicottville. Open Monday–Saturday 4:30–11, Sunday 4:30–10. A full-service restaurant with a reputation for excellence. For over 20 years Chef Ken Roush and his wife, Judy, have been serving locals and visitors such specialties as fresh seafood, pasta, steak, ribs, and veal.

NIGHTLIFE Some of the restaurants mentioned above are also popular watering holes with the après-ski crowd. Here are a few other popular night spots:

Gin Mill (716-699-2530), 20 Washington Street, Ellicottville. Kitchen open 11:30 AM–12 AM daily (bar until 2 AM). An Ellicottville hot spot since 1976, they are known for "good eatin' and drinkin'." Fifteen domestic and imported beers are on draft. Menu selections range from burgers and sandwiches to steaks.

Madigans (716-699-4455), 36 Washington Street, Ellicottville. Open 11:30 AM–2 AM daily. This bar/restaurant offers a selection of burgers, sandwiches, and other pub grub.

✷ Selective Shopping

ANTIQUES & **Bear Hollow Furniture and Antiques** (716-945-5229 antiques, 716-945-1739 furniture; www.bhollow.com), 4861 US 219, Great Valley. Open Tuesday, Wednesday, Friday, Saturday 10–5, Thursday 10–8. Bear Hollow is western New York's largest antiques co-op and new furniture store. They have everything you can think of, including books, dishes, home decor items, new and antique furniture, even a bargain corner.

& **Green Gable Village** (716-945-3600; www.greengablevillage.com), 4343 South Whalen Road (US 219), Great Valley. Open 1–5 daily. A 33,000-square-foot antiques mall with over 75 dealers. Located behind the shop is Yesterday and Today's Country Store (open 10–5), which features a large array of gift items, seasonal decorations, and antiques.

ART GALLERIES **Earth Arts** (716-699-2169; www.eartharts24.com), 24 Washington Street, Ellicottville. Open daily July–March 10–5; call for spring hours. Choose from distinctive contemporary fine crafts, jewelry, original art, stained glass, sculptures, and more.

Discover Ellicottville (716-699-8056), 18 Monroe Street at the Market Place, Ellicottville. Open Monday 10–4, Tuesday and Thursday 10–2, Friday and Saturday 10–6, Sunday 11–5. A unique basement art gallery featuring the work of local artists, including paintings, wood carvings, textiles, and poetry. Art workshops are also offered.

Monti Gallery (716-699-5544), 18 Monroe Street, Ellicottville. Open

Wednesday–Sunday 9–5, year-round. This shop features custom framing and artwork, including photos of the local Amish community. It is also the home of Blou, a Bondu collie well-known in the community for having donated over $2,000 of his own money to the Pet Emergency Fund of Western New York. Blou raises money through the sale of note cards with his picture, which are sold at the gallery.

FARM MARKETS ✿ **Pushes Cider Mill** (716-699-2938), NY 98, Great Valley. Open daily 10–5 mid-September–October 31. Watch cider being pressed from start to finish. Browse the gift shop for jams and jellies, fresh-baked goods, maple products, and more. The cider mill also has a farm animal petting zoo and picnic area.

✿ **Pumpkinville** (716-699-2994), 4844 Sugartown Road, Great Valley. Open daily 9 AM–7 PM mid-September–October 31. See *Family Fun.*

SPECIAL SHOPS

Ellicottville
Alexandra (716-699-5621), 10 Washington Street, Ellicottville. Open Monday–Saturday 10–6, Sunday 11–5. Choose from jewelry, scented candles, bath and beauty treats, pottery, jewelry, books, and more.

Daff (716-699-2293), 17-19 Washington Street, Ellicottville. Open Sunday–Thursday 10–5, Friday–Saturday 10–6. This shop, in one of Ellicottville's vintage buildings, features Western wear, hats, boots, quilts, leather clothing, sweaters, and accessories.

Ellicottville Pharmacy and Gift Shoppe (716-699-2384), 13 Washington Street, Ellicottville. Open Monday–Friday 9–6, Saturday 9–5, Sunday 10–3. A selection of country and Victorian gifts can be found along with a full service pharmacy.

Gado-Gado (716-699-2128), PO Box 102, Ellicottville Marketplace, Ellicottville. Open 10–6 daily. The owners of this unique shop travel to Indonesia and Bali twice a year to bring back a selection of clothing, jewelry, home decor, furniture, and other items. They also carry a selection of African imports.

✿ **Kazoo II** (716-699-4484), 18 Washington Street, Ellicottville. Winter hours: Monday–Thursday 10–6, Friday and Saturday 10–8; rest of year Monday–Thursday 10–5, Friday 10–6. Shop on two floors in this popular Ellicottville store. Downstairs, the Lion's Blue Mane, is a child's domain that includes all sorts of educational toys, plush animals, and other timeless toys. Upstairs, choose from jewelry, cards, mirrors, seasonal decorating items, ski- and snow-themed merchandise, candles, Frank Lloyd Wright books and stained glass, and much more.

Mud Sweat n' Gears (716-699-8300; www.mudsweatgears.com), 21 Washington Street, Ellicottville. Open Monday–Saturday 10–6, Sunday 10–5, extended hours during ski season. This shop carries ski and snowboard equipment, accessories, and clothing along with mountain bike sales and service. Ski, snowboard, and mountain bike rentals are available.

One of a Kind (716-699-5022), 22 Washington Street, Ellicottville. Open 10–5 daily. This shop specializes in French Country decor items, including cards, clocks, and unusual dishes and bowls.

Shhh (716-699-5586), 18 Monroe Street, Ellicottville. Open 10–5 daily. A collection of unique and unusual toys, puppets, and wind toys.

The Store (716-699-5622 www .thestoreellicottville.com), 5364 NY 242 East, Ellicottville. Open Monday–Saturday 7–5, Sunday 8–4. This former general store, built in 1870, specializing in beer, wine, and sausage-making supplies along with cheese, bison meat, local honey, books, and useful household items. Their restaurant is open daily for breakfast and lunch.

Ellicottville Ski Shops

There are also numerous ski shops in Ellicottville, including **Red Door Ski Shop** (716-699-2026), 11 Washington Street, Ellicottville, which has top of the line ski and golf apparel for men and women; **The City Garage** (716-699-2054 citygarage-evi.com), Monroe Street, Ellicottville, specializing in ski and outdoor wear; and **Greg Dekdebrun's Ski Shop** (716-699-2754 www.dekdebrun.com), 20 Washington Street, Ellicottville, a full-service ski shop.

Franklinville and Vicinity

This area is known as the Northern Ischua Valley Shopping trail (www .geocities.com/nivatrail)

Amish Treasures (716-676-2599), NY 16, two miles north of Franklinville. Open April–Dec. Wednesday–Sat 10–5, Sunday 12–5. Specializing in goods made by Old Order Amish craftspersons, including quilts, dolls, oak bentwood rockers, cedar chests, woodcrafts, and more.

Chickory Hill Country Store (716-676-9309), 9440 Laidlaw Road, Farmersville. Open year-round Saturday and Sunday 10–5; May–December also open Wednesday–Friday 12–5. A family-owned and operated country store off the beaten trail, offering unique and affordable gifts. Choose from candles, dolls, specialty foods, seasonal items, antiques, wood furniture, maple syrup, and more.

Heart of Franklinville (716-676-5167), 28 North Main Street (Route 16) Franklinville. Open Wednesday–Saturday 10–5, Sunday 1–5. Browse the entire house plus three barns full of antiques, Victorian gifts, country crafts, gourmet coffees, and garden statuaries.

Sweetbriar Farm Gift Shop (716-676-9140), 8435 NY 16, 2 miles north of Franklinville. Open Tuesday–Saturday 10–5, Sunday 12–5. A charming country store featuring Boyd's Bears, candles, florals, baskets, cards, decorative accessories, and primitive handicrafts.

✳ Special Events

January: **Blues Festival** (716-699-5046 or 800-349-9099; www.ellicott villeny.com), Ellicottville. Enjoy jazz and blues in various locations throughout the village.

March: **Mardi Gras Parade** (716-699-5046 or 800-349-9099; www .ellicottvilleny.com), Ellicottville. This event is one of the last parties of the ski season.

June: **Ellicottvillle Rodeo** (716-699-4839; www.ellicottvillerodeo.com), The third largest APRA-sanctioned rodeo in the Northeast.

July: **Cattaraugus County Fair** (716-938-9146; www.cattaragusco fair.com), NY 353, Little Valley. This has been a popular event for over 160 years. **Summer Festival of the**

Arts (716-699-5046 or 800-349-9099; www.ellicottvilleny.com), An annual art show held in Ellicottville.

October: **Ellicottville Fall Festival** (716-699-5046 or 800-349-9099; www.ellicottvilleny.com), Ellicottville. One of the largest fall festivals in western New York takes place on Columbus Day weekend. It includes a crafts show, live entertainment, and chair-lift rides at Holiday Valley.

November: **Ellicottville Christmas Open House** (716-699-5046 or 800-349-9099; www.ellicottvilleny.com), Christmas shop in the stores of Elli-cottville.

SALAMANCA

Prior to the early 1860s, the sole inhabitants of this area were Native Americans. Today, Salamanca is the only city in the United States located entirely on an trib-al reservation. The area was originally called Bucktooth, after an old Indian with crooked teeth who traded with early settlers. The name was later changed to Salamanca, to honor Don Jose de Salamanca, the Marquis of Salamanca, Spain, an early investor in the Atlantic & Great Western Railroad.

The city grew largely because of the development of railroads. The Atlantic & Great Western Railroad had its eastern terminus in Salamanca, and the city was on the main line of the Erie Railroad. The city was also served by the Buffalo, Rochester & Pittsburgh Railway, whose restored station now serves as the Sala-manca Rail Museum.

The region is also noted for its hunting and fishing, so it's a popular spot for outdoorsmen. Hiking and camping are also favorite pastimes because the area has large tracts of state forest, many with natural rock formations.

AREA CODE The area code is 716.

GUIDANCE Salamanca Area Chamber of Commerce (716-945-2034; www.cityofsalamanca.com), 26 Main Street, Salamanca 14779. Open Monday 9–12 Tuesday–Friday 9–5.

GETTING THERE *By car:* Salamanca can be reached from US 219 or NY 353. It can also be accessed off I-86, exits 20 and 21.

MEDICAL EMERGENCY Dial 911

✳ To See

MURAL The Clan Mother Bonds All Nations Mural, 54 Main Street, Sala-manca. This mural—painted in 1998 by Carson R. Waterman, one of the Seneca Nation's most renowned artists—depicts the face of a clan mother, who plays an important role in working toward peace among the clans. The date "1794" signi-fies when the Iroquois Confederacy signed the Canandaigua Treaty with the United States. The eight clans of the Seneca Nation are shown in the mural: the four of the Animal Group (Bear, Wolf, Turtle, and Beaver) and the four of the Bird Group (Hawk, Deer, Heron, and Snipe).

MUSEUMS AND HISTORIC HOMES **Salamanca Historical Society** (716-945-5825, director), 125 Main Street, Salamanca. Call for hours. The historical society, located in the old savings and loan building, exhibits photographs, books, and other artifacts related to Salamanca's history.

✔ ♿ **Seneca-Iroquois National Museum** (716-945-1738; www.sececamuseum .org), 794-814 Broad Street, Salamanca. Open Monday, Tuesday, Thursday, and Friday 10–5, Saturday 9–5, Sunday 12–5. Admission $4 adults, $3 seniors and students, $2 children 7–13. This museum houses exhibits depicting Native American history and culture in western New York. The Seneca Nation is known as the Keepers of the Western Door. Two reservations are located within Cattaraugus County—the Allegany Reservation, which includes the city of Salamanca, and the Cattaraugus Reservation in the northwest part of the county. Displays include a clan-animal display, a partial longhouse, and a log cabin, traditional crafts such as baskets and beadwork, and modern Iroquois art. There is a hands-on area for children, where they can learn more about Native American culture. A gift shop offers traditional and handmade crafts and artwork, as well as books, posters, T-shirts, and inexpensive children's souvenirs.

✔ ♿ **Salamanca Rail Museum** (716-945-3133), 170 Main Street, Salamanca. Open Monday–Saturday 10–5, Sunday 12–5 (closed Monday in April and October–December; Museum closed January–March). Donation. The Salamanca Rail Museum is a fully restored passenger depot built in 1912 by the Buffalo, Rochester, and Pittsburgh Railway. The museum contains photos, artifacts, and video presentations documenting a bygone era. When the building was first acquired in 1980, it had been vacant and vandalized since the 1960s. It has been restored to its original appearance, including red-oak wainscoting and a two-story skylighted ceiling. Everything in the museum is either a restored original or a duplicate based on the original plans. Visitors learn about the history of Salamanca as well as railroad history. Kids get to explore two cabooses and view a box car, coach, crew, and camp car. The gift shop offers a variety of railroad-related items.

THIS FULLY RESTORED 1912 DEPOT IS NOW THE SALAMANCA RAILROAD MUSEUM.

Christine A. Smyczynski

HISTORIC SITES **Allegany State Park Fire Tower**, Allegany State Park, Salamanca. The Summit Fire Tower in Allegany State Park was first built in 1926 and manned by the New York State Conservation Department from 1927 until 1970, when airplanes took over the task of watching for wildfires. A committee has been formed in recent years to restore this historic tower to its original condition for future generations to learn about the tower's history.

✷ To Do

CASINO GAMING **Seneca Allegany Casino** (716-945-3200; www.seneca alleganycasino.com), 777 Seneca Allegany Boulevard (right by I-86 exit 20), Salamanca. Open 24 hours. This 122,000-square-foot facility has over 1,700 real and video slot machines and 22 game tables as well as high-stakes bingo, an all-you-can-eat buffet room, and snack bar. Note: You must be 21 or older to enter the casino.

CROSS COUNTRY SKIING See **Allegany State Park** in *Green Space—Parks.*

GOLF **Elkdale Country Club** (716-945-5553; www.elkdalecc.com), NY 353, Salamanca. An 18-hole, par-70 course that includes an air-conditioned clubhouse, restaurant, and heated swimming pool.

MARINAS **Onoville Marina** (716-354-2615; www.onovillemarina.org), 704 West Perimeter Road, Steamburg. Open the first Friday in May–end of September. The Onoville Marina is located on the 12,000-acre Allegheny Reservoir, which has 91 miles of shoreline that includes secluded bays and campsites accessible only by boat. Facilities include 394 docks, camping facilities, picnic shelter, shower, and laundry. Boat rentals are available. Fishing licenses can be obtained at any county, town, or village clerk's office.

✷ Green Space

PARKS **Allegany State Park** (716-354-9121), 2373 ASP Route #1, Salamanca. Open year-round dawn–dusk. Admission: $7 parking fee. At 65,000 acres, Allegany State Park, which was dedicated in 1921, is the largest in the New York State Park System. Most of the park is primitive woodland adorning mountains, meadows, and streams. The park has two sand beaches (in the Quaker and Red House areas), 300 campsites, and 300 cabins, with about 150 of those cabins winterized. It has 90 miles of snowmobile trails, which double as horseback riding trails in the warmer months. There are also 18 hiking and nature trails and 35 miles of cross-country ski trails that can be used for hiking and biking in the summer. A park museum is located in the restored Old Quaker Store (716-354-2182).

Sycamore Street Park Sycamore Street (near the Allegheny River), Salamanca. It has one tennis court and two basketball courts.

Crowley Park North side of the Allegheny River, Salamanca. Enjoy ball fields, picnic tables, a playground, a skateboard ramp, horseshoe pits, and basketball courts.

Vet's Park, Broad Street, Salamanca. The park has a playground, basketball courts and football field.

WALKING AND HIKING TRAILS See *Parks*, **Allegany State Park**.

✳ Lodging

MOTELS AND HOTELS Bayview Lodge and Ice Cream Parlor (716-354-9295 or 716-354-2021), 767 West Perimeter Road, Frewsburg. Open year-round. This five-room hotel has a spectacular view of Onoville Marina. The ice cream parlor features a pirate ship deck. $50–$99.

The Dudley Hotel (716-945-2002), 132 Main Street, Salamanca. Open year-round. This restored circa 1901 hotel offers 30 clean and affordable standard guest rooms. $59.99/single, $10 each additional person, up to four per room.

Holiday Inn Express Hotel and Suites (716-945-7600), 779 Broad Street, Salamanca. This newly built hotel features a Southwestern theme. The lobby is dominated by a large stone fireplace and paintings by Seneca artist Carson Waterman. Each of the 68 guest rooms feature amenities like coffeemakers, hair dryers, irons, and dataports. The hotel also has an indoor pool and fitness center. A complimentary deluxe continental breakfast is served in the Great Room. $104–$179.

Myers Hotel and Steakhouse (716-945-3153), 460 Wildwood Avenue, Salamanca. Open year-round. A turn-of-the-20th-century hotel and restaurant, operated by Don Hammond and Rosalyn Hoag, that has been completely renovated. The six rooms have king-sized beds, private baths, air conditioning, and cable TV. $55–$65.

Mountain View Motel (716-945-2920), 888 Broad Street, Salamanca. Open year-round. A newly remodeled, family-oriented motel offering the lowest rates in town. Conveniently located near Allegany State Park and Seneca Gaming and Entertainment and only 15 minutes from Ellicottville. $38+.

BED & BREAKFASTS Harvest Moon (716-945-2200 or 866-302-2200), 145 Center Street, Salamanca. Open year-round. Innkeeper Jackie Kennedy offers four rooms that share a bath in this newly opened B&B. A full breakfast is served. $40.

TarryHere (716-945-3123; www .tarryhere.com), 141 Broad Street, Salamanca. Open year-round. Bob and Cheryl Pierce offer five elegantly decorated guest rooms in their newly opened inn. Three rooms have private baths, while the other two share. $60–$100.

OTHER LODGING

Campgrounds

Allegany State Park See *Green Space—Parks.*

✳ Where to Eat

DINING OUT The Red Garter Restaurant (716-945-2503; www .redgarterrestaurant.com), Parkway Drive (exit 21 off I-86), Salamanca. Open year-round Sunday 4–8, Monday–Thursday 4–9, Friday and Saturday 4–10. Enjoy fine dining with the most spectacular view east of the Mississippi. Menu selections include New York strip steak, prime rib, crab legs, BBQ ribs, chicken, seafood, including lobster, and pasta dishes. A raw bar is open during the summer months. The restaurant is located on the summit of Round Top Mountain. The original Red Garter restaurant was part of Ned Fenton's amusement park, Fentier Village, which was demolished about 30 years ago to make way for the Southern Tier Expressway.

EATING OUT CW's Bar and Grille in the Dudley Hotel (716-945-2002), 132 Main Street, Salamanca. Open 11–2 for lunch and 4–9 for dinner. Bar is open to 2 AM. This casual pub offers sandwiches and burgers for lunch and dinner entrées like prime rib and fish fry as well as daily specials.

Myers Hotel and Steakhouse (716-945-3153), 460 Wildwood Avenue, Salamanca. Open Sunday 8–9, Monday–Thursday 11–9, Friday and Saturday 11–10. Established in 1900, this small but popular establishment has a longstanding reputation for serving fine steaks. Six guest rooms are also available for overnight accommodations in this restored turn-of-the-20th-century hotel. See also *Lodging*.

Traders (716-945-4436), 15 Main Street, Salamanca. Open daily 7–9. Enjoy homemade diner-style food in this restaurant with upscale decor.

❋ Selective Shopping

ANTIQUES ❖ Salamanca Mall Antiques (716-945-5532 or 1-800-410-0273), 100 Main Street, Salamanca. Open 10–6 daily. More than 1,000 dealers display their wares in 80,000 square feet of display space located in a former shopping mall. Many of the smaller items are neatly displayed in glass cases. Choose from dishes, glass-ware, toys, books, and collectibles, along with furniture and other larger items.

SPECIAL SHOPS Hampshire Mills (716-945-3100), 890 Broad Street, Salamanca. Open Monday–Thursday and Saturday 10–6, Friday 1–8, Sunday 11–5. This unique shop has been operated by the same family for over 30 years. Items carried include home decor, cards, jewelry, candles, Native American art, gourmet foods, toys, clothing, and Salamanca-related items.

Note: Numerous Native American-run smoke shops and low-price gas stations are located throughout Salamanca.

❋ Special Events

March: **Maple Sugaring Demonstrations** (716-896-5200), Camp Allegany at Allegany State Park. Learn about the history of syrup making from the 1600s to the present. This is run by the Buffalo Museum of Science. Fee includes a pancake meal.

July: **Native American Powwow** (716-945-1738; www.sececamuseum.org), Salamanca. An annual festival, held the third week of July, highlighting Native American culture, crafts, food, and music, along with traditional dancing contests.

October: **Falling Leaves Festival** (716-945-3110), Salamanca. Food and craft vendors, parade, antique car show, and more.

OLEAN AND VICINITY

Olean, the largest city in Cattaraugus County, was founded in 1804 by Adam and Robert Hoops and originally called Hamilton, in honor of Alexander Hamilton. The town developed mainly because of its location on the Allegheny River. Approximately 90 percent of people heading west had to pass through Olean. The word *Olean* is Latin for "oil"—prior to the turn of the 20th century, the

largest oil producers in the world could be found in Olean and nearby Bradford,
Pennsylvania. In addition to oil production, Olean was known for the manufacturer of bicycles, autos, glass, wagons, and lumber. Many of the wealthy people who were involved in these industries resided in the Oak Hill District, which today runs from Union Street to 4th Street. Fortunately many of these lovely homes are still intact.

The Olean area is also home to St. Bonaventure University, established in 1856 as a private Franciscan college. This 500-acre campus features historic Florentine architecture. The St. Bonaventure Bonnies basketball team is in the Atlantic 10 Conference.

AREA CODE The area code is 716.

GUIDANCE Greater Olean Area Chamber of Commerce (716-372-4433; www.oleanny.com; e-mail: tourism@oleanny.com), 120 North Union Street, Olean 14760. Open Monday–Friday 8:30–4:30.

Chamber of Commerce of Olean and Vicinity (716-373-4230; www .oleanny.org), 319 North Union Street, Olean 14760. Open Monday–Friday 9–5.

Cattaraugus County Arts Council (716-372-7455; www.cattcountyarts.org), 80 North Fourth Street, Allegany 14706. Open Monday–Friday 12–5.

GETTING THERE *By car:* Olean can be reached via NY 16 or exits 25 and 26 off I-86.

MEDICAL EMERGENCY Dial 911.

Olean General Hospital (716-373-2600; www.ogh.org), 515 Main Street, Olean.

✳ To See

ART MUSEUMS ♿ **F. Donald Kenney Museum and Art Study Wing** (716-375-2494), Regina Quick Center for the Arts, St. Bonaventure University, St. Bonaventure. Open Tuesday–Sunday 1–5. Free admission This museum houses a permanent collection of Italian Renaissance paintings, Asian porcelain, Southwest pottery, and American paintings as well as traveling exhibits by visiting artists.

The Regina A. Quick Center for the Arts (716-375-2494), St. Bonaventure University, St. Bonaventure. The university's arts center has a 321-seat theater, art museum, and art study wing with instructional space.

MUSEUMS AND HISTORIC HOMES Fannie Bartlett Center (716-376-5642), 302 Laurens Street, Olean. Open Wednesday, Thursday, Saturday, and Sunday 1–5, Friday 1–7. Donation. The Bartlett House, an 1881 Victorian home, has nine rooms decorated with period furniture along with a Tiffany-style staircase window, seven unique fireplaces, and intricate detail work throughout. The home's carriage museum houses the **Olean Point Museum of Local History**, which displays artifacts and exhibits on Olean's history from 1804 until the present. The offices of the **Olean Historical Preservation Society** (716-373-0285) are located on the second floor of the Bartlett House. (Open Tuesday and Friday 1–3.)

Cutco/Ka-Bar Visitors Center (716-790-7000; www.cutco.com www.ka-bar .com), 1040 East State Street, Olean (exit 26 off I-86). Open Monday–Friday 9–5. The Ka-Bar company was founded during Olean's early days by European immigrants with skills in the cutlery trade. Ka-Bar knives were standard issue weaponry for American soldiers during World War II and still are today. Cutco kitchen knives are regarded as the world's finest cutlery.

✴ To Do

GOLF **Birch Run Country Club** (716-373-3113), Birch Run Road, Allegany. A 9-hole, par-35 semiprivate course.

St. Bonaventure Golf Course (716-372-7692), NY 417, St. Bonaventure. A 9-hole, par-35 course.

SNOWTUBING **O'Dea's Recreation Center** (716-373-5471), 3329 West River Road, Olean. Snow tubing season is weather dependent. Generally open Friday 5–9, Saturday 11–9, Sunday 11–7, Monday holidays 11–7, Christmas vacation 11–9. Three hours $12, unlimited $15. O'Dea's has one of the highest elevations and longest snowtubing runs in the region. A warming hut and snack bar are available. During the summer enjoy miniature golf and a driving range (open daily 8–9).

✴ Green Space

NATURE PRESERVES **Pfeiffer Nature Center** (716-373-1742 or 933-6063; www.pfeiffernaturecenter.org), 1974 Lillibridge Road, Portville. Open year-round Tuesday–Sunday 9–6. A nearly-200-acre nature center with 6 miles of nature trails. About 20 acres are old-growth forest made up of eastern hemlock, white pine, red oak, and American beech dating back 400 years. Guided nature walks are available. A 60-year-old log cabin on the property, constructed from American chestnut, is listed on the State and National Historic Registers.

PARKS **Rock City Park** (716-372-7790 or 1-866-404-ROCK), Rock City Road (NY 16, 5.5 miles south of Olean), Olean. Open 9–6 daily May 1–October 31; last admission at 5 PM) $4 adults, $3.75 seniors, $2.50 ages 6–12, under six free. Rock City Park, one of the largest exposures of quartz conglomerate, is sometimes called the eighth wonder of the world. The rock formations, believed to have once been on a prehistoric ocean floor, resemble a city of rocks several stories high. Native Americans used the area as a fortress. Visitors are amazed at some of the formations, including one boulder that weighs over 1,000 tons that balances precariously on another. Mountain laurel and wildflowers bloom in the spring and summer, while fall visitors are treated to magnificent fall foliage. Visit the park's museum to see photos of the park in days gone by and also view a video about the park. The gift shop carries many rock-related, items including precious minerals. A video is available for those unable to hike the trails.

Gargoyle Park, State Street, Olean. This town park is located along the Allegheny River.

WALKING AND HIKING TRAILS ₺ **Allegheny River Valley Trail** (716-372-4433), Along the Allegheny River from St. Bonaventure University to Olean. Allegany. A paved, multiuse 5.6-mile recreational trail, with spectacular views of the Allegheny River, that goes from the village of Allegany to Olean through the campus of St. Bonaventure University.

✳ Lodging

MOTELS AND HOTELS ₺ **Country Inn & Suites by Carlson** (716-372-7500 or 800-456-4000; www.country inns.com/olean), 3270 NY 417, Olean. Located near St. Bonaventure University, this motel has 77 guest rooms, an indoor pool, and complimentary breakfast. $67+.

₺ **Hampton Inn** (716-375-1000; www.hampton-inn.com), 101 Main Street, Olean. Seventy-six guest rooms are available at this hotel convenient to St. Bonaventure University. $79–$168.

BED & BREAKFASTS Gallets House Bed & Breakfast (716-373-7493; www.galletshouse.com), 1759 Lower Four Mile Road (CR 60), Allegany (2 miles from exit 24 off I-86). Open year-round. Enjoy overnight accommodations in a stately 1896 Victorian home furnished with antiques and original family photographs. Hosts Joan and Gary Boser offer five elegant guest rooms with private baths plus a three-bedroom carriage house suite perfect for families. The house was built by Gary Boser's great uncle and changed hands several times before being purchased by the Bosers in the late 1990s and restored to its Victorian splendor. The Sew Special gift shop, featuring handcrafted specialty gifts, is open to the public, as is a museum of interesting memorabilia from the past on the third floor, which is open by appointment. A full gourmet breakfast is served. $85–$135.

Old Library Bed & Breakfast (716-373-9804 or 877-241-4347; www.old libraryrestaurant.com), 120 South Union Street, Olean. Open year-round. Seven bedrooms and two suites are available in an 1895 Victorian inn managed by innkeeper Lori Dunn. All rooms have private baths, air conditioning, cable TV, and phones. A country breakfast is cooked to order daily. The inn is located in a historical section of downtown Olean, next to the Old Library Restaurant. It is not far from St. Bonaventure University. $75–$145. (*Note:* When coming to events at the university, make reservations well in advance, as rooms fill up quickly.)

✳ Where to Eat

DINING OUT Century Manor Restaurant (716-372-1864; www .centurymanor.com), 401 East State Street, Olean. Open Monday–Saturday 4–10, Sunday 4:30–9:30. This dining establishment—founded over 50 years ago in a building erected in the 1800s by a local lumber baron—is regarded as one of the finest steak and seafood establishments in the Southern Tier. Menu selections include a large selection of steaks and chops as well as seafood, chicken, and pasta dishes. They recently added an outdoor patio, dubbed "Coconuts at the Manor," which has a Caribbean theme, complete with a fire pit, palm trees, and tropical drinks. Century Manor also offers extended-stay accommodations on the second floor.

Lucia's (716-372-0039), NY 16 South, Rock City Hill, Olean. Open Tuesday–Sunday 5–9:30. This elegant restaurant is known for its Italian specialties.

& **Old Library Restaurant** (716-372-2226 or 877-241-4347; www .oldlibraryrestaurant.com), 116 South Union Street, Olean. Open Monday–Saturday 11–11, Sunday 11–10. Fine dining in casual yet elegant atmosphere in a circa 1910 building that served as the Olean Public Library from 1910 until 1974. It was saved from demolition in the early 1980s by the Marra family and opened as the Old Library Restaurant. The Marras have added many antiques to the restaurant's furnishings, including the long bar from Chicago's famous Cattleman's Restaurant, a popular watering hole for notorious figures of the 1920s and '30s. Keeping with the restaurant's library theme, the shelves are filled with books.

EATING OUT & **Beef & Barrel** (585-372-2785), 146 North Union Street, Olean. 11–10. This large steakhouse, decorated with wood throughout, features beef dishes, including beef on weck, hot roast beef dinners, and ground round along with soups, salads, sandwiches, and chicken entrées.

Breadstix Cafe (716-373-3321), 833 East State Street, Olean. Open 11–10. Specialties at this restaurant include prime rib, haddock fish fry, and Pittsburgh steak salad.

Dee's Eastside Restaurant and Coffee Shop (716-372-4595), 1695 East State Street, Olean. Open Sunday–Thursday 5 AM–3 PM, Saturday 5 AM–2 PM, Friday 5 AM–9 PM. This restaurant's menu features sandwiches, pizza, subs, fish fries, and more.

Don Lorenzos (716-373-0101), 128 West Main Street, Allegany. Open Sunday 11:30–9, Monday–Thursday 11–10, Friday and Saturday 11–10:30. Don Lorenzos serves up Mexican specialties along with American selections.

Jumpin' Juice and Java (716-375-JAVA), 317 North Union Street, Olean. Open Monday–Friday 6 AM–10 PM, Saturday 7 AM–10 PM, Sunday 7:30 AM–9 PM. Enjoy gourmet coffees, teas, smoothies, desserts, and more. They also have an art gallery and live entertainment.

Randy's Up the River (716-372-9606), South Nine Mile Road, Allegany. Open daily 11–midnight, bar until 2 AM. This restaurant, located in an 1860s stagecoach stop, is known for its steak dinners, jumbo wings, and Friday fish fry.

& **Spragues Maple Farms** (716-933-6637 or 800-446-2753; www .spraguesmaplefarms.com), 1048 NY 305, Portville (exit 28 off I-86 to NY 305). Open year-round Sunday–Thursday 7–8, Friday and Saturday 7–9. A large pancake house and restaurant, featuring an all-day breakfast with Sprague's 100 percent pure maple syrup. They also serve down-home country meals for lunch and dinner—including their special roast-turkey dinners from their own free-range turkeys raised on their farm—along with a Friday fish fry. Maple tours are offered during the maple sugaring season in early spring. A gift shop features maple products, gourmet foods, and country crafts.

✳ Entertainment

MUSIC Southern Tier Symphony (716-372-1110; www.southerntier symphony.org), PO Box 501, Olean. Performances take place in various venues throughout the Southern Tier, including Olean High School, Reg Lenna (Jamestown) Houghton College, and Genesee Valley High School (Belmont). A professional-grade orchestra presenting local and regional talent. See Web site for schedule; tickets can be purchased by mail at the above address.

The Bent Brass (716-933-7540). This group performs in a number of venues in Olean, including the village park, parades, and local nursing homes.

✳ Selective Shopping

ANTIQUES Cindy's Emporium and Antique Co-op (716-372-4111), 420 East State Street, Olean. Open Tuesday–Sunday 10–6. This store offers a unique shopping environment with a little bit of something for everyone. Owner Cindy Worth-Smith has created a great shop within this old grocery store warehouse featuring antiques, collectibles, furniture, and old and new merchandise. A small café serves coffee, tea, and espresso.

Country Gentleman Antiques (716-373-2410), 1562 Olean-Portville Road, Olean. Open Monday–Saturday 10–5, Sunday 1–5; closed Tuesday. A general line of antiques can be found in this store. Look for the stone front wall.

ART GALLERIES Little Apple Enterprises (716-373-7420), 209 North Union Street, Olean. Open Monday–Thursday 10–5, Friday 10–7, Saturday 10–4. This retail store operated by BOCES students features handcrafted items made by artisans in southwestern New York, including paintings, pottery, wood crafts, and jewelry, along with maple products and candy.

SPECIAL SHOPS Cindy's Craft Co-Op (716-372-1398; www.cccoop.com), 400 North Union Street, Olean. Open Monday–Saturday 10–9, Sunday 11–5. This newly redecorated store has a little bit of everything, including quilts, towels, pillows, pictures, baskets, furniture, candles, floral, collectibles, and birdhouses.

Country Christmas Shop (716-372-1993), 119 North Union Street, Olean. Open Monday–Saturday 10–5. It's Christmas year-round in this store located in an 1860 brick building that once housed a drugstore. Choose from dolls, teddy bears, and collectibles along with a variety of Christmas decorations and ornaments. Adele's Tea Room, located within the store, serves coffee, tea, bagels, and pastries.

ALLEGANY COUNTY

While most of New York was settled during the 1800s, Allegany County remained a wilderness area, so it isn't as highly developed as the rest of the state. Visitors will find an abundance of small villages and towns throughout the county, many retaining their Victorian charm of days gone by.

Allegany County is rich in rural heritage and scenic beauty. No matter what your interest—antiquing, hiking, skiing, hunting, or just enjoying nature—you'll be able to indulge it in Allegany County. The county offers several fine bed & breakfast inns as well as numerous country stores for your shopping pleasure. An annual county-wide artisans' studio tour takes place in October.

Love nature? Allegany County has lakes and streams, woodland trails, wildlife areas, equestrian farms, and more. There are 23 state forests, totaling over 46,000 acres. The county is also an angler's paradise, with trout and bass found in the Genesee River and Allen and Rushford Lakes. Cuba Lake is known for its perch and bass fishing. Deer hunters will be thrilled to know that Allegany has more bucks per square mile than any other county in the state. Turkey and other small game are also plentiful.

Incidentally, in case you're wondering, confusion abounds on the spelling of the county's name. While the county, village, and tribal reservation spell their name "Allegany," the river, reservoir, and mountain range is spelled "Allegheny." No one seems to know why the spelling is different. Either way, it's a translation from the original Seneca language meaning "land of beautiful water."

AREA CODE Allegany County has two area codes: 585 in the western and central portions, and 607 in the eastern part.

COUNTY-WIDE GUIDANCE Allegany County Tourism (585-268-7472 or 1-800-836-1869; www.alleganyco.com), **Crossroads Commerce & Conference Center,** 6087 NY 19, Belmont. Open Monday–Friday 8:30–4. This beautiful visitors center, which opened in the summer of 2004, is conveniently located just north of the I-86 Belmont exit. They have lots of brochures and knowledgeable tourism specialists to assist you.

Allegany County History and Genealogy Information, Web site www.usgennet.org/usa/ny/county/allegany

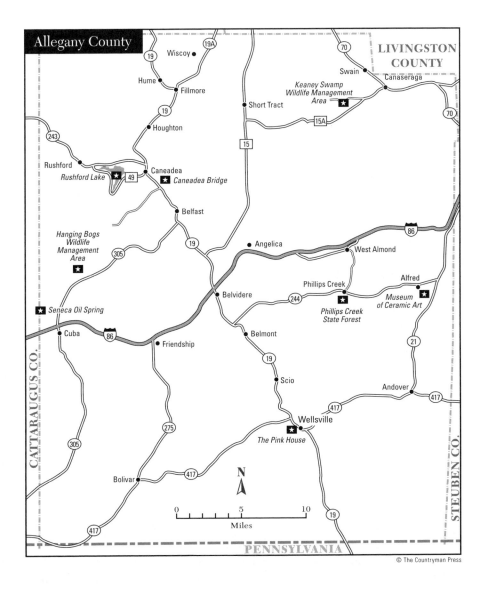

Allegany County

Wiscoy
Swain
Hume
Fillmore
Short Tract
Houghton
Rushford
Rushford Lake
Caneadea
Caneadea Bridge
Belfast
Hanging Bogs
Wildlife
Management
Area
Angelica
West Almond
Alfred
Phillips Creek
Belvidere
Museum
of Ceramic Art
Phillips Creek
State Forest
Seneca Oil Spring
Cuba
Belmont
Friendship
Scio
Andover
Wellsville
The Pink House
Bolivar
N
Keaney Swamp
Wildlife Management
Area
Canaseraga

LIVINGSTON
COUNTY

CATTARAUGUS CO.

STEUBEN CO.

0   5   10
Miles

PENNSYLVANIA

© The Countryman Press

NORTHERN ALLEGANY—Rushford, Caneadea, Belfast, Houghton, Swain, and Canaseraga

The northern portion of county is fairly rural with rolling hills. There are numerous nature areas to explore and several creeks that will delight anglers. Rushford Lake has a nice beach to cool off at on a hot summer day.

Canaseraga, in the town of Burns, is in a rural agricultural region that has fun things to do no matter what the season. In winter enjoy skiing. In spring observe migrating birds in many of the nearby state forests. Summer visitors can enjoy fishing, while fall foliage is the top autumn activity. Canaseraga, which comes from an Iroquois word meaning "among the elms," was first settled in 1809, when Samuel Boylan built the first house in the village. One unique aspect of this village is the "four-corners district" in the center of town, listed on the National Register of Historic Places. The entire downtown area burned in 1895 and was immediately rebuilt all at once. These buildings, all of the same architectural style, are all still intact.

Some of the smaller towns in this region include Caneadea and Belfast, both close to the Genesee Valley Greenway hiking trail; Houghton, home to Houghton College, a Christian liberal arts institution; and Swain, a ski resort town that has one of the best terrain parks in the East.

AREA CODE The area code for Rushford, Caneadea, Belfast, and Houghton is 585. The area code for Swain and Canaseraga is 607.

GUIDANCE Rushford Town Hall (585-437-2206), 8999 Main Street, Rushford. Open Monday, Tuesday, Thursday, Friday 8:30–4 (closed 12–1 for lunch), and Saturday 8:30–12.

Caneadea Town Hall (585-365-2928), 8911 Route 19, Caneadea. Open Monday–Friday 8:30–12 and 1–4:30.

Belfast Town Hall (585-365-2623), 9 Merton Avenue, Belfast. Open Monday, Thursday 8–12 and 1–4, Tuesday 9–12, and Wednesday 4–7.

Canaseraga Village Hall (607-545-8963; www.villageofcanaseraga.com), 10 Main Street, Canaseraga. Open Monday–Friday 8:30–12.

For comprehensive information on the area, go to: www.rushfordlakeguide.com.

GETTING THERE *By car:* Rushford, Caneadea, Houghton, and Belfast are accessed from NY 243 or NY 19, while Swain and Canaseraga are along NY 70. The Southern Tier Expressway (I-86) is located south of this area.

MEDICAL EMERGENCY Dial 911.

✳ To See

MUSEUMS AND HISTORIC HOMES Canaseraga Shawmut Station and Museum (607-545-6527), 2258 Ames Nichols Road (off CR 15A), Canaseraga. Open by appointment. An annual open house is held on the first Sunday in May. Dairy farmer Harvey Lacy, and his wife, Sue, run this museum that focuses on railroad and local history. The 1883 depot for the Pittsburgh, Shawmut, and Northern Railroad line was moved to the Lacys' farm several years ago since the old railroad bed runs through their property. The museum has a display of railroad memorabilia, local history, and agricultural collectibles.

HISTORIC DISTRICTS Canaseraga Four Corners Historic District. The "four corners" area in downtown Canaseraga is on the National Register of Historic Places. The entire downtown district burned in 1895 and was rebuilt all at once. All four corners are of the same era, and all buildings are still intact.

HISTORIC SITES The Caneadea Bridge, East River Road, Caneadea. This camelback construction bridge over the Genesee River was built in 1906 by the

☀ To Do

FISHING Good fishing spots can be found on **Caneadea Creek, Rush Creek, Wiscoy Creek,** and **Allen Lake**, with brown trout, rainbow trout, and bass the likely catch of the day. **Rushford Lake** is also popular for fishing, with fishing access points at Balcom Beach on the north side of the lake and near the dam off Dam Road. See also **Rushford Lake County Beach, Hanging Bog Wildlife Management Area,** and **Keaney Swamp Wildlife Management Area** in *Green Space*. Fishing licenses can be obtained at any town clerk's office. Out-of-state anglers can get a New York State special five-day license by contacting **New York State Department of Environmental Conservation** (Olean office 716-372-0888; www.dec.state.ny.us).

GOLF Allegheny Hills (585-437-2163), 9622 Hardy's Corner Road, Rushford. An 18-hole, par-70 public course.

Six S Golf Course (585-365-2201), 5920 CR 16, Belfast. A public 36-hole (par 72 for 18 holes) golf course with restaurant and RV park.

SCENIC AIRPLANE RIDES Just a "Plane" Bed & Breakfast (585-567-8338), 11152 NY 19A, Fillmore. Pilot Craig Smith offers scenic airplane rides (maximum three passengers) over Letchworth State Park and the surrounding countryside. See *Lodging—Bed & Breakfast.*

SKIING Swain Ski and Snowboard Center (607-545-6511; www.swain.com) Main Street, Swain. This family ski center has terrain for all levels of skiers, including a snowboard park. The Zero Gravity and Mini-G terrain parks are two of the best terrain parks in the East. Swain also has one of the largest base lodges in western New York that includes a restaurant, two bars, and a cafeteria. This is where four-time U.S. ski champion A. J. Kitt learned to ski.

Lifts: 5 (one surface lift, one double chair, and three quad chairs).

Trails: 21 (39 percent beginner, 28 percent intermediate, 33 percent expert).

Vertical Drop: 650 feet.

Snowmaking: 97 percent.

Facilities: Tubing also available.

Ski School: Downhill and snowboard lessons.

For Children: Child care and children's lessons available.

Rates: $17–$41.

☀ Green Space

BEACHES Rushford Lake County Beach, Rushford (on CR 49 about 2.5 miles south of Route 19). Park open dusk to dawn. Free admission. This Allegany County public beach is located on 4.5-mile-long Rushford Lake. The man-made lake is popular for sailing and motor boating, and is stocked for fishing by the NYS Department of Environmental Conservation. The beach is mainly grass with a small strip of sand near the water's edge, and the swimming area has a sand bottom. Park amenities include changing rooms, rest rooms, picnic tables, grills, and horseshoe pits.

NATURE PRESERVES The following are undeveloped areas—which means no amenities. For more info about these undeveloped tracts, contact **NYS Department of Environmental Conservation** (585-268-5392), 5425 CR 48, Belmont, NY 14813.

Hanging Bogs Wildlife Management Area New Hudson (exit 28 off I-86, to NY 305 and New Hudson Road). This 4,500-acre wildlife area features hiking trails, camping, cross-country skiing, snowshoeing, hunting, fishing, and trapping.

Keaney Swamp Wildlife Management Area About 6 miles southwest of Canaseraga, off CR 15B (Jersey Hill Road) and CR 15A (Fink Hollow Road). Some 708 acres of wetlands for bird-watching, hunting, fishing, and trapping. Black Creek runs through the area.

Moss Lake Nature Sanctuary (585-546-8030), Sand Hill Road, off NY 19, Caneadea. Open year-round. Open dawn to dusk. Free admission. An 81-acre kettle-hole bog surrounded by upland forest and oil fields. There are nature trails and picnic tables. This is a very popular place to hike and bird-watch. Locals recommend bringing along some stale bread to feed the catfish.

Rattlesnake Hill Wildlife Management Area. See *Dansville, Livingston County—Green Space.*

PARKS There are 23 state forests in northern Allegany County in which to enjoy camping, hiking, and other recreational activities. For a complete list, contact **NYS Department of Environmental Conservation** (585-268-5292; http://rin .buffalo.edu/s_gove/nys/dec9.html) or **Allegany Office of Tourism** (585-268-9229; www.alleganyco.com).

PONDS AND LAKES Allen Lake Recreational Area, Off CR 15, Allen. A remote man-made lake with fishing and nonmotorized boat access.

Rushford Lake, NY 243, Rushford. A 585-acre man-made lake with a public beach, picnic area, and public boat launch. Rushford Lake was built as a reservoir by Rochester Electric and Gas in 1929. It is now a privately owned lake managed by the Rushford Lake Recreation District.

WALKING AND HIKING TRAILS Genesee Valley Greenway. This trail will eventually extend 90 miles from Olean to Rochester. See complete description under *Green Space: Walking and Hiking Trails—Mount Morris, Livingston County.*

✳ Lodging

INNS AND RESORTS **The Inn at Houghton Creek** (585-567-8400; www.innathoughtoncreek.com), 9722 Genesee Street, Houghton. Seventeen clean and comfortable rooms with either a king or two double beds are available at this newly built year-round country inn, located within walking distance of Houghton College. Innkeeper Becky Samuels and her husband, David, live on premises. Amenities include complimentary hot morning beverages, cable TV, and free use of the pool and physical education center at Houghton College. $69 per adult, $5 each additional adult; children under 12 free (higher rates during college-event weekends).

Mountain Side Inn (585-476-5665; www.crawfordinns.com), Main Street, Swain. This year-round inn, operated by Jim and Teresa Crawford, is located at the base of Swain Ski Center. Several types of accommodations are offered, ranging from suites to an entire house with full kitchen facilities. $95–$350. Dining is available at the adjacent Sierra Restaurant.

BED & BREAKFASTS **Willard's Country Place** (585-365-8317), 7496 Crawford Creek Road, Caneadea. Hosts George and Marie Willard offer four guest rooms with shared baths in a century-old farmhouse tucked away on 150 rolling acres out in the country. A family-style country breakfast is served. They also operate a campground across the street. See *Other Lodging*. $40+.

Just a "Plane" Bed & Breakfast (585-567-8338), 11152 NY 19A, Fillmore. Open March–November 30. This 1926 Dutch Colonial home is located on the banks of the historic

JUST A "PLANE" BED & BREAKFAST OFFERS SCENIC AIRPLANE RIDES AS WELL AS ACCOMMODATIONS AT THEIR FILLMORE B&B.

Christine A. Smyczynski

Genesee Valley Canal. Craig and Audrey Smith have renovated each of the four guest rooms, which all have private baths, and decorated them with individual themes: the Americana Room, the Basket Room, the Mauve Room, and the Country Room, which has unique family heirloom twin beds and a "pig pen" bath. The inn is filled with quilts and baskets handcrafted by Audrey. The yard features a gazebo and a swing—a perfect place to sit and watch the sun set over the neighboring farm. Craig, a licensed pilot, offers scenic airplane rides (additional fee) over Letchworth State Park and the surrounding countryside. (Airplane rides are available to all interested parties, not just inn guests.) A full country breakfast includes homemade coffee cakes and jams. $55–$70.

Mill Creek Inn (607-545-8688; www.millcreekinnbedandbreakfast .com), 17 Mill Street, Canaseraga. Open year-round. Allan and Patty Nobles offer four guest rooms, one with a private bath and three that share a bath, in an 1863 Victorian home with wraparound porch located close to Swain Ski Center. You'll start your day with a homemade breakfast served in the dining room on fine china. $55–$65.

OTHER LODGING **Camping at Mariposa Ponds** (585-567-4211; www.mariposaponds.com), 7632 Centerville Road, Houghton. Open May 1–October 15. Seventy full hookup sites. Facilities include hiking trails, catch-and-release fishing, and an indoor pool. Tent sites $22, RV sites $22–$25.

Maple Creek Campground (585-476-2214; e-mail: maplecreek@yahoo.com), 10433 CR 16, Swain. Open year-round. Rustic camping, tepees, tents, and cabins located on state land. Tent sites $18, teepees $30, cabins $40.

Willard's Country Place (585-365-8317) 7496 Crawford Creek Road, Caneadea. Open May 15–October 15. Hosts George and Marie Willard operate this family-owned business on 150 rolling acres in the country. Thirty-five campsites are available, 20 with full hookups. Activities include catch-and-release fishing in their pond, a playground, farm animal display, and Saturday-afternoon hayrides. Tent sites $15, RV sites $18, cabins $35–$55.

✳ Where to Eat

EATING OUT **Ace's Country Cupboard** (585-365-2692), 40 Main Street, NY 19, Belfast. Open Sunday-Tuesday 6–3, Wednesday–Saturday 6–8. The menu features 30 different sandwiches, a half-dozen varieties of homemade soups, and entrées that include meat loaf, prime rib, and seafood. A fish fry is served Friday and Saturday. Save room for their homemade pies and desserts.

Canaseraga Hardware & Coffee Company (607-545-8828; www.canaseragacoffee.com), 63 Main Street, Canaseraga. Open Tuesday-Sunday 11–9, with later hours on weekends. This coffee shop is located in a historic 1895 hardware store, which appears very much as it did at the end of the 19th century, including the original wooden counters and wall shelves. The menu features locally roasted coffees, cappuccino, teas, gourmet snacks, and light fare like sandwiches and wraps. Gift items include hand-painted African items, locally made candles, pottery and gourmet food items. Live music is featured on Friday and Saturday evenings.

🍴 🍷 ♿ **Deb's Place** (585-567-4545), NY 19, Houghton. Open Monday–Saturday 7–8. Reasonably priced family fare is available at this neat, clean restaurant that has really good service. The restaurant, which resembles a Dutch Colonial barn, is nicely decorated in country style. The main dining room is located upstairs, but several handicapped-accessible tables are located on the first floor. Menu selections include eggs, pancakes, breakfast sandwiches, and breakfast burritos as well as hamburgers, salads, and specialty sandwiches for lunch. The best bet is the all-you-can-eat lunch bar, which features salads, soup, and two different hot entrées daily. Dinners include home-style favorites like broiled chicken, meatloaf, roast beef, and liver and onions.

🍴 🍷 ♿ **Jac-n-Mary's Rushford Family Restaurant** (585-437-LAKE), NY 243, Rushford. Open daily Memorial Day–Labor Day 11–9; winter hours Friday and Saturday 3-10, Sunday 7:30–9. A casual and cozy family restaurant featuring homemade pasta, BBQ ribs, shops, chicken, steaks, and more, including a full-service soup and salad bar. Enjoy their fish fry Friday and Saturday. The restaurant also has a tap room, with a band every Saturday and karaoke on Friday.

Sierra Restaurant (607-545-8909), Main Street, Swain. Open in winter 12–10 daily (bar until 2 AM); off season Wednesday 3–10, Thursday 4–10, Friday and Saturday 12–10. Enjoy fine dining at the base of Swain Ski Center. Menu selections include steaks, seafood, ribs, chicken, veal, and pasta as well as daily specials.

✷ Entertainment

MUSIC **Rushford Village Band** (585-437-2771). This community band, which was established in 1857, performs Saturday evenings in the gazebo on Main Street in Rushford. They can also be seen performing on their horse-drawn wagon in several parades around New York State and Pennsylvania.

✷ Selective Shopping

SPECIAL SHOPS **Allegany Log Homes** (585-567-2583; www.allegany loghomes.com) 9646 NY 19, Houghton. Open 1–4 Monday–Saturday. While the main focus of this business is selling log homes, they also have a small gift shop that has handmade items, local maple syrup, teas, honey, beeswax candles, soaps, jewelry, Christmas ornaments, and more. Five models of log homes are open for viewing, which are interesting to look at even if you aren't in the market for one.

Little Critters Country Store (585-365-9960; www.littlecrittersstore.com), 8788 NY19 (south of NY 243), Caneadea. Open Monday and Tuesday 10–5, Wednesday, Thursday, Saturday, and Sunday 10–6, Friday 10–7. This quaint little shop is jam-packed with all sorts of goodies, including Boyd's Bears, Yankee Candles, Department 56, and many more collectibles and gift items.

Red Barn Country Mall/Bears Repeating (585-365-2437), NY 19 at NY 243, Caneadea. Open Tuesday–Saturday 10–5. A large red barn filled with antiques and collectibles as well as vintage clothing and flea market items.

✷ Special Events

October: **Allegany Artisans Open Studio Tour** (800-521-0885; www .alleganyartisans.com). Countywide. Art lovers are invited to visit artisan's studios throughout Allegany County and neighboring Steuben County. Many of these studios are not normally open to the public.

CENTRAL ALLEGANY—Angelica, Alfred, Belmont, Cuba, and Friendship

Many of the buildings in Angelica, "a town where history lives," are listed on the National Historic Register. The town, incorporated in 1805, was named after Angelica Church, mother of Philip Church, who chose the site for the town in 1802. The tree-lined historic district of this planned community centers around Park Circle, the geographic center of the county. The park has a gazebo, roque court (similar to croquet), and a playground. Many of the homes in the community are built in the Classic Revival style, with Victorian-style homes added after the 1860s. In fact, there has been little new construction in town since the early 1900s. Today this quaint little village, which has a population of around 1,000, is a great place to shop for antiques and gifts, enjoy fine dining, or stay overnight in a romantic B&B. The village is so quaint and nostalgic, it was chosen by *Readers Digest* to be the setting of their 1997 holiday video, *An Old Fashioned Christmas*.

The village of Alfred, population approximately 4,000, is located in a valley in the foothills of the Allegany Mountains. Its downtown National Historic District is made up of well-maintained 19th- and early 20th-century Victorian homes. The first settlers, who were mainly Seventh-Day Baptists from Rhode Island and the Hudson Valley, arrived in 1807, following Native American trails to reach their destination. The town was named after King Alfred the Great of England—the evergreen-covered hills surrounding the community reminded the settlers of their homeland in Wessex, England, from where King Alfred ruled. Two institutions of higher learning are located in the community, Alfred State College and Alfred University, which is fitting since Alfred the Great was known as a patron of learning. Alfred University, founded in 1836, was one of the first coeducational, nonsectarian institutions of higher learning in the United States. Alfred State College, a two-year school, started as the NYS School of Agriculture in 1908 and joined the state system in 1948.

Belmont, the county seat for Allegany County, was laid out in 1833 and incorporated in 1853. It was originally called Philipsburg after Philip Church. The name was later changed in 1870 to Belmont—Italian for "beautiful mountain."

The four-block South Street Historic District in Cuba is one of the best preserved areas of architectural history in the country, displaying several types of Victorian architecture. Thirty-seven residential properties, built between 1840–1940, and three churches are listed on the State and National Historic Registers. In the late 1800s Cuba was a center for Temperance, a movement that opposed the abuse of alcohol. In the early 19th century, alcohol was the most abused drug; people in this country consumed more alcohol than any other nation. At one point Cuba was considered the Mecca for the abstinence movement, with a Temperance camp located on South Street. During the same time period, the area was also known for cheese manufacturing, due to the abundance of dairy farms in the area. Manufacturing cheese gave dairy farmers a more lucrative way to support their families, and cheese is still manufactured in the area today. Cuba was also the birthplace of Charles Ingalls, father of Laura Ingalls Wilder, author of the *Little House on the Prarie* books.

Friendship was first settled in 1805, with many of the early settlers coming from New England, particularly Connecticut. Officially formed in 1815, the town was originally called Fighting or Bloody Corners and Dog Town, due to its Wild West reputation and two battling factions in the area. The name Friendship was suggested by a man by the name of Davis since the skirmishers had resolved their differences prior to it becoming a township. According to local legend, the town is the birthplace of the Republican Party. Ashel Cole and other local citizens met in Friendship's Baptist Church in May 1854 and formed the antislavery party. Shortly after, the name "Republican" was suggested by Horace Greeley. The town, which today has seven churches and no bars, was one of the stops on the Underground Railroad. A well-known company headquartered in town is Friendship Dairy, which markets their products, including cottage cheese, butter, sour cream, and yogurt, throughout the East Coast.

AREA CODE The area code is 585, except for Alfred, which is 607.

GUIDANCE Allegany County Tourism (585-268-7472 or 1-800-836-1869; www .alleganyco.com), Crossroads Commerce & Conference Center, 6087 NY 19 (just north of the I-86 expressway) Belmont. Open Monday–Friday 8:30–4:00.

Town of Alfred (607-587-8524), 6340 Shaw Road, Alfred Station. Open Monday–Friday 9–12:30 and 1:30–4.

Alfred Business Association (607-587-8222; www.alfred.net), 43 North Main Alfred, NY 14802

Village of Angelica (585-466-7431), 79 Center Street, Angelica. Open Monday–Friday 9–4.

Town of Angelica (585-466-3280; www.angelica-ny.com/), Park Circle, Angelica. Open Tuesday–Thursday 3:30–6:30.

Belmont Town Hall (585-268-5522), 1 Schuyler Street, Belmont. Open Monday–Friday 8:30–12, 12:30–5 (Wednesday open 8:30–12 only).

Cuba Chamber of Commerce (585-968-5654 or 585-968-2140; www.cuba-ny .org), Barbara's Flower Shop, 56 West Main Street, Cuba. Open Monday–Friday 9–5 (Wednesday until noon), Saturday 9–1. Local tourism brochures can also be found at the **Cuba Pharmacy** (585-968-3111), 2 Center Street, Cuba; open Monday–Friday 9–7, Saturday 9–5, Sunday 9–1.

www.cubalakebook.com has interesting information on the town of Cuba.

Friendship Information (585-973-2481). Information by phone only.

GETTING THERE *By car:* Angelica, Exit 31 off the Southern Tier Expressway (I-86). For Cuba, exit 28 off I-86. For Friendship, exit 29 off I-86.

MEDICAL EMERGENCY Dial 911

Cuba Memorial Hospital (585-968-2000 or 866-412-CUBA), 140 West Main Street, Cuba.

✳ To See

ART MUSEUMS The Fountain Art Center (585-268-5951), 48 Schuyler Street, Belmont. Open Monday, Tuesday and Friday 10–12 and 2–4 and by chance or appointment. This art center, located in the historic former Belmont Hotel, features art exhibits and community art events, as well as classes at various times throughout the year.

Schein-Joseph International Museum of Ceramic Art (607-871-2421; http://ceramicsmuseum.alfred.edu), Binns Merrill Hall, Alfred University Campus, Alfred. Open Tuesday–Sunday 10–5. This 1,500-square-foot gallery on the Alfred University campus houses some 8,000 ceramic and glass objects, from small pottery shards unearthed from ancient civilizations to sculptures and contemporary pieces. Works displayed are by Alfred students as well as by national and international artists.

MUSEUMS AND HISTORIC HOMES **Allegany County Museum** (585-268-9293), Court Street, Belmont. Open Monday, Tuesday, Thursday, Friday 9–4. Located in a vintage church, this museum has a collection of pictures, local history, and genealogical research documents from 1806 to the present.

Cuba Historical Society Museum (585-968-2633), 12 Genesee Street, Cuba. Open Friday 2–4 or by appointment.

Friendship Free Library (585-973-7724), 40 West Main Street, Friendship. Be sure to stop by the library to see the exhibit on James Baxter, a Friendship native who developed classroom-style musical training. Baxter was also involved in the Underground Railroad.

Pittsburgh, Shawmut and Northern Railroad Historical Society (607-566-9598), Allegany County Fairgrounds, Angelica. Open first full week in June and by appointment. It is also open during the Allegany County Fair in July. This historical society focuses on preserving the history of this railroad line, which operated from the early 1800s until 1947. The museum has several railroad cars on display as well as a replica railroad station that contains photos and other memorabilia.

HISTORIC SITES **Block Barn,** South Street (NY 305), Cuba. This completely fireproof cement-block barn measuring 347 feet long by 50 feet wide was built in 1909 by William B. Simpson to protect his world-famous stallion "McKinney." It is currently home to Empire City Farms.

Seneca Oil Spring—Oil First Discovered near the (south) spillway end of Cuba Lake on the Oil Spring Indian Reservation. A historic marker indicates the place where oil was first discovered in the United States in 1627. The first

MEASURING 347 FEET LONG, THE 1909 BLOCK BARN WAS CONSTRUCTED OF FIREPROOF CEMENT TO HOUSE "MCKINNEY," A WORLD-FAMOUS RACEHORSE.

Christine A. Smyczynski

recorded mention of oil in North America was described by Franciscan Missionary Joseph De La Roche D'Allion.

Terra-Cotta Building, Main Street, Alfred. This small terra-cotta building built in the 1890s served as the office for the Celadon Tile Company and the "catalog" of their terra-cotta architectural products. This company mined shale from the glacial cuts north of Alfred and manufactured terra-cotta roofing and decorative tiles. More than 50 homes in the village are roofed with 100-year-old terra-cotta tiles.

Wellman Homestead, 50 West Main Street, Friendship. This 1835 building, which houses village offices, is on the National Register of Historic Places.

✴ To Do

CROSS-COUNTRY SKIING Phillips Creek State Forest, Water Wells (NY 244), 5 miles west of Alfred. This tract of some 2,700-acres of reforestation land offers several miles of cross-country skiing and horseback riding trails. For information, contact **NYS Department of Environmental Conservation** (585-268-5392).

FISHING Brown Trout can be found in **Black Creek** as well as a variety of fish in the **Genesee Rive**r. **Cuba Lake** features black crappie, large- and small-mouth bass, yellow perch, and walleye. The town of Almond, with its many creeks, is also a popular fishing area. Fishing licenses can be obtained at any town clerk's office. Out-of-state anglers can get a New York State special five-day license by contacting **New York State Department of Environmental Conservation** (Olean office 716-372-0888; www.dec.state.ny.us).

GOLF Serenity Hill Golf Course (585-973-8882), 6462 East Hill (CR 31), Friendship. Nine holes with two tees play to an 18-hole, par-72 course. **Vanderview Golf Course** (607-587-9727), 1960 Waterwells Road (off Vandermark Road), Alfred. A 9-hole, par-34 course.

WALKING TOURS A self-guided walking tour of **Alfred**, which highlights the many buildings in that village listed on the National Register of Historic Places, has been published by the **Alfred Historical Society.** You can pick up a copy of the guide at the Gallery Gift Shop or by calling the historical society (607-587-9319). Note as you walk around town that about 50 of these historic homes have roofs of 100-year-old terra-cotta tile;

THE TERRA COTTA BUILDING IN ALFRED—ALL TERRA COTTA ROOFING AND DECORATIVE TILES—WAS BUILT IN THE 1890S AS A "CATALOG" OF THE TILE COMPANY'S WARES.

Christine A. Smyczynski

manufacturing terra-cotta tiles was a big industry in the Alfred area in the late 1800s and early 1900s.

✳ Green Space

PARKS **Cuba Reservation State Park** (585-851-7200), NY 305, 2 miles north of Cuba. This undeveloped park features a boat launch on Cuba Lake as well as ice sailing in winter.

Island Park (585-973-7779), 31 West Water Street, Friendship. A small village park.

Park Circle (585-466-7431), Angelica. A small village park surrounded by historical buildings. Includes a gazebo, picnic tables, and a small playground.

PONDS AND LAKES **Cuba Lake.** When this lake was built in 1858, it was the largest man-made lake ever built, encompassing 500 acres and 7 miles of shoreline. It was built as part of the Genesee Valley Canal System that linked Olean and the Allegany River to the Erie Canal and Rochester. However, the canal was short-lived as railroads soon became the mode of transportation. After the closing of the canal, the lake became a popular spot with recreational boaters. The lake, which is the highest reservoir in the county, is known as one of the best bass fishing spots in Allegany County. There is public access to the lake by the spillway on the west end of the lake off South Shore Road. There is also fishing access on the west side of the lake near Rawson Road.

WALKING AND HIKING TRAILS **Genesee Valley Greenway.** This trail will eventually extend 90 miles from Olean to Rochester. See complete description in *Livingston County, Mount Morris—Green Space,* **Walking and Hiking Trails.**

✳ Lodging

INNS AND RESORTS **Saxon Inn** (607-871-2600; www.alfred.edu/ saxoninn), 1 Park Street, Alfred. Open year-round. The Saxon Inn, on the campus of Alfred University, offers 20 deluxe guest rooms, including six with fireplaces. Complimentary continental breakfast and access to Alfred University fitness center and pool are included. $93–$120.

BED & BREAKFASTS **Angelica Inn Bed & Breakfast** (585-466-3063; www.angelica-inn.com), 64 West Main Street, Angelica. Open year-round This large Victorian mansion set on 130 acres features three spacious guest rooms, plus one two-

bedroom suite that sleeps up to six people, all with antique furnishings, private baths, and working fireplaces. Innkeepers Mark Itzkowitz and Joel Kassirer have named each room after a notable person from Angelica's history. Two suites are available next door at the 1825 Country House. A full breakfast is included. $85–$125.

Country Cabin Manor B & B (607-587-8504; www.countrycabinmanor .com), 1289 NY 244, Alfred Station. Open year-round. Three guest rooms with private baths are offered by innkeeper Judy Burdick in this log home. The Country Elegance Suite has a king-sized bed and two-person whirlpool tub; the Country Garden

Suite features a queen-sized bed and gazebo-style decor, while the Country Cabin Room has twin beds and a rustic deep-woods theme. A full breakfast is included. $80–$125.

Park Circle Bed & Breakfast (585-466-3999 or 800-350-5778; www.park circlebedandbreakfast.com), 2 East Main Street, Angelica. Open year round. This Queen Anne Gothic–style home built in 1884 has been restored and tastefully decorated by innkeeper Jane Tylenda. It is listed on the National Register of Historic Places and was featured in the 1997 *Reader's Digest* video, *An Old Fashioned Christmas*. The inn features three large guest rooms with 10.5-foot-high ceilings and private baths. Two of the rooms overlook the park. A full hot breakfast includes omelets, eggs Benedict, and fresh fruit. $75–$95 (adults only).

CAMPGROUNDS **Evergreen Trails Campground** (585-466-7993; www .evergreentrails.com), 8403 CR15, Angelica. Open April 1–December 1. This campground features 23 log cabins in the woods along with trailer and tent sites. There are two catch-and-release fishing ponds and 5 miles of hiking trails. They also offer Sunday afternoon hayrides. Tent sites $20, trailer sites $22, cabins $50–$100.

Lake Lodge Camping (607-587-4705), Upper Campus Drive, Alfred. Open May–September. This campground features 60 sites with full hookups. Swimming, fishing, hunting, a playground, and recreational activities. It is popular with the college community. Tent and RV sites $12.

Maple Lane RV Park and Campground (585-968-1677; www.maple lanecamp.com), 5239 Maple Lane, Cuba. Open April 1–November 1.

Thirty-four camp and RV sites plus 3 cabins, 1 mile from Cuba Lake. Campsites $20, cabins $25.

McCarthy Ranch (585-567-4541), NY 210, Angelica. Open year-round. Activities include hiking, swimming, hunting, and fishing on seven ponds and 200 sites with full hookups. Tent and RV sites $12.

Mother's "Pickin Chickin" Lodge & Campground (585-268-7340), Ingraham Road (off NY 19), Belmont. Open year-round. Sites for tents and RVs. Campground amenities include hunting, fishing, cross-country skiing, snowmobiling, lodge with legal beverages, BBQ, and bluegrass music. Tents $10–$15, RVs $20.

ECO-RESORT **Pollywogg Holler Eco-Resort** (585-268-5819 or 800-291-9668; www.pollywoggholler.com), 6242 South Road, Belmont. Open year-round, , Pollywogg Holler is a Great Camp–style lodge featuring solar energy, organic gardening, a Sioux tepee, and gravity-fed spring water. Other amenities include sculpture gardens, a wood-fired Finnish-style sauna, gourmet brick-oven dinners, and breakfast. If you like nature, are ecology minded, and don't mind roughing it a bit, you will enjoy this unique resort, which is similar to going to summer camp: There are no private baths, only a community shower, and no flush toilets. Pollywogg Holler has been featured in several national travel magazines. $110–$170/person; extended-stay discounts available.

❋ **Where to Eat**

DINING OUT **American House & Hotel** (585-466-7784 or 1-800-924-5193), 128 West Main Street, Angelica.

Open for dinner Friday and Saturday 4–9, Sunday brunch 11–3. Allegany County's premier dining spot, featuring fish fry, prime rib, steaks, seafood, and Italian specialties. The 1882 building has undergone extensive renovations to make it a friendly, comfortable place to dine. Their legendary Sunday buffet brunch offers made-to-order eggs and omelets, carved roast beef, sausages, hash, biscuits, and many other selections, including a dessert table.

The Belvidere (585-268-5631), 5855 Old NY 19 (exit 30 off I-86), Belmont. Open for lunch Tuesday–Friday 11–2, dinner Thursday–Saturday 4–9. This casual restaurant is very popular with the locals. Dinner specials include Thursday Mexican night, Friday fish fry, and prime rib on Saturday.

Manhattan West (607-587-9363), 32 North Main Street, Alfred. Open for lunch Monday–Friday 11:30–2, dinner Sunday–Thursday 5–10, bar menu served Friday–Saturday 5–midnight. A popular upscale restaurant and bar.

Moonwinks Restaurant (585-968-1232; www.moonwinks.com), NY 305 North, Cuba. Open Monday–Wednesday 11–10, Thursday–Sunday 11–11. This restaurant/bar offers casual fine dining with menu selection like pasta marinara, chicken Alfredo, and "Oscar" specialties. They also serve filet mignon, rack of lamb, lobster tails, and steak. The lunch menu includes salads, sandwiches, and burgers as well as a variety of hot entrées.

The Stone House Restaurant (585-968-9773; www.thestonehouse restaurant.com), 46 Genesee Street, Cuba. Open Tuesday–Sunday for lunch 11–3, dinner 4–9; Sunday 1–8. Becky and Rich Lee's stone restaurant

was originally built in 1856 as a hardware store and gristmill. It is one of the last original commercial buildings still standing on what was the Genesee Valley Canal. Casual yet upscale, this restaurant features steaks, seafood, and chicken entrées, as well as many pasta dishes. The lunch menu features a variety of sandwiches and bread-bowl salads. A walk-up ice cream window features Hershey's hard ice cream.

EATING OUT Café Za (607-587-9673), 18 Church Street, Alfred. Open Monday–Thursday 11–3:30, 4:30–9; Friday–Saturday 4:30–10; closed Sunday. This café offers an eclectic menu that includes vegan and vegetarian specials.

Chesterfield Trading Inc. Bakery and Cafe (585-968-0960), 6 South Street, Cuba. Open Monday–Saturday 7–3:30. A very tiny café serving breakfast and lunch along with really good coffee, including espresso. Fresh baked goods include cakes, pies, pastries, and brownies.

✍ 🍴 **The Collegiate Restaurant** (607-587-9293), 7 North Main Street, Alfred. Open Monday–Friday 7–9, Saturday and Sunday 8–9. A casual family restaurant serving breakfast anytime, as well as lunch and dinners.

♿ ✍ 🍴 **Cruisers Café & Drive Thru** (585-968-3495), 5220 Maple Lane (NY 305), Cuba. Open seasonally. This café serves up pizza, wings, burgers, and subs, as well as ice cream treats.

Ginny's Creamery (585-466-3155), 27 West Main Street, Angelica. Open year-round. Monday–Thursday 6:30–2:30, Friday 6:30–7:30, Saturday–Sunday 7–2:30. This restaurant with a diner decor features cheeseburgers, hamburgers, and specialty sandwiches, like fried bologna and Reubens. It is home of the "Angelican foot long" (hot dog). They also serve ice cream May–September.

Heritage Coffee House (585-466-7844), 40 West Main Street, Angelica. Open Wednesday–Sunday 10–5. A relaxing place to rest and refresh after checking out Angelica's many shops. Enjoy a snack amid antiques and country decor. The coffeehouse is located adjacent to Heritage Antiques. See *Selective Shopping— Antiques.*

Heritage Sweets Bakery & Coffee-house (585-973-2444), 2 West Main Street, Friendship. Coffee and a variety of baked goods can be found here.

The Kopper Keg (585-968-1523), 11 East Main. Street, Cuba. Open Monday–Saturday 5:30 AM–8 PM, Friday 5:30 AM–9 PM, Sunday 7 AM–4 PM. This family restaurant is known for its good home cooking, including real potatoes and homemade soups and pies.

Miller & Brandes (585-973-2780 deli, 585-973-7688 store), Castle Garden Road, Friendship. Open Monday–Friday 6 AM–10 PM, Saturday and Sunday 7 AM–10 PM. A small convenience store that also has a popular deli known for sandwiches.

Nana's Pottery and Japanese Café (607-587-8335), 56 North Main Street, Alfred. Open Monday–Friday 8 AM–6 PM. This small restaurant specializes in healthy, natural, home-cooked Asian foods, including vegetarian dishes, salads, wraps, and soups as well as smoothies and a variety of teas. Nana is also a potter, so there is a small area in the front of the restaurant with pieces of her work displayed for sale.

☙ ✿ ♿ **Papi & Pati's Sundae Drive** (585-268-5521), NY 19, Belmont. Open April–Labor Day 10:30–8. Menu selection includes burgers, salads, and wraps as well as ice cream treats. They also have a miniature golf course.

Stage II: An American Bistro (585-968-8167), 2 West Main Street, Cuba. Open daily 11:30–9. This casual restaurant specializes in gourmet pizza, pasta, fresh seafood, and steaks.

♿ **Terra-Cotta Coffeehouse** (607-587-8800), 34 North Main Street, Alfred. Open 11 AM–1 AM. Terra-cotta is the decorating theme in this popular coffeehouse. The marble-topped bar has a terra-cotta front, which compliments the terra-cotta tile floor. Sculptures by local artists are also part of the decor. Several small chess board tables are at the rear of the room. The menu features specialty coffees, grilled and deli sandwiches, focaccia sandwiches, desserts, and smoothies.

☙ **Udder Restaurant** (585-973-7631), 14 West Main Street, Friendship. Open Monday–Friday 7–3, Saturday and Sunday 7 –2. Breakfast and lunch with a cow theme.

✳ Selective Shopping

ANTIQUES Anntiques (585-973-7921), 18 West Main Street, Friendship. Open Monday, Tuesday, Thursday–Saturday 11–5, Sunday 1:30–5. Owner Ann Wereley has a huge inventory of small items, including buttons, gadgets, jewelry, glass, and pottery. She also has a large collection of lamps.

The Browsing Barn, corner of Genesee Street (NY 305) and Woodruff Street, Cuba. Open Wednesday–Friday 11–5, Saturday

10–5. This unique country store in a barn features gifts, antiques, collectibles, Christmas items, furniture, and Amish-made goods.

Country Folk Antiques & Collectibles (585-973-2478), 39 Main Street, Friendship. Open 10:30–5 Thursday–Monday. General line of antiques, including furniture and lamps.

Heritage Antiques (585-466-3712 or 466-3549; E-mail: fleurettepeletier@ stny.rr.com), 42 West Main Street, Angelica. Open April–December, Wednesday–Sunday 10–5; January and March, Saturday and Sunday 10–5. This two-story, 5,000-square-foot multidealer shop features fine antiques and collectibles, including furniture, clothing, jewelry, silver, linens, books, and glassware. A small coffee shop is adjacent to the store.

Old Holley Farm Building (585-973-8838), 16 West Main Street, Friendship. Open by chance or appointment. Lots of "guy stuff," including tractors, steam engines, tools, and even marbles, as well as antiques, collectibles, and furniture.

Circus Barn (585-973-7921). This two-story barn behind Anntiques and Old Holley Farm has primitives, furniture, lots of chairs, and household items.

The Pink Church (same hours and phone as Anntiques), 39 West Main, Friendship. This 1850s country church with beautiful stained-glass windows is painted pink and loaded with quality antiques, including vintage clothing, books, furniture, linens, and Depression glass.

FARM MARKETS **All Decked Out** (607-276-6736), NY 21, Almond.

Open daily 10–6. Amish-made outdoor furniture, greenhouse, local produce. They carry only the finest Amish-made furniture handcrafted in New York, Pennsylvania, and Ohio.

Cuba Farm Market, Church and Main Streets, Cuba. Open late June–late October. This market features fresh in-season produce, baked goods, and more.

SPECIAL SHOPS

Alfred

The Bicycle Man (607-587-8835; www.bicycleman.com), 570 Main Street, Alfred Station. Open Wednesday–Saturday 10–6. This well-known bike shop located in an 1879 one-room schoolhouse specializes in recumbent bicycles. It has the largest selection of recumbent bikes in the Northeast.

Canacadea Country Store (607-587-8634), 599 NY 244, Alfred Station. Open daily 10–5:30. One of Allegany County's most unique places to shop, this 1858 general store features wooden floors and a terra-cotta roof. It has been operating as a gift shop since 1985. Browse three floors of gifts, antiques and foods, including Honey Pot candy made right in Alfred. Items carried include books, dishes, Yankee Candles, cards, Gund, Vera Bradley, pottery, bath and body, and gourmet food items.

Canacadea Sled Shop (607-587-9450; www.sledman2.com), 676 Tinker Town Road (NY 244), Alfred Station. Open by chance and appointment. This shop specializes in restored and original sleds.

The Gallery (607-587-9200; www .thegalleryalfred.com), 43 North Main Street, Alfred. Open Tuesday–Friday 10–5, Saturday 10–4. Enjoy browsing two floors of an 1840 Greek Revival–style building for unique gifts and handmade merchandise from local and national artists, including pottery, sterling silver jewelry, porcelain, and handblown glass. They also have gourmet foods, cards, accessories, fashions, toys, and more.

Angelica

Angelica Bakery (585-466-7602), 37 Main Street, Angelica. Though mainly a wholesale operation, they will sell you a loaf or two if come to their door. They are there Monday, Tuesday, Thursday, and Friday 9–2:30. Their products can be found in supermarkets in the region surrounding Angelica. This bakery is famous for its "salt-rising bread." Salt-rising yeast is formed when cornmeal and boiled milk are mixed and set aside to ferment. This natural fermentation process was used by pioneer women because yeast and baking powder were unavailable. The resulting bread has an almost cheesy taste and is best served toasted and topped with butter and/or cinnamon sugar.

Angelica Country Store & Annex (585-466-3040; dedeward@hotmail.com), 48–50 West Main Street, Angelica. Open Tuesday–Sunday 10–5. Gifts, antiques, collectibles, garden items, and custom stained glass on three floors in two buildings. The 1830 main building was originally a hardware store.

Angelica Main Street Gallery (585-466-7658), 39 West Main Street, Angelica. Open Wednesday–Sunday 10–5. Antiques, collectibles and fine arts are displayed in a vintage brick building.

Budinger's Shoppe (585-466-3112), 33 West Main Street, Angelica. Open Wednesday–Sunday 10–5. Candles, gifts, cards, antiques, and salt and pepper shakers are displayed in a vintage building that has the original embossed-tin ceiling.

The Doll House (585-466-3089), 44 West Main Street, Angelica. Open Wednesday–Saturday 10–4. Antique and modern dolls, bears, gifts, accessories, and a doll hospital.

F. Pelletier & Co. (585-466-3788 or 466-3549), 44 West Main Street, Angelica. Open March–December, Wednesday–Sunday 10–5; January and February, Saturday and Sunday 10–5. A home decor shop featuring lamps, clocks, giftware, linens, and floral arrangements.

The Old Garage (585-466-3258), 95 West Main Street, Angelica. Open year-round Wednesday–Sunday 10–5. This multidealer co-op shop housed in a former auto mechanic's garage deals in gifts, crafts, antiques, cards, furniture, and more.

The Village Mercantile (585-466-7726), 21 West Main Street, Angelica. Open Thursday–Sunday 10–5. A multidealer shop featuring antiques, arts, crafts, and gifts.

Belmont

Country View Crafts (585-268-7232), NY 244, Phillips Creek Road, Belmont. Open year-round Wednesday–Friday 12–4, Saturday 9:30–4, and by appointment. Specializing in Amish- and Mennonite-made items, including fine oak furniture, outdoor deck furniture, and many gift items.

Cuba

Barbara's Flower Shop (585-968-2140), 56 West Main Street, Cuba. Open Monday–Friday 9–5 (Wednesday until noon) Saturday 9–1. This shop features flowers and gifts. It's also where visitors can go to get information on the Cuba area.

Cuba Cheese Shoppe (1-800-543-4938; www.cubacheese.com), 53 Genesee Street, Cuba. Open daily 9–6, Saturday and Sunday 9–5. Cheese making has been part of this rural community for several generations. During the late 1800s Cuba was considered the cheese-making center of the world, with many cheese factories dotting the landscape. The Cuba Cheese Shoppe carries on that tradition. Here you can choose from over 200 varieties of gourmet cheese, including their award-winning white cheddar. Gift baskets are made while you wait. The shop also stocks other specialty cheeses, salt-rising bread, and gourmet gift items. They ship anywhere in the United States.

Garden Wall Studio (585-968-8118), 29 East Main Street, Cuba. Open Tuesday–Saturday 10–5. Gloria Iacono's shop has a large selection of stencils and supplies, custom picture frames, antiques, and handmade gift items.

The Gift Nook at Cuba Pharmacy (585-968-3111), 2 Center Street, Cuba. Open Monday–Friday 9–7, Saturday 9–5, Sunday 9–1. Choose from porcelain dolls, gifts, souvenirs, collectibles, and cards as well as birdhouses, lawn-and-garden items, nautical, and more. The gift shop is located in a full-service drugstore that also has local visitor information brochures.

❋ Special Events

June **Cuba Dairy Week** (585-968-2530), Fireman's Park, Center Street, Cuba. This annual event, which kicks off the summer season in Cuba, focuses on the region's dairy industry.

July: **Allegany County Fair** (716-466-8527), County fairgrounds, Angelica. Known as the "Fair with a Country Smile," the Allegany County Fair has been a summer tradition for over 160 years. **Friendship Freedom Fair** (585-973-2481), Friendship. This event, which takes place the last full weekend of July, features a parade, a car show, family activities, and more. **Summerfest** (585-968-5654 or 585-968-2140), Cuba. This village-wide festival features arts, crafts, and a "taste of Cuba."

August: **Angelica Heritage Days** (585-466-3712 or 585-466-3549), Park Circle, Angelica. This festival focuses on the history of Angelica. It features crafts, antiques, food, and entertainment.

October: **Allegany Artisans Open Studio Tour** (800-521-0885; www.alleganyartisans.com), Countywide. Art lovers are invited to visit artisan's studios throughout Allegany and neighboring Steuben County.

November–December: **Heritage Christmas** (585-466-3712 or 585-466-3549), Angelica. Browse in unique shops in a town where history lives. An annual Christmas angel postage cancellation takes place in early December at the Angelica post office (585-466-7689). On the Sunday before Christmas, luminaries are lit around the Park Circle. The evening features caroling, a live nativity, and refreshments.

Before the first settlers arrived in 1795, the area now known as Wellsville was a densely forested territory that was hunting and fishing territory for the Seneca Indians. Some of the earliest trades included making maple sugar and palm-leaf hats as well as fur trading. Later lumbering was added. Wellsville was incorporated in 1857 and grew rapidly following the discovery of oil in 1879. By 1884 there were 55 saloons and six "houses of ill fame." Wellsville became, and still is, the most populous town in Allegany County. Located just 10 miles north of the Pennsylvania border, this safe, family-oriented community is the cultural and employment center of Allegany County. One of Wellsville's most famous residents was George "Gabby" Hayes, who was born outside the town in 1885. Hayes appeared in over 200 western movies, more than any other Hollywood actor. He died in 1969 at the age of 83.

Andover was first settled in 1796 by Nathaniel Dyke and Stephen Cole. Other settlers soon followed and the town was incorporated in 1824. The name Andover was suggested by a settler who hailed from Andover, Vermont. The town grew quite a bit after the Erie Railroad came through Allegany County in 1851. Dairy farming was one of the principal occupations in the early days. Today Andover is home to numerous artisans' studios, which are open during the Allegany County Artisans Tour each October.

Bolivar was first settled by Timothy Cowles in 1819. The township was formed in 1825 and named to honor General Simon Bolivar, the heroic South American liberator. In the early days settlers made their living as farmers, loggers, and tanners. But when oil was discovered in the nearby town of Wirth in 1881, Bolivar quickly became a boom town. At one point it was one of the wealthiest communities in the state.

AREA CODE The area code is 585, except for Andover, which is 607.

GUIDANCE Town of Andover (607-478-8446; www.andoverny.com), 22 East Greenwood, Andover 14806. Open Monday, Friday 8–12, Tuesday, Thursday 4–6.

Allegany Arts Association (585-593-1183 or 585-593-0918), Wellsville. Contact by phone only. This association has information on the arts in the Wellsville area and Allegany County.

Town of Wellsville (585-593-1780; www.townofwellsville.org), 156 North Main Street, Wellsville. Open Monday–Friday 8–12, 1–4. The town and village offices are in the same building.

Village of Wellsville (585-593-1121; www.wellsvilleny.com), 156 North Main Street, Wellsville. Open Monday–Friday 8–12, 1–4. The town and village offices are in the same building.

Wellsville Chamber of Commerce (585-593-5080; www.wellsvilleareachamber.com), 114 North Main Street, Wellsville. Open Monday–Friday 8:30–4, closed 1–2 for lunch.

THE PINK HOUSE

One of the most fascinating structures in Wellsville is the world-famous "Pink House," one of the finest examples of Italianate architecture in the nation. The 18-room mansion, the most photographed building in Allegany County, was built in 1869 for Edwin Hall and is currently owned by his great-grandsons. It is not open to the public, but you can view it from the corner of West State Street and Brooklyn Avenue.

Two tragic stories associated with the Pink House add to its intrigue. The first concerns the drowning of Hall's two-year-old granddaughter in the fountain on the front lawn. Hall witnessed the tragedy from the front porch but was unable to help because he was paralyzed. He later had the fountain filled in. The second story concerns Hall's marriage to Antoinette Farnum. Years before the marriage, Hall had fallen in love with Antoinette's sister, Frances; however, her father disapproved of him and forged letters to each of them, breaking off the relationship. Several years later he ran into Frances and her father the day before she was to wed another. He greeted Frances so coldly that she became greatly upset. That night Hall dreamed of Frances calling his name before throwing herself into a pool of water. He awoke that morning to learn that Frances had drowned herself in a stream during the night. Hall eventually married her sister, Antoinette, and built the Pink House for her. According to local legend, Frances's spirit walks through the house and plays the piano.

BUILT IN 1869, THE PINK HOUSE IS ONE OF THE FINEST EXAMPLES OF ITALIANATE ARCHITECTURE IN THE COUNTRY.

Christine A. Smyczynski

GETTING THERE *By air:* **Wellsville Municipal Airport** (585-593-3350), Tarantine Road, Wellsville. While this airport—the only one in Allegany County—does not have scheduled commercial service, they do offer chartered service.

By car: The Southern Tier Expressway, I-86, runs east/west through Allegany County, NY 19 is the major north/south route.

MEDICAL EMERGENCY Dial 911

Jones Memorial Hospital (585-593-1100; www.jmhny.org), 191 North Main Street, Wellsville.

✳ To See

ARCHITECTURE Wellsville is noted for its many Victorian and Greek Revival homes built during the town's oil and logging booms. Be sure to visit the **David A. Howe Public Library** (155 North Main Street) and the **post office** (40 East Pearl Street).

MUSEUMS AND HISTORIC HOMES **Dyke Museum** (585-593-1404; www .usgennet.org/usa/ny/county/allegany), 116 East Dyke Street, Wellsville. Open Wednesday 1–4, May–October and by appointment. This museum has a collection of artifacts from Wellsville's early settlers and local business memorabilia as well as local genealogical research documents.

Mather Homestead (585-593-1636), 343 North Main Street, Wellsville. Open by appointment or by chance. Donation. Visitors can roam the first floor of the 19th-century house and examine the artifacts, which range from a glass vase from 1500 B.C. to paintings by area artists. Other items include clocks from the 1930s and 1940s, a kitchen from the 1930s, and lots of musical instruments. Visitors are allowed to touch many of the items. A 1937 Cord automobile housed in the garage is also part of the museum's collection.

Pioneer Oil Museum (585-928-1344), Main Street, Bolivar. Open Monday–Friday 10–4, Memorial Day–Labor Day. Admission: $3. This museum houses a collection of artifacts used in the oil business in Allegany and Cattaraugus Counties, including a collection of photographs dating from the 1870s to the present. The museum focuses on the "oil boom" that took place in Bolivar in April 1881: When oil was struck, close to 10,000 people converged on this quiet farm town in a matter of weeks.

✳ To Do

FISHING The **Genesee River,** which runs through Wellsville, is a popular fishing spot. Fishing licenses can be obtained at K-Mart in Wellsville or at any county, town, or village clerk's office. Out-of-state anglers can get a New York State special five-day license by contacting **NYS Department of Environmental Conservation** (Olean office, 716-372-0888; www.dec.state.ny.us).

GOLF **Bolivar Golf Club** (585-928-1266), Halls Road and NY 417, Bolivar. An 18-hole, par-72 course.

Wellsville Country Club (585-593-6337), Riverside Drive, Wellsville. A semi-private 18-hole, par-71 course.

❋ Green Space

PARKS **Greenwood Hill Farm** (607-478-5171; www.greenwoodhill.com), 7 Pleasant Avenue (off NY 417), Andover. Open May–August, Thursday and Friday 12–5, Saturday and Sunday 10–7; Saturday and Sunday 12–5 in fall and spring; closed in winter. A privately owned, family-run park open to the public that offers hiking, picnicking, farm buildings, and farm animals. Horse-drawn wagon tours are available.

Island Park (585-593-1121), NY 417, Wellsville. A 7-acre village park with a playground and picnic area.

❋ Lodging

INNS AND RESORTS **Hilltop Lodge** (585-928-1040 or 1-800-479-1042; www.hilltoplodge.net), 8015 Messer Hill Road, Bolivar. Open year-round. This historic redwood lodge with 20 guest rooms is located on a mountaintop 2,217 feet above sea level. The five original lodge buildings were built in 1928 by oil millionaire William Addison Dusenbury. Each room has two double beds, a private bath, and a TV. Host Rick Fontana, a trained chef, offers a deluxe three-day, two-night package that includes meals for $129. Rooms are also available for $50/night without meals.

♿ **Wellspring Nature Center Inn and Retreat** (716-498-0005, cell phone or 585-593-6988; www.well springinn.com), 1483 River Road, Wellsville. Open year-round. This is a place to escape the pressures of everyday life. David and Janice Porter designed and built this woodland retreat on 85 acres—with no phones, no TVs, and no computer hookups for when you really need to get away and contemplate life. Amenities include two private suites and a separate sleeping porch that share a common sitting room with a stove, sink, microwave, and refrigerator. Each

room has its own private bath; one bath is handicap accessible. Many of the pieces of hardwood furniture at the inn have been handcrafted by David using native Allegany hard- and softwoods. Guests have the option of ordering a hospitality basket filled with homemade baked goods, eggs, and more for you to prepare for breakfast the next morning. Guests have use of four hiking trails with varying degrees of difficulty as well as a seven-circuit labyrinth. $85–$150; $95–$185 with hospitality basket.

MOTELS AND HOTELS **Best Value Inn** (585-593-2494 or 1-877-595-7087; www.bestvalueinn.com), 3186 Andover Road (NY 417 East), Wellsville. A small chain motel offers 19 rooms, each with a refrigerator, microwave, and coffeemaker. A continental breakfast is included. $39–$55.

Long-Vue Motel (585-593-2450; www.longvuemotel.com), NY 417 West, Wellsville. This motel has air-conditioned 19 rooms, including some suites, all with VCRs and complimentary movies. Independently owned and operated. $54–$135.

Microtel Inn and Suites (585-593-3449; www.microtelinn.com), 30 West

Dyke Street, Wellsville. A newly built chain motel that has 60 units, including some suites. A free continental breakfast is included. $39–$89.

OTHER LODGING **Riverside Park Campground** (585-593-3856), 3277 Riverside Drive (NY 19), Wellsville. Open April 15–October. Activities include fishing on the Genesee River and hiking. Tent sites $10/night, $50/week, RV sites $15/night, $75/week.

✳ Where to Eat

DINING OUT ✍ ♿ **The Beef Haus** (585-593-6222; www.beefhaus.com), 176 North Main Street, Wellsville. Open Monday–Saturday 11:30–9:30, Sunday 11:30–3. This establishment is a Wellsville tradition dating back to 1978, with the restaurant at its current location since 1984. Over 500 pounds of beef get served weekly, including their beef on weck on freshly made rolls. Lunch selections include soups, salads, burgers, grilled chicken, sandwiches, and wraps as well, as roast beef sandwiches and beef on weck. The dinner menu features pasta dishes, roast beef dinners, steak, ribs, seafood, and chicken entrées. A kids' menu is available.

♿ **L'Italia** (585-593-2223), 105 North Main Street, Wellsville. Open Tuesday–Thursday 11–10, Friday and Saturday 11–11. This restaurant, in a vintage building with high tin ceilings and ceiling fans, offers fine Italian American cuisine in a casual yet elegant atmosphere. Choose from hot sandwiches, a variety of gourmet pizzas, salads, and classic Italian entrées.

EATING OUT ✍ ♿ **Club Boomers Pit Stop Grill** (585-593-7506; www .club-boomers.com), 4193 NY19,

Scio. Open Tuesday–Sunday at 11 AM. A family-friendly entertainment complex that opened in 2001 features a 3,200-square-foot restaurant, a 2,400-square-foot dance club, an 1,800-square-foot video arcade, and even a petting zoo. Menu selection include subs and burgers, including the one-pound "Big Boomer." Several vintage cars are on display, including a 1957 Chevy Bel-Air Tudor, a 1971 Mustang Mach 1, and a 1981 gull-winged DeLorean coupe.

♿ **The Dill Pickle Restaurant** (585-593-9889), Andover Road (NY 417), Wellsville. Open Monday–Wednesday 7–8, Thursday and Friday 7–9, Saturday 8–9; closed Sunday. This restaurant features daily specials as well as a fish fry everyday.

♿ ✍ **Modern Diner** (585-593-9842), 73 Main Street, Wellsville. Open for breakfast, lunch, and dinner Monday–Wednesday 5–7, Thursday and Friday 5–8, Saturday 5–7, Sunday 5–2. A small, classic diner in downtown Wellsville that serves some of the best burgers in town.

♿ **Stars & Stripes Café** (585-593-7330) 4270 Bolivar Road, Wellsville. Open Sunday–Monday 7–3, Tuesday and Wednesday 7–7, Thursday–Saturday 7–8. Known for their homemade food and desserts, this restaurant has a soup and salad bar, daily specials, and a Friday fish fry. They offer discounts to veterans and senior citizens.

♿ **Sweet Attitudes** (585-593-1901 or 877-593-1901; www.sweetattitudes .com), 95 North Main Street, Wellsville. Open Tuesday–Saturday 9–5 (Thursday until 7). This coffeehouse features handmade chocolates, cappuccino, espresso, and gourmet coffee.

&. **The Texas Hot Restaurant** (585-593-1400), 132 North Main Street, Wellsville. Open 6–11:45. This restaurant, housed in a vintage building, has been known since 1921 for their Texas hot chili sauce. Everything on the menu is homemade. Selections include standard breakfasts, hamburgers, hot and cold sandwiches, and, of course, their famous Texas hots. Dinner entrées include roast beef, fresh roast pork, meat loaf, steak, chops, and seafood, as well as daily specials.

✳ Entertainment

MUSIC **Wellsville Performing Arts Orchestra** (585-593-0118), Wellsville. This group, which has been performing for 17 years, usually gives two performances each year: one at Wellsville High School and the other at one of the local restaurants.

PROFESSIONAL SPORTS **Allegany County Nitros** (585-593-3144; www .wellsville-nitros.com). Season: June and July. Baseball games are played at the Scio High School Field, 3968 Washington Street, Scio. This team plays in the New York Collegiate League.

✳ Selective Shopping

ANTIQUES **The Andover House** (585-593-3947 or 607-478-5014), 21 Main Street, Andover. Open Saturday and Sunday 10–5. This shop has fine antique furniture and collectibles, including a large collection of ceramic art. They specialize in Glidden Pottery, very popular from 1942–1956, and ceramic art from Alfred.

Kailbourne Antiques (585-610-0798 or 585-593-5240), 95 North Main Street (lower level), Wellsville. Open Tuesday, Thursday–Saturday 10:30–4.

Specializing in quality American country and formal furniture, cut glass, china, flow blue, and textiles.

Rev's Needful Things (585-593-3133), 95 North Main Street, Wellsville. Open Tuesday–Saturday 10:30–4. This shop carries a general line of antiques from smalls to furniture. Choose from dishes, artwork, glassware, wicker, and caned furniture.

SPECIAL SHOPS **Fisher's Pharmacy and the Other Side** (585-593-2611), 138 North Main Street, Wellsville. Open Monday–Wednesday and Friday 8:30–7, Thursday 8:30–8, Saturday 9–5, Sunday 10–1. This pharmacy seems to have more gift items than drugstore items. Choose from Yankee Candles, Wellsville souvenirs, Boyd's Bears, whole-bean gourmet coffee, home decor, pottery, glassware, and more. A full-service drugstore is located in the back.

The Flower Garden Gift Shop (585-593-5528), 2780 Hollsport Road, Wellsville. Open Tuesday–Friday 10–6, Saturday 10–4. Browse through an 1830s farmhouse filled with country and primitive treasures. Choose from candles, pottery, baskets, flags, kitchen decor, floral arrangements, cards, lamps, and more.

The General Store (585-593-1051), 163 North Main Street, Wellsville. Open Monday–Friday 9–5 (Thursday 9-8), Saturday 9–3. This store has a little bit of everything, from groceries to clothing and even printer cartridges.

Main Street Emporium (607-478-5009), 44 South Main Street, Andover. Open Tuesday–Friday 10–5, Saturday 10–3. Cards, gifts, and more are sold in an old-fashioned dry goods store.

✳ Special Events

April: **Great Wellsville Fishing Derby** (for information, contact Gary Balcom, Steuben Trust Bank: 585-593-0100), Genesee River near Island Park, Wellsville. More than 2,000 anglers compete for cash prizes.

Late June–August **Music on the Lawn** (585-593-5300), David A. Howe Library, 155 North Main Street, Wellsville. Concerts on the lawn of the library every Thursday evening, weather permitting.

July: **Wellsville Balloon Rally** (800-836-1869; www.wellsville.net), Island Park, Wellsville. One of the longest-running hot-air balloon events in the Northeast, this rally features more than 40 hot air balloons from all over the U.S. and Canada.

October: **Ridgewalk and Run** (585-593-5080; www.ridgewalk.com) Wellsville. A walking/running event combining exercise with fall foliage.

Allegany Artisans Open Studio Tour (800-521-0885; www.allegany artisans.com) Countywide. Art lovers can visit artisans' studios throughout Allegany County and neighboring Steuben County.

MONROE COUNTY

Monroe County—established in 1821 from part of Ontario County—has many attractions and activities for residents and visitors alike. The hub of the county is Rochester, the state's third largest metropolitan area and a high-tech manufacturing city recognized internationally for its skilled workforce. It is equally well known for its cultural and historical attractions such as the George Eastman House, Strong Museum, and Susan B. Anthony House. The county has numerous historical museums, including Genesee Country Village in Mumford, one of the largest collections of historic buildings in the nation.

Monroe County also has numerous recreational attractions, including the Erie Canal, which is popular with recreational boaters as well as walkers and bicyclists who can enjoy the paved towpath that follows the canal. Lake Ontario as well as Irondequoit Bay are renowned for sportfishing. The county has several wildlife sanctuaries, over 11,000 acres of parkland, and more than 45 golf courses.

CITY OF ROCHESTER

Rochester, on Lake Ontario, is the third largest urban area in New York and the 79th largest city in the United States, with just over 1 million people in the metro area. It is the western gateway to the Finger Lakes Region.

The first white settlers came to the area in 1788. Much of the land was swampy and infested with rattlesnakes. The first gristmill was built by Ebenezer Allan just south of High Falls on the Genesee River. In 1810 Col. Nathaniel Rochester and his partners purchased this mill, and several more were constructed, giving the city the nickname of "flour city." Rochester is also known as the "flower city," thanks to the park system and gardens created by George Ellwanger and Patrick Barry. After the completion of the Erie Canal in 1825, Rochester became a real boom town. In addition to the flour mills, the garment industry was a major trade, especially during the Civil War, when uniforms were in great demand.

Many notable people called Rochester their home, including Frederick Douglass, the famous orator and abolitionist, who lived here from 1847–1872. Douglass made many important speeches, published *The North Star,* an abolitionist

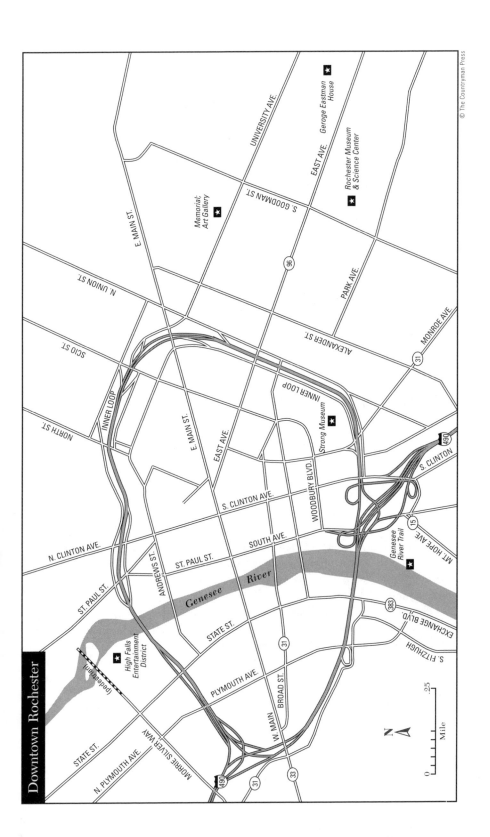

Downtown Rochester

★ George Eastman House

★ Rochester Museum & Science Center

UNIVERSITY AVE.

EAST AVE.

S. GOODMAN ST.

★ Memorial; Art Gallery

E. MAIN ST.

N. UNION ST.

PARK AVE.

ALEXANDER ST.

96

MONROE AVE.

31

SCIO ST.

NORTH ST.

INNER LOOP

E. MAIN ST.

EAST AVE.

INNER LOOP

★ Strong Museum

WOODBURY BLVD.

S. CLINTON AVE.

490

S. CLINTON

N. CLINTON AVE.

SOUTH AVE.

15

MT. HOPE AVE.

★ Genesee River Trail

ST. PAUL ST.

ANDREWS ST.

ST. PAUL ST.

Genesee River

STATE ST.

383

EXCHANGE BLVD.

S. FITZHUGH

High Falls Entertainment District ★

(pedestrian)

STATE ST.

N. PLYMOUTH AVE.

MORRIE SILVER WAY

PLYMOUTH AVE.

BROAD ST.

W. MAIN

31

490

31

33

N

0   .25
Mile

© The Countryman Press

newspaper, and made the Underground Railroad a successful route to freedom for many African-American slaves.

Another famous Rochester citizen was Susan B. Anthony, who advocated women's rights—especially the right to vote. She was arrested in 1872 for the crime of voting in a presidential election. Her home is now a National Historic Landmark as well as a museum. Several well-known industries were founded in Rochester during the late 19th and early 20th centuries, including Bausch & Lomb, Eastman Kodak, and Xerox.

Rochester was recently named one of "America's 10 Best Cities for Families" by *Child* magazine, and the city's Strong Museum is one of the top children's museums in the country. There are many activities for young families to choose from: parks, beaches, boat tours, and festivals. Rochester is also rich in cultural attractions, including museums, historic sites, art galleries, and theaters.

The downtown area can be divided into several distinct districts. The **Center City** is the heart of the legal, financial, and government sectors as well as home to several cultural attractions, including the Strong Museum and Geva Theatre. The Genesee River runs through the center of town, with several vehicle and pedestrian bridges to view the river from. The **High Falls Entertainment District** is located near 100-foot High Falls in the Genesee River gorge. It features a visitors center with interactive exhibits, restaurants, nightclubs, and Frontier Field just across the street. A laser light show takes place at High Falls during the summer months. The **St. Paul Quarter,** along the Genesee River's east bank, was once was the center of Rochester's garment district. The vintage warehouses and commercial buildings now house nightclubs and trendy dining spots. Rochester's **East End** is the cultural district, with the Eastman School of Music and Theatre located here as well as many fine restaurants and nightclubs. Just a little farther down East Avenue is the George Eastman House Museum and the Rochester Museum & Science Center, as well as many large mansions built in the early 1900s. Monroe Avenue and Park Avenue are the city's main shopping areas, with many unique shops and restaurants mixed in with well-kept Victorian homes. The **Corn Hill District** just south of downtown features architecturally interesting older homes and mansions. This community of restored Victorian and Queen Anne–style homes was Rochester's first residential neighborhood.

Far away from the hustle and bustle of downtown, yet still part of the city, is the **Harbor District** (www.harbordistrict.com), which includes the village of Charlotte, Port of Rochester, and Ontario Beach Park. In this area, where the Genesee River empties into Lake Ontario, you can visit a lighthouse, go to the beach, take a harbor cruise, and eat in one of the area's many waterfront restaurants.

AREA CODE The area code in Rochester is 585.

GUIDANCE Rochester Convention and Visitors Bureau (585-546-3070 or 1-800-677-7282; www.visitrochester.com), 45 East Avenue, Rochester. Open Monday–Friday 8:30–5, Saturday 9–5 (10–4 November–April), Sunday 10–3.

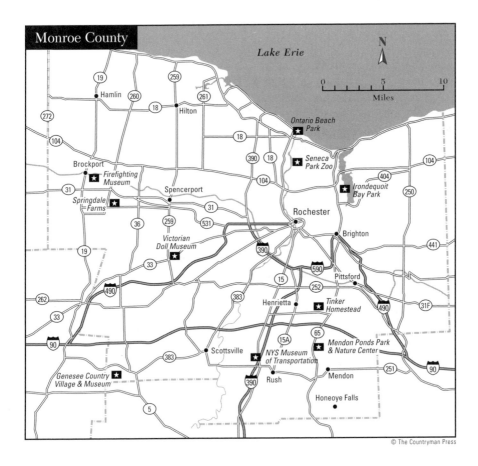

Monroe County

Lake Erie

N

0   5   10
Miles

19 259
Hamlin 260
18
Hilton 261

272
104

Brockport
Firefighting
Museum
31
Springdale
Farms
Spencerport
36 259 531
31

Victorian
Doll Museum
33
19

262
33
490

90

383
Scottsville
383
Genesee Country
Village & Museum
Rush
390

Ontario Beach
Park

18

390 18
Seneca
Park Zoo
104

Rochester

Brighton
441

390

590
Pittsford

15
252

Henrietta
Tinker
Homestead
490
31F

15A
65
Mendon Ponds Park
& Nature Center

NYS Museum
of Transportation
Mendon
251
90

Honeoye Falls

404
Irondequoit
Bay Park
250

104

© The Countryman Press

Downtown Guides Information Center (585-232-3420; www.rochester
downtown.com), 120 East Main Street (corner of St. Paul), Rochester. Open
Monday–Friday 8:30–5:30, Saturday 10–4. Downtown Guides, easily spotted in
their teal and khaki uniforms, complete with Aussie-style hat, can be found on
the streets and skyway system of Rochester. (Guides operate Monday–Thursday
8:30 AM–5:30 PM, Friday 8:30 AM–9 PM and Saturday night 5–9 PM.) They can
provide you with area information and directions, and recommend restaurants.
The center has maps and downtown specific information as well as regional
information.

City of Rochester City Hall (585-428-7000; www.ci.rochester.ny.us), 30 Church
Street, Rochester. Open Monday–Friday 9–5.

County of Monroe (585-428-5301; www.monroecounty.gov), 39 West Main
Street, Rochester. Open Monday–Friday 8–5.

Arts & Cultural Council for Greater Rochester (585-473-4000; www.arts
rochester.org) 277 North Goodman Street, Rochester. Open Monday–Friday

9–5. This organization offers grants and advocacy for Rochester area artists and art organizations, as well as organizes community cultural events.

Landmark Society of Western New York (585-546-7106 or 1-888-546-3849; www.landmarksociety.org), 133 South Fitzhugh Street, Rochester. Open Monday–Friday 9–4. Guides to walking tours of Rochester's historic districts are available either at their offices or online.

New York State Thruway Information Center. This information center, at the Scottsville rest stop, eastbound between the Leroy exit (47) and I-390 exit (46), has lots of Rochester and Finger Lakes Region information.

Useful Rochester Web sites:

www.movingtorochester.org.

www.rbjdaily.com (business information).

GETTING THERE *By air:* **Greater Rochester International Airport** (585-464-6020; www.rocairport.com), 1200 Brooks Avenue, Rochester 14624 (exit 18 off I-390).

By bus: NY State Trailways and Greyhound Bus Terminal behind Midtown Plaza.

By car: NYS Thruway Exits 47 (I-490), 46 (I-390) or 45 (I-490) The I-490 feeds into the "Inner Loop" which circles around the Central City area.

By train: **Amtrak** (585-454-2894 or 800-872-7245) 320 Central Avenue, Rochester.

By ferry: **Canadian American Transportation System "The Breeze"** (585-663-0790 or 877-825-3774; www.thebreeze.com), 1000 North River Street, Rochester. A high-speed caamaran ferry, The Spirit of Ontario, a 284-foot, 750 passenger luxury ship, which can also accommodate 220 vehicles, began service in 2004 from the port of Charlotte. However, operations are currently suspended due to a variety of factors. The ferry is slated to be up and running in spring 2005. Check with local media or the **Rochester Convention and Visitors Bureau** (585-546-3070, 800-677-7282; www.visitrochester.com) 45 East Avenue for current updates.

GETTING AROUND *By car:* The "Outer Loop" consists of I-390 to the west and I-590 to the east and travels around the city through the suburbs. I-490 leads to the "inner loop," which rings the downtown area.

By bus: **Regional Transit System (RTS)** (585-288-1700 or 800-288-3777; www.rgrta.org), 1372 East Main Street, Rochester. There are numerous bus routes throughout the city, including service to the suburbs.

By taxi: Taxi service can be found outside the airport, bus station, and train station.

By foot: **The "Skyway,"** a climate-controlled system of walkways, connects major buildings, hotels, and the convention center in downtown Rochester. It has underground, street-level, and aboveground components. Look for the blue Skyway signs to follow the system, which centers around Main, Broad, and Court Streets, as well as South and Clinton Avenues.

By bicycle: There are many bike trails throughout the metro area. See *Green Space—Hiking and Biking Trails.* Contact the **Rochester Bicycling Club Hotline,** 888-857-8198, for up-to-date information.

MEDICAL EMERGENCY Dial 911.

Highland Hospital (585-473-2200), 1000 South Avenue, Rochester.

Monroe Community Hospital (585-274-7100), 435 East Henrietta Road, Rochester.

Park Ridge Hospital (585-723-7000), 1555 Long Pond Road, Rochester.

Rochester General Hospital (585-338-4000), 1425 Portland Avenue, Rochester.

Strong Memorial Hospital (585-272-2100), 601 Elmwood Avenue, Rochester.

✳ To See

ARCHITECTURE AND SCULPTURE Prominent Rochester architects include Andrew Jackson Warner, who designed **St. Bernard's Seminary** (2260 Lake Avenue, now used for senior housing), the **Powers Building** (see below), which had the first elevator in Rochester, and the **High Victorian Gate House** in Mount Hope Cemetery. Another prominent architect was J. Foster Warner, who designed the fireproof 1893 **Granite Building** (130 East Main Street), the 1892 Richardsonian-Romanesque **Wilson Soule House** (1050 East Avenue), and the **George Eastman House.** The city also boasts the **Boynton House** at 16 East Boulevard, a Prairie-style home with 220 leaded-glass windows, designed by noted architect Frank Lloyd Wright, and built in 1908 for lantern manufacturer Edward Boynton. The home is a private residence.

Mercury, next to Aqueduct Park along the Genesee River off East Main Street in downtown Rochester. This 21-foot, 700-pound copper statue of the Roman god of commerce was originally installed on the smokestack of William Kimbal's tobacco factory in 1881. The Kimbal factory was demolished in 1951 to make room for the Rochester Community War Memorial Arena, the present site of the Blue Cross Arena. The statue was placed into storage until 1974, when it was installed on the Aqueduct/West Group building, across the street from its original site.

The Wings of Progress, atop the Times Square Building, 45 Exchange Boulevard, was designed by Ralph Walker in the 1920s. It has been said that Walker got the inspiration for the design from four sea shells he saw while walking along the beach.

Powers Building, 16 West Main Street. Originally constructed in 1869, additions were made in 1874, 1880, 1888, and 1891. This building was constructed in layers because the building's owner, Daniel Powers, wanted to have the tallest building in Rochester. As other buildings were built taller, Powers commissioned his architect, Andrew Jackson Warner, to keep adding floors. Local folklore says that the building is haunted.

Rochester City Hall, 30 Church Street. This Richardsonian-Romanesque–Revival–style building was built in the early 1890s.

St. Luke's Episcopal Church, 17 South Fitzhugh Street. This 1824 Gothic-Revival church is the oldest building in Rochester.

ART MUSEUMS & **Memorial Art Gallery** (585-473-7720; www.mag.rochester.edu), 500 University Avenue, Rochester. Open Tuesday 12–4, Wednesday–Friday 10–4, Thursday until 9, Saturday 10–5, Sunday 12–5. Admission: $7 adults, $5 over 61 and college students, $2 children 6–18; Thursdays from 5–9, general admission is $2. Located on the campus of the University of Rochester, this gallery features 5,000 years of art, including works by some of the great masters such as Monet, Cezanne, Matisse, and Homer. The gallery also has a gourmet restaurant, gift shop, and a sculpture garden.

Rochester Contemporary (585-461-2222; www.rochestercontemporary.org), 137 East Avenue, Rochester. Open Wednesday and Friday 1–6, Thursday 1–7, Saturday and Sunday 1–5. Free admission. Formerly the Pyramid Arts Center, Rochester Contemporary has been promoting contemporary art in upstate New York for over 25 years. The center features exhibits, educational programs, film and lecture series, and a variety of multimedia programs.

CEMETERIES **Mount Hope Cemetery** (585-428-7999 or 585-461-3494: www.fomh.org), 791 Mount Hope Avenue (Mount Hope and Elmwood Avenue), Rochester. Tours Sunday May–October at 2 and 3. Themed monthly tours are also conducted (www.fomh.org/tour/theme.htm) Mount Hope, established in 1838, was the first municipal Victorian cemetery in America. The 196-acre cemetery is much more than just a burial ground; it's also a park (set in a geological formation of eskers, ridges, and kettles—deep holes left by glaciers), a sculpture gallery, a museum, and a garden. Notables buried here include Frederick Douglass, who played an important role in the operation of the Underground Railroad; Susan B. Anthony, crusader for women's rights; and city founder Nathaniel Rochester. (For more information, read *Mount Hope America's First Municipal Victorian Cemetery* by Richard Reisem, Landmark Society of Western New York, 1994.)

SUFFRAGETTE SUSAN B. ANTHONY TAKES TEA WITH ABOLITIONIST FREDERICK DOUGLASS IN THIS PARK DOWN THE STREET FROM HER HOME.

Christine A. Smyczynski

MUSEUMS AND HISTORIC HOMES & ◎ **Susan B. Anthony House** (585-235-6124; www.susanbanthonyhouse.org), 17 Madison Street, Rochester. Open Labor Day–Memorial. Day, Wednesday–Sunday 11-4; Memorial Day–Labor Day, Tuesday–Sunday 11–5; closed holidays. Admission: Adults, $6; over 62, $5; college students and children, $3. This National Historic Landmark redbrick circa 1850s house was the home of Susan B. Anthony from 1866 until her death in 1906. It was in this home that she planned the Women's Suffrage Movement, and it was the site of her arrest for voting in the 1872 presidential election. Fourteen years after her death, the 19th amendment was passed, giving women the right to vote. Today the home is filled with Victorian furniture, memorabilia, and displays on the Women's Suffrage Movement. If you have time, walk down the street to Susan B. Anthony Square Park to see the sculpture of Susan B. Anthony having tea with Frederick Douglass.

Campbell-Whittlesey House Museum (585-546-7029; www.landmarksociety .org), 123 South Fitzhugh, Rochester. Open Thursday and Friday 12–3. Admission $3 adults, $1 children 8–18. Closed January–February. This 1835 Greek Revival home is located in Corn Hill, Rochester's oldest neighborhood. Displays focus on the daily activities of a wealthy flour miller's household in the mid-1800s.

✎ ⛺ ♿ ✪ **George Eastman House, International Museum of Photography and Film** (585-271-3361: www.eastmanhouse.org), 900 East Avenue, Rochester. Open Monday–Saturday 10–5, Sunday 1–5. Admission: Adults, $8; over 59 and students, $6; children 5–12, $3; under 5 free. This 12-acre estate was the home of George Eastman, founder of Eastman Kodak. Eastman, who invented the Kodak camera in 1888 and the Brownie camera in 1900, brought photography to the common man. He, along with Thomas Edison, was also responsible for the invention of motion picture film. Since 1949 the mansion has housed the International Museum of Photography and Film. Millions of fascinating photographs and artifacts capture the 150-year history of photography. The children's discovery room is a hands-on space that explores the basic principles

GEORGE EASTMAN MADE A FORTUNE BY BRINGING PHOTOGRAPHY TO THE COMMON MAN; NOW HIS ROCHESTER ESTATE IS THE INTERNATIONAL MUSEUM OF PHOTOGRAPHY AND FILM.

Christine A. Smyczynski

of photography. Take a guided tour of the National Historic Landmark mansion, built between 1902–1905. This home, designed by prominent Rochester architect, J. Foster Warner, is the largest single-family residence ever built in Monroe County. It has 37 rooms, 13 baths, 9 fireplaces, and cost $300,000.

&. ♂ ♈ **Rochester Museum and Science Center** (585-271-4320; www.rmsc .org), 657 East Avenue, Rochester. Open Monday–Saturday 9–5, Sunday 12–5. Admission: adults, $7; senior citizens and college students, $6; children 3–18, $5; under 3 free. The Rochester Museum and Science Center features three floors of science and regional history, including many interactive exhibits that make learning fun. A visit to the Strasenburgh Planetarium (585-271-1880) will help children learn about the night sky. The museum offers a summer family-fun program that includes many hands-on activities.

&. ♂ ♈ **Strong Museum** (585-263-2700; www.strongmuseum.org), 1 Manhattan Square, Rochester. Open Monday–Thursday 10–5, Friday 10–8, Saturday 10–5, Sunday 12–5. Admission: Adults, $7; over 62, $6, college students and children 2–17, $5; under 2 free. The Strong Museum is the first in the country devoted to the study of play. Rated one of the nation's top ten children's museums by *Child* magazine, the Strong Museum is home to the world's most comprehensive collection of play-related artifacts. It is the first and only museum in the world to focus on the importance of play in learning, child development, and education. The Strong Museum is also home to the National Toy Hall of Fame, which honors classic toys that have been enjoyed for generations. Plan on spending the entire day, as there much to see and do. Visitors of all ages can enjoy kid-friendly, interactive displays and activities, and ongoing and changing exhibits, including their signature exhibit, "Can You Tell Me How to Get to Sesame Street?"

Woodside Mansion–Rochester Historical Society (585-271-2705; www .rochesterhistory.org), 485 East Avenue, Rochester. Open 10–4 Monday–Friday, Memorial Day–Labor Day; Sunday–Thursday 12–4, rest of year. This Greek Revival–style home, built 1839–1841, houses the collection of the Rochester

MARGARET WOODBURY STRONG

As a young girl in the early 1900s, Margaret Woodbury Strong, the only child of wealthy parents, traveled extensively, both abroad and in the United States. On these trips she collected many souvenirs, which sparked her interest in collecting. She continued to add to her collection after her marriage to Homer Strong in 1920. When they purchased a 30-room estate, "Tuckaway Farms," in 1937, Margaret began to greatly expand her collection of dolls, toys, doll houses, and household items, and she often invited visitors into her home to view her treasures. Unlike other wealthy women of her day, Margaret preferred to collect "Americana," or everyday items. When she died in 1969, there were over 500,000 items in her collection, including 27,000 dolls. It was this collection that formed the basis of the museum that she founded in 1968—"to educate, fascinate, and entertain."

Historical Society. Included in the collection are over 400 paintings of Rochester pioneers, textiles, and costumes, household and kitchen equipment and toys.

HISTORIC SITES & ♪ ⊤ **The Center at High Falls** (585-325-2030), 74-78 Browns Race, Rochester. May-October, Tuesday–Friday 10–4, Saturday and Sunday 12–4 (closed Sunday during winter months). Home to a New York State Heritage Area Visitors Center, High Falls Museum, an art gallery, and gift shop. The surrounding area has several shops, restaurants, and nightclubs.

Ellwanger Garden (585-546-7029; www.landmarksociety.org/museums/ ellwanger1.htm), 625 Mount Hope Avenue, Rochester. Open to the public during the Lilac Festival in May, and by appointment for groups only rest of year. Free admission to public during Lilac festival, fee charged for group tours. Fees vary according top group size. This garden was created in 1867 by horticulturist, George Ellwanger, whose skills helped Rochester earn the name "flower city."

High Falls Historic District. A National Register Historic District where visitors can see the old mills and factories that made the city first in flour production in the world over 150 years ago. From the 850-foot-long Pont-de-Rennes pedestrian bridge, visitors can view High Falls, named the best city waterfall in America.

PRESERVATION DISTRICTS Visitors can get information on the various preservation districts in Rochester from either the **Rochester Convention and Visitors Bureau** or the **Landmark Society of Western New York.** See *Guidance.*

East Avenue Preservation District. At one point there were over 100 stately mansions and estates spanning 3 miles along tree-lined East Avenue. Thankfully, a number of them remain. The largest and best known is the George Eastman house (see *Museums and Historic Homes*).

Corn Hill District. Corn Hill Neighbors Association (585-262-3142; www .cornhill.org), 133 Fitzhugh Street, Rochester. Rochester's first residential neighborhood, this area—once referred to as the "ruffled-shirt district"—was home to Rochester's wealthiest 19th-century citizens. It is the site of a popular annual art festival.

High Falls Historic District. This area is filled with 19th-century factory buildings which now house a visitors center, restaurants, and clubs.

Maplewood Historic District. There are 234 historic homes and three parks in this neighborhood.

Mount Hope Preservation District. The center point of this district is Mount Hope cemetery, America's first municipal cemetery.

St. Paul Quarter. Once the center of Rochester's bustling garment district, now home to restaurants and nightclubs.

State Street National Register Historic District. Between 107 and 173 State Street there is a row of 19th-century commercial buildings that were once part of Rochester's market area.

LIGHTHOUSES Charlotte/Genesee Lighthouse (585-621-6179; www.frontier net.net/~mikemay), 70 Lighthouse Street, Rochester (off Lake Avenue at the end of Lake Ontario State Parkway, behind Holy Cross Church). Open Mother's Day–mid-October Saturday and Sunday 1–5. This 40-foot Medina sandstone lighthouse was built in 1821 when commercial ship traffic to the Port of Rochester increased. It is the second oldest lighthouse in the Great Lakes Region. The lighthouse, which is on the National Register of Historic Places, has four-foot-thick walls and a winding wrought-iron staircase. The adjacent keeper's cottage was built in 1863. The light was removed from service in 1881. In the 1960s it was facing the wrecker's ball—until a successful letter-writing campaign by students at Charlotte High School saved it from demolition. It is currently owned by Monroe County and is operated by the Charlotte-Genesee Lighthouse Historical Society, which runs the museum and gift shop as well as offering weekend tours of the tower.

✳ To Do

BOAT EXCURSIONS Canadian American Transportation System See *Getting There—By Ferry.*

The Harbor Town Belle (585-342-1810 or 800-836-8930; www.harbortown belle.com), Departs from Charlotte Pier at the Port of Rochester, near the Ontario Beach Carousel. May–December, weather permitting. Cruise Lake Ontario, Irondequoit Bay, or the Genesee River on an authentic eighty-foot paddlewheeler. This boat was constructed by Al Gilbert between 1995-98.

Corn Hill Waterfront and Navigation Foundation (585-262-5661; www.sampatch.org), 250 Exchange Boulevard (Corn Hill), Rochester. Season May 1–November 15. Cruise times vary throughout the season. See Web site or call for specifics. Cruise the Genesee River on the **Mary Jemison,** a replica of a 19th-century packet boat, which departs from Corn Hill Landing on the Genesee River in downtown Rochester. A second vessel, the **Sam Patch**, which cruises the Erie Canal, departs from the Schoen Place dock in the Village of Pittsford (See *Boat Excursions* listed under Pittsford). The mission of this foundation is promote the historic significance of the Genesee River and the Erie Canal in the Rochester area. The boats travel the routes of the early settlers and offer a glimpse into the history of the Erie Canal and the Genesee River.

WHO WAS SAM PATCH?
On Friday, Nov. 13, 1829, thousands of spectators gathered to see famous daredevil Sam Patch take his final leap of the season at the 100-foot High Falls on the Genesee River. Sam—who was known to jump from everything and anything—was quite a showman. He dressed in bight silk clothing and had a pet bear he kept on a leash. But it turned out that that November night was to be Sam's last leap ever. He jumped 125 feet from a tower into the dark water and never emerged. His body was found the following spring in the Genesee River.

✪ **Seabreeze Amusement Park** (585-323-1900; www.seabreeze
.com), 4600 Culver Road, Rochester. Mid-May–mid-June, open weekends only;
mid-June–Labor Day, open daily 12–10. Wristbands for rides and water park:
$17.95, $13.95 under 48 inches; general admission to grounds $7 (does not allow
use of water park). Individual amusement rides tickets can be purchased by gen-
eral-admission patrons. Located on the shores of Lake Ontario, Seabreeze is a
popular summertime destination. Enjoy more than 75 rides and water park
activities in a venue that just the right size for families. Rides include four roller
coasters, a wooden carousel, a log flume with the steepest drop in the world, as
well as water slides and the raging river water ride. There are also games, gift
shops, and live entertainment. The park opened in 1879 as a picnic grove at the
end of a steam railroad line. It is the fourth-oldest amusement park in the
nation. In 1900 a carousel was added to the park, and by the 1920s the park had
four roller coasters, live thrill acts, and the world's largest saltwater swimming
pool. Over the years new rides and attractions have been added.

&. ✪ **Seneca Park Zoo** (585-336-7200; www.senecaparkzoo.org), 2222 St. Paul
Boulevard, Rochester. Open 10–4 daily, except for the zoo's annual fund-raiser
day in June. The Seneca Park Zoo, which opened in 1894, is one of Rochester's
most popular attractions. The facility, owned and operated by Monroe County,
has exhibits that include New York's only African elephants and the only Eurasian
Arctic wolves in captivity in the United States, as well as the ever-popular polar
bears and sea lions.

FISHING Rochester Fishing Hotline (585-987-8800). The Genesee River at
the lower falls is a popular spot for salmon fishing. Lake Ontario is also a popular
fishing spot, either from shore or from a boat. A fishing access site to the Genesee River, operated by the NYS Department of Environmental Conservation,
can be found at 5800 St. Paul Boulevard. It is open year-round, with plenty of
parking. Fishing licenses can be obtained at many town clerk's offices and at
most bait and tackle shops.

GOLF Throughout the Rochester Area there are numerous private courses as
well as several public courses. Here are a couple of them:

Genesee Valley Golf Course (585-424-4920), 1000 East River Road, Rochester.
An 18-hole, par-71 county course located in scenic Genesee Valley Park.

Latta Lea Par 3 (585-663-9440), Latta Road, Rochester. A 9-hole, par-3 private
course open to public.

GUIDED TOURS The Underground Railroad Tours by Akwaaba (585-482-
5192; E-mail: akwaaba1@usa.net), 181 Royleston Road, Rochester. Tours are
available year-round but take place primarily during May–October. This full-
service tour operator offers walking tours as well as bus tours, ranging from two
hours to three days, that bring historical events and personalities to life. You can
"meet" such people as Frederick Douglass, Harriet Tubman, and even Susan B.
Anthony, who offered shelter to fugitives seeking to escape slavery. Be sure to
pick up the brochure "Rochester, New York, African American Historical and

Cultural Guide" for detailed information on African American history in the Rochester area.

✳ Green Space

BEACHES ✐ ♿ **Ontario Beach Park** (585-256-4950), Lake and Beach Avenues (along Lake Ontario), Rochester. Open dawn to dusk. Free admission This beach has one of the best natural sand beaches along the Great Lakes. During the summer in the early 1900s the Ontario Beach Amusement Park located here, dubbed the "Coney Island of the West," drew about 50,000 people per day, some from as far away as Pittsburgh. It still is a very popular place, with its pristine sand beach, large park with a playground, a historic carousel, and a long pier to fish off and stroll on. It is adjacent to the Port of Rochester and the ferry to Toronto. See *Parks* and also *Getting There—By Ferry*.

NATURE PRESERVES **Rochester Civic Garden Center** (585-473-5130; www .rccg.org), Highland Park, The Castle, 5 Castle Park (off Reservoir Avenue), Rochester. Open Tuesday–Thursday 9:30–3:30, Saturday 9:30–12:30, closed holiday weekends. Located at the historic Warner Castle in Highland Park, the Garden Center is the Horticultural Education Center for the Genesee Region. Visitors can tour the castle, view art exhibits, do research in the library, and visit the surrounding gardens.

PARKS Over 3,500 acres of green space adorn the city of Rochester, with 28 parks located within the city limits. Four parks in the Rochester area as well as a parkway system were designed by renowned landscape architect **Frederick Law Olmsted.** Rochester was the last municipal park system designed by Olmsted, considered "the Father of Landscape Architecture." These parks include:

ONTARIO BEACH HAS ONE OF THE BEST NATURAL SAND BEACHES IN THE GREAT LAKES REGION.
Christine A. Smyczynski

Genesee Valley Park (585-256-4950), 200 Elmwood Ave at Wilson Boulevard, Rochester. This 800-acre park, the oldest in Monroe County, has 70,000 trees planted by Olmsted. Park facilities include soccer and cricket fields, softball diamonds, hiking and biking trails, cross-country skiing, picnic areas, playgrounds, access to the Genesee River, Erie Barge Canal, and Red Creek, for canoeing and fishing as well as two 18-hole golf courses and a driving range.

Highland Park (585-256-4950), 450 Highland Avenue, Rochester. This 150-acre park was dedicated in 1890.

It features more than 1,200 lilac bushes of 500 varieties as well as magnolia, horse chestnut, and rhododendron. The park is the oldest public, planned arboretum (tree garden) in the United States. A pansy bed, with over 10,000 plants, is planted each season. The park's 1911 glass-walled **Lamberton Conservatory** (585-256-5878; open 10–4 daily) contains tropical and seasonal plants. Also in Highland Park is **Warner Castle**, a popular spot for wedding photos. The Gothic-style mansion was once the home of newspaper editor Horatio Gates Warner. The **Highland Park Bowl** is an outdoor amphitheater for concerts, Shakespeare in the Park, and Movies in the Bowl.

Maplewood Park (585-647-2379), Lake Avenue, Rochester. This Olmsted-designed city of Rochester park has one of the nation's largest rose gardens, with over 3,000 rose bushes adorning 14 acres of gardens on its manicured rolling hills. It has scenic views of two waterfalls in the Genesee River as well as hiking trails, a fishing pond, and a play area. The rose bushes are usually in full bloom the second week of June.

Seneca Park and Zoo (585-256-4950), St. Paul Street, Rochester. This park was originally called North Park and later renamed Seneca, meaning "stone," to recognize the area's Native American heritage and the stone in the river gorge. The 297-acre park, located next to the Genesee Gorge, is comprised of forested and open areas. Several hiking trails meander through the park, and there are numerous picnic areas. Points of interest include a trout lake, which was created by damming a natural spring. The lake featured swan boat rides in the early 20th century. Another point of interest is the Seneca Park Zoo, which was established in 1894 (see *Family Fun*).

OTHER ROCHESTER PARKS Aqueduct Park. Located just off Main Street on the west side of the Genesee River, downtown Rochester. This park overlooks the former Erie Canal aqueduct, on which the Broad Street Bridge is built.

Cobbs Hill Park, Culver Road and Norris Avenue, Rochester. This 109-acre treed park features walking trails, sports fields, picnic areas, playgrounds, and lilacs.

Genesee Crossroads Park, Andrews Avenue at Front Street, near High Falls along the Genesee River in downtown Rochester. This park is popular with downtown workers and features noontime concerts during the summer.

Genesee Gateway Park, Mount Hope Avenue at Gregory Street. Situated along the Genesee River just south of downtown, this park has a small playground and fishing access.

Manhattan Square Park (585-428-7541), 353 Court Street, Rochester (by the Strong Museum). Facilities include a water-play area, playground, and picnic areas as well as an ice rink in the winter. Live entertainment is featured during the summer.

✐ ⅙ **Ontario Beach Park** (585-256-4950), 4800 Lake Avenue near Beach Avenue, along Lake Ontario, Rochester. This 39-acre park, the most heavily used in Monroe County, is reputed to have one of the best natural sand beaches along the Great Lakes. In addition to the beach (open June–Labor Day), there is a bathhouse, concession stand, fishing pier, performance pavilion, public boat launch, and a historic 1905 Dentzel menagerie carousel, one of only six remaining such carousels in the United States. The park is the site of special events and concerts throughout the spring, summer, and fall.

Upper Falls Terrace Park. Located along the Genesee River with view of High Falls.

Washington Square Park .10 St. Mary's Place by Geva Theatre. A quiet green space with a beautiful monument to Abraham Lincoln.

MONROE COUNTY PARKS In addition to city parks, there are 21 county parks in Monroe County, many in Rochester. For a list, contact 585-256-4950; www .monroecounty.gov; 171 Reservoir Avenue, Rochester.

WALKING AND HIKING TRAILS Genesee Riverway Trail. A 13-mile paved trail that follows the Genesee River and links downtown Rochester to the Genesee Valley Park. This trail, intended for walking, running, biking, skating, and cross-country skiing, will eventually go from the Genesee Valley Park to Lake Ontario. **Highland Park** has paved walkways through the lilacs, gardens, and trees. **Maplewood Park** features hiking trails with views of the Genesee River Gorge, Lower Falls, and Middle Falls. **Seneca Park** features a 2-mile trail through wilderness areas with dramatic views of the Genesee River (see *Parks*).

The "Secret Sidewalk," located near Ontario Beach Park, can be accessed between the driveways of 490 and 510 Beach Avenue (off Lake Avenue) This public walkway along the shore of Lake Ontario offers a great view of the lake and of the many gardens along the path. It leads back to Beach Avenue next to 720 Beach. Leashed pets are OK on the path, provided you clean up after them, but bicycles are not allowed.

WATERFALLS High Falls. This 96-foot waterfall in the heart of Rochester, just a few blocks from Main Street, can be viewed from the pedestrian bridge that crosses the gorge or from the overlook area on the east side of the Genesee River, just off St. Paul Street. See also *High Falls Historic District*.

✳ Lodging

INNS AND RESORTS Crescent Beach Hotel (585-227-3600), 1372 Edgemere Drive (on Lake Ontario; I-390, exit 26, to Island Cottage Road to Edgemere Drive), Rochester. Since the early 1800s there have always been hotels and inns on this property. Since the 1980s the Crescent Beach Hotel has been operating as a popular restaurant. In addition to the restaurant, they will soon be offering overnight accommodations in a newly

built section with 38 standard guest rooms and suites. See also *Dining Out*.

The Inn on Broadway (585-232-3595 or 877-612-3595; www.innon broadway.com), 26 Broadway, Rochester. Built in 1929 as the University Club of Rochester, this restored building has been converted into a luxury urban inn offering 23 guest rooms and suites. Rooms feature Egyptian-cotton sheets, towels from Christy's of

England, and queen or king featherbeds. Many of the rooms also include Jacuzzi tubs and fireplaces. A complimentary breakfast is served in their restaurant, Tavern 26. $150+.

HOTELS ♿ **Clarion Riverside Hotel** (585-546-6400 or 888-596-6400; www.riversideclarion.com), 120 East Main Street, Rochester. The largest full-service conference hotel in Rochester, the Clarion Riverside has 466 guest rooms, a full-service restaurant, and over 100 retail stores. It is connected to the Rochester Riverside Convention Center. $71–$139.

♿ **Crowne Plaza Rochester** (585-546-3450; www.rochestercrowne.com), 70 State Street, Rochester. Right in downtown Rochester, close to the nightlife entertainment districts, and a two-block walk from the Blue Cross Arena. Each of the 363 guest rooms include two phones, coffeemakers, dataports, and irons, as well as use of the indoor fitness center and heated outdoor pool. The hotel's River Club Restaurant overlooks the Genesee River. $59–$99.

♿ **Hyatt Regency Rochester** (585-546-1234; www.rochester.hyatt.com), 125 East Main Street, Rochester. In the heart of downtown Rochester, this elegant hotel offers 336 guest rooms, including 18 luxury suites. Amenities include a fully equipped health club and a heated indoor pool. $79–$195.

♿ **Strathallan Hotel** (585-461-5010; www.strathallan.com), 550 East Avenue, Rochester. Located in the heart of Rochester's museum district, the Strathallan is the city's only all-suites, full-service hotel, which includes a four-diamond restaurant. The inn features 156 spacious suites, all with such amenities as refrigerators, microwaves, hair dryers, and irons. $169–$179.

BED & BREAKFASTS **Dartmouth House Inn** (585-271-7872; www.DartmouthHouse.com), 215 Dartmouth Street, Rochester. This historic 1905 English Tudor located in the Park–East Avenue cultural district was originally built for Edward Savage, a Rochester native and inventor, who was America's top toy designer in the 1930s. Four specious guest rooms include private baths, period antiques, and fireplaces. It is the only bed & breakfast in Rochester with whole-house central air. The third floor Canterbury Suite features two bedrooms and a full kitchen. Innkeepers Ellie and Bill Klein have stocked each room with little things that will make your stay enjoyable, such as extra-bright lightbulbs for reading. The inn is within walking distance of the George Eastman House and several other museums and antiques shops. Start your morning with a candlelit four-course gourmet breakfast served on fine china and Ellie's Depression glass collection. $110–$170.

The Edward Harris House Bed & Breakfast (585-473-9752 or 800-419-1213; www.edwardharrishousebb), 35 Argyle Street (between East Avenue and Park Avenue), Rochester. This 1896 home was originally built by lawyer Edward Harris as a wedding present for his daughter. Innkeepers Susan and Manny Alvarez offer five spacious, beautifully decorated guest rooms furnished in period antiques; three include fireplaces, and all have private baths. A full gourmet breakfast is served in the formal dining room or in the landscaped backyard garden. $125–$150.

428 Mt. Vernon (585-271-0792 or 800-836-3159; www.428mtvernon .com), 428 Mt. Vernon Avenue, Rochester. This Victorian home on 3 wooded acres adjacent to Highland Park is a perfect place for a relaxing getaway. It offers a country atmosphere, yet it's close to city restaurants and attractions. Innkeepers Philip and Claire Lanzatella offer seven rooms with Victorian furnishings and private baths. Breakfast is cooked to order. $110–$125.

✳ Where to Eat

Note: See also restaurant listings for communities just outside the city—for example, Irondequoit and Pittsford— because they are just a short drive from the downtown area.

DINING OUT

East End and Vicinity

Bacco's Ristorante (585-442-5090), 263 Park Avenue, Rochester. Open for lunch Tuesday–Friday 11:30–2:30, dinner Tuesday–Saturday 5–10. Northern Italian dishes are made to order and served with bruschetta and homemade bread in a cozy atmosphere. The restaurant, located in the heart of Park Avenue, also has an extensive wine list.

 ♿ **The Grill at Strathallan** (585-454-1880; www.grill175.com), 550 East Avenue, Rochester. Open for breakfast Monday–Friday 6:30–10; lunch Monday–Friday 11:30–2; dinner Monday–Thursday 5–10, Friday and Saturday 5–11; Sunday brunch 11:30–2. Enjoy fine dining at Rochester's only four-diamond restaurant, which features four-course meals and world-class wine. The Grill is the winner of *Wine Spectator*'s "Best of Award of Excellence." The seasonal

menu features inventive American cuisine, with choices like peach-lacquered duck breast and dry-aged strip steak.

♿ **Restaurant 2 Vine** (585-454-6020; www.2vine.com), 24 Winthrop Street (off East Avenue), Rochester. Open for lunch Monday–Friday 11–3, dinner Monday–Saturday 4–12. Serving French and Italian bistro fare in relaxed, casual surroundings—a renovated 1890s garage in the East End entertainment district—this restaurant has the reputation as one of Rochester's finest dining spots. Everything is freshly made, including the seafood, which is flown in daily from a small artisan fish house in Boston. Fresh, organic local produce is used, so the menu changes seasonally.

♿ **The Rio Bamba** (585-244-8680; www.theriobamba.com), 282 Alexander Street, Rochester. Open Monday–Saturday 5:30–10:30. This restaurant features French-inspired cuisine in a restored "grande dame" Rochester restaurant. Menu selections include sesame seed-crusted salmon and roasted Maine lobster. Prix fixe tasting menu also available.

Along Lake Ontario

♿ **Bellanca's Bootlegger** (585-663-8488), 4768 Lake Avenue, Rochester. Open Tuesday–Sunday 4:30–10. This lakeside restaurant, which serves American and Italian cuisine, offers casual fine dining with lake and harbor views.

Cavacori's Restaurant (585-663-8050), 4669 Lake Avenue, Rochester. Open 4–9 daily. Located across the street from the ferry terminal, this restaurant specializes in Italian and American cuisine.

& **The Crescent Beach Hotel** (585-227-3600), 1372 Edgemere Drive (on Lake Ontario), Rochester). Open for lunch Monday–Saturday 11-3; dinner Monday–Friday 4–9, Saturday 4–10, Sunday 1–9; Sunday brunch 10:30–2; call for winter hours. Hotels and inns have been on this Lake Ontario site since the early 1800s. The current building, constructed in the 1980s, offers fine lakefront dining, as well as a manicured garden terrace overlooking the lake during the summer months. See also *Lodging*.

✗ **Harborside Café Steak House** (585-865-8563), 4705 Lake Avenue, Rochester. Open Sunday 4–8, Monday–Thursday 4–9, Friday and Saturday 4–10. This restaurant is one of the best kept secrets in the Charlotte area. The menu features steaks as well as pork chops, chicken specialties, Friday-night seafood specials, and prime rib on Saturday.

Mr. Dominic's at the Lake (585-865-4630; www.mrdominics.com), 4699 Lake Avenue, Rochester. Open for lunch Tuesday–Friday 11–2, dinner Monday–Saturday 4:30–9:30, Sunday 3–9. Located across from the ferry terminal, this restaurant is noted for its Italian dishes, seafood, and steaks.

Downtown and Vicinity
& **Max of Eastman Place** (585-697-0491; www.maxofeastmanplace.com), 27 Gibbs Street (off University Avenue), Rochester. Open for lunch Monday–Friday 11:30–2:30, dinner Monday–Thursday 5–10, Friday and Saturday 5:30–11. Menus change weekly in this innovative restaurant operated by Chef Anthony Gullace.

Lola Bistro and Bar (585-271-0320), 630 Monroe Avenue, Rochester. Open 5 PM–2 AM daily. This small,

intimate bistro features gourmet seafood as well as sandwiches and salads. They are well-known for their crème brûlée.

EATING OUT

East End and Vicinity
Charlie's Frog Pond (585-271-1970), 652 Park Avenue, Rochester. Open Monday–Friday 7–10, Saturday 8–10, Sunday 8–3. This casual, tiny, bistro-style restaurant is an inviting spot with its bright yellow wallpaper with black and white frogs. Known for its frittata made with Italian sausage, peppers, and onions, the restaurant also features lunch and dinner specials that change daily, so be sure to check the blackboard. The tables are really close together, so be careful what you say; it's an interesting place to eavesdrop. During the warmer months there are tables outside along the sidewalk. It is really busy on Sunday mornings for breakfast.

The Dutch Market and Cafe (585-271-6110), 257 Park Avenue, Rochester. Open Tuesday–Friday 10–5:30, Saturday 9–5. This restaurant offers a taste of the Netherlands and Indonesia for breakfast, lunch, and afternoon tea. The gift shop carries Delft pottery, Dutch, and Indonesian foods, and spices, as well as 30 varieties of black licorice.

Edibles Bar and Restaurant (585-271-4910; www.ediblesrestaurant.com), 704 University Avenue, Rochester. Open daily for lunch 11–2:30, dinner 5–9. Enjoy a drink in their intimate foyer bar or sample a tapas platter, lobster ravioli, or handmade pierogi in the restaurant.

First Taste Grill (585-271-6220), 653 Park Avenue, Rochester. Open Monday 11–4, Tuesday–Saturday

11–10, Sunday 9–4. This small, intimate café offers fresh-made, from-scratch foods, including Cajun and grilled sandwiches. Eat indoors or outside on tables along the sidewalk. Note the bike racks along this stretch of Park Avenue. It's a bicycle-friendly neighborhood.

Jine's Restaurant (585-461-1280; www.jinesrestaurant.com), 658 Park Avenue corner of Berkeley Street, Rochester. Open Monday–Saturday 7–10, Sunday 7–8. Rated one of the best casual restaurants in Rochester. Specialties include spanakopita, scallops Marsala, and homemade soups and quiches. It is very popular, especially on Sunday mornings for breakfast. You can eat outdoors in the warmer months.

Park Place Deli (585-442-4986), 657 Park Avenue (corner Berkeley), Rochester. Open Monday–Friday 7–9, Saturday 7–6, Sunday 7–4. This deli, which does a big take-out business, is known for their super wraps as well as deli sandwiches. They also have breakfast specials served Saturday and Sunday. If you want to eat in, there are several small tables inside as well as tables along the sidewalk.

Along and Near Lake Ontario

✍ ఉ **Abbotts Frozen Custard** (office 585-865-7400; www.abbotts frozencustard.com), 4791 Lake Avenue, Rochester. Open seasonally February–October; hours vary each month. This local restaurant, specializing in frozen custard and sundaes, has over 20 Monroe County locations. It has been voted Rochester's #1 frozen custard.

✍ ఉ **LDR Char Pit** (585-865-0112), 4753 Lake Avenue, Rochester. Open year-round Sunday–Thursday 7–9,

Friday and Saturday 7–9:30. This casual restaurant, which has been here since 1945, specializes in steak sandwiches. They cut and grind their own beef for hamburgers, too.

✍ **Leadbelly Landing** (585-663-3210), 4776 Lake Avenue. Open year-round 11 AM–2 AM. This restaurant proclaims it's noted for "warm beer, lousy food, and ugly women." Don't believe 'em. They serve the usual beach restaurant fare like burgers, wings, wraps, salads, and sandwiches as well as a fish fry every day and plenty of ice cold beer to wash it down. Two huge outdoor decks overlook the Port of Rochester and the only take-out seafood window in Charlotte. Live entertainment is featured in the evening.

Ɣ **Nola's BBQ Restaurant and Bar** (585-663-3375; www.nolasbbq .com), 4775 Lake Avenue, Rochester. Open Monday–Thursday 11–9, Friday–Saturday 11–11, Sunday 12–8. This restaurant specializes in New Orleans BBQ as well as gumbo, jambalaya, voodoo chicken, and crawfish tails. All meats are smoked on-site in their smoke shack. They have several outdoor patios as well as an indoor dining room and bar, serving up specialty and frozen drinks. Musical entertainment is featured in the evening.

✍ ఉ **Pats Coffee Shop** (585-663-4990), Ontario Beach Park, Rochester. Open daily at 11 AM from Memorial Day through Labor Day Weekend. Since 1954 this family-owned and operated shop has been serving up hot dogs, burgers, homemade Italian sausage, ice cream, and more.

ఉ ✍ **Pelican Nest Restaurant** (585-663-5910; www.pelicansnestrestaur ant.com), 566 River Street (off Lake

Avenue on the Genesee River), Rochester. Open seven days 11 AM– 2 AM, late April–mid-November. This waterfront restaurant is located just 100 yards from the ferry terminal, with free shuttle service to and from the ferry. Come by car or come by boat, as guest dockage is available. The menu will appeal to everyone from kids to senior citizens. Selections include everything from burgers, salads, wraps, and wings, to crab legs and prime rib. A fish fry is served Wednesday and Friday. A DJ spins tunes Monday–Saturday starting at 8 PM.

Downtown and Vicinity

& **Beale Street Cafe** (585-271-4650; www.bealestreetcafe.com), 689 South Avenue, Rochester. Open for lunch 11:30–4, dinner 4–10. Combining New Orleans with Texas, this restaurant's specialties include BBQ and Cajun dishes, including jambalaya, veggie Creole, blackened prime rib, and chicken étouffée.

Barrister's Pub (585-232-2240), 36 West Main Street, Rochester. Coffee bar open Monday–Friday 7:30 AM– 11 AM, restaurant open Monday– Friday 11:30 AM–9 PM. Furnished with cherry-wood paneling and brass fixtures, this eatery—voted Rochester's best downtown pub—has a gourmet coffee bar along with a large lunch and dinner menu served in the dining room. Menu selections include American, Mexican, and vegetarian dishes.

& **Dinosaur Bar-B-Que** (585-325-7090; www.dinosaurbarbque.com), 99 Court Street (corner of South Avenue on the Genesee River), Rochester. Open Monday–Thursday 11 AM– 12 AM, Saturday 11 AM–1 AM. Winner of the *Democrat and Chronicle* Read-

er's Choice Award for the best BBQ in Rochester. Enjoy BBQ along with Cajun and Cuban specialties served up with live blues at this genuine honky-tonk rib joint. Feel free to bring your "hog"—there's ample motorcycle parking out front.

& **Nathaniel's Pub** (585-232-8473), 251 Exchange Street, Rochester. Open Monday–Friday 11 AM–2 AM, Saturday and Sunday noon–2 AM. Casual pub food is served here, including sandwiches, wraps, burgers, salads, and wings, as well as dinner entrées after 5 PM. This upscale pub with a sports theme, located in the historic Corn Hill district, has a great view of the Rochester skyline.

& **The Olive Tree** (585-454-3510; www.olivetreerestaurant.com), 165 Monroe Avenue, Rochester. Lunch Monday–Friday 11:30–2, Dinner Monday–Saturday 5–9. Since 1979 the Olive Tree has been downtown Rochester's number one Greek restaurant. The menu can best be described as nouvelle Greek cuisine, healthy as well as tasty. The restaurant is housed in a circa 1864 building that was awarded an Excellence in Design for its renovations by the American Institute of Architects.

& **Triphammer Grill** (716-262-2700; www.thetriphammergrill.com), 60 Browns Race (at the Center at High Falls), Rochester. Lunch Monday–Friday 11:30–2:30, dinner Monday–Thursday 5–10, Friday– Saturday 5–11 Enjoy a view of the High Falls Gorge while dining on steaks, seafood, and poultry, as well as vegetarian and low fat entrées. The wine list features New York State wines, as well as selections from California, France, and Australia. A popular spot to dine prior to, or after events at nearby Frontier Field.

South of Downtown

The Distillery (585-271-4105; www.thedistillery.com), 1142 Mount Hope Avenue, Rochester. Open Monday–Saturday 11 AM–1 AM, Sunday 12 PM–1 AM. This restaurant is popular for food, drinks, sports, and fun. With sports broadcasted on 32 large-screen monitors, it's considered one of the best sports bars in Rochester. The restaurant features a microbrewery on premises and a large outdoor deck. Menu selections include soups, salads, pasta, pizza, burgers, sandwiches, and grilled foods as well as daily specials.

& **Highland Park Diner** (585-461-5040; highlandparkdiner.com), 960 South Clinton Avenue, Rochester. Open Sunday 8–3, Monday–Saturday 7:30–10. Rochester's last classic art deco diner, circa 1940—many architectural experts consider it to be one of the most beautiful diners in America—serves real food, real well at real prices. They have one of the best vanilla milkshakes in the city of Rochester.

East of Downtown

Lorraine's Food Factory (585-442-6574; www.lorrainesfoodfactory.com), 777 Culver Road, Rochester. Open Monday–Wednesday 11–6, Thursday–Saturday 11–10, Sunday 8–3. This restaurant, owned by Lorraine Serpe since 1984, is popular with touring celebrities; photos and other memorabilia can be found on the walls. They serve sandwiches, steaks, burgers, pasta, seafood, wraps, pizza, homemade soups, salads, vegetarian dishes, and more. Be sure to save room for their special cheesecake brownie.

✳ Entertainment

MUSIC AND DANCE **Eastman School of Music** (585-274-1100; www.rochester.edu/eastman), 26 Gibbs Street, Rochester. The Eastman School of Music, part of the University of Rochester, is recognized as one of the finest music schools in the world. It was established in 1921 by George Eastman, founder of Eastman Kodak. Over 700 concerts, many of them free, are presented by its students each year.

Garth Fagan Dance (585-454-3260; www.garthfagandance.org), 50 Chestnut Street, Rochester. This renowned dance company, which tours internationally, offers classes as well as a full-week season of performances each fall. Artistic director Garth Fagan won a Tony Award in 1998 for his choreography of the Broadway production *The Lion King*.

Rochester City Ballet (585-461-2100; www.rochestercityballet.org), 1326 University Avenue Rochester. This company performs the Nutcracker with the RPO as well as offering classes and summer workshops.

Rochester Chamber Orchestra (585-663-4693 www.roch.com/rco), This professional ensemble has four programs each year at Hochstein Performance Hall, 50 North Plymouth Avenue, which is connected with the **Hochstein Music School** (585-454-4596; www.hochstein.org), a community music school.

Rochester Philharmonic Orchestra (585-454-2100, 454-7311; www.rpo.org), 108 East Avenue, Rochester. The Rochester Philharmonic Orchestra, founded by George Eastman in 1922, has a reputation as one of America's great orchestras.

Performances take place October through May at the Eastman Theatre (60 Gibbs Street) and during the summer at the Finger Lakes Performing Arts Center in Canandaigua.

THEATERS **BlackFriars** (585-454-1260; www.blackfriars.org), 28 Lawn Street, Rochester. Theater season runs September–May plus one summer production. A community theater that offers classic plays as well as original productions.

Dryden Theatre (585-271-4090) at the George Eastman House, 900 East Avenue, Rochester. Screenings of art and classical films.

♭ **Downstairs Cabaret Theatre** (585-325-4370. www.downstairs cabaret.com), 20 Windsor Street, 172 Main Street and 540 East Main Street, Rochester. Year-round. A low-budget yet high quality theater company that features in-house as well as touring productions.

♭ **Geva Theatre** (585-232-4382; www.gevatheatre.org), 75 Woodbury Boulevard, Rochester. Productions take place year-round. The Geva, the most attended professional regional theater in the state, offers a wide variety of theater performances from world premiers to American classics.

The Little Theatre (585-258-0444; www.little-theatre.com), 240 East Avenue, Rochester. This downtown theater specializes in first-run American independent and foreign films. Their cozy café offers dinners, coffees, New York State wines, and regional beers.

Rochester Broadway Theatre League/Auditorium Center (585-325-7760; www.rbtl.org), 100 East Avenue, Rochester. Broadway touring productions, concerts, and other special events.

Shipping Dock Theatre (585-232-2250; www.shippingdocktheatre.org), 151 St. Paul Street, Rochester. This company offers thought-provoking and imaginative plays.

NIGHTLIFE Three main nightclub districts are located in and around the downtown Rochester area: East End, High Falls, and St. Paul Quarter.

East End
Numerous nightspots can be found in the East End district, which centers around East Avenue and Alexander Street. **Milestones Restaurant and Music Room** (585-325-6490; www .milestonesmusicroom.com; 170 East Avenue) features live bands every night of the week. **Karma 355** (585-454-7010; 355 East Avenue) has a New York City-like atmosphere. It is connected to **Barfly** (585-232-5630; 359 East Avenue). **The Whiskey Bar & Lounge** (585-232-7550; 315 Alexander Street) has dancing plus karaoke on Tuesday nights. **Club Rain** (585-232-1340; 360 Monroe Avenue) features rain falling into troughs between the dance floor and bar. **The Alexander Street Pub** (585-262-3820; 291 Alexander Street) and **The Jungle** (585-546-2211; 289 Alexander Street) are good places to dance. **Tonic** (585-325-7720; www .tonicusa.com, 336 East Avenue) features a Soho-style loft restaurant as well as a nightclub. **The Old Toad** (585-232-2626; 277 Alexander) is known for its English pub atmosphere. The **Blue Room** (585-232-2230; 293 Alexander) is known for its martinis, including the Ovaltini, a unique creation made with, what else, Ovaltine!

High Falls

The High Falls district, overlooking High Falls in the Genesee River, offers several restaurants and bars, including the **Empire Brewing Company** (585-454-2337; 300 State Street), which features a microbrewery. & **Jillians** (585-454-6530; 61 Commercial Street; Sunday–Wednesday 11 AM–12 AM, Thursday–Saturday 11 AM–2 AM) is more than a restaurant/nightclub. Housed in a circa 1890s railway powerhouse, it's a unique entertainment center with a 10-table billiard room, bowling lanes, and a dance club.

St. Paul Quarter

The St. Paul Quarter, located near the west bank of the Genesee River, has several nightspots, including **Club Industry** (585-262-4570; 155 St. Paul Street) which features hip-hop, reggae and R&B. The **Toasted Head Bar & Grill** (585-232-4305; 187 St. Paul Street) features high-end beer. The **Tapas 177 Lounge** (585-262-2090; 177 St. Paul Street) features Latin and Salsa music.

PROFESSIONAL SPORTS **Rochester Americans Hockey Club** (585-454-5335; www.amerks.com), Blue Cross Arena at the Rochester War Memorial, 100 Exchange Street, Rochester. One of the oldest minor-league teams in the nation, they are a franchise of the Buffalo Sabres.

Rochester Brigade Arena Football (585-292-1530; www.rochesterbrigade .com), Blue Cross Arena at the War Memorial, 100 Exchange Street, Rochester.

Rochester Knighthawks Lacrosse (585-454-5335; www.knighthawks .com), Blue Cross Arena at the War Memorial, 100 Exchange Street, Rochester. This National Lacrosse League central Division team plays box lacrosse December through April.

Rochester Raging Rhinos Soccer (585-454-5425; www.rhinossoccer .com), Frontier Field, 1 Morrie Silver Way, Rochester. They are currently building a downtown stadium of their own at 333 North Plymouth.

Rochester Rattlers Lacrosse (585-454-5425; www.rochesterrattlers.com), Frontier Field, 1 Morrie Silver Way, Rochester. Major league lacrosse in July and August.

Rochester Red Wings Baseball (585-454-1001; www.redwingsbaseball .com). Professional baseball has been played in Rochester since 1877. The team, a Triple-A farm team of the Minnesota Twins, has been known as the Red Wings since 1929. Rochester was recently named the best city in the minor leagues by Baseball America. Games are played at **Frontier Field** (585-423-9464) 1 Morrie Silver Way, Rochester.

✳ Selective Shopping

ANTIQUES **Antiek Journeys** (585-271-8890; www.antiekjourneys.com), 340 Culver Road, Rochester. Open Tuesday–Thursday 10:30–6, Friday and Saturday 10:30–5, Sunday 11–4. Browse through 14,000 square feet of fine imported European antiques, including furniture, lighting, accessories, and art at Rochester's largest one-dealer independently owned shop.

Antiques & Old Lace (585-461-1884; www.antiquesandoldlace.com), 1290 University Avenue (near Culver Road), Rochester. Open Monday–Saturday 11–6. A 4,000-square-foot shop with 15 dealers offering a wide assortment of antiques and collectibles.

Gutenberg Books (585-442-4620), 675 Monroe Avenue, Rochester. Open Monday–Saturday 11–6 (Thursday until 8). This shop specializes in rare and used books, photographs, and ephemera.

Lakeside Floral & Antique Gallery (585-663-2990), 4419 Lake Avenue, Rochester. Open daily 9–6. This shop combines a complete floral shop, specializing in fresh flowers as well as silks, with an antique gallery featuring fine antiques, including art, pottery, jewelry, china, glass, and vintage textiles.

Rochester Antique Market & Galleries (585-262-4643), 155 Monroe Avenue, Rochester. Open Monday–Saturday 10–6, Sunday 12–6. Find a large selection of quality items at this 8,000-square-foot consignment market.

Shady Lady & Lamp Doctor (585-458-1731), 1171 Lyell Avenue (NY 31), Rochester. Open Monday–Saturday 10–5:30. Specializing in Victorian lamps and lampshades as well as lamp parts and accessories.

Talulah Petunia's (585-244-7720), 39 South Goodman Street, Rochester. Tuesday–Saturday 11–6. European antiques, gift items, and home decor.

Yankee Peddler Bookshops (585-271-5080), Village Gate Square, 274 North Goodman Street, Rochester. Open Monday–Saturday 11–6, Sunday 12–5. Thousands of used and rare books can be found in this unique shop, the largest and oldest antique bookshop in the Rochester area.

ART GALLERIES Artisan Works (585-288-7170; www.artisanworks .net), 565 Blossom Road, Suite L, Rochester. Open Monday–Saturday 11–6, Sunday 12–5. This large gallery has one of the most diverse art collections in the region. Numerous resident artists work on their latest creations in their on-site studios.

Craft Company No. 6 (585-473-3413; www.craftcompany.com), 785 University Avenue, Rochester. Open Monday–Saturday 10–6 (Thursday until 9), Sunday 11–5. Located in a renovated Victorian firehouse, this gallery is considered one of the top American craft galleries in the U.S. It has eight rooms and an outdoor courtyard with a variety of handcrafted items displayed, including furniture, jewelry, pottery, blown glass, home decor, and garden art.

&. **The Creator's Hands** (585-235-8550; www.thecreatorshands.com), 336 Arnett Boulevard, Rochester.

CRAFT COMPANY NO. 6 IS CONSIDERED ONE OF THE TOP AMERICAN CRAFT GALLERIES.

Christine A. Smyczynski

Open Monday–Saturday 10–6 (Thursday until 8), Sunday 12–6. Since 1979 this shop has been filled with items that touch the mind and heart, including calligraphy, spiritual gifts, decorative religious items, gift books, and Rochester-related gift items. About 90 percent of the merchandise is handcrafted by artisans from the United States and Canada.

Genesee Center for Arts, Education and New Ideas, Inc. (585-244-1730; www.geneseearts.org), 713 Monroe Avenue, Rochester. Galleries open Monday–Friday 11–6, Saturday and Sunday 12–5. Facilities include a community darkroom and exhibit galleries that focus mainly on photography and pottery.

Oxford Gallery (585-271-5885; www.oxfordgallery.com), 267 Oxford Street (at Park Avenue) Rochester. Open Tuesday–Friday 12–5, Saturday 10–5. The Oxford Gallery is one of the oldest and most prestigious galleries in Rochester. It has the works of over 100 regional and national artists, including paintings, prints, and sculptures.

FARM MARKETS ♿ **The Rochester Public Market** (585-428-6907), 280 North Union Street (two blocks north of East Main Street), Rochester. Open year-round Tuesday and Thursday 6–1, Saturday 5–3. Choose from fresh produce, meat, ethnic delicacies, craft items, and more. The market was recently included on a list of the top farmers' markets in the world.

SPECIAL SHOPS

Monroe Avenue

Monroe Avenue from Averill Avenue to Dartmouth Street features Greenwich Village–style shops and restaurants. Some of the shops include:

Juliana's (585-271-1830), 2209 Monroe Avenue, Rochester. Open Monday–Friday 10–5:30, Saturday 10–5. Specializing in couture and bridal fashions.

Oxford Square Shopping District, Monroe Ave, between I-490 and Goodman (contact Oxford Square Society for the Preservation of Diversity, 675 Monroe Avenue, Rochester 14607). This area offers a shopping experience that includes unique stores, ethnic restaurants, antiques, coffeehouses, and more. This friendly shopping area is considered the mall alternative.

Park Avenue

Park Avenue, from Alexander Street to Culver Road, is known for its boutiques and specialty shops. Below are just a few.

Jembetat Gallery (585-442-8960 or 800-688-6254; www.jembetat.com) 645 Park Avenue, Rochester. Open Monday–Friday 11–6, Saturday 10–5, Sunday 10–1 or by appointment. The name is a West African word for replanting; this store offers museum-quality African art, original jewelry, tribal masks, wooden bowls, drums, and beads.

Parkleigh (585-244-4842; www.parkleigh.com), 215 Park Avenue Rochester. Open Monday–Friday 10–9, Saturday 10–6, Sunday 10–5. This unique gift shop, which started out as a pharmacy in 1960, features perfumes, cosmetics, clothing, gifts, and more.

Stever's Candies (585-473-2098; www.steverscandy.com), 623 Park Avenue, Rochester. Open Monday–Saturday 10–6; closed Sundays and the month of July. Stever's has been making the best homemade candy in

Rochester since 1946, when Douglas Stever and his wife, Hilda, started their first small shop. Unlike large manufacturers, Stever's candies are made fresh daily in small batches, using Doug Stever's original recipes. Choose from chocolates, nuts, mints, novelty items, sugar-free candy, and more.

Village Gate Square (585-442-9061), 274 North Goodman Street, Rochester. Hours vary according to individual establishment. This building, once a printing factory, has been turned into a complex of shops, art galleries, and restaurants.

✳ Special Events

May: **Lilac Festival** Highland Park (585-256-4960; www.lilacfestival.com). More than 500 varieties of lilacs are in bloom on over 22 acres of Highland Park. Activities include entertainment, craft shows, and international foods.

June: **Rochester International Jazz Festival** (585-234-2002; www.rochesterjazz.com). Various venues throughout downtown Rochester, including the Eastman Theatre, Max of Eastman Place, and Milestones Music Room. National and International musicians converge on Rochester for this eight-day event. **Maplewood Rose Festival** (585-428-6690; www.cityofrochester.gov), Maplewood Park. This festival focuses on the more than 5,000 roses in historic Maplewood Park.

July: **Rochester Musicfest** (585-222-5000; www.rochestermusicfest.com). A two-day musical celebration in Genesee Valley Park. This is one of the more popular regional rhythm-and-blues musical festivals in the country. **Corn Hill Arts Festival** (585-262-3142; www.cornhill.org), A juried art show with over 450 artists and crafters in the historic Corn Hill district, one of Rochester's oldest residential neighborhoods. **Monroe County Fair** (585-334-4000; www.mcfair.com), Dome Center. A traditional country fair with rides, agricultural exhibits, and entertainment.

August: **Park Avenue Summer Art Fest** (585-244-0951; www.rochesterevents.com). This festival, which takes place in the trendy Park Avenue neighborhood, features, musical entertainment, arts and crafts, shopping, and dining. **PGA Championship** (800-742-8258; www.pga.com), Oak Hill Country Club.

September: **Clothesline Arts Festival** (585-473-7720; mag.rochester.edu), Memorial Art Gallery. One of the oldest and largest juried art shows in the United States.

October: **Rochester River Romance** (585-428-6690; www.cityofrochester.gov). A party along Rochester's many waterways, including hiking, boating, and a regatta.

November: **High Falls Film Festival** (585-258-0481; www.highfallsfilmfestival.com). Films shown at the Little Theater (240 East Ave.) and the Dryden and Curtis Theatre at the George Eastman House (900 East Ave.). This film festival features works by women in film and video, including features and documentaries.

WESTERN AND NORTHWESTERN MONROE—
Greece, Gates, Spencerport, and Brockport

Determined to find a water passage to the East through North America, the French explorer La Salle passed through the area now known as Greece in 1669. The first permanent settlers arrived in 1792 and the town was established in 1822. Originally called Northampton, the name Greece was chosen because of sympathy toward the Greeks, who were then fighting for independence from Turkish rule. The town remained largely agricultural until the 20th century, when Kodak became the region's major employer. Greece is the largest suburb of Rochester, covering 26,742 acres. It is home to the University of Rochester, the oldest major learning center in the area. The area is also a popular nature and recreational area, with 8 miles of shoreline on Lake Ontario and with Braddock Bay State Fish and Wildlife Management Area, one of the area's prime wildlife habitats.

The town of Gates was named after General Horatio Gates, a Revolutionary War hero who defeated the British at the Battle of Saratoga. When incorporated in 1813, it included what is now the city of Rochester and the town of Greece, but annexations over the years gradually reduced Gates to its present size of 15 square miles, the smallest town in Monroe County. The town, which is 90 percent developed, is home to the Monroe County Airport.

Early pioneers arrived in Spencerport in 1802, most settling south of the present-day town. Austin Spencer, for whom the town is named, came to the area in 1808. When the Erie Canal was built, the Spencer family's 180-acre farm was bisected by the canal, so it was divided into lots and sold to settlers. The village, located in the town of Ogden, was originally named Spencer's Basin and later changed to Spencerport. By the 1880s it was a thriving community, yet it still maintained its rural nature. While today it is a more residential area, many small shops are still located near the canal.

Settlers first came to the Brockport area in 1802, when a road was cut through the wilderness from LeRoy. Named after one of the village founders, Hiel Brockway, who arrived in the area in 1817, the village saw rapid growth in the early 1820s, when the Erie Canal was being constructed and many industries developed, including manufacturers of farm implements, shoes, pianos, and small appliances. The mechanical reaper for harvesting wheat, invented in 1831 by West Virginia native Cyrus McCormick, was first manufactured by the Globe Iron Works in Brockport. The reaper was first used to harvest wheat on the Brockport farm of Frederick Root. Today Brockport's historic commercial district, with several boutiques and restaurants, is popular with recreational boaters and tourists. Many of the Victorian structures along Brockport's Main Street, a designated historic district, were built during the canal's construction period.

AREA CODE The area code is 585.

GUIDANCE Village of Brockport (585-637-5300; www.brockportny.org), 49 State Street, Brockport. Open Monday–Friday 8:30–4:30.

Town of Clarkson (585-637-1130; www.clarksonny.org) 3710 Lake Road, Clarkson. Open Monday–Friday 8–4.

Town of Gates (585-247-6100), 1605 Buffalo Road, Gates. Open Monday–Friday 9–5.

Town of Greece (585-225-2000; www.townofgreece.org, www.greeceny.gov), 1 Vince Tofany Boulevard, Greece. Open Monday–Friday 9–5.

Greece Chamber of Commerce (585-227-7272; www.greecechamber.org), 2496 West Ridge Road, Suite 201, Greece. Open Monday–Thursday 9–5, Friday 9–4.

Town of Hamlin (585-964-8981; www.hamlinny.org), 1658 Lake Road, Hamlin. Open Monday–Friday 8–4.

Town of Hilton (585-392-4144), 59 Henry Street, Hilton. Open Monday–Friday 9–5.

Town of Ogden (585-352-2100; www.ogdenny.com), 269 Ogden Center Road, Ogden. Open Monday–Friday 9–5.

Town of Parma (585-392-9462; www.parmany.org), 1300 Hilton-Parma Corners Road, Parma. Open Monday–Friday 8–4.

Spencerport Chamber of Commerce (585-349-1488; www.spencerport chamber.org), PO Box 7, Spencerport, NY. Obtain information by phone or through their Web site.

Village of Spencerport (585-352-4771; www.vil.spencerport.ny.us), 27 West Avenue, Spencerport. Open Monday–Friday 9–4:30.

Town of Sweden (585-637-2144; www.townofsweden.org), 18 State Street, Brockport. Open Monday–Friday 9–5.

GETTING THERE *By bus:* **RTS bus service** (585-288-1700 or 888-288-3777; www .rgrta.com), from downtown Rochester includes #14 (Greece), #20 (Brockport/ Spencerport), #76 (Gates/Ogden/Chili), and #96 (Hilton/Hamlin/Clarkson).

By car: Spencerport and points west are accessible from I-531 as well as via NY 104. Greece is accessible by I-390, NY 104, and the Lake Ontario State Parkway, which parallels Lake Ontario.

By Air: **Ledgedale Airpark Airport** (585-637-5050), a small landing strip located 3 miles southeast of Brockport. See also *Getting There—Rochester.*

MEDICAL EMERGENCY Dial 911.

Lakeside Memorial Hospital (585-637-3131), 156 West Avenue, Brockport.

✳ To See

MUSEUMS AND HISTORIC HOMES Capen Hose Co. and Firefighting Museum (585-637-4713, 585-637-2512 or 585-637-6445), 237 Main Street, Brockport. Open by appointment only. This 1904 fire station houses hundreds of firefighting artifacts as well as several pieces of vintage firefighting equipment, including an 1847 Selye & Porter hand pumper, a 1880 S. M. Stewart hose carriage, a 1876 Silsby steamer, and a 1930 Seagrave pumper.

The Greece Historical Society (585-225-7221), 595 Long Pond Road, Rochester. Open Sunday 2–4:30.

Morgan-Manning House (585-637-3645), 151 Main Street, Brockport. Open by appointment only. This 1854 dwelling houses the Western Monroe Historical Society. It was the home of Dayton Morgan, who, with William Seymor, developed a reaper industry on the Erie Canal. Morgan's eldest daughter lived here until her death in 1964. A candlelight Christmas celebration takes place the first weekend of December. This open house features handcrafted items made by local artisans.

HISTORIC SITES **"A Walking Tour of Brockport" brochure,** available at the village offices (49 State Street) describes the Historic Landmark homes located throughout the village, many built in Victorian style in the late 1800s and early 1900s. The 45 Victorian-era commercial buildings lining Main Street from the Erie Canal to State Street comprise a designated Historic District.

Spencerport, Pathways to the Past (585-352-2141 for info on guided tours). A self-guided tour pamphlet can be found near the gazebo along the canal. Exhibits along this tour consist of photographs depicting life in old Spencerport. The pamphlet describes the photos in further detail.

✳ To Do

FAMILY FUN ✇ **Springdale Farms** (585-352-5320 or 352-5315; www.springdale farm.org), 696 Colby Street, Spencerport. Open year-round Monday–Saturday 10–4, Sunday 12–4. Free admission. Springdale Farms was a typical family farm in the early 1800s. This 200-acre working demonstration farm, within Northampton Park, is part of the Monroe County Parks system. Springdale features historic farm buildings, a variety of farm animals, crops, a pond, and hiking trails, as well as a robotic milking parlor and visitors center. The park also has a picnic pavilion and a playground.

GOLF **Braemar Golf Course** (585-352-5360), 4704 Ridge Road, Spencerport. An 18-hole, par 72 private course open to the public.

Salmon Creek Country Club (585-352-4300), 335 Washington Street, Spencerport An 18-hole, par-72 private club open to the public.

✳ Green Space

PARKS **Braddock Bay State Fish and Wildlife Management Area,** 432 Manitour Beach Road (along Lake Ontario), Hilton. Open dawn to dusk. Free admission. This is a popular spot to view over 100,000 hawks, owls, and other birds of prey that migrate to this area in the spring. The refuge has the only hawk-banding station in the United States that is open for regular visitation.

Clyder Carter Memorial Gazebo, Along the Erie Canal in downtown Spencerport. A great place to overlook the canal and the site of concerts every Sunday evening during the summer.

Greece Canal Park (585-256-4950), 241 Elmgrove Road, Greece. This 577-acre county park is bordered on the south by the Erie Canal. Facilities include picnic areas, softball and soccer fields, and playgrounds, as well as hiking and cross-country trails.

Hamlin Beach State Park (585-964-2462 www.nysparks.state.ny.us), 1 Camp Road, Hamlin. Open 6–11 year-round for day use; camping April–November. Parking fee April–Memorial Day and Labor Day–November $6, Memorial Day–Labor Day $7, free rest of year. This New York State park is located on the south shore of Lake Ontario, about 25 miles west of Rochester. It has 264 trailer and tent campsites, picnic facilities, ten miles of hiking and nature trails, fishing, and a sandy beach. Campsites are $19/night. A prominent feature of the park is a bluff called Devil's Nose, which serves as a landmark for sailors as they pass to the north.

Northampton Park (585-256-4950), 696 Colby Street, Spencerport. Open dawn to dusk. This 973-acre Monroe Country park features a downhill ski slope with tow rope, a model-airplane field, the Ogden Historical Society's Pulver House, hiking trails, and Springdale Farm, a working, active farm. See *Family Fun*.

WALKING AND HIKING TRAILS Erie Canal Heritage Trail. Portions of this 850-mile trail, which follows the old Erie Canal towpath, are located in Monroe County. The trail currently winds from Lockport to Palmyra. Eventually it will go from Albany to Buffalo, like the original Erie Canal.

✳ Lodging

INNS AND RESORTS Adams Basin Inn (585-352-6784 or 888-352-3999; www.adamsbasininn.com), 425 Washington Street (NY 36), Adams Basin. (Note: The lift bridge over the Erie Canal on NY 36 just south of the inn's driveway is usually closed to traffic in the summer months. It is currently closed for repairs until 2007; access NY 36 via NY 104.) Open year-round, except for three weeks in January. The Adams Basin Inn is the only intact original tavern on the Erie Canal. The post-and-beam section of the inn, which was built by Marcus Adams, dates back to 1810. Adams Basin was the stopping point on the canal to exchange mules; it was also a popular port for the shipment of apples. The Ryan family acquired the property in 1890, added the Greek Revival portion of the structure, and operated it

as a tavern until 1916. When Mrs. Ryan died in 1922, her husband and son left everything in the house untouched. The dining room table was still set from the day she died when her son passed away 50 years later. The property was then purchased and converted into a bed and breakfast inn. Today owner and innkeeper Halya Sobkiw offers four antiques-furnished rooms with private baths. A full gourmet breakfast included Halya's signature dish, baked eggs with mushroom sauce, which is featured in *The Best of American Country Inns Bed & Breakfast Cookbook*. $95–$115.

MOTELS AND HOTELS Numerous chain motels are represented in Gates and Greece, especially near the airport and along Ridge Road. There are also some hotels in Brockport. Below are just a few:

☗ **Holiday Inn Express** (585-395-1000), 4908 Lake Road, Brockport. This hotel with 41 standard rooms has a free continental breakfast. $89–$139.

Comfort Inn Central (585-436-4400), 395 Buell Road, Gates. This 73-room hotel is located across the street from the Rochester–Monroe County Airport. $64–$94.

Marriott Airport Hotel (585-225-6880), 1890 Ridge Road West, Greece. This seven-story, 210-room hotel has a heated indoor pool, exercise room, and video library. $94–$129.

BED & BREAKFASTS **The Victorian Bed & Breakfast** (585-637-7519; www.victorianbandb.com), 320 Main Street, Brockport. Open year-round. Five guest rooms are available in Sharon Kehoe's National Historic Register, 1890 clapboard Queen Anne Victorian home, located just three blocks from the Erie Canal and Brockport's downtown shopping district. Each room, which is nicely decorated in Victorian style, has a private bath, phones and cable TVs. A full breakfast is offered each morning. $75-95.

OTHER LODGING

Campsites
See Hamlin Beach State Park in *Green Space.*

❋ **Where to Eat**

DINING OUT ♿ **Apple Tree Inn** (585-637-6440), 7407 West Ridge Road, Brockport. Open for lunch Tuesday–Sunday, dinner Thursday–Saturday. Housed in a historic brick 1839 farmhouse, this restaurant serves a variety of dishes, including soups, salads, and sandwiches for lunch. They are famous for their chicken potpie. Dinner selections include seafood, pasta, steak, chops, and poultry. A kids' menu is available.

♿ **Lamplighter Restaurant** (585-225-2500; www.lamplighterrestaurant.com), 831 Fetzner Road, Greece. Open for lunch Tuesday–Friday 11:30–2; dinner Monday–Saturday 4:30–10; closed Sundays except for holidays. Menu selections include seafood, beef, chops, and Italian dishes. One of their specialties is Portofino, a combination of lobster, shrimp, scallops, and crab sautéed in white wine and served with black olives and artichoke hearts over a bed of pasta.

Stuey's (585-352-9100), 94 Union Street, Spencerport. Open Monday–Saturday 11:30–8, Sunday 12–8. Enjoy full, sit-down dinners and lunches in a publike atmosphere with a view of the Erie Canal.

EATING OUT ♪ **Abbotts and Costello's** (585-352-9750), 138 South Union, Spencerport. Open Memorial Day–Labor Day 10–10, rest of year 11–7. A small corner ice cream parlor with black-and-white checkered floors and an outdoor deck overlooking South Union Street. They serve Abbott's frozen custard as well as hot dogs and hamburgers. It is part of a regional chain.

♪ ♿ **Choo Choo's Express** (585-352-4422; www.choochoosfun.com), 5138 West Ridge Road (NY 104), Spencerport. May–October, open Monday–Saturday 12–8, Sunday 1–7; November–April, open Thursday–Saturday 12–8, Sunday 1–7. A unique eatery featuring grilled food, kids' meals, and ice cream as well as their specialty, Cincinnati-style chili served over spaghetti. Be sure to ride their quarter-mile train with 29 realistic, life-size dinosaurs along the tracks. Special events take place during the year, including a haunted train ride at Halloween and the Winter Wonderland Express during the holiday season.

Gallery Restaurant Lounge and Party House (585-637-0200), Market Street, Brockport. Open Monday–Thursday 11:30–8:30, Friday–Saturday 11:30–9, Sunday 11:30–8. A casual seafood and steak eatery located along the canal.

Java Johns (585-352-9333), 123 South Union Street, Spencerport. Open Monday 7–3, Tuesday–Thursday 7–10, Friday–Saturday 7–midnight. A large coffeehouse with bright-yellow walls serving up soups, sandwiches, and pastries along with coffee. Live musical entertainment Friday and Saturday evenings.

Java Junction, 56 Main Street, Brockport. Open Monday–Thursday 7–10, Friday 7–11, Saturday 8–11, Sunday 8–6. A coffee roastery and bakery.

Lady Victoria's Tea Parlor (585-349-0002), 138 South Union Street, Spencerport. Tuesday–Saturday 8:30–4. A tearoom and parlor open for breakfast, lunch, dinner, and teas.

Mythos Café (585-637-2770), 77 Main Street, Brockport. Open Monday–Saturday 11–9. Greek and Mediterranean food served in a casual atmosphere.

Red Bird Tea Shoppe (585-637-3340), 88 Main Street, Brockport. Open Tuesday–Saturday 10–5, Sunday by chance. Tea and light refreshments, such as scones and biscuits, are served in this elegant tearoom located within the Tea for Two Antique Shop. See *Selective Shopping—Antiques.*

🍴 ♿ ❀ **Schallers** (585-865-3319), 965 Edgemere Road, Greece. Open year-round Sunday–Thursday 10:30–10, Friday–Saturday 10:30–11. This popular hot dog and hamburger joint, which has been at this spot since 1962, has the best hot sauce in the Rochester area. Other locations are at 2747 West Henrietta Road in Brighton and 559 East Ridge Road in Irondequoit.

✳ **Entertainment**

THEATERS **Strand Theater** (585-637-3310) 93 Main Street, Brockport. A historic 1916 landmark theater that now shows first-run movies on three screens.

✳ **Selective Shopping**

ANTIQUES ♿ **The Carriage Place Crafts & Antiques Co-op** (585-637-6224; www.thecarriageplace.8m.com), 6000 Sweden-Walker Road, Brockport. Open Thursday–Sunday 10–4. This shop, located amid the farmlands surrounding Brockport, features a large variety of antiques, furniture, primitives, florals, gifts, books, collectibles, and handcrafted items.

Craft Antique Co-op (585-368-0670; www.craftantiqueco-op.com), 3200 Ridge Road, Greece. Open Thursday–Sunday 10–5. This is more than a store; it's a destination. Over two hundred shops are located in the largest crafts and antiques co-op in New York—two floors of quality antiques, collectibles, primitives, and handcrafted items. Grammy G's Café, in the rear of the co-op, serves soups, salads, sandwiches, and desserts.

Special sales and events take place throughout the year. For a holiday treat, stop by during their annual Dickens Christmas Festival in November and December, where Dickens's England is recreated with decorations, costumes, and entertainment. You can even chat with Bob Cratchet and Tiny Tim.

Jill's Antiques & Collectibles and Yesterday's Antiques (585-637-5560; www.jillsantiques.com), 65 Main Street, Brockport. Open Tuesday–Friday 10:30–6, Saturday 10:30–5, Sunday 12–4. A general line of antiques can be found at these two stores, housed in a historic Main Street building.

& **Liberty Hollow** (585-349-4500), 4975 Ridge Road, Spencerport. Open seven days 10–5. Jam-packed with all sorts of primitive decor items, furniture, and country crafts, this shop just goes on and on. Browse through over 15,000 square feet of antiques, collectibles, and gifts, including Boyd's Bears, Willow Tree Angels, quilts, linens, and furniture.

& **Ridge Antiques** (585-352-4721), 5236 Ridge Road, Spencerport. Open 10–5; closed Monday and Wednesday. For over 31 years the Agostinelli family has offered quality antiques. This shop consists of three buildings of furniture, accessories, and small antiques.

Stony Point Antiques (585-392-5551), 1225 Hilton–Parma Center Road (at NY 18 and 259), Parma Center (north of Spencerport). Open Thursday–Saturday 10–5, Sunday 12–5. Dealing in antiques, collectibles, furniture, horse-drawn vehicles, china, toys, paintings, and jewelry since 1970.

Tea for Two Antiques and The Red Bird Tea Shoppe (585-637-3340), 88 Main Street, Brockport. Open Tuesday–Saturday 10–5, Sunday by chance. Two shops in one. Browse through antique glass, brass, china, crystal, and lace; then enjoy a spot of tea along with light refreshments like scones, biscuits, and fruit spreads.

SHOPPING MALLS **The Mall at Greece Ridge Center** (585-225-0430 www.greeceridgecenter.com), NY 104 (Ridge Road West) just west of I-390, Greece. Open Monday–Saturday 10–9, Sunday 12–5. This sprawling complex, with over 150 stores—including the Bon Ton, Kaufmann's, JC Penney, and Sears—is one of the largest shopping centers in upstate New York. There are also many chain retailers located along NY 104 in this area.

SPECIAL SHOPS **Afrikamba Curios, Inc.** (585-349-2999), 85 South Union (Spencer's Landing), Spencerport. Open Wednesday and Friday 11:30–4:30, Thursday 11:30–6, Saturday 10–2. This unique store specializes in handcrafted items imported from Africa, including wildlife collectibles, jewelry, home decor, and musical instruments.

American Accents (585-352-1920), 5319 Ridge Road West, Spencerport. Open Monday, Tuesday, Thursday–Saturday 10–5, Sunday 12–4. This shop features three floors of merchandise in a vintage red barn. Choose from furniture, country decor items, and accessories.

& **The Apple Tree** (585-637-9110), 7397 Ridge Road, Brockport. Open Tuesday–Friday 11–5, Saturday 10–5,

Sunday 12–4. This large store features 14,000 square feet of furniture as well as gifts, decorative accessories, garden accents, and candles. Fine dining is available in the adjacent **Apple Tree Inn Restaurant** (see *Where to Eat—Dining Out*).

Bittersweet (585-637-4774; www .brockport.net/bittersweet), 41 Main Street, Brockport. Open Monday–Thursday 10–6, Friday 10–8, Saturday and Sunday 10–5. This unique store with the big wooden door is located in a former bank building and still has the original counters, wooden floors, and stenciling around the high ceilings. They carry distinctive jewelry and clothing as well as country decor items, birdhouses, candy, and more.

The Bunny Patch (585-352-0606), 93 South Union Street, Spencerport. Open Tuesday–Friday 10–6, Saturday 10–5. This shop features country crafts and gifts, including Beanie babies, toys, decorative items, and more.

Country Treasures (585-637-5148), 27 Market Street, Brockport. Open Monday–Friday 10–6:30, Saturday 10–5, Sunday 12–4. Everything to decorate a country home, including a large selection of folk art and primitive home accessories, curtains, period and reproduction stencils, candles, linens, pottery, and rugs.

The Hollyday Shop (585-352-1020), 1835 North Union Street, Spencerport. Open Monday, Wednesday, Friday, and Saturday 10–5, Tuesday and Thursday 10–7, Sunday 12–4. Rochester's finest Christmas specialty store carries a complete collection of Dept. 56 Collectibles, Santas, snowmen, ornaments, nativity sets, and much more.

Lift Bridge Book Shop (585-637-9200; www.liftbridgebooks.com), 45 Main Street, Brockport. Open Monday–Friday 9:30–8, Saturday 9:30–5:30, Sunday 12–5. This large store features two floors of quality books and educational toys, including many books on New York State and the Erie Canal.

Mes-Sage Christian Books and Gifts (585-637-7180), 83 Main Street, Brockport. Open Monday–Thursday 10–6, Friday 10–8, Saturday 10–5. A variety of Christian books, cards, and gifts can be found here.

The Posh Princess (585-637-6330), 9 Market Street, Brockport. Open Tuesday–Saturday 11–6, Sunday 12–4. This shop has jewelry, purses, scarves, and trendy accessories for princesses of all ages.

Seaward Candies (585-637-4120) 7 Main Street, Brockport. Open Monday–Saturday 11–7, Sunday 12–5. This store is known as the sweetest shop in Brockport. In 1976 Donna Seaward starting making candies in her home kitchen. The candies are still made by hand today in an addition built onto the Seaward home. The shop also carries Clarendon Cheesecake, fudge, maple syrup, and ice cream.

Sweet Herbs n' Sundry (585-637-7690; www.shnsundry.bitstation.com), 5384 Brockport-Spencerport Road (NY 31), Brockport. Open Wednesday–Thursday 10–5, Friday and Saturday 10–6, Sunday 12–5. This cozy little shop features antiques, quilts, linens, folk art, dried flowers, birdhouses, and assorted sundries.

Union Street Primitives (585-352-1589), 104 South Union Street, Spencerport. Open Wednesday–

Saturday 10–5, Sunday 12–4. Shop in one of Spencerport's original buildings and choose from country furniture, folk art, primitives, dolls, bears, dried floral wreaths, and one-of-a-kind treasures. Most of the items are handmade locally.

Unique Gift Boutique (585-637-9150), 71 Main Street, Brockport. Open Monday–Friday 10:30–6, Saturday 10:30–5. A large selection of gift items, including Boyd's Bears, Precious Moments, Ty, Disney, Mary Engelbreit, and greeting cards.

The Unique Shop (585-352-1350), 130 South Union Street, Spencerport. Open Monday–Friday 10–6, Saturday 10–5 (open Sunday 12–5, November and December only). All sorts of unique items can be found in this shop, including Dept. 56 Villages, Snowbabies and ornaments, Harbour Lights, Precious Moments, cards, collectible dolls, and Spencerport posters.

✳ Special Events

June: **Spencerport Fireman's Carnival** (585-349-1488; www.spencer portchamber.org), Spencerport. This popular annual event features a kiddie parade as well as a fireman's parade, carnival rides, games, and food. **Concerts on the Canal** (585-352-4771), At the Clyde Carter Memorial Gazebo by the Erie Canal, Spencerport. Sundays at 6:30 PM June–August. Free musical entertainment by the canal.

July: **Canal Days** (585-349-1488; www.spencerportchamber.org), Spencerport. A two-day festival that began in 1981 that takes place the last weekend in July and attracts thousands of visitors, features arts, crafts, music, classic car show, street dance, fireworks, and water events.

October: **Hilton Apple Fest** (585-234-3378; www.hiltonapplefest.org), West Avenue (NY 18). between Heinz and Henry Streets, Hilton. This event, which takes place the first weekend of October, has been celebrating the apple harvest season and providing free family entertainment since 1981. Over 200 craft vendors, plus a car show, kids activities, food vendors, and musical entertainment.

December: **Christmas by the Canal** (585-349-1488; www.spencerport chamber.org), Spencerport. This annual event, which takes place the first Sunday of December, features children's activities, entertainment, horse-drawn sleigh rides, and caroling.

NORTHEASTERN MONROE COUNTY— Irondequoit and Webster

Irondequoit—the name comes from the Iroquois word meaning "where the land meets the water"—is surrounded by three waterways: the Genesee River, Lake Ontario, and Irondequoit Bay. The town of 53,000 has a diverse population, covering all ages and ethnic backgrounds. Given the town's location, it's a popular place for boating, fishing, and other water activities. It is also home to Seabreeze, one of the oldest family-owned amusement parks in the country.

The history of Irondequoit can be divided into four phases. During the first phase the land was controlled by the Seneca. While they didn't have any permanent villages established, it was a popular fishing and hunting ground, but the Seneca considered it to be an unhealthy place due to the marshy conditions that attracted fever-carrying mosquitoes. The second phase began after the American Revolution, when two war veterans purchased a large tract of land. Settlement was slow due to the swampy conditions and the presence of bears, wolves, and rattlesnakes, but once the swamps were drained, the land was found to be good for farming; some of the major crops included peaches, melons, and grapes.

The town's third phase began in the 1870s with the development of rail and trolley lines. Resorts along the Lake Ontario shore attracted thousands of summertime visitors. The best known resort was Sea Breeze, which was owned by the railroads. An amusement park by the same name still exists in the area today. With the advent of the automobile, the fourth phase began. Many of the farmers sold the land to returning World War II vets for housing, and the area turned into a bustling suburban community.

The town of Webster, named for American statesman Daniel Webster, started out as an agricultural community. In the late 1800s over 400 farms dotted the area, producing apples, pears, and peaches—apple drying was one of the main industries up until World War II. The town was once home to the world's largest basket-making factory. Today the Webster area is best known as the home of Xerox Corporation's research and manufacturing facilities.

AREA CODE The area code is 585.

GUIDANCE Webster Chamber of Commerce (585-265-3960; www.webster chamber.com), 26 East Main Street, Webster. Open Monday–Friday 9–4.

Town of Webster (585-872-1000; www.ci.webster.ny.us), 1000 Ridge Road, Webster. Open Monday–Friday 9–5.

Village of Webster (585-265-3770; www.villageofwebster.com), 28 West Main Street, Webster. Open Monday–Friday 8–4:30.

Town of Irondequoit (585-467-8840; www.irondequoit.org), 1280 Titus Avenue, Irondequoit. Open Monday–Friday 8:30–4:30.

GETTING THERE *By bus:* **RTS bus service** (585-288-1700 or 888-288-3777; www.rgrta.com), from downtown Rochester includes #30, #35, #40, and #45 (Webster).

By car: For Irondequoit, take the NYS Thruway (I-90) exit 45 (I-490) to I-590 north. For Webster take Thruway exit 45 (I-490) to exit 29 (NY 96) to NY 250 north. Webster and Irondequoit can also be reached via NY 104.

MEDICAL EMERGENCY Dial 911.

✳ To See

MUSEUMS AND HISTORIC HOMES Irondequoit's Pioneer Home (585-336-7269; www.ggw.org/IHSociety), 1280 Titus Avenue (town hall campus, behind the gazebo), Irondequoit. Open Sunday 2–4 April–September. Free admission.

The Pioneer house is also open during the July 4th celebration and the first Sunday in December for the town's tree lighting. This saltbox-style home, built in 1830, is furnished with many original pieces, including some of the original glass windows. The first owner of the home was believed to be a farmer, his wife, and their seven children. Some of the home's features include a shelf chimney, which starts three-quarters of the way up the wall, and a wall of bricks between the inside and outside wall—referred to as "noggin"—to keep the house insulated. One room of the museum, which was established in 1995, has a display of a mid-1800s kitchen, with walls finished with lath, plaster, and horsehair. Another room has changing exhibits about Irondequoit.

Webster Museum and Historical Society (585-265-3308), 18 Lapham Park, Webster. Open Sunday, Tuesday, Thursday 2–4:30 Exhibits depict the history of Webster.

✶ To Do

FAMILY FUN **The Golf Tee** (585-872-1390; www.thegolftee.net), 1039 Ridge Road, Webster. Open April–October 11–dusk. An 18-hole miniature golf course; also batting cages, a driving range, and video games. An ice cream shop and bakery are next door.

ON THE SHORES OF LAKE ONTARIO, SEABREEZE AMUSEMENT PARK IS GREAT FOR SUMMERTIME FAMILY FUN.
Christine A. Smyczynski

Seabreeze Amusement Park (585-323-1900; www.seabreeze.com), 4600 Culver Road, Rochester. See *Family Fun—City of Rochester*.

FISHING **Irondequoit Bay** is a popular fishing spot. Access points include **Irondequoit Bay State Marine Park** and **Irondequoit Bay Park West**. See *Green Space—Parks*.

GOLF **Durand-Eastman Park** (585-342-9810). See *Green Space—Parks*.

Webster West Golf Course (585-265-1307), 440 Salt Road, Webster. A private 18-hole, par-70 course open to the public.

✶ Green Space

NATURE PRESERVES **Helmer Nature Center** (585-336-3035), 154 Pinegrove Avenue, Irondequoit. Open daily dawn to dusk. This 45-acre nature preserve, founded in 1973, offers a wide range of educational programs along with nature trails.

PARKS **Durand-Eastman Park** (585-342-9810), On Lake Ontario 7 miles north of Rochester off I-590. Open daily 10–11. The original 484 acres of this park were donated to the county by George Eastman and Dr. Henry Durand. The park, which now encompasses about 1,000 acres, includes an 18-hole golf course, hiking trails, and small lakes and ponds. It also features 5,000 feet of shoreline along Lake Ontario. An arboretum in the northeast section of the park features rare and exotic species from around the world (info: 585-266-1372), as well as a large collection of flowering crab apple trees. The fall foliage is spectacular. Camp Eastman, which has two lodges and three cabins available for rental, is located within the park. This is the site of the annual Oktoberfest.

Irondequoit Bay State Marine Park (585-964-2462 www.nysparks.com), Culver Road and I-590, Irondequoit. Open dawn to dusk. This is a popular spot for fishing and boating. A seasonal bridge allows vehicle traffic between Irondequoit and Webster during the winter months. During the fishing and boating season the bridge is swung open to allow boat traffic to move freely from the bay to Lake Ontario. Several casual restaurants are located near the park on what is referred to as "hot dog row." Seabreeze Amusement Park is nearby.

Irondequoit Bay Park West, Just north of Empire Boulevard, Irondequoit. A 147-acre undeveloped county park with 2,000 feet of waterfront frontage on the west shore of Irondequoit Bay. Popular for hiking and fishing.

North Ponds Park (585-872-2911), 1000 Ridge Road (NY 104), Webster. This 55-acre park is known for its summer swimming area and nature trail. It also has several shelters, a beach volleyball court, and snack bar.

Veterans Memorial Park, North Avenue, Webster. A small village park with a gazebo and benches, the site of summer events and concerts.

Webster Arboretum (585-234-4622; www.websterny.com/arboretum), 1700 Schlegel Road (PO Box 372), Webster. This 32-acre site, about 2 miles from Lake Ontario, features perennials, butterfly and hummingbird gardens, a rose garden, a large children's garden, hiking trails, an exhibit room, and rest rooms.

Webster County Park (585-256-4950) 999, Lake Road, Webster. This 550-acre park on the shores of Lake Ontario offers a great view and a fishing pier as well as 41 campsites available May–October. Other park facilities include picnic areas, sports fields, and hiking trails as well as cross-country skiing and sledding in winter.

PONDS AND LAKES **Irondequoit Bay.** Sailing, fishing and waterskiing are popular activities in the bay.

Lake Ontario. This region borders Lake Ontario. Irodequoit Bay has an outlet to the lake right near Seabreeze Amusement Park.

✳ Lodging

MOTELS AND HOTELS ♿ **Holiday Inn Express Irondequoit** (585-342-0430), 2200 Goodman Street North (off NY 104), Irondequoit. This small-scale hotel has amenities that include a small indoor pool. $79–$109.

&. **Webster Fairfield Inn by Marriott** (585-671-1500), 915 Hard Road, Webster. This hotel has 63 standard rooms plus an indoor pool. $104–$119.

✳ Where to Eat

DINING OUT **Castaways on the Lake** (585-323-2943; www.castaways onthelake.com), 244 Lake Road, Webster. Open Tuesday–Thursday 4–9, Friday 11:30–10, Saturday 12–10, Sunday 1–9. Extended hours during summer months. This restaurant, which caters to all—couples, families and seniors—has a spectacular view of Lake Ontario from their lakeside heated canopy decks. You can also dine inside in their nautical-themed dining room. Start your meal with bruschetta, crab cakes, or their signature clam chowder. Lunch selections include salads, wraps, hot sandwiches, and seafood entrées. For dinner, chose from pasta, salads, chicken, prime rib, steak, and seafood. Musical entertainment is featured weekends in summer.

Hedges Nine Mile Point Restaurant (585-265-3850), 1290 Lake Road, Webster. Open for lunch Tuesday–Friday 11:30–2, dinner Tuesday–Saturday 5:30–9, sometimes later on Friday and Saturday. Closed mid-December–March. An upscale restaurant—with gardens, patios, and gazebos overlooking Lake Ontario—that features steak and seafood. Your hosts, the Nowrocki-Swift families, have been operating restaurants in the Webster area for five generations.

EATING OUT

Irondequoit

Ｙ **Froggy's on the Bay** (585-288-1080; www.froggysonthebay.com), 1129 Empire Boulevard (NY 404), Irondequoit. Open seasonally. Menu items at this bar/restaurant include steak, ribs, seafood, prime rib, and a Friday fish fry. Dine indoors or on the deck overlooking the Irondequoit Bay area.

𝄢 **Irondequoit Hots** (585-266-3670), 635 Titus Avenue, Irondequoit. Open Monday–Thursday 8 AM–1 AM, Friday and Saturday 9 AM–4 AM, Sunday 11 AM–1 AM. This fast-food joint, known as the "Home of the Big Plate," specializes in hot dogs, cheeseburgers, and Texas plates. They also serve frozen custard.

Seabreeze Area

Several casual, seasonal restaurants—referred to as "Hot Dog Row"—are located near Seabreeze Amusement Park and Irondequoit Bay State Marine Park. These include:

𝄢 &. ● **Bill Gray's Restaurants** (corporate offices 585-787-0150 www.billgrays.com), 4870 Culver Road. This regional restaurant features cheeseburgers, hamburgers, pulled pork, Buffalo chicken sandwiches, and more. This location opened in 1965. They have numerous other locations in the Rochester area.

𝄢 &. ● **Don's Original,** 4900 Culver. This hot-dog joint, started by Don Barbato, is famous for ground round and frozen custard. Two other locations are at 2545 Monroe Avenue in Brighton, and 2055 Nine Mile Point Road in Penfield

𝄢 &. ● **Vic & Irv's Refreshments** (585-544-7680), 4880 Culver Road. Since 1934 they have been known for their steaks and ground rounds.

Other restaurants near Seabreeze include:

Churi's (585-339-9250), 4615 Culver Road. Open Thursday–Saturday

11:30–8:30, more days and hours during summer. This tiny restaurant serves authentic Thai food as well as 37 flavors of ice cream.

Nick's Seabreeze Inn (585-323-1950) 4581 Culver Road, Rochester. Open for lunch Monday–Friday 11:30–3, dinner Monday–Thursday 4–9, Friday and Saturday 4–10, Sunday 12–8. This family-owned Italian restaurant features an antipasto bar with hot and cold food. Dinner selections include veal, chicken, steaks, and pasta.

Y **The Reunion Inn** (585-323-9899), Culver Road (across from Seabreeze), Rochester. Open year-round for lunch Monday–Friday 11:30–2, dinner Tuesday–Saturday 5–9:30. This busy bar and restaurant serves lunches, dinner, and late-night snacks. Menu selections include wings, ribs, steak, and a Friday fish fry.

Y **Shamrock Jack's** (585-323-9310), 4554 Culver Road, Rochester. Open year-round for lunch Monday–Friday 11:30–2:30, Saturday 12–4, dinner Monday–Thursday 5–9, Friday–Saturday 5–10, Sunday 12–9. This bar and restaurant features steak and seafood, as well as a late-night menu and musical entertainment.

Webster

✿ & **Atlantic Family Restaurant** (585-671-2149), 888 Ridge Road, Webster. Open Monday–Saturday 6–midnight, Sunday 6–10. This restaurant has some of the best made-from-scratch food in Monroe County. Specialties include moussaka, spinach lasagna, fresh seafood, and daily specials.

Bazil: A Casual Italian Kitchen (585-679-2006), Empire Boulevard (on Irondequoit Bay), Webster. Open for lunch Monday–Friday 11:30–2, dinner 5–9, Saturday 12–11, Sunday 12–9. This newly opened branch of a popular eatery (the original is on East Henrietta Road) serves traditional Italian entrées in a casual relaxed setting. They also serve a variety of stone-oven pizza, soups, and salads. Their lunch buffet features a different hot entrée every day as well as Italian dishes and salads. A 186-slip marina is located next to the restaurant. For more upscale Italian dining, visit Mario's Via Abruzzi in Brighton, near Pittsford, owned and operated by the same family.

✿ & **Charlie's** (585-671-4320), 1843 Empire Boulevard, Webster. Open daily 10–10, Friday and Saturday until 11. This casual burger restaurant was opened by Charlie Riedel in 1969. They also have restaurants in Canandaigua, Victor, and Ontario.

✿ **Rubinos Italian Deli** (585-265-0870), 24 East Main Street, Webster. Open Monday–Saturday 10–8. This small deli features pizza, subs, wings, wraps, and pastas. They have several booths indoors and tables outside on the sidewalk. Take-out is available.

Streppas Bistro (585-265-2264), 30 East Main Street, Webster. Open for lunch Monday–Friday 11–2, dinner Monday–Thursday 5–8, Friday and Saturday 5–9. This restaurant features pastas and seafood as well as deli sandwiches, burgers, hot sandwiches, and a Friday fish fry.

Village Bakery Café (585-265-2630), 32 East Main Street, Webster. Open Tuesday–Wednesday 9–8, Thursday 9–11, Saturday 8–11, Sunday 8– 2. This café features fresh hot bread, stoned-baked pizza, hot and cold subs, calzones, wraps, and fresh-roasted turkey, roast beef, and baked ham. They also have a selection of cookies and pastries.

✳ Selective Shopping

ANTIQUES All That Jazz Antique and Collectible Co-Op (585-224-0340), 1221 Empire Boulevard (one mile east of I-590), Webster. Open Monday–Saturday 10–5, Sunday 11–5. This is the largest antique co-op in Monroe County that's strictly antiques and collectibles. There are over 150 dealers in 10,000 square feet, with everything from smalls to furniture.

SPECIAL SHOPS Allyson's (585-265-0730), 11 East Main Street, Webster. Open Tuesday–Friday 10–5:30, Saturday 10–3. Choose from a large selection of fine gift items, including Dept. 56 Villages, crystal, china, picture frames, Red Hat Society merchandise, wedding and baby gifts, and nautical items. The shop is located in the 1906 former Jayne and Mason Bank, the first state bank in New York.

Cranberry Cottage (585-872-2010), 30 North Avenue, Webster. Open Tuesday–Saturday 10–5. This tiny cottage is filled with folk art, primitives, and country decorating items as well as homespun fabrics, patterns, and books.

House of Guitars, Inc. (585-544-3500), 645 Titus Avenue, Irondequoit. Open Monday–Saturday 10–9, Sunday 1–5. Since 1964 this store has been billed as the world's largest music store. Bands from all over the world shop here, through several floors of new, used, and vintage musical instruments, as well as four million albums, tapes, and CDs. Be sure to check out some of their rock-star memorabilia, including hundreds of autographs, John Lennon's military jacket from Sgt. Pepper, and even Elvis Presley's leather pants. Some people consider this store "cooler than Hollywood."

&. ✿ **House of Plates** (585-265-3201), 36 East Main Street, Webster. Open Monday–Wednesday 10–5, Thursday 10–7, Saturday 10–5. This store carries limited-edition collectors plates, collectible dolls, fine glassware, and a few inexpensive novelty items.

&. ✿ **Piccadilly's Toy Shoppe** (585-671-2160; www.piccadillystoys.com), 1223 Bay Road, Webster. Open Monday–Wednesday 9–6, Thursday and Friday 9–8, Saturday 9–5, Sunday 12–4; extended hours before Christmas. This shop has a nice selection of educational and fun toys for kids of all ages.

Rozmataz (585-671-0820), 1201 Bay Road, Webster. Open Monday 10–2, Tuesday–Friday 10–5, Saturday 10–4. Art, custom framing, gifts, jewelry, and cards.

✳ Special Events

September: **Oktoberfest** (585-336-6070; www.irondequoit.org/events/oktober.htm), Irondequoit. This annual event offers two weekends of food and entertainment.

Penfield, Perinton, Fairport, East Rochester, and Pittsford

The town of Penfield, incorporated in 1810, was first visited by early explorers like La Salle because of its proximity to Lake Ontario and Irondequoit Bay. Daniel Penfield, the town's founder, and his wife, Mary, were among the first settlers. Many mills were built in this area along Irondequoit Creek, which runs into Irondequoit Bay. Fishing was also one of the early industries. Later the town was known for mining of building materials. In 2001 Penfield became one of the first towns in Monroe County to adopt an "Open Space Plan" to preserve farmlands and wetlands to be used for agriculture, green space, and parkland.

The town of Perinton, which encompasses the village of Fairport, first settled by Glover Perrin and his family, was incorporated in 1812. Many of the early settlers became farmers, millers, blacksmiths, and tavern keepers. The opening of the Erie Canal aided in the development of Perinton, especially the village of Fairport, which served as a port for farmers to bring their goods for shipment. Perinton is now known as a "trail town" due to its large number of hiking and biking trails. It was named one of the top ten trail towns in 1996 by the American Hiking Association and the National Parks Service.

The village of Fairport got its name from a traveler who stopped at Mallet's Tavern in what was originally called Perrinsville along the Erie Canal in 1825. As he took his rest and refreshments, he was overheard to comment, "This is truly a fair port." A few decades later when the village was incorporated in 1867, the traveler's observation became the name of the town. Fairport later became a booming industrial town, although some might argue that the town's most enduring claim to fame is the lift bridge over the Erie Canal—the only lift bridge in the world built on a bias. The south end is higher than the north end. It is built in a way that no two angles in the bridge are the same, and no corners on the bridge floor are square. It has been featured in *Ripley's Believe It or Not* 16 times! Fairport's The Village Landing and Packetts Landing complexes along the canal, houses, shops, restaurants and businesses of interest to recreational boaters. Although recently constructed, these structures maintain the ambiance of a 19th-century canal village.

The small, 1-mile-square village of East Rochester, founded in 1897, features an unusual neighborhood, "Concrest." These villa-style poured-concrete duplexes were built as housing for factory workers nearly a century ago.

Hundreds of years ago, what is now the village of Pittsford was the Big Spring rest stop on a major Iroquois trade route. In 1687 the Marquis Denonville and his army camped by the spring on their way to battle the Iroquois Confederacy. Although Pittsford is the oldest of Monroe County's 10 villages, the area didn't really become a thriving community until the late 1700s. The first settler, Israel Stone, built a log home here in 1789. Pittsford is the site of Monroe County's first school (1794), library (1803), permanent church (1807), post office (1811), and newspaper (1815). Originally called Northfield and later Boyee, Pittsford was named after Pittsford, Vermont, the hometown of Col. Calib Hopkins, one of the town's early supervisors and a War of 1812 hero. With the opening of the Erie Canal, the village became a busy shipping port. The arrival of the railroad in 1840 also helped increase village growth. It is also rumored that the area played a role in the Underground Railroad. In the late 1800s many wealthy Rochester residents built country estates in this area, and Pittsford is still an upscale residential community, with many well-preserved historic homes and gardens as well as restaurants, shops, and boutiques along the canal. It has one of the best preserved collections of 19th-century structures in the area. Visitors can even enjoy a sightseeing cruise on the Erie Canal. A paved trail for walkers, joggers, bicyclists, and in-line skaters runs beside the canal.

GUIDANCE **Village of East Rochester** (585-586-3553; www.eastrochester.org), 120 Commercial, East Rochester. Open Monday–Friday 8:30–4:30.

Village of Fairport (585-223-0313; www.village.fairport.ny.us), 31 South Main Street, Fairport. Open Monday–Friday 8:30–4:30.

Town of Perinton (585-223-0770; www.perinton.org), 1350 Turk Hill Road, Fairport. Open Monday–Friday 9–5.

Town of Penfield (585-340-8600; www.penfield.org), 3100 Atlantic Avenue, Penfield. Open Monday–Friday 9–5.

Pittsford Chamber of Commerce (585-234-0308; www.pittsfordchamber.org), PO Box 576, Pittsford. Information can be obtained by phone or through their Web site.

Town of Pittsford (585-248-6200; www.townofpittsford.com), 11 South Main Street, Pittsford. Open Monday–Friday 9–5.

Village of Pittsford (585-586-4332; www.villageofpittsford.org), 21 North Main Street, Pittsford. Open Monday–Friday 7:30–4.

GETTING THERE *By bus:* **RTS bus service** (585-288-1700 or 888-288-3777; www.rgrta.com) from downtown Rochester includes #21 (Fairport), #22 (Penfield), and #92 (Perinton/Bushnell's Basin/Lyons).

By car: NYS Thruway (I-90) exit 45 (I-490); then take NY 96 to NY 250. Fairport is accessible from NY 250 or 31F; Pittsford can be reached via NY 96.

MEDICAL EMERGENCY Dial 911.

✳ To See

MUSEUMS AND HISTORIC HOMES **Fairport Historical Museum** (585-223-3989), 18 Perrin Street, Fairport. Open year-round Tuesday 2–4, Thursday 7–9, and Sunday 2–4. Free admission. Displays include a collection of regional artifacts, photos, and documents, including a Victorian parlor, early kitchen, country store, and changing displays of local interest.

✳ To Do

BICYCLING **Towpath Bike** (585-381-2808; www.towpathbike.com), Schoen Place, Pittsford. This business offers bicycle rentals by the hour or day, as well as bikes for sale.

BOAT EXCURSIONS & *The Colonial Belle* (585-223-9470; www.colonialbelle .com), 400 Packetts Landing (at Main Street), Fairport. May–October, Tuesday– Saturday 12 (lunch), 2:30, 6 (dinner), Sunday 12 and 3 (dinner). Cruise the most picturesque section of the Erie Canal on the largest tour boat operating on the historic canal. The boat, which can hold up to 246 passengers, has a fully enclosed lower deck with a full-service bar and dining area as well as an open-air upper deck for scenic viewing.

Sam Patch (585-262-5661; www.sampatch.org), Schoen Place, Pittsford. Season May 1–November 15. Cruise times vary throughout the season. See their Web site, or call for specifics. Cruise the canal on a 54-foot replica of a 19th-century packet boat. The vessel is operated by the **Corn Hill Waterfront and Navigation Foundation**, which also offers cruises on the *Mary Jemison,* departing from downtown Rochester (See Rochester, *To Do—Boat Excursions*). The mission of this foundation is to promote the historic significance of the Genesee River and the Erie Canal in the Rochester area. The boats travel the routes of the early settlers and offer a glimpse into the history of the Erie Canal and the Genesee River.

FAMILY FUN & 🌀 **Long Acre Farms and the Amazing Maize Maze** (315-986-4202; www.longacrefarms.com), 1342 Eddy Road, Macedon. Open May– October. Located just east of Rochester in neighboring Wayne County, Long Acre Farms is a regional agri-tourism destination—more than a farm, it's "agri-tainment." The farm features a corn maze to get lost in—but with an interactive, two-way communications system, you are never really lost. Visitors can also get fresh, in-season produce at their farm market and ice cream from their ice cream shop. The adjacent **Finger Lakes Aerosport Park** (www.fingerlakes aerosportpark) is the only aerotow hang-gliding park in the state.

GOLF **Island Valley Golf Course** (585-586-1300), 1208 Fairport Road (NY 31F), Fairport. A 9-hole, par 35 public course.

Lodge at Woodcliff (585-381-4000; www.woodclifflodge.com), 199 Wood-cliff Drive, Fairport. This semiprivate 9-hole, par-35 course has mature fair-ways, challenging greens, and spectac-ular scenery. See also *Lodging* and *Where to Eat.*

Shadow Pines Golf Club (585-385-8550), 600 Whalen Road, Penfield. An 18-hole, par-72 private course open to the public.

WINERIES & **Casa Larga Vineyards** (585-223-4210; www.casalarga.com), 2287 Turk Hill Road, Fairport. Open Monday–Saturday 10–6, Sunday 12–6.

CRUISE THE ERIE CANAL ON THE *SAM PATCH,* A REPRODUCTION PACKET BOAT.

Christine A. Smyczynski

Tours are offered on weekends March–Memorial Day, and daily Memorial Day–Thanksgiving weekend. Private tours can also be arranged for groups. The Rochester area's only winery specializes in winemaking from graft to glass. The winery started out in 1974, when Andrew Colaruotolo planted the vineyard's first 5 acres. Since 1978 the Colaruotolo family has been producing award-winning wines and champagnes, and what began as a hobby has grown to a 40-acre estate winery that has won over 200 awards in state, regional, and international competition. The impressive winery—named after Mr. Colaruotolo's grandparents' vineyard in Italy—is set high on a hill overlooking the surrounding vineyards. The building includes a gift shop and tasting room.

✳ Green Space

NATURE PRESERVES **Thousand Acre Swamp Sanctuary,** Jackson Road, near Penfield Center Road, Penfield. Contact The Nature Conservancy (585-546-8030), 315 Alexander Street, Rochester. Open during daylight hours spring, summer, and fall. Free admission. More than 500 species of plants live within this 457-acre sanctuary, as well as 147 species of birds and numerous animals. Why is it called the Thousand Acre Swamp? Because it has been called that from the days of the early American settlers. Guided hikes are offered from April until the end of October.

PARKS **Ellison Park** (716-256-4950), Blossom and Landing Roads, Penfield. Open dawn to dusk. This wooded park in northeastern Monroe County features Fort Schuyler, erected in 1938 to commemorate a colonial trading post built in this area in 1721. Park visitors can glimpse some of the remnants of the lost city of Tryon—the dream city of Salmon Tryon—which unfortunately declined after his death in 1807. There are several hiking trails through the park, as well as a disc golf course, tennis courts, softball diamonds, and picnic areas. It's a popular place to walk your dog. Cross-country skiing and sledding are favorite winter pastimes. **Ellison Wetlands Park**, located just north of Ellison Park, offers canoe and kayak access to Irondequoit Bay.

Irondequoit Bay Park East, Smith Road, Penfield. Open dawn to dusk. A 182-acre undeveloped county park with 2,000 feet of waterfront frontage. It is popular for hiking and fishing.

Kennelley Park, South bank of the Erie Canal on Main Street, Fairport. The gazebo in this park, named after long-time Fairport mayor Vincent Kennelley, is the site of summer concerts.

Lock 32 State Canal Park, NY 65 by the Erie Canal, Pittsford. This park's centerpiece is lock 32 of the Erie Canal.

Potter Memorial and Park, West Church Street, Fairport. The former home of investor Henry Potter now serves as a community meeting room. The surrounding grounds include a park and playground.

Powder Mills Park, (585-256-4950), NY 96, Perinton. Open dawn to dusk. Free admission. This Monroe County Park features steep hillsides, creekside meadows, and wetlands. Activities include a playground, hiking, volleyball, and trout fishing as well as sledding and cross-country and downhill skiing (tow rope). The **Powder Mills Fish Hatchery** (585-586-1670) is located in the park.

Tryon Park, off Tryon Road, Brighton. Open dawn to dusk. This 82-acre undeveloped park features hiking trails.

WALKING AND HIKING TRAILS Crescent Trail Association (585-234-1621; www.ggw.org/ctha), PO Box 1354, Fairport. The Crescent Trail is a 26-mile-long footpath in the Town of Perinton. The association offers guided hikes as well as maps for self guided hikes. Maps can be obtained at **Perinton Town Hall** (585-223-0770) or **Fairport Library** (585-223-9091).

Erie Canal Heritage Trail, Fairport. A popular place to hike, bike, and in-line skate along the former towpath of the Erie Canal, this trail runs along the canal from Lockport to Palmyra and will eventually extend east all the way to Albany.

Thomas Creek Wetland Walk, Lifebridge Lane East, Fairport. Open dawn to dusk. A 13-ace recreational and historical site that encompasses Thomas Creek and Irondequoit Creek. The wetlands walk features an elevated boardwalk and observation platform.

Town of Perinton. This town, with its 40 miles of hiking and nature trails, has been named one of the top-ten trail towns by the American Hiking Society.

✳ Lodging

INNS AND RESORTS ♿ **Brookwood Inn Pittsford** (585-248-8000 or 800-396-1194), 800 Pittsford-Victor Road, Pittsford. This inn features 108 spacious guest rooms and suites, some with whirlpool tubs. It also has an indoor heated pool and exercise facilities. Located near the Erie Canal and village retail shops and restaurants. $79–$139.

♿ **The Lodge at Woodcliff** (585-381-4000 or 800-365-3065; www.woodclifflodge.com), 100 Woodcliff Drive, Rochester (Fairport). Two-hundred suites and guest rooms, including 12 Jacuzzi suites, are available at this premier resort set high on a hilltop. Amenities include a heated indoor/outdoor pool, a complete fitness center and a 9-hole golf course. $175–$350.

MOTELS AND HOTELS ♿ **Penfield Courtyard by Marriott** (585-385-1000), 1000 Linden Park, Rochester.

This hotel has 96 standard hotel rooms. Amenities include a small heated indoor pool, whirlpool, and exercise room. $99–$134.

Renaissance Del Monte Lodge (585-381-9900; www.delmontelodge.com or renaissancehotels.com/rocdl), 41 North Main Street, Pittsford. Near the historic Erie Canal, the area's only luxury hotel offers 99 spacious guest rooms that feature European down comforters and pillows, mini-bar with refrigerator, irons, fitness center, and indoor pool. The hotel's Erie Grill restaurant serves fine American cuisine. $179–$194.

BED & BREAKFASTS Canal Lamp Inn (585-381-4351; www.canallampinn.com), 27 North Main Street, Pittsford. Open year-round. Keith and Beth Miller's historic brick home is located on 1.5 acres along the Erie Canal. The oldest home in the village of Pittsford, the inn is decorated with antiques and reproduction pieces and also has the original flooring and woodwork. The decor features lots of Mary Engelbreit designs. Each of the four guest rooms has a private bath. The Main Street Room, which has a Victorian bay window overlooking Main Street, has a canopy bed with a lace bedspread. The Zornow Room, named after the home's original owner, overlooks the canal and has a king-sized bed and two-person Jacuzzi tub in the bath. The Agate Room, named after the home's second owner, has a queen bed and an unusual sink in the bath. The Canal View Room, which also has a queen bed, features a rainforest shower head in the bathroom. Rooms include a full breakfast that usually features quiche, mini waffles, pancakes, and fresh fruit. It is within walking distance to restaurants and boutiques. $95–$125 weekdays, $105–$150 weekends.

Clematis Inn (585-388-9442), 2513 Penfield Road, Fairport. Open year-round. Innkeeper Theda Ann Burnham offers three rooms in a historic 1900 home, once home of James George and his brother, David. They owned George Brothers Nursery, which primarily grew the clematis vine—and hundreds of these beautiful vines still bloom in the inn's yard from spring through autumn. Each of the three guest rooms have a beautiful clematis flower painted on the bedroom door. The Nellie Moser and the Ramona rooms share a bath, while the Mrs. Cholmondeley room has its own private bath complete with a restored claw-foot tub. Breakfast—served either in the dining room or solar room, or even brought to you in bed—includes freshly ground cof-

fee, homemade breads, and hot entrées. $80–$110.

Esten-Wahl Farm Bed & Breakfast (585-388-1881; www.estenwahlfarm.com), 4394 Carter Road, Fairport. Open year-round. Carol Santos offers two large guest rooms, each with a queen bed and private bath, in her 19th-century farmstead, as well as a two-bedroom cottage next to the pool and tennis court that is fully handicapped accessible. The 30-acre farm, which was founded in 1827 by Henry Esten and worked for three generations of his family, has retained its original appearance, making it a getaway to the country, yet it's only 20 minutes from downtown Rochester. Breakfast is served each morning in the Victorian dining room. $80–$90 rooms, $125–$240 weekend rate, cottage.

Twenty Woodlawn Bed & Breakfast (585-377-8224; nycanal.com/bandb/woodlawn/woodlawn.html), 20 Woodlawn Avenue, Fairport. Open year-round. Bill and Connie Foster offer two antiques-furnished guest rooms in this 1882 Victorian home. One room has a private bath; the other shares with Bill and Connie. The Rose Room features imported English floral wallpaper and a rosebud chandelier, while the Morning Room features an antique iron bed and furnishings. It's just a few blocks from Fairport's Main Street. $75–$90.

✳ Where to Eat

DINING OUT Aladdins Natural Eatery (585-264-9000), 8 Schoen Place, Pittsford. Open Monday–Thursday 11–9, Friday and Saturday 11–10, Sunday 12–9. This canalside restaurant features Rochester's finest Mediterranean cuisine, including hummus, tabouli, and falafel as well as gyros and souvlaki.

&. The Clark House at Shadow Pines (585-385-3700; www.234golf .com), 600 Whalen Road, Penfield. Open Tuesday–Saturday 5–9. Enjoy contemporary gourmet entrées in a historic landmark home. This house, which has three fireplaces, is part of the original 1832 homestead of Alpheus Clark, the son of the first settler in Penfield.

&. Crystal Barn (585-381-4844; www .crystalbarn.com), 2851 Clover Street, Pittsford. Open for lunch Monday– Friday 11:30–2, dinner Monday– Saturday 5–9, Sunday 4–9. Enjoy traditional gourmet cuisine and original culinary creations in an 1860 Victorian country barn decorated with crystal chandeliers. Menu selections range from classic American and Continental cuisine to contemporary creations. Specialties include spanakopita, beef Wellington, rack of lamb, prime rib, and seafood. The Crystal Barn is a member of the Rochester Landmark Restaurant group, which consists of restaurants located in historically significant buildings

&. The Grill & Tap Room at Shadow Lake (585-385-2011; www.234 golf.com) 1850 Five Mile Line Road, Penfield. Open for lunch Monday– Friday 11:30–2:30, dinner Tuesday– Saturday 5–9:30. Enjoy dining on steak and fresh seafood while overlooking the lake and golf course in this classic American steakhouse.

&. ✍ Harbor House Café (585-223-7280), 400 Packett's Landing, Fairport. Open Tuesday–Saturday lunch 11:30–2:30, dinner 5–10; Sunday 10–2. This restaurant offers family dining with a view of the Erie Canal. Lunch entrées include salads, sandwiches, and wraps, while dinner features dishes like filet mignon, roasted chicken, and grilled swordfish. A children's menu is available.

Hicks & McCarthy Café (585-586-0938), 23 South Main Street, Pittsford. Open Monday–Thursday 7:30–9, Friday and Saturday 7:30–9, Sunday 8–2:30. Afternoon tea served Wednesday–Saturday by reservation. This elegant café features a variety of salads, specialty sandwiches, wraps, and seasonal entrées for lunch. Dinner entrées include lobster ravioli, Atlantic salmon, beef bourguignon, and almond-crusted chicken breast.

&. Horizons (585-381-4000; www .woodclifflodge.com), The Lodge at Woodcliff, 199 Woodcliff Drive, Fairport. Open daily for breakfast 6:30–10:30, lunch 11:30–2, and dinner 6–9 (until 10 Friday and Saturday.). This upscale restaurant offers the most spectacular view in the Rochester area. The menu features American cuisine spiced up with international accents. Dishes include maple bourbon pork chop, barbecued salmon and, Hungarian veal paprikash.

&. Legends Grill (585-264-9880; www.legendsgrillpenfieldny.com), 1778 Penfield Road, Penfield. Open for lunch Tuesday–Friday 11:30–2:30, dinner, Tuesday–Saturday 5–10, Sunday 4–9. This contemporary restaurant offers creative American cuisine, including fresh seafood, Black Angus beef, rack of lamb, roast duck, and more.

Mario's Via Abruzzi (585-271-1111 www.Mariosviaabruzzi.com), 2740 Monroe Avenue (at the I-590) Brighton, near Pittsford. See listing under Brighton.

Richardson's Canal House (585-248-5000), 1474 Marsh Road, Pittsford. Open for dinner Monday–Saturday 6–9. One of the few surviving taverns on the Erie Canal, this inn was restored in 1978 and has been placed on the National Register of Historic Places. The menu consists of a prix-fixe, three-course dinner, featuring French and American regional cooking. Dine by the fireplace or on the canalside terrace, surrounded by antiques and artifacts.

Schoen Place Prime Rib & Grill (585-586-5286), 50 State Street, Pittsford. Open Monday–Thursday 4:30–10, Friday-Saturday 4:30–11. This casual fine-dining eatery, across the street from the Erie Canal, specializes in prime rib, lobster tails, crab legs, fish, and chicken.

Simply Crepes (585-383-8310), 7 Schoen Place, Pittsford. Open Tuesday–Saturday 7 AM–8 PM, Sunday 7 AM–3 PM. This nicely decorated restaurant features a large variety of crepes, from appetizers to dessert, and everything in between, as well as soups and salads.

EATING OUT & **Fairport Village Coffee** (585-377-5880), 120 Fairport Village Landing, Fairport. Open Sunday 9–5, Monday–Thursday 7:30–9, Friday 7:30–5, Saturday. 8–5:30. A small café, located next to the library, specializing in gourmet coffees, light lunches, and fresh baked goods.

Fairport Village Inn (585-388-0112; www.fairportvillageinn.com), 103 North Main Street, Fairport. Open Sunday 12–9, Monday–Tuesday 11:30–9, Wednesday–Saturday 11:30–10. This historic inn was originally built in the 1880s as John Ryan's Pub. Menu selections include sandwiches, chicken, seafood, and New York strip steak.

Liftbridge Café (585-377-7770), 6 North Main, Fairport. Open seasonally May 1–September, for lunch and dinner. This café offers dining overlooking the canal and the liftbridge.

Linburgers (585-388-9420), 2157 Penfield Road, Penfield. Open Monday–Thursday 11–9, Friday and Saturday 11–10, Sunday 12–8. This restaurant features 50 varieties of gourmet burgers, including the high-class East Avenue topped with caviar, the meat loaf burger, and the Hawaiian burger topped with pineapple. They also serve sandwiches and salads.

& ✍ **Riki's Family Restaurant** (585-388-0139), 25 North Main Street, Fairport. Open Monday–Friday 6–9, Saturday and Sunday 6–3. This large family-friendly restaurant, located in the circa 1930 Fairport Hotel, features breakfast selections as well as a large selection of sandwiches. They also have homemade soups, some Greek food, and a children's menu. Dinner selections include steak, turkey, meat loaf, and seafood.

& ✍ **The Village Coal Tower** (585-381-7866; www.thecoaltower.com), Schoen Place, Pittsford. Open Monday–Friday 7–8, Saturday and Sunday 8–8. The coal tower, center point of this family restaurant, was built in the early 1900s to store coal for boats on the Erie Canal and local residents. The building originally opened as a restaurant in 1976. The menu features soups, salads, cold and hot sandwiches, and gourmet burgers as well as chicken entrées, meat loaf, oven-roasted turkey, daily specials, and a Friday fish fry.

✳ Entertainment

MUSIC Penfield Symphony Orchestra (585-872-0774; www.penfieldsymphony.org), 1587 Jackson Road, Penfield. This orchestra has been performing for 50 years. They perform a four-concert season of classical music. Most performances take place at the **Browncliff Community Church,** 2530 Browncroft Boulevard, Penfield.

NIGHTLIFE Taylor's Disco Nightclub (585-381-3000), 3300 Monroe Avenue, Pittsford. Open Thursday 8:30 PM–1 AM, Friday–Saturday 8:30 PM–2 AM. Casual yet elegant nightspot for the over-30 crowd features hits from the '70s and '80s.

THEATER Nazareth College Arts Center (585-389-2170; www.nazedu.com/dept/artscenter), 4245 East Avenue, Rochester. This college performing-arts center offers a wide variety of dance, theater performances, children's programs, and more.

✳ Selective Shopping

ANTIQUES

East Rochester

Antique Mall of Rochester (585-586-7340 or 585-233-5153), 400 West Commercial Street (exit 24 off I-490 E), East Rochester. Open Tuesday–Saturday 11–5. This 4,000-square-foot shop features quality antiques from 50 dealers, including china, crystal, sterling, and art glass.

Rodi's Antiques (585-218-4090), 159 West Commercial Street (I-490 East Rochester exit), East Rochester. Open daily 9–4. Specializing in black amethyst glass and Depression glass.

Fairport

For general information on Fairport antiques and merchants: 585-377-4140; www.fairportmerchants.com. Two retail complexes are located along the canal, Packets Landing and Fairport Village Landing.

Fairport Antiques/Rainy Day Mercantile (585-377-4140; www.fairportantiques.com, www.rainydaymercantile.com, www.fairportanderiecanalshop.com), 62 North Main Street, Fairport. Open Monday–Saturday 10–5, Sunday 12–4. Two shops in one, an antiques shop and a gift shop. Choose from quality antiques from 16 vendors as well as candles, books, maps, Erie Canal–related items, and more.

Millstone Block (585-377-4710), 9 North Main Street, Fairport. Open Monday–Wednesday 10–5, Thursday 10–7, Friday 10–5, Saturday 10–4, Sunday 12–4. Used books, vintage treasures, and new gifts.

Echoes of Time (585-586-5310), 17 South Main Street, Pittsford. Open Monday–Saturday 11–5. This shop features period furniture, Oriental carpeting, antique lighting, art, and gifts.

Leah Grace Antiques (585-385-2860), 56 North Main Street, Pittsford. Open Monday–Saturday 10–6. Antiques, country primitives, furniture, books, art, and more can be found at this shop.

ART GALLERIES Austin Harvard Gallery (585-383-1472; www.austinharvardgallery.com), Northfield Common, 50 State Street, Pittsford. Open Monday–Saturday 10–5. Local and international artists have work displayed here. Custom framing is available.

Mostly Clay (585-381-9990), 7 Schoen Place, Pittsford. Open Monday, Wednesday, Thursday 10–6, Tuesday 11–6, Friday 10–8, Saturday 10–5, Sunday 12–5. This shop features pottery by local artists as well as jewelry, candles, and leather.

SPECIAL SHOPS

Fairport

& **Best Friends Gifts & Antiques** (585-377-5820), Fairport Village Landing on South Main Street, Fairport. Monday–Saturday 10–5 Candles, collectibles, books, furniture, casual clothing, and antiques in a friendly shopping environment.

Candy Caboose Fudge Factory (585-377-3275), 52 Railroad Street, Fairport. Open Monday–Friday 11–6, Saturday 10–4. This small shop specializes in homemade fudge, including sugar-free, handcrafted chocolates and gift baskets.

Candy Nation (585-377-0030), 20A Fairport Village Landing, Fairport. Open Monday, Tuesday, Wednesday, and Friday 10–5, Thursday 10–6, Saturday 10–4:30; extended hours November and December. A large selection of specialty candies and candymaking supplies.

Diane Prince Country Furniture and Gifts (585-388-0060; www.diane princefurniture.com), 23 Liftbridge Lane East, Fairport. Open Monday–Saturday 10–5. This two-story shop has everything you need to decorate your country home, including sofas, chairs, painted furniture, and dining room and bedroom sets. Diane also carries beautiful home accessories and gifts, including Irish-made Nicholas Mosse Pottery, and Dedham, Rowe, and Bennington Pottery.

Lombardi's (585-388-1330; www .lombardisgourmet.com), 124 North Main Street, Fairport. Open Monday–Friday 9–7, Saturday 9–6, Sunday 11–3. This shop specializes in gourmet imports and specialty items, including pottery, china, and bakeware as well as imported coffees, fresh pastas, oils, and vinegars. They can also custom make gourmet gift baskets.

Mulberry's (585-377-2560), 15 North Main Street, Fairport. Open Tuesday–Saturday 10–5, Sunday 12–4. A country gift shop carrying seasonal decorating needs, painted glassware, candles, primitive items, and more.

The Toy Soldier (585-223-6170), 16 West Church Street, Fairport. Open Monday–Saturday 10–5:30, Sunday 12–4. A vintage house full of classic and educational toys for imaginative play.

& **Village Gifts Street of Shops** (585-377-7710), 5 Liftbridge Lane East, Fairport. Open Tuesday–Saturday 10–5, Sunday 12–4. Two floors of gifts and home decor, including primitives, baskets, soap, jewelry, and florals.

& **Windy Acres** (585-377-2207), 2518 Huber Road (off Penfield Road NY 441) Fairport. Open Friday–Saturday 10–5. This old barn of a country shop features handcrafted furniture as well as antiques, folk-art Santas, Christmas decorating items, and more. Look for the stone fence and wooden lampposts.

Pittsford

The village boasts two boutique shopping areas, **Northfield Common** and **Schoen Place.** Both are located along the historic Erie Canal and feature distinctive shops and restaurants.

Larger chain retailers can be found just west of the village in Pittsford Plaza, 3349 Monroe Avenue (NY 31).

Northfield Common (www.north fieldcommon.com), 50 State Street (NY 31) at Schoen Place by the Erie Canal, Pittsford Village. This quaint New England–style complex with more than 25 shops and restaurants was once a lumberyard. Several of the businesses are located in the original lumber sheds, which have been remodeled. A newly constructed building at 45 Schoen Place also has several shops. The following is a selection of the shops at the common:

Archipelago (585-248-2450), 50 State Street, Pittsford. Open Tuesday–Saturday 11–5, Thursday until 8. A unique shop focusing on distinctive lamps and lampshades along with antiques, accessories, and items from local artists.

Beads 'N Things (585-586-7230; www.beadsnthings-ny.com), 50 State Street, Pittsford. Open Tuesday–Wednesday 12–5, Thursday 10:30–5:30, Friday and Saturday 10:30–5. All sorts of ready-to-wear beaded jewelry as well as a large selection of beads to make your own items.

Bearly Country (585-381-5540; www.bearlychristmas.com), 45 Schoen Place, Pittsford. Open Monday–Saturday 11–5:30. Choose from country gifts and antiques as well as a large selection of collectible teddy bears.

Brambleberry Barn (585-383-5630; www.brambleberrybarn.com), 45 Schoen Place, Pittsford. Open Tuesday–Thursday 10–6, Friday and Saturday 11–8, Sunday 12–6; also open Mondays from Halloween–Christmas and Memorial Day–Labor Day. They specialize in custom gift baskets,

gourmet foods, aromatherapy products, and distinctive gift items.

Harmony in Wood (585-381-1992), 50 State Street, Pittsford. Open Monday–Saturday 10–5, Thursday until 7, Sunday 12–4. Fine wooden gifts created by over 450 American and Canadian artists. Choose from jewelry boxes, salad sets, cutting boards, desk accessories, toys, jewelry, home decor, and more.

Kookla's Miniature World (585-383-0330), 50 State Street, Pittsford. Open Monday, Tuesday, Friday, Saturday 10–5. This store specializes in miniature and dollhouses.

The Pedestal (585-381-7640; www .pedestalgifts.com), 50 State Street, Pittsford. Open Monday–Wednesday 10–6, Thursday–Saturday 10–8, Sunday 12–4. This unique shop features gifts, music boxes, gourmet foods, and jewelry.

The Topiary (585-586-3540), 50 State Street, Pittsford. Open Monday–Saturday 10–4:30. Fresh floral arrangements and gift items are sold here.

Schoen Place. Stroll along the canal towpath, feed the ducks, and check out the specialty shops and restaurants of Schoen Place. A few are:

Naples Creek (585-586-9070 www.naplescreekshoestore.com), Shoen Place, Pittsford. Open Monday–Saturday 10–7, Sunday 10–5. This shop specializes in shoes, jewelry, and small leather goods.

✿ **Port of Pittsford** (585-383-9250 or 1-888-343-7678), 7 Schoen Place, Pittsford. Open Monday–Saturday 10–7, Sunday 10–6. This unique shop located along the Erie Canal (right where the *Sam Patch* boats dock) features gifts, gourmet food items, toys, and the area's largest selection of

Rochester and Erie Canal souvenirs. They also have a large selection of Lang items.

Along Main Street and State Street:

The Black Sheep (585-248-3960), 34 South Main Street, Pittsford. Open Monday–Saturday 10–5 (Thursday until 7). This shop has upscale children's clothing and accessories.

Deco-Tude (585-586-4360), 15 South Main Street, Pittsford. Monday 12–5, Tuesday–Saturday 10–5:30. A gallery featuring home decor, jewelry, and gift items crafted by some 20 local artisans.

Ewe Two (585-264-9670), 15 South Main Street, Pittsford. Open Monday–Saturday 10–5, Thursday 10–7. This store has upscale clothing and accessories.

L'avant Garbe (585-248-0440 www .lavantgarbe.com), 19 State Street, Pittsford. Open Monday–Saturday 10–6 (Thursday until 8), Sunday 12–5. For upscale women's clothing and accessories as well as Trish McEvoy cosmetics and Darphin skin-care products.

Pendleton Shop (585-264-0010) 1 South Main Street, Pittsford. Open Monday–Friday 10–6, Saturday 10–5. Woolen clothing from Pendleton Mills.

Secret Garden Gifts (585-383-9130), 39 South Main Street, Pittsford. Open Monday–Saturday 10–5. This nicely decorated, small yet elegant shop has unique gift items, cards, and accessories.

Sissy's (585-383-8512), 15 South Main Street, Pittsford. Open Monday–Saturday 10–5. Women's clothing, accessories, and gifts. Upstairs the **Country Gallery** (585-381-2161),

features home-decor items and a designer service.

SJ's (585-248-0640), 25 South Main Street, Pittsford. Open Monday–Saturday 10–5. Specializing in upscale women's clothing and accessories, they are known for their silver and designer jewelry.

Suzanne's Distinctive Fashions (585-383-1810), 40 State Street, Pittsford. Open Sunday–Friday 10–5 (Thursday until 6), Saturday 10–6. This shop carries exclusive fashions and accessories, from casual sportswear to evening wear.

Up the Creek (585-381-3550), 28 South Main, Pittsford. Open Monday–Saturday 9–5:30 (Thursday until 7:30). Upscale men's clothing and accessories.

✳ Special Events

June: **Canal Days** (585-234-4323; www.fairportcanaldays.com), Fairport. One of western New York's premier festivals draws more than 400 arts and crafts exhibitors from all over the United States. Over 75,000 visitors attend the annual two-day event, held the first weekend of June. **Summer Concerts** (585-340-8651), Veterans Memorial Park, Atlantic Avenue, Penfield. Over 20 musical events are planned in this series, which takes place from June–September.

Positively Pittsford (585-234-0308; www.pittsfordchamber.org), Main Street, Pittsford. This event features musical entertainment along Main Street, a regatta on the Erie Canal, and a chicken BBQ.

July: **Hill Cumorah Pageant** (315-597-5851; www.hillcumorah.org), NY 21, Manchester. The annual Church of the Latter-Day Saints religious pag-

eant, a major regional event, takes place in Manchester in Ontario County, with several related religious sites near Palmyra in Wayne County. The Hill Cumorah Pageant is one of America's largest outdoor theatrical performances. **Penfield Independence Day Celebration** (585-340-8651), Harris-Whalen Park, Penfield Road, Penfield. This annual two-day celebration, held on the evenings of July 3 and July 4, features kids activities, food vendors, musical performances, and fireworks on the 4th.
Buffalo Bills Parade (585-234-0308; www.pittsfordchamber.org), Main Street, Pittsford. The Buffalo Bills football team has their training camp at St. John Fisher College in Pittsford, and this annual parade features members of the team. **Concerts on the Canal** (585-234-0308; www.pittsfordchamber.org), along the south side of the canal near Main Street, Pittsford. Concerts take place every other Friday evening during July and August.

August: **Penfield Country Fair Days** (585-340-8651), Historic Four Corners (Penfield and Five Mile Line Roads), Penfield. Events include crafts, food, arts, and family activities.

September: **Pittsford Celebrates** (585-234-0308; www.pittsford chamber.org), Main Street, Pittsford. An annual fall festival featuring musical entertainment, special sales in the village shops, and more.

December: **Candlelight Night** (585-234-0308; www.pittsfordchamber.org), Main Street, Pittsford. This event, which takes place the first Tuesday in December, features holiday lights, special sales in the village shops, horse-drawn wagon rides, and caroling.

SOUTHERN MONROE COUNTY—Rush, Mendon, Honeoye Falls, Henrietta, and Brighton

Rush, one of the smallest towns in Monroe County, is mainly an agricultural area. The first settler to the area (which was originally called Hartford) was Col. William Markham, a Revolutionary War veteran from Maryland. The town of Rush was incorporated in 1813, and Markham was named first supervisor. No one can be certain where the name Rush came from. Some say it's named after a plant called bull rush, which grew along Honeoye Creek. Farmers used to bring their cattle along the creek in winter to eat the plant. Some speculate that the town might be named to honor Dr. Benjamin Rush, a surgeon who served under George Washington during the Revolutionary War and a signer of the Declaration of Independence. One of Rush's most famous citizens was Al Mattern, a left-handed pitcher known for his spitball, who played for the Boston Nationals in the early 1800s.

The town of Mendon was first settled in 1791 and incorporated in 1813. Many of the first pioneers who came to farm the land came from Mendon, Massachusetts, and they named their new home after that town. There are many nice older homes in the town, including 10 cobblestone buildings. Mendon

Ponds Park and Nature Center is a designated National Natural Landmark because of its glacial land forms.

The name Honeoye Falls comes from the Seneca word *Honeoye*, meaning "where the finger lies." Legend has it that two Seneca tribesmen were fighting in this area, and one man's finger was severed, yet he continued to fight and won the battle. Later when he told the tale, he referred to the area as the place where the finger lies on the ground. The town began as Norton Mills, named after the gristmill erected here by Zebulon Norton in 1791. The village expanded during the late 19th century with the coming of the railroad. Many of the structures erected during this time that are still standing are listed on the National Register of Historic Places. One such building is the Mendon Town Hall, which was originally built as a mill in 1827, then rebuilt in 1885 after a fire. Several historical markers are located next to the town hall by the overlook next to the falls.

The town of Henrietta, incorporated in 1818, is considered the crossroads of Monroe County since it is the geographic center. The land was part of the 1788 land sale that opened up western New York to settlement after the Revolutionary War. Known as the Phelps and Gorham Purchase, Oliver Phelps and Nathaniel Gorham purchased nearly 3 million acres of wilderness land at five cents an acre. Originally under the jurisdiction of Pittsford, the town was named Henrietta to honor Henrietta Laura Pulteney, Countess of Bath, the daughter of Sir William Pulteney, a major British investor in the land purchase. While farming was the major occupation in the early days, today Henrietta is home to several major Fortune 500 industries as well as the campus of Rochester Institute of Technology (R. I. T.) and the Tinker Nature Center.

Brighton, which has a current population of about 35,000, was incorporated in 1814, with the first settlers arriving about 1790. Early industries in the town—named after Brighton, England—included brick making and nurseries. Until the 20th century this area was mainly rural and agricultural. Today it is a suburban residential community.

AREA CODE The area code is 585.

GUIDANCE Town of Rush (585-533-1312; www.rushconnections.com), 5977 East Henrietta Road, Rush. Open Monday–Friday 8:30–4:30, Thursday until 6. This is the smallest town in Monroe County.

Town of Mendon (585-624-6060; www.townofmendon.org), 16 West Main Street, Honeoye Falls. Open Monday–Friday 8:30–4:30. The town hall, right by the falls in Honeoye Creek, was originally built as a mill and remodeled into a town hall in the 1980s.

Village of Honeoye Falls (585-624-1711), 5 East Street, Honeoye Falls. Open Monday–Friday 9–4:30.

Town of Henrietta (585-334-7700; www.townofhenrietta.org), 475 Calkins Road, Henrietta. Open Monday–Friday 9–5.

Town of Brighton (585-784-5250; www.townofbrighton.org), 2300 Elmwood, Brighton. Open Monday–Friday 9–5.

By bus: **RTS bus service** (585-288-1700 or 888-288-3777;
www.rgrta.com) from downtown Rochester includes #24 (RIT), #26 Henrietta),
and #91 (Avon/Rush/ Honeoye Falls).

By car: NYS Thruway (I-90) to I-390 south to exit 11 will take you toward Rush,
Mendon, and Honeoye Falls. Take I-390 north to exits 12–15 to access Henrietta
and Brighton.

MEDICAL EMERGENCY Dial 911.

✳ To See

ART GALLERIES **Mill Art Center and Gallery** (585-624-7740), 61 North Main
Street, Honeoye Falls. Open Monday–Saturday 9–5. This gallery is located on
the second floor of Honeoye Falls historic lower mill. Artwork by local artists is
displayed, and art classes are offered to both adults and children.

MUSEUMS AND HISTORIC HOMES **New York Museum of Transportation**
(585-533-1113; www.nymtmuseum.org), 6393 East River Road (1 mile north of
NY 251, exit 11 off I-390), West Henrietta. Open year-round Sunday 11–5 or by
appointment for large groups. Admission May–October $6 adults, $5 seniors
65+, $4 children 3–15; rest of year $3 adults, $2 children under 12. A scenic 2-
mile rail ride (May–October) takes visitors between the New York Museum of
Transportation Museum and the nearby **Rochester and Genesee Valley Railroad Museum** (585-533-1431; www.rochnrhs.org), open mid-May–October.
These two museums focus on the transportation and railway history of the Genesee Valley. Exhibits include rail cars, vintage vehicles, and a 1918 Erie Railroad
depot. You can also enjoy historic films in the video gallery, see a large operating
HO layout, and view photos outlining the history of rail transportation in the
Genesee Valley. Purchase admission tickets to both museums at the New York
Museum of Transportation because the RGVRM is only open when the Museum
of Transportation is open.

Peacock Oriental Antiques Museum (585-624-7740), 61 North Main Street,
Honeoye Falls. Open Tuesday–Sunday 9–5. Free admission. This unique museum features over 700 Chinese, Japanese, and peacock artifacts from 206 B.C. to
World War II., including a "poison teapot." This museum is the collection of
Anne Peacock-Jacobs, who has been collecting oriental antiques for over 40
years. The collection includes smoking equipment, dolls, toys, wood carvings,
and jewelry. The museum's library has over 500 books on Oriental antiques.

Stone-Tolan House (585-546-7029 www.landmarksociety.org), 2370 East
Avenue, Brighton. Open Friday and Saturday 12–3; closed January–February.
Admission: $3 adults, $ 1 children 8–18. The Stone-Tolan house is the oldest
home in Monroe County, built in 1792 with additions made in 1805. The Stone
family managed this frontier tavern, which played host to such notable visitors as
Aaron Burr, Marquis de Lafayette, Mohawk Chief Joseph Brant, and Louis
Philippe, later the King of France. Tour the home along with an orchard, smoke-
house, privy, and kitchen garden.

Tinker Homestead and Farm Museum (585-359-7042), 1525 Calkins Road, Henrietta. Open year-round Tuesday–Sunday 10–4. This 1830s farmstead, on the National Register of Historic Places, is located within the 68-acre **Tinker Nature Park** (see *Green Space*). The homestead was owned by six generations of the Tinker family from 1812 until 1991, when it was sold to the town of Henrietta. The cobblestone home, an architectural style unique to western New York, was completed in 1830. The interior of the home has been restored to its early 20th-century Victorian style. A farm museum on the grounds gives an overview of the growth of agriculture in western New York plus an extensive collection of farm implements.

EXHIBITION SPACE **The Dome Center** (585-334-4000; www.domecenter.com), 2695 East Henrietta Road, Henrietta. The Dome Center is a multipurpose exhibition and event center for Monroe County. Numerous events, trade fairs, concerts, sports events, and more are held here. The Monroe County Fair (www.mcfair.com) is held on the grounds in July.

✳ To Do

GOLF **Wild Wood Country Club** (585-334-5860), 1201 West Rush Road, Rush. An 18-hole, par-71 private course open to the public.

GUIDED TOURS ♿ **Custom BrewCrafters Inc**. (585-624-4386; www.custom brewcrafters.com), 93 Paper Mill Street, Honeoye Falls. Open for retail sales Monday–Thursday 5–8, Friday 3–8, Saturday 11–6, Sunday 12:30–5; tours and tastings Saturday and Sunday. Rochester's only true microbrewery creates over 50 custom-made ales for western New York restaurants.

✳ Green Space

PARKS **Harry Allen Park,** NY 65, Honeoye Falls. This small park on the banks of Honeoye Creek features a gazebo and new playground. It is located adjacent to the town's historical museum, which is open Sunday afternoons.

Mendon Ponds Park and Nature Center (585-256-4950; www.monroecounty .gov/documentView.asp?docID=33), 3914 Clover Street, Honeoye Falls. Open daily 6–11. The 2,500-acre Mendon Ponds Park is the largest park in the Monroe County park system, with some 20 miles of multiuse trails. It is a designated National Natural Landmark because of its glacial land forms, which include kames, eskers, and kettles. The kettle referred to as the "Devil's Bathtub" is a meromictic lake, a deep body of water surrounded by high ridges. It is one of only a handful of such lakes in the world, and people from all over the country come here to see it. Park facilities include picnic areas, hiking trails, fishing access, boat launches, and two sledding hills. The park's 550-acre **Mendon Nature Center** features 7 miles of trails, wildlife, and plant life.

Tinker Nature Park–Hansen Nature Center (585-359-7044; www.ggw.org/ hansen), 1525 Calkins Road, Henrietta. This 68-acre handicapped-accessible park offers a variety of nature programs as well as animal displays plus a 1.2-mile hiking trail and a 0.5-mile nature trail.

WATERFALLS **Honeoye Falls** This picturesque waterfall is located next to Mendon Town Hall on Main Street.

✳ Lodging

MOTELS AND HOTELS Several chain hotels are located in this area near I-390. These include:

Hampton Inn Rochester South (585-272-7800), 717 East Henrietta Road, Brighton. This hotel has 112 standard rooms. $104–164.

Courtyard by Marriott Brighton (585-292-1000), 33 Corporate Woods, Brighton. This hotel has 137 standard rooms and 12 suites. Amenities include a video library, video games, an outdoor heated pool, and an exercise room. $99–134.

Comfort Suites of Rochester (585-334-6620), 2085 Hylan Drive, Henrietta. This 66 room hotel has a heated indoor pool and whirlpool. $69–109.

Radisson Hotel Rochester Airport (585-475-1910), 175 Jefferson Road, Henrietta. This four-story hotel has 171 standard rooms. Amenities include a heated pool, video library, on-site restaurant, and a free newspaper.

✳ Where to Eat

DINING OUT **Mario's Via Abruzzi** (585-271-1111 www.mariosvia abruzzi.com), 2740 Monroe Avenue (at the I-590), Brighton. Monday–Thursday 5–10, Friday 5–11, Saturday 4:30–9, Sunday brunch 10:30–2, dinner 4–9 Rochester's best-known Italian restaurant has been owned and operated by the Daniele family for over 20 years. Dine on traditional Abruzzese entrées such as homemade gnocchi, "thousand" layer lasagna, and pollo prosciutto. The restaurant has won the Wine Spectator Award of Excellence several years in a row. Strolling accordion players are featured on Saturday. For more casual Italian dining visit Bazil, also owned and operated by the Daniele family. They have two locations, one in Henrietta and one in Webster.

⭤ ✿ 🐾 🍸 **The Brewery** (585-624-7870), 8 West Main Street, Honeoye Falls. Open Monday–Saturday 10:30–10, Sunday 10:30–9 (bar open later). This casual restaurant in the heart of the village features both a nice indoor dining room and a warm-weather dining patio that overlooks Honeoye Creek and the waterfall. The menu features salads, sandwiches, and beef on weck, as well as steak and chicken entrées.

The Cartwright Inn (585-334-4444; www.thecartwightinn.com), 5691 West Henrietta Road, Henrietta. Sunday 12:30–8:30, Monday–Thursday 11:30–9:30, Friday and Saturday 11:30–10. This restaurant has been voted one of Rochester's finest seafood and prime rib houses. Casual fine dining is also offered on the patio in summer, with live jazz and blues on Friday and Saturday.

Golden Dynasty Restaurant (585-442-6340; www.golden-dynasty.com), 1900 South Clinton Avenue, Brighton. Open Monday–Thursday 11:30–9:45, Friday and Saturday 11:30–10:45, Sunday 12–9:45. This elegantly casual restaurant is one of the more popular Chinese restaurants in the Rochester area.

⭤ **Phillips European** (585-272-9910; www.phillipseuropean.com), 26 Corporate Woods, Rochester. Open Monday–Saturday 11–10. This family-owned restaurant features fine dining in European style. The restaurant, which originally opened in 1984 on South Avenue, had one of the first cappuccino makers in the city. They use only the freshest ingredients. Lunch features soups, salads, and sandwiches. The dinner menu includes veal, pork, beef, chicken, and seafood. Over 30 desserts are baked daily, including crème brûlée, cheesecake, and cookies.

The Shanghai Chinese Restaurant and Party House (585-424-4000; www.shanghaichinese.com), 2920 West Henrietta Road, Henrietta. Open Sunday 11:30–10, Friday and Saturday 11–11. Rated the best Chinese restaurant in the Rochester area by *Interstate Gourmet*. Choose from Szechwan, Cantonese, and Mandarin cuisine, plus exotic drinks.

Tokyo Japanese Restaurant & Steak House (585-424-4166; www .restaurantpix.com), 2930 West Henrietta Road, Henrietta. Open Monday–Thursday 11:30–10, Friday and Saturday 11:30–11. Partake in a taste of Japan with choices like teriyaki, tempura, sukiyaki, shabu bento, and traditional hibachi. Sushi, steak, and seafood also available.

Yangtze Asia Buffet and Bistro (585-427-2178), 1100 Jefferson Road, Henrietta. Open daily 11–9:30. This sizeable restaurant features the area's largest Asian buffet. Choose from authentic Chinese and Thai appetizers and soups, sushi, and Nigre and Mongolian BBQ as well as a selection of healthy foods. They also have a large selection of ice creams and cakes.

Juniper Beans (585-582-1830), 61 North Main Street, Honeoye Falls. Open Monday–Thursday 7–3, Friday and Saturday 7–10. This unique

antiques-filled bistro is located on the first floor of a historic stone 1830s mill building. The menu, featuring seasonal and local products, includes salads, paninis, and wraps as well as daily specials. **The Mill Art Center** (see *To Do—Art Galleries*) is located on the second floor, while the third floor features the **Peacock Oriental Museum** (see *Museums*).

EATING OUT **Bazil: A Casual Italian Kitchen** (585-427-7420; www.bazil restaurant.com), 749 East Henrietta Road, Henrietta. Open for lunch Monday–Friday 11:30–2, dinner 5–9, Saturday 12–11, Sunday 12–9. This restaurant serves traditional Italian entrées in a casual, relaxed setting. They also have a variety of stone-oven pizza, soups, and salads. Their lunch buffet features a different hot entrée everyday as well as Italian dishes and salads.

✳ Entertainment

MUSIC **Brighton Symphony** (585-777-8145 or 585-248-0680; www .brightonsymphony.org), Brookside School, 220 Idlewood Road, Rochester. This group of 55 volunteer musicians gives eight concerts per year.

NIGHTLIFE **The Pulse Dance Club** (585-436-7573; www.feelmypulse.com), 1509 Scottsville Road (near R.I.T.) Rochester. Thursday 10 PM–2 AM, Friday–Saturday 9 PM–2 AM. This dance club features a 20-foot rotating dance floor, the largest in New York and the second largest in the world. It has two chrome hydraulic dance cages that lift dancers above the crowd. The **Steel Music Hall** (585-436-7573; www .steel musichall.com), in the same building, features live local and national musical acts. See their Web site or call for concert dates.

✳ Selective Shopping

ANTIQUES **Green Door Antiques**
(585-271-2460 or 800-754-9633;
www.greendoorantiques.com), 1534
Monroe Avenue, Brighton. Open
Wednesday, Friday, Saturday 11–4
(closed Saturday July and August)
Specializing in quality 19th- and early
20th-century antiques, including
china, cut glass, Christmas ornaments,
sterling and flatware, and hollow
ware.

Mantegna (585-624-3432), 22 North
Main Street, Honeoye Falls. Open
Tuesday–Friday 10–4, Saturday
9–noon. A red barn full of antiques
and restored furniture plus furniture
refinishing, chair caning, repairs, and
reupholstery.

Windsor Cottage (585-442-6530),
1704 Monroe Avenue, Brighton.
Open Tuesday–Saturday 10–5:30.
New and used furniture and decorative accessories in a specialty consignment shop.

SPECIAL SHOPS ♿ **The Flower Mill**
(585-624-1930 or 888-624-1930), 11
East Street, Honeoye Falls. Open
Monday–Saturday 9–6. This small
florist offers natural floral designs as
well as bath and body products, gifts,
jewelry, and candy.

Liberty Cottage (585-624-5270;
www.libertycottage.com), 9 North
Main Street, Honeoye Falls. Open
Tuesday–Saturday 10–5. A quaint
store, with tin ceilings and period
lighting, is located in part of a 1902
hotel. The shop specializes in country
and primitive items as well as supplies
and patterns for "old-fashioned"
stitchery and crafts like rag weaving
and redwork, which were popular in
the 1800s and are now making a comeback. They also carry Lang products,
candles, linens, and more. Owner
Nancy Noonan makes wool jackets
and appliquéd sweatshirts to order.

♿ **The Write Book and Gift Shop**
(585-624-4560; www.writebook
andgifts.com), 19 North Main Street,
Honeoye Falls. Open Monday–Friday
9–7, Saturday 10–7. This shop features the latest books, as well as
unique gifts that celebrate reading
and writing. A small café in the front
of the store offers patrons coffee,
muffins, and cookies. Writing classes
are given in an upstairs classroom.

✳ Special Events

June: **Festival on the Green** (585-
624-1711), Honeoye Falls. This festival held in Harry Allen Park features
crafters and food vendors as well as
musical entertainment.

July: **Monroe County Fair** (585-
334-4000; www.mcfair.com), Dome
Center, 2695 East Henrietta Road,
Henrietta. This fair, which began as a
cattle show in 1823, focuses on promoting agriculture and technology as
well as building community. It has
been in its present location since
1947. The fair features agricultural
displays, family educational programs,
midway rides, stock car races, live
entertainment, and more.

SOUTHWESTERN MONROE COUNTY—Chili, Churchville, and Mumford

The Town of Chili is fairly rural, but slowly growing. Several historic buildings are located along Union Street. A doll museum is located in North Chili.

Churchville, in the town of Riga, features the landmark Star of the West Milling Company at 35 South Main, the only flour mill still operating in the Rochester area. They process 60 million pounds of flour annually.

Mumford, a quaint town near the Livingston County border, is home to Genesee Country Village, the third largest collection of historic buildings in the United States.

AREA CODE The area code is 585.

GUIDANCE **Town of Chili** (585-889-3550; www.townofchili.org), 3333 Chili Avenue, Chili. Open Monday–Friday 9–5.

Town of Riga (585-293-3880; www.townofriga.org), 8 Main Street, Churchville. Open Monday, Tuesday, Thursday, Friday 9–4, Wednesday 9–5.

Village of Churchville (585-293-3720), 21 East Buffalo, Churchville. Open Monday–Friday 8:30–4.

Town of Wheatland (585-889-1553; www.townofwheatland.org). The hamlet of Mumford, home of Genesee Country Village, is located in this town.

GETTING THERE *By bus:* **RTS bus service** (585-288-1700 or 888-288-3777; www.rgrta.com) from downtown Rochester includes #95 (North Chili/Churchville/Bergen/Batavia).

By car: Exit 47 off NYS Thruway (I-90). Mumford: Take NY 19 south to North Road, and follow signs to Genesee Country Village. Churchville/Riga: Take exit 3 off I-490. Chili: Take exit 4 off I-490.

MEDICAL EMERGENCY Dial 911.

✳ To See

MUSEUMS AND HISTORIC HOMES ✐ **Genesee Country Village** (585-538-6822; www.gcv.org), Flint Hill Road, Mumford. Open May, June, and September, Tuesday–Sunday 10–4; July and August, Tuesday–Sunday 10–5. Admission: $12.50 adults, $9.50 seniors and students, $3 children 4–16. Step back in time at Genesee Country Village, the third largest collection of historic buildings in the nation. All the period structures on the site have been moved to the museum from various locations throughout western and central New York. Visit 57 restored and fully furnished buildings in this recreated 1800s community, and watch craftsmen demonstrate such 19th-century occupations as weaver, potter, and cabinetmaker. Be sure to wear comfortable shoes—touring the 200-acre site takes at least five hours. Also on the grounds are an antique carriage museum, a gallery of sporting and wildlife arts, and the **Genesee Country Nature Center** (see *Green Space*).

Victorian Doll Museum (585-247-0130), 4332 Buffalo Road (NY 33), North Chili. Open February–December, Tuesday–Saturday 10–4:30. More than 3,000 dolls are on permanent display at this unique museum, located in a historic "red building" built in the early 1900s. The collection ranges from antique dolls from the 1860s to present-day Madame Alexander Dolls. Curator Linda Greenfield, a recognized expert in doll restorations, also operates a "doll hospital" on the premises, where she restores antique and newer dolls for individuals and museums. There is also a doll gift shop, offering a variety of books, paper dolls, and new dolls priced from $5 to $300-plus.

✳ Green Space

NATURE PRESERVES **Genesee Country Nature Center** (585-538-6822; www.gcv.org), 1410 Flint Hill Road, Mumford. Open May–October, Tuesday–Friday 10–4; November–April, Thursday–Friday 10–4; January and December, weekends 10–4. A diversity of plants and wildlife can be found in the fields and woodlands that boarder Genesee Country Village. This 175-acre nature center has 5 miles of hiking trails—the Lower Meadow Trail is especially suited to visitors who prefer a shorter walk on level ground. Indigenous water plants are displayed in the water gardens, which includes a flowing stream. Inside the interpretive building, view exhibits that describe plants, animals, and geological formations. Visitors can also examine coral fossils and see amphibious pond life. The nature center is involved in a nesting program, helping birds with populations in decline.

PARKS **Black Creek Park** (585-256-4950), Chili-Riga Townline Road, Chili. Open dawn to dusk. This 1,500-acre Monroe County park has two small ponds as well as Black Creek running through its undeveloped hilly areas. The park's wide paths are perfect for hiking, horseback riding, or cross-country skiing. The park also has a model-airplane field and picnic areas.

Churchville Park (585-256-4950), Kendall Road, Churchville. Open dawn to dusk. This 742-acre county park features a 9-hole golf course with pro-shop, plus softball and soccer fields, playgrounds, a skating rink, and a boat launch on Black Creek.

Hubbard Park, NY 259, North Chili. A town park with playground equipment and sports fields.

Oatka Creek County Park (585-256-4950), Union Street (off NY 383), Wheatland. This 461-acre undeveloped park, which has Oatka Creek running through it, is a popular place for fly casting for trout.

WALKING AND HIKING TRAILS **Genesee Valley Greenway** (585-658-2569), Parts of this former transportation corridor—used by the Genesee Valley Canal during the mid-1800s and later by the railroads—runs through the southwestern part of Monroe County. The portion of the trail known as the Dumping Hill Lock Trail, off Morgan Road in Scottsville, takes you past one of the best preserved locks from the old canal system. See also *Green Space—Walking and Hiking Trails* for *Mount Morris, Livingston County.*

Lehigh Valley Trail Park, Open dawn to dusk. This park, which runs parallel to NY 251, has many access points just south of that road. This 15-mile linear park, popular for hiking, biking, and cross-country skiing, begins at the Genesee River and travels through Rush and Mendon to the Ontario County Line.

✳ Lodging

BED & BREAKFASTS **Genesee County Inn** (585-538-2500; www.geneseecountryinn.com), 948 George Street, Mumford. Open year-round. Innkeeper Kim Rasmussen runs this peaceful B&B just down the road from Genesee Country Village. Nine elegant, antiques-filled guest rooms, all with private baths and some with fireplaces, are available in this 1833 inn, which served the community as a mill for 100 years before transforming into a bed & breakfast in 1982. The guest rooms feature Amish quilts on the beds and hand stenciling on the walls. Walk off your gourmet breakfast by strolling the 8 acres of beautiful grounds that surround the inn. $95–$175.

OTHER LODGING **Genesee Country Campground** (585-538-4200), 40 Flint Hill Road, Caledonia. Open May–October 31. This campground offers spacious drive-thru wooded sites and large grassy tent areas. Amenities include a rec room, playground, shuffleboard, basketball court, and hiking trails. $22, includes water and electric.

✳ Where to Eat

EATING OUT **Jitters Café** (585-594-3922), 4357 Buffalo Road (NY 33), North Chili. Open Monday–Friday 6–10, Saturday 7–10, Sunday 9–3. This small café features coffee, cappuccino, gourmet sandwiches, homemade soup, and desserts.

Leaf & Bean Coffee Company (585-889-8270), 3187 Chili Ave (NY 33A), Chili Center. Open Monday–Friday 6:30–10, Saturday 7:30–10, Sunday 8–10. The best place to go for coffee in Chili Center. Live music is featured on weekends.

Sals Birdland Restaurant (585-544-4171; www.salsbirdland.com), 1300 Scottsville Road in Chili, 309 Ridge Road, and 534 Lake Avenue. Open Monday–Thursday 11 AM–10 PM, Friday and Saturday 11 AM–1 AM, Sunday 1 PM–9 PM. Chicken wings are their specialty as well as Sal's Sassy Sauce. This restaurant chain, founded in 1974 by Sal Nalbone, features chicken and rib dinners.

✳ Selective Shopping

SPECIAL SHOPS **Amish Outlet & Gift Shop** (585-889-8520), 3530 Union Street (NY 259), North Chili. Open Monday–Friday 10–6, Saturday 10–5, Sunday 11–4. This 12,000-square-foot store has reasonably priced quality indoor and outdoor furniture, playground equipment, and sheds along with candles, lace, ornaments, gourmet foods, and other gift items.

The Glue Factory (585-594-0857), 3252 Union Street (NY 259), North Chili. Open Monday–Friday 10–8, Saturday 10–5, Sunday 12–5. A 5,500-square-foot store full of collectibles, candles, pottery, florals, books, lamps, and seasonal decorations. The store has a large porch with plenty of comfortable rocking chairs—perfect for husbands to sit and relax while their wives shop. The store was named first runner-up in the 2002 National Retailer of the Year content by *Country Business* magazine.

McKenzie's Mercantile (585-538-2038), Main Street, Mumford. Open Tuesday–Sunday 11–5. A large selection of country wares for the garden and home can be found at this store in a former firehouse. Choose from folk art, pottery, lamps, art prints, antiques, candles, and more.

Tin and Brass Works (585-538-2160), Corner of Main and State Street, Mumford. Open Wednesday–Friday 11–5:30, Saturday 11–5, Sunday 11–5:30. Tinsmith Bob Beltz, who is one of the resident tinsmiths at nearby Genesee Country Village, creates all sorts of tin and brass items for the home. His wife, Jo, compliments his wares with an array of handcrafted quilted items.

✳ Special Events

December: **Yuletide in the Country** (585-538-6822; www.gcv.org), Genesee Country Village, Mumford. Step back into the 19th century to discover Victorian holiday traditions when the decorated historic village comes alive for the holiday season.

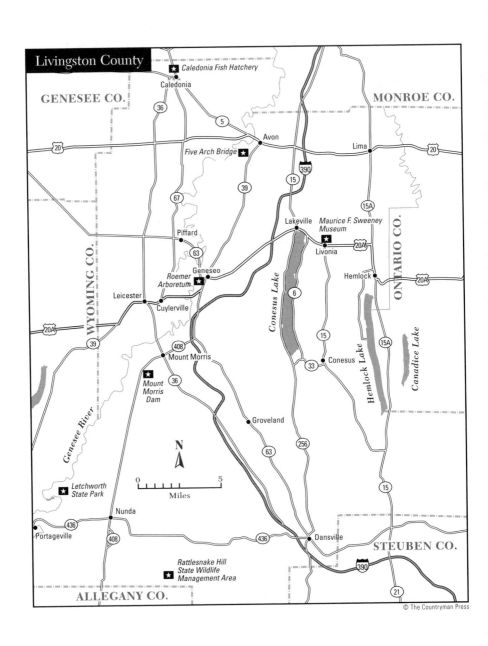

Livingston County

Caledonia Fish Hatchery

Caledonia

GENESEE CO.   MONROE CO.

36

5

20   Lima   20

Avon

Five Arch Bridge

390

39

15

67

15A

Piffard   Lakeville   Maurice F. Sweeney
                                                        Museum

63   Livonia   20A

Roemer
Arboretum   Geneseo   Hemlock   20A

Leicester   6

Cuylerville

20A   15

39   15A

408

Mount Morris   33   Conesus

Mount
Morris   36
Dam

Groveland

63   256

N

0 |‑‑‑‑‑‑‑| 5
        Miles

Letchworth
State Park

Nunda

436   15

Portageville

408   436   Dansville   STEUBEN CO.

Rattlesnake Hill   390
State Wildlife
Management Area

21

ALLEGANY CO.

Genesee River

Conesus Lake

Hemlock Lake

Canadice Lake

WYOMING CO.

ONTARIO CO.

© The Countryman Press

LIVINGSTON COUNTY

Experience a relaxing pace when you visit Livingston County. Bordered on the west by Letchworth State Park—"the Grand Canyon of the East"—and on the east by two of the Finger Lakes—Conesus and Hemlock—this western Finger Lakes county also has many small villages that offer unique shopping, dining, and lodging. Many sites of historic significance can be found here, including Red Cross Chapter Number 1, established by Clara Barton in Dansville; Mount Morris, the birthplace of Francis Bellamy, author of the "Pledge of Allegiance"; and Geneseo, a designated National Historic Landmark village.

Livingston County was incorporated in 1821, formed from parts of Ontario and Genesee Counties. It was named to honor Chancellor Robert R. Livingston, who helped draft the Declaration of Independence and the New York State Constitution. He was also one of the principal negotiators of the Louisiana Purchase. Before the Revolutionary War, this area was inhabited by the Seneca tribe; then in 1779 General John Sullivan's army arrived in the area and destroyed the Seneca village. This was the only Revolutionary War "battle" fought in Livingston County.

One of the county's most significant historical events was the Big Tree Treaty in 1797, in which the Seneca relinquished their land in exchange for reservations.

AREA CODE The county-wide area code is 585.

COUNTYWIDE GUIDANCE Livingston County Chamber of Commerce (585-243-2222 or 800-538-7365; www.livingstoncountychamber.com), 4560 Millennium Drive, Geneseo. Open Monday–Friday 8:30–4:30.

Routes 5 and 20 (www.routes5and20.com). This route, which was originally a Native American foot trail, has been referred to as an authentic American Road. In the 1700s the pioneers widened the trail, and soon communities grew along the route. Once cars became the mode of transportation, it was one of the most traveled east-west highways in the state, until the New York State Thruway was built. Today it provides a scenic byway for travelers seeking a slice of Americana. A publication outlining this driving tour can be obtained at the Livingston County Chamber of Commerce.

Genesee Valley Council on the Arts (585-243-6785; www.gvcaonline.org), Building 4, Apartment 1, Livingston County Campus, Mount Morris. Dedicated to supporting and promoting arts and culture in Livingston County. Events are listed on their Web site.

NORTHERN LIVINGSTON COUNTY — Caledonia, Lima, and Avon

Prior to the arrival of white settlers in 1795, the area now known as Caledonia was referred to as *Gan-e-o-di-ya* ("small clear lake") and *Na-gan-oose* ("clear running water") by the Turtle tribe of the Seneca. The area was a favorite camping ground, with such wildlife as deer and bear, and fruits like plums and grapes being plentiful. In 1799 the first Scottish settlers arrived in the area, and in 1806 the name was changed to Caledonia, which means "New Scotland." The first fish hatchery in the United States was started in Caledonia by Seth Green in 1864.

Lima, a village of historic homes surrounded by farmland, sits at the intersection of NY 15A and Routes 5 and 20. Considered the "Crossroads of Western New York," it was founded in 1788, near the crossing of two main Indian trails and the former site of a major Native American village. It was originally called Charleston and renamed Lima in 1808 by Paul Davidson, who was originally from Old Lyme, Connecticut. Lima was also home to the Genesee Wesleyan Seminary, one of the first coeducational schools in the country. The school closed in 1941, and since 1951 it has been the campus of the Elim Bible Institute.

In the past Avon was known for the sulphur spring and spas that attracted tourists to its many hotels. Today it is a bedroom community for Rochester and the location of Livingston County's major employer, Kraft Foods. The Avon plant is the only place where the company produces Cool Whip, making the town the "Cool Whip Capital of the World."

GUIDANCE **Town of Lima** (585-624-7911; www.townoflima.org), 7329 East Main Street, Lima. Open Monday, Tuesday, Thursday, Friday 8–12, and 1–4; Wednesday 9–12. In the same building as village offices.

Village of Lima (585-624-2210; www.crossroadscouncil.org), 7329 East Main Street, Lima. Open Monday, Tuesday, Thursday, Friday 8–12 and 1–4; Wednesday 9–12. In the same building as town offices.

Town of Caledonia (585-538-4927; www.cal-mum.com), 3109 Main Street, Caledonia. Open Monday, Tuesday, Thursday, Friday 8:30–12 and 1–4; Wednesday 8:30–12.

Village of Caledonia (585-538-6565), 3095 Main Street, Caledonia. Monday–Friday 8–12 and 1–4.

Town of Avon (585-226-2425; www.avon-ny.org), 27 Genesee Street, Avon. Open Monday, Tuesday, Thursday, Friday 8–4; Wednesday 8–12.

Village of Avon (585-226-8118), 74 Genesee Street, Avon. Open Monday–Friday 8–4.

GETTING THERE *By bus:* **Livingston Area Transportation Service** (585-335-3344), PO Box 355, Dansville. This public transportation service operates throughout Livingston County on a limited scheduled and call-for-ride service.

By car: This area can be reached from exit 10 off I-390; Routes 5 and 20 also travel through the towns.

MEDICAL EMERGENCY Dial 911.

✳ To See

MUSEUMS AND HISTORIC HOMES **Avon Historical Society** (585-226-2794, 585-226-8290; www.avonhistorical.org), 27 Genesee Street, Avon. Open by appointment only.

Big Springs Museum (585-538-9880; www.cal-mum.com), 3095 Main Street (Village Office Building), Caledonia. Open Sunday 1–4. This museum focuses on local history and heritage. Big Springs was an ancient Indian campsite on the Niagara Trail. The earliest white tourist came to the area in 1615, and the first Scottish settlers arrived in 1799. The region was the terminus of the Pioneer Railroad in 1838.

Caledonia Library (585-538-4512; www.cal-mum.com/library.htm), 3108 Main Street, Caledonia. Established 1873, the library is housed in an 1826 stone building that served the town as an early post office, bank, and apothecary shop.

Tennie Burton Museum (585-582-1130), NY 15A, Lima. Open Sunday 2–4 June–September. Displays on the history of the "Crossroads of Western New York."

HISTORIC SITES *A Walk Around Lima* A self-guided walking tour brochure of the many architecturally and historically significant buildings in Lima is available for $1 at the **Lima Pharmacy** (585-582-1140), 1923 Lake Avenue, Lima.

5 Arch Bridge, NY 39, Avon. This unique bridge was built in 1856–57 by the Genesee Valley Railroad to span the Conesus Outlet. The limestone bridge with five distinctive arches is 200 feet long and 12 feet wide. Avon was a railroad hub connecting Buffalo, Rochester, Corning, and Hornell, with 13 runs daily between Rochester and Mount Morris. This section of the rail line was abandoned in 1941, and the rails were removed. A small park is located beside the bridge.

Elim Bible Institute, College Street, Lima. The Greek Revival–style College Hall was completed in 1851. It is located next to the 1842 Genesee Wesleyan Seminary building, which serves as classrooms and dormitories.

Lima Bank Vault, South side of East Main Street, Lima. This vault commemorates the first bank robbery in Livingston County, which took place in the Bank of Lima on February 6, 1915.

Soldier's Monument, Caledonia. This monument in the center of town was dedicated in 1900 by then-governor of New York Theodore Roosevelt.

☀ To Do

AUTO RACING Limerock Speedway (585-538-2597), Flint Hill Road, Caledonia. Microsprint racing at New York's finest eighth-mile oval track.

FISHING Try your luck in **Oatka Creek,** which can be accessed on NY 36 near the junction of NY 383. Fishing licenses can be obtained at most town clerk's offices and most retail stores that sell fishing gear.

GOLF Caledonia Country Club (585-538-9956), 303 Park Place, Caledonia. An 18-hole, par-72 course open to the public Monday and Tuesday. It's the finest golf course in Livingston County and one of the top 25 Rochester-area golf courses.

Lima Golf & Country Club (585-624-1490), 2681 Plank Road, Lima. A 36-hole, par-72 course. Facilities include club rental, driving range, lessons, pro shop, carts, and restaurant.

GUIDED TOURS ☙ NYS Fish Hatchery (585-538-6300; www.dec.state.ny.us), 16 North Street, Caledonia. Open to the public 8–4 daily. Tours by appointment only Monday–Friday 9–3. Founded in 1870 by Seth Green, the "Father of Fish Culture," this was the first fish hatchery open in the entire western hemisphere. Many of the buildings are the original structures. The purpose of a fish hatchery is to raise fish to restock local streams and lakes with native species and to enhance recreational fishing. New York runs 12 hatcheries throughout the state. The Caledonia site raises primarily brown trout.

☀ Green Space

GARDENS Linwood Gardens (585-584-3913), York Road (off NY 36, northwest Livingston County), Linwood. The gardens are open to the public for two weekends each year in late May and early June. This garden estate, built between 1901 and 1910 by William Henry Gratwick II as a county home, is listed on the New York State Register of Historic Places. Maintained by Gratwick's granddaughter, Lee, the estate has close to 400 tree peonies along with numerous other plantings, fountains, and statues.

NATURE CENTERS Twin Cedars Environmental Area (585-226-2466), 6274 East Avon–Lima Road, Avon. Open year-round Monday–Friday, 8–4:30. Free admission The center includes 1.7 miles of trails, a 20-acre fishing pond, and an exhibit center.

PARKS Avon Driving Park, End of Spring Street, Avon. This park, which now has baseball diamonds, playground, and picnic pavilion, was once a pony-trotting area. At the turn of the 20th century it was the site of a sulphur spring and several hotels that accommodated guests who traveled here for the water's curative powers.

Mark Tubbs Park, Off Ziegler Road, Lima. Facilities include picnic area, sports fields, playgrounds, and paved trails; also the site of a summer concert series.

Park Circle, Routes 5 and 20, Avon. This small park with a gazebo in the center of town, along the newly renovated Main Street, is the site of the annual Avon Corn Festival.

✳ Lodging

INNS AND RESORTS The American Hotel (585-624-9464), 7304 Main Street, Lima. Open year-round. This Lima landmark has been owned and run by the Reynolds family since the 1920s. While they are best known for the variety of homemade soups served in their dining room, the family also offers overnight accommodations. The rooms are clean, comfortable, and decorated nicely, though they are a bit old fashioned: Six of the seven rooms have only sinks and showers and share a toilet down the hall. The seventh room has a private bath. $40–$50.

Avon Inn (585-226-8181; www .avoninn.com), 55 East Main Street, Avon. Open year-round, except first two weeks in January. Owner Linda Reusch Moran offers 14 air-conditioned rooms with private baths in this 1829 Greek Revival structure that's on the National Register of Historic Places. Built originally as a residence, the inn was operated in the late 1800s as a water-cure health center. Many notables were guests at the Avon Inn, including George Eastman, Henry Ford, Thomas Edison, and Katherine Hepburn. A self-service breakfast bar, featuring cereals, muffins, and beverages, is available to overnight guests. The inn's dining room is open to the public Wednesday–Sunday for dinner and Sunday breakfast buffet (see *Dining Out*). November 15–April 15 $65–$95, April 16–November 14 Monday–Thursday $65–$95, Friday–Sunday $75–$115.

BED & BREAKFASTS Charlton Bed & Breakfast (585-226-2838 or 1-800-667-6545; www.charltoninn.com), East Main Street (look for the driveway with carriage wheels), Avon. This 1894 mansion, built by famed Rochester architect J. Foster Warner, is set on 450 acres of farmland and offers year-round country elegance and hospitality in its four antiques-filled guest rooms. The master suite features a private bath, fireplace and garden view; the other rooms share baths. Hosts Pat and Joe Tuchrello serve a full country breakfast as well as a complimentary cheese and fruit platter in the evening. The inn, set back from the road amid beautiful gardens, is a popular setting for weddings. High tea, which includes teas, sandwiches, and sweets, is offered on select dates. $95–$150.

White Oak Bed & Breakfast (585-226-6735; www.whiteoakbandb.com), 277 Genesee Street, Avon. Open year-round. Three nicely decorated guest rooms with private baths are available in this elegant Second Empire Victorian home, which was constructed as a summer residence in 1850 for Asahel Wadsworth. Two of the rooms feature antique claw-foot tubs in the baths. Innkeeper Barbara Herman offers guests a snack upon arrival and a full country breakfast in the morning. $95-105.

OTHER LODGING Genesee Country Campground (585-538-4200), 40 Flint Hill Road, Caledonia. Open May 1–October 31. A 75-site campground with grassy and shaded areas. Amenities include a playground, basketball court, recreation room, and hiking trails. $22/night includes water and electric.

❋ Where to Eat

DINING OUT Avon Inn (585-226-8181; www.AvonInn.com), 55 East Main Street, Avon. Open Easter–November, Wednesday–Friday 4:30–9, Saturday 5–9, Sunday 9–1 breakfast buffet, 1:30–8 dinner; November–Easter open Friday–Sunday; call for hours. This 1829 Greek Revival structure, which is on the National Register of Historic Places, offers dining in their elegant dining room. Entrées include seafood, prime rib, poultry, beef, pasta, and country classics like chicken and biscuits and roast leg of lamb.

Springbrook Inn (585-538-2990), 26 North Street, Caledonia. Open for lunch Tuesday–Saturday 11:30–2; dinner Tuesday–Thursday 4:30–9, Friday–Saturday 4:30–10, Sunday 1–8; Sunday brunch, 10:30–2. Enjoy gracious dining in an 1818 inn whose prominent visitors in the past included Theodore Roosevelt. Specialties are steak and seafood.

The Village Inn (585-538-9530), 3137 Main Street, Caledonia. Open for lunch Tuesday–Saturday 11–2, dinner Tuesday–Thursday 4:30–9:30, Friday–Saturday 4:30–10, and Sunday 4:30–8. This restaurant, located in a vintage brick building, is noted for its fine dining. Choose from seafood, surf and turf, beef dishes, and more. A lunch buffet is served Monday–Friday, and early-bird dinner specials are offered daily.

EATING OUT The American Hotel (585-624-9464), 7304 Main Street,

Lima. Monday–Wednesday 11:30–9, Thursday 11:30–4, Friday and Saturday 11:30–8. This circa 1860 hotel, a Lima landmark, has been run by the Reynolds family since the 1920s. The hotel is noted for over 60 varieties of homemade soups, with usually a half dozen soups to chose from each day (the most requested is split pea). Another specialty: speidie sandwiches made with marinated chicken or pork and served topped with cheese and onions. See also *Lodging*.

Aunt Denise's Donut Den (585-732-0102), 7305 East Main Street, Lima. Open for breakfast Monday–Saturday 5–11. A small café offering coffee, donuts, bagels, and muffins.

Cozy Kitchen, 3103 Main Street, Caledonia. Open Friday 6–2, Saturday 6–noon, Sunday 7–noon. Breakfast and lunch are served in this small country restaurant with walls adorned with red-and-white checked wallpaper.

✿ ❦ **Crossroads Restaurant** (585-624-1590), 7281 West Main Street, Lima. Open Monday–Thursday 11–8:30, Friday 11–10, Saturday 11–9, Sunday 12–8. This family restaurant, which also has an adjacent taproom, features soups, salads, and specialty sandwiches for lunch as well as prime rib, chicken veal, seafood, and Italian entrées for dinner.

Iroquois Hotel (585-538-6331), 224 North Street, Caledonia. Open for lunch Monday–Saturday, dinners Friday evening. Casual dining in a former hotel dining room. Lunch selections include soups, sandwiches, and burgers. The Friday dinner menu includes a fish fry, sirloin steak, scallops and other seafood entrées, and chicken.

🍴 🌿 **Peppermints Family Restaurant** (585-226-2702), 244 East Main Street, Avon. Open daily 6–11 for breakfast, lunch, and dinner. A popular, reasonably priced family restaurant, with selections like roast chicken, Yankee pot roast, prime rib, and a Friday fish fry. Breakfast is served all day.

🍴 ♿ 🌿 **Tom Wahl's** (585-226-2420), 283 East Main Street, Avon. Open Sunday–Thursday 10:30–9, Friday–Saturday 10:30–10. Since 1955 Tom Wahl's has been a popular Finger Lakes destination for burgers, hot dogs, and chicken fingers. Enjoy quality food in this large restaurant with a 1950s diner theme, sporting old-time photos of Avon. Their special root beer, which can be ordered in a frosted glass mug, is worth the trip. Several other locations of this restaurant can be found throughout the region.

Town & Country (585-538-2150), 3013 Main Street, Caledonia. Open Monday–Saturday 5:30–9, Sunday 5:30–8. A small casual, family-style restaurant serving breakfast, lunch, and dinner.

✳ Selective Shopping

ANTIQUES **Another Time** (585-538-9730; www.boycetime.com), 3164 State Street (Route 5), Caledonia. Open Monday–Saturday 11–5:30. This shop, located in an 1897 building, features antiques and decorative items, including glass, china, textiles, vintage clothing, and furniture. The building, originally an undertaking business, later housed a meat market and five-and-dime store. It still has the shelving and cases from the five and dime, along with the original pressed tin decorative ceiling. All remnants of the undertaker are gone.

Avon Antiques and Artisans Mall (585-226-2906), 65 East Main Street (Routes 5 and 20), Avon. Open Wednesday–Saturday 10–5, Friday until 7. More than 40 vendors, featuring crafts, antiques and art are located in this 6,000 square foot complex, which is right next door to the historic Avon Inn.

Caledonia Antiques and More, LLC (585-538-2350; www.caledonia antiques.com), 3113 Main Street, Caledonia. Open 10–5 Tuesday–Sunday. More than 30 dealers offer fine antiques and collectibles on three floors of this vintage building.

Crossroads Country Mall (585-624-1993), 7348 East Main Street, Lima. Open October–May, Monday–Friday 11–5, Saturday–Sunday 10–5; June–September, daily 10–5. More than 50 dealers have quality antiques and collectibles displayed in 7,000 square feet on two floors in this former church. Choose from furniture, glassware, jewelry, primitives, used books, toys, and vintage clothing.

Curious Goods (585-538-6775 or 585-533-9048), 3133 Main Street, Caledonia. Open Friday–Sunday 12–5. A general line of quality antiques in a vintage building.

Fox Farm Antiques (585-226-6160; www.foxfarmantiques.com), 4127 Telephone Road, (US 20, 1 mile west of Route 5) Caledonia. Open Monday–Friday 1–5, Saturday–Sunday 11–5. At 14,000 square feet and three full floors, this is the largest single-owner antiques emporium in the area. Choose from furniture, lamps, china, glass, books, textiles, and more.

Lima Antiques (585-624-4700), 1804 Rochester Street (NY 15A) Lima. Open daily 11–5. This shop features a selection of small antiques, glassware, jewelry, collectible glassware, pottery, and china.

The Stray Cat Antiques & Gifts (585-538-2300), 3141 State Street, Caledonia. Open Thursday–Sunday 10–5. Cat-related items are prominent in this shop, located in an old stone building at the traffic circle. Two small tables in front of the store let shoppers relax and enjoy coffee, tea, or cookies.

SPECIAL SHOPS Country Depot (585-538-6610), 226 North Street (NY 36N) Caledonia. Open Tuesday–Saturday 10–5, Sunday 11–4. A vintage, rustic train station filled with handmade articles, hand-painted items, collectibles, candles, and other gift items.

Debue's Book Shop (585-624-3730), 7310 East Main Street, Lima. Open Monday, Wednesday–Saturday 11–5. An inventory of over 20,000 used and out-of-print books, plus a selection of recent books. They also have collectible postcards and ephemera along with decorative folk-art items painted by the owner's wife.

Food for the Soul, 7303 East Main Street, Lima. Open Monday, Wednesday, and Friday 3–6. A Christian bookstore that also carries CDs and videos.

Gigglin' Pig (1-800-649-2930; www .gigglinpig.com), 3090-3092 Main Street, Caledonia. Open Monday–Saturday 9–5, Sunday 12–5.They have one of the largest selections of country wares and Amish handcrafted furniture in the area. If you only have time to shop in one store, this is the place to come. Housed in two buildings, this shop has new Amish-made furniture, candles, country decor, linens, yard ornaments, seasonal decorations, and much more. The shop's historic Keith House, a stone building erected in 1827, served the area as an early tavern, post office, and bank.

Knit one, Scrapbook Too (585-538-2639 www.countryatheartcrafts.com), 3096 Main Street (Route 5), Caledonia. Open daily 11–5, extended holiday hours. Knitting supplies, yarn, scrapbooking supplies, and handmade gifts. Knitting and scrapbooking lessons are offered.

Kurt's Trains and Hobbies (585-538-2960), 3133 Main Street, Caledonia. Open Monday, Thursday, Friday 6–9, Saturday 10–5, Sunday 12–5. Specializing in model trains and accessories.

Lima Pharmacy (585-582-1140), 1923 Lake Avenue, Lima. Open Monday–Thursday 9–6, Friday 9–7, Saturday 9–3. This store has more than just pharmacy items. Choose from gift items, hardware, school supplies, toys, and more.

McKenzie's Mercantile (585-538-2038), 1013 Main Street, Mumford. Open Tuesday–Sunday 11–5. A large selection of country wares for the garden and home can be found at this store located in a former firehouse. Choose from folk art, pottery, lamps, art prints, antiques, candles and more.

1788 Gift Country (585-624-3950), 7308 East Main Street, Lima. Monday–Friday 10–5, Saturday 10–4. This shop offers a large variety of gift items, including Ty plush animals, porcelain dolls, pottery, items relating to local history, cards, lighthouses, doll furniture, and much more. **Traditional Cupola & Millwork**, which specializes in custom designed woodwork, weathervanes and cupolas is located within this store.

Tin and Brass Works (585-538-2160), Corner of Main and State Street, Mumford. Open Wednesday–Friday 11–5:30, Saturday 11–5, Sunday 11–5:30. Tinsmith Bob Beltz, who is one of the resident tinsmiths at nearby Genesee Country Village, creates all sorts of tin and brass items for the home. His wife, Jo, complements his wares with an array of quilted items.

✳ Special Events

July: **Lima Crossroads Festival** (585-582-1481), Throughout the village of Lima. A summertime celebration of Lima's heritage.

August: **Livingston County Fair** (585-538-2168; www.caledoniafair .org), PO Box 85, 310 Leicester Street, Caledonia. A small agricultural fair that features displays plus fun activities for the entire family. **Avon Corn Festival** (585-226-8485), Park Circle, Avon. This day-long event, which takes place the second Saturday of August, features crafts, artisans, musical entertainment, and food vendors.

CENTRAL LIVINGSTON COUNTY—Mount Morris, Cuylerville, Geneseo, Piffard, Lakeville, Livonia, Conesus, and Hemlock Lakes

The first permanent white settler in Mount Morris was William Mills, who was dedicated to developing the region and was instrumental in establishing Livingston County. The name of the town honors Robert Morris, a land speculator, referred to as the "financier of the American Revolution." Mount Morris is the birthplace of Francis Bellamy, the author of the "Pledge of Allegiance." The town is also the site of the Mount Morris Dam, built in the late 1940s and early 1950s to prevent flooding in the Genesee Valley region. It has been aptly named "Best Town by a Damsite."

The village of Geneseo, which was designated a National Historic Landmark in 1991, was first settled in 1790. *Ge-ne-se-o* is a Seneca name meaning "beautiful valley." Leading architects consider the streets of Geneseo a museum of historic buildings, from Federal style to Colonial Revival. The two mansions occupying either end of Main Street were built by brothers James and William Wadsworth, the founders of Geneseo. Their descendants still live in the homes. Another Geneseo landmark is the bear fountain, found in the center of Main Street. Geneseo was named the Livingston County seat in 1821 and incorporated in 1832. The town is home to SUNY Geneseo.

Piffard and Culyerville are two of the small agricultural towns in the area. Piffard is best known for the Abbey of the Genesee, a religious community that makes the locally popular Monks' Bread found in western New York supermarkets.

Livonia, whose name was derived from a Russian province, was first settled in 1783 by Solomon Woodruff. Today Livonia is a popular vacation area, with many cottages dotting the shoreline of nearby Conesus Lake. Livonia is also known as the birthplace of Irving "The Deacon" Crane, seven-time world billiard champion, the only man to win world championships in four different decades. The small village of Lakeville is at the northern end of—appropriately—Conesus Lake.

The town of Conesus, founded in 1820, was named after the Seneca word *Ga-ne-a-sos*, which means "long string of berries." The area surrounding Hemlock Lake was a popular fishing area for the Seneca Nation prior to western settlement. The first settler, Philip Short, arrived in 1795, with other settlers to follow in the early 1800s. In the 1850s what is now route 15A was a wooden-plank toll road between Rochester and points south. By the 1870s Hemlock Lake was a popular summer vacation destination, with more than 100 cottages, five hotels, a railroad station with four trains daily to Rochester, sawmills, and five steamboats operating on the lake. Then a cholera epidemic and fires forced the nearby city of Rochester to find a clean and reliable water supply. Hemlock Lake was chosen for the purity of the water and the fact that the water could be gravity fed. The city obtained rights to the lake, and eventually all the hotels, cottages, and other structures were torn down. The lake is now the main source of drinking water for Rochester, and the area is a quiet, rural bedroom community.

GUIDANCE Livingston County Chamber of Commerce (585-243-2222; www.fingerlakeswest.com), 4560 Millennium Drive (in the Oak Valley Inn), Geneseo. Open Monday–Friday 8:30–4:30.

Hemlock Area History (www.wemett.net). A very interesting Web site with information on the Hemlock area and local genealogy.

Livonia Area Chamber of Commerce (585-346-2620; www.livoniachamber .com), Contact by phone only.

Town of Livonia (585-346-2157), 35 Commercial Street, Livonia. Open Monday–Friday 8–4:30.

Village of Mount Morris (585-658-4160; www.villageofmountmorris.com), 117 Main Street, Mount Morris. Open Monday–Friday 9–5.

Town of Geneseo (585-243-0722), 119 Main Street, Geneseo. Open Monday–Friday 8:30–4:30.

Town of Conesus (585-346-3130), 6210 South Livonia Road, Livonia. Open Monday and Wednesday 8–4, Thursday 9–1, first and third Tuesday 5–7.

GETTING THERE *By car:* This region is easily reached off I-390—Geneseo and Livonia from exit 8 and Mount Morris from exit 9. This area can also be reached from the west via the NYS Thruway (I-90) Batavia exit #46 and following NY 63 to Geneseo, NY 63 to NY 36 to Mount Morris, or US 20A out of Geneseo to the Livonia area.

MEDICAL EMERGENCY Dial 911.

✳ To See

ART MUSEUMS Lederer Art Gallery (585-245-5657), 1 College Circle, Geneseo. Open when college is in session 2–5 daily and Thursday 12–8. Changing exhibits by students, faculty, and alumni of SUNY Geneseo.

Lockhart Gallery (585-245-5448), 26 Main Street, Geneseo. Open when college is in session 2–5 daily, Thursday 12–8. This museum has a variety of exhibits by students, faculty, and alumni of SUNY Geneseo.

HISTORIC SITES **Abbey of the Genesee** (585-243-0660; geneseeabbey.org), 3258 River Road, Piffard. Bread store open 8–11 AM, 1:30–3:30 PM and 5:30–6:30 PM. The Abbey of the Genesee is a community of Contemplative Monks that belong to the Order of Cistercians of the Strict Observance, better known as Trappists, whose daily life consists of prayer, spiritual readings, and manual labor. The fruit of their manual labor is known as Monks' Bread, which is sold in stores in Buffalo, Rochester, and Syracuse—and right here at the abbey in the bread store. The recipe for the bread, which comes in five varieties, was created by Brother Sylvester, and the sale of this bread has supported the abbey since 1955. Along with the bread store, there is also a bookstore—and, of course, the church is open for prayer.

Mount Morris Dam (585-658-4790; www.lrb.usace.army.mil/brochure/mmd .html), William B. Hoyt II Visitors Center, 1 Mount Morris Dam, Mount Morris. Open daily mid-January–mid-November 8–4; tours Monday–Thursday at 2 and Friday–Saturday at 11 and 3. (Note: Anyone going on a dam tour must provide identification. Purses, backpacks, and bulky jackets are not permitted in the dam for security purposes.) Mount Morris Dam is located deep in the Genesee River Gorge, known as the Grand Canyon of the East. It is the largest dam of its type east of the Mississippi River. The 1,028-foot-long, 790-foot-high dam, operated by the U.S. Army Corps of Engineers, was constructed from 1948 to 1952 as a result of the Flood Control Act of 1944. The dam provides protection to farmland, residential areas, and businesses in the Genesee River Valley. Before the

MOUNT MORRIS DAM IS THE LARGEST DAM OF ITS TYPE EAST OF THE MISSISSIPPI.

Christine A. Smyczynski

dam was built, major floods ravaged the area about every seven years. Information about the dam's history and operation can be found in the state-of-the-art, 5,400-square-foot visitors center near the dam.

MUSEUMS AND HISTORIC HOMES **Livingston County Historical Society** (585-243-9147; www.livingstoncountyhistoricalsocity.org), 30 Center Street, Geneseo. Open May–October Thursday and Sunday 2–5 (also open Tuesday during July and August). The collections of the Livingston County Historical Society, including tools, household items and Native American artifacts, are housed in a 1838 cobblestone schoolhouse. The society, founded in 1876, is one of the oldest organizations of its kind in western New York. A separate shelter on the grounds houses a preserved section of the "Big Tree," a giant oak famous locally in the 1800's.

Livonia Area Preservation and Historical Society (Maurice F. Sweeney Museum) (585-346-4579), 10 Commercial Street, Livonia. Open Friday and Saturday 10–2. Free admission. This museum, housed in an 1871 building, contains a collection of antique tools, 19th-century medical instruments, domestic goods, and war memorabilia, along with information on local history.

Gen. William Mills Mansion (585-658-3292), 14 Main Street, Mount Morris. Open June–October Friday–Sunday 12–4 or by appointment. Donation. This restored 1838 Federal-style brick house, listed on the National Register of Historic Places, was the home of Gen. William Mills, the founder of Mount Morris. The 14-room mansion features an elegant staircase and an open hearth and bake oven.

1941 Historical Aircraft Group Museum, (716-243-2100; www.1941hag.org), Geneseo Airport (off NY 63), Geneseo. Open daily 10–4. Admission: $4 adults, 12 and under free admission. The 1941 Historical Aircraft Group is dedicated to restoring and flying vintage aircraft and preserving aviation history. They currently have seven planes fully restored and on display on airport grounds. Call for tours and information on events.

Tired Iron Tractor Museum (585-382-3110 or 585-382-9736), US 20A, Cuylerville. Open by appointment. Admission: $4. Over 100 tractors, trucks, and horse-drawn equipment as well as photos, toys, and a replica of an old-fashioned kitchen are on display at this unique museum.

WALKING TOUR A **walking tour brochure** published by the Association for the Preservation of Geneseo is available from the **Livingston County Chamber of Commerce**. This brochure describes notable homes on and near Main Street. Geneseo, a designated National Landmark Village, is one of the most pleasant small towns in western New York to walk around in, with its Victorian architecture, tree-lined streets, and views of the surrounding countryside.

WINERIES **Deer Run Winery** (585-346-0850; www.deerwunwinery.com), 3772 West Lake Road, Geneseo. Open year-round Saturday–Sunday 12–5; may be open additional days, depending on time of year. George and Joan Kuyon launched this winery on the west side of Conesus Lake in 2003. Wines include

Water Tower White, a blend of seyval blanc and vidal blanc, and Runway Red, a red table wine.

& **Eagle Crest Vineyards** (585-346-2321), 7107 Vineyard Road, Conesus. Open year-round Monday–Friday 8:30–4:30. This vineyard was established in 1872 by Bishop Bernard McQuaid, the first Catholic bishop of Rochester, and still produces altar and table wines using the original barrels, casks, and fermentation tanks. The wine is produced according to Cannon Law, with no additives or sugar. The label reads *O-neh-da,* the Seneca word for Hemlock Lake. The vineyard also markets several wines to the general public, which are available for purchase in the winery's tasting room.

✳ To Do

AUTO RACING **New York International Raceway Park** (585-382-3030; www.nyrip.com), 2011 New Road, Leicester. Season April–October. Hosts IHRA and NHRA drag-racing events on Saturdays and Sundays during the season. See Web site, or call for specifics.

FISHING **Long Point Park, Conesus Lake State Park, Hemlock Lake, Hemlock Creek, Genesee River.** More information on these fishing areas can be obtained from the **NYS Department of Environmental Conservation** (www.dec.state.ny.us). Note that access to Hemlock Lake is by permit only, which can be obtained free by sending a SASE to: City of Rochester, Watershed Permit, 7412 Rix Hill Road, Hemlock, NY 14466. There is also a kiosk set up near the lake where you can obtain a permit on the spot.

GOLF **Beards Creek** (585-382-4653), 2261 Pine Tavern Road, Leicester. A 9-hole, par-35 challenging course with many natural hazards.

Livingston Country Club (585-243-4430), Lakeville Road, US 20A, Geneseo. An 18-hole, par-72 course with pro shop and restaurant.

Old Hickory (585-346-2450), 6655 Big Tree Road, Livonia. An 18 hole, par-72 course.

MARINAS **Jansen Marina, Inc.** (585-346-2060; www.Jansenmarina.com), 5750 East Lake Road, Conesus.

Leisure Time Marina (585-346-2260; www.Leisuretimemarine.com), 5364 East Lake Road, Conesus.

Lakeville Marina Service (585-346-6010), 5942 Vanzandt Road, Livonia.

Richard's Marine Service (585-346-5307), 4087 East Lake Road, Livonia.

✳ Green Space

GARDENS **Spencer J. Roemer Arboretum** (585-245-5448), 1 College Circle, Geneseo. Open dawn to dusk. Over 70 species of trees, shrubs, and wildflowers are located on 20 acres on the South Campus of SUNY Geneseo near NY 20A and 63. Included are several oak trees over 200 years old and walnut trees over 100 years old.

PARKS Al Lorenz Park, Murray Hill Road, Mount Morris. Open dawn to dusk. This park in the north section of Mount Morris features walking trails, picnic pavilions, and a large playground.

Bellamy Memorial Park, Lackawanna Avenue, Mount Morris. Open dawn to dusk. This 19-acre recreational park has a playground, basketball courts, and baseball and soccer fields. It also has one of the few historical baseball grandstands in existence.

Conesus Lake State Park (585-493-3600 www.nyspark.com), East Lake Road, Livonia. Open mid-April–mid-Oct. Open dawn to dusk. This park has a boat launch, picnic tables, and rest rooms.

Hemlock Town Park, NY 15A, Hemlock. Open dawn to dusk. This park overlooks Hemlock Lake. It has a playground, rest rooms, pavilion, and picnic tables.

Letchworth State Park (585-493-3600), 1 Letchworth State Park, Castile. Open dawn to dusk. Bordering Livingston County on the west is Letchworth State Park, known as the Grand Canyon of the East for its 600-foot deep gorge.

THE GENESEE RIVER RUNS THROUGH LETCHWORTH STATE PARK, GOING OVER 20 DIFFERENT WATERFALLS

Christine A. Smyczynski

The Genesee River goes over 20 different waterfalls, including three major ones, as it snakes through the gorge in the park. Some 66 miles of hiking trails criss-cross the 14,350-acre, 17-mile-long park, and there are also trails for horseback riding, biking, snowmobiling, and cross-country skiing. Campers love this park for the 270 campsites and 80 cabins. Naturalists and guides are on hand to give lectures and conduct workshops on the park's history, geology, flora, and fauna. William Pryor Letchworth, a Buffalo businessman, gave the original 1,000 acres of the park to the state by in 1859. Located within the park is the Glen Iris Inn, formerly Letchworth's country home. During the summer months two pools are open for swimming as are the picnic areas and playgrounds. In the winter, visitors enjoy ice skating, snowmobiling, cross-country skiing, snowtubing, and horse-drawn sleigh rides. Deer and turkey hunting are permitted in-season.

Long Point Park, West Lake Road, Geneseo. Open dawn to dusk. This site of a former amusement park, Long Point offers access to Conesus Lake, picnic facilities, and fishing sites. Other park features include swimming and miniature golf.

Vitale Park, NY 20A, Lakeville. Open dawn to dusk. A public park on the northern shores of Conseus Lake.

WALKING AND HIKING TRAILS Genesee Valley Greenway Friends of the Genesee Valley Greenway (585-658-2569; www.fogvg.org), PO Box 42, Mount Morris, NY 14510. Access off NY 36 just south of Mount Morris. This multiuse trail, which will eventually extend 90 miles from Rochester to Olean, was created along the former railbed of the Pennsylvania Railroad and the canal towpath left from the Genesee Valley Canal of 1840–78. This level trail can be used for hiking, biking, and in some sections horseback riding and snowmobiling. Maps can be obtained by contacting FOGVG.

Finger Lakes Trail. Finger Lakes Trail Conference (585-658-9320; www.finger lakestrail.org), 6111 Visitors Center Road, Mount Morris, NY 14510. The Finger Lakes Trail is an 800-mile hiking trail system that runs from Albany west into the Finger Lakes region, where it has several branches. A narrow footpath designed for hiking, the trail is often hilly. Maps can be purchased through the above address.

PONDS AND LAKES Two of the smaller western Finger Lakes, **Conesus Lake** and **Hemlock Lake,** are located in eastern Livingston County. Conesus Lake, which is about 8 miles long, has two public parks—Vitale Park on the northern tip and Long Point on the western shores. Hemlock Lake has a public park with picnic tables and hiking trails. Conesus, east of NY 256 and south of US 20A near Lakeville, is well developed and busy, while Hemlock Lake, which runs parallel to NY 15A, has an undeveloped shoreline. Access to Hemlock Lake is by permit only, which can be obtained for free by sending a SASE: to City of Rochester, Watershed Permit, 7412 Rix Hill Road, Hemlock, NY 14466. Permits are also available at a kiosk set up near the lake. Only rowboats, canoes, and very small motorboats (less than 7 HP) are permitted on Hemlock Lake since it supplies water to Rochester. There is a nest of bald eagles at the south end of the lake, plus hiking trails along the lake shore.

✳ Lodging

INNS AND RESORTS Oak Valley Inn (585-243-5570; www.oakvalley inn.com), 4562 Millennium Drive, Geneseo. In the mid 1800s this building served as the almshouse for the poor. In 1990 the structure was restored and turned into an inn of distinction. The inn offers 13 guest rooms with private baths and air-conditioning, some with fireplaces and whirlpool tubs. The two-room, two-story honeymoon suite features a king-sized bed, fireplace, two-person shower, and whirlpool tub. Innkeepers Keith and Marilyn Hollis serve breakfast each morning. $60–$195.

MOTELS AND HOTELS Country Inn & Suites by Carlton (585-658-4080; www.countryinns.com), 130 North Main Street, Mount Morris. A newly built motel with 60 rooms located an eighth mile from the entrance to Letchworth State Park. Amenities include an indoor pool, exercise room, and complimentary continental breakfast. $85–$144.

🐾 **The Greenway Motel** (585-658-4500; www.greenwaymotel.com), Mount Morris–Sonyea Road (NY 36), Mount Morris. Twenty-three quiet, comfortable, air-conditioned rooms in a country setting are available just 2 miles from Letchworth State Park and directly across the street from the Genesee Valley Greenway Trail. $55–$65, $10 each additional person.

BED & BREAKFASTS Allan's Hill Bed & Breakfast (585-658-4591; wwwbbonline.com/ny/allanshill), 2513 Sand Hill Road (off NY 408 S), Mount Morris. Open year-round. Joyce and George Swanson's 1830 country home is located on 16 acres

of land overlooking a small pond. They offer one large room with a private bath. An additional bedroom is available if your party requires more than one room. A full breakfast is served. $70–$80.

Allegiance Bed & Breakfast (585-658-3524; www.allegiancebandb.com), 145 Main Street, Mount Morris. This elegant, fully restored, 29-room Victorian mansion, originally built in 1838 by Reuben P. Wisner, offers nine uniquely furnished guest rooms, each with a private bath. The inn, situated on 1.4 landscaped acres, features original hardwood floors, crystal chandeliers, and period furnishings. Your hosts Steven Luick and Glenda Giles-Luick serve daily breakfast either in the dining room or the fully enclosed sunroom. $100–$75.

Annabel Lee Bed & Breakfast Inn (585-243-9440; www.theannabelee .com), 16 Main Street, Geneseo. Open year-round. Mark and Kristen Scoville offer five guest rooms in this 1889 Victorian inn on Geneseo's historic Main Street. Each room has a private bath, cable TV, and a phone. Robert's Room has a sleigh bed, fireplace, and bay window, while Hans's Room has a mahogany queen bed and a view of Main Street. Anna's Room has a king bed and sunset view, and the cozy Hummingbird's Nest has a queen bed. The inn's largest room, the Garden Suite, offers a king bed, Jacuzzi, and gas fireplace. A Jacuzzi on the third floor is available to all guests on a sign-up basis for an additional charge. $100–$165.

East Lake Bed & Breakfast (585-346-3350 or 866-222-1544; www .eastlakebb.com), 5305 East Lake Road, Conesus. Open year-round. Innkeepers Charlotte and Dennis

Witte offer four guest rooms in a Prairie-style cottage whose wraparound porch has a great view of Conesus Lake. Each room has a queen-sized bed and private bath. The Romance Room, decorated in shades of yellow and pink, features a fireside whirlpool tub and a second-floor deck. The Interlude Room, decorated in an apple blossom and lilac theme, has an in-room Jacuzzi and fireplace. The Garden Room is decorated with a gazebo theme and has a lake-view deck. The Study has a private entrance and lake view. A full country breakfast is included with all rooms. $100–$189.

MacPhail House Bed & Breakfast (585-346-5600; www.MacPhail House.com), 5477 Lakeville Road (US 20A, 1 mile east of exit 8 off I-390), Geneseo. This year-round, small country inn, about a mile from Cone-

sus Lake, features a pair of two-room suites with private baths. Innkeeper Scottie Macphail Emery has bedecked her 1818 farmhouse with antiques, rare books, and other memorabilia, including several Christmas feather trees, one decorated with the annual White House ornaments. A full breakfast is served. $85+.

The Silver Tendril Bed & Breakfast (585-243-3912; www.Silver Tendril.com), 3054 Main Street (NY 36), Piffard. Open year-round. Gary and Shirley Cox offer two unique guest rooms in a well-preserved 1827 Federal-style brick home, decorated with a grape-and-wine theme. The Monet room, with its queen-sized bed and private bath, features replicas of works by the 19th-century master. The Shaker room has a king-sized bed and Shaker reproduction furniture. The grounds feature Gary's 150-vine

BUILT IN 1838, THE ALLEGIANCE BED & BREAKFAST OFFERS UNIQUE AND ELEGANT ACCOMMODATIONS TO GUESTS

Christine A. Smyczynski

vineyard, flower gardens, and a pond. About 30 years ago Gary started making wine as a hobby. He has perfected the craft, and guests at the inn get to sample his award-winning wines. A full breakfast is served in the dining room. Supervised children 13 and older. $85.

OTHER LODGING Conesus Lake Campground (585-346-5472; www .gocampingamerica.com/conesuslake), 5609 East Lake Road, Conesus. Open May 15–October 15. This 100-site campground features an indoor pool, fishing, playground, and game room.

❋ Where to Eat

DINING OUT Big Tree Inn (585-243-5220; www.bigtreeinn.com), 46 Main Street, Geneseo. Open for lunch Tuesday–Saturday 11:30-2, dinner Tuesday and Wednesday 4–8, Friday and Saturday 4–10. Fine dining in a relaxed atmosphere in a historic 1833 inn named after a great oak tree that once stood near Geneseo. Samuel Clemens and President Theodore Roosevelt are some of the notable guests who have dined here. Dinner selections include steaks, chops, salmon, and pasta. For lunch choose from homemade soups or favorite sandwiches like a Reuben or Monte Cristo.

Club 41 (585-243-4828), 41 Main Street, Geneseo. Open daily at 4, Sunday at noon. Fine tavern-style dining in a historic landmark structure.

Conesus Inn (585-346-6100, www .conesusinn.com), 5654 East Lake Road, Conesus. Open Sunday 4–7, Tuesday–Thursday 5–7, Friday–Saturday 5–9. Closed January 1–April 1. This restaurant has lovely stained-glass windows over the bar and a great view of Conesus Lake. The menu features prime rib, seafood, lobster, crab, and shrimp.

Dominic's Restaurant (585-658-4430), 27 Chapel Street, Mount Morris. Open Monday–Friday 11–11, Saturday 5–11. Serving the finest Italian cuisine in Livingston County, including homemade pasta and veal dishes, as well as seafood, steak, and chicken.

Fratelli's (585-346-6160), NY 15 near NY 256, Lakeville. Open for lunch Tuesday–Friday 11–3, dinner Tuesday–Sunday 3–9. A casual restaurant that serves the best authentic Italian food in Lakeville.

Genesee River Restaurant (585-658-2949; www.geneseeriver restaurant.com), 134 North Main Street, Mount Morris. Open daily for lunch 11–3, dinner 5–9; Sunday brunch 11–2. This popular restaurant, originally known as the Genesee River Hotel, has been operated by the same family for over 40 years. The lunch menu features salads, sandwiches, and burgers, while the dinner menu offers more substantial entrées like New York strip steak, prime rib, seafood platter, and a variety of chicken, pork, and pasta dishes.

Mills Race Restaurant (585-658-9470; www.villageofmountmorris .com/millsracerestaurant.htm), 10 Mill Street, Mount Morris. Open for lunch Wednesday–Friday 11:30–1:30, dinner Tuesday–Saturday 4–8:30, Sunday 4–7:30. The menu features steaks, fresh seafood, and Italian-American cuisine. They are famous for their decadent desserts.

The National Hotel (585-382-3130), 2827 Main Street, Cuylerville. Open Wednesday and Thursday 5–9, Friday and Saturday 4:40–10, Sunday 3–9. The National Hotel was originally built as a stagecoach stop in 1837 and called the National Exchange. Shortly after that, abolitionist Trusall Lamson purchased it, and it became an important stop on the Underground Railroad until the 1850s. It later served the town as a tavern and dance hall, town hall, and whiskey distillery. Today proprietors Art and Violet Allen offer dining selections that include prime rib, filet mignon, veal parmigiana, and assorted chicken and seafood dishes.

Yard of Ale Canal House Inn (585-243-3380), NY 63, Piffard Open for lunch Tuesday–Saturday 11:30–2, Sunday brunch 10:30–2, dinner Sunday 12–8, Tuesday–Thursday 4:30–9, Friday–Saturday 4:30–10. Enjoy casual fine dining in a historic restaurant that dates back to the days of the Genesee Valley Canal.

EATING OUT Bank Street Bagel Café (585-245-9080), Main Street at Bank, Geneseo. Open Monday–Saturday 7–4, Sunday 8–3. This café features gourmet coffee, bagels, gourmet sandwiches, and soups.

Bob's Dugout (585-658-2880), 39 Mill Street, Mount Morris. Open seasonally. This casual hot dog stand features charbroil foods and ice cream.

🍴 ♿ **Brian's USA Diner** (585-658-9380; www.briansusadiner.com), 5524 Mount Morris Road, Mount Morris. Open for breakfast, lunch, and dinner Sunday–Thursday 5:45–8, Friday and Saturday 5:45–9. This busy diner, formerly the Loafing Tree Restaurant, offers home cooking just like Grandma's. Come hungry, because portions are extra-large. Menu selections

include burgers, wraps, salads, diner-style diners such as mile-high meat loaf and country fried steak, Italian dishes, seafood, and steaks. Take-out is available. Located close to the Mount Morris entrance of Letchworth State Park.

🌹 🍴 **Geneseo Family Restaurant** (585-243-3240), 105 Main Street, Geneseo. Open Monday–Saturday 7–8, Sunday 7–2. This family-style restaurant features standard American fare with really quick service and reasonable prices.

Leaning Tower (585-658-3600), 25 Main Street, Mount Morris. Open Monday–Thursday 11–10, Friday and Saturday 11–midnight, Sunday noon–10. The best place for pizza, subs, wings, and salads in Mount Morris.

🍴 🌹 **Lee's Famous Hot Dogs,** NY 15A by the bridge, Hemlock. Open year-round Monday–Saturday 10:30–2:30. Don't be fooled by appearances. This postage-stamp-sized eatery, which is just a little bit bigger than a hot dog vendor's cart, serves some of the best burgers and dogs in the area. Lee Wemett, a large, friendly man with a long red ponytail, started this business in 1991, at the Hemlock Fair and decided to set up shop year-round in "downtown" Hemlock. You can take out or eat in; the stand has two tables in the attached shed and picnic tables outside. (Lee sets up heaters in the shed in the winter months.) If you're looking for information on the Hemlock area, Lee's the man to see. His Web site (www.wemett.net) has information on the Hemlock area as well as the history of neighboring towns and Wemett family genealogy dating back to 1350.

Leisure's Restaurant and Banquet Facility (585-346-2120), NY 15 and

US 20A at Bronson Hill Road, Lakeville. Open daily 6–8, Friday and Saturday until 9:30. This casual family restaurant features a luncheon buffet Monday–Friday as well as breakfast and dinner daily.

Miceli's Main Street Deli (585-243-9100), 82 Main Street, Geneseo. Open Monday–Friday 9–8, Saturday and Sunday 10–8. This small, quaint café overlooking Main Street features homemade soups, salads, subs, and sandwiches.

❀ **Minnehans Family Restaurant and Fun Center** (585-346-6167), Corner of US 20A and NY 256, Lakeville. Open Monday–Saturday 8 AM–10 PM. This casual restaurant serves up hot dogs and burgers as well as ice cream treats. They have a miniature golf course, go-carts, batting cages, and an arcade.

The South End Cafe (585-658-3060), NY 36 (next to the Greenway Motel), Mount Morris. Open Monday–Saturday 11–11. This small yet busy café specializes in gourmet burgers, salads, and deli sandwiches. They offer daily specials, including a fresh haddock fish fry on Friday.

❈ Selective Shopping

ANTIQUES **Allegiance Antiques** (585-658-5470), 35 Main Street, Mount Morris. Open Monday–Saturday 9:30–5. A nicely displayed selection of furniture, quilts, glassware, books, paintings, and more. (Look up at the original pressed tin ceilings.)

Red Gables Antiques (585-346-6490), 5812 Big Tree Road (US 20A), Lakeville. Open Thursday–Sunday 11–5. This shop has a general line of antiques.

SPECIAL SHOPS **Atties** (585-243-1380), 109 Main Street, Geneseo. Open Monday, Wednesday, Saturday 10–5; Tuesday, Friday 10–6; Thursday 10–8. They carry a huge selection of children's special-occasion clothing.

B & D Art and Framing (585-243-3060), 118 1/2 Main Street, Geneseo. Open Tuesday–Friday 10–5, Saturday 10–2. This tiny shop specializes in custom framing. They also carry a selection of posters, gift items, antiques, and art prints, including pen-and-ink drawings of local buildings by co-owner/artist Donna Kelsey.

♿ **Chocolate Bar** (585-346-9680), 5812 Big Tree Road, Lakeville. Open Tuesday–Thursday 11–7, Friday and Saturday 11–10, Sunday 9–5. This shop features a coffee and tea bar, as well as real hot cocoa and pastries. You can also purchase 25 flavors of truffles, 27 flavors of filled chocolates, 6 flavors of fudge, and sugar-free chocolates.

♿ **1812 Country Store** (585-367-2802; www.1812countrystore.com), 4270 NY 15A, Hemlock. Open Tuesday–Saturday 10–5, Sunday 12–5. Browse inside an 1812 barn for antiques, gifts and home decor. You can find reproductions, quilts, primitive items, candles, cards, lampshades, baskets, and textiles. The store also has an old-fashioned "penny candy" counter and New York State cheddar cheese.

Pictures & Presents (585-243-5376 www.picturesandpresents.com), 53 Main Street, Geneseo. Open Monday–Friday 10–6, Saturday 10–5, Sunday 12–4. Handcrafted jewelry and pottery, cards, photo supplies, and custom framing.

Pots 'o Paint (585-243-5380), 61 Main Street, Geneseo. Open Monday

4–10, Tuesday–Friday 12–8, Saturday 11–8, Sunday 1–5. A pottery shop where you get to be the artist. Choose from over 150 items to paint. When you're done, leave your creation with the staff, and they'll glaze it and fire it in the kiln. You pick up the finished product a few days later.

Touch of Grayce (585-243-4980), 65 Main Street, Geneseo. Open Monday–Saturday 10–6, Thursday until 7, Sunday 12–4. This shop, located in a historic building with a pressed tin ceiling and vintage ceiling fans, has a nice selection of books, cards, toys, puzzles and more.

Seasonal Gift Shop (585-658-4522), 2562 Perry Road (off NY 36 between Leicester and Mount Morris), Mount Morris. Open all year Monday–Friday 10–6, Saturday 10–5, Sunday 10–4. Located down a country road and up a winding driveway, this shop features 15 rooms full of unique gift items, including Amish furniture, baskets, tinware, candles, figurines, homespun fabrics, wreaths, and a year-round Christmas room. This shop is well worth the trip.

& **Victorian Rose** (585-658-3330), 3134 NY 408, Mount Morris. Open daily 10–6. This unique shop takes you back to the turn of the 20th century. Choose from a selection of all new Victorian-inspired gifts, crafts, and candles plus Victorian reproduction furniture. The shopkeeper is even dressed in Victorian style!

✳ Special Events

May: **Fire on the Genesee** (585-493-3600), Letchworth State Park. Civil War encampment and battle re-enactments.

July: **Conseus Lake Ring of Fire** (585-346-3130). Public viewing at Long Point Park or Vitale Park. This annual event, which takes place on July 3rd, kicks off the summer season. It began in 1922 as a fireworks display but, when fireworks were banned during World War II, cottage owners turned to flares to light up the night sky. Each property owner lights flares at 10 PM and the "ring of fire" lasts for about a half hour. Since there are no gaps on this ring of fire, it is one of the most impressive events of this type in the Finger Lakes region. The best places for public viewing are from Long Point Park or Vitale Park. **History of Flight Airshow,** Geneseo (585-243-2100; www.1941hag.org) Geneseo Airport, just west of the village. Admission: $7. An air show featuring vintage planes, warplanes, and experimental aircraft. **Highbanks Celtic Gathering** (585-493-3600), Letchworth State Park. Highland games, Celtic crafts, bagpipes, and more. **Livingston County Hemlock Fair** (wwwhemlockfair.org), NY 15A, north end of Hemlock Lake. This "Little World's Fair" has taken place in the Hemlock area since 1857. The fairground was placed on the National Register of Historic Places in 2000. **Mount Morris Italian Festival** (585-658-3132), Bellamy Park, Mount Morris. Celebrate Old-World customs, Italian food, music, and family activities.

August: **Stone Tool Technology Show** (585-493-3600), Letchworth State Park. Flint knapping, toolmaking, 19th-century mountain-men encampment.

September: **Finger Lakes Fiber Arts Festival** (www.gyhg.org/ fest.html), Hemlock Fairgrounds,

NY 15A, Hemlock. An annual event featuring items made from natural fibers, workshops, and demonstrations.

October: **Genesee Valley Hunt Races** (585-243-3949), The Nations Farm, Nations Road (off NY 39, just north of the village), Geneseo. The nation's second-oldest fox hunt features steeplechase races, carriage races and a parade.

December: **Mills Mansion Christmas Open House** (585-658-3292), 14 Main Street, Mount Morris. Holiday decorations, music, and refreshments.

SOUTHERN LIVINGSTON COUNTY—Dansville and Nunda

Dansville, located in the Genesee Valley, is surrounded by farmland and rolling hills. The city was founded by and named after Daniel Faulkner in 1795. Dansville's primary claim to fame began in 1858, with the establishment of the renowned "Our Home on the Hillside," a water-cure and health institute operated by Dr. Caleb Jackson that rivaled some of the finer European health resorts, and attracted the rich and famous from around the world. Clara Barton was one such patron. In 1873, exhausted and in need of rest following the Civil War, she sought out Dr. Jackson's care—and Dansville became home to America's "Angel of the Battlefield." While recuperating, Clara wrote to the head of the Red Cross in Geneva, asking to establish the International Red Cross in America, which she did in 1881. The health facility thrived for several decades, then began a decline in 1914. In 1929 it was purchased by health faddist Bernarr MacFadden and became known as the Physical Culture Hotel, offering exercise opportunities and therapeutic treatments. Many a celebrity visited the facility when they needed to get away from it all. The operation thrived, even surviving MacFadden's death in 1955. But the doors to the spa closed permanently in 1971, and the property, located on East Hill, is now privately owned and off-limits to the public. Today Dansville offers visitors picturesque streets and social, cultural, and recreational activities, including the New York State Festival of Balloons on Labor Day Weekend.

Nunda, founded in 1808, was originally part of Allegany County. The name comes from *Nunda-wa-ono,* a Seneca tribe that once lived in the area. In the Seneca language, Nunda means "where the valley meets the hills." The village then expanded when the portion of the Genesee Valley Canal from Rochester to Mount Morris was completed. The canal, which eventually connected Olean to Rochester, came to the Nunda by 1851. The arrival of the railroad also helped the area south of the village, known as Dalton or Nunda Station, to become a thriving community. In the late 1880s a highly ornamental commercial building known as the Union Block was built. This structure, which is now being renovated, was place on the State and National Registers of Historic Places in 1999.

The transportation corridor, once the location of the Genesee Valley Canal and later the Pennsylvania Railroad, is being transformed by the state into the

Genesee Valley Greenway, a 90-mile multiuse trail for biking, hiking, cross-country skiing, horseback riding, and snowmobiling.

GUIDANCE **Dansville Area Chamber of Commerce** (585-335-6920; http://dansville.lib.ny.us, www.dansvilleny.net), 126 Main Street, Dansville. Open Monday–Friday 10–1.

Town of Nunda (585-468-2215), 1 Mill Street, Nunda. Open Monday–Friday 9–12 and 1–4:30.

GETTING THERE *By air:* **Dansville Municipal Airport** (585-335-2076; www.dansville.lib.ny.us/airport.html), Exit 5 off I-390. This facility, operated by Sterling Airways, is favored by glider pilots and balloonists. See also *Getting There—Rochester.*

By car: Exits 4 and 5 off I-390.

MEDICAL EMERGENCY Dial 911.

Nicholas Noyes Memorial Hospital (585-335-4240; www.noyes-health.org), 111 Clara Barton Street, Dansville.

✳ To See

MUSEUMS AND HISTORIC HOMES **Clara Barton Chapter #1 American Red Cross** (585-335-3500; http://dansville.lib.ny.us/clara.html), 57 Elizabeth Street, Dansville. Open Monday–Friday 9–1. The first chapter of the American Red Cross was established in Dansville by Clara Barton in 1881. This house, donated to the American Red Cross in 1949 by the Noyes family, serves as a museum as well as the offices for Chapter #1.

Dansville Area Historical Museum (585-335-8090), 4 Church Street, Dansville. Open first and third Saturdays of the month from 10–3, and by appointment. Displays depict the history of southern Livingston County.

Nunda Historical Society (585-468-5420; www.nundahistory.org), 24 Portage Street, Nunda. Open by appointment. This museum has displays and artifacts from the Nunda and Dalton area.

✳ To Do

GOLF **Brae Burn Recreation Center** (585-335-3101), Red Jacket Street, Dansville. This 9-hole, par-34 golf course also has an outdoor snack bar and pro shop.

Triple Creek (585-468-2116), 8793 NY 408, Nunda. An 18-hole, par-69 course.

Woodlyn Hills (585-468-5010), 8780 NY 408, Nunda. Open April–October. An 18-hole, par-70 course with snack shop, full pro-shop and banquet facilities.

HORSEBACK RIDING **Dan Mar Ranch** (585-468-2679; www.danmarranch.com), 2278 NY 436, Nunda. Open by appointment. Their 80-foot by 168-foot indoor riding arena can rented by the day, week, or month. They also have lessons, stables to board horses, and host a variety of equestrian events throughout the year.

✳ Green Space

NATURE PRESERVES Rattlesnake Hill Wildlife Management Area (585-226-2466; www.dec.state.ny.us/Web site/reg8/wma/rattlesnake.html), NY 436 and CR 9, Dansville. Open dawn to dusk. Free admission A 5,100-acre area located about 8 miles west of Dansville, popular for hiking, bird-watching, horseback riding, cross-country skiing, snowshoeing, hunting, and fishing. About one-third of this undeveloped land is located in neighboring Allegany County. Abundant wildlife can be found here, including deer, turkey, beaver, and many other species. It has also been reported that there are indeed some rattlesnakes in the more remote areas of the preserve.

PARKS ⅋ Stony Brook State Park (585-335-8111; www.nysparks.com), 10820 Route 36 South, Dansville. Open dawn to dusk mid-April–late October. Admission: Memorial Day–Labor Day $7/car, off-peak $6/car. This picturesque park's terrain consists of hilly woodlands along with a deep gorge with three waterfalls. Hiking and nature trails are located along the gorge. The 0.75-mile long Gorge Trail descends down 250 steps into the gorge, passing three waterfalls. Both the West Rim Trail and East Rim Trail follow the upper edge of the gorge. The 577-acre park also has picnic areas, tennis courts, 125 tent and trailer campsites, and two stream-fed pools. See *Other Lodging*.

WALKING AND HIKING TRAILS See **Stony Brook State Park.**

✳ Lodging

MOTELS AND HOTELS Logan's Inn (585-335-5840; www.logansinn.com), 106 Clara Barton Street, Dansville. Thirty-one quality guest rooms plus an indoor pool and exercise room. Convenient to I-390 expressway. $50–$72.

OTHER LODGING

Campgrounds
Skybrook Campground (585-335-6880), 10861 McCurdy Road, Dansville. Open May 1–October 1. A family-oriented full-facility campground with 500 sites.

⅋ Stony Brook State Park Campground (585-333-5530; www.nysparks.com), 10820 NY 36 South, Dansville. Open dawn to dusk mid-April–late October. This state park has 125 campsites, including several prime creekside sites, but no electric, water, or sewer hookups. Showers and toilets are available. Creekside sites $19.75/night, $17 each additional night; all other sites $15.77/night, $13 each additional night. See also *Parks*.

Sugar Creek Glen Campground (585-335-6294; www.sugarcreekglen campground.com), 11288 Poag's Hole Road, Dansville. Open late April–mid-October. A beautiful 131-site campground with five waterfalls, including one that's illuminated at night. The campground has two stocked fishing ponds, wooded hiking trails, and family activities.

✳ Where to Eat

DINING OUT **The Old Madrid** (585-335-7220), 130 Main Street, Dansville. Open Monday–Friday 11:30–2, Tuesday–Saturday 5–10, Sunday 12–6. This restaurant features steak, ribs, seafood, chicken, and veal entrées as well as a Wednesday night all-you-can-eat prime rib and shrimp buffet.

EATING OUT **Bill's Restaurant** (585-468-3475), 83 Mill Street, Nunda. Open Tuesday–Sunday 11–9. This restaurant is known for its salad bar.

Java Jungle (585-335-3250), 148 Main Street, Dansville. Open Monday, Wednesday, Friday 6 AM–8 PM; Tuesday, Thursday, Saturday, and Sunday 6 AM–2:30 PM. This small restaurant with a jungle theme features numerous breakfast selections, including eggs, omelets, and specialty pancakes, along with sandwiches, salads, and wraps for lunch.

Shirley's Café (585-335-2551), 161 Main Street, Dansville. Open Monday and Tuesday 4:30–1, Wednesday–Friday 4:30–7, Saturday and Sunday 4:40–noon. This small bakery and café features a variety of items, including all-you-can-eat spaghetti.

✐ ♿ ♞ **Sunrise Restaurant** (585-335-5169), 186-188 Main Street, Dansville. Open for breakfast, lunch, and dinner Monday–Thursday 5:30–9, Friday and Saturday 6–10, Sunday 6:30–9. This family restaurant offers a variety of menu items that include pasta specialties, stir fries, fresh haddock, and Cajun chicken as well as a variety of sandwiches. They have both senior citizens and kids' menus. Finish off you meal with one of their homemade cakes or pies.

✳ Entertainment

THEATERS **Star Theatre** (585-335-6950), 144 Main Street, Dansville. A 1921 restored art deco theater that offers movies and live entertainment.

✳ Selective Shopping

SPECIAL SHOPS ♿ **The Book Den** (585-335-6805), 174 Main Street, Dansville. Open Tuesday–Saturday 10–5. Choose from new and preread books, plus comics, magazines, cards, candy, music, and gifts.

Byrnes Pharmacy (585-468-2416), 12 North State Street, Nunda. Open Monday 9–7, Tuesday–Friday 9–6, Saturday 9–3. Specializing in Nunda-area products, including locally made Maple Spring Farm Honey, Once Again nut butters, and famous Nunda mustard. They also carry a selection of books on local interest.

♿ **Earth, Moon & More** (585-335-6570), 160 Main Street, Dansville. Open Monday–Wednesday 11–7, Thursday and Friday 11–8, Saturday 11–7. New Age products and services, including herbal teas, yoga books, crystals, and aromatherapy.

Robins Nest (585-335-4770), 202 Main Street, Dansville. Open Monday–Friday 10–5, Saturday 10–4, Sunday 11–4. This shop, in a vintage brick house, features two floors of country decorating items, including candles, florals, painted items, and unfinished and finished Amish furniture.

♿ ✐ **Trading Company & Dansville Stationers** (585-335-8520), 178 Main Street, Dansville. Open Monday–Friday 9–5:30, Saturday 9–3. This distinctive Main Street shop, sporting

BALLOONISTS FROM ALL OVER THE COUNTRY CONVERGE ON DANSVILLE EVERY LABOR DAY WEEKEND FOR THE NEW YORK STATE FESTIVAL OF BALLOONS.

Christine A. Smyczynski

Welch's Wicks & Wares Antiques (585-476-2630; www.welchs-wicks .com), 9630 Chidsey Road, Dalton. Open by appointment. Cindy and Fran Welch's shop specializes in 19th-century lighting, with over 750 antique lamps and hard-to-find parts. They also offer their customers custom sewing, including alternations and repairs.

Welch's the Journey Continues (585-468-2320; www.welchs-wicks .com), 3 North State Street, Nunda. Open Monday–Friday 10-4, Saturday and Sunday 10-2. This unique shop specializes in quilting supplies, cottage-industry products, locally made Nunda mustards and Once Again nut butters, antiques, unusual gifts, and New Age items. They also offer machine quilting services and classes.

✳ Special Events

May: **Dogwood Festival** (585-335-2170; www.dansvilleny.net), Downtown Dansville. A week-long festival featuring a parade, music, historic displays, carnival rides, and more.

August: **Poag's Hole Hillclimb** (585-335-9260; www.poagshole.com), 10401 Poags Hole Road, Dansville. A professional motorcycle hill climb. **New York State Festival of Balloons** (585-335-9640), Dansville Airport. More than 50 hot-air balloons converge on Dansville each Labor Day Weekend for this annual extravaganza.

hardwood floors and a pressed tin ceiling, has a large variety of unusual gifts, toys, cards, notepads, and more. Come here for animal-shaped staplers, scrapbooking accessories, Crabtree & Evelyn products, and kites. It is a truly unique, old-fashioned shopping experience.

STEUBEN COUNTY

The area that came to be known as Steuben County was occupied by Native Americans until 1789, when the first permanent settlement was established by Frederick Calkins. Established in 1796 from part of Ontario County, the county is named after Baron Von Steuben, a Prussian who has been credited with teaching military skills to General George Washington's forces. After leaving the military service, he took up residence in New York State and was a prominent citizen.

Steuben County, the seventh-largest county in New York, has a landscape dominated by farms, woodlands, and gently rolling hills. Agriculture is the most important industry, with the primary crops being potatoes, celery, onions, cabbages, and apples, as well as buckwheat. It is home to one of the most popular tourist attractions in the state, the Corning Museum of Glass, plus numerous wineries that can be found along the shores of Keuka Lake.

NORTHERN STEUBEN COUNTY—Bath, Hammondsport, Prattsburgh, Arkport, Canisteo, and Hornell

Bath, the county seat, was founded in 1793 by Col. Charles Williamson, land agent for the Pulteney estate, and was the first planned community in western New York. The center of the village has two historic districts listed on the National Register of Historic Places. Pulteney Park, in one of those districts, was the first clearing in Steuben County. The county fair, which takes place in Bath, has been held since 1819, making it the oldest county fair in America.

Captain Shethar first purchased land in 1796 in what now is the village of Hammondsport, on the southern tip of Keuka Lake. The land was later sold to William Root, who in turn sold it to Lazarus Hammond, after whom the village was named. The first grape cuttings in the area were planted by Reverend Bostwick in 1829. Today the village is surrounded by hundreds of acres of vineyards and a dozen wineries and is known as the "Champagne Center of America." One of Hammondsport's most famous sons was Glenn Curtiss, the aviation pioneer, whose life and work are chronicled in the Glenn Curtiss Aviation Museum. Curtiss, who began his career as a motorcycle builder and racer, was known as the

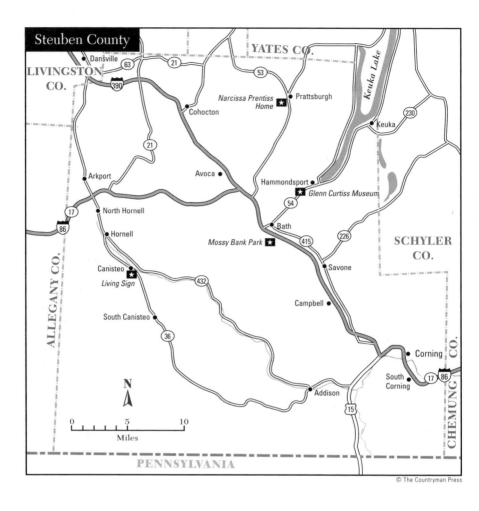

"fastest man on earth." The first flying school in the nation, the Curtiss School of Aviation, was located here, and the U.S. Navy's first aviator was trained at that school. Many important early aeronautical developments can be attributed to Glenn Curtiss. At one point, the Curtiss Aeroplane and Motor Co. was the largest aircraft engine producer in the world. During World War I, a number of Curtiss "Jenny" planes were produced in Hammondsport.

Canisteo, formed in 1796 as a French settlement, is one of the oldest towns in Steuben County. It is well known for its Native American lore. Its world-famous living sign, made up of 260 Scotch pine trees, was once noted in *Ripley's Believe it or Not.*

Hornell, incorporated in 1852, known as the Maple City because of its many maple trees, is named after Judge George Hornell, who settled in the area in 1792. In the past, it was a small railroad and farming town. The arrival of the Erie Railroad in the mid-1800s brought prosperity to the area, which lasted until the 1970s, when other forms of transporation for moving goods, such as trucks and air freight, became more popular than the railroads. The Canisteo River, which has caused numerous floods over the years, flows through the town, which has a population of about 13,000.

AREA CODE The area code for the county is 607.

GUIDANCE **Greater Bath Area Chamber of Commerce** (607-776-7122; www.bathnychamber.com), 10 Pulteney Square West, Bath. Open Monday–Friday 9–4.

Bath Tourist Information Booth, Corner Liberty Street and NY 54N, Bath. Open daily late June–Labor Day 9–5. Open weekends only Memorial Day–late June and Labor Day–Columbus Day.

Hammondsport Chamber of Commerce and Visitors Center (607-569-2989 www.hammondsport.org), 47 Shethar Street (at the Village Square), Hammondsport. Open summer Monday–Saturday 10–4, Sunday 11–3. Winter hours Monday–Friday 10–2.

Hornell Area Arts Council (607-324-3822), 20 Broadway, Hornell. Open Monday–Friday 9–1.

Hornell Tourist Information Booth, NY 36 and Webbs Crossing, Hornell. Open Memorial Day–Labor Day Monday–Friday 9–5, Saturday–Sunday 10–4.

Hornell Area Chamber of Commerce (607-324-0310 or 877-467-6355; www.hornellny.com), 40 Main Street, Hornell. Open Monday–Friday 8:30–5–3

GETTING THERE *By air:* **Hornell Municipal Airport** (607-324-2742), Hornell. The largest airport in Steuben County, with a paved 3,400 foot runway.

By car: Northern Steuben County is easily accessible from both I-390 and I-86.

MEDICAL EMERGENCY Dial 911.

Street James Mercy Hospital (607-324-8000), 411 Canisteo Street, Hornell.

Ira Davenport Memorial Hospital (607-776-8500), 7571 NY 54, Bath.

✳ To See

MUSEUMS AND HISTORIC HOMES ♿ **Glenn Curtiss Museum** (607-569-2160; www.linkny.com/curtissmuseum), 8419 NY 54, Hammondsport. Open January–March: Thursday–Saturday 10–4, Sunday 12–5; April: Monday–Saturday 10–4, Sunday 12–5; May–October: Monday–Saturday 9–5, Sunday 11–5; November–December: Monday–Saturday 10–4, Sunday 12–5. Admission: $6 adults, $4 seniors, $3.50 students 7–18, children under 6 free, $17/family rate. The Curtiss Museum houses a collection of early aircraft, motorcycles, bicycles, and household furnishings that belonged to the Curtiss family. In the early 1900s, motorcycle daredevil Glenn Curtiss, a Hammondsport native, turned his bicycle shop into the world's largest aircraft firm. Considered the father of naval aviation, Curtiss was issued the first pilot's license in the United

States, and his work and inventions changed the world. To find the museum, just look for the 1943 Curtiss-Wright C-46 Commando, on permanent display outside the building.

Narcissa Prentiss Home (607-522-3599), 7225 Mill Pond Road, Prattsburgh. Open June–August Saturday and Sunday 1–4. This museum is housed in the restored home of Narcissa Prentiss (1808–1847), pioneer and missionary. Narcissa was born in Prattsburg in 1808 and became a schoolteacher. But she dreamed of becoming a missionary, and in 1836 she married Dr. Marcus Whitman, who was also interested in missionary work, and together they traveled west to the Oregon Territory to minister to Native Americans. Narcissa and Eliza Spalding, who was traveling with her husband and the Whitmans, were the first two women to journey the Oregon Trail. After arriving in what is now Washington State, they set up a school and other facilities in their mission. At first the natives welcomed them, but after 11 years, resentment toward the missionaries grew. When many Indians died in an epidemic, they blamed the doctor. He and Narcissa were murdered, along with 12 others.

Steuben County History Center (607-776-9930), 2 Cameron Street, Bath. Open Monday–Friday 10–3. Housed in the historic circa 1831 Magee House, the historical society has a collection of documents and artifacts pertaining to the history of Steuben County.

HISTORIC SITES World-Famous Living Sign. Located on the hillside behind the Canisteo Elementary school on Greenwood Street. Some 260 10-foot-tall Scotch pine trees spell out Canisteo. Each letter is about 30 feet wide and 70 feet long. The sign was designed and planted by Harry Smith and Ed Childs in 1933. The property was sold to the school district in the 1950s, and part of the purchase agreement included a perpetual-care contract for the school to take care of the sign. The sign has been featured in *Ripley's Believe it or Not.*

WINERIES Keuka Lake Wine Trail (800-440-489; www.keukawinetrail.com), There are nine wineries along the shores of Keuka Lake on this trail. Special events take place at the wineries throughout the year.

AVIATION PIONEER GLENN CURTISS WAS A HAMMONDSPORT NATIVE.
Christine A. Smyczynski

Bully Hill Vineyards (607-868-3210; www.bullyhill.com), 8843 Greyton H. Taylor Memorial Drive, Hammondsport. Open Monday–Saturday 9–5, Sunday 11–5. Bully Hill, established in 1958, was the first small estate winery in the Finger Lakes since Prohibition. The hill the winery is located on was named Bully Hill by British settlers in 1797 in memory of a hill back in England. The winery is noted for innovative top quality wines and grape juice, plus the fun, interactive atmosphere on their tours and in the tasting room. (If you're lucky, Bully Hill's Phil will conduct your wine tastings.) Wines from Bully Hill have comical labels and unique names like Love My Goat Red. The wine shop sells a large selection of their wines. From April–November lunch is served daily in the Bully Hill Restaurant, as is dinner on Friday and Saturday evenings. The **Greyton H. Taylor Wine Museum**, which displays 18th-century winemaking equipment and accessories, is open daily 9–5 May–October. Three gift shops are located at the museum, with everything from upscale home decor to glow-in-the-dark underwear.

Christine A. Smyczynski

ESTABLISHED IN 1958, BULLY HILL WAS THE FIRST SMALL ESTATE WINERY IN THE FINGER LAKES SINCE PROHIBITION.

Chateau Renaissance Wine Cellars (607-569-3609; www.winesparkle.com), 7494 Fish Hatchery Road, Bath. Open Monday–Saturday 10–5, Sunday 12–5. Sparking wines are handmade one bottle at a time at this winery, which is built in a Normandy-style architecture, reflecting the heritage of winemaker Patrick DeMay. They specialize in *méthode champenoise*, the French technique of making sparkling wine.

Dr. Konstantin Frank's Vinifera Wine Cellars (607-868-4884, 800-320-0735; www. drfrankwines.com), 9749 Middle Road, Hammondsport. Open Monday–Saturday 9–5, Sunday 12–5. This winery, which produces New York State's most award-winning wines, was founded in 1962 by the legendary Dr. Konstantin Frank, the first person to successfully grow vinifera grapes in the northeastern United States. Dr. Frank died in 1985, but his son and grandson continue on the tradition of fine winemaking. Dr. Frank's has been named the greatest wine producer in the Atlantic Northeast by *Wine Report 2005*. One of the winery's most unusual wines is rkatsiteli, made from a spicy grape that originated on Mount Ararat over 5,000 year ago. Its sister winery, **Chateau Frank**, is noted for the production of sparkling wines, including their signature brut Champagne.

Heron Hill Winery (800-441-4241; www.heronhill.com), 9249 CR 76, Hammondsport. Open Monday–Saturday 10–5, Sunday 12–5. Enjoy tours and wine tastings in their vaulted tasting room at this award-winning winery overlooking Keuka Lake. The spacious grounds are a perfect spot to enjoy a picnic and a bottle of wine, and the winery's lookout tower is a great place to view the surrounding countryside. Musical entertainment and other events are scheduled every weekend June 1 through the end of October. A gift shop with distinctive items and a deli are also located at the winery.

Pleasant Valley Wine Company & Great Western Visitors Center (607-569-6111), 8260 Pleasant Valley Road (CR 88), Hammondsport. Open January–March, Tuesday–Saturday 10–4; April–December, 10–5 daily. Tour eight historic stone buildings, which are listed on the National Register of Historic Places, at this first winery established in 1860—the first winery bonded in the United States. The winery is noted for its sparkling wines and is the largest bottle-fermented Champagne producer in the East. It also has the world's most comprehensive winery visitors center. Free wine tastings and tours plus the unique Theater in a Wine Tank.

Ravines Wine Cellars (607-292-7007; www.ravineswinecellars.com), 14110 NY 54, Hammondsport. Open April–mid-December Friday, Saturday, and Monday 10–5, Sunday 12–5. This boutique winery, owned by French-trained winemaker, Morton Hallgren, is located on the eastern side of Keuka Lake. The winery specializes in ultrapremium vinifera wines, which include Riesling, chardonnay, pinot noir, Meritage, and a house white.

✳ To Do

BOAT EXCURSIONS *Keuka Maid* **Dinner Boat** (607-569-2628; www.keuka maid.com), NY 54, Hammondsport. Open May–November. Lunch and dinner cruises are offered on Keuka Lake aboard a 107 by 40-foot boat that can hold almost 500 passengers. The largest boat of its kind in a self-contained lake, it offers three dining levels, with dancing on the first and second decks. The first deck is handicapped accessible. Sunday brunch and moonlight cruises also available.

GOLF Bath Country Club (607-776-5043), 330 May Street, Bath. An 18-hole, par-72 rolling-to-hilly course open to the public.

Hornell Country Club (607-324-1735), 473 Seneca Road, Hornell. A public 18-hole, par-71 hilly course.

Twin Hickory Golf Course (607-324-1441), 1799 Turnpike Road, Hornell. An 18-hole, par-72 rolling, hilly course.

FISHING Keuka Lake is noted for its trout, perch, bass, and other lake fish. The **Conhocton River,** which runs near Bath, is good for trout fishing, while nearby **Lake Salubria** is noted for bass fishing. For more fishing information, check out www.fish steubencounty.com.

New York State Fish Hatchery (607-776-7087), Fish Hatchery Road, Bath. Open Monday–Friday 8–3:45,

KEUKA LAKE IS NOTED FOR ITS GREAT FISHING.

Christine A. Smyczynski

group tours by appointment. See rainbow trout in various stages of development at the fish hatchery.

MARINAS **Keuka Bay Marine Park** (607-569-2777), NY 54A, Hammondsport. Open seven days June–August A full service marina close to Hammondsport's Village Square.

SCENIC DRIVES **NY 54A** has been named one of the 15 most scenic drives in the world by the in-flight magazine of British Airways.

✳ Green Space

NATURE PRESERVES **Mossy Bank Park and Nature Center** (607-776-3811), Off County Road 10, Bath. Open dawn to dusk. At 1,600 feet above sea level, this park offers a panoramic view of the village of Bath and the valley beyond.

PARKS & **Birdseye Hollow Park & State Forest** (607-776-2165), 7291 Coon Road, Bath. Open dawn to dusk. This park includes a 200 foot handicapped-accessible fishing pier, picnic tables, grills, playground, and 2 miles of hiking trails.

& **Pulteney Park**, Bath. Located in the center of the village, this park is the site of the first clearing in Steuben County.

& **Hammondsport Park and Beach**, Water Street, Hammondsport. Stroll a boardwalk along Keuka Lake is lined with benches, plus boat docks and a guarded swimming area.

✳ Lodging

INNS AND RESORTS **The Park Inn Restaurant** (607-569-9387; www .fingerlakes-ny.com/parkinn), Village Square, Hammondsport. John Jensen's 1861 country inn has five beautifully restored guest suites, each with private bath, air conditioning, and distinctively decorated. A full breakfast is served. The restaurant also serves lunch and dinner year-round. $79–$89, $59 off-season.

Pleasant Valley Inn (607-569-2282; www.pleasantvalleyinn.com), 7979 NY 54, Hammondsport. This 1848 chef-owned Victorian country inn features four air-conditioned guest rooms with private baths and queen-sized beds. Innkeepers Tom and Marianne Simons serve breakfast on the porch, which overlooks vineyards. Candle-light dinners served Thursday–Sunday in the Victorian dining room. $98.

Village Tavern Restaurant & Inn (607-569-2528; www.villagetaverninn .com), 30 East Mechanic Street (Village Square), Hammondsport. Paul Geisz and his sister, Suzanne, operate this popular bar and restaurant that also has overnight accommodations. Four suites are located above the restaurant. Two are two-bedroom suites that have a sitting room, full bath, and a half kitchen. The other two suites are one-bedroom efficiencies with full kitchens. $79–$159. Additional accommodations are available at the **Champagne House**, just down the road on a quiet side street. Each of these four rooms has a queen-sized bed, fireplace, private bath, and private entrance. $79–$109. See also *Dining Out*.

MOTELS AND HOTELS Hammond-sport Motel (607-569-2600), William and Water Street, Hammondsport. Open April–November. This motel overlooks Keuka Lake and is within walking distance of the beach and boat docks. Amenities include air-condition-ing, phones, and cable TV. $66–$73.

Old National Hotel (607-776-4104), 13 East Steuben Street, Bath. Open year-round. This historic hotel, built in 1869, has 24 clean and comfortable guest rooms remodeled with modern amenities. The hotel is located across from historic Pulteney Square. $51–$60.

Vinehurst Inn Rooms & Suites (607-569-2300; www.vinehurstinn .com), NY 54, Hammondsport. This motel features 25 large rooms as well as three suites with themed motifs: winery, nautical, and Adirondack cabin. Continental breakfast served daily. Two two-bedroom apartment suites are also available. $65–$109.

Additionally, several national chain motels/hotels are located in the area:

Bath Super 8 (607-776-2187), 333 West Morris Street, Bath. This motel has 50 standard rooms. $56–$86.

Comfort Inn (607-324-4300), 1 Can-isteo Square, Hornell. This hotel has 62 standard rooms and a small heated indoor pool. $79–$125.

Days Inn (607-776-7644), 330 West Morris Street, Bath. This hotel has 104 standard rooms and an indoor heated pool. $75–$89.

BED & BREAKFASTS Abundant Grace Bed & Breakfast (607-292-3148), 1266 NY 54, Hammondsport. Open year-round. Eric & Kelley Carv-er's antiques-furnished 1870s con-verted barn with three guest rooms is located in a rural setting, midway between Hammondsport and Penn Yan. Each room is air-conditioned and has a private bath. Breakfast is served. $85–$110.

Amity Rose Inn Bed & Breakfast (800-982-8818; www.amityroseinn .com), 8264 Main Street, Hammond-sport. Open May–November. This charming 1900s home is located near the southern tip of Keuka Lake. Four elegant rooms, named after innkeep-ers Ellen and Frank Laufersweiler's daughters and granddaughter— Emma, Ellen, Dawn, and Hannah— offer private baths and air conditioning. Two of the rooms have whirlpool soaking tubs and fireplaces. A full breakfast is served. $95–$125.

Blushing Rose Bed & Breakfast (607-569-2687 or 866-569-2687), 11 William Street, Hammondsport. Open May–November. Dick and Pat Leonberger's romantic blush-colored 1843 Italianate home, just a half block from Keuka Lake's public beach, fea-tures four rooms with private baths. A hot sit-down breakfast is served. $105–$120.

The Captains Cottage (607-569-2157), 69 Shethar Street, Hammond-sport. Open year-round. Innkeepers Jerry and Judi Ross offer two rooms with private baths in this nautical-themed cottage in the heart of Ham-mondsport, right next to the opera house. One room features a king-sized captain's bed, while the other has a double bed and a small porch. $90–$95.

18 Vine Inn & Carriage House (607-569-3039; www.18vine.com), 18 Vine Street, Hammondsport. Open year-round. This 1860s Colonial Revival house was once the home of a prominent champagne maker.

Innkeeper George Powell offers four elegant rooms with private baths. Afternoon tea is served on the veranda overlooking the pool, and a full breakfast is served. $85–$135.

Feather Tick 'N Tyme Bed & Breakfast (607-522-4113; www.bbny fingerlakes.com), 7661 Tuttle Road, Prattsburgh. Open year-round. Deb and Ruth Cody offer four bedrooms—two with private baths, two share a bath—in an elegant 1890s Victorian country home set on 80 acres. This lovely home, with its wraparound porch and unique split staircase, won Honorable Mention in the 1996 *Better Homes and Gardens* Renovator's Contest. The scent of fresh thyme can be detected when you stroll along the walk, and you can watch hummingbirds sip nectar in the flower garden. A full-course breakfast, including freshly baked muffins and breads, is included. $80–$100.

J. S. Hubbs Bed & Breakfast (607-569-2440; www.jshubbs.com), 17 Shethar Street, Hammondsport. Open year-round. This 1840 Greek Revival "ink-bottle" house has been owned by the same family since 1894. Walter and Linda Carl offer three antiques-furnished guest rooms plus one two-room suite. All have private baths and queen-sized beds. The inn, which still has the original wallpaper in the foyer, was named after Walter's maternal grandfather, J. S. Hubbs. $89–$99.

Patchwork Peace Bed & Breakfast (607-566-2443; www.patchwork peace.com), 4279 Waterbury Hill, Avoca. Open year-round. Hosts Bill and Betty Mitchell offer four rooms in a comfortable home on a 300-acre working farm. The farmhouse, built in 1925, features natural wood floors and woodwork. Heirloom quilts adorn the house. One room has a private bath, while the other three share a bath. $40–$75.

CAMPGROUNDS **Hickory Hill Family Camping Resort** (800-760-0947 or 607-776-4345; www.hickoryhill campresort.com), 7531 Mitchellsville Road, Bath. Open May 1–October 31. This 200-acre campground resort has 185 campsites plus 13 cabins and cottages. Cottages have full bathrooms and all the amenities of home. They also have more rustic log cabins in the woods. Also enjoy include two swimming pools, a rec room, miniature golf, a playground, and hiking trails.

Kanakadea Recreation Facility (607-324-0539), CR 66, Hornell. Open mid-April–late November. The facility, which has 70 sites (40 RV and 30 tent), offers hiking trails, fishing, and a boat launch. $13 no-electric sites, $15 electric sites; two-week rate $150 no electric, $174 electric.

Sun Valley Campsites (607-545-8388; www.sunvalleycampsites.com), 10740 Poags Hole Road, Arkport. End of April–mid-October. A family-oriented campground with 295 sites. Amenities include modern rest room and shower facilities, swimming, fishing in a stocked stream, a recreation hall, an ice cream shop, and hiking trails. $25 night, $198 season.

Tumble Hill Campground (716-384-5248), 10551 Atlanta Back Road, Cohocton. Open May 1–October 1. This campground, located just 2 miles from I-390, offers large wooded private sites with hook-ups. There are 40 campsites for both tents and RVs plus two rental units (one trailer and one cabin). $18 tent sites, $25 full hookups; call for trailer and cabin rates.

✳ Where to Eat

DINING OUT Bully Hill Restaurant
(607-868-3210; www.bullyhill.com),
G. H. Taylor Memorial Drive (at the
Bully Hill Winery), Hammondsport.
Open April–December, lunch daily
11:30–4, dinner Friday and Saturday
5–9. The dishes in this unique restaurant can be described as wholesome,
delicious, and healthy—and, of
course, they taste best accompanied
by a glass of Bully Hill wine. Owner
and chef Lillian Taylor is committed
to serving the freshest ingredients
available. Enjoy dining indoors on
copper-topped tables or outdoors on
the deck overlooking the grounds. See
also *Wineries*.

Club 57 (607-324-5174), Hornell-
Arkport Road, Hornell. Open Monday–Thursday 11:30–10, Friday–
Saturday 11:30–11, Sunday 11:30–9.
An upscale restaurant offering ostrich
filets and burgers along with other
entrées. They are known for their
Rico chicken sandwich, a marinated
boneless chicken breast with special
Cajun-style seasoning, charbroiled
and served on a hard roll with dill
dressing. Another specialty is baby
back ribs.

Italian Villa (607-324-1143), Seneca
Street, Hornell. Open Monday–Saturday 11–11. As you might expect, this
restaurant specializes in Italian cuisine.

✐ ⑂ ♞ **Old National Hotel** (607-
776-4104), 13 East Steuben Street,
Bath. Open Monday–Friday 6 AM–
12:30 AM, Saturday–Sunday 8 AM–
12:30 AM. This historic hotel offers
both a spacious dining room and a full
taproom with a vintage bar. The lunch
menu features sandwiches and salads,
while dinner selections include steaks,

pork chops, chicken entrées, and
seafood. They also have a children's
menu and serve breakfast anytime.

Park Inn and Restaurant (607-569-
9387), 37 Shethar Street, Hammondsport. Monday–Saturday 11–11,
Sunday 4–9. Casual dining selections,
including wings, salads, sandwiches,
burgers, soups, salads, and daily specials are served in the dining room of
this 1861 hotel. See also *Lodging*.

✐ **Ruperts on the Lodge** (607-324-
3000), NY 36, Hornell. Open Tuesday–Saturday 4–11, Sunday brunch
10–2. This very popular casual fine
dining restaurant specializes in steaks
and seafood. They also have pasta,
veal, chicken, and sandwiches as well
as a kids' menu.

Three Birds Restaurant (607-868-
7684), 144 West Lake Road (NY 54A),
Hammondsport. Open daily in summer for lunch and dinner, weekends
only in winter. This Victorian restaurant, located on the shore of Keuka
Lake, offers a progressive American
menu with an emphasis on French-
inspired sauces. Selections include
roasted veal tenderloin, pan-seared
salmon, and grilled hanger steak.

✐ ⑂ ♞ **Village Tavern Restaurant
& Inn** (607-569-2528; www.village
taverninn.com), 30 East Mechanic
Street (Village Square), Hammondsport. Open 11:30–9 daily. This three-
diamond rated restaurant has the
Finger Lakes finest seafood, shellfish,
pasta, and steaks for dinner as well as
a lunch menu that features a variety
of sandwiches, pastas, vegetarian dishes, and daily specials. Their award-
winning wine list features close to 200
local wines, including 40 poured by
the glass. They also serve over 130
draft beers, including numerous Belgian ales. The Village Tavern is the

recipient of the New York State Wine & Grape Foundation Restaurant of the Year Award along with *Wine Spectator* awards. They were recently mentioned in *Time* magazine as *the* place to eat in the Finger Lakes Region. See also *Lodging*.

EATING OUT The Corner Deli at Heron Hill (607-868-3455 or **1**-800-441-4241, ext. 21; www.heronhill .com), 9249 CR. 76, Hammondsport. Lunch selections include gourmet sandwiches, wraps, soups, and salads plus desserts.

🌶 ♿ 🐾 **Crooked Lake Ice Cream Parlor** (607-569-2751), 35 Shethar Street (Village Square), Hammondsport. Open Monday–Saturday 7–7, Sunday 7–5. Breakfast, lunch, and dinner are served in this 1940s-style ice cream parlor, along with an assortment of ice cream favorites.

Lakeside Restaurant and Tavern (607-868-3636; www.lakeside-restaurant.com), 800 West Lake Road, Hammondsport. Open for lunch 11–4 Wednesday–Sunday and 5–9 for dinner. Extended hours in summer. They are noted for burgers and their Friday fish fry.

Liberty Street Café (607-776-0311), 100 Liberty Street, Bath. Open Monday–Friday 7–5, Saturday 8–1. This café features gourmet and specialty coffees as well as panini sandwiches, wraps, homemade soups, gelato, desserts, and more.

Maloney's Pub Ltd. (607-569-2264; www.maloneyspub.com), 57 Pulteney Street (Village Square), Hammondsport. Open Monday–Friday 3 PM– 1 AM, Saturday–Sunday noon–1 AM. Enjoy dining in an authentic Irish pub atmosphere. Choose from light snacks and sandwiches along with Irish

beers, stouts, and spirits.

Union Block Café (607-569-2244), 31 Shethar Street (in the basement of Browsers), Hammondsport. Open Sunday–Thursday 7–4, Friday–Saturday 7–5. This tiny basement café serves espresso, cappuccino, chai, latte, smoothies, and other specialty beverages along with breakfast sandwiches, French toast, salads, wraps, panini sandwiches, and croissandwiches.

✴ Selective Shopping

ANTIQUES Antiques at the Warehouse (607-569-3655), 8091 CR 88, Hammondsport. Open weekends only April–September. Enjoy browsing for antiques in a former coal and grain warehouse.

Antiques on Broadway (607-324-9464), 38 Broadway, Hornell. Open Wednesday–Saturday 10–1. Antiques and collectibles.

Cat's Cradle, 14 Seneca Street, Hornell. Open Tuesday–Saturday 10–5. Antiques and collectibles.

Bilby's Antiques (607-776-6826), 6730 Salubria Road, Bath. Open Monday–Saturday 9–3. Carries a general line of antiques.

Erie Line Antique Center (607-324-4074), 103–113 Main Street, Hornell. Open Tuesday–Saturday 10–5, Sunday 12–4. Browse through 8,000 square feet of antiques and collectibles from the 1800s–1960s at this multidealer co-op in the former Tuttler & Rockwell Department Store building.

Grove Springs Antiques (607-569-2926), 9502 Grove Springs Road, Hammondsport. Open daily 10–5. This shop carries quality antiques plus art glass.

The Hummingbird Emporium Antiques (607-295-7900), 28 Main

Street, Arkport. Open Monday–Saturday 9–6, Sunday 10–5 A shop that has a variety of antiques and gift items.

Opera House Antiques (607-569-3525), 61-63 Shethar Street, Hammondsport. Open May–December, daily 10–5; January–April, Saturday and Sunday only. A multidealer shop in a historic 100-year-old opera house located near the village square. Choose from country furniture, primitives, jewelry, linens, and glass.

Over the Bridge Antiques and Such (607-569-2708), 54 Pulteney Street (NY 54A), Hammondsport. Open May–November, daily 10–5; January–April, Saturday and Sunday only. This 15-dealer co-op features toys, prints, enamel- and graniteware, Depression glass, and more.

Warriner's Antiques (607-698-2204), 5059 NY 248, Canisteo. Open April–December Monday–Saturday 10–6, Sunday 12–4. Antiques, gifts, and fresh produce in-season.

Wild Goose Chase II Antiques (607-868-3945; www.winetiqueweekend.com), 10266 CR 76, Hammondsport. Open April–October 11–5 daily. General antiques can be found in this vintage vineyard barn overlooking Keuka Lake.

ART GALLERIES Keuka Moon (607-734-9780), Water Street, Hammondsport. Open May–October 11–5 daily. The gallery, the summer art studio of W. F. Hopkins, a Hudson River School painter, is located at the historic train station at the south end of Keuka Lake. The gallery features the major works of Finger Lakes artists, including paintings, art glass, and mixed media.

Mud Lust Pottery (607-569-3068; www.mudlustpottery.com), 59 Shethar Street, Hammondsport. Open Monday–Friday 12–5, Saturday 10–4. Pottery handcrafted in the Finger Lakes region is featured in this shop.

CRAFTS Creations Plus (607-776-3258), 7200 Knight Settlement Road, Bath. Open Monday–Saturday 10–7. Country furniture and other unique handcrafted items, including stoneware pottery, water fountains, and one-of-a-kind lamps.

✳ Special Shops

Browsers (607-569-2497), Village Square, Hammondsport. Open Monday–Thursday, Saturday and Sunday 9–5:30, Friday 9–7. Two floors of merchandise, including men's and ladies' sportswear, candles, gifts, gourmet foods, home decor, bath and body, books, glassware, Red Hat Society items, toys, and Keuka Lake merchandise. The Union Block Café in the basement serves coffees, teas, and goodies.

The Cinnamon Stick (607-569-2277; www.cinnamonstick.com), Village Square, Hammondsport. Open 9–5 daily. An old-fashioned store featuring gourmet foods and coffee, country accessories, Boyd's Bears, pottery, candles, glassware with grape motifs, Red Hat Society items, and Keuka Lake photos plus a second-floor Christmas loft with Dept. 56, Christopher Radko, Byers Choice, and more.

The Grapevine (607-569-2105), 68 Shethar, Hammondsport. Open daily 10–5. This shop features floral items, gifts, and local souvenirs, including Hammondsport T-shirts.

Park Pharmacy (607-569-2800; www.parkpharmacy.com), 27 Shethar Street, Hammondsport. Open Monday–Friday 8:30–6, Saturday 9–5,

Sunday 9–3. A full-service pharmacy with a small card and gift shop.

Scandia House (607-569-3070), 64 Shethar, Hammondsport. Open Monday, Wednesday–Saturday 10–5, Sunday 11–3. This upscale shop features fine gifts and home decor along with clothing and women's accessories. Upstairs they have Norwegian sweaters and Tommy Bahama men's clothing.

✳ Special Events

July: **Keuka Lake Arts Show** (607-776-7774), Hammondsport. This is one of the longest running art shows in the state.

August: **Steuben County Fair** (607-776-4801), Steuben County Fairgrounds, 15 East Washington Street, Bath. This fair, which began back in 1819, features a midway, agricultural exhibits, musical entertainment, and more. **Festival of Crafts** (607-569-2989), Village Square, Hammondsport. For over 25 years this event has attracted some of the area's finest craftspeople, who display and demonstrate their wares.

CORNING AND ELMIRA

The Chemung River Valley, where Corning and Elmira are now located, was once home to the Iroquois. During the American Revolution, they sided with the British, so George Washington ordered the destruction of their villages. After the Iroquois left, the first white settlers arrived. One of the first was Charles Williamson, who purchased 100 acres of land and built a better road to the area.

Corning is named after Erastus Corning, a real estate developer from Albany. Corning never actually lived in the city, but the town was named after him in hopes that he'd invest money in the growing community—which he did. The city has been dubbed the Crystal City because of the Corning Museum of Glass, a top upstate New York tourist destination. The Corning Glass Works was first established in 1868 by Amory Houghton, previously the proprietor of the Brooklyn Flint Glass Works. By the 1880s the company was the major manufacturer of lightbulbs and has expanded over the years to produce numerous functional and decorative glass items. Corning is also noted for its restored 19th-century buildings along the Historic Market Street district, which has over 100 stores, art studios, and restaurants.

Although Elmira is located in neighboring Chemung County, information on attractions in that city is included in this chapter since it is just a short drive from the Corning area. Elmira is known as the Soaring Capital of America, so be sure to visit the National Soaring Museum. One can even take a ride on a sailplane at the Harris Hill Soaring Company. Author Samuel Clemens, a.k.a. Mark Twain, wrote many of his well-known works here. Clemens's wife, Olivia, was an Elmira native, so the couple spent their summers here. His study is now located on the campus of Elmira College.

AREA CODE The area code is 607.

GUIDANCE Corning Information Center (607-962-8997 or 866-INFO-CNG; www.corningfingerlakes.com, www.corningny.com), 1 Baron Steuben Place (corner of Market Street), Corning. Open Monday–Wednesday 10–6, Thursday–Friday 10–8, Saturday 10–6, Sunday 11–5.

Corning's Gaffer District Festivals and Promotions (607-974-6436; www .gafferdistrict.com), Their Web site has information on events in downtown Corning. *Gaffer* is a 16th-century term referring to the head of an organized group of laborers. The term is also used to designate a master glassblower.

Finger Lakes Wine Country Visitors Center at Corning Museum of Glass (607-974-6786), I-86 Exit 46. Open daily 9–5 (until 8, July and August).

Chemung County Chamber of Commerce (607-734-5137; www.chemung chamber.org), 400 East Church Street, Elmira. Open Monday–Friday 8:30–5.

The Arts of the Southern Finger Lakes (607-962-5871; www.earts.org), 32 West Market Street, Corning. Open Monday–Friday 9–5.

GETTING THERE *By air:* Elmira-Corning Regional Airport (607-739-5621), Exit 51 off I-86.

By bus: **Corning-Erwin Area Transit System (CEATS)** (607-734-5211), 1201 Clemens Center Parkway, Elmira. Five routes service Corning and vicinity.

By car: I-86/NY17 runs right through Corning and Elmira.

MEDICAL EMERGENCY Dial 911 **Ambulance** (607-936-4177), **Police** (607-962-2451), **Fire** (607-962-3151).

Corning Hospital (607-937-7200 www.corninghospital.com), 176 Denison Parkway Extension, Corning.

❋ To See

ART MUSEUMS ⅙ **Arnot Art Museum** (607-734-3697; www.arnotartmuseum .org), 235 Lake Street, Elmira. Open Tuesday–Saturday 10–5, Sunday 1–5. Admission: $5 adults, $4.50 seniors and students, $2.50 children 6–12, $12.50 family rate. A collection of 17th- to 20th-century sculptures and paintings, along with changing exhibits.

171 Cedar Arts Center (607-936-4647; www.171cedararts.com), 171 Cedar Street, Corning. Gallery open Monday–Friday 2–7, Saturday 9–2. This community arts organization, which first opened in 1968, offers changing exhibits plus numerous classes.

Rockwell Museum, (607-937-5386; www.rockwellmuseum.org), 111 Cedar Street, Corning. Open July–Labor Day Monday–Saturday 9–8, Sunday 11–8; rest of year Monday–Saturday 9–5, Sunday 11–5. Admission: $6.50 adults, $4.50 children. The Rockwell Museum, in Corning's restored 1893 city hall, contains the collection of the Robert Rockwell family, featuring the most comprehensive collection of western art in the U.S. The museum houses works by Frederic Remington, C. M. Russell, and many other artists who portray the wildlife, scenery, Native Americans, and cowboys of the western frontier. The museum, which was established in 1976, also exhibits over 2,000 colored glass pieces designed by Frederick Carder, who cofounded Steuben Glass Works in 1903. Other displays include antique toys, dolls, doll furniture, and model trains.

MUSEUMS AND HISTORIC HOMES

Corning
Benjamin Patterson Inn Museum (607-937-5281; www.corningny.com/bpinn), 59 West Pulteney Street, Corning. Open Monday–Friday 10–4, March–December. Life in the 1800s is depicted at this complex: the Benjamin Patterson Inn (1796), a 1784 settlers' cabin, a 1787 one-room schoolhouse, and a replica blacksmith's shop. Benjamin Patterson was the first innkeeper in Corning. The inn sits on its original site; the other buildings in the museum complex were brought from other communities. After the Industrial Revolution, the inn became a private home and changed hands several times; by the 1970s it stood in disrepair. After the massive flood in June 1972, in which the inn was filled with 6 feet of mud and water, funds were raised by concerned citizens to restore the inn and make it a museum. It is now home to the Corning–Painted Post Historical Society and serves as a living reminder of history brought to life.

⛄ **Corning Museum of Glass** (607-937-5371; www.cmog.org), I-86, exit 46, Corning. Open daily July–Labor Day 9–8, rest of year 9–5. Admission: $12, under 17 free. Corning Museum of Glass is one of New York's most popular attractions and a one-of-a-kind educational experience for your family. The museum houses the most celebrated collection of glass in the world, with over 30,000 objects representing 3,500 years of glass craftsmanship. The Glass Innovations Center contains a theater and hands-on exhibits presenting historic innovations in glass science and technology. The always-popular Hot Glass Show demonstration of glassblowing is performed seven days a week. Visitors can even try their hand at hot glass work at the Walk-in Workshop. (Be sure to make reservations for these workshops early in the day because they are very popular. Some are designed for the whole family, while other workshops are restricted to teens and adults.) The museum's enormous gift shop has all sorts of glass treasures for sale.

THE CORNING MUSEUM OF GLASS HOUSES THE MOST CELEBRATED COLLECTION OF GLASS IN THE WORLD.
Christine A. Smyczynski

Elmira

Chemung County Historical Museum (607-734-4167; www.chemungvalley museum.org), 415 East Water Street, Elmira. Open Tuesday–Saturday 10–5, Sunday 1–5. The museum, in a historic restored bank building, features a Mark Twain room with many personal artifacts from Samuel Clemens, a.k.a. Mark Twain, who spent his summers in Elmira. Twain's wife, Olivia, was an Elmira native.

Elmira College (607-735-1941; www.elmira.edu\academics\ar_marktwain .shtml), 1 Park Place, Elmira. Open mid-June–Labor Day. Mark Twain's study, where he wrote many of his famous works, has been relocated to the campus of Elmira College and is open to visitors.

Wings of Eagles Discovery Center (formerly the National Warplane Museum) (607-739-8200; www.wingsofeagles.com), 17 Aviation Drive, Elmira/Corning Regional Airport, Horseheads. Open Monday–Friday 10–4, Saturday 9–5, Sunday 11–5. Admission: $7/adults, $5.50/seniors, $4/children, under 6 free, $18/family. This educational institution collects, preserves, and exhibits military aviation memorabilia and aircraft. The museum has two 30,000-square-foot hangers, one for display and one for aircraft restoration and maintenance. Vintage warplanes are restored to flying condition by museum volunteers. Aircraft from World War I to Desert Storm are on display. There are also in-depth displays, interactive exhibits, a theater, and a library for research. You can even arrange for a 30 minute "Flight of a Lifetime" on the museum's World War II classic B-17 "Fuddy Duddy," one of only a few of these planes still flying.

& **National Soaring Museum** (607-734-3128; www.soaringmuseum.org), 51 Soaring Hill Drive, Elmira. Open daily 10–5; shorter hours in winter. Admission: $6.50 adults, $5.50 seniors and children 5–17. AAA discount available. The National Soaring Museum in the "Soaring Capital of America" is home to the largest collection of gliders and sailplanes in the world. Visitors can experience flight in a soaring simulator and can design and land a sailplane using the museum's interactive computers. An aviation day camp is held in July for children ages 10–16. Sailplane rides are offered seasonally at the adjacent **Harris Hill Soaring Company** (607-734-0641).

HISTORIC SITES

Corning
"Little Joe." This distinctive 197-foot white tower with a glassblower painted on its side houses thermometer tube machinery built in 1912 for the Corning Glass Works. When it was built, it replaced hand-drawn thermometer technology. Although it is no longer used, it has become a Corning landmark.

Corning Clock Tower. The tower, in Centerway Square on Market Street, was built in 1883 as a memorial to Erastus Corning, the city's founder. The tower is 50 feet high and its bell weighs 1,400 pounds. The clock, which has the original mechanism, still keeps time.

Market Street. This four-block area, which features buildings constructed in the late 1800s, was named a historic district in 1974 and placed on the National

Register of Historic Places. This area has numerous specialty shops and restaurants.

Elmira

Woodlawn Cemetery (607-732-0151) ,1200 Walnut Street, Elmira. Open dawn to dusk. Mark Twain was laid to rest in this cemetery in 1910.

Woodlawn National Cemetery (607-732-5411), 1825 Davis Street, Elmira. Open dawn to dusk. Veterans cemetery from Civil War to present.

Near Westside Historic District (office 607-733-4924; 353 Davis Street, Elmira; office hours Monday–Friday 8–4). This 22 block historic district, listed on the National Register of Historic Places, has the largest concentration of Victorian-era homes in New York. Guided tours are offered, along with self-guided walking tour maps. The area has many specialty and antiques shops.

✳ To Do

FAMILY FUN ↑ **Corning Planetarium** (607-962-9100; www.corningplanetarium .com), 1 Academic Drive (Corning Community College), Corning. Open the first and third Friday evening of each month. Admission: $7 adults, $6 seniors, $5 youths 3–17, $15 family pass (two adults and two children). This facility presents multimedia planetarium shows.

The Fun Park (607-936-1888; www.corningny.com/funpark), 11233 East Corning Road (NY 352), Corning. Open daily late June–early December; seasonal hours rest of year. Enjoy indoor and outdoor miniature golf, bumper boats, a climbing wall, a driving range, and more.

Hands-on Glass Studio (607-962-3044; www.handsonglass.com), 124 Crystal Lane, Corning. Open year-round by appointment. Instructional glassmaking classes for all ages and levels of experience.

FISHING (866-946-3386; www.fishsteubencounty.com) See Web site for information on fishing and hunting in Steuben County.

GOLF **Corning Country Club** (607-936-3392), NY 353, Corning. An 18-hole, par-70 course that's home to the LPGA Corning Classic in May.

Indian Hills Golf Club (607-523-7315), 150 Indian Hills Road, Painted Post. An 18-hole, par-72 course plus a 6-hole, par-3 course. Facilities include club rental, driving range, lessons, pro shop, and restaurant.

Mark Twain Golf Course (607-737-5770), 2275 Corning Road, Elmira. An 18-hole, par-72 course.

Pinnacle Golf Course (607-359-2767), 1904 Pinnacle Road, Addison. A challenging 9-hole, par-30 course. See **Pinnacle State Park** in *Green Space—Parks*.

GUIDED TOURS **The Elmiran Trolley** (607-734-5137; www.chemungchamber .org), Departs from the Riverview Holiday Inn, 760 East Water Street, Elmira. Operates Memorial Day–Labor Day. A 60-minute narrated historical tour of

Elmira that focuses on Civil War history, Victorian homes, and sites that inspired Mark Twain.

✳ Green Space

NATURE PRESERVES Spencer Crest Nature Center (607-962-2169; www .spencercrest.org), 2424 Spencer Hill Road, Corning. Open dawn to dusk. This 250-acre nature center has two ponds, 7 miles of hiking trails, a stream, and a museum of natural systems with changing displays.

Tanglewood Nature Center and Museum (607-732-6060; www.tangle-wood .org), 246 West Hill Road, Elmira. Nature center open Tuesday–Saturday 10–4, trails open dawn to dusk. The center features nature trails through an evergreen plantation. The museum has nature displays, hands-on specimens, and wildlife observation windows.

PARKS Pinnacle State Park (607-359-2767; www.nysparks.state.ny.us), 1904 Pinnacle Road, Addison. Open dawn to dusk. This park offers breathtaking view of the Canisteo River Valley. Features include a 9-hole golf course, 11 miles of cross-country skiing and hiking trails, a picnic area, fishing pond, and hunting.

✳ Lodging

MOTELS AND HOTELS Radisson Hotel Corning (607-962-5000; www.radisson.com/corningny), 125 Denison Parkway, Corning. This modern hotel is located just steps away from historic Market Street. It offers 177 large guest rooms and suites, a heated indoor pool, and an exercise facility. $100–$160.

Staybridge Suites by Holiday Inn (607-936-7800), 201 Townley Avenue, Corning. This hotel next to the Corning Museum of Glass features studio, one-, and two-bedroom suites with fully equipped kitchens. It is perfect for families. A generous continental breakfast is served. Amenities include a 24-hour fitness center, indoor pool, and outdoor basketball court. $119–$199.

BED & BREAKFASTS Hillcrest Manor (607-936-4548; www .corninghillcrestmanor.com), 227 Cedar Street, Corning. Open year-round. Innkeepers Dick Bright and Kyle Goodman offer five luxurious air-conditioned guest rooms with private baths, in their 1890 Greek Revival mansion with a huge veranda. The inn has seven working fireplaces located throughout as well as beautiful woodwork. The 900-square-foot first-floor suite features a fireplace and private balcony. The second-floor hallway is adorned with artwork from the Pacific Northwest and cabinets full of Steuben glass. A formal candlelight breakfast, with beverages served in Steuben glass stemware, is offered each morning. Children 12 and older permitted. $125–$165.

Rosewood Inn Bed & Breakfast (607-962-3253; www.rosewoodinn .com), 134 East First Street, Corning. Open year-round. This beautiful inn is within walking distance of Market Street. Innkeepers Suzanne and Stewart Sanders offer seven Victorian rooms with private baths. Each room has its own theme, including the Jenny Lind Room with a canopy-style bed, the Frederick Carder Room with a Carder chandelier in the sitting room, and the Lewis Caroll Room with its Alice in Wonderland Theme. Each bed is dressed with 300-count lace linens, and the baths offer imported towels from Christies in London and pure glycerin soap. The home, which was built in 1855, has all the original floors, glass, and doorknobs; it hasn't been restored, just beautifully maintained. The guest parlor features a fireplace and a collection of antique Steuben glass. A full formal breakfast is served on English bone china. Afternoon tea is also served. $95–$185.

Villa Bernese Bed & Breakfast (607-936-2633; www.bedbreakfast corning.com), 11866 Overlook Drive, Corning. Open year-round. Tony and Marianne Spycher offer Swiss hospitality along with four luxurious guest rooms with private baths in this villa set high on a hill overlooking the Chemung River Valley. The first thing you'll notice when you arrive is the view—it is absolutely breathtaking. The inn has several patios and balconies where you can sit and enjoy the scenery. The largest room in the inn features a canopy bed and a large bathroom with a Jacuzzi tub. The Spychers have 13 acres along the ridge, with hiking trails for guests to explore. The grounds surrounding the villa are beautifully landscaped. A full breakfast is served in either the dining room or outdoors on one of the patios. $110–$150.

OTHER LODGING Ferenbaugh Campsites (607-962-6193; www .ferenbaugh.com), 4682 NY 414, Corning. This campground features 145 campsites. Amenities include a pool, game room, hiking trails, golf and planned activities.

✷ Where to Eat

DINING OUT Hill Top Inn (607-732-6728 or 1-888-444-5586; www.hill-top-inn.com), 171 Jerusalem Hill Road, Elmira. Open April–October Monday–Saturday 5–9; closed November–March except for private parties. Casual indoor and outdoor dining over looking scenic Elmira. This restaurant is home of the world's largest wreath and shamrock. Entrées include fresh seafood, steaks, lamb and more.

London Underground Café (607-962-2345; www.londonunderground cafe.com), 69 East Market Street, Corning. Open Monday–Thursday 11:30–9, Friday and Saturday 11:30–9:30. Enjoy dining on three levels in an air-conditioned historic Market Street building. The menu features contemporary American cuisine, including New York strip steak, rack of lamb, duck breast, and Champagne scallops. For lunch, choose from wraps, sandwiches, and salads such as a pan-fried goat cheese and Thai curry salad.

& **Three Birds Corning** (607-936-8882), 73-75 Market Street, Corning. Open Monday–Thursday 5–9, Friday and Saturday 5–10. This restaurant serves progressive American fare with European-style service. They also offer a five- or seven-course Chef's Table, pairing each course with a selected wine from their extensive list, for groups of four to eight people. Dinner entrées include pancetta-wrapped beef tenderloin, pan-seared chicken roulade, and oven-roasted New Zealand rack of lamb.

EATING OUT ♿ ♨ ✆ **Aniello's Pizza** (607-962-2060), 68-70 East Market Street, Corning. Open Monday–Thursday 11–12, Friday–Saturday 11–1, Sunday 11–11. This is one of the most popular pizzerias in Corning. Choose from a large variety of pizza as well as subs, calzones, salads, and homemade soups.

Beauregards Bakery & Café (607-962-2001), 28 West Market Street, Corning. Open Monday–Friday 7–4, Saturday 12–4. This small café and bakery features sandwiches and soups for lunch, but they are best known for their desserts like Black Forest cheesecake, bread pudding, rice pudding, and tortes. They will also cater your private tea party for 8-12 guests.

Bento Ya Masako (607-936-3659), 31½ East Market Street, Corning. Open Tuesday–Friday 1–2:30. This Asian restaurant, located on the second floor, offers authentic Japanese box lunches to eat in or take out. A different menu is featured daily, including sushi, tempura, and yakitori.

♿ ♨ **DeClementes Deli & Restaurant** (607-937-5657), 30 West Market Street, Corning. Open daily 7–4. This small restaurant and New York–style deli features soups, sandwiches, Italian specialties, beef, and chicken entrées.

♿ **The Gaffer Grille & Tap Room** (607-962-4649), 58 West Market Street, Corning. Open for lunch Monday–Friday 11:30–4:30, dinner Monday–Saturday 4:30–10. Taproom open Monday–Saturday 11:30 AM–1 AM. This unique restaurant features a traditional as well as a seasonal menu in a Victorian atmosphere. The decor features sculptures and artwork by local artists. The taproom offers casual dining.

♿ ✆ **Market Street Brewing Company and Restaurant** (607-936-BEER; www.936beer.com or www.marketstreetbrewpub.com), 63–65 West Market Street, Corning. Open Tuesday–Saturday 11:30 AM–1 AM. The only microbrewery in Corning, this restaurant features fresh brews on tap that compliment their large, varied menu. The family-friendly eatery has a rooftop patio, which is a great spot to dine in the warmer months.

♿ ♨ ✆ **Old World Cafe & Ice Cream** (607-936-1953), Market Street at Centerway, Corning. Open Monday–Wednesday 10–6, Thursday–Friday 10–7, Saturday 10–5. This café features a lunch menu that includes grilled panini, soups, and sandwiches along with an old-fashioned Victorian ice cream parlor that serves Purity ice cream. They also sell gourmet specialties, gift baskets, books, and coffee.

♿ ♨ ✆ **Sorge's** (607-937-5422), 66-68 West Market Street, Corning. Open daily 7–10. This restaurant, which is the finest Italian restaurant in the Corning area, was established in 1951 by Renato and Loretta Sorge. They are known for their authentic, homemade Italian dishes. Choose from spaghetti, ravioli, cavatelli, and more, as well as traditional American dishes like steak and seafood.

✳ Entertainment

THEATERS **Clemens Center for Performing Arts** (800-724-0159; www.clemenscenter.com), 207 Clemens Ctr. Parkway, Elmira. This restored 1925 vaudeville theater is the region's performing arts center, presenting drama, music, and dance throughout the year.

PROFESSIONAL SPORTS Elmira Jackals (607-734-PUCK; www.jackalshockey.com), 155 North Main, Elmira. Hockey is played October–April in the Coach USA Center in downtown Elmira.

Elmira Pioneers (607-734-1270; www.elmirapioneers.com), 546 Luce Street, Elmira. May–September. Member of the Northeast League of Independent Professional Baseball.

✳ Selective Shopping

ANTIQUES 94 West Antiques (607-936-2468), 94 West Market Street, Corning. Open Monday–Saturday 11–5, Sunday 1–5. An elegant shop featuring period furniture, cut glass, 1950s collectibles, and more.

Carder Steuben Glass Shop (607-962-7807), 5 West Market Street, Corning. Open Monday–Saturday 10–5. Specializing in Carder-Steuben glass, antiques, and Navajo rugs.

Market Street Antiques & Collectibles (607-937-5546), 94 and 98 East Market Street, Corning. Open Monday–Saturday 10–5. Co-op of 35 dealers, featuring a large selection of antiques and collectibles.

ART GALLERIES The Clay Pot (607-962-7250), 62 West Market Street, Corning. Open Tuesday–Thursday 11–5, Friday–Saturday 11–7, Sunday 12–4. Watch pottery being made, available for purchase. Lessons are offered.

Lost Angel Glass Studio (607-937-3578; www.lostangelglass.com), 79 West Market Street, Corning. Open Monday–Friday 8–5, Saturday 10–6, Sunday 12–5. A gallery filled with colorful handblown glass. Watch the

artists at work in the studio Monday–Friday.

Noslo Glass Studio (607-962-7886), 89 West Market Street, Corning. Open Monday–Saturday 10–5. Unique handblown glass sculpture created by Lewis Olson.

Steuben Glass Gallery (607-937-5371; www.cmog.org), 1 Museum Way (at the Corning Museum of Glass), Corning. Open daily 9–5. Handcrafted exquisite glass pieces created at the Steuben factory.

Vitrix Hot Glass Studio (607-936-8707; www.vitrixhotglass.com), 77 West Market Street, Corning. Open Monday–Friday 8–6, Saturday 10–6; April–December open until 8. Watch contemporary glass items being blown in the studio, located in the historic Hawkes Crystal Glass Building. All the blown-glass pieces sold in the shop are made in their studio.

West End Gallery (607-936-2011; www.westendgallery.net), 12 West Market Street, Corning. Open Monday–Saturday 10–5, Sunday 12–5. Fine-art gallery in a restored 1920s-era speakeasy, featuring sculptures, watercolors, and oil paintings from more than 30 artists.

SPECIAL SHOPS

Corning

Historic Market Street (607-937-5427), Corning. Numerous boutiques, restaurants, and galleries line this unique street with 19th century architecture, listed on the National Register of Historic Places. Some of the stores on the street are:

Bacalles Glass Shop (607-962-3339), 10 West Market Street, Corning. Open Monday–Saturday 11–5. This shop features very nice glass items, including dishes, vases, ornaments, and picture frames.

Brown Bag Gifts (607-962-6504), 72 East Market Street, Corning. Open Monday–Wednesday 10–6, Thursday–Saturday 10–8, Sunday 10–3. This unique shop features all sorts of gifts and unusual items, including jewelry, lamps, candles, floral, gourmet foods, greeting cards, cat items, and more.

Connors Market Street Mercantile (607-937-4438), 16 East Market Street, Corning. Open Monday–Wednesday, Saturday 10–6; Thursday 10–8; Sunday 12–5. This country store in the city, complete with old-fashioned ceiling fans, has a wide variety of items, including home decor, bath and body products, cards, books, collectible dolls, puzzles, Boyd's bears, Byers Choice figures, and Corning souvenirs.

The Glass Menagerie (607-962-6300; www.corningmenagerie.com), 37 East Market Street, Corning. Open Monday–Saturday 10–5:30, Sunday 12–5. If it's related to glass, you'll find it here: glass paperweights, kaleidoscopes, stained-glass ornaments, and more. They are well-known for their large selection of over 200 kaleidoscopes, ranging in price from $8 to $4,000. The shop's owner is also a magician; during the summer months he performs tricks for visitors.

Groners: The Biggest Little Store in Corning (607-936-4044), 80 West Market Street, Corning. Open Monday–Saturday 9–4. This store, a Market Street fixture since 1959, carries a little bit of everything: hardware, housewares, gift items, art supplies, crafts, and more.

☙ **Imagine That** (607-937-4242; www.imaaginethatkids.com), 86 West Market Street, Corning. Open Monday–Wednesday 10–6, Thursday 10–8, Saturday 10–5, Sunday 10–4. This children's boutique has all sorts of distinctive upscale clothing, gifts, and toys for that special child in your life.

Just Relax (607-962-1262), 44 West Market Street, Corning. Open Monday–Wednesday and Saturday 10:30–5:30, Thursday–Friday 10:30–7. This shop specializes in gifts to de-stress your life, including soaps, candles, gift baskets, and gourmet foods.

☙ **Le Toute Sweet** (607-937-3872; www.letoutesweet.com), 38 East Market Street, Corning. Open Monday–Saturday 10–6, Sunday by chance. A sweet shop filled with all sorts of candy confections and treats.

Wild Birds Unlimited (607-937-5593; www.wbu.com), 28 East Market Street, Corning. Open April–December Monday–Wednesday and Saturday 10–6, Thursday–Friday 10–8, Sunday 12–5; January–March Monday–Friday 10–6, Saturday 10–5. Everything you need to feed and enjoy birds in your own backyard. Choose from bird feeders, birdhouses, birdbaths, a variety of seeds, books, and CDs, along with garden accents.

Elmira and Vicinity
The Christmas House (607-734-9547; www.christmas-house.com), 361 Maples Avenue, Elmira. Open late June–mid-January Monday–Thursday 10–5:30, Friday 10–9, Saturday 10–5, Sunday 12–5. An 1894 Victorian mansion housing a large Christmas specialty shop.

Oldies But Goodies (607-562-7416), NY 352 and Carpenter Road, Big Flats. Open Monday–Saturday 9:30–6. This country store has over 35 rooms of treasures from candles and antiques to furniture and stuffed animals.

✳ Special Events

July: **Chemung County Fair** (607-734-1203; www.chemungcounty fair.com), Chemung County Fairgrounds, between South Main and Grand Central Avenue, Horseheads. This fair—around for over 160 years—features agricultural exhibits, arts and crafts, floral displays, livestock exhibits, 4-H, live entertainment, and James E. Strates Show rides and midway. **Finger Lakes Wine Festival** (607-535-2481; www.flwinefest.com), Watkins Glen International Raceway, 2790 CR 16, Watkins Glen. More than 60 wineries participate in this annual event that features crafts, music, food, and wine tastings. **ARTSfest** (607-937-6292), Market Street, Corning. This event features an outdoor fine arts display, crafts, entertainment, food, hands-on kids' activities, and wine tasting.

August **Race Fever** 607-974-6436; www.gafferdistrict.com), Market Street, Corning. A downtown street party celebrating Nextel Cup racing.

This event features racing displays, drivers, food, and entertainment.

September: **Crystal City Jazz & Wine Festival** (607-974-6436; www.gafferdistrict.com), Market Street, Corning. The downtown Gaffer District comes alive with jazz and wine tasting. Local and regional jazz talents are featured in Centerway Square in the center of the district.

November–December: **Christmas Arts & Crafts Festival** Corning (607-936-4686; www.corningartsandcrafts.com), Corning Community College, Chemung Street, Corning. Sponsored by the Corning Area Chamber of Commerce. **Crystal City Christmas** Corning (607-974-6436; www.gafferdistrict .com), Market Street, Corning. This holiday family getaway offers three weekends of parades, festivals, entertainment, Santa, skating, and shopping. The first weekend features a Parade of Lights; the second weekend, known as Sparkle, includes carriage rides, crafts, and food. The third weekend, Sounds of the Season, features carols, folk tunes, and traditional holiday songs. **Holiday Home Tour** (607-733-4924), Elmira. Tours of Victorian homes in the Near Westside neighborhood.

ONTARIO COUNTY

Established in 1789, Ontario County is considered the "mother county" for all of western New York because all 13 counties featured in this book were formed from the 6 million acres of land that once made up Ontario County. As the region's population increased, the New York State Legislature subdivided the land to create new counties: Steuben in 1796, Genesee in 1802, Livingston and Monroe in 1821, and Yates in 1823. Some of these counties were further subdivided to create the remaining counties. (See *Western New York History: a Brief Overview* in the introduction to this book for more information on the beginnings of western New York.)

Ontario County is referred to as "Lake County" by its tourism office because five of the Finger Lakes—Hemlock, Canadice, Honeoye, Canandaigua, and Seneca—are located either within the county or along its borders. Whether you like boating, fishing, swimming, or just enjoy lake views, you'll appreciate Ontario County's abundance of water. The county also has over a dozen parks, nine public golf courses, and numerous hiking and biking trails.

For those who prefer less strenuous activities, the county has numerous museums and historical sites, including Ganondagan State Historic Site in Victor, which is a National Historic Landmark, and the Ontario County Courthouse in Canandaigua, where Susan B. Anthony stood trial for voting in the 1872 presidential election. Those interested in horticulture will want to check out Canandaigua's 50-acre Sonnenberg Gardens.

For more relaxing pursuits, Ontario County has several wineries that produce award-winning wines as well as numerous shops that can be found in historic Victorian-era buildings.

AREA CODE The area code in the western part of the county is 585; in the eastern part it's 315.

COUNTYWIDE GUIDANCE Canandaigua Wine Trail (877-FUN-IN-NY; www.canandaiguawinetrail.com or www.canandaiguawinetrailonline.com), Several wineries can be found along this trail on the western edge of the Finger Lakes Wine Region. This resource can help you plan your route by showing you which winery is where.

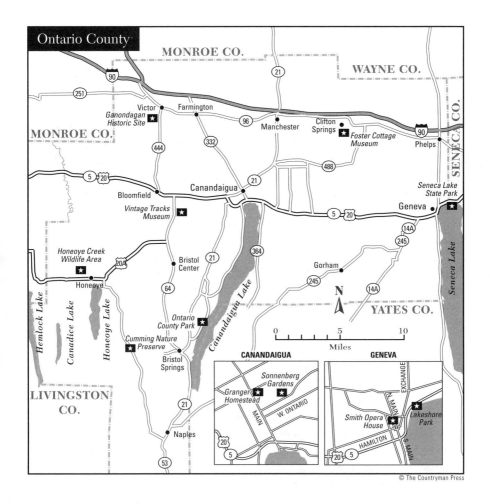

© The Countryman Press

Finger Lakes Visitors Connection (1-877-FUN-IN-NY or 877-386-4669; www.tourismny.com), 20 Ontario Street, 5 Lakes Suite, Canandaigua. Open Monday–Friday 8:30–4:30. Located in a brick house behind the Ontario County Courthouse, this information center has brochures and information about the entire county. (Note: Since they are located in a historic district, they don't have a sign on the building)

NORTHERN ONTARIO COUNTY—Clifton Springs, Farmington, Manchester, Victor, and Phelps

The area around Clifton Springs was first settled by Benjamin Shekell around 1800. The area developed slowly until the 1860s, when Dr. Henry Foster arrived to start the Clifton Springs Water Cure facility. Believing that the water held a curative power, visitors were drawn to the natural sulphur springs that flowed there, and travelers arrived by train and stagecoach from all over the eastern

United States. The village has retained much of its Victorian charm, with large restored mansions on East Main Street and numerous shops located in vintage buildings, including the restored Foster and Pierce Blocks.

The town of Farmington, home to Finger Lakes Gaming and Race Track, is largely a farming community with a growing number of small businesses.

The nearby town of Manchester saw its first settlers around 1773, but the village was not actually incorporated until almost 100 years later, when the Lehigh Valley railroad was built through the village. The name Manchester was chosen because local leaders thought that the town's many mills and factories would rival the industrial city in England with the same name. The railway expanded the village's freight transfer yard in 1914, and at one point it was considered the world's largest freight transfer yard. The village even had a semi-professional baseball team in the late 1800s, the Manchester Railroaders, which was one of the top teams in the northeast.

The area now known as the town of Victor was the site of the principal Seneca Nation village of Gannagaro. In July 1687 this village was invaded by the French Army under the Marquis Denonville and destroyed. The area where the village once stood is now a Ganondagan National Historic Site. After the Revolutionary War, the first settler, Enos Boughton, arrived in 1788 and others soon followed. The village was originally called Boughton Town, but in 1812, the name was changed—perhaps somewhat ironically—to Victor, to honor Claudius Victor Boughton, a War of 1812 hero. It was officially incorporated in 1879. Agriculture was an important early industry; with mills and factories springing up in Victor and nearby Fishers. One prominent early company was Locke Industries whose founder, Fred Locke, invented the high-voltage porcelain insulator. Today Victor, located close to the New York State Thruway, is home to many small business and high-tech manufacturing companies as well as Eastview Mall, the largest shopping center in the Finger Lakes. Many interesting architectural gems can be found throughout the town, including numerous homes of cobblestone construction.

Phelps, which was established in 1855, has lots of cobblestone buildings, as well, including an all-cobblestone farm located just east of town on NY 96. And a historical marker marks the spot next to a small waterfall where the first gristmill was built in Phelps by Seth Deane in the late 1700s. The village has a unique stone World War I memorial erected in 1921.

AREA CODE The area code in the western part of this region is 585; in the eastern part it's 315.

GUIDANCE **Village of Clifton Springs** (315-462-5151; www.cliftonsprings ny.org), 1 West Main Street, Clifton Springs. Open Monday–Friday 8–5.

Town of Farmington (315-986-8100; www.townoffarmingtonny.com), 1000 County Road 8. Open Monday–Friday 8–4:30.

Town of Phelps (315-548-5691 www.phelpsny.com), 79 Main Street, Phelps. Open Monday–Friday 9–4.

Village of Manchester (585-289-4340) 8, Clifton Street, Manchester. Open Monday–Friday 9–5.

Victor Chamber of Commerce (585-742-1476; www.victorchamber.com), Brochures from the Victor Chamber of Commerce are available at the **Act 2 Consignment Shop,** 31 East Main Street, Victor. Open Monday–Saturday 10–5.

Town of Victor (585-742-5000; www.victorny.org), 85 East Main Street, Victor. Monday–Friday 9–4:30.

Village of Victor (585-924-3311), 60 East Main, Victor. Monday–Friday 8:30–4:30.

GETTING THERE *By air:* See *Getting There Rochester.*

By car: All these towns are not far from the NYS Thruway (I-90): Victor exit 45, Farmington exit 44, and Manchester exit 43. Phelps and Clifton Springs are located on NY 96 between exits 42 and 43. NY 96 runs parallel to the NYS Thruway (I-90) and connects all the above mentioned towns.

MEDICAL EMERGENCY Dial 911

Clifton Springs Hospital and Clinic (315-462-9561; www.cliftonspring hospital.org), 2 Coulter Road, Clifton Springs.

✳ To See

ARCHITECTURE **Stone Acres Farm,** NY 96 east of Phelps. This Thoroughbred horse farm is made entirely of cobblestones, including the barns. It is private property, so view it from the road.

MUSEUMS AND HISTORIC HOMES **The Foster Cottage Museum** (315-462-7394; www.fostercottage.org), 9 East Main Street, Clifton Springs. Open Thursday–Saturday 10–3. Free admission. Learn about the history of Clifton Springs at this historic 1854 Victorian home, once the residence of Dr. Henry Foster, founder of the Clifton Springs Water Cure. This sulphur-cure therapy made the town a vacation destination at the turn of the 20th century.

Hill Cumorah Visitors Center and Historic Sites (315-597-5851; www .hillcumorah.com), NY 21 (I-90 exit 43), Manchester. Open November–March Monday–Saturday 9–5, Sunday 1–5; April–May Monday–Saturday 9–6, 1–6; June–August Monday–Saturday 9–7, Sunday 11–7; September–October Monday–Saturday 9–6, Sunday 1–6. Free admission. A visitor's center and various sites significant to the Church of Latter-Day Saints (Mormons) contain exhibits on the history of the church, which was founded in this area by Joseph Smith. Nearby is the site of the annual Hill Cumorah Pageant held in July. See *Special Events.*

Phelps Historical Society (315-548-4940), 66 Main Street, Phelps. Open Thursday and Friday 10–2 or by appointment. Free admission. The museum has information on local history, railroad and baseball exhibits, a unique two-story brick outhouse, and genealogy records.

Valentown (585-924-2645; www.Valentown.org), Valentown Square, Fishers (off NY96, across from Eastview Mall). Open seasonally May–October Sunday 12–4, and by appointment. The home of the Victor Historical Society, this three-story wooden building was built in 1879 as a shopping and community center by Levi Valentine. He built it next to the site where the Pittsburgh, Shawmut & Northern Railroad line was suppose to be built. Unfortunately, the railroad was constructed about 40 miles south of here and never reached the site. Valentown was used for a variety of businesses throughout the years. In the 1940s, it was turned into a museum by J. Sheldon Fisher. An annual antiques show, a fund-raiser for the historical society, takes place in summer.

HISTORIC SITES ✪ **Ganondagan State Historic Site** (585-924-5848; www .ganondagan.org), 1488 NY 444, Victor. Open Wednesday–Sunday 9–5, mid-May–October; trails open year-round 8–sunset. Admission: $2 adults, $1 seniors and students. This 277-acre historic site, designated a National Historic Landmark in 1964, was the location of a 17th-century Seneca village and sacred burial ground known as the Town of Peace. The village, which had about 150 bark longhouses and a population of 4,500 people, was attacked and destroyed by the French in 1687. The visitors center has exhibits on the Seneca clan system, works by Seneca artists, and a video on the history of the site. A full-size replica of a Seneca bark longhouse is open for tours. The grounds include three hiking trails: Our Mother Trail, the Trail of Peace, and the Granary Trail.

✷ To Do

GOLF Auburn Creek Driving Range (585-924-7570), 7331 Victor-Mendon Road, Victor. This driving range includes grass and matted teas, putting and chipping greens, target greens, night lights, and covered stalls.

Parkview Fairways (585-657-7539), 7100 Boughton Road, Victor. An 18-hole, par-72 course with driving range. Lessons offered; junior golf camp.

Ravenwood Golf Club (585-924-5100; www.ravenwoodgolf.com), 929 Lynaugh Road, Victor. An 18-hole, par-72 course with large putting surfaces and rolling fairways. It was selected by *Golf Digest* as one of the top-five new public golf courses in 2003.

Victor Hills Golf Club (585-924-3480) 1,450 Brace Road, Victor. This club has 36 holes, plus a 9-hole executive course. The course is easily accessible and has a lot of variety.

Winged Pheasant Golf Links (585-289-8846), 1433 Sand Hill Road, Shortsville. An 18-hole, par-70 course in a forest setting; full-service restaurant and snack bar.

HORSE RACING AND GAMING ♿ **Finger Lakes Gaming & Race Track** (585-585-924-3232 or 800-875-7191; www.fingerlakesracetrack.com), 5857 NY 96, Farmington. Open 10 AM–2 AM, seven days. The Finger Lakes Race Track opened in 1962, and in 2004 more than 1,000 video gaming machines in over 28,000 square feet were added to the facility. You can play in any denomination, from a nickel to $10, in the gaming room, which has a Finger Lakes winery theme. There are several dining options here, too, from upscale to casual. Thor-

oughbred racing takes place here Friday–Tuesday afternoons, April–December.
(Note: Patrons must be a minimum of 18 to play on the gaming floor or wager on races.)

✳ Green Space

PARKS Boughton Park (585-742-7028), Off Phillips Road, Victor. Open dawn to dusk. Park accessible by permit only. Permit can be obtained at Victor, Bloomfield or West Bloomfield town halls. Fishing, hiking trails, and a picnic area.

WALKING AND HIKING TRAILS Auburn Trail (Victor Hiking Trails), 85 East Main Street, Victor. An 8-mile trail from Fishers to Victor along the former Rochester and Auburn railroad corridor. This trail passes through a tunnel under the Thruway.

Ontario Pathways Rail Trail (585-234-7722; www.ontariopathways.org), NY 96 (just east of NY 488), Phelps. This 3-mile multipurpose trail follows an abandoned railroad bed through beautiful countryside and scenic woodlands.

Victor Hiking Trails System (585-234-8226; www.victorhikingtrails.org), 85 East Main Street, Victor. There are over 18 miles of foot trails throughout the town of Victor. These trails offer easy walking and biking and former railway beds, which connect with parks.

Note: More information on these and other Ontario County trails can be found on the **Ontario County Web site** (www.visitfingerlakes.com/outdoors).

✳ Lodging

MOTELS AND HOTELS ♿ **Hampton Inn** (585-924-4400 www.rochester hamptoninn.com), 7637 NY 96, Thruway exit 45, Victor. Stay in one of 123 spacious rooms, including 55 suites, decorated with Mission-style furniture. The hotel, which is located in a parklike setting, has such amenities as a free continental breakfast, indoor pool, and fitness center. $113–$149.

♿ **Microtel** (585-924-9240 or 800-278-8884), 7498 Main Street (NY 96) Victor. This motel offers 99 guest rooms with one or two queen-sized beds. A complimentary continental breakfast is served. $49–$69.
Note: Other chain hotels and motels are located near I-90 exits 44 (Victor/Farmington) and exit 43 (Manchester).

BED & BREAKFASTS Safari House Bed & Breakfast (585-924-0250; www.safarihouse.com), 950 Deer Crossing, (off NY 251), Victor. Open year-round. Lilo and Don Nibbelink offer two spacious suites and one smaller room in this secluded air conditioned B&B on a wooded, 12-acre paradise. The grounds feature swans, deer, ducks, mink, and wild turkeys as well as a 31-station self-guided nature trail and Japanese garden. The Honeymoon Suite features a king-sized brass bed, fireplace, and Jacuzzi; the Valentine Suite features a queen-sized bed, fireplace, and heart-shaped Jacuzzi. The Safari Room, decorated in an African safari motif, features a single four-poster bed and private bath. A full made-to-order breakfast is served. Eat in the Asian-themed dining room, or have breakfast served in your room. They will even serve you breakfast in bed! $95–$195.

Yorkshire Inn (315-548-YORK; www.theyorkshireinn.com), 1135 NY 96, Phelps. Doug and Kathe Latch are the innkeepers in this 1796 inn that started out as a farmhouse and was converted to a stagecoach stop in the early 1800s. The inn has two guest rooms with private baths, satellite TV, broadband Internet connections, and oversized showers. They have plans to add an adjoining room to one of the rooms to accommodate larger families. A spacious deck overlooks the property. The full breakfast may include favorites like French toast casserole, lemon-cheese strudel, and Belgian waffles, plus fresh fruits, juice and coffee. Mid-June–October 31 $99; rest of year $79.

OTHER LODGING

Campgrounds
Cheerful Valley Campground (315-781-1222; www.gocamping america.com/cheerfulvalley), 1412 NY 14, Phelps. Open April 15–October 15. One hundred campsites with hookups can be found at this camp-ground located on 100 acres in a river valley. Amenities include a swimming pool, horseshoes, shuffleboard, fish-ing, and planned activities.

Junius Ponds Cabins & Camp-ground (315-781-5120), 1475 Town-line Road, Phelps. Open April 15–October 30. One hundred RV sites, 25 tent sites, and four cabins are offered on shaded and open sites. It has a pool, playground, and showers.

✳ Where to Eat
DINING OUT **DiPacific's Restaurant** (585-924-3634), Victor-Manchester

Road (corner of NY 96 and 332), Farmington. Open daily 11–9. Enjoy fine Italian dining at this restaurant, located opposite the Finger Lakes Race Track.

The Historic Phelps Hotel (315-548-5200), 90 Main Street, Phelps. Open Monday–Thursday 4:30–9, Friday and Saturday 4:30–10, Sun-day 1–8. Menu selections include Friday fish fry, prime rib on Saturday, and a traditional turkey dinner on Sunday.

Warfield's Restaurant and Bakery (315-462-7184; www.warfields.com) 7 West Main Street, Clifton Springs. Open for lunch Tuesday–Saturday 11–2:30, dinner Tuesday–Thursday 5–8, Friday and Saturday 5–9, Sunday brunch 11–2. An impressive 1871 building houses this fine-dining desti-nation. The interior features brick and oak walls and tin ceilings. The exterior is surrounded by a beautiful English garden. The menu features country fare with Asian and European accents. They make their own pasta and sausages, smoke their own meats and seafood, and bake bread fresh daily. Their signature desserts include Warfield's red grits, made with rasp-berries, tapioca, and Grand Marnier, and Warfield's crème brûlée, rumored to be the best in upstate New York. The second-floor banquet room fea-tures an 1800s English pub bar. The restaurant also has an award-winning bakery offering specialty breads, cookies, and pies.

EATING OUT ⅋ **Brown Bag Deli** (315-462-7609), 14 East Main Street, Clifton Springs. Open Monday–Fri-day 7:30–3:30. This café, located in a historic building with tin ceilings, is open for breakfast and lunch.

&. ♂ ❦ **Burger King** (585-924-7073), 600 Rowley Road (at NY 96), Victor. While we don't ordinarily review fast-food chains, this Burger King deserves a mention because of its unique decor. It looks like an ordinary Burger King from the outside, but once you step inside, you'd swear you were in a 1950s diner, complete with a Wurlitzer jukebox spinning '50s tunes, posters of Elvis and James Dean on the walls and even booths that have tail fins.

&. **Cole & Parks Bakery, Café & Coffee Co.** (585-924-8710), 607 Rowley Road (NY 96 and Main Street) Victor. Open Monday–Thursday 6:30–8, Friday 6:30–10:30, Saturday 7–7:30, Sunday 7–6. This renovated 1813 building houses an upscale, elegant café that serves coffee beverages and fresh baked goods like cookies, scones, and muffins, along with soups, panini sandwiches, wraps, and ice cream. They even have a drive-through if you're running late for work. Or come here after dinner for your dessert and coffee.

Coffee Creek, 116 Main Street, Phelps. A cozy Internet cafe serving gourmet coffee, pastries, and sandwiches.

The Grind Coffeehouse and Café (585-924-9160), 54 West Main Street, Victor. Open Monday–Friday 6:30–4, Saturday 7–4, Sunday 8–4. A small coffee café in the heart of Victor offering gourmet javas and light fare.

Mickey Finn's Restaurant and Tavern (585-924-0530; www.mickey finns.com), 14 Railroad Street, Victor. Open Monday–Saturday 11–10:30 (bar until 12 AM) Sunday 4–10. Located in a circa 1880 brick building once part of the Victor Flour Mill complex, this restaurant's original brick walls are enhanced by natural-oak booths, Tiffany lamps, and a stone fireplace. The extensive menu features salads, sandwiches, and homemade soups for lunch, along with dinner entrées like steak, chicken, seafood, and vegetarian dishes. They have 18 draft beers, which are served in frosted mugs.

&. ♂ ❦ **Papa Jacks Ice Cream** (585-924-1460), 265 West Main Street (NY 96), Victor. Monday–Friday 11–9, Saturday–Sunday 12–9. This popular burger and ice cream place recently moved into this new, larger location.

&. **Talk of the Town Cafe** (315-462-CAFE), 12 West Main Street, Clifton Springs. Open Monday–Friday 7:30–7, Saturday 8–3, Sunday 9–1. This cute little café serves up bagels, soups, salads, wraps, and sandwiches as well as 20 flavors of gourmet coffee, smoothies, and 27 flavors of ice cream.

✴ Selective Shopping

ANTIQUES &. **Antique Emporium of Farmington** (585-398-3997; www .antiqueemporium.com), 1780 Rochester Road, Farmington. Open daily 10–5. An 11,000-square-foot multidealer antiques mall with a large selection of Victorian furniture, art glass, fine china, pottery, toys, silver, and primitives. They have a comfortable sitting area stocked with magazines and tourism information—a good place to leave your spouse while you shop.

Black Sheep Antiques (315-462-9338), 18 East Main Street, Clifton Springs. Open Thursday and Saturday 11–5, Sunday 12–4. This shop specializes in primitives, textiles, timepieces, and stoneware.

Country Road Antiques (585-526-6970), 2481 CR 20, Phelps. Open

Monday–Saturday 10-5. A small country shop specializing in refinishing.

The Cobblestore (585-742-1930; www.cobblestore.westernny/com), 6452 Victor-Manchester Road (NY 96), Victor. Monday–Saturday 11–6, Sunday 12–5, closed Wednesday. This unique shop, housed in a circa 1835 cobblestone building listed on the National Register of Historic Places, has one of the region's largest selections of dog- and animal-related antiques. The collection includes everything from furniture to fine porcelain, including "Tails of Yesteryear" animal art. They also have an extensive collection of rare lithophanes and porcelain figures.

&. **Ontario Mall Antiques** (585-398-0240), 1740 Rochester Road (NY 332), Farmington. Daily 10–6. This 50,000-square-foot antiques mega mall has over 600 dealers and the best prices anywhere. They even have a small sitting area near the front of the store stocked with magazines, coffee, and cookies—especially nice if you are shopping with a spouse or friend who doesn't share your passion for antiques. The mall has handicapped-accessible rest rooms.

Victor House Antiques (585-924-4260; www.victorhouseantiques.com), 72 West Main Street, Victor. Open Wednesday–Saturday 11–5, Sunday 12–4. A multidealer shop with a large variety of antiques and collectibles.

SHOPPING MALLS &. **Eastview Mall** (585-223-4420; www.eastviewmall.com), 7979 Pittsford-Victor Road (NY 96), Victor. The region's largest mall has over 1 million square feet of shopping, including five major department stores and more than 160 shops.

SPECIAL SHOPS Act 2 Consignment Shop (585-924-7260), 31 East Main Street, Victor. Open Monday–Saturday 10–5, Thursday until 7. This shop offers new and gently used clothing, antiques, and other items. They also have a handy display of brochures on the Victor area.

Cedar Hollow Mercantile (585-742-5460), 7353 Victor-Pittsford Road (NY 96), Victor. Open daily 12–5. Located in a log cabin, this shop features unique gifts for the home and cottage, including pottery, potpourri, artwork, Christmas items, jewelry, and gourmet foods.

SHOP FOR CANINE AND OTHER ANIMAL-RELATED ANTIQUES IN A COBBLESTONE BUILDING ON THE NATIONAL REGISTER OF HISTORIC PLACES.

Christine A. Smyczynski

Country Corner (315-548-3855), 247 West Main, Phelps. Monday–Friday 10–6, Saturday 9–5 This shop carries a complete line of Boyd and Ty Beanie Babies, Byers' Choice carolers, Willow Tree Angels, flags, candles, art prints, candy and more.

The Ivy Thimble (585-742-2680; www.ivythimble.com), 5 Railroad Avenue (at the Train Depot), Victor. Open Monday–Wednesday 9:30–5, Thursday 9:30–7, Friday and Saturday 9:30–4. This store carries over 1,200 bolts of fabric along with quilting supplies and patterns. They also carry a large selection of candles, painted items, jewelry and accessories, home decor, and more.

& **Mead Square Pharmacy** (585-924-7970); 53 West Main Street, Victor. Open Monday and Wednesday 9–8; Tuesday, Thursday, Friday 9–7; Saturday 9–5. The gift shop in this pharmacy carries a variety of items, including Ty Beanie Babies, greeting cards, and specialty foods.

A Patch of County (585-398-2913), 1734 Rochester Road (NY 332), Farmington. Open Tuesday–Sunday 10–5:30; closed January and February. Shop for unique gifts in a restored 1936 brick farmhouse. They carry a large collection of Cat's Meow collectible plus home decor items, Christmas ornaments, jewelry, kitchen gadgets, baskets, toys, miniatures, photos, and Boyd's plush animals.

& **Peirce's Antiques and Gifts** (315-548-GIFT), 2 West Main Street, Clifton Springs. Open Monday–Friday 10–5, Saturday 10–3, Sunday 12–3. Located in the historic Pierce Block, this shop specializes in hand-painted furniture, locally handcrafted items, antiques, country accessories, and year-round Christmas things.

& **Rose Petal Gift Shop** (315-462-7699), Main Street, Clifton Springs. Open Monday–Friday 10–5:30, Saturday 10–3. This gift shop carries cards, gifts, Ty plush, and Clifton Spring merchandise.

Whitson Pharmacy (315-548-9454), 110 Main Street, Phelps. Open Monday–Friday 9–8, Saturday 9–5. Choose from distinctive gifts, candles, Red Hat Society items, jewelry, postcards, and Phelps merchandise.

✳ Special Events

July: **Hill Cumorah Pageant** (315-597-5851: www.hillcumorah.com), NY 21, Manchester. The Hill Cumorah Pageant is one of America's largest outdoor theatrical performances. Since 1937 members of the Church of Jesus Christ of Latter-Day Saints (Mormons) have presented this annual event. Using elaborate costumes, state-of-the-art lighting, and special effects and digital sound, performers on a nine-level stage tell the history of the Latter-Day Saints. **Phelps Sauerkraut Festival** (315-548-2222; www.phelpssauerkrautfestival.com), Village of Phelps. This festival commemorates when Phelps was one of the largest producers of sauerkraut in the country. Events include cabbage-head decorating and cutting of the sauerkraut cake, along with rides, games, live music, crafts, and more.

August: **Sulphur Spring Festival** (315-462-8202; www.cliftonspring chamber.com/ssf.htm), Along Main Street and next to Sulphur Creek, Clifton Springs. The town was known for its natural sulphur springs "water cure" in the 1800s, and the festival celebrates this legacy. Enjoy historic house tours, arts and crafts, classic cars, antiques, entertainment, and more. **Valentown Antique Peddlers Market** (www.valentown.org) Historic Valentown (NY 96, across from Eastview Mall), Victor. Over 100 quality dealers; proceeds benefit Historic Valentown and the Victor Historical Society.

September: **Hang Around Victor Day** (585-742-1476 www.victorchamber .com), Victor. This annual event, sponsored by the Victor Chamber of Commerce, features local artisans, craftsmen, antique dealers, live entertainment, food vendors, and more.

WESTERN ONTARIO COUNTY—Bloomfield

The town of East Bloomfield was settled in 1799 by Deacon John Adams and his family, who came from New England. Agriculture was the main industry in the early days, with wheat and corn being the primary products. In the early 1800s Oliver and Herman Chapin developed the Northern Spy apple in their orchards on Boughton Road, and the apple industry became prominent.

Education was important to the early settlers, so in 1838 the East Bloomfield Academy was built. It first served the community as a private school, then became a public school in 1876. It closed in 1909, and today the building, which is on the State and National Registers of Historic Places, is used by the local historical society.

Today, the Bloomfield area has a large concentration of antiques stores, known as the Bloomfield Antique Country Mile—which is actually more like 3 miles. With over a dozen shops, you can find everything from early American antiques and primitives to retro items.

The town is also home to the country's largest Antique Wireless and Radio Museum, located in the historic Bloomfield Academy building. And the nearby Vintage Tracks Museum has more than a hundred antique tractors on display.

AREA CODE The area code in this region is 585.

GUIDANCE Village of Bloomfield (585-657-7554; www.bloomfieldny.org), 12 Main Street, Bloomfield. Open Monday–Thursday 9–12:30 and 1–4.

Town of East Bloomfield (585-657-6515), PO Box 85, 99 Main Street, East Bloomfield. Monday–Friday 8:30–4:30.

Town of West Bloomfield (585-624-2914), 9053 Routes 5 and 20, West Bloomfield. Open Monday–9:30–12 and 1–4:30, Thursday until 6:30.

Walking Tour of East Bloomfield can be found on www.bloomfieldbuzz.com.

GETTING THERE By air: *See Getting There—Rochester.*

By car: Bloomfield is located along Routes 5 and 20, which is off I-390.

MEDICAL EMERGENCY Dial 911

✳ To See

MUSEUMS AND HISTORIC HOMES **Bloomfield Academy Museum/East Bloomfield Historical Society** (585-657-7244), 8 South Avenue, Bloomfield. Open Tuesday–Friday 1—2; closed January and February. This 1838 brick schoolhouse houses a museum with information on local history. The **Antique Wireless Association Communications Museum** (585-657-6260; Saturday 2–4 June–August, Sunday 2–5 May–October; free admission), is located on the second floor of the Bloomfield Academy Museum. This museum houses one of the largest collections in the United States of early communications apparatus, including telegraph, radio, and television.

Vintage Tracks Museum (585-657-6608), 3170 Wheeler Station Road, Bloomfield. Open May–November Saturday and Sunday 11–4 and by appointment; July and August Thursday–Monday 12–4. Admission: $4. This museum features more than 100 tractors and machines from the early 1900s, including machines made by Caterpillar, John Deere, and American Tractor.

West Bloomfield Historical Society (585-624-2458), 8966 Routes 5 and 20, West Bloomfield. Open Monday 6:30–8:30 PM or by appointment. Historical information on West Bloomfield can be found in this former church building.

✳ Green Space

PARKS **Elton Park,** Routes 5 and 20 (near South Avenue), Bloomfield. A colonial village green with a Civil War monument dedicated in 1868.

✳ Lodging

See listings under **Canandaigua** and **Victor.**

THE BLOOMFIELD ACADEMY MUSEUM OFFERS LOCAL HISTORY, PLUS THE ANTIQUE WIRELESS ASSOCIATION COMMUNICATIONS MUSEUM ON THE SECOND FLOOR.
Christine A. Smyczynski

✱ Where to Eat

DINING OUT **Cheap Charlie's Restaurant and Lounge** (585-657-6812), 8 Elm Street (NY 444), Bloomfield. Open Monday–Thursday 11–9, Friday and Saturday 11–10, Sunday 11–8. Specializing in steaks, seafood, sautés, and prime rib.

The Holloway House Restaurant (585-657-7120; www.thehollowayhouse.com), Corner Routes 5 and 20 and South Avenue, Bloomfield. Open April–December Tuesday–Saturday 11:30–2 and 5–9, Sunday 12–7:30. In 1808 blacksmith Peter Holloway built this stagecoach tavern, which is now listed on the National Register of Historic Places. Menu selections feature roast turkey, Angus beef, fresh seafood, and homemade desserts.

EATING OUT ♿ **Jean's Village Restaurant** (585-657-7510), 7 Main Street, Bloomfield. Open Monday–Saturday 5:30–2, Sunday 6–1. Enjoy breakfast and lunch in a family restaurant and coffee shop just a few blocks from Routes 5 and 20

BLOOMFIELD IS NOTED FOR ITS CONCENTRATION OF ANTIQUES SHOPS.
Christine A. Smyczynski

✱ Selective Shopping

ANTIQUES Numerous antique shops can be found in **Bloomfield,** located 6 miles west of Canandaigua on Routes 5 and 20. Please note that 5 and 20 is a very busy highway with a 55 MPH speed limit in many places. Plan on driving from store to store, as it would not be safe to walk along or cross this road. You can visit the shops virtually at www.bloomfieldantiquemile.com.

♿ **Bloomberry Junction,** formerly Alan's Antique Alley (716-657-6776), 6925 Routes 5 and 20, Bloomfield. Open summer daily 10–5, winter daily 11–5. The wares of over 130 dealers are displayed in 10,000 square feet, including a large selection of furniture.

♿ **Bloomfield Antique Market** (585-657-4260; www.bloomfieldantiquemarket.com), 6980 Routes 5 and 20, Bloomfield. Open daily 11–5. This shop has a large selection of furniture, along with china, glassware, paintings, and other collectibles.

The Furniture Doctor (585-657-6941), 7007 Routes 5 and 20, Bloomfield. Open Monday–Saturday 9–5, Sunday 11–4. Specializing in fine furniture, custom upholstery, refinishing, and antiques.

♿ **One Potato Two Shop** (585-657-7446; www.onepotatotwoshop.com) 6900 Routes 5 and 20, Bloomfield. Open Monday–Saturday 10–5, Sunday 11–5. Over 60 quality dealers in 6,000 square feet display a large variety of period furniture, antique furnishings, timeless treasures, and gourmet foods.

& **Peddlers's Antiques and Collectibles** (585-657-4869), 3170 Wheeler Station Road, Bloomfield. Open daily 10–5. Forty-five dealers showcase their wares in this 10,000-square-foot shop. Choose from jewelry, smalls, furniture, and more. The **Vintage Tracks Tractor Museum** is located behind this shop (see *To See—Museums and Historic Homes*).

& **Rooster Cove Antiques** (585-624-2090), 8524 Routes 5 and 20, West Bloomfield. Open 10–5 Wednesday–Monday. A small shop with a variety of antiques and collectibles.

Sean Fagan Old & Rare Books (585-657-7096 www.faganbooks.com), 6883 Routes 5 and 20 Bloomfield. Open Friday–Sunday 11–6. A large selection of old and rare books.

CRAFTS **The Wizard of Clay Pottery** See listing under Honeoye.

SPECIAL SHOPS **Troll Mountain Mystic Gift Shoppe** See listing under Honeoye.

Twigs & Berries Designs (585-657-4150), 38 State Street, East Bloomfield. Open Tuesday–Saturday 10–4. Chose from antiques, home furnishings, fabrics, and accessories.

✳ Special Events

July: **Bloomfield Antique Show and Sale** (585-657-7664; www.bloomfield antiquemile.com), Elton Park, Routes 5 and 20 (near South Avenue), Bloomfield. An outdoor show with over 60 dealers, plus sales at all the antiques shops along the Bloomfield Antique Country Mile.

CENTRAL ONTARIO COUNTY—Canandaigua and Vicinity

Canandaigua: The name means "chosen place" from the Native American word *Kanandarque*, and it was the site of a principal Seneca village. It was on November 11, 1794, at Treaty Rock, that the Canandaigua Treaty between the United States government and the six nations of the Iroquois was signed. It is one of the longest-standing treaties between Native people and the government. Article One of the treaty states that "peace and friendship are hereby firmly established, and shall be perpetual, between the United States and the Six Nations." The first white settlers arrived in 1789 and laid out the town at the north end of Canandaigua Lake. It has been the county seat since its founding.

Canandaigua is a fairly urban area compared to the rest of Ontario County. The nearby town of Farmington, once a rural farm community, is now home of the Finger Lakes Gaming and Race Track. Downtown Canandaigua, which features the widest Main Street in the nation, has many unique boutiques and restaurants. Of course, the biggest attraction in the area is Canandaigua Lake. At 16 miles long and about 262 feet deep, it affords many recreational opportunities, from boating and swimming to fishing and waterskiing. Many of the region's wealthiest executives have large summer estates along the shores of Canandaigua Lake.

Rushville, several miles south of Canandaigua near the Yates County border, is rich in Native American history. Nundawao (South Hill) is considered the birthplace of the Seneca Nation. Marcus Whitman, a pioneer missionary, was born here. Whitman and his wife, Narcissa Prentiss, played an important role in the opening of the Oregon Trail— Narcissa was one of the first white women to travel the trail—and encouraged settlement in Oregon region.

AREA CODE The area code for Canandaigua is 585.

GUIDANCE **Canandaigua Chamber of Commerce** (585-394-4400; www .canandaigua.com), 113 South Main Street, Canandaigua. Open Monday–Friday 9–5; also open Saturday, Sunday, and holidays 10–4 from Memorial Day–Columbus Day.

City of Canandaigua (585-396-5000; www.ci.canandaigua.govoffices.com), 2 North Main Street, Canandaigua. Open Monday–Friday 9–4:45.

Finger Lakes Visitors Connection See *Countywide Guidance* at the beginning of this chapter.

Town of Canandaigua (585-394-1120; www.townofcanandaigua.org), 5440 Routes 5 and 20, Canandaigua. Open Monday–Friday 8–4.

Historic Downtown Canandaigua (585-396-0300; www.downtowncanandaigua .com) 115 South Main Street, Canandaigua. Information on shops, galleries, restaurants and festivals in Downtown Canandaigua. Open Monday–Friday 9–12.

GETTING THERE *By air:* **Canandaigua Airport** (585-393-1470). Land on this small airstrip, or see *Getting There—Rochester.*

By car: Take I-90 to exit 44 and head south on NY 332 or exit 43, then south on NY 21.

GETTING AROUND *By bus:* **County Area Transit System CATS** (800-667-CATS), 2450 Brickyard Road, Canandaigua. This transportation system runs between Canandaigua and Geneva and Canandaigua and Victor.

By taxi: **Canandaigua Cab** (585-394-9370) **Pat's Taxi** (585-394-1620), **Tom's Taxi** (585-396-0770) **Spot Hop** (585-394-4400), Operates daily in July and August. Free narrated transportation between some local attractions, including Roseland Waterpark, Kershaw Park, historic downtown, Inn on the Lake, Steamboat Landing, Sonnenberg Gardens, and Ontario County Historical Society.

MEDICAL EMERGENCY Dial 911.

F. F. Thompson Hospital (585-396-6000), 350 Parrish Street, Canandaigua.

✳ To See

ART MUSEUMS **South Bristol Cultural Center, Inc.** (585-396-9504; www .southbristolculturalcenter.com) 5323 Seneca Point Road, Canandaigua. Open

Wednesday–Saturday 10–5, Sunday 1–4. A gallery of works by local artists plus art classes and special events.

MUSEUMS AND HISTORIC HOMES Granger Homestead and Carriage Museum (585-394-1472 www.grangerhomestead.com), 294 North Main Street, Canandaigua. Open mid-May–mid-October Tuesday–Friday 1–5; also open Saturday and Sunday 1–5 June 1–August 31. Admission: $5 adults, $4 seniors, $1 children 7–16. The Federal-style Granger Mansion, built in 1816 by Gideon Granger, the first U.S. postmaster general, is restored and open to the public for tours. The carriage museum in the rear of the property has over 40 horse-drawn conveyances used in the 19th century.

Ontario County Historical Society (585-394-4975 www.ochs.org), 55 North Main Street, Canandaigua. Open Tuesday–Saturday 10–4:30, Wednesday until 9. Admission: $2. The Ontario County Historical Society was formed in 1902 to preserve the county's heritage. The 1914 Georgian Revival structure houses permanent and changing exhibits about the history of Ontario County as well as a genealogy research archive. Each historical society in Ontario County has an exhibit about their museum in this facility. A small gift shop has books on local history as well as walking tour brochures of historic downtown Canandaigua.

Trail of Remembrance, American Legion Post #256, 454 North Main Street, Canandaigua. Markers along this outdoor memorial trail highlight over 250 years of military history in the United States, from colonial wars until the present time.

HISTORIC SITES Ontario County Courthouse (800-654-9798; www.ontario ny.com), Main Street, Canandaigua. This courthouse was the site of Susan B. Anthony's famous trial in 1872 for voting in a presidential election. At that time, women did not have the right to vote, and the well-known suffragette was arrested for casting a ballot. See also **Susan B. Anthony House**, listed under *Monroe County—City of Rochester,* **Museums.**

✳ To Do

AUTO RACING Canandaigua Speedway (585-394-0961 or 315-834-6606 www.canandaiguaspeedway.com), Ontario County Fairgrounds, Townline Road (CR 10), Canandaigua. Open mid-April–Labor Day. DIRT motorsports racing every Saturday night. The half-mile clay oval track is one of the most revered on the circuit.

BALLOONING High Hopes Balloon Co. (585-377-7768; www.highhopes balloon.com). Take a hot-air balloon ride over the Finger Lakes Region. Launch sites are in Canandaigua, Conesus Lake, and Victor.

BOAT EXCURSIONS *Canandaigua Lady* (585-394-5365; www.steamboat landingonline.com), 169 Lakeshore Drive, Canandaigua. Open June–October for lunch, supper, and fine-dining cruises, as well as sightseeing and specialty cruises. Times and prices vary; call for schedule. Enjoy elegant dining and/or sightseeing on the only replica 19th-century paddlewheel steamboat in the Finger

Lakes region. The 150-passenger boat was built in 1984 and started sailing on Canandaigua Lake in 1989.

Captain Gray's Boat Tours (585-394-5270 www.captgrays.com). Boats depart from City Pier at the south end of Main Street and from the Inn on the Lake, 770 Main Street. Times and prices vary; call for schedule. Enjoy a great view of the lake and the surrounding countryside when you cruise with Captain Gray. The one-, two-, or three-hour tours also include tidbits of local heritage, from the days of the Seneca Nation to the glory days of the steamboat era.

FISHING **Canandaigua Lake** is stocked annually with lake trout and brown trout, while rainbow trout can be found in **Naples Creek,** at the southeast end of Canandaigua Lake near Naples, which has six fishing access points. Fishing licenses can be obtained at city or town halls and at sporting goods and large department stores. The **Canandaigua Lake Trout Derby** (585-394-4400) takes place the first weekend in June. Fishing takes place throughout Canandaigua Lake. Weigh stations are set up by the Canandaigua Inn on the Lake at the north and of the lake and at Jensen's Marina in Woodville at the south end of the lake. Cash prizes are awarded with a top prize of $1,000.

FAMILY FUN ✪ **Abbey Farm** (585-526-5420; www.abbeyhistoricalfarm.org), 1862 Routes 5 and 20, Stanley (between Canandaigua and Geneva). Open 10–5 Tuesday–Saturday and by appointment. Kids of all ages will enjoy a hands-on experience feeding farm animals, milking, candle dipping, and spinning on a historical Victorian farm. History comes alive as you learn about farm life in the late 1800s. (They also run a bed & breakfast. See *Lodging—Geneva*.)

✪ **Roseland Waterpark** (585-396-2000; www.roselandwaterpark.com), 250 Eastern Boulevard, Canandaigua. Open mid-June–Labor Day daily 11–7. Admission: $26.95, $12.95 under 48 inches. A 58-acre family-oriented water park that includes a giant wave pool, Adventure River, tube rides, body flumes, a children's area, and a 30-acre private lake.

GOLF **Bristol Harbour Golf Club & Resort** See listing in *Southern Ontario County*.

CenterPointe Golf Course (585-394-0346) 1940 Brickyard Road (off NY 332), Canandaigua. An 18-hole, par-71 course with a full-service restaurant and snack bar.

MARINAS **Canandaigua Lake State Marine Boat Launch** (315-536-

SEE CANANDAIGUA LAKE FROM THE DECK OF THE *CANANDAIGUA LADY,* A REPLICA 19TH-CENTURY PADDLEWHEELER.
Christine A. Smyczynski

launch at the north end of the lake.

See also **Kershaw Park** and **Onanda Park** in *Green Space.*

WINE TASTING **Finger Lakes Wine Center** (585-394-9016; www.fingerlakes winecenter.com), 151 Charlotte Street, Canandaigua. Open daily 11–4 May– Columbus Day. Features tastings and sales of New York State wine from 35— and counting!—Finger Lakes wineries. Part of **Sonnenberg Gardens** (see *Green Space*).

✳ Green Space

BEACHES **Butler Beach** (585-396-2752), West Lake Road, Canandaigua. A free beach on the west side of Canandaigua Lake

Deep Run Park (585-396-4000), East Lake Road, Canandaigua. A free beach on the east shore of Canandaigua Lake.

Kershaw Park. *See Parks.*

GARDENS **Sonnenberg Gardens**, (585-394-4922; www.sonnenberg.org), 151 Charlotte Street, Canandaigua. Open May–Columbus Day daily 9:30–4:30, until 5:30 July and August. Admission: $10 over age 12, $9 seniors and AAA members, children 12 and under free. Sonnenberg Gardens features 50 acres of gardens, a turn-of-the-20th-century conservatory, plus a Victorian mansion. Two miles of pathways link various themed gardens, including Japanese, butterfly, rose, and Italian. The 1887 40-room, three-story mansion, listed on the National Register of Historic Places, is built in the Queen Anne style. It was the summer home of Frederick Ferris Thompson and his wife, Mary Clark, whose main residence was in New York City, where Frederick was director of a successful 19th century bank—today known as Citibank. Finger Lakes Wine Center is adjacent to the gardens. See "Wine Tasting."

HIKING AND BIKING TRAILS **Ontario Pathways** (585-394-7968; www.ontario pathways.org), 200 Ontario Street, Canandaigua. Ontario County has 23 miles of "rails to trails" for biking, cross-country skiing, snowshoeing, horseback riding, and walking/running located between Canandaigua and Seneca Lakes.

Finger Lakes Trail Conference (585-288-7191 or 585-658-9320; www .fingerlakestrail.org). Contact them for maps and information on the various hiking trails throughout the Finger Lakes region. The main trail, which is 562 miles long, connects the Catskill Mountains with the Allegany Mountains. The trail and its six branches pass through many remote sections of New York's southern tier. One of the branches of this trail in Ontario County is the Bristol Trail, which goes from Bristol to Hammondsport. Trailheads are marked with a 1-foot-square yellow sign with a green FLT logo.

PARKS **Canandaiqua City Pier,** Off Lakeshore Drive, next to Kershaw Park. On a summer day the Canandaigua City Pier is both a good place for a walk and a popular place to fish. Walk all the way to the end for a scenic view of Squaw Island and the well-known boathouses. These historic boathouses were built in 1903 and are often the subject in photographs and paintings by local artists. A small store, ice cream shack, and rest rooms are located along the pier.

Kershaw Park (585-396-5060 or 585-396-5082; www.ci.canandaigua.ny.us), Lakeshore Drive, Canandaigua. Open dawn to dusk. This 8-acre park at the north end of Canandaigua Lake offers a sandy beach for swimming, walking trails, scenic views, picnic areas, and a playground.

Onanda Park (585-396-2752 or 585-394-1120), West Lake Road (8 miles south of Canandaigua), Canandaigua. Open dawn to dusk. This park has 7 acres along the Canandaigua Lake, plus another 73 acres of panoramic uplands—*Onanda* is an Indian word meaning "tall fir" or "pine." Amenities include swimming, picnic areas, hiking trails, a playground, sports fields, and fishing access. Eight lakeside cabins are available for overnight accommodations.

Pierce Park in Cheshire (585-394-1120), Goodale Road (NY 21S), Canandaigua. Playgrounds and picnic pavilions.

Squaw Island, North end of Canandaigua Lake, just off the City Pier. This 0.5-acre island, one of the few islands in the Finger Lakes region, is the smallest state-managed land in New York. It was a refuge for Seneca women and children during the Sullivan Expedition. Back then it was 2 acres, but over the years, natural and manmade erosion have reduced it to its present size.

PONDS AND LAKES Canandaigua Lake, the fourth largest of the Finger Lakes, is known as the "chosen spot." The area is considered the legendary birthplace of the Seneca Nation. The lake is 16 miles long, 262 feet deep, and is a popular spot for trout and bass fishing as well as other water-related recreational activities.

✳ Lodging

INNS AND RESORTS ♿ 🐾

Canandaigua Inn on the Lake (585-394-7800; www.visitinnonthe lake.com or www.hudsonhotels.com), 770 South Main Street, Canandaigua. This waterfront resort and conference center features 134 deluxe guest rooms, many with lake views, an indoor/outdoor pool, a spa and fitness center, and a restaurant and lounge. It is the finest waterfront conference center in the Finger Lakes Region. $89–$144.

♿ 🐾 **Finger Lakes Inn** (585-394-2800, 800-727-2772; www.finger lakesinn.com), 4343 Routes 5 and 20,

Canandaigua. This motor inn on 10 landscaped acres features 124 clean, comfortable rooms, some with kitchenettes. They also have several family-sized suites. Amenities include a heated outdoor pool, picnic area, cable TV, and a free continental breakfast. The inn is within walking distance of the Finger Lakes Performing Arts Center. $53–$80.

MOTELS AND HOTELS Canandaigua Motel (585-394-4140; www .canandaiguamotel.com), 4232 Routes 5 and 20, Canandaigua. This motel offers 30 clean, comfortable rooms, including two Jacuzzi rooms and four two-room suites that are perfect for families. $45–$85.

Econo Lodge (585-394-9000 or 800-797-1222; www.hudsonhotels.com), 170 Eastern Boulevard, Canandaigua. This motel with 64 well-appointed rooms is conveniently across the street from Roseland Waterpark. $39–$89.

BED & BREAKFASTS **Chosen Spot Bed & Breakfast** (585-393-1407; www.thechosenspot.com), 5395 Routes 5 and 20, Canandaigua. Open year-round. Tom and Priscilla Corbett's 1850 country inn has three rooms offering feather beds, private baths with whirlpool tubs, and computer hookups. They also have an extra room so that can share a bath with any of the other rooms if you have a larger party traveling together. The inn is located on part of the original Oliver Phelps property. A full breakfast is included $100–$140.

Habersham Country Inn (585-394-1510 or 800-240-0644; www.habershaminn.com), 6124 Routes 5 and 20, Canandaigua. Open year-round. Sharon and Ray Lesio operate this 1840 Federal-style antiques-furnished inn on 10 scenic acres. Three of the five guest rooms have private baths, including one suite with a Jacuzzi tub and fireplace; the remaining two rooms share a bath. The property includes a stocked pond and a barnyard with miniature horses. A full country breakfast is served. $85–$185.

Morgan Samuels Inn (585-394-9232; www.morgansamuelsinn.com), 2920 Smith Road, Canandaigua. Open year-round. Morgan Samuels Inn, owned by John and Julie Sullivan, is an 1810 stone mansion with

five guest rooms and one suite situated on 46 private acres. Each room has a fireplace and a private bath. The inn, which has a dramatic 2,000-foot tree-lined driveway, was voted Most Romantic Inn on the Eastern Seaboard in 1999 by *Bon Appetit* magazine and has received the prestigious four-diamond designation from the AAA. Innkeeper Brad Smith serves a gourmet breakfast by candlelight. $119–$295 (rates vary according to season).

Bed & Breakfast at Oliver Phelps (585-396-1650 or 800-724-7397; www.oliverphelps.com), 252 North Main Street, Canandaigua. Open year-round. Innkeepers John and Joann Button offer three guest rooms with private baths plus a two-room family suite with a shared bath. All rooms in this 1800s Federal-style house are furnished in period antiques. The inn is conveniently located on Canandaigua's historic Main Street, close to downtown shopping, restaurants, and the Sonnenberg Gardens. It's about a 1-mile walk to Canandaigua Lake. Accommodations include a delicious full breakfast—served in a dining room with 11-foot ceilings—that includes homemade baked goods, fresh fruit, and hot entrées like stuffed French toast or strata. $110–$160.

Sutherland House Bed & Breakfast (585-396-0375 or 800-396-0375; www.sutherlandhouse.com), 3179 NY 21S, Canandaigua. Open year-round. Innkeepers Gary and Bonnie Ross offers five spacious and luxurious guest rooms with private baths in this lovely Victorian inn, which is hand stenciled throughout. The home was built in 1885 by Henry Sutherland, vice-president of the Canandaigua Tin

Company. Three of the rooms have double Jacuzzi tubs. All rooms include cable TV, air conditioning, and access to a video library and complimentary soda and water. Lillian's Lodge, at the back of the house, is decorated with a grape-arbor theme and features four floor-to-ceiling windows. $100–$190.

Thendara Inn and Restaurant (585-394-4868; www.thendarainn .com), 4365 East Lake Road, Canandaigua. Open Memorial Day to Halloween. Owners Bill and Tracy Pellicano, along with innkeeper Lorie Leonard, offer four guest rooms in this lavish 1900 Victorian located lakeside on nine acres. Each room, which has a private bath, phone, TV, and air-conditioning, is furnished with turn-of-the-century antiques. The President's Room has a Jacuzzi under a skylight, while the other three rooms have lake views. A homemade breakfast is served in the dining room, on the sun porch, or out on the patio. $189–$250. See also *Where to Eat— Dining Out*.

OTHER LODGING Cottages, condos, cabins, and luxury homes are available for rental throughout the entire Finger Lakes Region. One of the larger rental agencies is **Rental Plus** (888-414-5253; www.rentalplus.com), which specializes in lakeside vacation rentals.

✳ Where to Eat

DINING OUT Lincoln Hill (585-394-8254; www.lincolnhill.com), 3365 East Lake Road, Canandaigua. Open Tuesday–Saturday 5–9. This restored 1804 farmhouse has six dining rooms and three covered decks and porches and features a continental menu that changes with the seasons. The restaurant's gardens are filled with herbs, vegetables, and flowers. It's a popular spot to dine before or after a performance at the adjacent Finger Lakes Performing Arts Center.

Nicole's Lakefront Dining Room at the Inn on the Lake (585-394-7800 or 800-228-2801; www.visitinnonthe lake.com), 770 South Main Street, Canandaigua. Open Monday–Saturday, breakfast 6:30–11, lunch 11–4, dinner 5–10; Sunday, breakfast 6:30–12, lunch 12–4, dinner 5–9. This lakefront restaurant offers traditional menu items like roast breast of duck and filet mignon, along with such seasonal specialties as blueberry-marinated pork chops. For lunch choose from salads, sandwiches, and entrées, including their specialty, Louisiana stew.

Polimenis (585-394-1410), 26 Lakeshore Drive, Canandaigua. Open Sunday–Thursday 7–8:30, Friday–Saturday 7–9. For over 60 years Polimenis has been serving Italian American dishes and seafood. This large restaurant is right across the street from Canandaigua Lake and has a wonderful view. The menu also includes salads, sandwiches, burgers, and an assortment of hot entrées, including daily specials.

Steamboat Landing (585-396-7350; www.steamboatlandingonline.com), 215 Lakeshore Drive, Canandaigua. Open May–November, Sunday–Thursday 11–9, Friday–Saturday 11–10; November–April, Friday and Saturday 12–10, Sunday 12–7. This 120-seat restaurant on the north shore of Canandaigua Lake features exposed wood beams, two-story windows, and a huge fireplace. The timbers used in construction of this eatery were salvaged from the Welland Canal in Ontario, Canada, when the wooden lock gates were replaced with steel and concrete. The extensive menu features many regional dishes and Finger Lakes wines. A more casual menu is featured on the outdoor patio.

Thendara Inn and Restaurant (585-394-4868; www.thendarainn .com), 4365 East Lake Road, Canandaigua. Open in summer Monday–Saturday 5–9, Sunday 4–8; open Friday and Saturday evenings during winter. All tables overlook the lake at this elegant restaurant located in a restored 1900 Victorian mansion. The menu features steak, salmon, and veal. See also *Lodging—Bed & Breakfasts*.

rant at Thendara (585-394-4868; www.thendarainn.com), 4365 East Lake Road, Canandaigua. Open summer for lunch and dinner. This casual lakeside restaurant features hot and cold sandwiches, wraps, salads, and a variety of entrées.

Catskill Bagel & Deli Co. (585-394-5830), 103 South Main Street, Canandaigua. Open Monday–Friday 10–3. This café has homemade bagels, bread, rolls, muffins, and cookies as well as soups, salads, and sandwiches.

Casa de Pasta (585-394-3710; www .casa-de-pasta.com), 125 Bemis Street, Canandaigua. Open Tuesday–Thursday 5–9, Friday and Saturday 5–10, Sunday 5–9. Located on a back street, this restaurant is one of

ENJOY A MEAL AND A VIEW OF CANANDAIGUA LAKE AT THE BOAT HOUSE RESTAURANT AT THENDARA.

Christine A. Smyczynski

the town's most popular eateries. Homemade Italian cuisine is prepared using only the finest ingredients. Start out your meal with fried calamari, antipasto, soup, or one of their house salads. Entrées include homemade lasagna, shrimp scampi, and braciola as well as steak, chicken, and veal dishes.

El Rincon Mexicano (585-394-3580), 5 Beeman Street, Canandaigua. Open Monday–Thursday 12–8, Friday and Saturday 12–9, Sunday 4–8. All dishes in this authentic Mexican restaurant are prepared with traditional ingredients imported from Mexico. Menu selections include tacos and burritos, soups, and combination plates.

🍴 **Lauren's Café** (585-393-9360), 76 South Main Street, Canandaigua. Open Monday–Friday 7–3, Saturday 8–3, Sunday 8–1. This small, narrow bakery and café is located in a historic building with a tin ceiling. Breakfast selections include omelets, breakfast wraps, eggs Benedict, and pancakes. For lunch, choose from burgers, chicken fingers, wraps, salads, sandwiches, and soups.

&. 🍴 🐾 **The Muar House Café** (585-394-6020), 169 Lakeshore Drive, Canandaigua. Open daily 7 AM–10 PM. Known as the sweetest spot in town, this café serves gourmet coffees, home-baked pies, cakes, cookies, and muffins. They are probably best known for their homemade ice creams and gelatos. The café overlooks the lake at the east end of Kershaw Park.

The Pickering Pub (585-396-9060 www.pickeringpub.com), 170 South Main Street, Canandaigua. Open Monday–Friday 11:30 AM–1 AM, Saturday 11:30 AM–2 AM. This casual eatery features traditional pub grub like sandwiches, chicken, burgers, wings, and Mexican fare. They also have a kids' menu.

Rose Corner Bakery & Restaurant (585-396-0500), 151 South Main Street, Canandaigua. Open Monday–Wednesday 7–4, Thursday–Saturday 7–8:30, Sunday 7–1. Serving all homemade food, including breads, pies, pastries, and cookies.

✳ **Entertainment**

THEATERS **Finger Lakes Performing Arts Center** (585-325-7760; www.fingerlakes.edu/flpac), Lincoln Hill at Finger Lakes Community College, Canandaigua. The summer home of the Rochester Philharmonic Orchestra, this performing arts center has outdoor covered and lawn seating for concerts.

✳ **Selective Shopping**

ANTIQUES **Antiques Unlimited** (585-394-7255), 168 Niagara Street, Canandaigua. Open Monday–Saturday 10–5, Sunday 12–5. This multidealer antiques center is housed in a restored 19th-century railroad building. Over 50 dealers offer fine antiques, furniture, stoneware, garden items, paintings, primitives, textiles, and early accessories.

The Carriage Factory Antiques (585-526-6076), 2348 Routes 5 and 20, Stanley (between Canandaigua and Geneva). Open seven days 10–5. A large multidealer shop with a selection that includes furniture, glassware, jewelry, coins, books, primitive tools, and many odd and unusual items.

Cuddeback Antique Center (585-394-2297), 47 Saltonstall Street (off Main), Canandaigua. Open daily 10–5. Browse through 10,000 square feet of period antiques in a restored

1875 schoolhouse. This is one of the oldest antiques centers in New York.

Nino's Antiques (585-526-6800), 2625 Main Street (NY 245), Gorham. Open Thursday–Saturday 11–4, Sunday 12–4. This store has been in business for over 30 years, offering gift items, furniture, household goods, lighting, and more in an old-fashioned country store atmosphere.

ART GALLERIES **Gallery on Main Street** (585-394-2780 www.down towncanandaigua.com), 131 South Main Street, Canandaigua. Open Tuesday–Saturday 10–5. Local artists' co-op, featuring paintings, sculpture, woodworking, jewelry, and more.

Christopher Wheat Gallery (585-396-1180), 92 South Main Street, Canandaigua. Open Monday–Friday 10–5, Saturday 10–4, Sunday 12–4. The gallery features watercolors and oils, focusing on local landscapes and coastal Maine, by Canandaigua native Christopher Wheat.

CRAFTS **The Gift Garden** (585-396-0330; www.winelamps.com), 116 South Main Street, Canandaigua. Open Monday–Friday 10–6, Saturday 10–5. This shop features handcrafted items made locally, including jewelry, pottery, painted items, florals, and candles.

FARM MARKETS **Hanna Junction Farm & Craft Market** (585-0394-7740; www.hannajunction.com), 4375 NY 21 North, Canandaigua. Open mid-April–mid-December, Saturday 8:30–5. Over 100 vendors sell their wares under one roof. Choose from farm-fresh produce, meats, cheeses and jams along with handmade furniture, quilts, jewelry, southwestern items, and more.

Canandaigua Vicinity (outside of downtown)

The Cheshire Union Gift Shop & Antique Center (585-394-5530), 4244 NY 21 South, Canandaigua. Open daily 10–5, Thursday and Friday until 8. Shop in the former Cheshire Union School building built in 1915. On the ground floor the **Company Store** offers groceries and auto supplies and foods from the **Schoolhouse Deli**, which is known for soups, sandwiches, pizza, and ice cream. Upstairs in the **Cheshire Union Gift Shop**, choose from unique gifts, including candles, books, folk art, jewelry, gourmet foods, and hand-painted grape-patterned crystal wine glasses and accessories. There is also a selection of antiques, including lamps, glassware, and pottery. The store also has a complete line of Lang merchandise.

Clement's Country Store (585-229-4201; www.clementscountrycorner .com), 4501-4503 Bristol Valley Road (NY 64), Canandaigua. Open Monday–Saturday 8–8, Sunday 8–7. This circa 1800 shop feature wines, antiques, candies, and homemade baked goods.

The Five Seasons (585-396-2021 wwwfiveseasonsgifts.com), 1901 Rochester Road (NY 332), Canandaigua. Open Saturday–Monday 10–5, Tuesday–Friday 10–8:30. Two floors of unique gifts are displayed inside a beautiful log building. Choose from clocks, candles, gifts, collectibles, and even fresh fudge.

Spring Valley Garden Center and Gift Shop (585-396-1460), 3100 CR 10 (just north of Routes 5 and 20), Canandaigua. Open Monday–Saturday 9–6, Sunday 9–5. This full-service garden center, located in a brick house dating back to the 1800s, also features a selection of gifts and home decor.

Downtown Canandaigua

Cats in the Kitchen (585-394-3994), 367 West Avenue, Canandaigua. Open summer, Tuesday–Saturday 11–5, Sunday 12–5; spring and fall, Wednesday–Sunday 12–5; winter, weekends only. This quaint shop features new, handcrafted, and vintage goods for cat lovers and cooks.

Celebration Gifts (585-394-5630; www.celebrategifts.com), 198 South Main Street, Canandaigua. Open Monday–Saturday 10–5. Unique and affordable gifts, including Yankee Candles, Boyd's Bears, Heritage Lace, Willow Tree Angels, wreaths and garlands, bath and body products, and Christmas ornaments.

& **Country Ewe** (585-396-9580 or 888-708-0820; www.countryewe.com), 79 South Main Street, Canandaigua. Open Monday–Friday 9:30–8, Saturday 9:30–5, Sunday 11–4. This 4,000-square-foot store offers classic apparel, including sportswear and outerwear for the entire family. They specialize in hand-knit sweaters from around the world along with jewelry, Finger Lakes souvenirs, and gift items.

& **Coyote's Den Games and Gifts** (585 394-0510; www.coyotesden online.com), 100 South Main Street, Canandaigua. Open Monday–Saturday 10–8, Sunday 11–4. The largest selection of local history books and postcards in Ontario County. They also carry candles and incense, Warhammer, Pokemon, sports cards, collectibles, and more.

Finger Lakes Wine Center at Sonnenberg Gardens (585-394-4922; www.fingerlakeswinecenter.com), 151 Charlotte Street, Canandaigua. Open daily 11–4 May–Columbus Day. Sample and purchase wines from 35 (and counting) Finger Lakes wineries. Gourmet foods, too.

& **Flowers by Stella-Main Store and Greenhouse** (585-394-1830; www.flowersbystella.com), 1880 Rochester Road (NY 332), Canandaigua. Open Monday–Friday 8–6, Saturday 8–5, Sunday 10–5. This large florist and greenhouse can fulfill all your floral and gift-giving needs, including custom arrangements, a garden store, and lots of gift items. A smaller shop is located in downtown Canandaigua.

& **Flowers by Stella-Downtown** (585-394-5535; www.flowersbystella.com), 168 South Main Street, Canandaigua. Monday–Wednesday 9–6, Thursday–Friday 9–7, Saturday 9–5, Sunday 11–3. You'll find a lot more than just flowers in this large shop. Choose from all sorts of silk arrangements, Americana items, candles, stationery, plush animals, and gift items, including some with nautical, golfing, and fishing themes. Owners Stella and Russell Pennise also have a year-round Christmas room in the back and a large selection of Canandaigua merchandise.

The Harvest Mill (585-394-5907), 40 Parrish Street, Canandaigua. Open Saturday 10–5, Sunday 12–5. Early-American and country furniture and accessories are displayed in a restored cider mill.

The Jewel Box (585-396-3059), 235 South Main Street, Canandaigua. Open Tuesday 10–5, Wednesday 12–8, Thursday 11–8, Friday 10–5, Saturday 9–3. This shop features hand-painted capes, scarves, and sarongs, plus unique jewelry, fine art, handcrafted ironwork, and a large selection of other gift items.

Kathryn's (585-394-2290), 106 South Main Street, Canandaigua. Open Monday–Tuesday and Saturday 10–6, Wednesday–Friday 10–8. Kathryn Bascom's distinctive shop features upscale home decor, jewelry, lingerie, and more. The Boleslawiec stoneware is imported from a small village in Poland, where each piece is individually crafted and hand painted.

The Little Peddler (585-393-5620), 80 South Main Street, Canandaigua. Open Wednesday–Saturday 10–5. Choose from gift items such as candles, florals, furniture, wooden items, greeting cards, home accessories, and jams and jellies.

Renaissance, the Goodie II Shoppe (585-394-6528), 56 South Main Street, Canandaigua. Open Monday–Wednesday and Friday 9:30–6, Thursday 9:30–8, Saturday 9:30–5:30. This landmark store features classic gifts, housewares, accessories, stationery, and whimsical items along with gourmet foods, local-interest books, jewelry, soaps, and garden items. The store's Christmas Shoppe is open August–December.

✿ **Sweet Expressions** (585-394-5250; www.sweetexpressionsonline .com) 169 South Main Street, Canandaigua. Open Monday–Tuesday 9:30–6, Wednesday–Friday 9:30–8, Saturday 9:30–5, Sunday 11–3. Satisfy your sweet tooth with a large selection of fine chocolates and gourmet foods as well as New York State and Finger Lakes products.

This-n-That Boutique (585-396-0420), 145 South Main Street, Canandaigua. Open Monday–Friday 10–6, Saturday 10–5. This shop carries an extensive array of home decor and gifts, including jewelry, lighthouses, wine accessories, Red Hat Society merchandise, and candles.

✿ **Unique Toy Shop** (585-394-2319), 120 South Main Street, Canandaigua. Open Monday–Friday 9:30–8, Saturday 9:30–5:30, Sunday 12–4. This store has a large selection of quality and educational toys—including Brio, Lamaze Infant, and Ty—as well as games and books.

✳ **Special Events**

July: **Ontario County Fair** (585-394-4987; www.ontariocountyfair.org), Ontario County Fairgrounds, Townline Road, Canandaigua. An agricultural fair that—like any good county fair—also features midway rides and entertainment. **Canandaigua Art Festival** (585-394-7110). Along Main Street in downtown Canandaigua. An exhibit by over 200 art and craft vendors.

August: **Pageant of Steam** (607-243-7634; www.pageantofsteam.org), Gehan Road, Canandaigua. A display of early 1900s tractors and farm machinery. **Cheshire Union Antique Show** (585-394-5530), 4244 NY 21 South, Canandaigua. Over 100 dealers display early American furniture, folk art, stoneware, and more at this antiques center.

October: **Haunted Gardens** (585-394-4922), Sonnenberg Gardens, Canandaigua. The gardens are decked out for Halloween and haunted by ghouls and ghosts.

Geneva was once the site of the elite Seneca village, or "castle," of Kanadesaga, which was burned to the ground by patriot soldiers during the Revolutionary War. The Seneca village of Ganechstage was also located in the Geneva area. After the war, white settlement began, and land agent Charles Williamson oversaw the construction of the early hamlet, which was built on a hill overlooking Seneca Lake. The area attracted plantation owners and wealthy families, influencing Geneva's architecture.

The Ontario Glass Manufacturing Company operated in Geneva in the early 1800s. Other initial occupations included farming and industries related to agriculture. Steamboat building also took place here, as steamboats plied the lake between 1828 and 1906, when the railroad became a popular mode of transportation.

In the early 19th century, Geneva was the commercial center of the state as well as a mecca for higher education and women's rights. In 1849 Elizabeth Blackwell received the first medical degree ever conferred on a woman, from Geneva Medical College located on South Main Street. Hobart College for men was founded in 1822 and William Smith College for women in 1908. Today they operate as a single coeducational institution—and the major employer in the Geneva area.

Geneva is the most culturally and racially diverse community in Ontario County since many former migrant workers have settled here. It is also a major tourist destination, attracting visitors with numerous wineries surrounding Seneca Lake, elegant architecture, recreational activities on the water, and many cultural events and festivals. It is also considered the lake trout capital of the world.

The historic downtown district has seen numerous improvements in the last few years, including new sidewalks and decorative Victorian lampposts. The South Main Historic District has many nicely restored homes and row houses.

AREA CODE The area code is 315.

GUIDANCE Geneva Chamber of Commerce (315-789-1776 or 877-5-GENEVA), 35 Lakefront (Routes 5 and 20) Geneva. Open year-round Monday–Friday 9–5; Memorial Day–Columbus Day also open Saturday–Sunday 10–4.

City of Geneva (315-789-2603; www.geneva.ny.us), 47 Castle Street, Geneva. Open Monday–Thursday 9–3:30, Friday 9–4.

Geneva Improvement District (315-789-0102), This organization publishes a directory and map of downtown Geneva that highlights area businesses and services.

GETTING THERE *By air:* See Getting There Rochester.

By car: Geneva is accessible off I-90 exit 42 to NY 14 south. The other main road to Geneva is Routes 5 and 20.

Geneva General Hospital (315-787-4000; www.flhealth.org), 196 North Street, Geneva.

✳ To See

MUSEUMS AND HISTORIC HOMES **Balmanno Cottage** (315-789-5151; www
.genevahistoricalsociety.com), 583 South Main Street, Geneva. Open Sunday
1:30–4:30 July–August and by appointment. This 1830s Gothic Revival–style cottage features fine furnishings and terraced gardens.

Mike Weaver Drain Tile Museum/John Johnson House (contact Rose Hill
Mansion 315-789-3848), NY 96A (0.5 mile south Routes 5 and 20), Geneva.
Open May 1–October 31 by appointment only. Over 350 styles of drain tiles,
from 100 B.C. to the present, are displayed in the 1821 Johnson house. John
Johnson introduced tile drainage for farms in 1835 and promoted the concept in
America.

Prouty-Chew Museum/Geneva Historical Society (315-789-5151; www
.genevahistoricalsociety.com), 543 South Main Street (NY 14 at Routes 5 and
20), Geneva. Open Tuesday–Friday 9:30–4:30, Saturday 1:30–4:30. Donation.
Open Sunday during July and August. Period rooms and exhibits on local history
are on display in this 1829 Federal-style home built by Charles Butler. The
home was purchased by and donated to the historical society by Mr. Beverly
Chew, a great-grandson of Phineas Prouty, who owned the home from 1842 until
1902. The museum shop sells local history publications and related items.

❂ **Rose Hill Mansion** (315-789-3848; www.genevahistoricalsociety.com), NY
96A (1 mile south Routes 5 and 20), Geneva. Open Monday–Saturday 10–4,
Sunday 1–5. Admission: $3 adults, $2 seniors and students 10–18, under 10 free.
This 1839 manor, an architectural treasure and a designated National Historic
Landmark, is one of the finest examples of Greek Revival architecture in
America. Tour guides in period costumes take visitors through the 21
rooms furnished in antiques and
reproductions. The home is named
for Robert Seldon Rose, who erected
Rose Hill Farm, now used as the
reception center. The mansion was
built by Gen. William Kerley Strong,
who later sold it to Robert Swan, a
prominent farmer who installed a tile
drainage system on the farm, which
resulted in tremendous crops.

HISTORIC DISTRICTS **South Main
Street Historic District.** Located on
NY 14 just north of Routes 5 and 20,
near the Ontario County Historical

THE SOUTH MAIN STREET HISTORIC DISTRICT IS CONSIDERED ONE OF THE ARCHITECTURAL GEMS OF THE FINGER LAKES REGION.

Christine A. Smyczynski

Society. The South Main Street Historic District is considered one of the architectural gems of the Finger Lakes region. There are many early 1800s homes, buildings, and churches along here, including colorful row houses built in the 1820s. The **Chapman House** at 562 South Main is the oldest house in Geneva. It was built for the Reverend Jedediah Chapman in 1802 and is now a private residence. A self-guided walking tour brochure of the district can be obtained at the historical society or the chamber of commerce.

HISTORIC SITES **Smith Opera House** (315-781-5483 or 866-355-5483; www .thesmith.org), 82 Seneca Street, Geneva. This local treasure was built in 1894 by Geneva philanthropist, William Smith. The first production on its stage was *The Count of Monte Cristo* in October 1894, starring James O'Neill, father of playwright Eugene O'Neill. The Smith Opera House later operated as a movie palace from the 1920s until the late 1970s. It has since been restored and is listed on the National Register of Historic Places. See also *Entertainment*.

WINERIES **Amberg Wine Cellars** (585-526-6742; www.ambergwine.com), 2200 Routes 5 and 20, Flint. Open year round Monday–Saturday 10–6, Sunday 12–6. A small family-owned and operated winery. The Amberg family cultivates their vineyards to produce the finest grapes available. The fermentation process combines Old-World tradition and modern technology to produce their award-winning wines. Sampling is available in their spacious salesroom, which carries wines along with wine accessories and gift items. The art gallery features the works of Finger Lakes artists. They even have a play area for kids.

Belhurst Winery at Belhurst Castle (315-781-0201; www.belhurstcastle.com), 4069 NY 14 South, Geneva. Open daily 10–8 year-round. This brand new wine-tasting room and gift shop is located in Belhurst Castle's new Vinifera Inn. See *Lodging*.

Billsboro Winery (315-789-9571; www.billsboro.com), 4760 West Lake Road (NY 14), Geneva. Open Tuesday–Sunday 12–6. Producer of artisan vinifera table wines, including chardonnay, pinot noir, and cabernet franc.

✳ To Do

CROSS-COUNTRY SKIING See *Green Space*, Seneca Lake State Park.

FAMILY FUN ✒ **Abbey Farm** (585-526-5420; www.abbeyhistoricalfarm.org), 1862 Routes 5 and 20, Stanley. Open Tuesday–Saturday 10–5 and by reservation. Experience life on a working 1800s farm. Visitors can touch and feed farm animals, help with haying and milking, and learn an old-time skill like spinning or candle dipping. Group tours can be arranged. They also have a bed & breakfast inn; see *Lodging*.

FISHING **Seneca Lake,** annually stocked with hatchery-reared trout and salmon, is known as the Lake Trout Capital of the World. Fishing licenses can be obtained at city or town halls and at sporting goods and large department stores. On Memorial Day weekend the **National Lake Trout Derby/Finger Lakes**

Sports-O-Rama (315-781-2195; www.flsor.com, PO Box 586, Geneva) takes place.

GOLF **Big Oak Public Golf Course** (315-789-9419), 33 Packwood Road, Geneva. An 18-hole, par-70 course with snack bar.

Seneca Lake Country Club (315-789-4681), NY 14 South, Geneva. Open April–October. An 18-hole, par-72 course with full-service restaurant and a great view of Seneca Lake.

MARINAS **Lakeshore Park** (315-789-1776), Routes 5 and 20, Geneva. This boat launch is located on Seneca Lake.

Roy's Marina (315-789-3094), 4398 Clark Point Road (NY 14), Geneva. This boat launch on Seneca Lake offers complete marine services as well as rentals.

See also *Green Space—Seneca Lake State Park.*

✳ Green Space

PARKS **Lakeshore Park** (315-789-1776), Routes 5 and 20, Geneva. Open dawn to dusk. Located along Seneca Lake, this park has picnic facilities, fishing access, a walking trail, and a visitors information center.

Pulteney Park, South Main Street (NY 14), Geneva. Laid out in 1794, this park in the South Main Historic District was originally the village green at the center of Geneva. By 1800 many businesses surrounded the green; then the row houses were built in the 1820s. The business district later shifted closer to the waterfront, where present downtown Geneva is located. The statue in the park's fountain is a symbol of peace.

Seneca Lake State Park (315-789-2331 or 607-387-7041), 1 Lakefront Drive (Routes 5 and 20, north end of lake), Geneva. Open year-round. Admission: $7 parking fee. This 141-acre New York State park, located 1 mile from Geneva, has a marina for both seasonal and transient boaters, picnic areas, showers and rest rooms, a hike and bike path, cross-country skiing in winter, a playground, fishing access, a boat launch, and a large area for kite flying. It also has a "sprayground"—a perfect spot for kids to cool off on a hot summer day. The park was first developed as a city park in 1922 and later transferred to the state.

PONDS AND LAKES **Seneca Lake** is 36 miles long and 632 feet deep, the deepest of the Finger Lakes. The lake was named in honor of the Seneca Nation of Indians, who inhabited this area hundreds of years ago. At night, a drumlike beating can be heard across the lake. Native American legend claims that the sound is the beat of ancestors' drums; scientists say the beating is the sound of escaping natural gas deposits from beneath the waters of the lake.

WALKING AND HIKING TRAILS For the best views of Seneca Lake's northern shore, start walking east on the trail at **Lakeshore Park** near the chamber of commerce visitors center. The trail will continue into **Seneca Lake State Park.** There is also a sidewalk along NY 14 (south of Routes 5 and 20) that offers lake views from high on a hill. Sit on one of the several benches located along this stretch of sidewalk and enjoy the vista.

❇ Lodging

INNS AND RESORTS Belhurst Castle and White Springs Manor (315-781-0201; www.belhurstcastle.com), 4069 NY 14 South, Geneva. Open year-round. This Richardson Romanesque-style stone castle overlooking Seneca Lake has been voted one of the Most Romantic Places in New York State. Built between 1885 and 1889 as a private residence, it has been a casino, a speakeasy, a restaurant, and now an elegant country inn and restaurant. The castle features 11 guest rooms with private baths; several have fireplaces. The spacious Tower Suite in the castle's turret features a large bathroom with Jacuzzi tub. A complimentary wine spigot is located on the castle's second floor, and a continental breakfast is served.

The attached **Vinifera Inn,** which opened in summer 2004, features 20 suites with lake views, king-sized beds, Jacuzzi tubs, and gas fireplaces. There's also a wine-tasting room—featuring wines from Belhurst's own vineyard—a gift shop, a casual pub-like restaurant, and a ballroom. Belhurst Castle also has an elegant restaurant open to the public serving lunch, dinner, and Sunday brunch (see *Dining Out*). $125–$320.

The nearby Georgian Revival–style mansion, **White Spring Manor**, also operated by Belhurst Castle, offers 12 well-appointed guest rooms plus a one-story house. Many of the rooms feature gas fireplaces and Jacuzzi tubs. A continental breakfast is served at Belhurst Castle. $125–$275.

&. **Geneva on the Lake Wine Country Villa & Resort** (315-789-7190 or 800-3-GENEVA; www.geneva onthelake.com), 1001 Lochland Road (NY 14), Geneva. Open year-round. This Italian Renaissance villa, listed on the National Register of Historic Places, offers 30 suites and studios, all with kitchens and some with whirlpool tubs and fireplaces. Modeled after Villa Lancellotti in Frascati, Italy, it was originally built as a private residence in 1914, then later used as a monastery from 1949–1974 by the Capuchin monks. In 1981 it was converted to a resort hotel. All accommodations in this four-diamond luxury resort are furnished with Stickley, except for the two-bedroom Classic Suite, which is appointed in Chippendale furnishings, and the Loft Suite, furnished in Mission cherry. Geneva on the Lake has been voted one of the 10 most romantic inns in the United States by *American Historic Inns*. A four-course dinner is served in the Lancellotti dining room. $225–$1,200.

&. ❀ **Ramada Inn Geneva Lakefront** (315-789-0400 or 800-990-0907; www.ramada.com), 41 Lakefront Drive (Routes 5 and 20), Geneva. Open year-round. This 148-room inn, which also has several suites, offers views of Seneca Lake. Amenities include an indoor pool, workout room, and the popular lakefront Pier House Restaurant. $89–$170.

BED & BREAKFASTS ⚘ **Abbey Farm** (585-526-5420; www.abbeyhistorical farm.org), 1862 Routes 5 and 20, Stanley (between Geneva and Canandaigua). Open year-round. Dave and Deb Abbey offer three guest rooms with private baths in this late-1700s restored farmhouse. The Victorian Suite features a king-sized bed and private sitting area, while Grandma's attic has two twin brass beds. The rustic Homesteader Room has a queen-sized bed and en suite air tub (similar to a Jacuzzi but with numerous smaller jets). Guests can help with the farm chores if they want to. A full country breakfast is served. $85–$110. See also *For Families*.

Bragdon House Bed & Breakfast (315-781-1772; www.bragdonhouse .com), 527 South Main Street, Geneva. Open year-round. Innkeeper Pam Prober offers three rooms with private baths—the two upstairs rooms have views of the lake. The 1907 home was designed by Claude Bragdon, a noted Rochester-area architect, for Thomas Hoskins, mayor of Geneva. The inn is located in Geneva's historic district and is near Hobart and William Smith Colleges. A full breakfast, which may include homemade specialties like bread pudding and eggs Benedict, is served. $90–$125.

The Farr Inn Bed & Breakfast (315-789-7730 or 877-700-FARR; www.thefarrinn.com), 164 Washington Street, Geneva. Open year-round. Cristina and Fernando Diaz offer three rooms in this 1929 English Tudor home that has been renovated to replicate a tea planter's bungalow of Ceylon. Cristina (who was born in Sri Lanka) and Fernando (a native of Mexico) have combined multicultural items to create a unique and restful inn. The common room features a 400-year-old chest from Sri Lanka and a carved wooden table that was presented to Cristina's family by the prime minister of Sri Lanka. Elephants, which in Sri Lanka are

thought to bring luck, are a recurrent decorating theme throughout the inn. Each of the three guest rooms are dedicated to a deceased love one. One room is dedicated to Cristina's uncle Tiger, who was a tea planter in Sri Lanka. The room has an Asian feel, with lots of elephant motifs. This room shares a bath with Kathy's Korner, dedicated to Cristina's sister, who loved the Adirondacks and whimsical things. The third room is dedicated to Fernando's father, Don Chevo, and has a Mexican theme. Breakfast may include their signature dish, Popocatepetl, better known as The Volcano: a big fluffy pancake topped with whipped cream and strawberries. Fernando's specialty is gorditas, a pocket sandwich stuffed with beans and cheese. They will also serve more traditional fare like eggs and toast, and will gladly tailor their menu to guests dietary needs. $85.

✍ **Gentle Giants Bed & Breakfast** (315-781-2723; www.gentlegiants.pair .com), 1826 CR4, Geneva. Open year-round. Two guest rooms with private baths are available in Bill and Glenda Nash's 1856 Italianate Victorian, located on a large farm with registered Belgian horses, or "gentle giants." The larger Blue Room has a stenciled floor, while the other room features two single beds and a country birds theme. Children will enjoy seeing the farm and petting the horses. Enjoy breakfast in their formal dining room or in the large kitchen. $75–$85.

Gorham House Bed & Breakfast (585-526-4402; www.gorham-house .freeyellow.com), 4752 East Swamp Road, Gorham. Open year-round. Southwest of Geneva, innkeepers Nancy and Al Rebmann offer three guest rooms in their 1887 country-colonial farmhouse on 5 acres. The inn is decorated in Victorian style and features three large porches for your relaxing pleasure. The Rose Suite features a private bath, and the antique double bed is decorated with a handmade quilt. The large Master Room features a queen bed and antique cross-stitch pictures on the wall. It shares a bath with the Impatiens and Lace Room, which features a unique scrolled-iron antique double bed. A gourmet breakfast is served. $99–$129.

Lafayette Bed & Breakfast (315-781-0068 or 866-781-0068; www .layfayettegenevany.com), 107 Lafayette Avenue (off Main Street), Geneva. Open year-round. Shirley and Jack Camp offer three rooms in an Italianate-style home that's over 100 years old. The downstairs room has a private bath and a private outdoor deck, while the other two rooms, located upstairs, comprise a family unit that shares a bath. A full breakfast that always includes fresh fruit and a hot dish is offered. $95–$105 single room, $170–180 two-room unit.

OTHER LODGING

Cottage Rentals

Cesco Properties (315-789-2817; E-mail: lcecere@rochester.rr.com), 3514 East Lake Road, Geneva. This company handles cottage rentals along Seneca Lake.

✳ Where to Eat

DINING OUT **Belhurst Castle** (315-781-0201; www.belhurstcastle.com), 4069 Route 14 South, Geneva. Open for breakfast Sunday–Saturday 8–10, lunch Monday–Saturday 11–2, Sunday brunch 11–1:45, dinner Monday–

Saturday 5–9, Sunday 4–9. This elegant restaurant, located in an 1885 castle overlooking Seneca Lake, features entrées like prime rib chop, rack of lamb, and osso buco. See also *Lodging*.

KYO Asian Bistro (315-719-0333), 486 Exchange Street, Geneva. Open Monday–Thursday 5–9, Friday and Saturday 5–10. This Asian restaurant specializes in creative fusion cuisine, including Thai crab cakes, Korean barbecue, Japanese sushi and sashimi, noodle dishes and hot pots, and KYO's tempura and drunken duck.

✐ ♿ ♨ **Nonna's Trattoria** (315-789-1638), 1 Railroad Place, Geneva. Open for lunch Monday, Wednesday–Friday 11:30–3:30; dinner Monday, Wednesday–Thursday 4:30–9:30, Friday and Saturday 4:30–10, Sunday 4–9. *Nonna* means "grandmother" in Italian and *trattoria* means "small family restaurant"—so eating here is like going to visit your Italian grandma. They serve homemade Italian dishes in a friendly, casual atmosphere. They are known to have the best sauce in Geneva. The menu also features steaks, prime rib, seafood, and veal. The same family also operates Uncle Joe's Pizzeria in Geneva.

Pasta Only's Cobblestone Restaurant (315-789-8498; www.pasta onlyscobblestone.com), Routes 5 and 20 (at CR 6), Geneva. Open for lunch Tuesday–Friday 11:30–2, dinner daily 5–9. Enjoy Northern Italian cuisine in a historic farmhouse and tavern. Eat outdoors on the porches or inside by the fireplace. Menu selections include wood-grilled steaks and chops, pasta with fresh sauces, and seafood brought in from Boston. The wine list offers a large selection of Finger Lakes wines and champagne.

The Pier House Restaurant at the Ramada Inn (315-789-5677), 41 Lakefront Drive, Geneva. Open for breakfast 6:30–11, lunch 11–3, dinner 5–10 (Friday and Saturday until 11). Menu selections include steaks and prime rib, served with an extensive list of Finger Lakes wine.

EATING OUT **Flour Petal Café** (315-781-2233), 34 Linden Street, Geneva. Open Monday–Wednesday 9–6, Thursday and Friday 9–7:30, Saturday 8–6. This small, antiques-decorated café on a one-way side street is known for desserts and homemade pies. They also serve cappuccino, latte, chai, smoothies, homemade soup, wraps, and sandwiches.

♪ ৬ ৠ **Osmens Family Restaurant** (315-789-7673), 813 Routes 5 and 20, Geneva. Open 7–9 daily. This large, clean family restaurant has the usual fare like salads, burgers, hot and cold sandwiches, traditional entrées, and Italian specialties. They also have daily specials that include shrimp scampi, BBQ pork chops, and prime rib. A kids' menu is available, and they offer a 10 percent senior discount.

♪ **Ports Cafe** (315-789-2020; www.portscafe.com), 4432 West Lake Road (NY 14), Geneva. Open for lunch and dinner Wednesday–Saturday. Dine overlooking the lake out on the deck or indoors. This casual restaurant features an extensive Finger Lakes wine list. Menu selections include steaks, mixed grills, pastas, salads, finger foods, and burgers. A kids' menu is available.

The Sweet Life Bakery & Café (315-789-0874 or 866-58-SWEET), 551 South Exchange Street, Geneva. Open Monday–Friday 7:30–5:30, Sat-

urday 8–1. Their motto is: Life is short, just eat dessert. Choose from pies, cheesecake, cookies, pastries, and bagels as well as soups, salads, and gourmet coffees.

♪ **Uncle Joe's Pizzeria** (315-781-1199), 99 North Genesee Street, Geneva. Open Monday, Wednesday–Friday at 11, Saturday and Sunday at 4:30. Since 1978 the Cosentino family has been serving pizza in Geneva. The menu now includes a variety of pizzas, salads, subs, sandwiches, pastas, and calzones. If you want more upscale Italian dining, visit their other restaurant, Nonna's Trattoria.

♪ ৠ **Wyatt's** (315-781-3222), 143 Wadsworth Street, Geneva (located in the Shops at the Station off Exchange Street). Open Sunday–Thursday 11 AM–10 PM, Friday and Saturday 11 AM–3 AM. They are known to serve the best burgers in Geneva as well as an assortment of sandwiches, Zweigles hot dogs, Friday fish fry, and "garbage plates." It's the best seat in the house when a train travels through town, as it's located in an old railroad depot.

✳ Entertainment

NIGHTLIFE Popular nightspots in downtown Geneva include **Castaways** (315-789-0300; 93 Seneca Street) and **Jelly Beans** (315-781-2126; 459 Exchange Street); both also serve a variety of sandwiches, salads, and entrées for lunch and dinner. **Parker's Grill and Tap Room** (315-789-4556; 100 Seneca Street) is a family-friendly restaurant by day and a hot nightspot by night.

THEATERS **Smith Opera House** (315-781-5483 or 866-355-5483; www.thesmith.org), 82 Seneca Street,

Geneva. This 1894 historic theater, one of only 304 remaining single-theater movie palaces in the country, presents live performances and second-run movies on a 40-foot screen. The theater is listed on the National Register of Historic Places. See also *Historic Sites*.

✳ Selective Shopping

ANTIQUES Another Man's Treasures, 20½ Linden Street, Geneva. Open Monday–Saturday 9:30–5:30. This shop features eclectic home decor, sports collectibles, and handmade jewelry.

The Carriage Factory Antiques (585-526-6076), 2348 Routes 5 and 20, Stanley (between Canandaigua and Geneva). Open daily 10–5. A multidealer shop featuring furniture, glassware, jewelry, coins, books, primitive tools, and other collectibles.

Rose Hill Antique Consignment Shop Rose Hill Mansion (315-789-3848; www.genevahistoricalsociety .com), NY 96A (1 mile south of Routes 5 and 20), Geneva. Open May–October Wednesday–Saturday 11–4, Sunday 1–5; also open Monday and Tuesday July and August. Browse through fine furniture, antiques, and collectibles. Proceeds benefit the Geneva Historical Society.

Timeless Collectibles/The Treasure Shop (315-789-5747), 471 Exchange Street, Geneva. Open Monday–Friday 11–5. This shop is a treasure trove of country and primitive antiques and collectibles.

FARM MARKETS ௮ Red Jacket Orchards Fruit Outlet (315-781-2749 or 800-828-9410; www.redjacket orchards.com), 957 Routes 5 and 20, Geneva. Open daily 8–7, until 6 in winter. Red Jacket Orchards has been growing fruit in the Geneva area since 1917. This outlet store offers orchard-fresh fruit in a unique refrigerated walk-in fruit cellar, including apples and cider year-round. In-season summer fruits and vegetables are also available as well as a variety of jams, jellies, honey, cheeses, syrups, sauces, and fruit butters.

SPECIAL SHOPS The Attique (315-781-0529), 266 Hamilton Street, Geneva. Open Monday–Thursday 10–6, Friday 10–8, Saturday 10–5, Sunday 12–4. This store is jam-packed with unique gifts and treasures such as antique reproductions, Yankee Candles, jewelry, pottery, Boyd's Bears, home and garden decor, lamps, quilts, country items, and wine accessories.

The Book Nook (315-781-6665; www.thebooknook.info), 508 Exchange Street, Geneva. Open Monday–Friday 10–6, Saturday 10–2. This shop has new and used books, including a selection of children's books.

Don's Own Flower Shop (315-789-2554; www.donsownflowershop.com), 40 Seneca Street, Geneva. Open Monday–Friday 8:30–5:30, Saturday 9–4. There's a lot more than just fresh flowers in this shop, located in a historic 1838 building with tin ceilings. From 1840–1976 it was operated as the J. West Smith Dry Goods Store, which at one point was the oldest and largest dry-goods store in the nation. The shop has a nice selection of unique gifts, including pottery, dried florals, grape-decorated items, cards, candles, glassware, Platters chocolate, Crabtree & Evelyn, and gourmet foods.

Earthly Possessions (315-781-1078; www.agirlstore.com), 70 Seneca Street, Geneva. Open Tuesday–Thursday 10:30–5:30, Friday 10:30–7:30, Saturday 11–5. A unique collection of handmade gifts, handcrafted jewelry by owner Yvette Ortiz, candles, accessories, and bath and body products, including handmade soaps. This is definitely a girly store!

Farmhouse Primitives (315-789-4220), 23 Seneca Street, Geneva. Open Monday–Friday 10–6, Saturday 10–5, Sunday 12–4. You'll want to decorate your home in country style after visiting this unique shop. Choose from country furniture, pottery, candles, and home accessories.

Guards Cards (315-789-6919), 60 Seneca Street, Geneva. Open Monday–Saturday 9–5:30, Sunday 12–4. This unique shop, with the atmosphere of a 1920s drugstore, features crystal, Department 56, clocks, pewter, garden items, cards, Mary Engelbreit merchandise, pottery, and Geneva merchandise.

Lake City Hobby (315-789-6397), 501 Exchange Street, Geneva. Open Monday–Saturday 10–5, Thursday until 9. This tiny shop has a large selection of model trains and train-related items. They specialize in Lehigh Valley.

Yarn Shop of Geneva (315-789-7211), 513 Exchange Street, Geneva.

Open Monday–Saturday 11–4. Choose from a large selection of yarn and knitting supplies.

✴ Special Events

June: **Medley of Taste** (315-781-5483, 866-355-5483; www.thesmith.org), Hobart and William Smith Colleges, Geneva. A fund-raiser for the Smith Opera House features over 50 food and wine vendors from the Finger Lakes region.

July: **Italian Festival** (Sons of Italy 315-781-2242), Geneva. A summertime festival with entertainment, rides, games, and lots of Italian food.

July–August: **Geneva Summer Arts Festival** (315-781-5483 or 866-355-5483; www.genevarts.com), Geneva. An array of theater, music, and visual arts takes place throughout the city over the course of several weeks.

Concerts by the Lake (315-789-5005), Geneva Lakefront Park. Free summertime concerts along the lake sponsored by the Geneva Recreation Department.

August: **Seneca Lake Whale Watch** (315-781-0820; www.senecalakewhalewatch.com), Geneva Lakefront Park. One of the area's most unique lakeside events. Activities include live music, food, and fun and games, including "watching for whales."

SOUTHERN ONTARIO COUNTY—Naples, Bristol, and Honeoye, including Honeoye and Canadice Lakes

Naples, near the south end of Canandaigua Lake, is one of the more scenic areas in Ontario County. First settled in 1789 by Samuel Reuben and Levi Parrish and their families, the town has many of its original homes and features an early 1800s Main Street. The economy of this area is based mainly on vineyards, wine, and grape juice. The area also has a thriving artists community, with artists displaying their work at seasonal festivals and at the Naples Valley Arts and Crafts Village, open Saturdays May–October. Perhaps the best time to visit Naples is during the annual Grape Harvest Festival in September, when you can celebrate the harvest and sample a famous Naples dessert, grape pie. Over 10,000 grape pies are baked by dozen of Naples-area bakers during the six-week grape-harvest season, and it's estimated that over 70,000 grape pies are sold in Naples annually.

When soldiers from General Sullivan's army traveled through what is now Bristol, they were impressed with the land and later returned as settlers. The area was purchased by Bristol County, Massachusetts, and many early pioneers came from that state to farm the land. Other early industries included lumbering and tanneries. Today this area is home to several popular resort destinations, including Bristol Mountain Ski Resort and Bristol Harbor Golf Resort.

Honeoye is located on an ancient Native American site. Many summer cabins and lodges are located along the lake, as are the homes of year-round residents. Picnicking and swimming are popular at Sandy Bottom Park.

AREA CODE The area code is 585.

GUIDANCE Town of Bristol (585-229-2400; www.townofbristol.org), 6740 CR 32, Bristol. Open Monday–Friday 8–4:30.

Village of Naples (585-374-2435), 106 South Main Street, Naples. Open Monday–Friday 8–4:30.

www.naplesvalleyny.com. This site has lots of tourism information and links.

A **visitors information kiosk** is located in front of **Nimble Needles,** 196 North Main Street.

GETTING THERE *By air:* See *Getting There—Rochester.*

By car: From the north, take the NYS Thruway (I-90) to either exit 43 or 44, and head into Canandaigua. From there, take Routes 5 and 20 west. For Naples take NY 21 south, for Bristol take NY 64 south, and for Honeoye and Canadice, take NY 64 to US 20A. From the south, take I-390 to exit 3, and proceed north on NY 21 for Naples or Bristol; take NY 15 to 15A to Honeoye and Canadice.

MEDICAL EMERGENCY Dial 911.

✳ To See

MUSEUMS AND HISTORIC HOMES Naples Historical Society, Morgan Hook and Ladder, 5 Mill Street, Naples. Open by appointment. The Morgan Hook

and Ladder, which houses the Naples Historical Society, is on the State and
National Register of Historic Places. It was built in 1830 as a private residence
and later became a boarding house and then village offices. The hook and ladder
company acquired it in 1891 and added the tower. Another historic building in
Naples is the **Old Grist Mill,** located behind the firehouse. It has memorabilia
from the Naples area and is open by appointment. Contact Mr. Vierhile at Vierhile Appliances (585-374-2560).

WINERIES Arbor Hill Grapery and Winery (585-374-5817 or 800-554-2406;
www.thegrapery.com or www.arborhillwinery.com), 6461 NY 64, Bristol Springs,
Naples. Open May–December, Monday–Saturday 10–5, Sunday 11–5; weekends
only January–April. The Brahm family offers a large selection of their award-winning wines, along with grapes and fruit produced in the Finger Lakes, in this complex of antique buildings just down the street from Bristol Mountain Ski Resort.
The **Arbor Hill Wine and Gift Shop** offers New York State wine and cheese to
taste and buy plus wine glasses and other accessories. The **Arbor Hill Grapery**
showcases Arbor Hill jams, jellies, and preserves plus sauces, vinegars, mustards,
and dressings, all made by the Brahm family. The famous Naples grape pie is also
available for sale, frozen baked or unbaked, as well as quarts of grape-pie filling.

Widmer Wine Cellars (585-374-6311, 800-836-LAKE; www.widmerwine.com),
1 Lake Niagara Lane, Naples. Open year-round 12–4 daily. Tours and tastings at
1, 2, and 3. This century-old winery was founded in the 1800s by Swiss winemaker John Jacob Widmer and his wife, Lisette. Tours take visitors from the fields to
the wine cellars where the juice is made. The aging cellars contain over 10,000
gallons of wine in wooden casks. Widmer produces over 50 different wines and is
the largest winery in the eastern United States. They are also the producer of
Manischewitz, the world's largest producer of kosher wines. Their sister winery,
Pleasant Valley Wine Company in Hammondsport in Steuben County, produces
Great Western champagnes. After
your tour, sample wines in their tasting room. The gift shop carries a large
selection of wines and champagnes as
well as jams, jellies, and gourmet
foods.

TOUR THE FIELDS TO THE WINE CELLARS
AT WIDMER WINE, THE LARGEST WINERY
IN THE EAST.

Christine A. Smyczynski

✳ To Do

CROSS COUNTRY SKIING See **Cummings Nature Center** in *Green
Space—Nature Preserves.*

FISHING **Honeoye Lake** is best
known for walleye, and largemouth
and smallmouth bass. Because of its
shallow depth, it's also a great place
for ice fishing in winter. **Canadice
Lake** is best known for smallmouth

bass, while **Hemlock Lake** (on the border of Ontario and Livingston Counties) is stocked with a variety of fish year-round. Fishing licenses can be obtained at city or town halls and at sporting goods and large department stores.
Canandaigua Lake Fishing Access Site (585-226-2466), NY 215, Naples. Fishing access site at the south end of Canandaigua Lake.

GOLF **Bristol Harbour Golf Club & Resort** (585-396-2460 or 800-288-8248; www.bristolharbour.com), 5410 Seneca Point Road, Canandaigua (Bristol). An 18-hole, par-72 course with snack bar and full-service restaurant. Lodging on site and cross-country skiing in winter. Jack Nicklaus set the course record for Bristol Harbor Golf Club on August 14, 1978, shooting a 67. See *Lodging*.

Reservoir Creek Golf Club (585-374-8010; www.rcgolf.com), 8613 Cohocton Street, Naples. An 18-hole, par-71 wooded and classic link course, with a full-service restaurant, the Creek Café, which has indoor and outdoor seating.

MARINAS **Honeoye Lake Boat Launch State Park** (585-335-8111), US 20A, Honeoye. Open May–November. Boat launch site for all boats, including power-boats, as well as fishing access. Ice fishing in winter.

SKIING **Bristol Mountain** (585-374-6000; www.bristolmt.com), 5662 NY 64, Canandaigua. Bristol Mountain boasts the tallest vertical rise in the region and spectacular views of the Bristol Hills.

Lifts: 5 (one rope tow, two double chairs, one triple chair, one high-speed quad).

Trails: 22 (20 percent beginner, 60 percent intermediate, 20 percent expert).

Vertical Drop: 1,200 feet

Snowmaking: 93 percent (120-inch average annual snowfall).

Facilities: The Sunset Lodge offers food service, a children's area, lockers, a repair shop, and overnight ski storage.

Ski School: Lessons available for adults and children.

For Children: Children's programs and child care available.

Rates: $12–$43.

✳ Green Space

BEACHES **Sandy Bottom Beach** (585-229-5757), off US 20A, Honeoye. This beach features a boardwalk, picnic areas, playground, shuffleboard court, and fishing access.

NATURE PRESERVES **Cumming Nature Preserve**, (585-374-6160; www .rmsc.org), 6472 Gulick Road, Naples. Open Wednesday–Saturday 9–5. This 900-acre environmental center, operated by the Rochester Museum and Science Center, features 6 miles of themed walking trails. The Conservation Trail communicates forest conservation, the Pioneer trail features a reconstructed 18th-century homestead, the Helen Gordon Trail is an outdoor art gallery, and the Beaver Trail introduces cycles of nature. Also on the grounds is a pond with an observation platform for bird- and nature watching. The visitors center has multimedia theater presentations, nature art, and hands-on exhibits. During the winter months there are 15 miles of cross-country trails as well as two walking/snowshoe trails.

Hi-Tor Wildlife Management Area (585-226-2466), NY 245 and 21, Naples. Open dawn to dusk. A 6,100-acre nature preserve. Boating, canoeing, hiking, and nature studies are popular pastimes. The uplands of the area include gorges and scenic waterfalls.

Honeoye Creek Wildlife Area (585-226-2466), CR 37, Honeoye. Open dawn to dusk. This wildlife area has 1,717 acres for wildlife observation, bird-watching, and hiking.

Stid Hill Wildlife Area (585-226-2466), NY 64 (near CR 34), Naples. Open dawn to dusk. An 847-acre wildlife area.

PARKS **Harriet Hollister Spencer State Park** (585-335-8111; www.nysparks .com), Canadice Hill Road, Honeoye. Open dawn to dusk. Enjoy picnic areas as well as hiking and biking trails. Deer hunting is permitted in season.

Ontario County Park (585-374-6250), 6475 Gannett Hill Road (NY 64 near NY 21), South Bristol. Open mid-May–mid-October 9–9. Free admission. This 410-acre park is best known for the "Lookout" on the top of Gannett Hill that, at 2,256 feet above sea level, gives visitors a bird's-eye view of the surrounding hills. The park also has hiking trails, playgrounds, picnic areas, and fishing ponds.

Sandy Bottom Park (585-229-5757), off US 20A, Honeoye. A 50-acre park with picnic facilities and swimming.

PONDS AND LAKES **Canadice Lake** means "long lake", which is a humorous twist since the lake—the smallest of the Finger Lakes—is only 3 miles long. Canadice, along with nearby **Hemlock Lake** (Livingston County) supplies the water for the city of Rochester, so the shoreline is undeveloped, and there are limitations as to the size of recreational boats permitted. **Honeoye Lake,** which means "lying finger," is one of the prime fishing spots in the Finger Lakes. Only 30 feet deep, it freezes quickly in the winter, making it a popular spot for ice fishing, skating, and ice boating.

✳ Lodging

INNS AND RESORTS **The Inn at Bristol Harbour** (585-396-2200 or 800-288-8248; www.bristolharbour .com), 5410 Seneca Point Road, Canandaigua. Open year-round. Thirty rooms in an Adirondack-style inn with a view of Canandaigua Lake. Each room has a balcony and fireplace. Amenities include a pool and spa, tennis, 18-hole golf course, pro shop, and restaurant. $89–$229. *See To Do—Golf.*

MOTELS AND HOTELS **Naples Hotel & Restaurant** (585-374-5630; www .thenapleshotel.com), 111 South Main Street, Naples. Five renovated rooms and suites with private baths, along with casual fine dining, are available in this 1895 hotel owned by mother and son, Lynn and Jason Randall. When it was built, it was considered the finest brick hotel in Ontario County. The Niagara Room features a king-sized bed and Jacuzzi, while the Victorian Cabernet Room overlooks Main Street. The Asian-decor Sake room is a two-room suite with a queen bed. The Delaware room has a queen bed, and the Catawba Room features a Victorian claw-foot tub. $75–$125.

BED & BREAKFASTS Bristol Views Bed & Breakfast (585-374-8875; www.bristolviews.com), 66932 CR 12, Naples. Year-round. Henry and Barb Owens are the innkeepers of Naples's newest inn, located in the circa-1870 Hawkins homestead. The inn has a view of Canandaigua Lake, a 50-foot waterfall in the backyard, and an outdoor hot tub. Each of the four air-conditioned guest rooms has satellite TV and a private bath, including one with a large Jacuzzi tub. The first-floor room is wheelchair accessible. A full breakfast is served. $95–$150.

Chambery Cottage (585-393-1405; www.chamberycottage.com), 6104 Monks Road, Canandaigua. Open year-round. Experience a taste of Europe when you stay at the Chambery Cottage. Terence and Zora Molkenthin offer four rooms with private baths in this 100-year-old farmhouse. The French-country decor reflects French influences as well as Eastern and Western Europe, from Prague to Vienna. A full breakfast is included. $119–$189.

Cheshire Inn (585-396-2383; www.cheshireinn.com), 6004 NY 21, Naples. Open May–October. Laura Moats is the innkeeper of this large, comfortable 1830 farmhouse with five guest rooms and a view of Canandaigua Lake. Four of the rooms have

private baths, the fifth is an extra room usually used by additional family members renting one of the other rooms. A full breakfast is served. $85–$125.

The Filigree Inn (585-229-5460; www.filigreeinn.com), 5406 Bristol Valley Road (NY 64), Canandaigua. Open year-round. Don and Connie Simmons offer four suites in this inn located less than 1 mile from Bristol Mountain Ski Resort. Each 750-square-foot suite, named after one of the innkeepers' granddaughters, has a fluffy feather bed and features a full kitchen, living room with sofa bed, fireplace, Jacuzzi, and a private bath and deck. $140–$160.

The Grapevine Inn (585-374-9298; www.grapevineinnbb.com), 182 North Main Street, Naples. Year-round. This English Tudor Victorian home was built in 1923 by William Widmer, son of the founder of Widmer Winery. Innkeepers John and Bonnie Steff offer two guest rooms in this unique home, which has the original woodwork and 900 panels of leaded glass throughout. The three-room Widmer Suite, which was the master bedroom for the Widmers, has 650 square feet of space, including a private bath with the original fixtures. The Garden Room has a queen-sized bed, private bath, and the original paint on the walls. A Jacuzzi is available for all guests, and a full breakfast is served. Summer $110-140, winter $100–$125.

Greenwoods Bed & Breakfast (585-229-2111 or 800-914-3559; www.greenwoodsinn.com), 8136 Quayle Road, Honeoye. Open year-round. This 6,000-square-foot log home overlooking Honeoye Lake will remind you of a Adirondack great camp. Innkeepers Mike and Lisa Ligon offer five luxurious rooms that feature queen-sized feather beds and private baths. Some rooms include fireplaces. The house has three decks, a porch overlooking the lake, and a garden Jacuzzi tub to relax in at the end of the day. A full breakfast is served in the breakfast room overlooking the gardens. $99–$159.

Monier Manor (585-374-6719; www.moniermanor.com), 154 North Main Street, Naples. Open year-round. Bruce and Donna Nichols Scott offer four large, upscale guest rooms in this recently renovated 1850 Italianate Victorian home that's within walking distance of the village. Each professionally decorated room has a queen four-poster bed, private bath, CD player, satellite TV, and fireplace. One room's bath features a deep "soaking tub." The inn's hardwood floors are adorned with Oriental rugs; the parlor has the original marble fireplace with gas logs, and the dining room has huge built-in bookshelves. Outdoors, a large hot tub seats eight. A full gourmet breakfast with both hot and cold items is served. $125–$165, with slightly reduced rates midweek.

Naples Valley Bed & Breakfast (585-374-6397), 5851 CR 12, Naples. Open year-round. Innkeeper Nadina Stevens has three guest rooms, that share two baths, in her antiques-filled country inn that has a view of Canandaigua Lake. Two of the rooms have king-sized beds (one with an electric fireplace), while the third has two twins and a sleeper sofa plus an electric fireplace. The common room features a working cobblestone fireplace along with books and a TV. A full gourmet breakfast is prepared. $85.

The Vagabond Inn (585-554-6271; www.thevagabondinn.com), 3300 Sliter Road, Naples. Five luxurious guest rooms are available in Celeste Wiley's 7,000-square-foot secluded inn, which has been a popular year-round getaway destination for over 20 years. From the minute you enter the 80-foot great room with its two massive stone fireplaces, you'll know that you are staying at an inn of distinction. It is known as one of the most romantic destinations in the Finger Lakes, so it's a perfect place to honeymoon or celebrate an anniversary. Two rooms have canopy beds, and there are fireplaces and Jacuzzi tubs in some rooms. The Mahogany Room has its own private outdoor hot tub. Each room has its own private bath and spectacular views of the surrounding mountains. The inn has a fully equipped guest kitchen and a gas grill outside. A beautiful in-ground swimming pool is open May–Labor Day. The inn also features an exclusive crafts gallery—named one of the top 100 American crafts galleries in 2001—that features works by artisans from across the country. $115–$225. The inn also has a three-bedroom retreat house available for $400/night.

OTHER LODGING Bristol Woodlands Campground (585-229-2290; www.bristolwoodlands.com), 4835 South Hill Road, Canandaigua. Open May–October. This campground, about 10 miles south of Canandaigua, has 58 RV sites and 23 tent sites plus a rental cabin on 100 acres with panoramic views. Facilities include a pool, fishing pond, playground, and picnic pavilion. Tent and RV sites with full hookups $22–$32, cabin $48.

✷ Where to Eat

EATING OUT &. **Bob & Ruth's Vineland Restaurant** (585-374-5122), Corner NY 245 and 21, Naples. This landmark restaurant is open daily 7–8 March–November. Enjoy a view of the surrounding vineyards while dining on traditional fare.

&. **The Grainery** (585-374-8220), Main Street, Naples. Open for breakfast and lunch Tuesday–Sunday 6:30–4, Friday and Saturday until 2. Enjoy gourmet coffee and other beverages along with panini sandwiches, wraps, soups, bagels, desserts, and breakfast specials.

Hovey House Café & Bakery (585-374-5850), 6459 NY 64 (at Arbor Hill Commons), Bristol Springs. Open May–October Thursday–Sunday 7–2; also open Wednesday July and August. This bakery café in an 1800s home serves traditional breakfast fare, like eggs and pancakes, along with lunch items like hot and cold sandwiches, wraps, soups, and salads.

Naples Hotel & Restaurant (585-374-5630 www.thenapleshotel.com), 111 South Main Street, Naples. Open for lunch Monday–Saturday 11–2, dinner Tuesday–Saturday 5–8, Sunday 12–6. Live music on weekends. The menu features pasta to prime rib and everything in between, including sandwiches, salads, wraps, and burgers for lunch, and sirloin, salmon, chicken, and veal for dinner.

Redwood Restaurant (585-374-6360), 6 Cohocton Street (NY 21 and 53), Naples. Open year-round Sunday–Thursday 6–8, Friday and Saturday till 9. This family restaurant is the home of the original grape pie.

✷ Entertainment

THEATERS **Bristol Valley Theatre** (585-374-9032; www.bvtnaples.org) 151 South Main Street, Naples. Show times are Thursday–Saturday at 8 and Sunday at 2. A professional summer-theater company located in an old church, they offer a variety of plays during the season.

✷ Selective Shopping

ART GALLERIES **The Brown House Gallery** (585-374-5129), 107 North Main Street, Naples. Open Tuesday–Saturday 10–5. A variety of artwork with a local motif.

CRAFTS ✐ &. **Naples Valley Arts & Crafts Village** (585-374-5110; www.naplesartsandcrafts.com), 191 South Main Street (NY 21), Naples. Open Saturday–Sunday 10–6 mid-May–October. Free admission and free parking. Arts, crafts, and fresh produce are offered in this early 1900s-style village that features over 72 shops and artists' cabins. There is a food court with several restaurants, a courtyard with live entertainment, and a tiki bar with wine, beer, shrimp, oysters, and clams. Demonstrations of jewelry making, candle carving, metalsmithing, and more along with kids' activities, a golf driving range, and special events throughout the season.

The Wizard of Clay Pottery (585229-2980; www.wizardofclay.com), 7851 US 20A, Honeoye. Open daily 9–5 year-round. Inside a geodesic dome, the Wizards—father-and-son team Jim and Jamie Kozlowski—bring pottery to life. The pottery studio goes through over 100,000 pounds of clay each year and is best known for its Bristoleaf pieces, which are decorated with impressions of real leaves.

They are also known for their Crystalline glazed pieces, which have a jewel-like shimmer.

SPECIAL SHOPS Arbor Hill (585-374-2870; www.thegrapery.com), 6461 NY 64, Bristol Springs. See *To See—Wineries.*

Classics Timeless Treasures (585-374-5650), 199 North Main Street, Naples. Open Monday–Saturday 10–5, Sunday 12–5. Things of timeless quality include clothing and accessories, home decor, gifts, Christmas decorations, and garden items.

Joseph's Wayside Market (585-374-2380), 201 South Main Street (NY 21) Naples. Open May–October daily 8:30–7. Since 1955 the Joseph family has offered fresh produce and flowers as well as baked goods, grape products, jams, jellies, and gift items.

Monica's Pies (585-374-2139; www.monicaspies.com), 7599 NY 21, Naples. Open year-round 9–5 daily. This business is famous for grape pies, available year-round, along with a variety of other fruit pies. They also carry jams, jellies, relishes, grape-pie filling, and gift baskets. Products can also be ordered through their Web site. (*Note:* Pies are purchased whole, no slices. If you can't wait to sample yours, bring plastic cutlery and paper plates.)

Naples Pharmacy (585-374-2080), 105 South Main Street, Naples. Open seven days 9–9. Gift shop, cards, candy, Naples souvenirs, and more along with a full-service pharmacy.

Nimble Needles (585-374-6070), 196 North Main Street, Naples. Open Tuesday and Thursday 9–6, Wednesday 9–9 or by appointment. This needlework shop is located in an 1870 one-room schoolhouse.

Timberwood (585-374-5660), 197 North Main Street, Naples. Open May-December Monday–Saturday 10–5, Sunday 12–4. Hand-crafted Amish and Mennonite furniture and gifts, including candles, baskets, and toys.

Troll Mountain Mystic Gift Shoppe (585-229-2672), 5142 Pinewood Hill Road, Honeoye. Open Wednesday–Sunday 12–5. A 5-foot troll and 9-foot wizard overlook the array of goods offered here. Choose from collectible dolls, home decor, lamps, Beanie Babies, jewelry, clothing, handblown glass, and, of course, a large selection of trolls and gnomes.

Winderwood Country Store (585-374-8504), 4934 NY 245, Naples. Open daily 9–8; call first on summer weekends and Mondays. Unique gifts for the home and garden, including spinning wheels and yarns.

✳ Special Events

September: **Grape Festival** (585-374-2240; www.naplesvalleyny.com), Throughout village of Naples. This annual event features grape recipes, grape stomping, winery tours and tastings, arts and crafts, musical entertainment, family activities, and more.

October: **Naples Valley Flea and Craft Festival** (585-374-2757), Memorial Town Hall, Main Street, Naples. View the works of 200 regional artists amid the fall foliage. You can also enjoy wagon rides, chairlift rides at Bristol Mountain, and winery tours.

YATES COUNTY

Yates County was established in 1823 out of part of Ontario County. Primarily an agricultural area, it is dotted with many farms and farm markets as well as vineyards and wineries. Yates County is the largest grape-growing county in the United States outside of California and is home to more wineries than any other county in New York State. If you are looking for an old-fashioned kind of vacation that takes you back to nature, Yates County is the perfect spot. With its abundance of beaches, hiking trails, and water recreation areas, along with museums, it's a great place to leave the fast-paced world behind. Some of the local shops carry goods made by the many Mennonite settlers to the region. Yates is a fairly small county, just over 338 square miles and about 20 miles from border to border, which means you can see a lot of what the county has to offer in just one day. The two larger towns are Penn Yan, the county seat, and Dundee, which is close to several wineries. The county is bordered by two of the Finger Lakes—Seneca and Keuka—which give the county the perfect climate for growing grapes.

Penn Yan, which was incorporated in 1833, got its interesting name as a compromise between its early Pennsylvania and Yankee settlers. The village, which has two lakeside parks, was mentioned by Norman Crampton in his 1995 book, *The 100 Best Small Towns in American* (Prentice Hall). Birkett Mills, located in downtown Penn Yan, is the largest producer of buckwheat products in the world. Penn Yan has a downtown historic district, with many unique shops and restaurants. A walking-tour guide can be obtained from the Yates County Chamber of Commerce (see *Guidance*).

The nearby village of Dresden, named after the city in Germany, is one of the smallest and the oldest incorporated villages in New York. Designed in 1814 and incorporated in 1867, it is the only planned community in Yates County. It is the birthplace of Robert Ingersoll, noted agnostic and writer. The area is known for its fishing access to Seneca Lake as well as its boat launches and beaches.

The village of Dundee, named after Dundee, Scotland, features unique architecture that takes you back in time. The first settler to the area was Isaac Stark who arrived here from New Jersey in 1807. The village was first known as Stark's Mill, after the mill that Stark built, and later Harpending's Corners after Samuel Harpending, who arrived here in 1811; it was incorporated in 1848. This rural

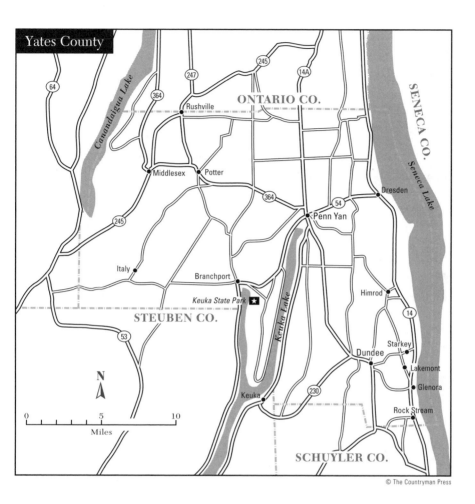

Yates County

© The Countryman Press

village, which is surrounded by farmland in the heart of the Finger Lakes region, is near wineries and recreational activities. It was once the blackberry capital of the world—blackberries were used for dyes by meat processors for the USDA stamp of approval. Today the village is home to Northland, a large producer of grape juice and other fruit-based products.

AREA CODE The area codes in Yates County are 315 and 607.

GUIDANCE Chamber of Commerce of Yates County (315-536-3111 or 800-868-9283; www.yatesny.com), 2375 Route 14A, just south of Penn Yan. Open Monday–Friday 8–5. Also open seasonally Saturday 10–4.

Finger Lakes Tourism Alliance (800-530-7488 or 315-536-7488; www.finger lakes.org) Publishes numerous guides for the Finger Lakes region, including a fishing guide.

Village of Dresden (315-536-2477), 1 Firehouse Avenue, Dresden. Open Monday–Friday 9–4.

Village of Dundee (607-243-5551), 12 Union Street, Dundee. Open Monday–Friday 9–4:30.

Village of Penn Yan (315-536-3015), 3 Maiden Lane, Penn Yan. Open Monday–Friday 8–4:30.

GETTING THERE *By air:* **Penn Yan Airport and Flying Club** (315-536-4471; www.senecafoods.com), 2521 Bath Road, Penn Yan 14527. Runway for small private planes. Scenic flights offered.

By car: NY 364 or NY 14A will take travelers into Penn Yan from Routes 5 and 20. NY 54 and 54A circle Keuka Lake. NY 14A will take travelers from Routes 5 and 20 into Dundee.

MEDICAL EMERGENCY Dial 911

Soldiers and Sailors Memorial Hospital (315-531-2000 www.flhealth.org), 418 North Main Street, Penn Yan.

✳ To See

ART MUSEUMS **Yates County Arts Center** (315-536-8226; www.ycac.org), 119 East Elm Street, Penn Yan. Open Tuesday–Friday 12–4, Saturday 9–3. This center features art exhibits, events, workshops, and classes.

MUSEUMS AND HISTORIC HOMES **Agricultural Memories Museum** (315-536-1206), 1110 Townline Road, Penn Yan. Open June–October Sunday 1–4 or by appointment. Admission: $4 adults, $1 children 2–12, under 2 free. This museum contains artifacts relating to agricultural history, including gasoline engines, horse-drawn carriages, antique tractors, and toys.

Dundee Area Historical Society (607-243-7047), 26 Seneca Street (off NY 14A), Dundee. Open May–October Tuesday–Friday 1–5, Saturday 8:30–12:30. Free admission. An 1890 brick schoolhouse with displays of antiques, memorabilia, and local history.

Historic Main Street Walking Tour. Many historic structures are located in Penn Yan. A brochure giving an overview of these buildings can be obtained at the **Chamber of Commerce of Yates County** (see *Guidance*).

Oliver House Museum (315-536-7318; www.yatespaStreetcom), 200 Main Street, Penn Yan. Open Monday–Friday 9:30–4:30; also open Saturday 10–2 July and August. This 1882 former home of Dr. Oliver houses the area's historical society. Collection includes articles associated with Jemima Wilkinson along with genealogical and local history. It is home to the **Yates Historical Society** (315-536-3032).

Robert Green Ingersoll Museum (315-536-1074; www.secularhumanism.org/ingersoll), 61 Main Street, Dresden. Open May 30–October 31 Saturday and Sunday 12–5. Donation: $1. This home was the birthplace of Robert Green Ingersoll, a famed and often controversial 19th-century agnostic orator and political speech-maker. The Civil War hero and attorney also championed causes such as racial equality and women's rights. The museum includes displays of local history.

HISTORIC SITES Garrett Memorial Chapel (315-536-3955), 1228 East Bluff Road, Bluff Point. Open July 4–Labor Day Tuesday–Thursday 1–4. Services are held in the chapel on Sundays at 9 AM during the summer. This stone chapel in the woods was built in 1931 by Mr. and Mrs. Paul Garrett, a wine magnate, as a memorial to their son Charles, who died at age 28 of tuberculosis. (*Note:* It is not handicapped accessible, and there are no rest rooms available)

WINERIES Keuka Lake Wine Trail (800-440-4898; www.keukawinetrail.com), 2375 NY14A, Penn Yan. The nine wineries along picturesque Keuka Lake are on this wine trail.

&. **Anthony Road Wine Company** (315-536-2182 or 800-559-2182; www .anthonyroadwine.com), 1225 Anthony Road (off CR 14), Penn Yan. Open year-round Monday–Saturday 10–5, Sunday 12–5. Enjoy a taste of award-winning wines amid landscaped gardens and a scenic view of Seneca Lake. This winery has been creating their distinctive wines since 1973.

Barrington Cellars/Buzzard Crest Vineyards (315-536-9686; www .barringtoncellars.com), 2772 Gray Road, Penn Yan. Open Monday–Saturday 11–5:30, Sunday 12–5:30; November–May, Saturdays only. This small family-owned winery, located in a 100 year old farmhouse, specializes in Labrusca and French-American hybrid wines along with ice wines.

&. **Fox Run Vineyards** (315-536-4616 or 1-800-636-9786; www.foxrunvineyards .com), 670 NY 14, Penn Yan. Open year-round Monday–Saturday 10–6, Sunday 11–6. This winery, which has been recognized in this country and Europe for their award-wining wines, has been featured in articles in the *New York Times* and *Wine Enthusiast*. Their Riesling won a gold medal at Alsace's International Riesling Competition. Enjoy tasting their wines in a relaxed atmosphere over-looking Seneca Lake. The café at the winery serves lunch seven day a week and features gourmet soups, salads, and sandwiches. A large gift shop offers an assortment of wines and wine accessories.

Hunt Country Vineyards (315-595-2812 or 1-800-WINEBUY; www.hunt countryvineyards.com), 4021 Italy Hill Road, Branchport. Open Monday–Satur-day 10–5, Sunday 12–5. Tours and tastings are offered at this sixth-generation farm, considered by many to be one of the loveliest wineries in the Finger Lakes region. Art and Joyce Hunt produce a variety of red, white, and blush wines, including chardonnay, Foxy Lady, Hunter's Red, and Vidal Ice Wine.

Keuka Spring Vineyards (315-536-3147; www.keukaspringwinery.com), 273 East Lake Road (NY 54), Penn Yan. Open Monday–Saturday 10–5, Sunday 11–5. Premium wines are available at this historic 1840s homestead. Awards include the Governor's Cup for most outstanding wine. The grounds contain lovely gardens and a gift shop with regional gifts. The winery is located on one of the highest hillsides in the Finger Lakes.

&. **Prejean Winery** (315-536-7524 or 800-548-2216 www.prejeanwinery.com), 2634 NY 14, Penn Yan. Open year-round. April–December, 10–5:30, Sunday 11–5:30; December–March, 10–5, Sunday 11–5. Sample estate-grown wines in an air-conditioned tasting room overlooking Seneca Lake. The winery is surrounded by the 38-acre vineyard that the Prejean family planted in 1979. At Prejean the fruit is treated gently in the pressing process; pressing whole clusters produces wines that are fruitier and lively. They create premium wines, which have won numerous awards, from estate-grown chardonnay, Riesling, gewürztraminer, merlot, Marechal Foch, cabernet franc, and cabernet sauvignon grapes.

Rooster Hill Vineyards (315-536-4773; www.roosterhill.com), 489 NY 54, Penn Yan. Open May–October, Monday–Saturday 1–-5, Sunday 12–5. This small winery has a reputation for distinctive handcrafted wines using state-of-the art equipment. Tastings are offered in a Tuscan-style room and wraparound porch with a view of Keuka Lake. The atmosphere of the winery is informal, relaxed, and down-to-earth. Vintages include seyval blanc, Riesling, merlot, Silver Pencil, and Cayuga White.

Seneca Shore Wine Cellars (315-536-0882 or 800-LUV-VINO), NY 14 and Davy Road, Penn Yan. Open year-round Monday–Saturday 10–5, Sunday 12–5. This winery, producing wines since 1979, has a definite medieval theme. Forty-eight acres of vineyards surround the tasting room, which includes a deck with rocking chairs overlooking Seneca Lake.

Torrey Ridge Winery (315-536-1210; www.torreyridgewinery.com), 2770 NY 14, Penn Yan. Open June–November, Monday, Wednesday–Saturday 10–5, Sunday 11:30–5; December–May, Sunday, Monday, Wednesday–Friday 12–5, Saturday 10–5. Torrey Ridge is one of the newest and most modern wineries in the Finger Lakes region. Educational tours of the winery and honey production facility are offered as well as walks in the vineyard The second-floor tasting room has a panoramic view of Seneca Lake. The winery specializes in the production of premium wines. Their sister winery, **Earle Estates Meadery** is part of the Seneca Lake Wine Trail (see below).

Seneca Lake Wine Trail (877-536-2717; www.senecalakewine.com), 100 North Franklin Street, Watkins Glen. Twenty-one wineries are located along Seneca Lake, making it the largest community of wine producers in the entire United States. The following wineries are located on the western shores of the lake.

Arcadian Estates Vineyards (607-535-2068 or 800-298-1346; www.arcadian wine.com), 4184 NY14, Rock Stream. Open year-round Monday–Saturday 10–6, Sunday 12–6. Arcadian specializes in red wines. Enjoy wine tastings along with special weekend events in a 170-year-old barn.

Earle Estate Meadery (315-536-1210; meadery.com), 3586 NY 14, Himrod. Open June–November Monday, Friday, and Saturday 10–5, Sunday 12–5; December–May, call for hours. This winery, which was established in 1993, produces over 30 different honey wines, known as mead, along with fruit and grape wines. Tasting of their wines and meads is offered. Observe a beehive at work, and browse their unique gift shop.

Four Chimneys Farm Winery (607-243-7502; www.fourchimneysorganic wines.com), 211 Hall Road (off NY 14) Himrod. Open year-round Monday–Saturday 10–5; also Sunday 11–5 May–December. This winery—America's first organic wine producer— is located on a Victorian estate and has been named Most Picturesque Winery by *National Geographic* magazine. They produce dry to sweet certified organically grown grapes and fruit wines.

Fulkerson Winery (607-243-7883), 5576 NY 14, Dundee. Open year-round Monday–Saturday 10–5, Sunday 11–5. They offer an array of over 20 wines, including several dry reds and ice wines along with their specialty, Red Zeppelin.

& **Glenora Wine Cellars** (607-243-5511, 1-800-243-5513; www.glenora.com), 5435 NY 14, Dundee. Open daily 10–5. Enjoy a spectacular view of Seneca Lake as you sip fine wines and champagnes in Glenora's expansive tasting room. A small children's play area has been set up in the corner of the tasting room.

Keuka Overlook Wine Cellars (607-292-6877; www.keukaoverlook.com), 5777 Old Bath/Gardner Road, (CR 17/26), Dundee. Open 11–5 daily spring, summer, and fall. Keuka Overlook is located on one of the highest hillsides in the Finger Lakes region. Enjoy a panoramic view of Keuka Lake while sampling award-winning wines. A bed & breakfast inn is located on the grounds.

McGregor Vineyard Winery (607-292-3999 or 800-272-0192; www.mcgregor winery.com), 5503 Dutch Street, Dundee. Open seven days: April–October 10–6, December–March 11–5. This estate vineyard, established by the McGregor family in 1980, specializes in fine vinifera wines, including pinot noir, merlot, and Riesling. Enjoy tastings and a view of Keuka Lake.

Miles Wine Cellars (607-243-7742; www.mileswinecellars.com), 168 Randall Crossing Road, Himrod. Open year-round Monday–Thursday 10–4, Friday–Sunday 10–6. Sample estate-grown wine on the porch of a 200-year-old Greek Revival mansion.

Hermann J. Wiemer Vineyard (607-243-7971 or 800-371-7971; www.wiemer .com) NY 14, Dundee. Open January–March Monday–Friday 10–5; April–December Monday–Saturday 10–5, Sunday 11–5. This winery, designed by an award-winning team of Cornell architects, features a unique white cathedral-like interior. All the wines produced by Hermann J. Wiemer, who came to the United States from Germany in 1968, are produced from grapes grown on his 140-acre vineyard. Visitors can stroll the popular Vineyard Walk through the property.

Woodbury Vineyards (607-243-8925; www.woodburyvineyards.com), 4141 NY 14, Dundee. Open year-round, daily 10–6. Sample more than 20 varieties of wine in their spacious tasting room overlooking Seneca Lake.

WATKINS GLEN WINERIES (*Note:* Although Watkins Glen is in neighboring Schuyler County, these wineries are in close proximity to those mentioned above.)

Lakewood Vineyards (607-535-9252; www.lakewoodvineyards.com), 4024 NY 14, Watkins Glen. Open year-round Monday–Saturday 10–5, Sunday 12–5. The Stamp family, owners of Lakewood Vineyards, has been farming on the western shores of Seneca Lake for four generations. They are committed to producing grapes of the highest quality, using cutting-edge technology for their award-winning wines. Sample their wines in a chalet-style tasting room overlooking Seneca Lake.

Castel Grisch Estate Winery (607-535-9614; www.fingerlakes-ny.com/castel grisch), 3380 CR 28, Watkins Glen. Open daily year-round 10–5. This winery, founded by a Swiss family, is currently run by the Malina family, using Old-World traditions. In addition to tastings and a fabulous view, the winery has a Bavarian deli that features a full-service lunch Monday–Saturday plus a Sunday brunch. A German buffet dinner is served Friday and Saturday evenings 5–9.

✳ To Do

AUTO RACING Black Rock Speedway (607-243-8686; www.blackrockspeed way.com), 86 Main Street (NY 14A), Dundee. Season April–September. Sprint cars, super stocks, and pro trucks.

Watkins Glen International (607-535-2481; www.theglen.com) 2790 CR 16, Watkins Glen. This facility, one of the nation's premier road-racing tracks, offers exciting NASCAR racing May–September.

BOAT EXCURSIONS *Viking Spirit* **Cruise Ship** (315-536-7061; www.viking resort.com), 680 East Lake Road (NY 54) Penn Yan. Daily cruises during the summer. Cruise Keuka Lake in a climate-controlled ship with two open-air decks. The vessel was custom built by Ken Christensen and specifically designed to cruise Keuka Lake.

GOLF Lakeside Country Club (315-536-6251), 200 E. Lake Rd. (NY 54), Penn Yan. An 18-hole, par-72 private course that's open to the public. It has a pro shop, driving range, and full-service restaurant.

FAMILY FUN Keuka Karts Go-Kart Track (315-536-4833), 2245 NY 54A, Penn Yan. Open daily in summer, weekends in spring and fall. A family-owned and -operated attraction that features both single and double carts.

FISHING Keuka Lake is popular for bass, perch, trout, and salmon. Fishing licenses can be obtained at any town clerk's office as well as at **Beverage Barn,** Lake Street, Penn Yan and **Doug's Bait,** NY 54A, Penn Yan.

MARINAS AND BOAT LAUNCHES Basin Park Marina (315-595-8808; www .basinparkmarina.com), 46 West Lake Road, Branchport. Open dawn to dusk.

The Boat Yard (315-595-2295), 289 West Lake Road, Branchport. Open dawn to dusk.

East Bluff Harbor Marina (315-536-8236), 654 East Bluff Drive, Penn Yan. Open dawn to dusk.

Keuka Lake Marina (315-595-2806), 47 West Lake Road, Branchport. Open dawn to dusk.

Keuka Lake State Park boat launch (315-536-3666), 3370 Pepper Road, Bluff Point. Open dawn to dusk.

Morgan Marina (315-536-8166), 100 East Lake Road, Penn Yan. Open dawn to dusk.

North-End Marina (315-595-2853), 3553 West Lake Road, Branchport. Open dawn to dusk.

Penn Yan Boat Launch (315-536-3015), Corner of Water and Keuka Street, Penn Yan. Open dawn to dusk.

SCENIC DRIVES **NY 54A from Penn Yan to Branchport** has been called one of the most beautiful drives in the United States.

✳ Green Space

BEACHES See **Keuka Lake State Park** in *Parks*.

LAKES AND PONDS **Keuka Lake**—known as Crooked Lake—is the third largest lake in the Finger Lakes region. Its unique Y shape provides the 22-mile-long lake with 60 miles of shoreline. Anglers like the lake for bass, perch, trout, and salmon. It is also one of the cleanest lakes in the region.

PARKS **Keuka Lake State Park** (315-536-3666), 3370 Pepper Road, Bluff Point. Open dawn to dusk. Park facilities include a swimming beach on Keuka Lake, picnic areas, boat launch, docks, and hiking trails. The park also has 150 campsites.

Indian Pines Park (Village of Penn Yan, 315-536-3015), NY 54A, Penn Yan. Open dawn to dusk. A nice midsized park for picnicking and relaxing along the lake. Facilities include a beach and picnic pavilions

Red Jacket Park (Village of Penn Yan, 315-536-3015), NY 54, Penn Yan. Open dawn to dusk. A scenic park along Keuka Lake. Facilities include a beach and picnic pavilions.

WALKING AND HIKING TRAILS **Keuka Lake Outlet Trail** (800-868-9283), Friends of the Finger Lakes Outlet, PO Box 231, Penn Yan 14527. Trail guides can be obtained at the Yates County Historian Office, 110 Court Street, Penn Yan. or at the Chamber of Commerce of Yates County on NY 14A (see *Guidance*). This 7.5-mile mostly flat recreational trail goes from Dresden to Penn Yan. Considered one of the top 25 hiking trails in the Northeast, the trail follows the former towpath of the "Crooked Lake Canal," which ran between Keuka and Seneca Lakes in the mid-19th century. The towpath was later converted to a railroad, which operated until the tracks were washed away in a 1972 flood. Along the trail you'll see remnants of former sawmills, gristmills, and other industries that were located here in the 1800s and early 1900s. The Friends of the Outlet have developed and maintained the property since the early 1980s. Entrances to the trail can be found near the **Crossroads Ice Cream Shop** (315-531-5311) on Main Street in Dresden and near the **Little** League field on Elm Street (NY 54A) in Penn Yan. The Crossroads Ice Cream Shop offers bicycle rentals April–September. See *Where to Eat—Eating Out.*

✳ Lodging

INNS AND RESORTS Esperanza Mansion (315-536-4400; www.esperanzamansion.com), 3456 NY 54A, Bluff Point. Open year-round. This elegant mansion overlooking Keuka Lake—the largest house ever built in Yates County—was built in 1838 by one of the area's wealthiest citizens. The mansion, which has two verandas plus a covered patio with spectacular views, has been completely renovated into a luxurious inn offering nine spacious lake-view suites with private baths furnished in Victorian style with such touches as canopy and sleigh beds and period decorative fireplaces. Modern amenities include hair dryers, individual in-room heat and air conditioning, flat-screen cable TV, and high-speed Internet access. A complimentary bottle of Finger Lakes wine greets each guest. An additional 22 deluxe guest rooms are available at the adjacent Inn at Esperanza. A complimentary deluxe continental breakfast is offered to guests at both the mansion and the inn. A 1962 Silver Cloud Rolls Royce is available for guest rental. A casual, yet elegant restaurant on premises serves lunch and dinner. Mansion rooms $140–$285, inn rooms $89–$169.

The Inn at Glenora Wine Cellars (607-243-9500 or 800-243-5513; www.glenora.com), 5435 NY 14, Dundee. Open year-round. Stay in one of 30 spacious and bright rooms, furnished in Mission style, overlooking Seneca Lake. Each room includes a balcony or patio, private bath, and a complimentary bottle of Glenora wine. The inn, just steps away from wine tasting at the Glenora Wine Cellars, also has a gourmet restaurant with an extensive wine list. $99–$235.

Viking Resort (315-536-7061; www.vikingresort.com), 680 East Lake Road, Penn Yan. Open mid-May–mid-October. This family-oriented resort, with 1,000 feet of private lakeshore on Keuka Lake, offers apartments, suites, motel rooms, and cottages. Amenities include a swimming pool, hot tub, and boat slips as well as a nightly bonfire on the lake. The *Viking Spirit* tour boat has daily cruises. Rates range from $70 for a basic motel room to $520 for a cottage that sleeps 12. Weekly rates are also available.

MOTELS AND HOTELS The Showboat (607-243-7434), 3434 Plum Point Road, Himrod. Open May–October. This 45-room motel and adjacent restaurant are located right on Seneca Lake. Amenities include air conditioning, cable TV, and a pool. $60–$90.

STAY THE NIGHT—OR JUST FOR A FINE MEAL—AT THE ESPERANZA MANSION.
Christine A. Smyczynski

Branchport

Gone with the Wind Bed & Breakfast and Retreat Lodge (607-868-4603; www.gonewiththewindon keukalake.com), 453 West Lake Road, Branchport. Five luxurious guest rooms, some with private baths, are available in a historic 1887 stone plantation-style inn. A newly built log lodge has an additional five guest rooms. Hosts Robert and Linda Lewis serve a full breakfast with homemade baked goods. $85–$140.

10,000 Delights Bed & Breakfast (607-868-3731), 1170 West Lake Road, Branchport. Twelve rooms are available at this 50-acre estate that includes a Greek-Revival mansion, lake house, and luxury apartment. Also on the grounds is a Japanese tea-house over a 60-foot waterfall, beach, and paddleboats. Innkeeper Vera VanAtta serves a gourmet breakfast. $75–$135.

Penn Yan

Finton's Landing Bed & Breakfast on Keuka Lake (315-536-3146; http://home.eznet.net/~tepperd), 661 East Lake Road, Penn Yan. Open spring–fall. Innkeepers Douglas and Arianne Tepper offer four air-conditioned guest rooms with private baths in their waterfront Victorian home. This secluded getaway boasts a large front porch, a 165-foot beach on Keuka Lake, and a lakeside gazebo. Room include a two-course breakfast, served on the lake-view porch, weather permitting. $119–$159.

The Fox Inn (315-536-3101 or 800-901-7997; www.foxinnbandb.com), 158 Main Street, Penn Yan. Open year-round. Cliff and Michele Orr's 1820 Greek Revival inn, located in downtown Penn Yan, offers five antiques-furnished guest rooms with private baths. Amenities include a Victorian parlor with a billiard table, a turn-of-the-20th-century dining room with the original parquet floor, a 1926 slot machine, and a beverage center with wine and beer (it's one of the few B&Bs in the area with a liquor license). The Harry Fox Room, on the first floor, features a queen four-poster bed, TV/VCR, and private bath. Upstairs, the William Oliver Room, the inn's premier accommodation, overlooks Main Street and has a gas fireplace and a two-person Jacuzzi tub. The Lucy Fox Room, decorated in a dramatic pink-and-black theme, has a queen-sized canopy box, while the Dorothy Fox Room is decorated in county style. The William Fox Family Suite features two guest rooms that share a bath. Fox Inn has been rated one of the Top 50 Inns in America. All rooms include a gourmet home-cooked breakfast, including the

JUST STEPS AWAY FROM THE WINE TASTING ROOM AT GLENORA WINE CELLARS IS THEIR INN OVERLOOKING SENECA LAKE.

Christine A. Smyczynski

inn's special "Green Flannel Hash." $89–$159.

Los Gatos Bed & Breakfast (315-536-0686; www.losgatosbandb.com), 1491 NY 14A, Penn Yan. Open year-round. Innkeepers Burney and Susan Baron offer three rooms in this new B&B. The Grand Suite on the second floor offers a gorgeous view and a private balcony. Downstairs, the Sage Room features a sleigh bed, while the Blue Room is decorated with antiques. All rooms have queen-sized beds and private baths. A full breakfast is served in the gazebo by the pool or on the enclosed sun porch. $99–$149.

Merritt Hill Manor Bed & Breakfast (315-536-7682; www.merritthillmanor.com), 2756 Coates Road (off Merritt Hill Road, off 54A), Penn Yan. Open year-round. This 1822 Federal-style manor house overlooking Keuka and Seneca Lakes is located on 12 acres, with walking trails and an extensive garden. Each of innkeeper's Marc and Susan Hyser's five guest rooms has a private bath. The Isaac Hartshorn Room, named after the original builder, has a queen-sized bed, while the Leon Taylor Room, named after a prominent local businessman, has a king bed. The remaining three rooms are named after Marc and Susan's children; Robert Todd, Matthew Joseph, and Megan Elizabeth. A hearty country breakfast is served. An upscale gift and antiques shop is located next to the inn (see *Special Shops*). $130–$150.

Robertson House Bed & Breakfast (315-536-9273; www.robertson house.net), 107 Court Street, Penn Yan. Open year-round. Jane and Paul Boyd's circa 1830 house has four guest rooms with private baths, each room individually decorated in country style with antiques. Eleanor's Room is done in a grape motif. The Flag Room is patriotically decorated in red, white, and blue and has an annex room that can be used as a family suite. Martha's Room features a king-sized bed and a bath with a lady-slipper tub. The Welcome Wagon Room has a queen bed and primitive country motif. If you see something you like, make an offer; many of the antiques in the inn are for sale. The inn faces the town common off Main Street, and is close to downtown shops. They have a small antique shop which is open Friday and Saturday. $125–150

Tudor Hall B & B (315-536-9962; www.bbhost.com/tudorhall), 762 East Bluff Drive, Penn Yan. Open May–October. Don and Priscilla Erickson's elegant English Tudor on Keuka Lake features terraced gardens and a private beach. While at the inn, peruse a book from their library, play a tune on the baby grand piano, and enjoy a gourmet breakfast by candlelight. Each of the three guest rooms has its own private bath, cable TV, refrigerator, and coffeemaker. $135–$185.

Wagener Estate Bed & Breakfast (315-536-4591; www.wagenerestate .com), 351 Elm Street, Penn Yan. Open year-round. On a main road yet set back from the street on 4 acres, this B&B is close to wineries, shops, and restaurants and is within walking distance to town. The historic circa 1790 home, operated by innkeepers Lisa and Ken Greenwood and assistant innkeeper Jeremy Wilson, is furnished in period antiques and offers five rooms, one a suite. The Niagara Room features a queen canopy bed plus a twin. The Aurora Room, done in shades of blue, features a king bed and a pull-out sofa, while the Delaware Room has a queen bed and a twin along with a balcony. The Catawba Room has a queen bed, and the Seyval Concord suite has a queen bed and a pull-out sofa. All five guest rooms have private baths and include a full breakfast, which is served on the porch in nice weather. The inn is listed on the National and State Registers of Historic Places. $100–$130.

Dundee

Anna Rose Bed & Breakfast (607-243-5898 or 866-261-7673; www.annarose.com), 524 Rock Stream Road, Dundee. Open year-round. Innkeepers Ken and Sharon Miller offer six guest rooms in this 1927 three-story, 7,600-square-foot brick home on 5 country acres. Each tastefully decorated room has either a king or queen bed, and one room has a Jacuzzi. A full gourmet breakfast is served. On select Saturday evenings dinner is prepared for guests. $75–$195.

The 1819 Red Brick Inn (607-243-8844; www.bbonline.com/ny/redbrick), 2081 Route 230, Dundee. Open year-round. Wendy and Robert Greenslade offer five guest rooms, all with private baths, in this restored 1819 Federal-style home. The rooms are furnished with antique Victorian furniture and quilts, and the Tuttle Room, the inn's largest accommodation, features a working fireplace plus a small sitting area. The home is listed on both the State and National Register of Historic Places and is one of the finest examples of Federalist architecture in Yates County. $95–$115.

Keuka Overlook Bed & Breakfast (607-292-6877; www.keukaoverlook.com), 5777 Bath Road, Dundee. Open year-round. Enjoy Victorian elegance when you stay at this restored 1903 home that sits high on Barrington Hill with breathtaking views of both Keuka and Waneta Lakes. Innkeepers Bob and Terry Barrett have decorated each of the four guest rooms to represent one of the seasons. The Seneca Room has the colors of springtime; the Keuka Room, with its lake view, is decorated in summertime hues; the Waneta Room will remind you of harvest time; while the Lamoka Loft, with its queen-sized bed and view of two lakes, makes you think of winter. Each room has a private bath and a full breakfast is served. The entire home has decorations featuring a grape motif. $95.

South Glenora Tree Farm Bed & Breakfast (607-243-7414; www.fingerlakes.net/treefarm), 546 South Glenora Road, Dundee. Open year-round. Innkeepers Steve and Judy Ebert offer five beautiful guest rooms with private baths at this country retreat in the heart of the Finger Lakes. Rated three diamonds by AAA, the inn—created from two 1855 barns—is located on an active tree farm. It has three fireplaces and a wraparound porch with several gliders. One barn has four rooms, including the Cherry Room, which is handicapped accessible. The other barn has a large suite with a bedroom and sitting room plus a porch and balcony overlooking the property. A full country breakfast is served in the dining room. $125–$149.

Tobehanna Creek B & B (607-243-7616; www.linkny.com/~mherrick), 4229 Perry Hill Road (NY 226), Dundee. Open year-round. Innkeeper Peggy Herrick operates a peaceful inn in a restored 1830s farmhouse. Four air-conditioned guest rooms share two baths. The grounds have a 1-mile walking path, catfish pond, and a multitude of birdhouses and bird feeders. A full breakfast is served in the large country kitchen. $70–$80.

OTHER LODGING **Wigwam Keuka Lake Campground** (315-536-6352; www.wigwamkeukalake.com), 3324 Esperanza Road, Penn Yan. Open May 15–October 15. This secluded, quiet, family-oriented campground has tent and trailer sites as well as an authentic tepee, two cabins, and a RV camper to rent. Along with views of the lake, enjoy a swimming pool, fishing pond, playground, and planned activities. $18 tent sites, $23 trailer sites with water and electric, tepee $32.50, cabin $40, RV camper $60.

Rental Plus (315-536-2201 or 1-888-414-5253), 142 Lake Street, Penn Yan. They have an extensive listing of rental properties, including cabins and cottages, available by the day, week, or month, in the Finger Lakes region.

✳ Where to Eat

DINING OUT ✦ **Esperanza Mansion** (315-536-4400; www.esperanza mansion.com), 3456 NY 54A, Bluff Point. Open for lunch Monday–Saturday 11–2:30; dinner Monday–Thursday 5–9, Friday–Saturday 5–10; Sunday brunch 11–2:30. Reservations recommended during the summer and on weekends and holidays. Enjoy fine dining in an 1838 restored Greek Revival mansion overlooking Keuka Lake. Lunches include salads as well as entrées like chicken Oscar and crêpe wraps. Dinner selections include broiled lobster tail, prime rib,

and rack of lamb. More casual dining is available in the Mansion Tavern, where you can dine under a canopy overlooking Keuka Lake. See *Lodging*.

✦ ✦ **Serrasin's on the Lake** (315-536-9494; www.dineonthelake.com), 301 Lake Street (NY 54), Penn Yan. Open Monday–Saturday 11:30–9, Sunday brunch 11:30–3, Sunday dinner 3:30–9. Serving fine and casual American cuisine, including steak, chops, pasta, and salads. Lunch selections include soups, salads, sandwiches, and burgers; kids' menu available. Located at the north end of Keuka Lake with a spectacular view of the lake, 140 feet of beachfront, and docking for boats.

Veraisons Restaurant at the Inn at Glenora Wine Cellars (607-243-9500 or 1-800-243-5513; www.glenora .com), 5435 NY 14, Dundee. Open daily for breakfast 8–10, lunch 11:30–3, light fare 3–5, dinner Sunday–Thursday 5–9, Friday–Saturday 5–10. This restaurant overlooking Seneca Lake features regional cuisine prepared with a classical French influence. The decor features cherry wood, a cathedral ceiling, and a stone fireplace. Start your meal with Glenora's signature cabernet French onion soup. Diners include stuffed brace of quail, Veraisons scallops provençal, and Glenora vegetable lasagna.

EATING OUT

Dresden
✦ ✦ ✦ **Crossroads Ice Cream** (315-531-5311), 88 Main Street (at the intersection of NY 14 and 54), Dresden. Open daily 12–9 Memorial Day–Labor Day, 12–8 mid-April–Memorial Day and Labor Day–end of September. A popular place to stop for ice

cream, burgers, hot dogs, and other take-out foods. Near the entrance to the Keuka Outlet hiking and biking trail. They offer bicycle rentals April–September: $10/day, $3/hour.

Dundee

Classic Café (607-243-5111), 1 Main Street, Dundee. Open Monday–Saturday 7 AM–8 PM, Sunday 7 AM–3 PM. The menu features soups and pies made from scratch.

Penn Yan

Angel's Family Restaurant (315-536-4026), 5 Main Street, Penn Yan. Opens daily 5–9. This restaurant has a counter as well as several booths. The menu includes daily specials along with entrées like roast beef dinners, stuffed chicken breast, and fettuccini Alfredo.

Antique Inn (315-536-6576), 2940 NY 54A, Penn Yan. Open Sunday–Thursday 12–8, Friday–Saturday 11–9. A rustic-style restaurant with lunch and dinner menu specials like they had in the good old days, including soups, sandwiches, and salads.

The Haven Café (315-536-4033; www.thehavencafe.com), 20 Maiden Lane, Penn Yan. Open Monday–Thursday 7 AM–8 PM, Friday 7 AM–10 PM, Saturday 8 AM–10 PM. This café serves specialty coffee and beverages along with sandwiches, soups, salads, and more, including their signature chicken wraps.

Holly's Red Rooster (315-536-9800), 12 Maiden Lane, Penn Yan. Open Monday–Friday 11–9, Sunday 4–9. They have the best prime rib in Penn Yan as well as veal, chicken, and seafood entrées, and their wine list offers a large selection of Finger Lakes wines. The lunch menu includes burgers, sandwiches, soups, and salads.

& **Keuka Restaurant** (315-536-5852), 12 Main Street, Penn Yan. Open for lunch Monday–Saturday 11–3, dinner 4–9 (Friday until 10). A very nice family restaurant decorated with lots of wood and brick. Dinner selections include house specialties like ribs and kabobs plus pasta, beef, seafood, chicken, veal, and more. The lunch menu features burritos, seafood baskets, salads, burgers, and sandwiches.

Lamppost Restaurant (315-536-3529), 23 Main Street, Penn Yan. Open 7–3. Breakfast, lunch, and ice cream are served in this restaurant located in a historic building with a tin ceiling. All desserts are made in house, including their homemade hot fudge sauce.

✑ ❀ **Mac's Dairy Bar and Mini Golf** (315-536-3226), NY 14A, 1 mile south of Penn Yan. Open daily 11–9 March–October. They serve up soft-serve ice cream, frozen yogurt, sherbet, and hand-dipped Hershey's ice cream. You can also play 18 holes of miniature golf.

✑ & ❀ **Miller's Essenhaus** (315-531-8260), NY 14A, Penn Yan. Open Tuesday–Saturday 8–9, Sunday 11–4. Hearty, wholesome, family meals are served in this Mennonite-staffed restaurant. *Essenhaus* means "eating house," which is basically what one comes here to do. Enjoy home-baked breads, pies, and muffins along with homemade sauces, soups, and dressings at this large, clean country café. They also have a gift shop that features quilts and Amish- and Mennonite-made items and a take-out bakery. Be sure to try their sticky buns.

♂ ♣ **Penn Yan Diner** (315-536-6004), East Elm Street, Penn Yan. Open Tuesday–Saturday 7–7. This tiny diner was built and shipped by rail in 1925 from Galion, Ohio. The menu features old-fashioned home cooking, including homemade pies, pot roast, roast turkey, and baked ham, along with sandwiches and burgers. While waiting for your food, read the kitchen trivets and plaques that hang over the grill area and get a chuckle or two. Some examples: BOSS SPELLED BACKWARD IS DOUBLE SOB; and: HELEN WAITE IS OUR CREDIT MANAGER. IF YOU WANT CREDIT, GO TO HELEN WAITE.

♂ ♿ ♣ **Seneca Farms** (315-536-4066), NY 54A, Penn Yan. Open March–November seven days 10:30–9. This casual restaurant serves up fried chicken, burgers, ribs, and hot dogs along with shakes, sodas, and 50 varieties of homemade ice cream.

♂ ♿ ♣ **The Wagner Restaurant** (315-536-8062), 124 East Elm Street, Penn Yan. Open Monday–Saturday 5 AM–2 PM, Friday until 8 PM, Sunday 5 AM–1 PM. This restaurant is best known for their hot and cold lunch buffet and Sunday turkey dinners.

✴ Selective Shopping

ANTIQUES **Anglo American Antiques** (315-536-6906), 109 Main Street, Penn Yan. Open Monday–Saturday 10:30–3. They specialize in jewelry and dishes.

Neat Stuff Antiques (315-729-5780 or 607-522-3534), 104 Water Street, Penn Yan. Open Monday–Saturday 9–5, Sun. 9–3. A collection of general antiques, primitives, vintage clothing, jewelry, glassware, and other neat stuff.

Side Door Antiques (315-536-2101), 2223 Baker Road, Penn Yan. Open daily 10–5. Carries a general line of furniture and small items.

Spencer & French Antiques, etc. (315-536-7579), 107 Main Street, Penn Yan. Wednesday–Saturday. Specializing in primitives, glassware, pictures, furniture, and smalls.

Water Street Antiques (585-526-5865) 108 Water Street, Penn Yan. Open Monday 9–1, Friday–Saturday 10–5; other times by appointment. Specializing in small antiques.

FARM MARKETS **Yates Cooperative Farm and Craft Market**, Main Street, Penn Yan. Saturdays, June–October 7:30–noon. This weekly farm market includes fresh produce, baked goods, quilts, and other handmade items.

SPECIAL SHOPS

Branchport
Crooked Lake Mercantile (315-595-2233), NY 54A at the "Four Corners," Branchport. Open Monday–Saturday 8–6, Sunday 8–1. For baked goods, candles, flags, Keuka Lake sweatshirts, T-shirts, and birdhouses as well as take-out deli and groceries.

Dundee and Vicinity
Fall Bright The Winemakers Shoppe (607-292-3995; www .fallbright.com), 9750 Hyatt Hill, Wayne. Open September–October, Tuesday–Sunday 10–5; rest of year, Tuesday–Friday 10–4, Saturday by appointment. Choose from beer and winemaking supplies, including Finger Lakes grapes, available as juice or grapes.

Penn Yan (historic Main Street) and Vicinity

Birkett Mills (315-536-3311; www .thebirkettmills.com), 163 Main Street, Penn Yan. Open Monday–Friday 8–4. Birkett Mills is the largest producer of buckwheat products in the world, and many of their products are for sale at this location, which opened in 1797 and has been in continuous operation since. Be sure to take a look at the 28-foot griddle hanging on the side of the building, used to make a world's record pancake on September 27, 1987.

Coles Furniture and Decorative Accessories (315-536-3733), 123 Main Street, Penn Yan. Open Monday–Wednesday 9–5, Thursday–Friday 9–6, Saturday 9–4. Since 1931 this shop has carried fine furniture and home decor items.

Dried and True Shoppe (315-531-9228), 131 Main Street (lower level of Lown's House of Shops), Penn Yan. Open Tuesday-Saturday 9:30–5. Dried and silk floral arrangements along with reproduction furniture, folk art, Americana, and more.

East Hill Gallery (585-554-3539; www.rfag.org), 1445 Upper Hill Road, Middlesex (about 10 miles east of Penn Yan). Open May–October, Friday, Sunday, and Monday 1–5, Saturday 11–5 and by appointment. Quality American crafts are produced on site, including pottery, weaving, blown glass, furniture, and toys. This artists' guild, located on a 350-acre working farm, was started in 1957.

Frum Nature (315-536-2073), 101 Main Street, Penn Yan. Open Monday–Saturday 9–6, Sunday 10–4. Shop with nature in mind at this store featuring gifts, clothing, collectibles, gourmet foods, kitchen items, and handmade soaps, including locally made Holstein cow milk soap.

Heart Strings Gift Shop at Apple Barrel Orchards (315-536-8700), 2732 Wager Hill Road, Penn Yan. Open July–October daily 9–6, November–June 9–5. Choose from a large selection of gift items such as Precious Moments, Cherished Teddies, and Yankee Candles along with grape- and apple-themed items.

Henderson's Drug Store (315-536-4448), 126 Main Street, Penn Yan. Open Monday–Friday 8:30–7, Saturday 8:30–4. A full-service drugstore and pharmacy that also carries greeting cards and gifts.

&. **Loomis Barn and Country Shops** (585-554-3154; www.loomis barn.com), 4942 Loomis Road, Rushville (about 10 miles northeast of Penn Yan at the Ontario County border). Open Tuesday–Saturday 10–5:30, Sunday 12–4. Several unique shops and a restaurant are housed in this complex. **The Loomis Barn** features home furnishings, from sofas, chairs, and dining sets to Shaker and country reproductions, plus gifts, accessories, and accent pieces. **Colonial Bouquets** (585-554-3204; www.colonial bouquets.com) features dried flowers, herbal arrangements, wreaths, and garlands. When you're done shopping, take a break and stop for lunch in the **Corn House Café**, overlooking fields and a duck pond. Choose from homemade soups, specialty sandwiches or the entrée of the day.

Longs' Cards and Books (315-536-3131), 115 Main Street, Penn Yan. Open Monday–Thursday 8:30–6, Friday 8:30–8:30, Saturday 8– 6, Sunday 10–5. Specialize in greeting cards, books, and office supplies plus gift items, party goods, and local-interest books. The shop is housed in an 1864 former dry-goods emporium.

Lown's House of Shoppes (315-531-8343), 131 Main Street, Penn Yan. Open Monday–Saturday 9–6, Sunday 10–4. Browse through three floors of fine gifts and collectibles, including handcrafted wooden items, floral arrangements, candles, antiques, and Christmas decorations. The building, built in the late 1800s, houses one of the few Lamson Cash Carry Systems still existing in the United States.

Merritt Hill Manor Gift Shop (315-536-7682; www.merritthillmanor.com), 2756 Coates Road (off Merritt Hill Road, off 54A), Penn Yan. Open May–Christmas 10–5 daily, rest of year by appointment. This upscale shop next to Merritt Hill Manor Bed & Breakfast features oil paintings, seasonal merchandise, gifts, garden items, books, and more. See *Lodging*.

The Nest Egg (315-536-3488), 125 Main Street, Penn Yan. Open Monday–Wednesday 9–5, Thursday 9–7:30, Friday 9–6, Saturday 9–5, Sunday 11–4. This small shop features antique and new jewelry as well as local pottery, Yankee Candles, kids' items, home decor, and Vera Bradley designs.

The Quilt Room (315-536-5964; www.quiltroom.com), 1870 Hoyt Road, Penn Yan. Open Monday–Friday 10–4:30, Saturday 9:30–5. This shop specializes in handmade quilts and handcrafted items, candles, and gifts.

Roses and Oak Ranch (585-554-5409), 4169 Ferguson Corners Road, Rushville (about 10 miles northeast of Penn Yan at the Ontario County border). Open Thursday, Friday, and Sunday 12–4, Saturday 10–5. Amish handcrafted furniture and gift shop.

✒ **Weaver View Farms Country Store** (315-781-2571; www.weaver viewfarms.com), 1190 Earls Hill Road, Penn Yan. Open year-round Monday–Saturday 8–5. This annex attached to the back of an 1800s farmhouse, located on a 128-acre working dairy farm overlooking Seneca Lake, is filled with all sorts of country decor items including over 200 hand-stitched Amish quilts, stenciled items, pottery, candles, primitive and country items, cookbooks, homemade jams, baskets, Amish furniture, and wooden toys. Mennonite owner Pauline Weaver offers items made by family and friends as well as folks from neighboring Amish communi-

WINDMILL FARM AND CRAFT MARKET IN PENN YAN IS NEW YORK STATE'S FIRST AND LARGEST RURAL MARKET.
Christine A. Smyczynski

ties. It is the only store in the area that has such a large selection of Amish-made quilts. They also have over 2,000 quilting fabrics to choose from, along with quilting and sewing classes.

&. **Windmill Farm & Craft Market** (315-536-3032; www.thewindmill .com), 3900 NY 14A, Penn Yan. Open Saturdays 8–4:30 late April–mid-December. Windmill Farm, which first opened in 1987, is New York State's first and largest rural market. Over 250 vendors—in three buildings and along a street of shops on this 31-acre site—carry an assortment of goods from fresh produce to hand-made Amish and Mennonite craft items, baked good, furniture, and more.

✳ Special Events

July: **Yates County Fair** (315-356-3111 or 800-868-9283; www.yatesny .com), Old Route 14A, Penn Yan. A small fair featuring amusement rides, food vendors, agricultural displays, and entertainment. **Finger Lakes Wine Festival** (607-535-2481; www.flwinefest.com), Watkins Glen International Raceway, 2790 CR 16, Watkins Glen. More than 60 wineries participate in this annual event that features crafts, music, food, and, of course, wine tasting.

August: **Fine Arts and Wines** (www.ycac.org). Dozens of artists will be working and displaying their art at three wineries on the west side of Keuka Lake with proceeds to benefit arts in education.

INDEX

M